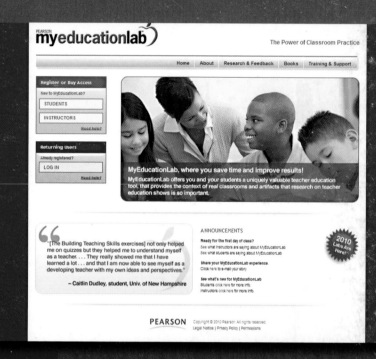

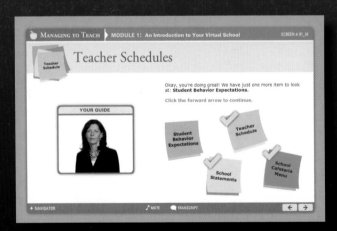

PEARSON myeducationlab™

Videos and Practical Tools for Your Classroom and Career!

MyEducationLab helps bring the classroom to life with a wealth of resources to help you prepare for practice teaching and the job of teaching itself.

Managing to Teach

An interactive, virtual learning environment, Managing to Teach has been designed to help teachers-in-training develop effective classroom management skills. Users will watch videos of classroom scenarios, complete interactive assignments, assume the role of decision maker in simulated teaching experiences, and receive valuable feedback from the Program Guide on their classroom decisions. Based on the three cornerstones of effective classroom management—prior planning, establishing constructive behaviours, and exhibiting desired modes of behaviour—**Managing to Teach** is the *MyEducationLab* resource that soon-to-be teachers have been waiting for!

Web Resources for Education in Canada

A comprehensive aggregation of provincial- and board-level links, a robust suite of weblinks will provide you and other students across the country with valuable information about programs and standards that will start you on the right path to becoming a teacher!

Career Resources

Access the Careers section of *MyEducationLab* to prepare your portfolio, sample a rich array of lesson plans, and learn more about getting a job in teaching

Save Time. Improve Results. www.myeducationlab.com

H10_210_BC

TEACHING STUDENTS WITH SPECIAL NEEDS IN INCLUSIVE SETTINGS

TOM E. C. SMITH ◆ **EDWARD A. POLLOWAY** ◆ **JAMES R. PATTON**
University of Arkansas   Lynchburg College   University of Texas

CAROL A. DOWDY ◆ **LAUREEN J. MCINTYRE** ◆ FOURTH CANADIAN EDITION
University of Alabama   University of Saskatechewan
at Birmingham

Pearson Canada
Toronto

Library and Archives Canada Cataloguing in Publication

Teaching students with special needs in inclusive settings/Tom E.C. Smith . . . [et al.].—4th Canadian ed.

Includes index.
ISBN 978-0-205-78146-1

1. Children with disabilities—Education.   2. Inclusive education. I. Smith, Tom E. C.

LC1203.C3T42 2011   371.9'046   C2010-906525-5

Original edition published by Pearson Education, Inc., Upper Saddle River, New Jersey, USA. Copyright © 2008 by Pearson Education, Inc. This edition is authorized for sale only in Canada.

ISBN 978-0-205-78146-1

Vice President, Editorial Director: Gary Bennett
Editor-in-Chief: Ky Pruesse
Acquisitions Editor: David S. Le Gallais
Marketing Manager: Loula March
Developmental Editor: Rema Celio
Project Manager: Cheryl Noseworthy
Production Editor: Melissa Churchill
Copy Editor: Sally Glover
Proofreader: Melissa Churchill
Manufacturing Manager: Jane Schell
Composition: MPS Limited, a Macmillan Company
Permissions and Photo Research: Joanne Tang
Art Director: Julia Hall
Cover Design: Anthony Leung
Cover Image: GettyImages

1 2 3 4 5   15 14 13 12 11
Printed and bound in USA.

Brief Table of Contents

Detailed Table of Contents

Preface

The delivery of services and supports to students with exceptionalities and other special needs in general classroom settings has increased significantly since the original edition of *Teaching Students with Special Needs in Inclusive Settings* was published. More and more schools are implementing inclusive education models each year. While the success of inclusion is difficult to validate due to inherent research problems and variant terminology, research tends to indicate that including students with exceptionalities and other special needs in general education classrooms proves beneficial both to these students and to students without exceptionalities. It is likely that the inclusion movement will continue to move forward if teacher training programs continue to address the need to better prepare general educators to deal effectively with students with diverse learning needs.

As with previous editions, we feel it is important to indicate our position on inclusion. When the movement first began, the general interpretation of inclusion was "all or none"—all students, regardless of the severity of their exceptionality, all of the time, in general education classrooms. As inclusion has been implemented, however, this all-or-none position has been moderated significantly. It is our belief that *inclusion* means that all children with exceptionalities *belong* with their typically achieving, chronological-age peers in the same classes, in the same school they would be attending if they did not have an exceptionality. However, it is also our belief that these students must be provided with appropriate educational opportunities. This could include the provision of supports in the general education classroom, but it may also mean the education of some students, at specific times during the day, in specialized settings where they can receive interventions that could not be provided as effectively in the general classroom setting.

It remains our strong belief that students with exceptionalities and other special needs must be provided educational services that are appropriate for them, as determined by professionals in consultation with parents and family members. The appropriateness of the services definitely includes the location of the educational program. Serving students based on educational need rather than clinical label or service delivery model should be the purpose of all special programming; individual student needs must remain the critical element in designing appropriate programs.

FEATURES OF THE FOURTH CANADIAN EDITION

Too often, special education in Canada is taught without reference to or acknowledgment of the substantial differences between the Canadian system of special education and that in the United States. Although Canada has been strongly influenced by the progression of special education services in the U.S., this country's provincial and territorial educational jurisdictions make it unique. Canada has 12 different approaches to special education definitions and service delivery. Currently, Nunavut uses the educational guidelines of the Northwest Territories, but we may soon be looking at 13 different models. A pre-service teacher in Canada needs to be aware of the range of services that exist throughout the country. Throughout this fourth Canadian edition, we highlight the differences and similarities across Canada. However, unlike some Canadian editions, this one strives to make pre-service teachers aware of the situation in the United States as well; instead of being limited to a review of Canadian services, this edition frequently contrasts the Canadian situation to the more generally recognized U.S. system of special education. In this way, students are best informed about current special education practices throughout North America.

References to Canadian research, statistics, and prevalence appear throughout the text. The perspective on multicultural education continues to be updated in each edition to provide the reader with more current views on approaches to the multicultural classroom. Personal Spotlights in every chapter feature Canadian teachers, parents, professionals in the community, and individuals with exceptionalities. Each chapter includes a list of recommended topical resources that are appropriate for Canadian teachers, including Canadian and international associations, books, videos, and resource guides. Similarly, each chapter provides a short description of recommended relevant websites with information and resources that will be helpful to Canadian teachers.

The Chapter Objectives are teaching and learning aids that outline the material to be covered in the chapter. Each opening vignette is a case study relating to the chapter's topic and is accompanied by Questions to Consider. After studying the chapter, students will be able to confidently answer all of those questions.

Margin notes are centred on four themes: Teaching Tips, Further Readings, Cross-References, and Consider This boxes. Each chapter also includes specific boxed features that highlight **technology, cultural diversity, inclusion strategies, and research-based evidence**. These features are intended to provide more depth to a specific topic than is found in the text.

Technology Today

Technology Today boxes feature practical information and discuss the ever-changing technology available to the teachers and students in today's inclusive classrooms.

- Developing an Effective Team Approach to Serve Students Using AAC in the Classroom p. 75
- Assistive Technology: Enhancing Quality of Life p. 193
- Pushing a Wheelchair p. 254
- Websites That Offer Curriculum, Strategies, and Interventions p. 282
- Virtual Technology in the Special Education Classroom p. 357
- Websites for Families of Children with Exceptionalities p. 399

Diversity Forum

Diversity Forum boxes provide in-depth information about how a teacher in an inclusive classroom can meet the needs of the culturally diverse students of today.

- Planning as a Team, Learning Together p. 10
- Considerations for Observing Linguistically Different Students p. 73
- ASD and Multiculturalism p. 207
- Issues to Consider before Referring Students from Culturally Diverse Backgrounds for Special Education Programs p. 293

Inclusion Strategies

Inclusion Strategies boxes provide practical strategies for implementing inclusion in the classroom.

- Using "People First" Language p. 5
- Classroom Ecological Inventory p. 17

- Components of a Behaviour Management Plan p. 174
- Teaching Science to Students Who Are Hearing Impaired p. 231
- Range and Types of Accelerative Options p. 274

Evidence-Based Practice

Evidence-Based Practice boxes highlight teaching strategies and suggestions supported by research.

- Increasing Peer Interactions for Students with Severe Disabilities Through Training for Paraprofessionals p. 44
- Music and Art Activities to Promote Friendship p. 44
- Teaching Strategies to Help Problem Listeners in the Classroom p. 68
- Evidence-Based Instruction: Sound Blending p. 98
- Part-by-Part Decoding Instruction when Pre-teaching Content Area Words p. 107
- First Step to Success: A Preventative Program for Behaviourally At-Risk Children (K-2) p. 166
- Circles of Friends in Schools p. 194
- Appropriate Adaptations for Students with ASD p. 210
- Teaching Self-Management Skills p. 213
- Physical Activity of Children with Visual Impairments p. 237
- Interventions for Students with Tourette Syndrome p. 256
- Goals for Curricula of Children Who Are Gifted p. 270
- Components of Effective Mentoring Programs for At-Risk Students p. 309
- Teaching Reading with Emphasis on Word Recognition p. 348
- Teaching Reading Comprehension p. 349
- Teaching Writing Skills p. 349
- Teaching Mathematics p. 352
- Teaching Social Skills p. 353
- Effective Grading Practices p. 370
- Parent-Delivered Interventions p. 405

Personal Spotlight

Personal Spotlight boxes highlight teachers, parents of students with special needs, and individuals with special needs, providing insight into the views of people who deal most closely with the challenge of inclusion.

- Speech-Language Pathologist Sharon Bond p. 77
- Alternate Education Teacher Heather Merasty p. 138
- Former Executive Director of Saskatoon Association for Community Living Jeanne Remenda p. 188
- Parent Education Facilitator Sue McCart p. 218
- Parents of Two Gifted Children Chad Coller and Danielle Gaudet p. 285

- Public Librarian Kim Hebig p. 310
- Clinical and Educational Audiologist Cassandra Grabowski p. 358
- University Professor Dr. Julie Corkett p. 380
- Special Education Teacher Cordell Osmond p. 408

SUPPLEMENTS

PEARSON
myeducationlab

Student Supplement

MyEducationLab Discover where the classroom comes to life! From video clips of teachers and students interacting to sample lessons and portfolio templates, MyEducationLab gives students the tools they will need to succeed in the classroom—with content easily integrated into existing courses. MyEducationLab gives students powerful insights into how real classrooms work and also gives them a rich array of tools that will support them on their journey from their first class to their first classroom.

Instructor Supplements

The fourth Canadian edition of *Teaching Students with Special Needs in Inclusive Settings* is accompanied by the following supplements, which all instructors will find helpful:

- The **Instructor's Manual** contains chapter overviews, discussion topics, handouts, and study guides.
- The **Test Item File** (in Microsoft Word format) consists of multiple choice, matching, short answer/short essay, and essay questions.
- There are approximately 30 to 50 **PowerPoint Slides** per chapter.
- Please note that all of these supplements are available online. They can be downloaded by instructors from a password-protected location on Pearson Education Canada's online catalogue (**vig.pearsoned.ca**). Simply search for the text, then click on "Instructor" under "Resources" in the left-hand menu. Contact your local sales representative for further information.

CourseSmart for Instructors

CourseSmart goes beyond traditional expectations, providing instant, online access to the textbooks and course materials you need at a lower cost for students. And even as students save money, you can save time and hassle with a digital eTextbook that allows you to search for the most relevant content at the very moment you need it. Whether it's evaluating textbooks or creating lecture notes to help students with difficult concepts, CourseSmart can make life a little easier. See how when you visit www.coursesmart.com/instructors.

CourseSmart for Students

CourseSmart goes beyond traditional expectations, providing instant, online access to the textbooks and course materials you need at an average savings of 60%. With instant access from any computer and the ability to search your text, you'll find the content you need quickly, no matter where you are. And with online tools like highlighting and note-taking, you can save time and study efficiently. See all the benefits at www.coursesmart.com/students.

ACKNOWLEDGMENTS

By the very nature of the Canadian special education situation, this book required the help and cooperation of every provincial and territorial Ministry of Education Special Education branch. We want to thank all those people who went out of their way to answer our questions and send us relevant materials. To all the individuals who shared their personal stories with us, we offer our most sincere appreciation and thanks.

We would like to thank the people who reviewed the previous edition or the manuscript for this edition and offered valuable suggestions:

Anna Bowles, University of Ottawa
Diane Galambos, Sheridan Institute of Advanced Learning & Technology
Thomas G. Ryan, Nipissing University
Angela Wilm, Lakeland College
Elsa Lo, Concordia University

We would also like to thank Pearson Education for the support provided to us during the completion of this project, particularly Duncan Mackinnon, David LeGallais, Rema Celio, Cheryl Noseworthy, and our copy editor, Sally Glover.

About the Authors

Tom E.C. Smith is currently Professor and Head of the Department of Curriculum and Instruction at the University of Arkansas. He has been on the faculties of the University of Arkansas at Little Rock, the University of Alabama at Birmingham, and the University of Arkansas for Medical Sciences. Prior to receiving his Ed.D. from Texas Tech University, Tom taught children with intellectual disabilities, learning disabilities, and autism at the elementary and secondary levels. President Clinton appointed him to three terms on the President's Committee on Mental Retardation. He has served as the Executive Director of the Division on Developmental Disabilities of the Council for Exceptional Children since 1996. Tom's current professional interests focus on legal issues and special education.

Edward A. Polloway is a Professor of Education and Human Development at Lynchburg College in Virginia, where he has taught since 1976. He also serves as Vice-President for Graduate Studies and Community Advancement. He received his doctoral degree from the University of Virginia and his undergraduate degree from Dickinson College in Pennsylvania. He has served twice as president of the Division on Developmental Disabilities of the Council for Exceptional Children and on the board of directors of the Council for Learning Disabilities. He also served on the committee that developed the 1992 definition of *mental retardation* for the American Association on Mental Retardation. He is the author of 12 books and 100 articles in the field of special education, with primary interests in the areas of learning disabilities and mental retardation.

James R. Patton is an Educational Consultant and Adjunct Associate Professor at the University of Texas at Austin. He received his Ed.D. from the University of Virginia, and is a former high school biology teacher and elementary-level special education resource teacher. He has taught students who were gifted and some who were gifted/learning disabled. James's professional interests include transition, life skills instruction, adult issues related to individuals with special needs, behavioural intervention planning, and classroom accommodations. He has served on national boards of the Division on Developmental Disabilities, the Council for Learning Disabilities, and the National Joint Committee on Learning Disabilities.

Carol A. Dowdy is Professor of Special Education at the University of Alabama at Birmingham, where she has taught since receiving her Ed.D. degree from the University of Alabama, Tuscaloosa. She was written eight books on special education and published 34 articles on learning disabilities. Carol has served on the national board of the Council for Learning Disabilities and the Professional Advisory Board for the Learning Disabilities Association of America, and she has worked closely with the federal department of Vocational Rehabilitation to assist in its efforts to better serve adults with learning disabilities.

Laureen J. McIntyre is an Associate Professor and Director of the Special Education Certificate program (an online teacher education program) in the Department of Educational Psychology and Special Education at the University of Saskatchewan. As an American- and Canadian-certified speech-language pathologist, Laureen worked in both community and school settings prior to completing her Ph.D. in Educational Psychology (specifically, Special Education) at the University of Alberta. Her research interests relate to how individuals with varied language and learning abilities are having their literacy needs met. Specific areas she explores related to this focus include: (1) how professionals' education, knowledge, and practice are impacting the language and learning abilities of individuals with exceptionalities; and (2) the development of language and literacy skills of individuals from diverse populations.

Chapter 1

Inclusive Education: An Introduction

Chapter Objectives

After reading this chapter, you should be able to

- describe the evolution of services for students with exceptionalities in Canada.

- describe some of the diversity evident in public schools as demonstrated by students with exceptionalities.

- describe the process for obtaining services for students with exceptionalities.

- discuss formal and informal assessment techniques.

- describe the role of the classroom teacher in assessment and in developing and using individualized education programs (IEPs).

Questions to Consider

1. How would Kevin's life have been different had he been born in the 1950s rather than in the 1980s?

2. Would a more inclusive placement during high school have had a positive or a negative impact on Kevin's future success?

3. What factors make inclusion successful for students with exceptionalities and for those without?

Kevin is 25 years old. He is intelligent, but has limited oral language skills and displays many characteristics expected of an adult with severe autism. When Kevin was three years old, he was diagnosed with autism. He was immediately enrolled in a preschool program for children with exceptionalities. At the age of six, Kevin transitioned to Kindergarten. He was in a self-contained special education classroom for children with severe exceptionalities from Kindergarten to Grade 2. Beginning in Grade 3, Kevin was included in a regular classroom for a small portion of each day. To the surprise of his parents and many teachers, he did better in his new placement than in the special education classroom. His behaviour, oral language skills, and general academic performance improved.

As a result of his success, Kevin's time in the inclusive setting was increased over the next several years until he was included for approximately 80 percent of the school day by Grade 6. Kevin continued to progress. However, when he went to junior high school, the amount of time Kevin spent in a special education setting increased; he was placed in some regular classes, mostly those with lower academic expectations. In high school, Kevin's placement in special education settings increased once again, primarily because of his difficulty with higher academic tasks. His individualized education program (IEP) focused on functional classes and pre-vocational activities.

Kevin completed his high school program at the age of 22 and began attending an adult day-service program. He recently moved to a group home for individuals with moderate to severe exceptionalities. Kevin's educational program provided him with many benefits. If he had been born 20 years earlier, he likely would not have had access to public education; in fact, his parents could have easily placed him in an institutional setting since there would have been no other programming options. Kevin would likely have benefited from being included in the regular classroom for a greater portion of the day in junior high and high school. However, his earlier inclusion helped improve his social skills and some of his basic academic abilities, which have assisted him in living semi-independently.

FURTHER READING

For a discussion of the issues of placement and programming in Canada as it relates to meeting the diverse needs of students with exceptionalities, review M.A. Williams and R.B. Macmillan's (2005) article "Litigation in special education: From placement to programming," in *Education Law Journal*, Volume 15 Issue 1, pp. 31–59.

Watch

Individuals with Disabilities Education Act (IDEA)

INTRODUCTION

As recently as the 1960s, many individuals with exceptionalities were separated from the general public, living and receiving their education in residential facilities. As people began to recognize the debilitating effects of institutionalization, the **normalization movement** emerged (Wolfensberger, 1972). Normalization proponents believed that all individuals, regardless of disability, should be provided with an education and a living arrangement as normal as possible. This conviction led to significant changes for individuals with special needs. People who had been institutionalized for years returned to their communities, and at the same time educational rights for individuals with special needs became a focus of the legal system.

In the United States, the *American Rehabilitation Act*, section 504 (1973), "guaranteed the rights of persons with handicaps in . . . educational institutions that receive federal moneys" (Stainback, Stainback, & Bunch, 1989). The *Education for All Handicapped Children Act* (PL 94–142) was passed by Congress in 1975, requiring each state to educate children with exceptionalities. This Act was re-authorized in 1990 under the title *Individuals with Disabilities Education Act* (IDEA). It states:

> *To the maximum extent appropriate, children with disabilities . . . are educated with children who are not disabled, and that special classes, separate schooling, or other*

removal of children with disabilities from the regular environment occurs only when the nature or severity of the disability is such that education in regular classes with the use of supplementary aids and services cannot be attained satisfactorily.

In Canada, the movement toward inclusion developed somewhat differently and progressed more slowly. Each province or territory has its own education act or school act governing education in schools within its jurisdiction, including special education services. A recent comparison of literature relating to disability legislation found that the U.S. has accumulated three times as much literature relating to trends and best practices in positive outcomes for individuals with exceptionalities as Canada over the past two decades (Kovacs-Burns & Gordon, 2010). This is not surprising, given that, unlike the U.S., Canada does not have federal legislation specific to education and disabilities. However, with Canada's adoption in 1982 of the *Constitution Act*, which includes the **Canadian Charter of Rights and Freedoms**—guaranteeing the rights of all individuals with exceptionalities—Canada became the first country in the world to enshrine the rights of people with exceptionalities in a constitution. The Charter of Rights and Freedoms, which came into effect in 1985, states in section 15.(1) that

> *Every individual is equal before and under the law and has the right to equal protection of the law without discrimination based on race, national or ethnic origin, colour, religion, sex, age, or mental or physical disability.*

Educational policy at every level (provincial or territorial and board or district) must abide by the Charter. Every province and territory has established its own policy documents, but all have moved steadily toward inclusion of students with special needs (Dworet & Bennett, 2002). Canadian proponents of inclusive education believe that students with exceptionalities, regardless of severity, should be included in the regular classroom (O'Brien, Snow, Forest, & Hasbury, 1989). They argue that educators are responsible for adapting the regular classroom to meet these students' needs. The provinces and territories adhere to the inclusive model to varying degrees, but all are committed to the principle of inclusion. As a teacher, you will need to learn the current special education guidelines and terminology for your own province or territory.

DEVELOPMENT OF SPECIAL SERVICES

Prior to the 1970s and the normalization movement, students with physical or intellectual disabilities were provided with services, albeit nearly always in self-contained, isolated classrooms. These students rarely interacted with their typically achieving peers, and their teachers did not routinely come into contact with other teachers in the school. In addition to being isolating for the students, the existing programs were small, and few students were served. Beyond such public school programs, children received services in **residential programs**. Typically, children with intellectual disabilities and sensory deficits were placed in these settings. These residential programs offered daily living supports as well as some education and training. In 1970, a report by Roberts and Lazure entitled "One Million Children: A National Study of Canadian Children with Emotional and Learning Disorders" called for integration and instruction based on learning characteristics, not categories. This landmark report, combined with Wolfensberger's work at the National

CONSIDER THIS

In Canada, education falls under provincial and territorial jurisdiction. What are the advantages and disadvantages of this system?

CONSIDER THIS

All children, even those with very different learning needs, have access to free educational services in Canadian public schools. How can these educational needs best be supported? Can this be accomplished in a fiscally responsible manner?

Figure 1.1 Historical Changes in Education for Students with Exceptionalities

From "Historic Changes in Mental Retardation and Developmental Disabilities," by E.A. Polloway, J.D. Smith, J.R. Patton, and T.E.C. Smith, 1996, *Education and Training in Mental Retardation and Developmental Disabilities, 31,* p. 9. Used by permission.

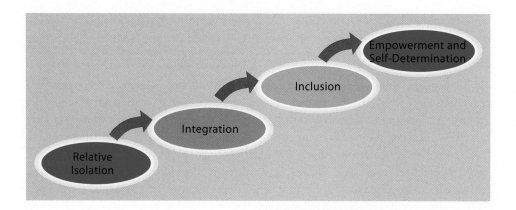

Institute of Mental Retardation in Toronto (Wolfensberger, 1972), which emphasized the importance of a normal environment for all individuals, contributed to changes in education in Canada in the 1970s.

Since the mid-1970s, services to students with exceptionalities have changed dramatically. Not only are more appropriate services provided by schools, they are also frequently provided in both resource rooms and in general or regular education classrooms through collaboration between special education and classroom teachers. Services for students with exceptionalities evolved in three distinct phases: (1) **relative isolation**, (2) **integration** (or **mainstreaming**), and (3) **inclusion**. In the relative isolation phase, students were either denied access to public schools or were permitted to attend in isolated settings. In the integration phase, which began in the 1970s, students with exceptionalities were mainstreamed, or integrated, into general education programs when they were considered ready to handle the general education program. Finally, the inclusion phase, introduced in the early 1980s, emphasized that students with exceptionalities should be fully included in school programs and activities. This phase differed from the integration phase in a small, but very significant, way.

While both integration and inclusion resulted in students with exceptionalities joining general classrooms, inclusion assumes that these students *belong* in general classrooms—in the integration phase, they were considered to be special education students who were placed in the general classroom part of the time. The importance of empowerment and self-determination for students with exceptionalities has been a focus of inclusion efforts in order to better prepare them for the highest degree of independence possible (Polloway, Smith, Patton, & Smith, 1996). Figure 1.1 depicts the historical changes in the education of students with exceptionalities in public education.

All children are eligible for public education in Canada; therefore, teachers in today's public schools must provide instruction and other educational services to meet the needs of a diverse student population. Teachers must develop ways to serve students with exceptionalities in general education environments. Traditionally, teacher education programs for classroom teachers have focused on teaching students who do not have learning or behaviour problems. However, today's teachers must be prepared to teach students with a variety of needs. Providing an appropriate education for a diverse group of students, including students with exceptionalities, is definitely challenging; however, it can also be exciting and highly rewarding.

STUDENTS WITH SPECIAL NEEDS

Many students do not fit the mould of the "typical" student. Those with identified exceptionalities, those who are classified as gifted and/or talented, and those who are "at risk" of developing learning and behavioural problems are among these "atypical" students.

It has been estimated that approximately 10 percent of school-age children in Canada have a recognized exceptionality. Another undetermined number experience learning and behaviour problems but have not been classified as having a disability. Still another group of students requiring special attention are those at risk of developing learning and behavioural problems. This group may include potential dropouts, students from minority cultures, students who are learning to speak English, students from low-income homes, students who abuse drugs or alcohol, students who become pregnant, and/or students from single-parent homes (Willms, 2002).

Such students, plus those who obviously need assistance but do not fit into any distinct group, comprise about half the population of public schools. Although many do not fit into the specific classification of "disabled"—and are therefore ineligible for special education services—school personnel cannot afford to ignore these students' special challenges.

Diversity among students in public schools represents the "norm" rather than the exception. If our public schools are to be effective, school personnel must address students' varying needs, identify students with learning and behavioural issues, and develop and implement appropriate educational programs for them. A first step for classroom

◄●─ **Simulate**

What Do You See?

Inclusion Strategies

Using "People First" Language

One of the results of the inclusion movement has been a change in the way individuals with exceptionalities are labelled. "People first" language communicates that having an exceptionality is only part of a person. It does not define the individual. The following list provides examples of "people first" language:

Say	Do Not Say
Person with a disability	The disabled person
Children with autism	Autistic children
Classroom for students with intellectual disorders	The mentally retarded classroom
Students with visual impairments	Blind students
Bus for students with disabilities	Special education bus
Individuals with disabilities	Disabled individuals
Disability or disabled	Handicap or handicapped
The boy with cerebral palsy	The crippled boy
The girl with a hearing impairment	The deaf girl
The student with a learning disability	The learning disabled student

teachers is to understand the types of student diversity they will encounter. See the Inclusion Strategies feature on using "people first" language for examples of how the labelling of individuals with exceptionalities has changed.

Students with Exceptionalities

👁️ **Watch**

Diverse Learners

One of the largest groups of students in the public school system with diverse learning and behavioural needs, and also the most visible, consists of students who have been formally classified as having **exceptionalities**.

The term *exceptional* describes individuals with diverse needs who differ from their typically achieving peers in some manner. Individuals with exceptionalities range from people with gifts and/or talents to people experiencing significant deficits in a variety of areas (i.e., academic deficits, physical impairments). Although the term *exceptionality* is used to describe individuals' areas of need, it also allows for the discussion of an individual's abilities. The term *disability* is more restrictive. A disability can be defined as "an inability to do something, a diminished capacity to perform in a specific way" (Hallahan & Kauffman, 2006, p. 7). *Disability* is frequently used when referring to specific categories of exceptionality (e.g., learning disability). Whenever possible we will use the term *exceptionality* rather than *disability* to emphasize that individuals with exceptionalities have areas of strength in addition to their identified areas of need.

Students with exceptionalities are defined differently in different provinces and territories. For example, the Ontario Ministry of Education defines an exceptional pupil as one "whose behavioural, communicational, intellectual, physical or multiple exceptionalities are such that he or she is considered to need placement in a special education program by a committee" (2001, p. A3). The British Columbia Ministry of Education defines students with special needs as those who "have difficulties of an intellectual, physical, sensory, emotional or behavioural nature, or have a learning disability or have exceptional gifts or talents" (2002). In Prince Edward Island, students needing special education services are described as "those students within the public school system whose educational needs require interventions different from, or in addition to, those which are needed by most students" (Prince Edward Island Education, 2001). In Saskatchewan, students are defined as having exceptional needs if they have been identified as having "physical, intellectual and learning disabilities, sensory impairments, social, emotional or behavioural challenges, and language delays and disorders" (Saskatchewan Learning, 2000). Similar definitions are found across the country and share the characteristic listing of exceptionalities and frequently the statement that the student needs special services.

One other approach to defining students with exceptionalities exists in some provincial and territorial education documents—namely, the absence of a definition! For example, in the *Education Act* (1995) of the Northwest Territories, no mention is made of what constitutes exceptionality. Instead, the Act focuses on the rights of all students to an inclusive education and support services to meet individual needs. However, even where provincial or territorial guidelines are not provided for identifying exceptionalities, practice at the school level often involves assessment for exceptionalities. Specific categories of exceptionality vary marginally in different jurisdictions, but the majority include the following categories:

- learning disabilities
- speech and/or language disorders

- intellectual disabilities
- emotional/behavioural disorders
- multiple disabilities
- auditory impairments
- orthopedic impairments
- other health impairments
- visual impairments
- autism spectrum disorders (ASD)
- fetal alcohol spectrum disorders (FASD)
- traumatic brain injury (TBI)

CONSIDER THIS

What characteristics do students with exceptionalities share with students from racial or cultural minorities? Are educational services offered to both groups of students in a similar fashion?

Many different types of students are found within these 12 categories. For example, the broad area of "other health impairments" includes students with cardiac problems, asthma, mental health disorders, and sickle cell anemia. Even the category of "learning disabilities" comprises an extremely heterogeneous group of students.

The fact that categories of exceptionality are composed of different types of students makes simple conclusions about them impossible. Students who need special assistance do not all fit neatly into categories of exceptionality. It is often difficult to know into which category a child would best fit. Consider a child with an attention-deficit disorder who has poor academic skills despite high intelligence, and often behaves disruptively. This child could be categorized by many provincial and territorial guidelines as having either a behavioural disorder or a learning disability—no jurisdiction has an attention-deficit disorder category.

The majority of students with exceptionalities experience mild disabilities and spend their school days in general education classrooms. A smaller number of students with more severe disabilities were more typically educated in segregated special education environments in the past. Today, however, students with more severe disabilities are frequently included in general education classrooms for part—or even all—of the time. The following section provides a brief overview of each of the major categories of exceptionality recognized in most schools.

Intellectual Disability The category of exceptionality that has been recognized for the longest time in most school districts is **intellectual disability** (Crane, 2002). Students with intellectual disabilities are usually identified through intelligence tests and measures of adaptive behaviour, which look at a person's ability to perform functional activities expected of age and cultural norms. By definition, such students score less than 70–75 on individual intelligence tests and have concurrent deficits in adaptive behaviour (American Association on Mental Retardation, 2002). Their general characteristics include problems in learning, memory, problem solving, adaptive behaviour, and social skills (Taylor, Richards, & Brady, 2005).

CROSS REFERENCE

For more information on specific exceptionalities, see chapters 3–11.

Learning Disabilities The category of exceptionality that accounts for more than 50 percent of all students served by special education is learning disabilities. This category is beset with problems of definition and programming, but continues to include more children than all other special education categories combined (Lyon et al., 2001; Smith, Dowdy, Polloway, & Blalock, 1997). In general, students with learning disabilities do not achieve commensurate with their abilities. According to the Learning Disabilities Association of Canada (LDAC), "Learning Disabilities are due to genetic and/or neurological factors or injury that alters brain functioning in a manner which affects one or more processes related to learning" (LDAC, 2002).

Emotional/Behavioural Disorders Students with emotional and behavioural disorders cause disruptions for themselves or others in their environment through inappropriate behaviours or expressions of emotion. Professionals serving children with these problems differ in their definitions of the problems and in the types of services they provide (Coleman & Webber, 2002). Partly due to the complexity of definition and the lack of agreement regarding appropriate intervention, students presenting behavioural challenges are frequently underserved.

Sensory Problems Some students have problems with sensory skills—their visual or auditory abilities. The majority of information provided by teachers is presented orally or visually; therefore, deficits in these areas can result in significant challenges. Visual impairment includes two subcategories: blindness and low vision. The category of auditory impairment covers both students who are deaf and students who are hard of hearing.

Orthopedic Impairments Many students experience problems related to their physical abilities. Cerebral palsy, spina bifida, amputations, and muscular dystrophy are a few examples. For these students, physical access to educational facilities and accommodation of problems with writing and manipulation are important concerns.

Other Health Impairments This category of exceptionality includes a wide variety of problems, including cardiac problems, acquired immune deficiency syndrome (AIDS), diabetes, epilepsy, and asthma. In some provinces, students with mental health conditions are also included in this category. For students with these exceptionalities, medical needs take precedence. School personnel must work closely with medical and other professionals to provide appropriate services.

CROSS REFERENCE

Information about autism can be found in chapter 8, which focuses on autism spectrum disorders and fetal alcohol spectrum disorders.

Autism Spectrum Disorders Autism is a lifelong disability that primarily affects communication and social interactions. Children with autism typically relate to people, objects, and events in abnormal ways; they insist on structured environments and display many self-stimulating behaviours (Tryon, Mayes, Rhodes, & Waldo, 2006). Autism spectrum disorders are not recognized as a separate category by most provinces and territories.

Traumatic Brain Injury Traumatic brain injury (TBI) was defined by Savage (1988) as an insult to the brain that often results in impaired cognitive, physical, or emotional functioning. Students with TBI are typically served under the category of exceptionality that relates to their functional limitations (e.g., intellectual disability for cognitive deficits or learning disabilities for erratic academic performance).

CONSIDER THIS

Why should students with severe exceptionalities not be served in institutional or segregated settings? Should some children be placed in such settings? Why or why not?

Fetal Alcohol Spectrum Disorders Fetal alcohol spectrum disorder is "an umbrella term [not a diagnostic term] used to refer to the damage or range of disabilities caused by alcohol consumption during pregnancy" (Saskatchewan Learning, 2004, p. 1.3). Fetal alcohol syndrome (FAS), partial fetal alcohol syndrome (pFAS), alcohol-related birth defects (ARBD), and alcohol-related neurodevelopmental disorder (ARND) are all disorders that may be included under this umbrella term (Saskatchewan Learning, 2004). Students with fetal alcohol spectrum disorders (FASD) are typically served under the category of exceptionality that relates to their functional limitations (e.g., intellectual disability for cognitive deficits or learning disabilities for erratic academic performance).

Speech and Language Disorders For some children, speech difficulties are a serious problem. Children with speech or language disorders are considered eligible for services under most provincial and territorial jurisdictions. Teachers must work closely with speech-language pathologists when dealing with this group of students. As language disorders are associated with many exceptionalities, including intellectual disabilities, emotional or behavioural disorders, learning disabilities, autism spectrum disorders, TBI, and fetal alcohol spectrum disorders, students with exceptionalities and their teachers frequently need support from a speech-language pathologist.

Students Classified as Gifted and/or Talented Some students differ from their peers by having above-average intelligence, learning abilities, and/or talents. These students, classified as gifted and/or talented, were traditionally defined and identified using intelligence quotient test scores (IQ scores). An IQ score of 120 or higher was the primary criterion for identifying a gifted and talented student. Current criteria are much broader. Although definitions vary, most focus on students who are capable of making significant contributions to society in a variety of areas that span academic endeavours, creativity, mechanical skills, motor skills, and skills in the fine arts.

Students at Risk of School Problems

Some students, who neither fit into a specific category of exceptionality nor have an above-average capacity to achieve academically, also experience difficulty achieving success at school. These students, classified as being at risk, manifest characteristics that could easily lead to learning and behaviour problems (Barr & Parrett, 2001). Those considered at risk include:

- students who are abused or neglected
- students who abuse drugs and alcohol
- students from minority cultures
- students living in poverty
- students who become pregnant
- students who speak English as a second language
- students who are in trouble with the justice system

CONSIDER THIS

Should students who are considered at risk of developing learning and behaviour problems be provided with special services? Why or why not?

These students may present unique problems for teachers, who must meet their educational needs in general education classrooms. For example, the number of students in our classrooms who are linguistically different (i.e., students who speak English as a second language or who have limited English proficiency) is on the rise. The Diversity Forum feature on the following page provides some suggestions for using collaboration to more effectively meet the needs of linguistically diverse students.

Students who are *at risk* need support to build **resiliency**. Educational programs must be modified to meet such needs since schools can be a necessary protective factor for vulnerable students.

OBTAINING SERVICES FOR STUDENTS WITH SPECIAL NEEDS

The majority of students who receive special education services are first identified by a regular classroom teacher. It is usually at the elementary level that a teacher initiates the process that will result in a student's receiving special education services. This process may involve a number of different school personnel depending on the situation and the specific school, as well as on the province or territory. Typically, a school team becomes involved. This team, referred to by different names, generally includes the regular classroom teacher, special education personnel (resource teacher, special education board or district consultant, school psychologist or guidance counsellor), the principal, and specific

Diversity Forum

Planning as a Team, Learning Together

Dinora is a seven-year-old student in Ms. Brown's Grade 2 classroom. Dinora's family moved from Mexico to Canada a year ago. Dinora continues to work on improving her English language skills and has recently been identified as having a learning disability. She began receiving reading instruction in Ms. Emerson's special education resource classroom earlier this month. Her IEP goals include letter recognition, recognizing letter–sound relationships, blending letter sounds, sight-word vocabulary development, and reading comprehension. Ms. Emerson does not speak Spanish; therefore, all instruction is provided in English. Given Ms. Emerson's limited experience with teaching English language learners (ELLs), Ms. Brown is concerned that Dinora will not benefit from her special education reading instruction.

This scenario documents the challenges of providing appropriate special education services for English language learners (ELLs) with exceptionalities when special educators are monolingual. Often, teachers are inadequately prepared to modify instruction to address the cultural and linguistic needs of their students. When used with ELLs with exceptionalities, special education interventions must provide appropriate language supports so that instruction is comprehensible (García & Dray, 2007; Santamaría, Fletcher, & Bos, 2002). Dinora's teachers understand the importance of collaboration, and they meet regularly to plan together (Delgado, 2006). As a result, they are able to learn from each other's expertise in working with ELLs with exceptionalities like Dinora. Ms. Emerson has spent time in Ms. Brown's class to model instructional adaptations that could support Dinora's reading during social studies, math,

and science. In turn, Ms. Brown has shared her knowledge of English as a second language (ESL) instruction and has suggested ways that Ms. Emerson could respond to Dinora's English proficiency level and simultaneously support her reading achievement in English. Through the assistance of an interpreter, both teachers have combined their efforts in communicating Dinora's progress to her mother. Through these facilitated conversations, Dinora's mother is able to actively participate in the decision-making process about the services her child should receive in school.

Questions

1. What factors contributed to successful collaboration between these two teachers?

2. In what other ways could general and special education teachers collaborate to increase Dinora's participation in the general education classroom during reading instruction?

3. What are other possibilities for collaboration between Dinora's teachers and the student's family?

References

García, S.B., & Dray, B. (2007). "Bilingualism and special education." In F. E. Obiakor (Ed.), *Multicultural special education* (pp. 18–33). Columbus, OH: Merrill.

Delgado, R. (2006). *Teachers' instructional practices when working with Latino English language learners with reading-related disabilities.* Unpublished doctoral dissertation, The University of Texas at Austin.

Santamaría, L.J., Fletcher, T.V., & Bos, C.S. (2002). "Effective pedagogy for English language learners in inclusive classrooms." In A.J. Artiles & A.A. Ortiz (Eds.), *English language learners with special education needs: Identification, assessment, and instruction* (pp. 133–157). Washington, DC: Center for Applied Linguistics and Delta Systems.

Figure 1.2 Steps from Pre-referral to IEP and Checklists of the Teacher's Responsibilities

From D.P. Hallahan, J.M. Kauffman & J.W. Lloyd. *Introduction to Learning Disabilities,* Second Edition, © 1999. Published by Allyn & Bacon, Boston, MA. Copyright © 1999 by Pearson Education. Reprinted by permission of the publisher.

STEPS LEADING TO THE IEP

1. A teacher notices that a student is having serious academic or behavioural difficulty.

2. The teacher consults the student's parents and tries the instructional or behaviour management strategies she or he believes will resolve the problem.

3. If the problem is not resolved, the teacher asks for the help of the school team.

4. With the help of the team, the teacher implements and documents the results of strategies designed to resolve the problem.

5. If the problem is not resolved after reasonable implementation of the team's suggestions, the teacher makes a referral for evaluation by the school psychologist.

6. The school psychologist evaluates the student.

7. With the results of the evaluation components in hand, the school team determines whether the student is eligible for special education.

8. If the student is found eligible, then an IEP must be written.

WHAT SHOULD I DO BEFORE MAKING A REFERRAL?

☑ Hold at least one conference to discuss your concerns with the parents (or make extensive and documented efforts to communicate with the parents).

☑ Check all available school records, and interview other professionals involved with the student to make sure you understand the student's history and efforts to help that have already been made.

☑ Ask the school team—or the principal, the school psychologist, and at least one other teacher who knows the student—to help you devise strategies to solve the problem.

☑ Implement and document the results of the academic and behaviour management strategies you have tried.

WHAT INFORMATION SHOULD I BE ABLE TO PROVIDE AT THE TIME OF REFERRAL?

☑ a statement of exactly what you are concerned about

☑ an explanation of why you are concerned

☑ detailed records from your observations of the problem, including samples of academic work

☑ records documenting the strategies you have used to try to resolve the problem and the outcomes of those strategies

medical or social service personnel, depending on the nature of the student's difficulty. While all of these individuals take part in the formal identification of the student, the process of obtaining services almost always begins with just the teacher. Ideally, this process should adhere to the steps outlined in Figure 1.2.

A variety of assessments are completed during the process of obtaining special services for a student.

ASSESSMENT PRACTICES

Assessment is the process of gathering relevant information to use in making decisions about students (Salvia & Ysseldyke, 2004). It is a dynamic, continuous process that guides and directs planning for students with suspected or known disabilities. Teachers play four

CONSIDER THIS

How can schools deal with the financial impact of special services for students with exceptionalities? Is there a limit to how much should be spent on a single child? This varies from province to province. Should it be the same across the country?

major roles in regard to school-based assessment and, as a result, need to have skills in all four areas:

1. Teachers are *consumers* of assessment information. In this role, they must be able to understand assessment information.

2. Teachers are *producers* of assessment information. They must be able to generate assessment information by administering tests, conducting observations, and so on.

3. Teachers are *communicators* of assessment information. They must be able to share assessment information with other team members (e.g., professionals, parents, and students).

4. Teachers are *developers* of assessment instruments. Most teachers will find that they have to create assessment techniques to accomplish some education-related tasks.

This information-gathering process should focus primarily on identifying the strengths of children considered *at risk*; appropriate adaptations can then be designed to facilitate student success in the inclusive environment of a general education classroom. Later, assessment will measure the success of instructional and behavioural interventions implemented in the general education classroom. Assessment can pinpoint problems that should be addressed; it does not necessarily lead to special education placement.

Purpose of Assessment

Watch

Assessment of Students with Special Needs

Assessment is critical in each of the major phases of the planning process. During the *screening* phase, including the steps of pre-referral and referral, the concerns expressed by teachers and parents are the result of their informal assessment of the student's lack of progress. Their concern comes from their observations and interactions with the student in the natural environment. When parents and teachers become concerned, they may consult others who have worked with the child and review previous records or current work. At this point these students are at risk for failure, and the first level of assessment for special education services has begun.

When a referral is made, the identification and *eligibility* phase of assessment begins. During this phase the child is formally evaluated to determine if he or she has an exceptionality and which special education services would be most appropriate. The student's intellectual ability, strengths, and needs are evaluated individually by trained professionals. These results are shared with the IEP team.

Assessment data are needed for *program planning*. Existing data are studied further, and new data may be collected to help the IEP team select goals and objectives or benchmarks, as well as identify the most effective methods of instruction to include in the IEP. After the IEP has been implemented, assessment is conducted to *monitor* and *evaluate* the student's progress.

Approaches to Assessment

Salvia and Ysseldyke (2004) identified four approaches used to gather information on students: (1) observation, (2) recollection (by means of interview or rating scale), (3) record or portfolio review, and (4) testing. Data collected through naturalistic *observation* can be highly accurate and can provide detailed, relevant information on how the student performs in the natural environment. The observer may be systematically looking for one or more specific behaviours, such as inattention or inappropriate comments. In this approach, the frequency, duration, and intensity of the behaviour(s) are usually recorded for study. The student's behaviour can then be compared to normal standards of his or her peers or to the individual's previous behaviour. Another method of collecting observational data is more anecdotal, in which the observer records any behaviour that seems significant. This type of data may be more subjective than the systematic recordings and is harder to validate. Observational data may also be collected using audio or video recordings.

In data collection involving *recollection*, individuals familiar with the student are asked to recall events and interpret behaviours. The most commonly used methods are interviews or ratings scales that can be obtained from students through self-report or from peers, family members, teachers, counsellors, or others. Through interviews, parents' concerns and preferences can be determined. Reactions to questions can be observed and, when appropriate, questions can be explored more thoroughly, since interviews are generally held in person. *Rating scales* offer a structured method of data collection that involves asking the rater to respond to a statement by indicating the degree to which an item describes an individual. When using rating-scale data, care should be taken to confirm the rater's ability to understand the scale and determine the possibility of bias in reporting.

Another important component of assessment is record or *portfolio review*. Existing information, such as school cumulative records, databases, anecdotal records, nonschool records, or student products (often found in a student's portfolio), should be reviewed carefully for insight into the student's needs and strengths. Usually, a school will consider the same kinds of records for each child being considered, to maintain consistency.

The most common method of gathering information is through student testing. **Testing**, whether formal or informal, is the process of presenting challenges or problems and measuring students' competency, attitude, or behaviours by evaluating their responses (Ysseldyke & Olsen, 1999).

Formal Assessment

Formal assessment instruments are generally available commercially. They typically contain detailed guidelines for administration, scoring, and interpretation, as well as statistical data regarding **validity**, reliability, and standardization procedures. They are most often **norm-referenced**; that is, the tests provide quantitative information comparing the performance of an individual student to others in his or her norm group (determined, for example, by age, grade, or gender). Test results are usually reported in the form of test quotients, percentiles, and age or grade equivalents. These tools are most useful early in an assessment procedure, when relatively little is known of a student's strengths and areas of need, and thus they may help identify areas in which informal assessment can begin. The ability to compare the student to his or her age and grade peers is also an advantage in making eligibility and placement decisions and fulfilling related administrative requirements. Table 1.1 is a useful assessment resource that shows the relationship across various types of scores obtained through standardized testing.

Professionals can make more informed decisions about the use of formal instruments if they study the instrument and become familiar with its features, benefits, and possible liabilities. One way to do this is to consult one or more resources on tests, such as the *Mental Measurements Yearbook* (Buros Institute at the University of Nebraska, n.d.).

◀●▬Simulate

Accountability

CONSIDER THIS

Test scores often confuse parents and cause great concern. The information in Table 1.1 will help you more accurately convey students' scores to parents and help them understand the meaning of those scores. Notice that the 50th percentile rank is in the nondeficit range. An indication of a mild disability begins with a score at the 16th percentile, and a moderate deficit begins with a score at the 5th percentile.

Table 1.1 Relation of Various Standard Scores to Percentile Rank and to Each Other

Percentile Rank	Standard Scores					
	Quotients	NCE Scores	T-scores	Z-scores	Stanines	Deficit
99	150	99	83	+3.33	9	
99	145	99	80	+3.00	9	
99	140	99	77	+2.67	9	
99	135	99	73	+2.33	9	
98	130	92	70	+2.00	9	
95	125	85	67	+1.67	8	
91	120	78	63	+1.34	8	none
84	115	71	60	+1.00	7	
75	110	64	57	+0.67	6	
63	105	57	53	+0.33	6	
50	100	50	50	+0.00	5	
37	95	43	47	−0.33	4	
25	90	36	43	−0.67	4	
16	85	29	40	−1.00	3	
9	80	22	37	−1.34	2	mild
5	75	15	33	−1.67	2	
2	70	8	30	−2.00	1	moderate
1	65	1	27	−2.33	1	
1	60	1	23	−2.67	1	severe
1	55	1	20	−3.00	1	

From "The Role of Standardized Tests in Planning Academic Instruction," by D.D. Hammill and B.R. Bryant, 1991. *Handbook on the Assessment of Learning Disabilities*, edited by H. L. Swanson (p. 377). Austin, TX: Pro-Ed. Copyright 1991 by Pro-Ed, Inc. Used by permission.

Although formal testing provides quantitative and sometimes qualitative data based on student performance, tests can obtain a measure of a student's best performance only in a contrived situation; they cannot broadly represent a student's typical performance under natural conditions. When considered in isolation, the results of formal tests can also result in lost data that can lead to poor decisions regarding placement and instructional planning. Rigid administration and interpretation of test results can obscure, rather than reveal, a student's strengths and areas of need. It has become increasingly apparent that traditional, formal approaches must be augmented with assessment techniques that more accurately represent a student's typical skills.

Informal Assessment

Informal tests and measurements are usually more loosely structured than formal instruments and are more closely tied to teaching. Tools such as these are typically devised by teachers to determine what skills or knowledge a child possesses. The key advantage of informal tests and measurements is the direct application of assessment data to instructional programs. By incorporating assessment results into the teaching program and monitoring student responses each day, teachers can more accurately assess changes in learning or behaviour.

Criterion-referenced assessment compares a student's performance with a criterion of mastery for a specific task, disregarding his or her relative standing in a group. Because the acquisition of skills can be clearly demonstrated with this type of informal assessment, it can be especially useful when documentation of progress is needed for accountability. As Taylor (2000) stresses, criterion-based assessments are quite popular because they focus attention on specific skills in the curriculum, provide measures of progress toward mastery, and assist teachers in designing instructional strategies. Traditionally, most criterion-referenced assessments have been produced by teachers, but recently, publishers have begun to produce assessment tools of this type.

One important and popular form of criterion-referenced assessment is **curriculum-based assessment**. Unlike norm-referenced tools, curriculum-based assessment uses the actual curriculum as the standard and thus provides a basis for evaluating and modifying the curriculum for an individual student (McLoughlin & Lewis, 2000). This type of assessment can have a role in many important tasks: identification, eligibility, instructional grouping, program planning, progress monitoring, and program evaluation. Curriculum-based assessment can focus attention on changes in academic behaviour within the context of the curriculum being used, thus enhancing the relationship between assessment and teaching (McMillan, Hellsten, & Klinger, 2011).

Curriculum-based measures can be developed through systematic analysis of a given curriculum, selection of specific items, and construction of assessment formats (e.g., questions, *cloze*—i.e., fill-in-the-blank—activities, and worksheets). Although manuals and other resources for developing curriculum-based instruments exist, they serve primarily as guides. Instruments used in the classroom should reflect the curriculum being followed there.

Alternative assessment procedures have emerged as dissatisfaction with group-administered standardized tests has increased. Two terms commonly used to describe these procedures are **authentic assessment** and portfolio assessment. These assessment methods use similar techniques, such as requiring students to construct, produce, perform, or demonstrate a task. These tasks are considered alternatives to typical testing, such as selecting from multiple-choice items, a technique commonly used on standardized, formal tests. An example of an authentic assessment would be assigning a student the task of asking for help from an individual whom he or she does not know. The individual being asked would be trained to evaluate the quality of the interaction and recommend the supports or accommodations that a student might need to improve the interaction (Ysseldyke & Olsen, 1999).

Ecological Assessment

Ecological assessment is another approach used with many types of informal assessment. As educational assessment has increasingly begun to reflect a trend toward appreciating the ecology of the student, data obtained are now more frequently analyzed in relation to the child's functioning in his or her various environments. Although a full discussion of ecological assessment is beyond the scope of this chapter, the following information

◄⊙│**Simulate**

Classroom Assessment

TEACHING TIP

When entering a new school system, ask the principal or a fellow teacher to describe the assessment instruments typically used. If curriculum-based assessments have not been developed, organize a grade-level team to begin this important process.

Curriculum-based assessment can focus attention on changes in a student's academic behaviour.

highlights some basic considerations, and the Inclusion Strategies feature on page 17 provides an example of a classroom ecological inventory.

The focus of ecological assessment is to set the evaluation process within the context of the student's environment. Its central element is functionality—how well the student functions in the current environment or the one into which he or she will be moving. This focus shifts a program's emphasis toward determining how to build on strengths and interests.

An emphasis on ecological assessment necessarily broadens the assessment process and offers professionals a way of validating findings. The following questions can help teachers better understand the child and why he or she is having difficulty succeeding in school. Answers should help educators develop a positive learning environment and identify specific strategies to reduce negative impacts on learning.

- In what physical environment does the child learn best?
- What is useful, debilitating, or neutral about the way the child approaches the task?
- Can the student hold multiple pieces of information in memory and then act upon them?
- How does increasing or slowing the speed of instruction affect the accuracy of a child's work?
- What processing mechanisms are being taxed in any given task?
- How does this student interact with a certain teaching style?
- With which professional has the child been most successful? What characteristics of that person seem to contribute to the child's success?
- What is encouraging to the child? What is discouraging?
- How does manipulating the mode of teaching (e.g., visual or auditory presentation) affect the child's performance? (Waterman, 1994, pp. 9–10)

Issues of Bias in Assessment

The importance of ensuring fair and equitable assessment procedures cannot be underestimated. The number of K–12 students from diverse cultures is expected to increase. This trend will present one of the greatest challenges for special educators—accurately assessing culturally and linguistically diverse students for disabilities (Council for Exceptional Children, 1997). Some norm-referenced standardized tests may be inherently discriminatory not only toward students from diverse cultural or linguistic backgrounds but also toward students from disadvantaged socio-economic groups. Teachers and other school personnel must be extremely cautious when interpreting standardized test scores for their students, since these scores may not reflect an accurate estimate of a student's abilities.

Many sources of possible bias can be found in the assessment process, ranging from administrative practices, such as proximity to student and physical contact, to gender of tester and testee, cultural and ethnic prejudice, and linguistic variance. This kind of information should be used when assessing all individuals whose differences might lead to test bias.

Of special concern is the accurate assessment of individuals who experience sensory or motor disabilities. For example, individuals who have hearing impairments may require a nonverbal test, whereas persons who have visual impairments require measures that do

Classroom Ecological Inventory

Special Education Teacher _____   Grade _____ Date _____

General Education Teacher _____   Number of Students in General Class _____

Student _____

PART 1: CLASSROOM OBSERVATION

Physical Environment

Directions: Please circle or provide the appropriate answer.

1. Is there an area for small groups?   Yes   No
2. Are partitions used in the room?   Yes   No
3. Is there a computer in the classroom?   Yes   No
4. Where is the student's desk located? (for example, front of room, back, middle, away from other students, etc.)
_____

Teacher/Student Behaviour

Directions for #1–#4: Please circle the appropriate answer.

1. How much movement or activity is tolerated by the teacher?   Much   Average   Little   Unclear
2. How much talking among students is tolerated?   Much   Average   Little   Unclear
3. Does the teacher use praise?   Much   Average   Little   Unclear
4. Was subject taught to the entire group or to small groups?   Entire   Small

Directions for #5–#7: Please provide an appropriate answer.

5. During the observation, where did the teacher spend most of the time? (for example, at the board, at teacher's desk, at student's desk) _____

6. What teaching methods did you observe while in the classroom? (for example, teacher modelled the lesson, asked students to work at board, helped small groups, helped individual students) _____
_____

7. How did the teacher interact with students who appeared to be low achieving or slower than their classmates? (for example, helped them individually, talked to them in the large group) _____
_____

Posted Classroom Rules

If classroom rules are posted, what are they?

Special Education   **General Education**

_____   _____

_____   _____

_____   _____

Is there any other pertinent information you observed about this classroom that would be helpful in reintegrating the student? (for example, crowded classroom)

_____

_____

(continued)

PART 2: TEACHER INTERVIEW

Classroom Rules	**Special Ed**	**General Ed**
1. During class are there important rules? (Yes or No)	_____	_____
2. If yes, how are they communicated? (for example, written or oral)	_____	_____
3. If class rules are *not* posted, what are they?	_____	_____
4. If a rule is broken, what happens? What is the typical consequence?	_____	_____
5. Who enforces the rules? (teacher, aide, students)	_____	_____

Teacher Behaviour

	Special Ed	**General Ed**
1. a. Is homework assigned? (Yes or No)	_____	_____
b. If so, indicate approximate amount (minutes) of homework, and	_____	_____
c. the frequency with which it is given.	_____	_____

Directions for #2–#4: Using a 3-point scale (1=Often, 2=Sometimes, 3=Never), rate each item according to frequency of occurrence in class. Place an asterisk (*) in the right-hand margin to indicate important differences between the special and regular education classrooms.

	Special Ed	General Ed
2. Assignments in Class		
a. Students are given assignments:		
• that are the same for all	____	____
• that differ in amount or type	____	____
• to complete in school at a specified time	____	____
• that, if unfinished in school, are assigned as homework	____	____
b. Evaluation of assignment:		
• teacher evaluation	____	____
• student self-evaluation	____	____
• peer evaluation	____	____
3. Tests		
a. Tests are		
• presented orally	____	____
• copied from board	____	____
• timed	____	____
• based on study guides given to students prior to test	____	____
• administered by resource teacher	____	____
b. Grades are:		
• percentages (for example, 75%)	____	____
• letter grades (for example, B+)	____	____
• both	____	____

	Special Ed	General Ed
4. Academic/Social Rewards		
a. Classroom rewards or reinforcement includes:		
• material rewards (for example, stars)	____	____
b. Classroom punishment includes:		
• time out	____	____
• loss of activity-related privileges (for example, loss of free time)	____	____
• teacher ignoring	____	____
• reprimands	____	____
• poorer grade, loss of star, etc.	____	____
• extra work	____	____
• staying after school	____	____
5. To what extent does each of the following contribute to an overall grade? Estimate the percentage for each so that the total sums to 100 percent.		
• homework	____	____
• daily work	____	____
• tests	____	____
• class participation	____	____

6. Please list skills that have been taught since the beginning of the school year (general education teacher only):

Skill	Will Reteach Later? (Yes or No)

From "Classroom Ecological Inventory," by D. Fuchs, P. Fernstrom, S. Scott, L. Fuchs, and L. Vandermeer, 1994, *Teaching Exceptional Children, 26,* 14–15.

not rely on object manipulation and do not include cards or pictures. An individual with a severe motor impairment may have limited voluntary responses and may need to respond via an eye scan or blink.

Students who have multiple disabilities compound the difficulties of administering the assessment task. For example, they may refuse to stay seated for an assessment session or may exhibit interfering self-stimulatory behaviour, such as hand flapping or rocking. Further, the language of the test itself may adversely affect the findings for students with receptive or expressive language disorders. That is, the test may measure students' understanding of language used in directions or descriptions within the measure rather than their level of functioning.

Considered collectively, these problem areas can make traditional testing procedures ineffective, resulting in discriminatory practices despite the best intentions of the tester. Implementing adaptations or accommodations appropriate to the needs of each student with an exceptionality greatly reduces this type of test bias (McMillan, Hellsten, & Klinger, 2011). Refer to Table 1.2 for a list of commonly used adaptations.

Table 1.2 Suggested Adaptations for Test Taking: Checklist

Behavioural and Environmental Adaptations

Distracted/off task
- Provide both written and verbal instructions
- Provide additional space between work areas
- Place student near teacher and/or in the front of the class
- Develop a secret signal for on-task behaviour
- Keep work area free from unnecessary materials (e.g., books, pencils)
- Provide positive feedback
- Enforce behaviour management system
- Seat apart from others

Completion of Task-Related Adaptations

Getting started and completing tasks
- Reduce length of test (e.g., select questions to be answered)
- Allow additional time
- Break test into shorter tasks (e.g., break every 10 minutes)
- Establish a reward system
- Set timer for designated amount of work time and allow student to take a one-minute break after the timer is complete
- Provide checklist of appropriate behaviours

Processing difficulties
- Allow use of manipulatives (e.g., counting blocks)
- Provide both written and verbal instructions

- Take frequent breaks
- Break test into shorter tasks
- Provide list of things to do

Difficulty keeping place when reading
- Provide large-print version
- Allow use of place keeper (e.g., bookmark, paper)
- Create version of test with fewer questions per page

Academic Adaptations

Difficulty with reading comprehension
- Identify key vocabulary (e.g., highlight or underline)
- Review key vocabulary
- Read questions or passages to student

Difficulty with writing
- Allow oral response
- Have proctor or teacher write student response
- Allow the use of computer or word processor

Difficulty with mathematics
- Have calculation read to student
- Allow the use of a calculator
- Break task into smaller parts
- Reduce the number of questions to be answered (e.g., answer only even-numbered questions)

From *Step-by-Step Guide: For Including Students with Disabilities in State and District-wide Assessments* (p. 29), by D.P. Bryant, J.R. Patton, & S. Vaughn, 2000, Austin, TX: Pro-Ed.

Nondiscriminatory assessment requires that data be gathered by a school team in a nondiscriminatory fashion, with an awareness of how bias could enter the decision-making process and with the knowledge of how to control it. This general admonition serves as a backdrop to more specific cautions on assessment procedures, as follows:

■ The assessment process should be initiated only when sufficient cause is documented.

■ Parents must consent to the assessment, and they have the right to participate in and appeal any determinations made and any program decisions that follow from assessment.

■ Assessments are to be undertaken only by fully qualified professionals.

■ Assessment procedures must be adjusted to account for specific exceptionalities in hearing, vision, health, or motor impairment.

■ Assessments should be adapted for individuals whose culture or language differs from the population upon whom the instruments were standardized.

■ Conclusions and recommendations should be made on the basis of multiple sources of data, including input from people directly acquainted with the person (e.g., parents) and direct observations of the student.

■ Periodic reassessments must be made (at least every three years) to re-evaluate previous judgments and to consider necessary programming changes.

The express purpose of undertaking assessment is to provide information that will lead to effective programming. Thus, the utility of the results is measured by how closely they ultimately relate to effective instruction.

Role of the Classroom Teacher

The list that follows suggests ways in which the general education professional can take an active role in the assessment process.

1. Ask questions about the assessment process. Special education teachers, school psychologists, speech-language pathologists, and other professionals should be committed to clarifying the nature of the assessments used and the interpretation of the results.

2. Seek help as needed in conveying information to parents. Special education teachers may offer you needed support during a conference.

3. Provide input. Formal test data should add to observations in the classroom about a student's ability, achievement, and learning patterns. When formal tests indicate higher abilities than observed in the classroom, re-evaluate your perceptions of the student's ability. A valid diagnostic picture should bring together multiple sources of data.

4. Observe assessment procedures. If time and facilities (e.g., a one-way mirror) permit, you will find that observing can be educational and can enhance your ability to take part in decision making.

5. Consider issues of possible bias. Formal assessments are often administered by an individual relatively unknown to the child (e.g., a psychologist); therefore, inadvertent bias factors between examiner and examinee may creep into the results. Conversely, classroom underachievement and behaviour can lead to bias as well. Work together with the psychologist and other professionals to ensure an unbiased process.

CONSIDER THIS

Do you feel that the role of the classroom teacher in the assessment process is realistic? In what areas do you feel comfortable participating? In what areas are you uncomfortable?

TEACHING TIP

When the results of standardized tests differ significantly from your observations of and experiences with a child, consult the examiner. Provide samples of the student's work or report your observations. Additional assessment may be necessary.

6. Avoid viewing assessment as a means of confirming a set of observations or conclusions about a student's difficulties. Assessment is exploratory and may not lead to expected results. Too often, after a student is judged ineligible for special services, various parties feel resentment toward the assessment process. Keep in mind that the purpose is to elicit useful information to help the student, not to arrive at a foregone decision about eligibility that may please the student, parent, or teacher.

INDIVIDUALIZED EDUCATION PROGRAMS (IEPS)

The results of assessment should be translated into educational plans for instructional goals. The *individualized education program (IEP)*—sometimes referred to in different provinces and territories as the individualized program plan (IPP), the individual student support plan (ISSP), or the personal program plan (PPP)—is a description of services planned for students with exceptionalities. The IEP is a requirement under most provincial and territorial jurisdictions (Smith & Foster, 1996).

The intent of this requirement is to place the focus of intervention on individual needs. The IEP itself is, ideally, developed by the school team. After analyzing relevant diagnostic data, the team writes an IEP reflecting the student's educational needs. In some provinces and territories, the IEP is required independent of any identification process. The overriding concept behind the IEP is that all educational programming should be driven by the needs of the student. If academic, behavioural, or social needs are identified, then goals need to be written to address these needs. In other words, services are determined by individual need, not by availability.

The IEP Team

The educational program, based on information collected during the comprehensive assessment, is developed by a group of individuals knowledgeable about the student (Gartin & Murdick, 2005). The participation of parents or guardians is critical (Lytle & Bordin, 2001), although schools may proceed to develop and implement an IEP if a parent does not wish to meet with the team. However, parents or guardians are uniquely qualified to provide important information during the development of an appropriate program for their child (Drasgow et al., 2001). School districts should ensure that the IEP team assembled for each student with an exceptionality includes the following:

1. The parents or guardians of the student

2. At least one general education teacher of the student (if the student is in general education classrooms)

3. A qualified special education teacher

4. A representative of the school district who is

   a. qualified to provide or supervise the provision of specially designed instruction to meet the unique needs of students with disabilities

   b. knowledgeable about the general education curriculum

   c. knowledgeable about the availability of resources of the school district

   d. able to interpret the instructional implications of evaluation results

◄⊙ Simulate

Accessing the General Education Curriculum

CONSIDER THIS

Should all students be required to have an individualized education program (IEP)? What would be the advantages, disadvantages, and general impact of such a requirement?

FURTHER READING

Access Alberta Education's guide, *Individualized Program Planning* (2006), for more information on creating and documenting individualized education programs (available at http://education.alberta.ca/admin/special/resources/ipp.aspx).

⊙ Watch

Kevin's IEP Meeting (Part 1)

Kevin's IEP Meeting (Part 2)

FURTHER READING

For further information on developing IEPs, review the resource guide entitled *Individual Education Planning for students with special needs: A resource guide for teachers (2009,)* available from the British Columbia Ministry of Education at www.bced.gov.bc.ca/specialed/docs/iepssn.pdf.

5. Other individuals who have knowledge or special expertise regarding the student, including related service personnel as appropriate (at the discretion of the parent or the school district)

6. The student, if appropriate

IEPs may serve varied purposes. For example, they can provide instructional direction. Well-written goals can help remedy an approach to instruction that consists of pulling together isolated or marginally related exercises. IEPs can also function as the basis of evaluation; annual goals then serve as standards against student progress and teacher effectiveness and efficiency can be judged. Finally, IEPs can improve communication among members of a team. IEPs should facilitate planning and program implementation among staff members, teachers, and parents, and, as appropriate, between teachers and students.

How, then, should teachers approach the task of formulating and using individualized education programs?

For the IEP process to function well, teachers must move beyond seeing IEPs as mere paperwork and view them as instruments that help tailor individual programs to address areas of instructional need. Teachers should use the plan as a foundation for teaching decisions. Only then can annual goals, which should serve as the basis for determining short-term objectives, be reflected in ongoing instructional planning. The discussion that follows illustrates the principles underlying the development of IEPs.

Three Key Components of an IEP

CONSIDER THIS

Some individuals are negative about the use and value of IEPs. Do you see a purpose in their development? How would you improve the process?

The major components in the IEP document that guide intervention are: (1) present levels of educational performance, (2) measurable annual goals, and (3) short-term objectives, or benchmarks. These three elements provide the foundation that directs the services that will be implemented.

The first component, *present level of educational performance*, provides a summary of assessment data on a student's current functioning, which subsequently serves as the basis for establishing annual goals. Therefore, the information should include data for each priority area in which instructional support is needed. Depending on the individual student, consideration might be given to reading, math, and other academic skills, written and oral communication skills, vocational talents and needs, social skills, behavioural patterns, study skills, self-help skills and other life skills, and motor skills.

Performance levels can be presented in various forms, such as formal and informal assessment data, behavioural descriptions, and specific abilities delineated by checklists or skill sequences. Functional summary statements of an individual's strengths and areas of need draw on information from a variety of sources rather than relying on a single source. Test scores in math, for example, might be combined with a description of how the child performed on a curriculum-based measure such as a computational checklist. In general, the phrasing used to define levels of performance should be positive and should describe things the child *can* do. For example, the same information is conveyed by the following two statements, but the first demonstrates a more positive approach: "The student can identify 50 percent of times table facts" versus "The student does not know half of the facts." Appropriately written performance levels provide a broad range of data from which to generate relevant and appropriate annual goals. In addition, Gibb and Dyches (2000) recommend that present levels of educational performance include some sense of how the

Parental involvement in the development of the individualized education program is both a requirement and an important aspect in the design of appropriate school programs.

exceptionality affects the student's involvement and progress in the general curriculum in addition to logical cues for writing the accompanying goals.

The second, and central, IEP instructional component is **annual goals**. Each student's goals should be individually determined to address unique needs and abilities. Goals should be reasonable projections of what the student will accomplish, since it is clearly impossible to predict the precise amount of progress a student will make in a year. In order to develop realistic expectations, teachers can consider a number of variables, including the chronological age of the child, the expected rate of learning, and past and current learning profiles.

Annual goals should be measurable, positive, student-oriented, and relevant (Polloway, Patton, & Serna, 2001). *Measurable* goals provide a basis for evaluation. Statements should use terms that denote action and can therefore be operationally defined (e.g., *pronounce*, *write*), rather than vague, general language that confounds evaluation and observer agreement (e.g., *know*, *understand*). Progress monitoring is a key component of the IEP. Often, schools might develop an IEP but fail to monitor adequately the student's progress (Etscheidt, 2006). *Positive* goals provide an appropriate direction for instruction. Avoiding negative goals creates an atmosphere conducive to good home–school relationships and makes it easier to chart student progress. Goals should also be *oriented to the student*. Developing the student's skills is the intent, and the only measure of effectiveness should be what is learned, rather than what is taught. Finally, goals must be *relevant* to the individual's actual needs in terms of remediation and other desirable skills.

Annual goals should subsequently be broken down into *short-term objectives*, given in a logical and sequential series to provide a general plan for instruction. Short-term objectives, the third major IEP component, can be derived only after annual goals are established. They should be based on a task-analysis process; skill sequences and checklists can be used to divide an annual goal into components that can be shaped into precise objectives. Each broad goal will generate a cluster of objectives. The four criteria applied to annual goals are also appropriate to short-term objectives. Since objectives are narrower

Table 1.3 Examples of Lark's IEP Goals and Objectives

Goal 2: Lark will follow school and team rules.

■ Objectives	■ Criteria	■ Evaluation Procedures
Lark will wear appropriate clothing to school.	0 occurrences per week of being sent home for dress code violations	Teacher observation using school dress code requirements
Lark will use appropriate language on the bus and at school.	0 occurrences per week of inappropriate language	Number of referrals to office or disciplinary actions for inappropriate language
Lark will talk respectfully to teachers and other school personnel.	0 referrals per week for inappropriate language	Number of referrals to office or disciplinary actions for inappropriate language

Goal 4: Lark will develop effective organizational and study skills.

■ Objectives	■ Criteria	■ Evaluation Procedures
Lark will record all class assignments in a daily planner.	90%	Daily checks by teacher and grandmother
Lark will complete and submit assignments.	4 of 5 days (80%) with 80% accuracy	Daily records in teacher grade books
Lark will attend and participate in the student homework support group.	6 of 8 times/month (75%)	Student self-evaluation and peer evaluations of participation

Adapted from *Collaboration for Inclusive Education: Developing Successful Programs* (p. 226), by C. Walther-Thomas, L. Korinek, V. McLaughlin, & B.T. Williams, 2000, Boston: Allyn & Bacon.

in focus, an objective's measurability should be enhanced with a criterion for mastery. For example, a math short-term objective might read, "Given 20 multiplication facts using numbers 1–5, John will give correct answers for 90 percent with no verbal cues from the teacher for four consecutive weeks." These benchmarks should be obtained from the general education curriculum being used by the student's typically achieving peers. A portion of an IEP containing annual goals, short-term objectives, and method of evaluation is presented in Table 1.3. Teachers should familiarize themselves with the format for IEPs used by their particular boards.

Role of the Classroom Teacher

It is essential that the classroom teacher take part in the IEP meeting so that the document reflects the student's needs in the inclusive classroom. Furthermore, the IEP itself should be referenced throughout the year. In particular, the teacher should keep the goal and objective clusters at hand so that the IEP can influence instructional programs.

An IEP's annual goals and short-term objectives should ultimately be reflected in instructional plans in the classroom. But short-term objectives are not intended to be used as weekly, let alone daily, plans. Teachers should refer to the document periodically to ensure that instruction is consistent with the student's long-term needs. When significant variance is noted, it may become the basis for a correction in instruction or perhaps a rationale for a change in the goals or objectives of the IEP. Figure 1.3 shows a sample IEP.

Teachers need to view IEP documents as tools for meeting students' individual needs. Unless guided by the rationale and spirit that informed the original development of the IEP concept, the process can degenerate into a mere bookkeeping activity. Instead, well-thought-out IEPs should form the foundation for individually designed educational programs for students with exceptionalities.

CONSIDER THIS

Do you think the IEP in Figure 1.3 is adequate for a student in a totally inclusive setting? What safeguards does it provide to ensure success?

TEACHING TIP

The IEP is a plan, not a contract. If teachers make good-faith efforts to implement IEPs, they cannot be held responsible for lack of progress. Ongoing communication with the IEP team is critical, and a revision of the IEP may be necessary.

Student Name _____ Year _____ Page _____

Area: General Classroom Placement

Annual Goal: _____ will maintain average or above-average grades in all general _____ grade academic classes.

Objectives:

1. _____ will participate in general class activities 5 of 5 days per week.

2. _____ will complete general class assignments on time 5 of 5 days per week.

3. _____ will complete homework assignments 4 of 5 days per week.

4. _____ will average 70 percent or higher on tests taken in the general academic classes.

5. _____ will self-evaluate progress by meeting with a resource teacher a minimum of once per grading period.

Type of Evaluation:

Projected Check Date
_____

Date/Degree of Mastery _____
_____

Progress will be monitored every nine weeks, and the report card will document the meeting of objectives.

Note: This student _____ does/ _____ does not require classroom modifications.

From N. Dunavant, 1993, Homewood School System, Birmingham, AL.

Figure 1.3 IEP for Student with Learning Disability in the General Education Classroom

SUMMARY

- As recently as the 1960s, students with exceptionalities were not provided services in regular schools.

- In Canada, the Charter of Rights and Freedoms, which is part of our Constitution, guarantees the rights of all people, including those with disabilities.

- Canada is the only country in the world that includes the rights of individuals with exceptionalities in its constitution.

- Education is the responsibility of the provinces and territories.

- All provinces and territories must adhere to the Charter of Rights and Freedoms and not discriminate on the basis of mental or physical disability.

- All provinces and territories are committed in principle to inclusive education.

- Services for students with exceptionalities have evolved significantly over the past 20 years.

- Current services for students with exceptionalities focus on inclusion—including students in general education classrooms as much as possible.

- Today's student population is diverse and includes students with a variety of exceptionalities.

- A sizeable percentage of students are at risk of developing problems, present learning or behaviour problems, or may be classified as having a disability.

- Although recognized categories of exceptionality exist, many students do not fit neatly into a specific one.

- Students who are at risk of developing problems and those considered gifted and/or talented also require special attention from school personnel.

- Assessment goes beyond testing, encompassing a broader range of methods that help define a student's strengths and problems. Assessment can lead to the development of educational interventions.

- Formal assessment is based on the administration of commercial instruments, typically for survey or diagnostic purposes.

- Informal assessment includes a variety of tools that can enhance a teacher's knowledge of students' learning needs.

- Curriculum-based measures are tied to the class curriculum and assess a student within this context.

- Ecological assessment places the evaluative data within the context of a student's environment.

- The control of bias in assessment is essential to accurate and fair evaluation.

- Classroom teachers may not administer formal assessments, but they contribute in important ways to any assessment process and should be informed about the procedure.

Weblinks

Council for Exceptional Children
www.cec.sped.org
This website, which provides information about a variety of exceptionalities, is an excellent starting point for all teachers working with children with exceptionalities or in a diverse classroom.

The Disability Resource Monthly WebWatcher
www.disabilityresources.org
This site, self-described as "a website for students that are studying in the field of exceptionality, as well as professionals working within it," is a resource centre providing information on other links, news, books, contacts, associations, and forums related to disability. The WebWatcher is a subject guide to all the resources related to exceptionalities that are available on the internet. Accessed by alphabetical listing, it is updated monthly and provides relevant sites by exceptionality.

The Special Education Yahoo! Subdirectory
http://dir.yahoo.com/Education/Special_Education
Many sites related to special education are listed in this directory. Although the majority of sites are U.S.-based, the material is highly relevant for all special education.

The Disabilities, Society and Culture, Yahoo! Subdirectory
http://dir.yahoo.com/Society_and_Culture/Disabilities
Recommended by Canada's *Ability Network* magazine, this directory of sites related to the society and culture of exceptionalities covers a huge range of issues. For example, some of the directories are relevant to independent living (44 websites); education (51 websites); children (31 websites); parental support, personal experiences, and specific exceptionalities (568 websites).

Instructor's Manual
http://news.yahoo.com/fc?tmpl=fc&cid=34&in=world&cat=disabilities_and_the_disabled
Instructor's Manual provides a summary of all recent news stories pertaining to individuals with exceptionalities. A quick browse on a regular basis will provide readers, especially professors, with the most current issues in the field and with good material for discussion in class.

Chapter 2
Designing Inclusive Classrooms

Chapter Objectives

After reading this chapter, you should be able to

- describe the different service delivery models used in meeting the needs of students with special needs
- describe the advantages and disadvantages of the service delivery models
- describe the role of special education and regular classroom teachers in the service delivery models
- describe methods that enhance the inclusion of students with exceptionalities
- delineate five critical dimensions of inclusive classrooms
- describe the roles of classroom management, curricular options, and accommodative practices in inclusive classrooms
- discuss the range of personnel supports in inclusive classrooms
- explain how to create and maintain successful inclusive classrooms
- describe methods of maintaining inclusive programs after their initiation

1. Do you think Ms. Jordan and Ms. Baker planned for this result?

2. Can events be planned to facilitate social interactions among students with and without exceptionalities in the classroom?

3. Who is responsible for facilitating the acceptance of students with exceptionalities into general education classrooms?

4. What are some other ways that Ms. Jordan could have encouraged the students in the class to accept Rhonda?

Libby is a popular, high-achieving student in Ms. Jordan's Grade 3 class. At the beginning of the school year, Rhonda, a new student, was placed in Ms. Jordan's classroom. Rhonda has cerebral palsy and a mild intellectual impairment. She rarely spoke, did not follow Ms. Jordan's directions very well, and had difficulty reading. Libby, and all the other students in the class, thought Rhonda was really odd and did not want anything to do with her in class, on the playground, or in the lunchroom.

Ms. Baker, the special education teacher, started working with Rhonda in the classroom to improve her reading skills. Libby and all her friends thought this proved that Rhonda was dumb and really did not belong in the class. About two weeks later, Ms. Baker asked if any of the students in Ms. Jordan's class wanted to be a peer tutor. None of the students knew what a peer tutor was but thought that it sounded pretty important. Libby volunteered. When Ms. Baker and Ms. Jordan met with Libby and discussed what it meant to be a peer tutor, they explained that Rhonda had some learning problems and needed some extra help in the classroom. Libby had not known she would have to work with Rhonda when she volunteered, but she decided to try it out for a little while.

When Libby began working with Rhonda, she discovered that she loved helping others. Libby also learned a very important fact that she quickly spread to all her classmates—Rhonda was okay. In fact, Rhonda was pretty cool. Getting to know Rhonda made Libby stop and think about people's differences. From then on, Rhonda was considered an equal by all the students in Ms. Jordan's class. The biggest step in facilitating her acceptance was to have one of the most popular students accept her as a fellow classmate.

INTRODUCTION

CONSIDER THIS

Think about the services that students with exceptionalities had when you were in school. Did you make contact and interact much with these students? Why or why not?

The idea of including students with special needs in general education classrooms continues to receive significant attention on a philosophical level. Inclusion is implemented for a variety of reasons, but chiefly to improve educational opportunities and social development (Salend, 2000; Wolfe & Hall, 2003) and to give all students equal opportunities. However, not enough attention has been focused on specific ways to implement inclusion successfully. Addressing the needs of a growing, diverse student population is a daunting task for today's schools. Adding students with exceptionalities to the mix only increases the challenges faced by general educators. This chapter discusses some of the key features of sound inclusive settings; it also addresses how to create and maintain these settings and the collaborative relationships that are critical to help them function well. We should note, however, that not all students' needs are best met in the regular classroom. Although the regular classroom is the starting place when considering the best environment in which to deliver a student's educational program, the continuum of placement options available to each student must be considered as part of team planning.

Terminology in special education can vary depending on the source. In this text, we define some commonly used terms as follows:

Placement: *Placement* can be used to describe the physical setting of a student's educational program, or it can refer to the educational program that has been created for a student. We use the term *placement* to refer to the physical environment in which a student is being educated, while the term *program* is used to refer to the child's educational program.

Accommodation: *Accommodation* refers to the "specialized support and services that are provided to enable students with diverse needs to achieve learning expectations. This may include technological equipment, support staff, and informal supports" (Saskatchewan Learning, 2000, p. 145).

Adaptation: This term will be used to refer to the "adjustments to curriculum content, instructional practices, materials or technology, assessment strategies, and the learning environment made in accordance with the strengths, needs, and interests of the learner" (Saskatchewan Learning, 2000, p. 145).

Modification: The term *modification* refers to changes in policy that will support students with exceptionalities in their learning (e.g., altering school curriculum or attendance policy).

EDUCATING STUDENTS WITH EXCEPTIONALITIES

The setting in which students with exceptionalities should receive educational and related services is a much-discussed, much-debated topic. In fact, as early as 1989, Jenkins and Heinen wrote that the issue has "received more attention, undergone more modifications, and generated even more controversy than have decisions about how or what these students are taught" (p. 516). The topic remains one of the key issues in the field of education for children with exceptionalities. Simply using the word *inclusion* "is likely to engender fervent debate" (Kavale & Forness, 2000, p. 279).

While still raging, the debate about where students should be educated has shifted in favour of more inclusion, which can be implemented in many different ways. Students might be placed in general education classrooms for most of the school day and "pulled out" periodically to be provided instruction in resource settings by special education teachers. Or they might be placed full-time in general education classrooms. In the latter case, special education teachers may go into general classrooms to work with students who are experiencing difficulties or to collaborate directly with classroom teachers in developing and implementing methods and materials that will meet the needs of many students. Schools use the model that best meets individual students' needs, as developed through the IEP process.

PROGRAMS IN WHICH STUDENTS RECEIVE INTERVENTION IN SPECIAL EDUCATION SETTINGS

Traditionally, students with exceptionalities received their educational programs in specialized classrooms, typically called self-contained special classrooms. Serving students with exceptionalities in special programs was based on the presumption that general educators did not have the skills necessary to meet the needs of all students with different learning needs (Shanker, 1994–1995). This placement option has been considered a "stage" in the movement from isolation for students with exceptionalities to inclusion (Safford & Safford, 1998). The result was twofold: students were removed from the general education environment, and their education was provided by specialists.

The Special Education Classroom Approach

In the special education classroom approach, students receive the majority of their educational program from a special education teacher specifically trained to serve the

CONSIDER THIS

What kinds of problems are created when students with exceptionalities enter and leave general education classrooms over the course of the day? How can teachers deal with these problems?

FURTHER READING

Read about fostering inclusive values in S.J. Salend's article, "Fostering Inclusive Values in Children: What Families Can Do," in Volume 37, Issue 1 of *Teaching Exceptional Children*, 2004 (pp. 64–69).

◄●┤**Simulate**

Addressing the Revolving Door

population of students with intellectual disabilities, learning disabilities, or some other specific exceptionality.

Self-contained special education classes were the preferred and dominant service model between 1950 and 1970 (Idol, 1983; Podemski et al., 1995; Smith, 1990; Smith et al., 1986). Special education teachers were trained to teach students with exceptionalities—but usually only students with one kind of exceptionality—in all subject areas. However, the primary focus was on a functional curriculum. Students placed in self-contained special education classrooms rarely interacted with their typically achieving peers, often even eating lunch alone. Likewise, the special education teacher interacted very little with typically achieving students or classroom teachers.

Many general education teachers liked the self-contained special class model because they did not have to deal with students who differed from their view of "typical" children. The role of classroom teachers in the self-contained model was extremely limited. They referred students to the special education program, but they rarely had to instruct them. Referrals primarily occurred in lower elementary grades, where the majority of students with exceptionalities are identified.

The movement away from special class programs has not been without dissent. Advocates for special classes have noted several problems with inclusion. Arguing against including all students with exceptionalities in general education classes, Fuchs and Fuchs (1994–1995) note that separate settings have several advantages:

- Education is provided by well-trained special educators.

- Education is selected from a variety of instructional methods, curricula, and motivational strategies.

- The system monitors student growth and progress.

CONSIDER THIS

Often, parents of students with intellectual disabilities are more supportive of inclusion than parents of students with less severe exceptionalities. Why do you think this is the case?

Between 1950 and 1970, children with exceptionalities were often educated in isolated, self-contained classes.

Regardless of these advantages, the self-contained model has many critics. The movement away from self-contained classrooms was sparked by several factors, including the following:

- Students served in special classes are isolated from their typically achieving peers.
- Students do not have "typical" role models.
- Students may be isolated from many of the activities that typically achieving students engage in.
- Special education teachers in special class models have limited interaction with general education teachers.
- Special education students are considered to "belong" to the special education teacher and program.
- Typically achieving students do not have the opportunity to interact with students with exceptionalities.
- Teachers are required to teach all areas rather than relying on colleagues with specialized expertise in selected areas.

Special classes, which segregate students with exceptionalities from their typically achieving peers, cannot be considered a "normal" school placement and were therefore criticized by adherents to the normalization philosophy of the 1970s. One way to implement the **normalization** philosophy was through inclusion, which resulted in the widespread reduction of special classes.

A final reason for the decline of the self-contained special class model was a growing awareness of the diversity of students with exceptionalities. Although the special class was the predominant model, the majority of students with exceptionalities served in special education had mild intellectual disabilities. As exceptional populations, such as students with learning disabilities or emotional problems, became recognized, the number of students needing special education grew significantly. The feasibility of serving all of these students in isolated special classes became less attractive. On the other hand, including these students in general classrooms came to be seen as beneficial for all (Wang, Reynolds, & Walberg, 1994–1995).

The Resource Room Model

The primary service delivery option used for most students with exceptionalities (except those with speech delays or disorders) is the resource room model. The **resource room** is a special education classroom. However, unlike the self-contained special class, students go to the resource room only for special instruction. Students who are served by the resource room model spend part of each school day with their typically achieving, chronological-age peers and attend resource rooms for special assistance in addressing their areas of difficulty (Friend & Bursuck, 2002).

Advantages of the Resource Room Model Several obvious advantages make the resource room model preferable to the self-contained special class. Most important, students with exceptionalities have an opportunity to interact with their chronological-age peers. Other advantages include the following:

- Students are more visible throughout the school and are more likely to be considered a part of the school community.

CROSS REFERENCE

Read chapter 6 to see how modelling appropriate behaviours can have an impact on students with serious emotional disturbances.

FURTHER READING

Consider some of the issues that arise in the training of pre-service teachers to teach in inclusive classrooms in P.J. Stanovich and A. Jordan's article, "Preparing General Educators to Teach in Inclusive Classrooms: Some Food for Thought," in *The Teacher Educator*, Volume 37, Issue 3, 2002 (pp. 173–185).

FURTHER READING

For an extensive discussion on normalization, read one of the early articles on European approaches and innovations in serving the handicapped, written by K.D. Juul and published in *Exceptional Children*, Volume 44, 1978.

- Students have the opportunity to receive instruction from more than one person.

- Students have the opportunity to receive instruction from "specialists" in specific academic areas.

- Special education teachers have the opportunity to interact with general education teachers and be an active part of the school staff.

Disadvantages of the Resource Room Model Despite the numerous advantages of the resource room model, this approach does not provide the ultimate answer to the complex question of where students with exceptionalities should be educated. Identifying students as needing special education and requiring them to leave the general education classroom, even for only part of the day, can be detrimental. Guterman (1995) found this concern to be one "unifying element" among students interviewed about their special education placement.

Dunn (1968) questioned the efficacy of serving students with exceptionalities in separate classes. His article, along with others, helped move the field from segregated to integrated services. Current research similarly questions the efficacy of resource room services. While there are many advantages to serving students with exceptionalities in this model, there are some obvious disadvantages, including the following:

- Pull-out programs are disruptive to the routine of the general classroom.

- Students who exit the classroom to receive specialized services may be ostracized.

- Communication between the resource room teacher and general classroom teachers, which must be mandatory for programs to be successful, is often difficult.

- Students may become confused if teachers use different strategies to teach similar content.

- Students may miss some favourite activities when they are pulled out for resource room instruction.

Role of Special Education Personnel In the resource room model, a key role of special education personnel is to collaborate with classroom teachers to deliver appropriate programs to students with exceptionalities. Special education teachers cannot simply focus on their students only when they are in the special education classroom. Close collaboration between the special education teacher and the classroom teacher must occur to ensure that students receiving instruction in both the special education and general education classrooms are not confused by contradictory methods, assignments, curricula, and so on. The special education teacher should take the lead in opening lines of communication and in facilitating collaborative efforts.

Role of the Classroom Teacher Unlike the special class model, the resource room model requires that classroom teachers play numerous roles related to students with exceptionalities. One primary role is referral. The majority of students with mild disabilities and other special needs are referred for services by classroom teachers. Students with mild intellectual disabilities, learning disabilities, and mild behaviour problems are usually in elementary classrooms before their problems become so apparent that they warrant a referral for special education. General education teachers are often the first to recognize that a student is experiencing problems that could require special education services.

FURTHER READING

Read about teachers' attitudes toward labelling in B. Norwich's "The Connotation of Special Education Labels for Professionals in the Field," in Volume 26, Issue 4 of the *British Journal of Special Education*, 1999 (pp. 179–183); and A. Weisel and H. Tur-Kaspa's "Effects of Labels and Personal Contact on Teachers' Attitudes toward Students with Special Needs," in Volume 10, Issue 1 of *Exceptionality*, 2002 (pp. 1–10).

Classroom teachers also play the important role of implementing interventions that can bring improvement in problem areas and thereby prevent unnecessary referrals. As a result, fewer students may be labelled with a disability and served in special education programs. Labelling students with exceptionalities has both identified advantages (e.g., access to funding) and disadvantages (e.g., stigmatization).

INCLUSIVE EDUCATION PROGRAMS

Just as full-time special class placement of students with exceptionalities received criticism in the early 1970s, resource room programs began to be criticized in the 1980s. Since the mid-1980s there has been a call for dismantling the **dual education system** (general and special) in favour of a unified system dedicated to meeting the needs of all students. Rather than spend much time and effort identifying students with special problems and determining if they are eligible for special education services, proponents of a single education system call for providing appropriate services to all students.

Inclusion Model

The model for more fully including students with special needs in general education programs, referred to as the inclusion model, has been defined in many different ways. Unfortunately, the term **full inclusion** was originally used, suggesting that all students with exceptionalities, regardless of the severity of the disability, be included full-time in general education classes (Kavale & Forness, 2000). This approach was advocated by several professional and advocacy groups, most notably the Canadian Association for Community Living (CACL), The Association for the Severely Handicapped (TASH), and The Arc (formerly the Association for Retarded Citizens). Their encouragement of full-time general education classroom placement for all students provoked much criticism and skepticism. In recommending such an approach, advocates were essentially asserting that there was no need for a continuum of placement options for students, since the least restrictive environment was always the general education classroom (Kavale & Forness, 2000).

Currently, the term **inclusion** is used to describe the movement to provide services to students with exceptionalities in general education settings (Smith & Dowdy, 1992). While acknowledging that a number of such students may require some services outside the general classroom, proponents suggest that all students with exceptionalities belong with their typically achieving peers. Smith (1995, p. 1) states that inclusion means

> *(1) that every child should be included in a regular classroom to the optimum extent appropriate to the needs of that child while preserving the placements and services that special education can provide; (2) that the education of children with disabilities is viewed by all educators as a shared responsibility and privilege; (3) that there is a commitment to include students with disabilities in every facet of school; (4) that every child must have a place and be welcome in a regular classroom.*

Although advocates of inclusion have articulated numerous reasons to support the model (e.g., Stainback & Stainback, 1984), many others oppose its implementation (e.g., Fuchs & Fuchs, 1994–1995). Several professional and advocacy groups support the continued use of a **continuum of services** model. These include the Council for Exceptional

FURTHER READING

Read several 1980s articles on the move to integration, including "Effective Special Education in Regular Classes," by M.C. Wang and J.W. Birch, published in *Exceptional Children*, Volume 52, 1984; and "Integration versus Cooperation: A Commentary," by Stainback and Stainback, published in *Exceptional Children*, Volume 54, 1987.

◉⃟ **Watch**

Tyler Lewis Talks about His Progress in the General Education Curriculum

CONSIDER THIS

How can terms such as *mainstreaming, inclusion,* and *full inclusion* complicate the planning of services for students with exceptionalities? What could be done to clarify terminology?

There are numerous advantages to including students with exceptionalities in general classrooms.

Children (CEC), the Canadian National Institute for the Blind (CNIB), the Family Network for Deaf Children, the Learning Disabilities Association of Canada (LDAC), and the Council for Children with Behaviour Disorders.

The continuum of services model, also termed *cascade of services model*, provides placement and programming options for students with exceptionalities along a continuum of least-to-most restrictiveness: "Students are given the opportunity to move sequentially between program alternatives as their needs change" (Saskatchewan Learning, 2000, p. 145). These options may range from regular classroom placement (less restrictive) to residential settings (most restrictive).

Watch

Inclusion in an Early Childhood Class

Advantages of Inclusion There are many advantages to inclusion, including opportunities for social interaction (Hunt et al., 2000), ease in accessing the general curriculum (King-Sears, 2001; Wehmeyer, Lattin, & Agram, 2001), academic improvement (Hunt et al., 2001), and positive outcomes for students with and without exceptionalities (Federico, Herrold, & Venn, 1999; Rieck & Wadsworth, 1999; Salend & Duhaney, 1999).

Although not mandatory, parental and teacher support for inclusion is very important. Parents may have differing views of inclusion. While they believe that it can provide some obvious benefits for their children, they also worry about their children being in integrated placements. The concept has simply "not been embraced by all parents" (Palmer, Fuller, Arora, & Nelson, 2001, p. 481).

Teachers, for the most part, have expressed support for inclusion. In a recent study, it was determined that both teachers and parents of children with and without exceptionalities generally supported inclusion both at the beginning and at the end of a school year in which inclusive practices were used. However, there were some differences in the support of these two groups, and both groups had a variety of concerns related to inclusion (Seery, Davis, & Johnson, 2000).

Disadvantages of Inclusion Just as there are many supporters of inclusion and many reasons for its implementation, there are also professionals and parents who decry the movement. Among the reasons for their opposition are the following:

1. General educators have not been involved sufficiently and are therefore unlikely to support the model. In addition, general educators may not have the knowledge or skills enabling them to make needed adaptations, accommodations, or modifications to a student's program.

2. General educators and special educators do not have the collaboration skills necessary to make inclusion successful.

3. Limited empirical data exist to support the model. Therefore, full implementation should be put on hold until sound research supports the effort.

4. Full inclusion of students with exceptionalities in general education classrooms may take away from students without exceptionalities and lessen their quality of education.

5. Current funding, teacher training, and teacher certification are based on separate education systems.

6. Students with exceptionalities do better when served in special education classes by special education teachers.

Although some of these criticisms may have merit, others have been discounted. For example, research indicates that the education of typically achieving students is not negatively affected by inclusion (National Study on Inclusion, 1995). Research provides support for the idea that inclusion works for most students with exceptionalities.

Role of Special Education Personnel In the inclusion model, special education personnel become much more integral to the broad educational efforts of the school. In the dual system, special education teachers provide instructional programming only to students identified with exceptionalities and determined eligible for special education programs under provincial or territorial guidelines. In inclusive schools, these teachers work with a variety of students, including those having difficulties but not identified specifically as having an exceptionality. The special education teacher works much more closely with classroom teachers in the inclusion model, resulting in increased opportunities for all students.

Role of the Classroom Teacher The role of the classroom teacher also changes dramatically in the inclusion model. Instead of focusing primarily on identification and referral, and possibly providing some instructional services to students with exceptionalities, teachers in the inclusive school become fully responsible for all students, including those with identified exceptionalities. Special education support personnel are available to collaborate on educational programs for all students, but the primary responsibility is assumed by the classroom teacher.

Classroom teachers play a vital role in the education of students with exceptionalities. They must be able to perform many different functions, such as the following:

- acting as a team member on assessment and IEP committees
- advocating for children with exceptionalities when they are in general education classrooms and in special programs
- counselling and interacting with parents of students with exceptionalities

FURTHER READING

For more information on teacher preparation relating to inclusion, read the 2003 special issue of *Exceptionality Education Canada*, Volume 13, Issue 1, "Preparing Canadian Teachers for Inclusion."

CONSIDER THIS

How can some of the problems caused by inclusion be addressed to facilitate success in school for all students?

Simulate

Supporting Beginning Special Educators

Watch

The Collaborative Process

Interview with an Intervention Specialist

- individualizing instruction for students with exceptionalities
- being innovative in providing equal educational opportunities for all students, including those with exceptionalities

✳ Explore

He's Just a Goofy Guy

Sharing responsibility among classroom teachers, special education teachers, and other specialists, such as reading teachers, is the key to providing effective educational programs for all students (Voltz, Brazil, & Ford, 2001).

In general, the classroom teacher controls the educational programs for all students in the classroom, including students with exceptionalities, students at risk for developing problems, and those classified as gifted or talented. The attitude of the teacher toward students and the general climate the teacher establishes in the classroom impact the success of all students, particularly those with exceptionalities.

METHODS THAT ENHANCE INCLUSION OF STUDENTS WITH EXCEPTIONALITIES

The concept of inclusion purports that students with special needs can be active, valued, and fully participating members of a school community in which diversity is viewed as the norm and high-quality education is provided through a combination of meaningful curricula, effective teaching, and necessary supports (Halvorsen & Neary, 2001). Anything less is unacceptable. Inclusion is distinctly different from the notion of integration or mainstreaming, in which students with special needs are educated in physical proximity to their chronological-age peers, yet without significant attention paid to the qualitative features of this arrangement. Both integration and mainstreaming begin with the notion that students with exceptionalities belong in special classes and should be integrated as much as possible in general classrooms. Inclusion, on the other hand, assumes that all students *belong* in the general education classroom and should be pulled out only when appropriate services cannot be provided in the inclusive setting. While seemingly a simple difference, these two approaches vary significantly (Halvorsen & Neary, 2001). Many factors are critical to the success of inclusion. Webber (1997) identified five essential features that characterize successful inclusion of students with special needs: (1) a sense of community and social acceptance; (2) appreciation of student diversity; (3) attention to curricular needs; (4) effective management and instruction; and (5) personnel support and collaboration. Voltz, Brazil, and Ford (2001) list three critical elements: (1) active, meaningful participation in the mainstream; (2) sense of belonging; and (3) shared ownership among faculty. Finally, Mastropieri and Scruggs (2001) add administrative support to the list.

When in place, the features noted by Webber (1997), Voltz et al. (2001), and Mastropieri and Scruggs (2001) make the general education classroom the best possible placement option for many students with exceptionalities. If these features are not present, however, the likelihood of inclusion being successful is significantly limited. The five dimensions for successful inclusion are discussed in the following sections.

TEACHING TIP

Teachers can create opportunities for students with exceptionalities to be active members of their classrooms with such methods as peer support systems.

Sense of Community and Social Acceptance

✳ Explore

Our Children Are Getting Less Attention

In desirable inclusive settings, every student is valued and nurtured. Settings such as this promote an environment in which all members are seen as equal, all have the opportunity to contribute, and all contributions are respected.

Students with special needs are truly included in their classroom communities only when they are appreciated by their teachers and socially accepted by their classmates. An understanding teacher more effectively meets students' instructional and curricular needs, and social acceptance among classmates contributes to students' self-perception of value. Meeting students' educational and social needs is critical to creating effective inclusive settings and responsible learning environments. It is imperative that we address the need for acceptance, belonging, and friendship (Murray & Greenberg, 2006; Voltz et al., 2001).

Teachers play a critical role in creating a positive classroom environment (Favazza, Phillipsen, & Kumar, 2000). Several factors controlled by teachers are essential to establishing a successful inclusive setting, including teachers' attitude, expectations, competence, collaborative skills, and support (Mastropieri & Scruggs, 2001; Salend, 1999).

Teachers must have a positive attitude about having students with special needs in their classrooms and must also have high expectations for those students' performance. Students often achieve at a level that is expected of them; if teachers expect less, they get less. A great deal of research has shown that teachers actually treat students whom they consider underachievers differently than they treat other students (Jones & Jones, 2007). Students are also aware of the support given by their teachers to students with exceptionalities, and they have a tendency to mirror these attitudes and behaviours. As a result, teachers "need to examine their own attitudes and behaviours as they relate to interactions with students and the acceptance of individual differences" (Salend, 1999, p. 10). If they are not supportive of the inclusion of these students, other students will detect this attitude and be less likely to accept them (Salend, 1999).

Teachers also need to have the skills necessary to meet the instructional needs of students with special needs (Mastropieri & Scruggs, 2001). Teaching all students the same way will not be effective for many.

Teachers must prepare students to interact with others whose physical characteristics, behaviours, or learning-related needs require special consideration. (Specific techniques for doing this will be presented later in the chapter.) Sometimes students need to be educated about diversity and exceptionalities to reduce the fear of differences. While teachers can serve as excellent role models for acceptance of diversity, they can also facilitate acceptance by orchestrating situations where students with and without exceptionalities interact.

In studying the importance of social relationships in the lives of students, Murray and Greenberg (2006) concluded that school personnel must develop intervention strategies to help students with exceptionalities develop better relations with their peers and with adults. Remember the chapter-opening vignette, where the teacher's actions resulted in a student without an exceptionality interacting positively with a student with an exceptionality.

When determining if the school promotes a sense of community and social acceptance, school personnel can ask the following questions (Voltz et al., 2001):

- Are students with exceptionalities disproportionately teased by other students?
- Do students with exceptionalities seem to enjoy being in the general education classroom?
- Do typically achieving students voluntarily include students with exceptionalities in various activities?

Watch

Attitudes and Dispositions

- Do typically achieving students seem to value the ideas and opinions of students with exceptionalities? Do students with exceptionalities seem to value the ideas and opinions of typically achieving students?

- Do students with exceptionalities consider the general education classroom to be their "real class"? Do they consider the general education teacher to be one of their "real teachers"? (p. 25)

Students also play a critical role in the success of inclusion. Both students with exceptionalities and typically achieving students must understand and accept diversity. Attitudes begin to develop in young children (Favazza et al., 2000); therefore, it is critical that teachers of young children create a positive, accepting attitude and model acceptance.

Students must achieve a level of interaction that leads to classroom communities where peer understanding and support are the norm. "The more consistently students receive the message that school is a place where everyone belongs and is cared for, will get needed support, and has something to contribute, the more likely it is that classroom programs will be effective" (Korinek et al., 1999, p. 5). Though 100 percent success cannot be guaranteed in making inclusion work in every classroom, well-prepared students and capable, optimistic, caring teachers can set the stage for a positive educational experience for each person in the class.

While students may naturally develop friendships and build a classroom community, teachers can do some things to facilitate the process. Friendship facilitation should be an integral part of both special education and general education teachers' roles in inclusive settings (Turnbull, Pereira, & Blue-Banning, 2000). Facilitation can occur through organized group activities, pairing students for various tasks, seating arrangements, buddy systems, and other methods.

Appreciation of Student Diversity

School personnel involved in the education of students with exceptionalities must have a positive attitude about serving this group. If teachers feel that they are being asked to do things that are unnecessary, the entire classroom climate may be affected. Teachers set the example for students in their classrooms by either accepting and supporting students with exceptionalities or rejecting them. Therefore, educators' philosophy regarding special education is critical to the success of these students.

All educational personnel need to be able to articulate their philosophy of education in general, as well as how it relates to children with special needs. A philosophy should include the purposes of general education, the purposes of special education, characteristics of educational programs that meet the needs of all children, and a personal vision translated into practical applications (Bates, 2000). In order to incorporate these ideas into a philosophy of education, Bates (2000) suggests teachers answer the following questions:

1. Who am I?
2. What do I value?
3. How do I define myself as an educator?
4. What is my vision of education?
5. How does education serve individuals and society?
6. How might my vision of education be implemented?

CONSIDER THIS

How likely is it that students with special needs will be successfully included if teachers leave peer acceptance of these students to chance? Why?

TEACHING TIP

When preparing a class for the inclusion of students with special needs, use a variety of techniques. Do not rely on only one method, such as a discussion or the showing of one film (e.g., use simulations, guest speakers, etc.).

CONSIDER THIS

Describe the ways in which today's school population can be diverse. What can school personnel do to show sensitivity to diversity?

These questions can be answered as they relate to education in general and to serving children with special needs in particular.

In addition to having a personal philosophy of education that forms the basis for meeting the needs of all children, including those with special needs, educators must be aware of the code of ethics that is used to govern meeting the needs of students with special needs. The Council for Exceptional Children (CEC), the primary professional group for special education personnel, has a code of ethics that could be adopted by all educators serving this group of students. All educators should adhere to professional ethics in meeting the needs of the diverse students in our schools.

In order to maximize learning, a teacher must understand each individual in the classroom as well as possible. The increasing diversity of today's classrooms makes teaching a complex activity that will likely only become more complicated in the future (Maheady, Harper, & Mallette, 2001). Educators must be sensitive to the cultural, community, and family values that can have an impact on a student's educational experience. For instance, the nature of teacher–student interactions may be affected directly by certain cultural factors, or the type of home–school contact will be dictated by how the family wants to interact with the school.

Different types of diversity exist within classroom settings. It is important to recognize and celebrate each one. Schwartz and Karge (1996) have identified the following types of differences: racial and ethnic diversity; gender and sexual orientation; religious diversity; physical, learning, and intellectual differences; linguistic differences; and behaviour and personality diversity. Although the following chapters focus on areas of exceptionality and, to a lesser extent, cultural diversity, teachers should consider the much broader range of individual variance.

Diversity is enriching. All students can flourish in an atmosphere in which diversity is recognized, opportunities exist to better understand its various forms, and differences are appreciated. Clearly, a classroom setting that champions differences provides a welcoming environment for students whose learning, physical, emotional, and social needs vary from those of their classmates. All students benefit from being in an inclusive classroom (Voltz et al., 2001). Students learn tolerance and the ability to accept differences in others, and are provided with opportunities to benefit from co-operative learning and other alternative instructional strategies.

Attention to Curricular Needs

Many discussions of inclusion lose track of an important consideration: what the student needs to learn. Teachers must examine the curriculum and ask what students are learning and how students with exceptionalities can access it (Pugach & Warger, 2001). If the individual curricular needs of a student are not being met, the curriculum must be adapted or the educational placement must be re-examined. Not meeting the curricular needs of students will definitely make it difficult for the student to learn, but it will also likely lead to behaviour problems (Jones & Jones, 2001). A student's learning and life needs should always be the driving force in programmatic efforts and decisions (Smith & Hilton, 1994). Good teachers vary their curricula to meet the needs of the students (Walther-Thomas, Korinek, McLaughlin, & Williams, 2000). While some students with exceptionalities included in general classrooms may be able to deal effectively with mainstream curricula, many need substantial modifications (Van Laarhoven, Coutinho, Van Laarhoven-Myers, & Repp, 1999). Fortunately, most curricular needs can be addressed within the context of the general education classroom.

FURTHER READING

Visit the CEC website to review the Code of Ethics for Educators of Persons with Exceptionalities: www.cec.sped.org/ps/code.html.

CONSIDER THIS

Can you imagine a situation in which a student with an exceptionality may not have his or her needs met in the general classroom setting? What would be an appropriate action in such a case?

Curricular concerns include two issues: (1) content that is meaningful to students in a current and future sense, and (2) approaches and materials that work best for them. Dealing with the first issue helps ensure that what students need to learn (i.e., knowledge and skills acquisition) is provided within the inclusive setting. The second issue involves choosing how to teach relevant content. Teachers can modify the academic level of the content and focus more on functional objectives, reduce the content to a manageable amount, and change how students are asked to demonstrate mastery of the curriculum.

Effective Management and Instruction

CONSIDER THIS

If examples of good inclusive classrooms are unavailable in a school board or district, how can teachers find such examples to observe?

CROSS REFERENCE

For more information on appropriate classroom management techniques for inclusive settings, see chapter 12.

CONSIDER THIS

How can appropriate adaptive or accommodative practices benefit all students, including those with special needs?

👁 **Watch**

Inclusion of Students with Hearing Impairments

Another essential component of successful inclusive settings is the effective management of the classroom and effective instruction that meets a wide range of student needs (Cangelosi, 2004; Voltz et al., 2001). These practices include four elements: (1) successful classroom management, (2) effective instructional techniques, (3) appropriate adaptive or accommodative practices, and (4) instructional flexibility. Successful inclusion is improbable without effective practices in these areas.

Successful Classroom Management Classrooms that encourage learning are characterized by sound organizational and management systems. Classroom management—including physical, procedural, instructional, and behavioural management—sets the stage for the smooth delivery of instruction. Effective classroom management is required if students are to benefit from any form of instruction, especially in inclusive classrooms where students display a wide range of diversity (Jones & Jones, 2001). Learning will not be optimal for any student without effective classroom organization and management.

Effective Instructional Techniques Teachers must feel comfortable using a wide variety of instructional techniques to meet the diverse needs of individuals in their classrooms (Voltz et al., 2001). Obviously, when instructional techniques are ineffective, successful inclusion will not occur. Students with exceptionalities, especially those eligible for special education services, by definition, have learning problems. As a result, effective instructional techniques must be used for these students to be successful. Mastropieri and Scruggs (1993) have summarized key elements of effective instructional practice: daily review, specific techniques for presenting new information, guided practice, independent practice, and formative evaluation. These concepts are addressed throughout the chapters of this book as they apply to children with various special needs. Chapters 13 and 14 specifically address instructional concerns in elementary and secondary classes, respectively.

Appropriate Adaptive or Accommodative Practices Some students require special adaptations to the physical environment, the curriculum, the way instruction is provided, or the assignments given to them. Chapters 3 to 11 provide examples of disability-specific adaptations and accommodations.

The critical concept of supports within classrooms refashions inclusion as "**supported education**" (Snell & Drake, 1994). Supports include adaptations, accommodations, and modifications to enhance learning and acceptance in the general education curriculum. As previously outlined, adaptations are changes in the manner in which students are taught. They include changes in instruction, assignments and homework, and testing. Accommodations refer to the specialized support and services provided to students to meet their educational needs. Modifications, on the other hand, generally refer to changes in policies that may affect students with exceptionalities. One example is altering the school curriculum or attendance policy. Whenever possible, adaptive and accommodative supports should be designed so that they benefit not only students with special needs, but other students in the class as well (Stainback, Stainback, & Wehman, 1997). The idea has merit for three primary reasons. First, it provides support to other students who will find the adaptations helpful. Second, this approach can minimize overt attention to the fact that a certain student needs special adaptations. Third, it enhances the likelihood that teachers will see the specific strategy as feasible, desirable, and helpful. The issue of equality or "fairness" often arises when teachers are considering the implementation of adaptations or accommodations for students with exceptionalities. It is important to remember that equity refers to an individual's receiving what he or she needs to succeed, and equality refers to everyone receiving the same thing (Lavoie, 1989). Teachers' making adaptations or accommodations for students with exceptionalities is an equity issue, and therefore teachers should not feel guilty about giving students what they need to succeed.

One support that can have a significant impact on the success of inclusion efforts is the use of **assistive technology**. Ranging from low-tech (e.g., optical devices) to high-tech (e.g., computer-based augmentative communication systems) applications, assistive technology can allow students with specific exceptionalities to participate fully, or even partially, in ongoing classroom activities.

Instructional Flexibility The ability to respond to unexpected and changing situations to support students with special needs is a key characteristic of responsible inclusive settings. Teachers must be flexible; they must be able to handle behaviour problems, to provide extra support during instruction, to modify assessment techniques, and to facilitate social interactions (Jones & Jones, 2007). Differentiated instruction has become an important focus for facilitating the success of students with exceptionalities in general education classrooms. Originally used as a tool for meeting the needs of gifted students, differentiated instruction is now considered an appropriate tool for meeting the needs of students with exceptionalities (van Garderen & Whittaker, 2006). Differentiated instruction can be described as planning and implementing curricula to address students' diverse learning needs. Table 2.1 provides an overview and examples.

Personnel Support and Collaboration

Students with special needs will require personnel supports to allow them to benefit from placement in inclusive settings, in addition to the instructional supports noted earlier (adaptive practices and assistive technology). Special education teachers, **paraeducators** (paraprofessionals or teacher aides), and other related service professionals such as speech-language pathologists, occupational and physical therapists, psychologists, counsellors, and audiologists are typically involved in providing supports to students with exceptionalities. They also assist general education teachers in inclusive settings through a variety of collaborative models, including collaboration–consultation, peer support systems, teacher assistance teams, and co-teaching. Table 2.2 summarizes these approaches. Equally important is administrative support for inclusion, as reflected by attitudes, policies, and practices at the district and individual school levels (Mastropieri & Scruggs, 2001; Podemski et al., 1995).

The use of co-operative teams to provide services to students with exceptionalities, especially students included in general education classrooms, has grown significantly over the past several years. A primary reason for this growth is the realization that it takes a

Guiding the School Counsellor

Working with Your School Nurse

The Inclusive Classroom

Table 2.1 Overview and Examples of Key Concepts for Differentiated Instruction

Elements	Examples
Content: What is taught and how access is given to the information and ideas that matter.	• Provide texts at varied reading levels • Provide organizers to guide note taking • Use examples and illustrations based on student interest • Present in visual, auditory, and kinesthetic modes • Provide materials in the primary language of second-language learners
Process: How students come to understand and "own" the knowledge, skills, and understanding.	• Vary the pacing of student work • Use co-operative grouping strategies (e.g., Think-Pair-Share, Jigsaw) • Develop activities that seek multiple perspectives on topics and issues • Highlight critical passages in a text • Give tiered assignments
Product: Student demonstration of what he or she has come to know, understand, and be able to do.	• Provide bookmarked internet sites at different levels of complexity for research sources • Develop rubrics for success based on both grade-level expectations and individual student learning needs • Teach students how to use a wide range of product formats (e.g., presentation software)
Affect: Student linking of thought and feeling in the classroom.	• Model respect • Help students examine multiple perspectives on important issues • Ensure consistently equitable participation of every student
Learning Environment: Classroom function and feeling.	• Rearrange furniture to allow for individual, small-group, and whole-group work • Have supplies and materials readily available (e.g., paint, paper, pencil) • Implement procedures for working at various places in the room and for various tasks

From "Planning Differentiated Multicultural Instruction for Secondary Classrooms," by D. van Garderen and C. Whittaker, *Teaching Exceptional Children, 44,* p. 14. Used with permission.

FURTHER READING

For more information on critical variables that must be in place for co-operative teams to be successful, refer to the article "Process Variables Critical for Team Effectiveness," by J.L. Fleming and L.E. Monda-Amaya, in Volume 22 of *Remedial and Special Education*, 2001 (pp. 158–171).

creative use of human resources to effectively implement an inclusion teaching model. As one study found, "Working as a team enables teachers to plan more effectively, to problem-solve more efficiently, and to intervene with a student throughout the school day" (Allsop, Santos, & Linn, 2000, p. 142). The inclusion of students with exceptionalities in general education classrooms presents an ideal opportunity for collaboration among educators. In an inclusive classroom, collaboration occurs when general classroom teachers collaborate with special education teachers "to design environments that ensure the academic and social success for all students" (Meadan & Monda-Amaya, 2008, p. 165). This collaboration occurs both formally, when teams are formed around a particular child, and informally, when two or more teachers or professionals get together to discuss how to meet a child's specific needs (Friend & Cook, 2009). Special education and general

Table 2.2 Types of Collaborative Efforts

Approach	Nature of Contact with Student	Description
Collaboration–Consultation	Indirect	General education teacher requests the services of the special education teacher (i.e., consultant) to help generate ideas for addressing an ongoing situation. The approach is interactive.
Peer Support Systems	Indirect	Two general education teachers work together to identify effective solutions to classroom situations. The approach emphasizes the balance of the relationship.
Teacher Assistance Teams	Indirect	Teams provide support to general education teachers. Made up of core members plus the teacher seeking assistance, this approach emphasizes analyzing the problem situation and developing potential solutions.
Co-Teaching	Direct	General and special education teachers work together to provide direct service to students. Using joint planning and teaching, the approach emphasizes the joint responsibilities of instruction.

From *Cooperative Teaching: Rebuilding the Schoolhouse for All Students* (p. 74), by J. Bauwens and J.J. Hourcade, 1995, Austin, TX: Pro-Ed. Used with permission.

education teachers must share knowledge of teaching strategies and curricula in order to implement effective instruction: "Through collaborative teaming, teachers set the stage for student achievement of goals" (Wolfe & Hall, 2003, p. 57).

The use of teacher aides to provide direct support to students with significant learning problems is increasing (Giangreco et al., 2001). In fact, it is "one of the primary mechanisms by which students with disabilities are being supported in general educational classes" (Cavkaytar & Pollard, 2009, p. 382). If their knowledge of working with students with exceptionalities is minimal, paraeducators must be trained and supervised carefully if they are to provide critical assistance to students in inclusive classrooms. (See the Evidence-Based Practice box "Increasing Peer Interactions for Students with Severe Disabilities through Training for Paraprofessionals" for tips on providing appropriate training.) The practice has great potential as long as proper safeguards ensure that paraeducators implement support services effectively. However, it is important to note when working with a teacher aide that it is the classroom teacher who remains primarily responsible for a student's educational program. The paraeducator provides assistance to the professional (e.g., classroom teacher or special education teacher), although their roles and responsibilities, expectations, and training may differ from school division to school division, and even from school team to team. In order to facilitate working relationships, and clarify what is expected of each team member, it is important for team members to familiarize themselves with existing teacher and paraeducator role and responsibility guidelines. Teachers should review and become familiar with existing guidelines in their school, school division, or provincial or territorial ministry of education.

Establishing a **circle of friends** for students can assist the development of a peer support network. Such a network is particularly important for students who are different and new to a classroom situation. Pearpoint, Forest, and O'Brien (1996) assert the following:

In the absence of a natural circle of friends, educators can facilitate a circle process, which can be used to enlist the involvement and commitment of peers around an

 Watch

Classroom Aides

CONSIDER THIS

How could the use of paraeducators or teacher aides be a detriment to the successful inclusion of students with special needs in a general education classroom?

FURTHER READING

For an example of established teacher and paraeducator role and responsibility guidelines, read the Saskatchewan Ministry of Education's (formerly Saskatchewan Learning) document *Creating Opportunities for Students with Severe and Multiple Disabilities* (see pp. 71–72) available at www.publications.gov.sk.ca/details.cfm?p=10114? StudentSupportServicesPublications.

TEACHING TIP

Provide opportunities for students with exceptionalities to act as full members of the classroom. Use methods such as peer support systems.

individual student. For a student who is not well connected or does not have an extensive network of friends, a circle of friends process can be useful. (p. 74)

The use of a circle of friends is further discussed in chapter 7. Friendships with typically achieving peers can be facilitated through fine arts. See the Evidence-Based Practice box "Music and Art Activities to Promote Friendship" for more information.

The five critical dimensions we have discussed—(1) a sense of community and social acceptance, (2) an appreciation of student diversity, (3) attention to curricular needs,

---

Evidence-Based Practice

Increasing Peer Interactions for Students with Severe Disabilities through Training for Paraprofessionals

Interactions between individuals with exceptionalities and their typically achieving peers can be increased by training paraprofessionals to facilitate such interactions. Following are four topics that might be included in the training activities:

1. *Enhancing paraprofessionals' perspective of their social interactions:* Ask paraprofessionals to complete a worksheet to reflect on their own social relationships and then on the social relationships of the students with whom they work.

2. *Establishing the importance of peer interactions:* Discuss the importance of peer interactions involving paraprofessionals.

3. *Clarifying the paraprofessional's role in facilitating interactions:* Use discussions about how paraprofessionals could facilitate interactions to help them understand this important role.

4. *Increasing paraprofessionals' knowledge base:* Present and discuss specific strategies for enhancing interactions. Present examples of such strategies.

From "Increasing Peer Interactions for Students with Severe Disabilities via Training for Paraprofessionals," by J.N. Causton-Theoharis and K.W. Malmgren, 2005, *Exceptional Children, 71,* pp. 431–444.

Evidence-Based Practice

Music and Art Activities to Promote Friendship

Teach students songs that deal with the theme of friendship, including recorded songs such as "Friends" (Buzzy Linhart and Moogy Klingman, 1976), "You've Got a Friend" (James Taylor, 1971), "That's What Friends Are For" (Carole Bayer Sager and Burt Bacharach, 1985), and "With a Little Help from My Friends" (John Lennon and Paul McCartney, 1967), and nonrecorded songs that appear in music books, such as "Best of Friends" (Stan Fidel and Richard Johnston, 1986).

■ Teach students group singalong songs.

■ Teach students songs that require two or more students to perform accompanying physical gestures and movements.

■ Teach students humorous songs.

■ Ask students to draw pictures of scenes depicting friendships.

■ Have students work on group art projects, such as a friendship mural, a friendship book with illustrations, and a friendship bulletin board.

■ Have students make silhouettes and collages of their friends.

■ Have students make friendship posters that include the qualities that contribute to making someone a good friend.

From "Facilitating Friendships among Diverse Students," by S.J. Salend, 1999, *Intervention in School and Clinic, 35,* p. 11. Used with permission.

(4) effective management and instruction, and (5) personnel support and collaboration—
are essential to making inclusive settings effective. Appropriate programming for students
with exceptionalities should always be based on an "individual student's needs as determined by an interdisciplinary team and represented by the student's IEP" (Smith &
Hilton, 1994, p. 8). Just as important, however, is the need to evaluate those instructional
settings on the basis of the five critical dimensions. Successful inclusion hinges on their
success.

✱ Explore

A Broken Arm

MAINTAINING EFFECTIVE INCLUSIVE CLASSROOMS

Setting up a responsible inclusive classroom does not guarantee that it will remain effective over time. Constant vigilance concerning the critical dimensions of inclusive settings
and ongoing re-evaluation of standard operating procedures can ensure continued success.
Both special education and general education teachers can become disenchanted with
the process and often burn out (Westling et al., 2006). This may be partly due to being
constantly asked by the educational system to do more.

Westling and colleagues (2006) describe a teacher support program designed to
provide the necessary supports for teachers involved in delivering services in inclusive
settings. The program was founded on five principles:

1. Teachers can help each other through collaborative problem solving as well as other
   types of mutual support, but can also benefit from additional expertise.

2. A support program for teachers should be available to all teachers but not required
   of any, should offer multiple types of support, and should allow for flexible
   participation.

3. A support program should provide valid information and assistance to deal with
   practical problems, and teachers should have the opportunity to specify the type of
   information or assistance they need and know how it should be delivered.

4. Support must be dissociated from evaluation or judgment.

5. A support program should not create additional problems or increase stress.

(Westling et al., 2006, p. 137).

This teacher support program provides for problem-solving meetings, electronic networking, information and materials searches, peer mentoring, on-site class consultation,
teacher release, and staff development workshops. An initial review of the program found
it to have a positive impact (Westling et al., 2006).

Maintaining flexibility contributes to long-term success. Rigid procedures cannot
adequately address the unpredictable situations that arise as challenges to management
and instruction. Unforeseen problems will inevitably surface as a result of including
students with special needs in general education classrooms. The more flexible a
school can be in dealing with new challenges, the more likely it is that responsible
inclusion will continue. For problem solving to be useful, teachers must have sufficient
time to meet and implement the proposed solution. Support from administrators
can be very helpful in this area. Principals who are supportive of inclusion and
team problem solving often find ways to alter schedules to allow for more teaming
opportunities.

FINAL THOUGHT

The concept of inclusion and its practical applications will continue to evolve as one of the changing dynamics in schools today. An inclusive classroom contains many students with diverse needs; therefore, teachers must be equipped to address an array of challenges. In order to do so effectively, teachers must create classroom communities that embrace diversity and are responsive to individual needs. Educators should actively collaborate with professionals (colleagues, support personnel) and engage in continuing education opportunities to expand their knowledge in the area of special education.

SUMMARY

- Although current services for students with exceptionalities focus on inclusion, a range of other services still exist in most Canadian schools.

- Key service delivery models are the self-contained classroom, the resource room, and the inclusive classroom.

- There are advantages and disadvantages for each model of service delivery.

- In the self-contained classroom model, special education teachers were trained to teach specific types of students, primarily based on clinical labels.

- In the self-contained classroom model, classroom teachers had a very limited role in special education.

- The role of the regular classroom teacher expands when a school progresses from the self-contained classroom model to an inclusive one.

- Inclusion of students with exceptionalities in general education classes has received more attention on a philosophical level than on a practical level.

- Five essential features must be in place to ensure maximum success of inclusion: a sense of community and social acceptance, appreciation of student diversity, attention to curricular needs, effective management and instruction of students, and access to adequate personnel support.

- The concept of inclusion affirms that students with exceptionalities can be active, valued, and fully participating members of the school community.

- Students with exceptionalities will be truly included in classrooms only when they are appreciated by their teachers and socially accepted by their classmates.

- Teachers play a critical role in the success of inclusion.

- The curricular needs of students must not be lost in the philosophical and political debate on inclusion.

- Effective classroom management is an important component in a successful inclusive classroom.

- Adaptive or accommodative practices that are good for students with exceptionalities are usually good for all students.

- Appropriately trained personnel, in adequate numbers, form a major factor in successful inclusion programs.

- Both staff and students must be prepared for inclusion.

- Once inclusion is initiated, it is important to monitor how well its five essential features are working together to ensure ongoing success.

Weblinks

Government of Alberta Learning Resources Centre
www.lrc.education.gov.ab.ca/pro/default.html
For resources on inclusion strategies for students with exceptionalities, visit the centre's site. All of the resources have been reviewed and approved by Alberta's Ministry of Education.

Alberta Ministry of Education, Special Education
http://education.alberta.ca/admin/special.aspx
Visit this website to gain more information on resources (videos, books, resource guides, and handbooks) for students with exceptionalities.

Chapter 3
Teaching Students with Communication Disorders

Chapter Objectives
After reading this chapter, you should be able to

- define the concept of communication and describe its major components, language and speech
- discuss communication disorders, including the different types of disorders and some of their characteristics
- describe various classroom adaptations and accommodations appropriate for students with speech and language disorders

Questions to Consider

1. Do children typically "grow out" of their speech and language difficulties?

2. How can Ms. Dunne revisit the subject of making a speech and language referral with Declan's parents?

3. Why would early intervention be important for a child like Declan? How might his speech and language difficulties impact his learning in the classroom?

■ describe typical speech and language development in children

■ discuss language differences that are due to culture and examine ways that teachers can deal with these differences

■ discuss augmentative and alternative communication techniques

Declan, an active five-year-old, is the youngest of three children. When Declan started Kindergarten, his parents reported to his teacher, Ms. Dunne, that he had some problems saying all of his sounds correctly in words, and that he used shorter sentences when speaking than either of his older brothers had at his age. However, they were not concerned because they had been told by their family doctor that Declan would "grow out" of these difficulties. As the school year has progressed, Ms. Dunne has not noticed any change in Declan's use of sounds, and he seems to also have difficulty following multi-step directions, initiating and maintaining interactions with his peers during free play activities, and learning new vocabulary words that are introduced during class activities. Ms. Dunne wants to refer Declan for a speech and language evaluation with the speech-language pathologist who provides services to the school. However, Declan's parents are reluctant to consent to the referral since they are sure he will "grow out" of his difficulties.

INTRODUCTION

For most of us, the ability to communicate is a skill we take for granted. Our communication is effortless and frequent. In one day, we might share a story with family members, discuss problems with our co-workers, ask for directions from a stranger on the street, and telephone an old friend. When we are able to communicate easily and effectively, it is natural to participate in both the commonplace activities of daily living and the more enjoyable experiences that enrich our lives.

However, when communication is impaired, absent, or qualitatively different, the simplest interactions may become difficult or even impossible. Moreover, because the communication skills that most of us use so fluently and easily almost always involve personal interactions with others, disorders in speech or language may result in social problems. For children, these social problems are most likely to occur in school. School is a place not only for academic learning, but also for building positive relationships with teachers and long-lasting friendships with peers. When a student's communication disorder, however mild, limits these experiences, makes him or her feel different and inadequate, or undermines confidence and self-esteem, the overall impact can be devastating.

Communication problems are often complex. There are many types of communication disorders, related to both speech and language. This chapter describes strategies that teachers can use with students who have such disorders. Suggestions will address specific communication disorders as well as associated problems in socialization and adjustment.

BASIC CONCEPTS ABOUT COMMUNICATION DISORDERS

Communication and Communication Disorders Defined

Speech and **language** are interrelated skills, tools that we use for communication. Heward (2003) defines the related terms this way:

> Communication is the interactive exchange of information, ideas, feelings, needs, and desires. It involves encoding, transmitting, and decoding messages. Each communication interaction includes three elements: (1) a message, (2) a sender who expresses the message, and (3) a receiver who responds to the message. . . . Language is a formalized code used by a group of people to communicate with one another. All languages consist of a set of abstract symbols—sounds, letters, numbers, elements of sign language—and a system of rules for combining those symbols into larger units. . . . Speech is the oral production of language. Although it is not the only possible vehicle for expressing language (e.g., gestures, manual signing, pictures, and written symbols can also be used), speech is the fastest, most efficient method of communication by language. . . . Speech is also one of the most complex and difficult human endeavours. (pp. 326–328)

Various cultures develop and use language differently, and the study of language is a complex topic. The **American Speech-Language-Hearing Association (ASHA)** (1982) includes the following important considerations in its discussion of language: (1) Language evolves within specific historical, social, and cultural contexts; (2) language is rule-governed behaviour; (3) language learning and use are determined by the interaction of biological, cognitive, psychosocial, and environmental factors; and (4) effective use of language for communication requires a broad understanding of human interactions, including associated factors such as nonverbal cues, motivation, and socio-cultural roles (p. 949).

Language development and use are complicated topics; therefore, determining what is *normal* and what is *disordered* communication is also difficult. According to Haynes and Pindzola (1998, p. 6), a communication difference is considered a disability in any of the following situations:

- The transmission and/or perception of messages is faulty.
- The person is placed at an economic disadvantage.
- The person is placed at a learning disadvantage.
- The person is placed at a social disadvantage.
- There is a negative impact upon the emotional growth of the person.
- The problem causes physical damage or endangers the health of the person.

In order to better understand communication disorders, it is helpful to be familiar with the dimensions of language and the terms used to describe related disorders.

Types of Communication Disorders

In its definition of communicative disorders, ASHA (1993) describes both speech disorders and language disorders. **Speech disorders** include impairments of *articulation*, *voice*, and *fluency*. **Language disorders** are impairments of *comprehension* or *use of language*,

CONSIDER THIS

How would your life be different if you could not talk, or if you could not write, or if you could not hear?

CONSIDER THIS

Have you been involved in a situation in which communication between two or more persons was so poor that problems resulted?

CROSS REFERENCE

See chapter 4 on learning disabilities, and consider the integral link between language disorders and learning disabilities. Also see Table 3.3: Linguistic, Social, Emotional, and Academic Problems Related to Language Disorders, presented later in this chapter.

TEACHING TIP

If a student in your class is experiencing speech or language difficulties, refer the student to your school's speech-language pathologist for an evaluation as soon as possible.

CROSS REFERENCE

Refer to chapter 9 for more information on auditory processing disorders, also termed central auditory processing disorders.

CONSIDER THIS

What are the advantages of serving most of the students with communication disorders in general education classrooms? When would pull-out services be appropriate?

regardless of the symbol system used. A language disorder may involve the *form* of language, the *content* of language, or the *function* of language. Specific disorders of language form include **phonologic**, syntactic, and **morphologic impairments**. **Semantics** refers to the content of language, and **pragmatics** is the system controlling language function. Figure 3.1 contains the definitions of communication disorders as described by ASHA. The terms in this figure will be discussed in more detail later in the chapter. The category of communication disorders is broad in scope and includes a wide variety of problems, some of which may overlap. For example, individuals can demonstrate speech and language difficulties in isolation (e.g., only demonstrate a moderate articulation disorder), in combination (e.g., demonstrate a moderate articulation disorder and a moderate receptive and expressive language disorder), and in association with other exceptionalities (e.g., identified with a moderate learning disability and a mild receptive and expressive language disorder).

Prevalence and Causes of Communication Disorders

After learning disabilities, speech and language disorders are the most common disability seen in the schools. In Canada, it is estimated that 5 to 10 percent of school-age children have some type of speech or language disorder (CASLPA, 2005). These students have impairments in their ability to send or receive a message, to articulate clearly or fluently, or to comprehend the pragmatics of social interactions. The majority of them also have other exceptionalities, such as learning disabilities, autism, or traumatic brain injury, so they are served under a variety of categories.

Identification and Assessment

Students with speech and language disorders receive services under a variety of categories depending on the appropriate provincial or territorial guidelines. The categories used in Yukon, Saskatchewan, and Alberta indicate the range. In Yukon, learning disabilities and speech and language impairments are combined under the heading of "communication exceptionality" (Yukon Education, Special Programs Services, 1995). In Saskatchewan, special education funding is no longer restricted to students who meet specific diagnostic criteria (Saskatchewan Learning, 2005). As of the 2005–2006 school year, eligible school divisions are provided with a fixed pool of funds that can be directed to support diverse student needs, including speech and language (Saskatchewan Learning, 2005). And in Alberta, a specific communication exceptionality category specifies the severity of a student's communication disorder (Alberta Learning, 2004). Regardless of the category, the focus across the country remains on providing services to students with language and speech disorders in the regular classroom wherever possible. The traditional model of pull-out services for speech and language therapy typically occurs only in cases where intensive, specific intervention is required.

SPEECH DISORDERS

This section of the chapter discusses speech disorders, including problems in *articulation*, *voice*, and *fluency*. The discussion includes: (1) a description and definition, (2) a brief explanation of causes, and (3) information related to identifying problems serious enough to require a referral for possible assessment or remediation. Next, suggestions for classroom teachers will be presented.

COMMUNICATION DISORDERS

A. A *speech disorder* is an impairment of the articulation of speech sounds, fluency, and/or voice.

1. An articulation disorder is the atypical production of speech sounds characterized by substitutions, omissions, additions, or distortions that may interfere with intelligibility.

2. A fluency disorder is an interruption in the flow of speaking characterized by atypical rate, rhythm, and repetitions in sounds, syllables, words, and phrases. This may be accompanied by excessive tension, struggle behaviour, and secondary mannerisms.

3. A voice disorder is characterized by the abnormal production and/or absences of vocal quality, pitch, loudness, resonance, and/or duration, which is inappropriate for an individual's age and sex.

B. A *language disorder* is impaired comprehension and/or use of a spoken, written, and/or other symbol systems. The disorder may involve (1) the form of language (phonology, morphology, and syntax); (2) the content of language (semantics); and/or (3) the function of language in communication (pragmatics) in any combination.

1. Form of Language
   a. *Phonology* is the sound system of a language and the rules that govern the sound combinations.
   b. *Morphology* is the system that governs the structure of words and the construction of word forms.
   c. *Syntax* is the system governing the order and combination of words to form sentences, and the relationships among the elements within a sentence.

2. Content of Language
   a. *Semantics* is the system that governs the meanings of words and sentences.

3. Function of Language
   a. *Pragmatics* is the system that combines the above language components in functionally and socially appropriate communication.

C. A *hearing disorder* is the result of impaired auditory sensitivity of the physiological auditory system. A hearing disorder may limit the development, comprehension, production, and/or maintenance of speech and/or language. Hearing disorders are classified according to difficulties in detection, recognition, discrimination, comprehension, and perception of auditory information. Individuals with hearing impairment may be described as deaf or hard of hearing.

1. *Deaf* is defined as a hearing disorder that limits an individual's aural/oral communication performance to the extent that the primary sensory input for communication may be other than the auditory channel.

2. *Hard of hearing* is defined as a hearing disorder, whether fluctuating or permanent, which adversely affects an individual's ability to communicate. The hard-of-hearing individual relies on the auditory channel as the primary sensory input for communication.

D. *Central auditory processing disorders* are deficits in the information processing of audible signals not attributed to impaired peripheral hearing sensitivity or intellectual impairment. This information processing involves perceptual, cognitive, and linguistic functions that, with appropriate interaction, result in effective receptive communication of auditorily presented stimuli. Specifically, CAPD refers to limitations in the ongoing transmission, analysis, organization, transformation, elaboration, storage, retrieval, and use of information contained in audible signals. CAPD may involve the listener's active and passive (e.g., conscious and unconscious, mediated and unmediated, controlled and automatic) ability to do the following:

- attend, discriminate, and identify acoustic signals;
- transform and continuously transmit information through both the peripheral and central nervous systems;
- filter, sort, and combine information at appropriate perceptual and conceptual levels;

(continued)

Figure 3.1 Definitions of Communication Disorders from ASHA

- store and retrieve information efficiently; restore, organize, and use retrieved information;
- segment and decode acoustic stimuli using phonological, semantic, syntactic, and pragmatic knowledge; and attach meaning to a stream of acoustic signals through use of linguistic and nonlinguistic contexts.

COMMUNICATION VARIATIONS

A. *Communicative difference/dialect* is a variation of a symbol system used by a group of individuals that reflects and is determined by shared regional, social, or cultural/ethnic factors. A regional, social, or cultural/ethnic variation of a symbol system should not be considered a disorder of speech or language.

B. *Augmentative/alternative communication* systems attempt to compensate and facilitate, temporarily or permanently, for the impairment and disability patterns of individuals with severe expressive and/or language comprehension disorders. Augmentative/alternative communication may be required for individuals demonstrating impairments in gestural, spoken, and/or written modalities.

From "Definitions of Communication Disorders and Variations," by the American Speech-Language-Hearing Association Ad Hoc Committee on Service Delivery in Schools, 1993, *ASHA, 35 (Suppl. 10)*, pp. 40–41. Reprinted by permission of the American Speech-Language-Hearing Association.

Figure 3.1 Continued

Articulation, Phonological, and Motor Speech Disorders

On their website, the Canadian Association of Speech-Language Pathologists and Audiologists (CASLPA) differentiates between the speech sound disorders of articulation, phonology, and motor speech. **Articulation disorders** are described to "occur when a person cannot correctly pronounce one or more sounds" (CASLPA, 2004). For example, an individual who only has difficulty pronouncing the *r* sound at the beginning of words may be described as having an articulation disorder. Phonological disorders involve more than the inability to correctly pronounce one or more sounds. Phonological disorders are "errors of many sounds that form patterns" (CASLPA, 2004). The patterns of sound errors differ in type and severity for each individual, while **motor speech disorders** are "articulation disorders caused as a result of neurological damage such as stroke or head injury" (CASLPA, 2004). Phonological and **articulation disorders** are the most common speech disorders, affecting about 10 percent of preschool and school-age children (ASHA, 2002). The ability to articulate clearly and use the phonological code correctly is a function of many variables, including a student's age, developmental history, oral-motor skills, and culture. Although some articulation and phonological errors are normal and acceptable at young ages, when students are older these same errors may be viewed as developmentally inappropriate and problematic. The most common types of articulation errors include **distortions**, **substitutions**, **omissions**, and **additions** (McReynolds, 1990; Van Riper & Erickson, 1996). (See Table 3.1.)

CONSIDER THIS

Think of all the young children you have encountered who have had articulation or phonological problems. Have most of the problems improved over time without intervention, or has intervention been required?

Causes of Problems in the Phonological System Articulation and phonological impairments can be either *organic* (i.e., having an identifiable physical cause) or *functional* (i.e., having no identifiable organic cause). When you encounter a child with articulation or phonological disorders, consider the child's environment. Some functional disorders may be related to the student's opportunities to learn appropriate and inappropriate speech patterns, including opportunities to practise appropriate speech, fluctuating

Table 3.1 The Four Kinds of Articulation Errors

Error Type	Definition	Example
Distortion	A sound is produced in an unfamiliar manner.	Standard: Give the pencil to Sally. Distortion: Give the pencil to Sally. (the /p/ is nasalized)
Substitution	Replace one sound with another sound.	Standard: The ball is red. Substitution: The ball is wed.
Omission	A sound is omitted in a word.	Standard: Play the piano. Omission: P_ay the piano.
Addition	An extra sound is inserted within a word.	Standard: I have a black horse. Addition: I have a balack horse.

Reprinted with the permission of Macmillan Publishing Company from *Human Communication Disorders, Third Edition,* by George H. Shames and Elisabeth H. Wiig. Copyright © 1990 by Macmillan Publishing Company.

hearing loss due to otitis media during early development, and the absence or presence of good speech models. Some functional articulation and phonological problems have causes that may be related to complex neurological or neuromuscular activities and might never be specifically identified. Differences in speech can also be related to cultural and linguistic factors. These differences typically do not constitute a speech disorder and will be discussed later in the chapter.

Organic articulation and phonological disorders are related to the neurological and physical abilities required in the process of producing speech sounds, which is a highly complex activity involving intricate, precise, and rapid coordination of neurological and muscular interactions. According to the American Psychiatric Association (2000), organic causes of speech impairments may include hearing loss, cleft palate, dental malformations, or tumours. Brain damage and related neurological problems may also result in motor speech disorders, such as verbal apraxia and dysarthria. The severity of articulation and phonological disorders can vary widely, depending in part on the causes of the disorders.

CROSS REFERENCE

Refer to chapter 9 for a detailed definition of *otitis media,* and to learn more about the impact of otitis media on speech and language development.

When Articulation and Phonological Errors Are a Serious Problem

We know the developmental patterns for normal sound production and can recognize children who are significantly different from the norm. The normal pattern of consonant sound production falls within relatively well-defined age limits (Sander, 1972). For example, children usually master the consonant *p* sound by age three but may not produce a correct *s* sound consistently until age eight. Although young children between ages two and six often make articulation or phonological errors as their speech develops, similar errors in older students would indicate a problem. At age three it might be normal for a child to say *wabbit* instead of *rabbit.* If a 12-year-old made the same error, however, it would be considered a problem, and the teacher should refer the student to a **speech-language pathologist** for evaluation. Figure 3.2 presents this pattern of normal development for the production of consonants among speakers of Standard American English.

For a general education teacher, judging a student's articulation or phonological errors requires looking at the big picture—that is, how well the student is doing in class and whether the articulation or phonological disorder is interfering with either overall

CONSIDER THIS

How could cultural differences have an impact on a child's development of the specific sounds listed in Figure 3.2?

Figure 3.2 Ages at Which 90 Percent of All Children Typically Produce a Specific Sound Correctly

Note: Average estimates and upper age limits of customary consonant production. The solid bar corresponding to each sound starts at the median age of customary articulation; it stops at an age level at which 90 percent of all children are customarily producing the sound. The Ø symbol stands for the breathed "th" sound, as in *bathroom*, and the ∂ symbol stands for the voiced "th" sound, as in feather (Smith and Luckasson, 1992, p. 168).

From "When Are Speech Sounds Learned?" by E.K. Sander, 1972, *Journal of Speech and Hearing Disorders, 37*, p. 62. Reprinted by permission of the American Speech-Language-Hearing Association.

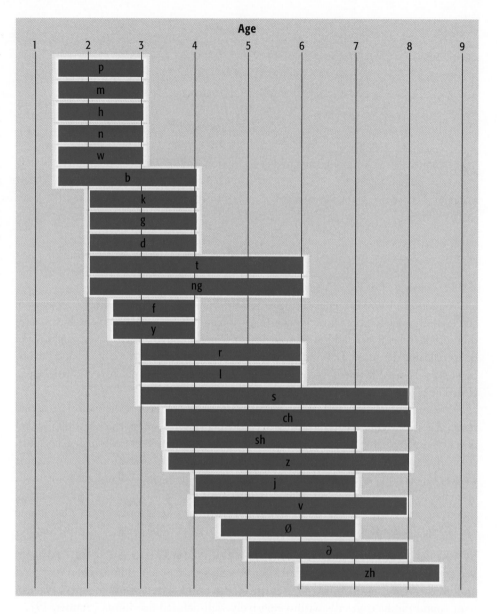

academic performance or social adjustment. A few common-sense considerations may give some insight into whether the student has a serious problem and what, if anything, should be done about it:

■ *Take note of how understandable the student's speech is.*
This factor may vary over time and across individuals. Sometimes, the context of the student's speech will make it easier for listeners to understand her or him. Some errors are easier to understand than others. For example, omissions are usually more difficult to understand than distortions or substitutions. Individuals who spend more time around the student, and who are more familiar with his or her patterns of error, will likely find the individual easier to understand. It is important to judge how understandable the student's speech would be if you were a stranger to whom he or she was speaking.

- *Consider how many different errors the student makes.*

  If the errors are consistent—that is, if the student repeats the same error rather than numerous different errors—he or she will be easier to understand. Peers and teachers will become familiar with these speech problems, and the student will have less of a problem relating to others. However, the problem should be addressed so that the student's speech is understandable to strangers.

- *Observe whether the articulation errors cause the student problems in socialization or adjustment.*

  If a student with articulation problems is ridiculed, excluded, or singled out because of a speech problem, then the teacher may want to refer the student for a speech-language evaluation. Likewise, if a student is reluctant to speak in class, or seems self-conscious or embarrassed by articulation or phonological errors, the general education teacher should seek an evaluation.

- *Consider whether the problems are due to physical problems.*

  If they are, be sure that the student is referred to a physician. Some articulation problems are due to malformations of the mouth, jaw, or teeth. When the problems are structural, such as cleft lip or palate, they can often be corrected surgically. Likewise, dental malocclusions (abnormal closures and fit of the teeth) can be corrected with orthodontic treatment.

The early identification of and intervention for speech or language disorders are extremely important in making effective gains. Do not wait to see if an individual will "grow out" of his or her difficulties. Refer the individual to a certified speech-language pathologist for an evaluation if parents or teachers have any concerns about the child's speech or language skills.

Voice Disorders

Voice disorders are abnormalities of speech related to volume, quality, or pitch. Voice problems are typically less common in children, and it is difficult to distinguish an unpleasant voice from one that would be considered disordered. People generally tolerate a wide range of voices. Our voices are related to our identities and are an integral part of who we are and how we are recognized; therefore, we usually allow for a wide range of individual differences in voice.

According to Heward (2003), there are two basic types of voice disorders: **phonation** and **resonance**. Phonation refers to the production of sounds by the vocal folds. Humans have two vocal folds, which are located in the larynx and lie side by side. When we speak, healthy vocal folds vibrate, coming together smoothly along the length of their surfaces, separating, and then coming together again. These movements are usually rapid and are partially controlled by the air pressure coming from the lungs. The rate of vibration controls the pitch of our voices (slow movements result in a low pitch, and a faster rate results in a high pitch). If a student's vocal folds are too tense or relaxed, or if the voice is produced by vibrating laryngeal structures other than the true vocal folds, the student might demonstrate a pitch disorder. Although pitch disorders occur infrequently in school-age populations, they can sometimes lead to devastating social and emotional consequences. If the vocal folds do not meet and close together smoothly, the voice is likely to sound breathy, hoarse, husky, or strained. Chronic hoarseness is the most

General classroom teachers should screen all students in their classes, especially during the early elementary grades, to determine which students have speech sound problems that might require intervention.

common voice disorder among children, affecting as many as 38 percent of the school-age population (Hooper, 2004).

Disorders of resonance involve either too many sounds coming out through the air passages of the nose (hypernasality) or the opposite—too little resonance of the nasal passages (hyponasality). People with hypernasality sound as though they are talking through their nose or with a "twang"; those with hyponasality sound as though they have a cold or a stuffy nose. Resonance is related to what happens to air that travels from the vocal folds into the throat, mouth, and nasal cavity; therefore, when there are abnormalities in any of these structures or in the associated musculature, resonance problems can result.

Causes of Voice Disorders Voice disorders can result from vocal abuse and misuse (such as shouting, screaming, talking loudly, making vocal sound effects, and throat clearing), trauma to the larynx from accidents or medical procedures, and congenital malformations of the larynx, nodules, or tumours. Disorders caused by abuse or misuse are the most common and most easily prevented voice disorders in school-age children. Common childhood health problems such as upper respiratory tract infections, allergies, asthma, and gastroesophageal reflux can worsen symptoms (Hooper, 2004). Voice disorders caused by abuse or misuse of the vocal folds affect boys more often than girls (ASHA, 2002). Sometimes, voice disorders are related to other medical conditions so that when students evidence a voice disorder, the speech-language pathologist will often refer them to an otolaryngologist (ear, nose, and throat doctor) for an examination. Some examples of organic problems related to voice disorders include congenital anomalies of the larynx, Reye's syndrome, juvenile arthritis, psychiatric problems, Tourette syndrome, physical trauma to the larynx, and cancer. Most of these conditions are relatively rare, so it may be more likely that the student's voice disorder is a functional problem, perhaps resulting from learned speech patterns (Hall, Oyer, & Haas, 2001).

When Voice Disorders Are a Serious Problem Classroom teachers can help prevent voice disorders among their students by modelling and promoting healthy vocal habits in the classroom, on the playground, and at home. A student suspected of having a voice disorder should be observed over the course of several weeks, since many symptoms of voice disorders are similar to other temporary conditions, such as colds, seasonal allergies, or minor respiratory infections (Hall et al., 2001). One way to get a meaningful measure of the student's speech during this time is recording him or her several times during the observation period. The recordings will be helpful to the speech-language pathologist and will provide a basis for comparison. Again, our voices are part of our identity, and, quite often, differences in voice quality, volume, or pitch may be considered part of who we are, rather than a problem that requires correction. Teachers might ask themselves the following questions before referring a student for evaluation of a voice disorder:

- Is the student's voice having such an unpleasant effect on others that the student is excluded from activities?
- Does the student habitually abuse or misuse his voice?
- Is there a possibility that the voice disorder is related to another medical condition?
- Does the student's voice problem make it difficult for others to understand him or her?
- Has there been a recent, noticeable change in the student's vocal quality?
- Might the voice quality be related to a hearing loss?

Articulation or phonological problems can result in problems in socialization or adjustment.

FURTHER READING

For more information on voice disorders, refer to the information sheet entitled "Questions/Answers about Voice Problems," found on the ASHA website at www.asha.org.

CONSIDER THIS

How can a student's voice quality affect classroom and peer acceptance? What are some things that teachers can do to influence student response?

Teachers should also monitor the quality of their own voices throughout the school year, since individuals in the teaching profession are more likely to develop voice problems than individuals in any other profession (Fritzell, 1996; Merrill et al., 2004).

Fluency Disorders

Fluency refers to the pattern of the rate and flow of a person's speech. Normal speech has a rhythm and timing that is regular and steady, but normal speech patterns also include some interruptions in speech flow. We all sometimes stumble over sounds, repeat syllables or words, mix up speech sounds in words, speak too fast, or fill in pauses with "uh" or "you know." Often, typical speech dysfluencies are related to stressful or demanding situations. When the interruptions in speech flow are so frequent or pervasive that a speaker cannot be understood, when efforts at speech are so intense that they are uncomfortable, or when they draw undue attention, then the dysfluencies are considered a problem.

Many young children, especially those between the ages of two and five, demonstrate dysfluencies in the course of normal speech development. That is, when children go through periods of rapid language development they may experience periods of nonfluency (ASHA, 2007). Parents and teachers may become concerned about young children's fluency problems, but most dysfluencies of early childhood begin to disappear by age five. The most frequent type of fluency disorder is **stuttering**, which affects about 4 to 8 percent of school-age children (CASLPA, 2005). Cluttering, another type of fluency disorder, occurs infrequently in school-age children. Disturbances of prosody and intonation are rare in children, and are often associated with other, more serious communication problems.

Fluency problems usually consist of blocking, repeating (e.g., M-m-m-m-mommy), or prolonging sounds, syllables, words, or phrases (e.g., Mmmmmmommy). In *stuttering*, these interruptions are frequently obvious to both the speaker and the listener. Often, they are very disruptive to the act of speaking, much more so than disorders of articulation or voice. When the speech dysfluencies occur, listeners may become uncomfortable and try to finish the speaker's words, phrases, or sentences. This discomfort is exacerbated when a speaker's stuttering is accompanied by gestures, facial contortions, or physical movements. Stuttering is a pronounced interruption of normal speech and has a profound impact on listeners. Therefore, the disorder receives a lot of attention, even though it is not as prevalent as other communication disorders.

Causes of Stuttering
Although many causes of stuttering have been suggested over the years, the current thinking among professionals in the field of communication disorders is that there may be many different causes of the disorder. Current theories regarding the possible causes of developmental stuttering include factors such as language development, motor skills, personality, and environment.

There seems to be no doubt that children who stutter are vulnerable to the attitudes, responses, and comments of their teachers and peers. When considerable attention is focused on normal dysfluencies or when students begin to have negative feelings about themselves because of their stuttering, they may become even more anxious and their stuttering may get worse. Most students who stutter would benefit from intervention by a speech-language pathologist if they hope to avoid a lifelong problem that will affect their ability to communicate, learn, work, and develop positive interpersonal relationships.

TEACHING TIP

In order to maintain a healthy voice and promote healthy vocal habits among their students, throughout the school day teachers can (1) continually drink water to ensure proper hydration, (2) decrease vocally abusive behaviours such as yelling or prolonged vocal use without rest, and (3) utilize an electronic voice amplification device in the classroom (personal or classroom system).

TEACHING TIP

Teachers who have students who stutter should attempt to reduce the stress on these students and create an accepting atmosphere (refer to the section entitled "Build a Positive Classroom Climate" for suggestions).

TEACHING TIP

When deciding whether to refer a child for a speech and language evaluation, teachers should keep a log to record instances of dysfluency and the activities occurring with the student and rest of the class when dysfluencies occur. They should also note circumstances in which dysfluencies do not occur.

When Fluency Disorders Are a Serious Problem Speech dysfluencies are a normal developmental occurrence for many children. However, some children will continue to experience these dysfluencies beyond their preschool and early school years. It would be difficult for a parent or teacher to determine whether the dysfluencies a child is demonstrating are normal nonfluencies. Therefore, parents and classroom teachers should refer any children experiencing dysfluencies to a speech-language pathologist for a speech and language evaluation. Teachers may wish to consider the following questions when monitoring a student's speech dysfluencies:

■ *Are the dysfluencies beginning to occur more often in the student's speech or beginning to sound more effortful or strained?*
Keep track of the quality of the student's speech and his or her periods of fluency and dysfluency on a calendar. This will provide concrete information as to whether dysfluencies are occurring more often, as well as whether the quality of the student's speech is changing (e.g., strained, effortful, etc.).

■ *Is there a pattern to situations in which the student is dysfluent?*
Collect information about the student related to his dysfluencies. With careful observation, teachers may be able to determine if a student's dysfluencies occur under specific conditions—that is, with certain individuals, in particular settings, or when in stressful situations.

FURTHER READING

For more information on fluency intervention and current research initiatives in Canada, visit the Institute for Stuttering Treatment and Research's (ISTAR) website at www.istar.ualberta.ca.

■ *Is the student experiencing social problems?*
Carefully monitor unstructured situations to determine the level of the student's acceptance by peers. Much of the socialization that occurs in school takes place in the cafeteria, on the playground, in the halls, on the bus, and in other nonacademic settings. When a student is not successfully relating to peers in these environments because of his or her dysfluencies, then the problem is likely to grow worse.

■ *Is the student concerned about his or her dysfluencies?*
Monitor the student's verbal interactions with others and note whether he or she is becoming more concerned or self-conscious about the dysfluencies. For example, individuals interacting with the student may inadvertently criticize his or her fluency skills and increase his or her awareness of the difficulties he or she is having speaking fluently (e.g., "Think about what you want to say first"; "Take your time").

■ *Is the student confident?*
Talk to the student to ascertain his or her level of confidence and self-esteem. One of the biggest problems facing children who stutter is the interactive effect of the disorder. The more they are dysfluent, the more anxious, fearful, or nervous they become when they speak, thereby increasing the likelihood of stuttering. Children caught in this cycle of behaviour may be so self-conscious that they avoid situations in which they are required to speak and thus become isolated from friends and teachers.

■ *Does the student avoid speaking because he or she is afraid of stuttering?*
Students may associate particular topics, words, or situations with increased dysfluencies. Monitor whether the student avoids speaking in certain situations, or avoids using certain phrases or words.

Classroom Adaptations and/or Accommodations for Students with Speech Disorders

Build a Positive Classroom Climate Regardless of the type of speech disorder that students in general education classes demonstrate, it is crucial that teachers make every effort to create a positive, accepting, and safe climate. The following points are helpful to remember when dealing with children who have articulation or phonological, fluency, or voice disorders:

- Talk with the student privately about his or her speech difficulties. Acknowledge your awareness of the difficulties the student is experiencing, and stress your belief that his or her speech will improve with practice.

- Encourage the student's family to actively support the student's educational and communication goals. Teachers and speech-language pathologists should ensure that a child's parents are an integral part of their child's educational and communication intervention program.

- Don't think of or refer to students with speech disorders in terms of their behaviours (i.e., they are "students," not "stutterers").

- Work closely with the speech-language pathologist, following suggestions and trying to reinforce specific skills.

- Encourage the student.

- Be positive.

- Accept the child just as you would any other student in the class.

- Model good speech and language skills for your students. Children can improve their speech and language skills by listening to good models.

- Provide lots of opportunities for students to participate in oral group activities.

- Give students plenty of chances to model and practise appropriate speech.

- Maintain eye contact when the student speaks.

- Be a good listener.

- Don't interrupt or finish the student's sentence.

- When appropriate, educate other students in the class about speech disorders and about acceptance and understanding.

Help Students Learn to Monitor Their Own Speech Students who have been working with a speech-language pathologist to improve their speech skills may be at a point in their intervention when they are ready to work on their speech skills at the conversational level. By using simple contract formats, teachers can help students focus on using the skills they learn in speech therapy. When students are aware of how to make sounds correctly, they can then practise, monitor their own performance, and earn reinforcement from the teacher or parents whenever specific criteria are met.

Work with Peers or Parents If students are to master speech skills, they will need to practise the skills taught by the speech-language pathologist on a regular basis in many different settings. One way for students to practise specific sounds is to perform exercises like those in Loehr's *Read the Picture Stories for Articulation* (Loehr, 2002; see Figure 3.3.)

> **TEACHING TIP**
>
> Self-monitoring strategies, such as record keeping, can facilitate a student's attempts to monitor his or her own speech.

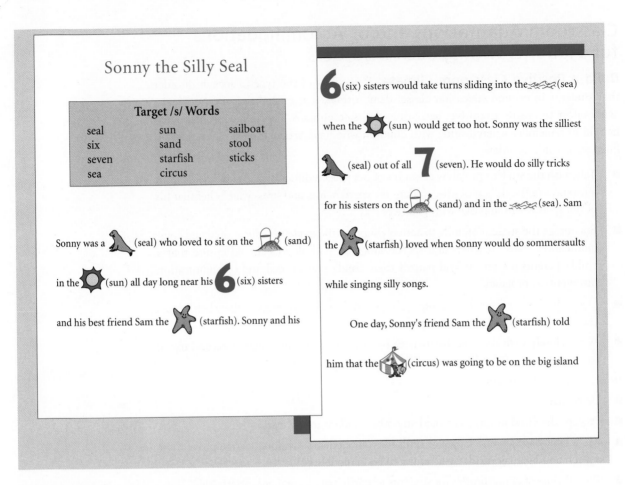

Figure 3.3 Sample Form for Articulation Practice

From *Read the Picture Stories for Articulation* (2nd ed., pp. 19–20) by J. Loehr, 2002, Austin, TX: Pro-Ed. Used with permission.

With a partner, students can use short periods of downtime, such as between or before classes, to work on their articulation. Students can also use these types of activities to work at home with their parents. First, the student is trained in the speech therapy setting on a specific phoneme in a particular word position in a key word—for example, the initial *s* sound in *seal*. After the student has reached 90 percent mastery of producing the *s* sound at the beginning of words, she or he then reads a story that contains words beginning with the *s* sound to a classmate or to his or her parents. Each practice session should take no more than five minutes and will provide students with practice that is simple and fun. In the classroom, both partners should be reinforced for their participation. However, it is important to note that every student who experiences articulation or phonological difficulties demonstrates individual strengths and needs. Parents and teachers should consult with a student's speech-language pathologist prior to implementing *any* type of speech practice activity in the classroom or at home.

Teach Students Their Own Strategies Many of the speech problems that students demonstrate while young can be corrected and modified with therapy. While the therapy is going on, the teacher and speech-language pathologist should focus on giving students strategies for successful learning. Students can use these strategies to maximize their academic and social strengths. Some of these strategies also require adaptations or accommodations on the part of the teacher in structuring situations and requirements.

- Encourage students to participate in groups in which responses do not have to be individually generated.

- Teach students to self-reinforce by recognizing when they are doing well and by self-appreciating.

- Let students practise skills with a friend in real situations so that they are not afraid or nervous when faced with the "real thing."

- Let students record their own speech and listen carefully for errors so that they can discriminate between correct and incorrect sounds.

- Help students come up with strategies for dealing with specific people or situations that make them nervous (e.g., walking away, counting to 10 before they speak, deep breathing, etc.).

Students with speech disorders can learn strategies that will help them maximize their social strengths.

LANGUAGE DISORDERS

Language is the system we use to communicate our thoughts and ideas to others. According to Lahey (1988), language is a code "whereby ideas about the world are expressed through a conventional system of arbitrary signals for communication" (p. 2). The interrelationships of what we hear, speak, read, and write become our format for sharing information.

For most of us, spoken language is the tool we use to communicate our ideas, but even the most articulate, fluent, pleasant speech would be useless without a language system that enables us to understand and be understood. Language is an integral component of students' abilities in reading, writing, speaking, and listening. Disorders of language may have a serious impact on academic performance. In recent years, the emphasis in the field of communication disorders has shifted away from remediation of speech problems to an increased focus on language disorders.

More important for classroom teachers, however, is that remediation of language disorders will often be as much their responsibility as it is the speech-language pathologist's. Although remediation of speech problems is often provided in a therapeutic setting, it is often then supported and reinforced by the classroom teacher. Teachers may, in fact, direct and manage their students' overall language development in collaboration with the speech-language pathologist and other special education staff. Recent research has proven that some types of language disorders are best treated collaboratively in the classroom (McGinty & Justice, 2006).

We know humans can communicate in several ways. We generally describe modes of communication as either **receptive language**, which involves receiving and decoding or

👁️ Watch

Norm-referenced Assessment

CONSIDER THIS

Try to go through a social situation without using oral language. Did you become frustrated when attempting to make your needs or ideas known to other people? How did you deal with the frustration?

CONSIDER THIS

Remember when some children with whom you are familiar began to talk. What were some of their first words? What factors influence a child's early oral language development?

interpreting language, or **expressive language**, which is the encoding or production of a message. Reading and listening are examples of receptive language; writing and speaking are forms of expressive language.

As with speech disorders, knowing the normal sequence of language development is important in working with students with language disorders. Some children may be delayed in their development of language but still acquire skills in the same sequence as other children. Other children may acquire some age-appropriate language skills but have deficits in other specific areas. Table 3.2 shows the normal patterns of language development for children with language disorders and children without language disorders. Although teachers may refer to these general patterns of language development to judge students' overall progress, teachers should not expect every child to follow this precise sequence on these exact timelines.

FURTHER READING

Learn more about promoting children's language and literacy development by visiting the Hanen Centre's website at www.hanen.org.

Table 3.2 Language Development for Children with Language Disorders and without Language Disorders

Language-Disordered Child			Normally Developing Child		
Age	**Attainment**	**Example**	**Age**	**Attainment**	**Example**
27 months	First words	*this, mama, bye-bye, doggie*	13 months	First words	*here, mama, bye-bye, kitty*
38 months	50-word vocabulary		17 months	50-word vocabulary	
40 months	First two-word combinations	*this doggie, more apple, this mama, more play*	18 months	First two-word combinations	*more juice, here ball, more TV, here kitty*
48 months	Later two-word combinations	*Mimi purse, Daddy coat, block chair, dolly table*	22 months	Later two-word combinations	*Andy shoe, Mommy ring, cup floor, keys chair*
52 months	Mean sentence length of 2.00 words		24 months	Mean sentence length of 2.00 words	
55 months	First appearance of -ing	*Mommy eating*	24 months	First appearance of -ing	*Andy sleeping*
63 months	Mean sentence length of 3.10 words		30 months	Mean sentence length of 3.10 words	
66 months	First appearance of is	*The doggie's mad*	30 months	First appearance of is	*My car's gone!*
73 months	Mean sentence length of 4.10 words		37 months	Mean sentence length of 4.10 words	
79 months	Mean sentence length of 4.50 words		37 months	First appearance of indirect requests	*Can I have some cookies?*
79 months	First appearance of indirect requests	*Can I get the ball?*	40 months	Mean sentence length of 4.50 words	

From "Language Disorders in Preschool Children," by L. Leonard, in *Human Communications Disorders: An Introduction* (4th ed., p. 179), edited by G. H. Shames, E. H. Wiig, and W. A. Second, 1994, New York: Macmillan. Copyright © 1994. Reprinted with permission of Merrill, an imprint of Macmillan Publishing Company.

Dimensions of Language

Earlier in the chapter, some terminology related to language disorders was introduced. In addition, we refer to the dimensions of language and their related impairments in terms of form, content, and function (or use). Students can demonstrate impairments in any or all of these areas.

Form *Form* describes the rule systems used in oral language. Three different rule systems are included when we discuss form: **phonology**, **morphology**, and **syntax**.

Phonology is the rule system that governs the individual and combined sounds of a language. Phonological rules vary from one language to another. For example, some of the guttural sounds heard in German are not used in English, and some of the vowel combinations of English are not found in Spanish. The ability to process and manipulate the phonological components of language has been shown to be a critical component in the development of early reading skills.

Morphology refers to the rule system that controls the structure of words. Free morphemes (morphemes are units of meaning) can stand alone in word formation (e.g., *stop*), while bound morphemes cannot stand alone (e.g., *un-*, *-ed*, *-ing*). The structures of words govern their meanings; therefore, comparative suffixes are important, such as *-er* or *-est*, and plural forms, such as the *s* that changes *book* to *books*. Hall et al. (2001) provide an example of how morphemes can change a basic word into similar words with many different meanings:

> The word "friend" is composed of one free morpheme that has meaning. One or more bound morphemes may be added, making "friendly," "unfriendly," "friendless," "friendliness," "fri.endship," and "friendlier." There are rules for combining morphemes into words that must be followed (e.g., "disfriend" is not an allowable word and thus has no meaning). (p. 61)

Syntax is the ordering of words in such a way that they can be understood. Syntax rules determine where words are placed in a sentence, and just like phonology, they vary from one language to another. Rules governing negatives, questions, tenses, and compound or simple sentences determine the meanings of word combinations. For example, the same words used in different combinations can mean very different things: *The boy hit the ball* is not the same as *The ball hit the boy*.

All of these rule systems affect how we use and understand language. Children's abilities to understand and correctly use rules related to form develop sequentially as their language skill develops. Language form is important not only in spoken language, but also in written language and in sign language systems, as well as in augmentative and alternative communication (AAC), discussed later in this chapter.

Content *Content* refers to the intent and meaning of language and its rule system; *semantics* deals with the meaning of words and word combinations. Without specific words to label and describe objects or ideas, our language would have no meaning. When students fail to comprehend concrete and abstract meanings of words, inferences, or figurative expressions, it is difficult for them to understand more subtle uses of language such as jokes, puns, similes, proverbs, or sarcasm. As children mature, they are better able to differentiate meanings of similar words, classify them according to similarities and differences, understand abstract meanings of words, and comprehend figurative language.

Use When we use language in various social contexts, we follow another set of rules: *pragmatics*. The purpose and setting of our communication as well as the people with

CONSIDER THIS

Language disorders and behavioural disorders frequently coexist. Refer to chapter 6 to learn more about emotional and behavioural disorders.

Watch

Introducing New Sounds

New Sounds and Review

TEACHING TIP

Teaching students appropriate social skills helps them understand how to modify their language in different social situations and when interacting with different speakers (i.e., friends versus unfamiliar others).

whom we are communicating determine the language we use. If children are to build and maintain successful relationships with others, it is important that they understand and effectively use skills appropriate to the context. For example, when children speak to adults, it is helpful if they use polite, respectful language; when they speak to their friends, they will most likely use less formal spoken language, demonstrate more relaxed body language, and take turns talking (Owens, 2008).

Causes of Language Disorders

Language disorders can occur due to medical problems (e.g., traumatic brain injury during or after birth, hearing loss) or can have no known cause (ASHA, n.d.). There is also substantial evidence for familial transmission of specific language impairment (SLI). The incidence in families with a history of SLI is estimated at 20 percent to 40 percent (Choudhury & Benasich, 2003). However, it is important to note that being unable to determine the exact cause of a language disorder does not adversely impact assessment or intervention efforts. Delayed language occurs when a child develops language in the same approximate sequence as other children, but at a slower rate. Causes of language delays include intellectual disability, hearing loss, or lack of stimulation or appropriate experiences.

Sometimes language development is interrupted by illness or physical trauma. This type of language problem is increasingly common among children as a result of traumatic brain injury (TBI). In general education classrooms, teachers may encounter any or all of these types of language disorders, ranging from very mild to severe.

Indicators of Language Impairments

Some teachers may have an overall sense that a student is demonstrating language problems; others may not notice anything amiss. Wiig and Semel (1984) identified some indicators of language problems by grade level:

- *Primary grades*:
  Problems following verbal directions
  Difficulty with pre-academic skills (recognizing sound differences)
  Phonics problems
  Poor word-attack skills
  Difficulties with structural analysis
  Problems learning new material

- *Intermediate grades*:
  Word substitutions
  Inadequate language processing and production that affects reading comprehension and academic achievement

- *Middle or junior and high school*:
  Inability to understand abstract concepts
  Problems understanding multiple word meanings
  Difficulties connecting previously learned information to new material that must be learned independently
  Widening gap in achievement when compared to peers

Teachers can also check for linguistic, social, emotional, and academic problems that are related to language disorders. These problems are shown in Table 3.3. In addition,

CROSS REFERENCE

Language disorders are integrally linked to autism spectrum disorders and fetal alcohol spectrum disorders. Refer to chapter 8 to learn more about disorders that are considered to be part of the autism and fetal alcohol spectrums.

TEACHING TIP

If you suspect a child of having language problems, keep a record of the problems to better determine if a referral for services is warranted. Always consult a speech-language pathologist if you are unsure if the difficulties observed necessitate a referral.

FURTHER READING

For more information on language disorders and learning disabilities, refer to the information sheet entitled "Language-Based Learning Disabilities" found on the ASHA website at www.asha.org.

Table 3.3 Linguistic, Social, Emotional, and Academic Problems Related to Language Disorders

Linguistic Problems	Language structure	Omissions and distortions of speech sounds
		Omissions of parts of words or word endings
		Sounds or syllables of words out of sequence
		Immature sentence structure
	Language meaning	Difficulty understanding directions and questions
		Confusion of basic concepts and ideas
		Limited vocabulary
		Literal interpretation of figurative language and jokes
		Poor word classification and association skills
	Language use	Difficulty beginning, maintaining, and ending conversations
		Difficulty taking turns in conversations and other classroom activities
		Difficulty understanding the listener's point of view
		Overuse of pauses, fillers, and repetitions in conversation
	Metalinguistics	Difficulty expressing ideas about language
		Poor phonemic awareness skills (rhyming, syllabification, phonics)
Social Problems	Conversational deficits	Poor eye contact
		Inappropriate comments and responses to questions
		Providing insufficient information when describing, relaying information, or giving directions
		Poor social language use (please, thank you)
	Social interaction issues	Poor sense of fair play
		Unable to set limits or boundaries
		Difficulty with new situations
		Difficulty expressing wants, needs, and ideas
Emotional Problems	Personal issues	Poor self-concept
		Low frustration level
		Perseverative and repetitious
	Emotional-interaction issues	Inability to accept responsibility
		Gullible
		Sensitive to criticism
		Poor coping strategies
Academic Problems	Classroom issues	Poor retention of learning
		Problems with organizing and planning
		Difficulty problem solving
		Left/right confusion
		Symbol reversals

(continued)

Table 3.3 Continued

	Difficulty expressing known information
	Poor generalization of knowledge to new situations
	Difficulty with higher-level thinking skills (deduction, inference)
	Poor judgment and understanding of cause and effect
	Inability to monitor and self-correct
	Poor memory
Metacognition	Inability to talk about academic tasks

Adapted from *Understanding Language Disorders: The Impact on Learning* (pp. 171–174), by V. L. Ratner and L. R. Harris, 1994, Eau Claire, WI: Thinking Publications. Reprinted with permission.

Figure 3.4 presents a checklist of behaviours that may indicate either speech or language problems. Children who have language disorders sometimes develop patterns of interaction with peers, teachers, and family members that may result in behaviour problems. These problems might seem to have nothing to do with language problems, but may in fact have developed in response to inabilities to read, spell, talk, or write effectively.

Figure 3.4 Teacher's Checklist of Behaviours That May Indicate Communication Disorders

STEPS LEADING TO THE IEP

SPEECH

- ☑ poor articulation
- ☑ different voice quality
- ☑ dysfluencies
- ☑ slurred conversational speech

LANGUAGE

- ☑ has problems following oral directions
- ☑ speech rambles; isn't able to express ideas concisely
- ☑ appears shy, withdrawn, never seems to talk or interact with others
- ☑ asks questions that are off-topic
- ☑ has a poor sense of humour
- ☑ has poor comprehension of material read
- ☑ doesn't plan ahead in pencil-and-paper activities
- ☑ takes things literally
- ☑ is not organized; appears messy
- ☑ doesn't manage time well; has to be prodded to complete assignments

Classroom Adaptations and Accommodations for Students with Language Disorders

Numerous strategies can be used in general education classrooms to improve students' language skills and to remedy language deficits. Consult with a speech-language pathologist and other special education personnel such as the resource room teacher to individualize classroom suggestions for students with language disorders. The following section presents some ways of structuring learning situations and presenting information to enhance communication.

Improve Students' Comprehension in the Classroom Clary and Edwards (1992) suggest some specific activities to improve students' receptive language skills:

- *Give students practice in following directions.*
  Begin with one simple direction, and then increase the length of the list of directions. Have a student perform a simple task in the classroom, such as closing the door, turning around, and so on.

- *Have students pair up and practise descriptions.*
  Place two students at a table separated by a screen. Place groups of identical objects in front of both students. Have one describe one of the objects; the other must determine which object is being described. Reverse roles with new sets of objects.

- *Let students work on categorizing.*
  Orally present a list of three words. Two should be related in some way. Ask a student to tell which two are related and why (e.g., horse, tree, dog). For younger students, start by having students compare and organize physical objects (e.g., plastic animals, plastic food) and pictorial representations of the objects (i.e., pictures cut out of magazines) before moving to orally presented words.

The Evidence-Based Practice box on page 68 provides some additional suggestions for teaching listening skills.

Give Students Opportunities for Facilitative Play This type of interaction provides modelling for students so that they can imitate and expand their own use of language. For example:

- The teacher models self-talk in a play activity. ("I'm making the cars go.")

- The teacher elicits comments from the student and then expands on them. ("Yes, the cars are going *fast*.")

- The teacher uses "buildups" and "breakdowns" by expanding on a student's ideas, breaking them down and then repeating them. ("Red car go? Yes, look at the red car. It's going fast on the road. It's going to win the race.") (Nowacek & McShane, 1993)

Encourage Students to Talk with Their Teachers and Peers Sometimes students who are reluctant to speak require encouragement. In addition to encouraging them with positive social interactions, teachers might also have to structure situations in which students must use language to meet some of their needs in the classroom.

✳ Explore

Leadership Roles Encourage Language in the Classroom

CROSS REFERENCE

When reading chapters 13 and 14, consider specific activities that could be used to teach listening skills to elementary students and secondary students.

Teaching Strategies to Help Problem Listeners in the Classroom

- Allow for clarification and repetition of questions during oral tests.
- Limit the use of figurative language and complex or passive sentences. When figurative language expressions are used (e.g., "He let the cat out of the bag"), provide explanations of the expressions' literal and figurative meanings.
- Be an interesting speaker—use gestures, facial expressions, movement, and variety in your voice.
- Encourage students to ask questions.
- Identify students who are having difficulty listening in class and pair them with "study buddies."
- Keep sentence structures simple and direct.
- Limit concentrated listening time to short intervals.
- Make simple adaptations in your classroom to improve acoustics (e.g., place felt pads on the bottoms of chair and desk legs to dampen their sound when they are moved).
- Reduce noise levels in the classroom during listening tasks.
- Refer students who are experiencing listening difficulties to an audiologist for a hearing assessment.
- Repeat and rephrase information for students.
- Seat students with listening difficulties strategically (e.g., away from classroom door, at front of classroom).
- Speak slowly, and pause between spoken thoughts.
- Use advanced organizers and preview questions to help focus listening.
- Use the blackboard and other visual aids (e.g., overhead projector, videos).

Adapted from *It's Time to Listen: Metacognitive Activities for Improving Auditory Processing in the Classroom* (2nd ed., pp. 9–15), by P. A. Hamaguchi, 2002, Austin, TX: Pro-Ed.

The strategies that follow should prompt students to use language when they might otherwise not.

- Place items out of reach so that the child has to ask for them.
- When a child asks for an item, present the wrong item (e.g., the child asks for a spoon and you present a fork).
- Give a child an item that is hard to open so that he or she has to request assistance.
- When performing a task, do one step incorrectly (e.g., forget to put the milk in the blender with the pudding mix).
- Make items difficult to find.
- Give a child an item that requires some assistance to work with (e.g., an orange that needs peeling).

CONSIDER THIS

What can you do as a classroom teacher to ensure that the speech and language skills students develop through the use of these strategies continue to improve in the classroom environment?

Use Naturalistic Techniques and Simulated Real-Life Activities to Increase Language Use Often, the most effective techniques for instilling language acquisition and use are those that will be easy for teachers to implement and easy for students to generalize to everyday situations. Teachers can encourage generalization by using naturalistic and situational strategies and real-life activities.

- *Naturalistic Techniques*
  Try cloze activities. ("What do you need? Oh, you need paint and a _____. That's right, you need paint and a brush.")

Emphasize problem solving. ("You can't find your backpack? What should you do? Let's look on the hook. Is your coat there? What did we do to find your coat? That's right, we looked on the hook.")

Use questioning techniques. ("Where are you going? That's right, you are going to lunch.")

■ *Simulated Real-Life Activities*

Let students simulate a newscast or commercial.

Have students write and follow their own written directions to locations in and around the school.

Play "social charades" by having students act out social situations and decide on appropriate responses.

Have one student teach an everyday skill to another (e.g., how to shoot a basket).

Using real telephones, give students opportunities to call each other, and to give, receive, and record messages.

Develop Students' Conversational Skills through Story Reading

McNeill and Fowler (1996) give some excellent suggestions for helping students with delayed language development. Since students with language development problems often do not get the results they want through their ordinary conversations, they need more practice. What better way to practise effective language skills than through story reading! Students of all ages enjoy being read to, whether individually or in small groups while students are young, or in larger classes when they are in intermediate or secondary grades.

McNeill and Fowler suggest four specific strategies for teachers to use when reading stories aloud:

■ Praise the students' talk.

■ Expand on their words.

■ Ask open-ended questions.

■ Pause long enough to allow students to initiate speaking.

In addition, they emphasize taking turns, so that students have an opportunity to clarify their messages, hear appropriate language models, and practise the unspoken rules of communication. McNeill and Fowler (1996) also recommend coaching parents in how to give their children opportunities to talk and how to respond when their children *do* talk. When parents pause, expand on answers, and ask open-ended questions that require more than just "yes" or "no" responses, they can become their children's best teachers.

Use Music and Play Games to Improve Language

Teachers should always try to have fun with students. Using music and playing games are two ways language can be incorporated into enjoyable activities.

■ *Music*

Use songs that require students to request items (e.g., rhythm sticks or tambourines passed around a circle).

Have picture symbols for common songs so that students can request the ones they like.

Use props to raise interest and allow students to act out the story (e.g., during "Humpty Dumpty" the student falls off a large ball).

Use common chants such as "When You're Happy and You Know It," and let students choose the action (e.g., clap your hands).

TEACHING TIP

In order to improve students' conversational skills, teachers can encourage their students to (1) use greetings or lead-ins when initiating a conversation (e.g., "Hi, how are you this morning?" or "How was . . . ?"); or (2) ask open-ended questions to maintain a conversational topic (e.g., "Oh you went to the mall. Then what happened?").

- *Games That Require Language Comprehension and Expression Skills*
  Play "Simon Says."
  Play "Musical Chairs," using words rather than music. (Pass a ball around a circle. When the teacher says a magic word, the student with the ball is out.)
  Use key words to identify and organize students. ("All of the boys with red hair stand up. Everyone who has a sister sit down.")
  Play "20 Questions." ("I'm thinking of a person." Students ask yes-or-no questions.)

Arrange Your Classroom for Effective Interactions For students who have speech or language difficulties, the physical arrangement of the classroom can contribute to their success. The following guidelines may improve students' language development:

- Give instructions and important information when distractions are at their lowest.
- Use consistent attention-getting devices, with either verbal, visual, or physical cues (e.g., switching off the classroom light, raising your hand in the air).
- Be specific when giving directions (e.g., "Please finish page 12 in your math book").
- Write directions on the chalkboard, flipchart, or overhead so that students can refer to them. For younger students, post picture cues in the room to remind students of the directions you have given them (e.g., picture of paintbrush to remind students they are to complete their painting project).
- Use students' names frequently when talking to them.
- Emphasize what you're saying by using gestures and facial expressions.
- Pair students up with buddies for modelling and support.
- Allow for conversation time in the classroom so that students can share information and ideas.
- Encourage students to use calendars to organize themselves and manage their time. (Breeding, Stone, & Riley, n.d.)

Use Challenging Games with Older Students Older students may require continued intervention to improve their language skills. However, the activities chosen must be appropriate and not seem like "baby" games. Thomas and Carmack (1993) have collected ideas to involve older students in enjoyable, interactive tasks:

- Read fables or stories with morals. Discuss outcomes, and focus on the endings.
- Do "Explain That." Discuss common idiomatic phrases, and help students discover the connection between the literal and figurative meanings (e.g., *She was on pins and needles*).
- "Riddlemania" presents riddles to students and has them explain what makes them humorous.
- Have "Sense-Able Lessons." Bring objects to see, taste, hear, and smell, and compile a list of students' verbal comments. (p. 155)

Modify Strategies to Develop Students' Learning Tools When facilitating language development for older students, help them develop their own strategies to use in challenging situations (Thomas & Carmack, 1993). Requiring them to use higher-order thinking skills will both require and stimulate higher-level language.

- Pair students to find word meanings. Use partners when working on categories such as synonyms or antonyms. Let students work together to master how to use a thesaurus.

- Teach students to categorize. Begin with concrete objects that they relate to easily, such as types of cars or names of foods, and then move to more abstract concepts, such as feelings or ideas.

- Play reverse quiz games like "Jeopardy!" in which students have to work backward to think of questions for answers. (pp. 155–163)

Work Collaboratively with the Speech-Language Pathologist LINC (Language IN the Classroom) is a program adapted for use in schools (Breeding et al., n.d.). The program's philosophy holds that language learning should occur in the child's most natural environment and in conjunction with other content being learned. The development of students' language should relate to their world and should be a learning experience, not a teaching experience.

The purpose of the program is to strengthen the language system of those students in general education classrooms who need to develop coping and compensatory skills to survive academically. Another goal is to transfer language learned from the therapy setting to the classroom, thereby allowing children to learn to *communicate*, rather than merely *talk*. The teacher and the speech-language pathologist must both be present for the approach to be successful. The two professionals work together to plan unit lessons that develop language skills in students.

Use Storytelling and Process Writing When children listen to and retell a story, they incorporate it into their oral language repertoire. Students can retell stories they have heard, tell stories from their own experience, and write down and illustrate their oral presentations. In process writing, students are instructed based on what they can already do. This and other balanced literacy approaches often allow students who have had negative language experiences to begin to succeed, to link written and spoken language, and to grow as communicators.

FURTHER READING

For articles related to language and literacy, review the journal *Language & Literacy: A Canadian Online E-Journal* (see www.langandlit. ualberta.ca).

LANGUAGE DIFFERENCES

Children's patterns of speech and use of language reflect their culture and may be different from that of some of their peers. It is important not to mistake a language *difference* for a language *disorder*, although a disorder must not be overlooked in a student with language differences. Variations in family structure, child-rearing practices, family perceptions and attitudes, and language and communication styles can all influence students' communication (Wayman, Lynch, & Hanson, 1990).

English Language Learners

Students who are English language learners (ELLs) often exhibit error patterns that can look like language disorders when they are in fact part of the normal process of second-language acquisition (Roseberry-McKibbin & Brice, 2002). It is crucial that teachers of students who are English-language learners recognize these patterns as language differences rather than communication disorders in order to avoid unnecessary referrals:

- Interference or transfer: Students may make errors in English form because of the influence of structures or patterns in their native language.

- Silent period: Children who are learning a new language focus on listening to and attempting to understand the new language before trying out what they have learned. This silent period may last as long as a year in very young children and as briefly as a few weeks or months in older children.

- Code switching or code mixing: Languages are blended in phrases or sentences such that students alternate between the two.

- Subtractive bilingualism: As students learn English, they can begin to lose skill and proficiency in their native language if it is not also supported and valued.

FURTHER READING

For more information on language development, difficulties, and disorders in culturally and linguistically diverse children, read *Language Disorders in Children: A Multicultural and Case Perspective*, written by C. Roseberry-McKibbin and published in 2007 by Allyn & Bacon.

Relationship between Communication Style and Culture

Culture has a strong influence on the *style* of communication. Many areas of communication style can be affected by factors such as gender, status, and age roles; rules governing interruptions and turn taking; use of humour; and how to greet or leave someone. Teachers must be aware of the many manifestations of culture in nonverbal communication, as well. Differences in rules governing eye contact, the physical space between speakers, use of gestures and facial expressions, and use of silence can cause dissonance between teachers and students of differing cultures. Walker (1993) has described how differences such as directness of a conversation, volume of voices, and reliance on verbal (low-context) versus nonverbal (high-context) parts of communication affect attitudes toward the speaker. Teachers can respond to cultural differences in several ways. These suggestions are adapted from Walker (1993) and should be helpful for teachers who want to enhance both overall achievement and communication skills with students who are culturally or linguistically different:

- Try to involve community resources, including churches and neighbourhood organizations, in school activities.

- Invite parents to visit your classroom in order to learn more about students' families and encourage parent participation in classroom and school activities.

- Allow flexible hours for conferences.

- Question your own assumptions about human behaviour, values, biases, personal limitations, and so on.

- Try to understand the world from the student's perspective.

- Ask yourself questions about an individual student's behaviour in light of cultural values, motivation, and world views, and how these relate to his or her learning experiences.

- Remind yourself and your students to celebrate and value cultural and linguistic differences among individuals in their school and community.

- Consult with a speech-language pathologist to understand how to differentiate between students who have language differences and students who have language disorders.

Multicultural Considerations in Assessment

Assessment in the area of communication disorders is often complicated, just as it is for students with other exceptionalities. Linguistic differences are a contributing factor. The number of students in our classrooms who are linguistically different and who require services in learning to understand and speak English is increasing. Language differences may affect a student's oral and written communication. Therefore, teachers should consult with personnel in special education, English as a second language (ESL), speech and language services, and bilingual education to obtain appropriate evaluation and programming services for these students. Observation is an important form of assessment, particularly when assessing students who are linguistically different. The Diversity Forum feature provides some suggestions for observing these children.

There are many considerations for assessment personnel who work with students with cultural or linguistic differences. The following suggestions may be useful for classroom teachers who suspect that students may have communication disorders:

- When screening with tests, always select tests that have the most valid items for the skills to be assessed.

- Consider procedural modifications, such as lengthening the time limit.

- Try to assess whether the minority child has had access to the information.

- Consider scoring the test in two ways, first as the manual indicates, then allowing credit for items that may be considered correct in the child's language system or experiences. (Record and report both ways, and indicate the adjustments.)

- Focus on what the child does well rather than on what he or she cannot do. (Toliver-Weddington & Erickson, 1992)

Because of the increasing number of students in public schools from cultural and linguistic minority groups, teachers are recognizing the need for information related to learning and communication styles as well as modifications to curriculum and instruction. Although many of these children will never be identified as having a communication disorder, teachers in general education must be aware that differences in language and culture may often affect a student's apparent proficiency in both oral and written communication.

FURTHER READING

For a discussion of current principles and methods related to nonbiased assessment of individuals who are English language learners, see C. Roseberry-McKibbon and L. O'Hanlon's (2005) article "Nonbiased assessment of English Language Learners: A tutorial" in *Communication Disorders Quarterly*, Volume 26 Issue 3, pp. 178–185.

TEACHING TIP

Remember the basic tenets of nondiscriminatory assessment when evaluating students with diverse cultural backgrounds or when reviewing assessment data that have already been collected (refer to "Multicultural Considerations in Assessment").

Diversity Forum

Considerations for Observing Linguistically Different Students

1. Identify exactly what is to be observed. Be specific and know what you are watching as a part of the ongoing behaviour stream in classroom settings.

2. Record the time, date, and duration of your observation.

3. Number your observations of the same children across days. Important here is a systematic context and an easy, readily available reminder that this is, for example, the third observation of Juan, Tom, Hector, and Zoraida.

4. Make notes of what you are observing in a descriptive, specific form that tells exactly what occurred. Also, jot down any unexpected events that happened during your observation.

   However, when taking notes of these occurrences, it is helpful to jot down that they were "unexpected."

5. Keep notes of your interpretations of what happened.

Augmentative and Alternative Communication (AAC)

According to ASHA (2004a), "Augmentative and alternative communication (AAC) refers to ways (other than speech) that are used to send a message from one person to another." The term **augmentative communication** denotes techniques that supplement or enhance communication by complementing whatever vocal skills the individual already has, such as gestures, facial expressions, and writing (ASHA, 2004a). Research has demonstrated that the use of communication devices does not inhibit the development of natural speech. Other individuals (e.g., those who are severely neurologically impaired and cannot speak) must use other techniques in place of speech—in other words, **alternative communication** (e.g., communication boards).

AAC is a multimodal system consisting of four components (symbols, aids, techniques, and strategies) that can be utilized in various combinations to enhance communication. Communication techniques used in AAC are usually divided into either *aided* or *unaided forms*. Unaided techniques include nonverbal methods that are used in typical communication and that do not require any physical object or entity in order to express information (e.g., speech, manual signs or gestures, facial communication). Aided communication techniques require a physical object or device to enable the individual to communicate (e.g., communication boards, charts, and mechanical or electrical devices). There are substantial numbers of individuals who lack functional speech because of intellectual disabilities, traumatic brain injury, deafness, neurological disorders, or other causes. Therefore, in recent years there has been an increased demand for augmentative and alternative communication. A student's communication skills and needs will change over time, as will the types of technology and methods available

FURTHER READING

In order to learn more about enhancing literacy development with students using augmentative or alternative communication approaches, review the article "Using Augmentative and Alternative Communication Approaches to Promote Participation of Preschoolers During Book Reading: A Pilot Study," in the journal *Child Language Teaching and Therapy* (volume 19).

The cultural background of a child will influence many aspects of the style of communication that is used.

to support communication. Thus, the educational team should continually monitor and regularly re-evaluate the usefulness of each AAC approach used by their students. The Technology Today feature lists some of the approaches and facilitating strategies for developing an effective team approach to serve students using AAC in the classroom.

Students who are unable to use spoken language to communicate may use a basic nonautomated communication device with no electronic parts; for example, a communication board or communication book containing symbols, words, and letters. Typically, this

Technology Today

Developing an Effective Team Approach to Serve Students Using AAC in the Classroom

Approach	Facilitating Strategies
Collaborative teaming	Regularly scheduled team meetings
	Clearly defined roles and responsibilities of team members
	Mutual respect among team members
	Effective communication among team members and a proactive approach
	Flexible interpretation of traditional roles of team members
Access to the curriculum	Working knowledge of the curriculum by all team members
	Assessment of the student's learning style by each member of the team
	Provision of vocabulary and support for use of the device across all classroom activities and school events
Cultivation of social supports	Facilitation of social interactions between the student and his or her peers
	Identification and use of natural supports in the classroom
	Training of peers as communication partners
	Fostering the independence and autonomy of the student
Maintenance and operation of AAC system	Familiarity with the basic maintenance, operation, and elements of the AAC device
	Knowledge of how to access help and additional resources as necessary
	Familiarity with the device and how to provide communication support
Building of a supportive classroom community	Use of co-operative learning strategies
	Team teaching between general and special education personnel
	Working together to support all students in the classroom
	Promoting appreciation of differences within the classroom

Adapted from "Professional Skills for Serving Students Who Use AAC in General Education Classrooms: A Team Perspective" (pp. 51–56), by G. Soto et al., 2001, *Language, Speech, and Hearing Services in the Schools, 32.*

Table 3.4 Electronic Communication Aids and Their Key Features

BigMack

A large, colourful, single message digitizer.

Record and re-record a message, song, sound, storyline, or choice of up to 20 seconds.

A picture or label can easily be stuck to the large button.

Can be accessed by pressing anywhere on the large button or by a separate switch.

Can be used as a switch to control other devices, toys, or appliances.

Lightwriter SL35

A compact, portable keyboard will speak what is typed into it.

Text messages are displayed on the two-way screen, and synthesized speech is used.

Can be customized for people with more complex needs.

Add-ons, such as key guards, can be purchased, and a range of models are available.

Keystrokes are reduced by using memory and word prediction.

ChatPC

Based on a palmtop Windows CE computer.

Housed in a durable case to give additional protection and additional amplification.

Has a colour touchscreen, and over a hundred pages of messages can be programmed.

An onscreen keyboard is available, and this speaks out what is typed into it.

3000+ symbols are supplied and can be supplemented with scanned or digital images.

Speech output can be digital or synthetic.

Changes can be made on the device or on a computer and then downloaded.

Dynavox 3100

Touchscreen device offers word layouts, symbol layouts, or a combination of both.

Many preprogrammed page sets, suitable for users with a wide range of ability levels.

Flexible layout can be thoroughly customized.

Symbol-supported word prediction encourages literacy.

DecTalk speech synthesis offers nine different voices.

Can be accessed via touchscreen, mouse, joystick, or switches.

Auditory and visual scanning modes are possible.

Built-in infrared for environmental controls and computer access.

---

kind of device will contain common words, phrases, or numbers that can be arranged in either an alphabetic or a nonalphabetic format. Nonautomated communication devices are easy to construct and can be modified to fit the student's vocabulary. Therefore, these devices are very useful in communicating with teachers, family members, and peers. There are several commercially available sets of symbols, including *The Picture Communication Symbols* (Mayer-Johnson, 2004), *The Oakland Picture Dictionary* (Kirsten, 1981), and the graphic database *Boardmaker* (Mayer-Johnson, 2004).

Electronic communication aids encompass a wide variety of capabilities, from simple to complex. Aids that produce voice are known as voice output communication aids or VOCAS. There are a large number of different voice output communication aids available that vary greatly in their level of sophistication and complexity (e.g., aids that speak on message, aids with keyboards). The voice output may be amplified or digitized, or may use synthetic speech. Often, a voice synthesizer is used to produce speech output, while written output is produced on printers or displays. Software, which is becoming increasingly sophisticated, can accommodate the many different needs of individuals who cannot produce spoken and/or written language. Some examples of electronic communication aids and their key features are shown in Table 3.4.

TEACHING TIP

The speech-language pathologist should always be consulted when selecting any type of technology for use with students with speech and language difficulties.

Enhancing Inclusive Classrooms for Students with Communication Disorders

The traditional service delivery model for speech and language intervention involved regular pull-out sessions in which speech-language pathologists worked with students in a setting outside the regular classroom. However, a combination of intervention approaches can be effective when providing speech and language services to students in public schools (i.e., combination of individual sessions and classroom consultation). Just as academic services to students with exceptionalities have become more and more integrated into general education programs, speech-language services are following a more inclusive model. This collaboration between the classroom teacher and special education staff might involve having the speech-language pathologist in the classroom to work with individual students, small groups, or the entire class. This could mean having the teacher and speech-language pathologist teach alternate lessons or portions of a lesson, or co-teach the same lesson at the same time. The Personal Spotlight on Sharon Bond describes how a speech-language pathologist views the importance of

Personal Spotlight

Speech-Language Pathologist Sharon Bond

Sharon Bond has been a speech-language pathologist (SLP) for over 30 years, working with preschool children, their families, and a variety of other professionals committed to community-based services. Sharon has a particular interest in the area of listening—specifically, the impact of listening behaviours on the expressive language of young children.

Sharon's professional career has involved working as both an urban SLP in the province of Alberta and a rural SLP in southern Saskatchewan. In her current position, Sharon is part of an interdisciplinary team that provides services to children, from birth to five years of age, and their families. In addition to a speech-language pathologist, this team includes an audiologist, a pediatrician, a nurse practitioner, and community health nurses. Sharon is also a clinical supervisor for student SLP practicums in

the Speech-Language Pathology and Audiology program at the University of Alberta.

Sharon's work with children who are experiencing communication delays and disorders is guided by a strong belief in family-centred practice. She believes children's communication concerns must be viewed in the context of their families and the interactions that take place with each member. The family must be considered an integral part of any assessment or treatment program. Family needs, timelines, concerns, beliefs, and culture must be taken into account. During treatment, family members should be provided with the information and skills that they need to facilitate the improvement of their child's communication skills. Sharon also believes that family involvement should continue to be emphasized when children with communication difficulties enter the school system.

CROSS REFERENCE

Refer to chapter 8 to read more about the use of facilitated communication with autism spectrum disorders.

collaboration, particularly the involvement of parents, in developing a child's speech and language skills.

As schools try to maximize the positive impact of professional collaboration, it is important to recognize and overcome the barriers inherent in the process. The barriers to greater collaboration among speech-language professionals and teachers can include the following:

- territorial obstacles (*"This is my job; that is your job."*)
- time concerns (*"When are general education teachers supposed to find the time to meet, plan, and modify?"*)
- terror (*"I'm afraid this new way won't work."*; Kerrin, 1996)

Fortunately, team members can use the following tips to overcome these obstacles:

- Try to be flexible and creative when scheduling conferences.
- Encourage everyone involved to ask questions.
- Invite speech-language professionals into the classroom.
- Ask for assistance in planning.
- Maintain open, regular communication.
- Keep an open mind, a co-operative spirit, and a sense of humour (Kerrin, 1996).

CONSIDER THIS

What are some of the advantages and disadvantages, to both the child and the general classroom teacher, of pull-out speech-language intervention?

FUTURE TRENDS

Several forces are changing the field of communication disorders in today's schools. First, general education teachers are likely to see more students with moderate to severe exceptionalities in their classrooms. The movement toward more inclusive environments for students will require classroom teachers to provide more classroom-based interventions for these students. Moreover, recent research suggests a shift away from standardized assessment instruments toward dynamic, authentic, and curriculum-based assessment methods. The observations and input of the classroom teacher play a crucial role in each of these assessment models.

As a result of expanding knowledge and skills among professionals trained in speech-language pathology, the scope of the profession's practice has been increasing and will continue to do so. In addition to providing services in the more traditional area of oral communication skills, speech-language pathologists now working in schools are often called on to have expertise in swallowing disorders, selecting AAC systems, providing intervention and recommending classroom modifications for children with traumatic brain injuries and other complex neurological disorders, and promoting and enhancing literacy skills. The caseloads of speech-language pathologists are continuing to grow, and there is an ever-increasing demand for services, especially in the area of language disorders. Although pull-out speech-language intervention is typically still offered, many services are delivered in an increasingly collaborative framework, with teachers and speech-language pathologists co-operating and sharing resources. In areas where shortages of qualified speech-language pathologists are particularly acute, schools will need to consider alternate methods of providing services to students with communication disorders. Some methods that might compensate for shortages in specialty personnel include the hiring of speech-language pathology assistants, flexible scheduling, cross-disciplinary service provision, peer tutoring, and increased use of natural supports. In Canada, another alternate method of service delivery being explored to address service delivery in remote areas with large caseloads or shortages of speech-language pathologists is treatment provided via telehealth (e.g., Jessiman, 2003; Kully, 2000).

The social trends that are shaping our society may have a great effect on the provision of speech-language therapy services in schools. These trends include an increasingly multicultural and multilinguistic society and the changing role of the school in the community.

Another area of change is the expected continuation of technological advances. Some of the improved technology has already been described here; however, it is virtually impossible to keep up with the rapid improvements in this area—improvements that will lead to increased opportunities for students with severe communication disorders to interact with family members, teachers, and peers, perhaps allowing them to participate in activities that would have seemed impossible 10 years ago.

SUMMARY

- Most people take the ability to communicate for granted.

- It is estimated that 5 to 10 percent of school-age children have some type of speech or language impairment.

- Communication problems result in difficulties in even simple interactions.

- Speech and language are interrelated skills that we use for communication.

- Speech disorders include impairments of fluency, voice, articulation, and phonology. Articulation and phonological disorders are the most common speech disorders.

- Voice disorders are related to volume, quality, or pitch.

- Language disorders are impairments of comprehension (receptive language) or use of language (expressive language); disorders may be related to the form (phonology, morphology, syntax), content (semantics), or use (pragmatics) of language.

- Language difficulties are integrally linked to a variety of disorders (i.e., autism spectrum disorders, learning disabilities, emotional and behavioural disorders).

- Building a positive classroom environment is an important accommodation for students with speech and language problems.

- Teachers can make numerous accommodations and modifications for students with language disorders.

- Some language difficulties may be due to the cultural or linguistic diversity of students.

- Technology, through augmentative and alternative communication, can greatly facilitate the language use of persons with speech and language problems.

Weblinks

American Speech-Language-Hearing Association
www.asha.org
This site provides parents and educators with valuable information and resources on communication disorders.

Canadian Association of Speech-Language Pathologists and Audiologists
www.caslpa.ca
This site gives the public information on the practice of speech-language pathology and audiology in Canada, and provides useful links to other websites (e.g., provincial speech-language and hearing associations).

Ontario Association for Families of Children with Communication Disorders (OAFCCD)
www.oafccd.com
The Association's website has a wonderful array of resources, related links, personal stories, supports, and information on children with communication disorders as well as on children's activities.

Ontario Association for Families of Children with Communication Disorders: Lanark, Leeds, & Grenville Chapter
www.oafccd.com/lanark
This is a particularly effective website with resources, information, chat rooms, inspirational poems, stories, quotes, excellent related links for education and families, and superb kid links. The site has won numerous awards.

Net Connections for Communication Disorders and Sciences
www.mnsu.edu/comdis/kuster2/welcome.html
This website has an excellent list of internet sources related to communication disorders. A teacher will be able to find information and strategies on all communication disorders, from stuttering or fluency disorders to ESL or voice disorders.

Chapter 4
Teaching Students with Learning Disabilities

Chapter Objectives

After reading this chapter, you should be able to

- identify the characteristics of learning disabilities

- discuss the impact of cultural diversity on identification and intervention for students with learning disabilities

- describe the criteria for eligibility for learning disability services

- discuss and compare the traditional approaches to intervention for individuals with learning disabilities at the preschool, elementary, and secondary levels

- describe the challenges faced by adults with learning disabilities

- make modifications in teaching methods and classroom management to address academic, social and emotional, and cognitive differences

Questions to Consider

1. What kind of documentation can Ms. Moore show Rebecca's parents to help make a case for her referral for a psycho-educational assessment?

2. What professionals should ideally be involved in the assessment of Rebecca's strengths and areas of need?

3. What are some of the potential consequences of not having a psycho-educational assessment completed to further investigate Rebecca's areas of strength and need?

Rebecca is currently in Grade 3. She pays attention in class and has a large group of friends with whom she socializes on a regular basis. Academically, she has above-average abilities in math but has always struggled in language arts–related areas. Specifically, Rebecca has difficulty decoding unfamiliar words, expressing herself in writing, and processing information she receives auditorially. In Grade 2, Rebecca's teacher broached the idea of referring Rebecca for psycho-educational testing to further investigate her academic difficulties. However, Rebecca's parents did not feel the referral was necessary. They reported that Rebecca has always been disorganized and unmotivated to complete tasks, and that she just needs to work harder to improve in school.

In the first few months of the new school year, Rebecca's Grade 3 teacher, Ms. Moore, also noticed Rebecca's reading, writing, and listening difficulties. In order to address some of these areas of concern in the classroom, Ms. Moore asked the special education teacher to help her come up with some adaptations she could implement. The two teachers worked together to find material Ms. Moore could use to review skills and phonemic elements Rebecca had not yet mastered. Rebecca also worked with a Grade 5 peer helper, who read with her one-on-one three days a week. Ms. Moore consistently restated oral instructions, continued to work on improving Rebecca's phonics skills, and encouraged her to predict unknown words based on meaning and evaluate whether the word she guessed fit with the rest of the words in the sentence. After two months, Ms. Moore has not seen an improvement in Rebecca's reading, writing, or listening skills. She knows she needs to meet with Rebecca's parents to revisit the topic of making a referral for psycho-educational testing to investigate Rebecca's difficulties, but she is unsure how she is going to convince them to make a referral when others have been unsuccessful.

CONSIDER THIS

Reflect on the students who were your classmates during elementary and secondary school. Do you remember any peers who had good academic abilities in some areas and low achievement in others? Were they ever accused of not trying or being lazy? They may have been misunderstood children with learning disabilities.

INTRODUCTION

Just as it is difficult to distinguish children with **learning disabilities (LD)** from their peers by looks, you cannot distinguish adults with learning disabilities from other adults. You may be surprised to find that many important and famous people have achieved significant accomplishments in spite of experiencing a severe learning disability. Adults with learning disabilities can be found in all professions. They may be teachers, lawyers, doctors, factory workers, or politicians! Read the vignette that follows, and see if you can identify the name of the individual with a learning disability.

During his childhood, this young man was an outstanding athlete, achieving great success and satisfaction from sports. Unfortunately, he struggled in the classroom. He tried very hard, but he always seemed to fail academically. His biggest fear was being asked to stand up and read in front of his classmates. He was frequently teased about his class performance, and he described his school days as sheer torture. His only feelings of success were experienced on the playing field.

When he graduated from high school, he didn't consider going to university because he "wasn't a terrific student, and never got into books all that much." Even though he was an outstanding high-school pole-vaulter, he did not get a single scholarship during his senior year. He had already gone to work with his father when he was offered a $500 football scholarship from Graceland College. He didn't accept that offer; instead he trained in track and field. Several years later, he won a gold medal in the Olympics in the gruelling decathlon event! In case you haven't guessed, this story is about Bruce Jenner.

Individuals with learning disabilities are often misunderstood and teased early in life for their inadequacies in the classroom. In order to succeed, they have to be creative and persistent. Adults with learning disabilities rely on sheer determination to overcome their limitations and focus on their talents.

Perhaps the most difficult aspect of understanding and teaching students with learning disabilities is that the disability is hidden. When students with obviously normal intelligence fail to finish their work, interrupt inappropriately, never seem to follow directions, and turn in sloppy, poorly organized assignments, it is natural to blame poor motivation and lack of effort—and even an undesirable family life.

However, lack of accomplishment and success in the classroom *does* have a cause; the students are not demonstrating these behaviours to upset or irritate their teachers. A learning disability is a cognitive disability; it is a disorder of thinking and reasoning. The dysfunction is presumed to be in the central nervous system, so its presence is not visible.

Individuals with learning disabilities experience the frustration of living with a disability that is not easily identified. Children with learning disabilities look like the other students in their grade. They can perform like the other students in some areas, but not in others. As illustrated in the chapter-opening vignette, a child with a learning disability may have good social skills and make good grades in math, but fail in reading. Another child with a learning disability may be able to read and write at grade level, but fail in math and get in trouble for misconduct. Students with learning disabilities also may perform inconsistently. They may, for example, know spelling words on Thursday and fail the test on Friday. Each individual identified with a learning disability will have unique strengths and areas of need.

In this chapter you will study the strengths and needs of children, youth, and adults who experience unexplained underachievement. Professionals from many fields have joined the search for a definition and the causes of these exceptionalities, as well as methods to identify affected children and to successfully accommodate or remediate aspects of their exceptionality. The answers are still evolving, but much progress has been made in this exciting field.

BASIC CONCEPTS ABOUT LEARNING DISABILITIES
Learning Disabilities Defined

Initial studies of children later described as having learning disabilities were done by physicians interested in brain injury in children. Over the years, more than 90 terms have been introduced into the literature to describe these children (Deiner, 1993). The most common terms include *minimal brain dysfunction (MBD)*, *brain damaged*, *central process dysfunction*, and *language delayed*. Separate definitions were also offered to explain each term, which only added to the confusion. The term *specific learning disabilities* was first adopted publicly in 1963 at a meeting of parents and professionals. Kirk (1962) developed the generic term *learning disabilities* in an effort to unite the field, which was torn between different theories on underachievement. The term was received favourably because it did not have the negative connotations of the other terms and did describe the primary characteristic of the children in question.

In the United States, the most widely used definition of *learning disabilities* is the one featured in the *Individuals with Disabilities Education Act* (IDEA). This definition, modified only slightly over the years, has been reformatted into the following three sections under the Act (2004):

■ *IN GENERAL: The term* specific learning disability *means a disorder in one or more of the basic psychological processes involved in understanding or in using language, spoken or written, which disorder may manifest itself in an imperfect ability to listen, think, speak, read, write, spell, or to do mathematical calculations.*

■ *DISORDERS INCLUDED: The term includes such conditions as perceptual disabilities, brain injury, minimal brain dysfunction, dyslexia, and developmental aphasia.*

■ *DISORDERS NOT INCLUDED: The term does not include a learning problem that is primarily the result of visual, hearing, or motor disabilities, of intellectual impairment, of emotional disturbance, or of environmental, cultural, or economic disadvantage.*

A majority of states use the IDEA definition, but it has been criticized for including concepts that are unclear or difficult to use to identify children with a learning disability (Swanson, 2000). For example, the concept of deficits in "psychological processes" has been interpreted in several ways, including perceptual-motor deficits, deficits in the process of taking in information, difficulty in making sense of information and expressing knowledge effectively, and deficits in cognitive processes, such as attention, memory, and metacognition (the way one thinks about and controls one's cognitive processing—e.g., self-monitoring, predicting, and planning). As a result, the U.S. Office of Education (USOE) did not include a measure of psychological processes when publishing the original criteria for identifying students with learning disabilities (USOE, 1977). The agency focused instead on identifying a discrepancy between a child's ability and his or her achievement in reading, math, written language, speaking, or listening. Most recently, the practice of documenting a discrepancy between IQ and achievement—for LD identification—has been made optional in the U.S. (IDEA, 2004).

In 2002, the Learning Disabilities Association of Canada (LDAC) defined *learning disabilities* as follows:

> *Learning disabilities refer to a number of disorders which may affect the acquisition, organization, retention, understanding or use of verbal or nonverbal information. These disorders affect learning in individuals who otherwise demonstrate at least average abilities essential for thinking and/or reasoning. As such, learning disabilities are distinct from global intellectual deficiency.*
>
> *Learning disabilities result from impairments in one or more processes related to perceiving, thinking, remembering or learning. These include, but are not limited to: language processing; phonological processing; visual spatial processing; processing speed; memory and attention; and executive functions (e.g., planning and decision-making).*
>
> *Learning disabilities range in severity and may interfere with the acquisition and use of one or more of the following:*
>
> ■ *oral language (e.g., listening, speaking, understanding);*
> ■ *reading (e.g., decoding, phonetic knowledge, word recognition, comprehension);*

- *written language (e.g., spelling, written expression); and*
- *mathematics (e.g., computation, problem solving).*

Learning disabilities may also involve difficulties with organizational skills, social perception, social interaction and perspective taking.

Learning disabilities are lifelong. The way in which they are expressed may vary over an individual's lifetime, depending on the interaction between the demands of the environment and the individual's strengths and needs. Learning disabilities are suggested by unexpected academic under-achievement or achievement which is maintained only by unusually high levels of effort and support.

Learning disabilities are due to genetic and/or neurobiological factors or injury that alters brain functioning in a manner which affects one or more processes related to learning. These disorders are not due primarily to hearing and/or vision problems, socio-economic factors, cultural or linguistic differences, lack of motivation or ineffective teaching, although these factors may further complicate the challenges faced by individuals with learning disabilities. Learning disabilities may co-exist with various conditions including attentional, behavioural and emotional disorders, sensory impairments or other medical conditions. (Learning Disabilities Association of Canada, 2002)

Although this definition has been accepted by LDAC and has influenced the definitions adopted by the individual provinces or territories, the actual process of identification of children with learning disabilities varies across the country.

Prevalence and Causes of Learning Disabilities

In today's schools, there are, by far, more students with learning disabilities than with any other exceptionality. In both Canada and the United States, it is estimated that approximately half of all exceptional students have learning disabilities (LDAC, n.d.; U.S. Department of Education, 2002). It is important to note:

It is difficult to establish the prevalence among Canadian children for many reasons, including lack of diagnosis and reluctance of parents to identify their children as learning disabled due to stigmatization. But the long-standing rate of 1 in 10 Canadians—although thought to be a low estimate—can most likely be applied to children as well as the population as a whole given that learning disabilities are lifelong. (Government of Canada, 2009, p. 24)

However, using data from the 2002/2003 National Longitudinal Survey of Children and Youth (NLSCY), 4 percent of Canadian children aged 8 to 11 years were identified with a learning disability in 2002 (Hou, Milan, & Wong, 2006).

Advances in methods that are reasonably reliable in detecting brain abnormalities, such as computerized imaging techniques, have led to the generally accepted view that learning disabilities are the result of differences in brain function or structure (Hallahan et al., 2005). The literature suggests several causes for neurological differences or dysfunction, primarily hereditary factors and trauma experienced before birth, during birth, and after birth. Following is adapted from a summary provided by Hallahan and colleagues (2005).

1. *Genetic and hereditary influences*: Many studies have cited the large number of relatives with learning problems in children identified with learning disabilities. Chromosomal

CROSS REFERENCE

Fetal alcohol spectrum disorder is discussed in more detail in chapter 8.

CONSIDER THIS

Often, parents will ask teachers what causes a learning disability. You might discuss some of the possible causes and suggest that a single cause is seldom identifiable for individual children. Reassure them that pinpointing the cause is not a factor in planning and implementing effective intervention strategies.

abnormalities and structural brain differences have also been linked to learning disabilities. Raskind (2001) describes the progress that has been made identifying the gene location for a learning disability in reading. Research in this area continues to show promise.

2. *Causes occurring before birth*: Learning problems have been linked to injuries to the embryo or fetus caused by the birth mother's use of alcohol, cigarettes, or other drugs such as cocaine and prescription and nonprescription drugs. The fetus, through the mother, is exposed to the toxins, which cause malformations of the developing brain and central nervous system. Although significant amounts of overexposure to these drugs may cause serious problems, such as intellectual disabilities, no safe levels have been identified. For more information, refer to the section "Fetal Alcohol Spectrum Disorders" (FASD) presented in chapter 8.

3. *Causes occurring during birth process*: Traumas during birth may include prolonged labour, anoxia, prematurity, and injury from medical instruments such as forceps. Although not all children with a traumatic birth are found to have learning problems later on, a significant number of children with learning problems do have a history of complications during birth.

4. *Causes occurring after birth*: High fever, encephalitis, meningitis, stroke, diabetes, head trauma, and pediatric acquired immune deficiency syndrome (AIDS) have been linked to learning disabilities. Malnutrition, poor postnatal health care, and lead ingestion can also lead to neurological dysfunction.

Advances in neurological research and the use of computerized neurological techniques such as computerized axial tomography (CAT) scans and positron emission tomography (PET) scans have made professionals more inclined to believe in a neurological explanation of learning disabilities. Widespread use of these tests to identify a learning disability, however, has not been forthcoming for several reasons: such procedures are expensive and invasive, and the documented presence of a neurological dysfunction does not affect how the child is taught (Hallahan et al., 2005). Neurological research is important to advance knowledge of this type of exceptionality and in the future may help determine the effectiveness of various treatment techniques. Studies are underway, for example, that monitor the impact of various reading interventions on the results of neuroimaging (Pugh et al., 2001). A neurophysicist has recommended using neuroimaging to identify young children with reading problems for treatment purposes, noting that learning to read can cause the brain to change and become like the brain of good readers (Richards, 2001). Perhaps one day brain imaging could be used to determine the best methods for teaching.

Characteristics of Students with Learning Disabilities

Learning disabilities are primarily described as a deficit in academic achievement (reading, writing, and mathematics) or language (listening and speaking). However, children with learning disabilities may have significant problems in other areas, such as social interactions and emotional maturity, attention and hyperactivity, memory, cognition, metacognition, motor skills, and perceptual abilities. As well, students with learning disabilities tend to be overly optimistic regarding some of their abilities, masking strategy and skill deficits. They may need more support in these areas than they report that they need (Klassen, 2002). Learning disabilities are presumed to be a central nervous system dysfunction, so characteristics may be manifested throughout the lifespan (preschool to adulthood) (Bender, 2001).

The most common characteristics of students with learning disabilities are described briefly in the following sections, concentrating on the challenges those characteristics may create in a classroom. Students with learning disabilities are a heterogeneous group. A single student will typically not have difficulties in all of these areas. In addition, a student with a learning disability may be average or above average in one or more of these areas and might actually exceed the abilities of his or her peers in that particular area. For example, a student with average or above-average abilities in math, metacognition, and social skills may experience limitations in reading, writing, and attention. Another student might have strengths in attention, writing, and reading, but be challenged in math, social skills, and metacognition. An understanding of the characteristics of each individual with learning difficulties will be important in developing pre-referral interventions, making appropriate referrals, and identifying effective adaptations and accommodations and intervention strategies. Figure 4.1 displays the possible strengths and areas of need of children with learning disabilities.

Academic Difficulties

During the elementary years, a discrepancy between ability and achievement begins to emerge in students with learning disabilities. Often puzzling to teachers, these students seem to have strengths similar to their peers in several areas, but their rate of learning in other areas is unexpectedly slower. In the vignette that began this chapter, Rebecca typifies a child with learning disabilities: above-average ability in math; seemingly average ability in language, attention, and social skills; and severe difficulties in reading, written expression, and listening.

The academic problems that serve to identify a learning disability fall into the areas of reading, math, and written expression. The most prevalent academic difficulty for students with learning disabilities is reading. However, this does not mean that a learning

TEACHING TIP

Just as students who demonstrate reading difficulties may have difficulties understanding and using language, students with receptive and expressive language difficulties may have difficulties reading. Consult with the speech-language pathologist and reading consultant in your school to determine whether students demonstrating reading or language difficulties require further assessments in either area.

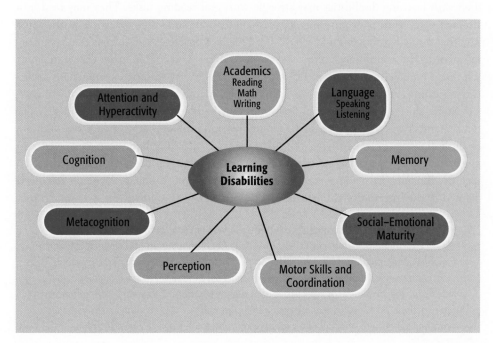

Figure 4.1 Areas of Possible Strengths and Needs of Students with Learning Disabilities

During Grades 2 through 6, academic problems begin to become obvious.

⬤─Watch

Learning Disabilities

disability is the same thing as a reading disability. Although people equate learning disabilities with reading disabilities, reading problems form only one type of academic learning disability. There are also spelling, writing, and mathematics disabilities, as well as nonacademic learning disabilities, such as perceptual, memory, and visual-motor disabilities. Lyon et al. (2001) reported that approximately 80 percent of children identified with a learning disability have primary difficulties in the area of reading and related language functions. Problems may be noted in *basic reading skills* and *reading comprehension*. Children with learning disabilities may struggle with oral reading tasks. They may read in a strained voice with poor phrasing, ignore punctuation, and grope for words in the same way that a much younger child would. Oral reading problems cause tremendous embarrassment to these children. Polloway, Patton, and Serna (2001) confirm that a student's self-image and feelings of confidence are greatly affected by reading experience. Difficulties in reading skills can also lead to acting-out behaviour and poor motivation.

Some children with learning disabilities may be able to say the words correctly but not remember what they have read. Comprehension problems may include one or more of the following: (1) identifying the main idea, (2) recalling basic facts and events in a sequence, and (3) making inferences or evaluating what has been read. A child with a specific difficulty in reading may be described as having **dyslexia**. Dyslexia has been defined by the International Dyslexia Association (IDA) as follows:

> *Dyslexia is a specific learning disability that is neurological in origin. It is characterized by difficulties with accurate and/or fluent word recognition and by poor spelling and decoding abilities. These difficulties typically result from a deficit in the phonological component of language that is often unexpected in relation to other cognitive abilities and the provision of effective classroom instruction. Secondary consequences may include problems in reading comprehension and reduced reading experience that can impede growth of vocabulary and background knowledge. (IDA, 2002)*

Another major academic problem area is mathematics. Students with learning disabilities may have problems in *math computation* or *math reasoning* (LDAC, 2002). These conceptual and skill areas include difficulties in the four operations, the concept of zero, regrouping, place value, basic math concepts (e.g., one-to-one correspondence, sets), and solving math problems. Children may have *abilities* in calculation but have *disabilities* in math reasoning; they may make many errors in calculations but be able to solve a math word problem. Often, the rate of response interferes with success in math; for example, a child may be able to perform the skill but be unable to complete the number of problems required during the time allowed. Robinson, Manchetti, and Torgesen (2002) proposed that for some children this math difficulty may be due to either problems in the phonological processing of the features of spoken numbers or failure to grasp meaningful aspects of numbers. They note that 43 percent of students with a math disability also have reading problems. It is hoped that math disabilities will soon be studied as intensely as reading disabilities. A disability in math may be referred to as **dyscalculia**.

Learning disabilities in the area of *writing* are beginning to receive more recognition as a potentially serious problem. The three main areas of concern are handwriting, spelling, and written expression, including mechanics and creativity. The impact of written language problems increases with a student's age because so many school assignments require a written product. A learning disability in writing may be referred to as **dysgraphia**.

Language Difficulties Individuals may demonstrate *oral expression* (speaking) or *listening comprehension* difficulties. These two areas control our ability to communicate with others, so any areas of need can have a major impact on quality of life—including life in a general education classroom! Common oral language problems include difficulty in retrieving words. This is often seen when children use a less appropriate word because the right word will not come to them. The response rate of children with learning disabilities may be slower than that of their typically achieving peers, and they may speak more slowly. If ample time is not allowed for a response, the student's behaviour may be misinterpreted as failure to understand or refusal to participate. Children with learning disabilities tend to use simpler, less mature language and confuse sequences in retelling a story. Listening problems also can be easily misinterpreted. A child with an exceptionality in listening demonstrates his or her difficulties in a negative way, for example, by failing to follow directions or by appearing oppositional or unmotivated. A teacher's careful observation and assessment of a student's language ability is therefore important for ensuring the student's success. Figure 4.2 provides examples of how speech can become "twisted" for students with receptive language (e.g., listening) deficits. These deficits may be referred to as auditory processing deficits.

CROSS REFERENCE

Refer to chapter 3 to review other language areas in which students with learning disabilities may demonstrate difficulties.

These are actual "mis-heard" sayings from an individual who has a receptive language/listening learning disability.

1. Rocker buy bay bee inner tree hops ["Rock-a-bye baby in the tree top"]
2. Turnip out fir play ["Turnabout is fair play"]
3. Roland's tone gadders nome hoss ["A rolling stone gathers no moss"]
4. Sinker's honkers sick spentz ["Sing a song of sixpence"]
5. Law tent britches full in town ["London Bridge is falling down"]

Figure 4.2 Family Air Sangs (Familiar Sayings)

Source: "Recognizing and Responding to Cultural Differences in the Education of Culturally and Linguistically Diverse Learners," by S.P. Chamberlain, 2005, *Intervention in School and Clinic, 40*(4), p. 207.

An area of concern, and a subject of current research pertaining to children with language-learning disabilities, is the use of language in social communication situations—i.e., **pragmatics**. Children with these exceptionalities are sometimes unsuccessful in fully participating in conversation. They may need extra time to process incoming information, may not understand the meaning of the words or word sequences, may change the subject of a conversation, may ask inappropriate questions, may miss nonverbal language cues (i.e., frowns), may not understand jokes, or may laugh inappropriately or at the wrong times. Group work is often difficult, as is giving or following directions. Language disabilities can contribute significantly to difficulties in other social situations.

Social-Emotional Problems Some children with learning disabilities have good social skills and are well-liked by their peers and their teachers. However, several characteristics of learning disabilities, like those noted in the area of language, can create difficulties in an individual's social and emotional life. Social skill deficits of children with learning disabilities may include resolving conflict, managing frustration, initiating or joining a conversation or play activity, listening, demonstrating empathy, maintaining a friendship, and working in groups. Establishing and maintaining peer relationships is often an area of difficulty for individuals with learning disabilities. When completing a review of the literature relating to social skills and peer relationships (peer status, friendship, peer victimization, and loneliness), Wiener (2004) found that "considerable research has documented the social skill deficits of children with LD and their difficulties with peer relationships. Although social skill deficits are associated with their problematic peer relationships, the data suggest that a multiple-risk model should be explored" (p. 29). That is, we should examine whether the presence of one or more risk factors (such as problematic parenting, comorbid ADHD) results in internalizing and externalizing behaviour problems (Wiener, 2004). Furthermore, about a third of students with learning disabilities have nonverbal or social disabilities (Morris, 2002). These students and those with attention deficit/hyperactivity disorder (AD/HD) have also been shown to have lower self-concept in academics and social relations (Tabassam & Grainger, 2002).

Often, positive interactions and exchanges of information do not occur between children with learning disabilities and their peers or teachers. Children with learning disabilities need more guidance and structure, particularly if they present with behaviour and language differences. Over time, these needs can create feelings of overdependency, and eventually "learned helplessness" can occur. Social deficits have even been known to lead to school failure (Bryan, Burstein, & Ergul, 2004), and, in turn, years of failure can eventually result in psychological problems, including feelings of anxiety, depression, inadequacy, frustration, and anger (Bender, 2002). Confusion and frustration can also result in aggressive behaviour (Allsopp, Santos, & Linn, 2000). By adolescence, a student's combined cognitive and language deficits can interfere significantly with deciding how to act in the new social situations brought about by increased independence. When interacting with typically achieving adolescents who have advanced language skills, students with exceptionalities may experience greater failure in communication and may suffer more rejection (Morris, 2002).

In summary, Wiener and Schneider (2002) found that learning disabilities are often linked with an increase in emotional distress. While emotional issues may mask or exacerbate a child's learning disabilities, positive emotional health can enhance the performance of students with learning disabilities. Teachers should, then, be sensitive to

CROSS REFERENCE

Often, students with learning disabilities have social-emotional problems and will present challenges in behaviour management in the classroom. Refer to chapter 6 for more information.

TEACHING TIP

Encourage students who have listening difficulties to ask questions when listening to a speaker (e.g., "You said to finish chapter 3. Does this mean we're supposed to answer the chapter questions?"). This can help students clarify the message a speaker is conveying.

emotional issues and take care to include students with learning disabilities in supportive situations, providing reinforcement for specific successes. General praise statements such as "Good work!" or "You are really smart" will not have much impact because they are not believable to the students. Commenting on or rewarding specific accomplishments is more effective. Additional examples of appropriate interventions are discussed later in this chapter and in future chapters.

Attention Difficulties and Hyperactivity Attention is a critical skill in learning. Children must be able to initiate attention, focus their attention in the appropriate direction, sustain their attention according to the task demands, and shift attention when appropriate. Difficulties in these areas can have an impact on all aspects of success in school. When children are "not paying attention," they cannot respond appropriately to questions, follow directions, or take notes during a lecture. The excess movement of a hyperactive student can draw sharp criticism when it negatively affects the learning environment. Social problems occur when the student interrupts others and does not listen to his or her peers. Students with attention problems often have trouble finishing assignments, or they rush through their work with little regard for detail. Estimates of the number of students with learning disabilities who have attention problems vary widely based on the stringency of the criteria used to define the attention deficit (Smith & Adams, 2006). However, the majority of individuals with learning disabilities do not have attention deficit disorders (Weber & Bennett, 1999). Attention deficits are covered more thoroughly in chapter 5.

CROSS REFERENCE

Students with learning disabilities may also have attention deficit/hyperactivity disorders. This topic is covered more extensively in chapter 5.

Memory Difficulties Students with learning disabilities have deficits in short-term memory, working memory, and long-term memory (Hallahan et al., 2005). Short-term memory problems show up when a child has difficulty repeating information heard less than one or two minutes earlier. Working memory problems occur when students are trying to take recent information and organize it for storage or link it to information previously stored in long-term memory to broaden their knowledge about a subject. Long-term memory problems relate to difficulties accessing information that has been stored and is typically available for access over a long period of time. Students may have problems with auditory or visual memory. Work by McNamara and Wong (2003) confirms that students' memory problems have a negative impact on everyday tasks and situations as well as on academic demands. Teachers and parents may also report that memory skills are inconsistent—for example, a student with a learning disability may know the multiplication facts on Thursday but fail the test on Friday. The good news is that when children with learning disabilities are taught memory strategies, they make substantial gains at all grade levels (Scruggs & Mastropieri, 2000).

TEACHING TIP

Help students with memory difficulties remember and follow oral directions by breaking up longer directions into multiple steps (e.g., "Turn to page 12 in your math book; complete questions 1, 3, and 5; hand in your work.").

Cognition Difficulties Cognition refers to the ability to reason or think (Hallahan et al., 2005). Students with problems in this area may make poor decisions or frequent errors. They may have trouble getting started on a task, have delayed verbal responses, require more supervision, or have trouble adjusting to change. Understanding social expectations may be difficult. They may require concrete demonstrations. They often have trouble using previously learned information in a new situation.

Metacognition Difficulties Hallahan et al. (2005) refer to **metacognition** as "thinking about thinking." Metacognitive deficits include the inability to control and direct one's own attention and mental processes (Wong, 2004). Students with problems in this area might have difficulty focusing on listening, purposefully remembering important information, connecting that information to prior knowledge, making sense out of the new information, and using what they know to solve a problem. They often lack strategies for planning and organizing, setting priorities, and predicting and solving problems. An important component of metacognition is the ability to evaluate one's own behaviour and behave differently when identifying inappropriate behaviours or mistakes.

Perceptual Differences Perceptual disorders affect the ability to recognize stimuli being received through sight, hearing, or touch and to discriminate between and interpret the sensations appropriately. A child with a learning disability might not have any problems in these areas, or he or she might have deficits in any or all of them. Identification of deficits and training in the perceptual processes was emphasized in the early 1970s; however, it is no longer a prominent consideration in the education of children with learning disabilities.

Motor Skills and Coordination Problems This area has also been de-emphasized in the identification of an intervention for children with learning disabilities because it is not directly related to academics. However, it is common for children with learning disabilities to display problems in gross motor areas; they often cannot throw and catch a ball or may have a clumsy gait. Common fine motor deficits include difficulties with cutting with scissors, buttoning clothing, and handwriting. Occupational therapists refer to this profile as a developmental coordination disorder (DCD) and for more than a decade have acknowledged the overlap between this disorder and learning disabilities (Martini, Heath, & Missiunia, 1999). Consideration of motor skills and coordination is important in the selection of a vocational program and ultimately in the identification of a career.

Identification, Assessment, and Eligibility

In the United States, the federal Office of Education specified criteria for identifying a learning disability (USOE, 1977), stating that there must be a "severe discrepancy" between achievement and intellectual ability. Similarly, the Learning Disabilities Association of Canada definition (LDAC, 1987, 2002) indicates that individuals with learning disabilities will have potentially average or above-average intelligence with delays in specific areas (e.g., reading, writing, or arithmetic). Recently, however, policy-makers in the United States have begun to emphasize the importance of developing a "genuine science" for dealing with learning disabilities (Elksnin et al., 2001). The recent reauthorization of IDEA (2004) reflected the thinking that significant changes were needed in the policies used to identify and serve students with learning disabilities; specifically, requiring documentation of a discrepancy between achievement and IQ was determined to be unnecessary and insufficient for identifying individuals with specific learning disabilities (SLD). Stanovich (2005) believes that a reliance on the use of a discrepancy definition in the field of learning disabilities is flawed. "The persistence of the discrepancy concept in LD signals that the field is not ready to put itself on a scientific footing and that it will continue to operate on the borders of pseudoscience" (Stanovich, 2005, p. 103). The use of a discrepancy model has been supplemented or replaced in many states by the responsiveness-to-intervention (RTI) model. IDEA describes this approach "as a process that determines if a child responds to scientific, research-based intervention as a part of the evaluation procedures." The model is based on the assumption that a student with exceptionalities will make satisfactory progress when given intensive, well-designed instruction (National Joint Committee on Learning Disabilities, 2005). This is a pre-referral intervention implemented in the general education classroom; it is predicted to reduce the number of special education referrals using a problem-solving approach rather than a mathematical discrepancy formula.

Lyon and colleagues (2001) propose that the RTI model applied to students with reading deficits could reduce the number of students with reading problems by up to 70 percent. Schools have been strongly encouraged to adopt this model based on the premise that it would result in earlier identification of children who may need special education services and offer more timely and effective support for all students experiencing academic difficulties, especially in the early elementary school years. However, not all professionals and parents are in full support of this model. Researchers believe there are a number of questions that need to be addressed before RTI will be successful (e.g., intensity of intervention, professional(s) best placed to deliver intervention, etc.; Fuchs, Fuchs, McMaster, Yen, & Svenson, 2004; Fuchs, Mock, Morgan, & Young, 2003; Fuchs, 2003; Vaughn & Fuchs, 2003). Figure 4.3 presents some of the pro and con arguments being made in the debate over the replacement of the discrepancy clause with the RTI model.

The U.S. National Research Center on Learning Disabilities and the six regional research centres in the United States are charged with identifying best practices in the RTI model, including identifying model programs.

((•—[Listen

Leonard Baca on RTI and Cultural Considerations

Figure 4.3 Issues Raised at the LD Summit and in the Literature

With the negative impact often created by the use of a learning disabilities label (Higgins, Raskind, Goldberg, & Herman, 2002), some feel it is critical that we apply the label only to those who are truly learning disabled. Others have asked why students with specific learning disabilities are any more entitled to resources than those who struggle for other reasons or who are just slow (Finn, Rotherham, & Hokanson, 2002). MacMillan and Siperstein (2001) suggest that public schools are using low achievement alone without considering the discrepancy from aptitude, essentially making learning disabilities a "category of failure" or low achievement. Kavale and colleagues (2006) suggest that without the discrepancy factor, the existence of learning disabilities as a category is endangered. However, he contends that determining discrepancy should be only one component of the assessment process. Wise and Snyder (2001), primarily focusing on reading, recommend the use of clinical judgment to determine disability and to identify the most effective instructional interventions. Other researchers also studying reading found that students with low achievement had scores that were higher than students with learning disabilities, especially on timed measures requiring skills in comprehension. Their research suggests that students with learning disabilities may be the lowest of the low achievers. Still others suggest that it is the lack of response to intervention that separates learning disabilities from other low-achieving groups, and they recommend that this be considered in identification (Fuchs, Fuchs, Mathes, Lipsey, & Roberts, 2001). Kavale and colleagues (2006) warn that using the RTI model to identify students with learning disabilities creates the potential for "diagnostic chaos." They propose that, at best, the RTI model will identify students at such risk for reading failure that they will require intensive intervention to have any chance for success. Conversely, Francis and colleagues (2005) purport that the weakness of using a discrepancy score is that the measurement is of one point in time, using norm-referenced testing that has low reliability, whereas the RTI uses behaviours related to classroom performance and has more reliability than the norm-referenced testing.

In 2001, over 100 000 Canadian children aged 5 to 14 were reported to have learning disabilities, representing 64.9 percent of children with exceptionalities in this age group (Statistics Canada, 2001a). Among these school-age children with exceptionalities, boys (68.9 percent) were more likely to have a learning disability than girls (58.0 percent; Statistics Canada, 2001a). The percentage of children identified as having a learning disability varies from province to province, and even from school division to school division, depending on the identification procedures being used. Ultimately, teachers in Canadian schools need to familiarize themselves with the criteria used in their province and school division. A teacher must be aware of characteristics of students with learning disabilities to know when he or she might want to further document a student's strengths and areas of need for a possible referral to the school psychologist or school team.

Difficulty of Identifying Preschool Students with Learning Disabilities

The criteria for determining a learning disability (USOE, 1977) mainly involve academic and language deficits that emerge in the elementary years; therefore, the identification of exceptionalities and the delivery of special education services for preschool children have been difficult and often controversial (Jenkins & O'Connor, 2001). One approach described by Hallahan and colleagues (2005) has been to identify students with a generic label, such as "developmental delay." In this model, students are determined to be at risk for school failure and receive assistance with the language, academic, or motor skills in which they are generally found to be lagging behind as compared to their peers. The advantage of this approach is that it helps a large number of students if the criterion is a small developmental delay. However, if a significant delay is required in order to be eligible for services, the students with potential learning disabilities may be excluded. That is, it is much easier to identify an intellectual impairment using more stringent criteria and less easy to identify the more subtle indicators of a learning disability.

The alternative to the generic approach is the identification of the specific disability. Mercer and Pullen (2005) describe several issues that make this approach difficult. The greatest complication is the tremendous differences in children's growth and maturation—differences that are normal and that may not represent a learning disability. Mercer and Pullen (2005) and Hallahan and colleagues (2005) offer caution against early identification of learning disabilities. One concern is the difficulty in diagnosis that results from the inadequacy of assessment tools and procedures for this age group. Young children may have language and other skills that are lower than expected based on IQ, but it is difficult to determine whether these are the result of a learning disability, a maturational lag, or the effect of diverse educational experiences, language, or culture. An additional concern is the risk of diagnosing a learning disability where none exists, thus labelling and burdening the child unnecessarily. However, this argument does not address the equal risk of failing to diagnose and appropriately assist a student who needs special educational services; such a student may, too, be burdened by difficulties and failure that could have been avoided.

✱ Explore

Is This Child Mislabelled?

Critics call current practice for learning disabilities identification the "wait and fail" effect as the gap or discrepancy between ability and achievement becomes large enough to be labelled a severe discrepancy that warrants services (MacMillan & Siperstein, 2001). Lyon et al. (2001) concluded that a child must be nine years old before discrepancy between IQ and achievement can be measured reliably. Thus, under the discrepancy model, potentially life-changing failure occurs for several years. Lyon et al. further suggest that early intervention can be so critical for exceptionalities in the area of reading that children with a strong family history of attention difficulties or reading failure should be labelled at risk and placed in a preventive intervention program to strengthen their areas of weakness. Hammill (2004) identifies the following skills as effective screening items for identifying young children at risk for future reading failure (i.e., children who have difficulties mastering these skills are deemed at risk): "Handling books; copying letters and numbers, writing their names; distinguishing print from nonprint markings; naming and writing letters and numbers; knowing the meaning of a few abbreviations and acronyms; discriminating among letters, numbers, and words; identifying and spelling some preprimer words."

CULTURAL AND LINGUISTIC DIVERSITY

Learning disabilities are found in approximately 5 percent of the school-age population, and the number of school-age children with cultural and language diversity is growing steadily; many children will inevitably fall into both groups. Although the issues related to educating all culturally diverse children apply to the population of children with learning disabilities as well, the existence of a learning disability does present additional challenges in assessment for identification, program planning, instructional implementation, and personnel preparation. Much of the literature on special education supports the idea that there is an overrepresentation of culturally and linguistically diverse learners. Chamberlain (2005) suggests that this is due to multiple variables, some of which, like poverty, are beyond the realm of education; others, like inadequate instruction and assessment practices, should be addressed.

Accurately identifying a learning disability in the presence of cultural diversity is no small challenge. School personnel must carefully determine that the differences related to diversity are not the primary cause of a student's learning difficulties. In other words, the student's learning difficulties must be significantly different when compared to peers in age, grade, and culture. In Canada, we have a large multicultural population, two official languages, and second-language immersion programs in our education systems. These factors make the identification and instruction of students with learning disabilities a complex endeavour.

Gregory (2004) reports that too often a diagnosis of a learning disability is based on intelligence and achievement tests administered in English, without considering cultural and language differences. The discrepancy model is considered especially problematic when applied to culturally and linguistically diverse students because of their problems in using standardized tests. The referral itself may be made because a teacher has been ineffective in teaching a student who comes from another culture or who understands little of the language of the classroom. In this case, the child's failure to make progress may not be the result of a learning disability but may be due to the failure of the education system to respect and adequately respond to cultural and language differences (Garcia & Guerra, 2004). Chamberlain (2005) refers to these as "cultural clashes" and suggests teachers sometimes expect less from students from diverse cultural backgrounds and view special education as the most viable placement option for them. As a result, a disproportionate number is referred for assessment and ultimately funnelled into special education settings. However, it is certainly possible that a child at a low socio-economic level or who is an English language learner could have a central nervous system dysfunction that results in a learning disability. Fuchs, Mock, Morgan, and Young (2003) propose the RTI pre-referral

Understanding and speaking a language other than English may have a significant impact on the assessment process. Inappropriate referrals, identification of an exceptionality, or inappropriate programming might result.

Figure 4.4 Addressing Cultural and Linguistic Diversity in the Assessment Process

From: "Recognizing and Responding to Cultural Differences in the Education of Culturally and Linguistically Diverse Learners," by S.P. Chamberlain, 2005, *Intervention in School and Clinic,* *40*(4), p. 207.

Following are recommendations for anyone involved in the assessment of students. These were compiled by Chamberlain (2005) from a variety of sources.

1. Understand nondiscriminatory assessment practices. Bias may occur when English tests are used for students more fluent in another language, when tests have items that are biased, and when eligibility is determined using tests covering material the student has not had an opportunity to learn.

2. Rely less on norm-referenced data and more on comprehensive sets of data, such as curriculum-based assessment techniques that measure directly what is being taught in the classroom.

3. Support well-designed pre-referral intervention to lessen the number of referrals and lead to properly identified students' receiving special education services.

4. Advocate for students by using a comprehensive set of assessment procedures, being alert for the possibility of bias, and validating the results of norm-referenced tests.

TEACHING TIP

Teachers can use holistic approaches to literacy development to address students' varied linguistic needs (e.g., utilize thematic literature units to integrate language teaching across the curriculum; assign daily journal entries to encourage daily writing practice).

CONSIDER THIS

According to Lyon's (2001) study, intervention in reading skills in Grades 1 to 3 is critical. Should all students who are behind their peers in reading ability be helped during these years? What are possible positive and negative outcomes of providing a "special education" program for these children at risk for later failure?

model as a promising approach to reduce the overrepresentation of culturally and linguistically diverse students in special education. In this model, underachievement is addressed by more intense instruction with ongoing monitoring of progress by a team of individuals and a variety of nonstandardized measurement techniques. Recommendations for anyone involved in the assessment of culturally and linguistically diverse students are presented in Figure 4.4.

When a student is determined eligible for special education services, the process of designing and implementing an appropriate educational plan is critical. Teachers may be uninformed about the short- and long-term goals held by families from different cultures. Therefore, family participation and ongoing communication about progress are essential. Consulting with the student's family, members of the community (e.g., community leaders from different cultural backgrounds), and professionals in the school (e.g., colleagues, principal) can assist the classroom teacher in developing and implementing appropriate educational programming for culturally and linguistically diverse students.

STRATEGIES FOR CURRICULUM AND INSTRUCTION

Over the years, treatment procedures for individuals with learning disabilities have been a source of controversy. In the 1970s, for example, advocates for perceptual training of auditory and visual processes debated those who promoted direct instruction in the deficit academic area(s) (Engelmann & Carnine, 1982). A convincing article by Hammill and Larsen (1974) analyzed research showing that perceptual training did little to improve basic academic skills. This triggered a move toward a skills approach in which direct instruction was implemented in the areas of academic deficit. More recently, language, social-emotional, and cognitive-metacognitive areas have received positive attention. Many approaches have gained acceptance as research-based methods for improving the skills and developing the abilities of children and adults with learning disabilities. Other nontraditional approaches have been proposed and some even have a large following, although they may not be supported by research (Silver, 2003). Teachers need to be well informed on all approaches so that they can provide objective information to parents who seek to understand and address their child's difficulties. The following section discusses the accepted traditional approaches for each age level and provides a brief overview of some of the nontraditional approaches.

Traditional Approaches

In a review of various treatment approaches, Elksnin et al. (2001) conclude that no single approach to learning disabilities can be cited as the best. They suggest that each model has a "partial view of the truth," and "each individually is too narrow to be useful for all students" (Elksnin et al., 2001, p. 189). Many of the following approaches adhere to these time-tested principles and are research-based. They all can be implemented in a general education classroom and may also benefit many typically achieving students. The strategies are discussed according to age levels—preschool, elementary, secondary, and adult. The largest section concerns the elementary school student; however, many elementary-level techniques are equally effective at the secondary level.

Preschool Services In addition to the controversy surrounding assessment and identification of learning disabilities in preschool children, much has been written for and against the educational effectiveness and cost-effectiveness of early intervention programs. Bender (2001) summarizes research in this area by stating that early intervention for some preschool children with learning disabilities—particularly those from low socioeconomic minority groups—is effective.

Mercer (2005) provides an overview of the curriculum models primarily used in preschool programs for children with learning disabilities. These include developmental, cognitive, and behavioural models. The **developmental model** stresses provision of an enriched environment. The child is given numerous experiences and opportunities for learning. Development is stimulated through language and storytelling, field trips, and creative opportunities. These activities are particularly effective with diverse learners (Craig, Hull, Haggart, & Crowder, 2001).

The **cognitive model** (or constructionist model) is based on Piaget's work. Stimulating the child's cognitive or thinking abilities is the primary focus. Activities are designed to improve memory, discrimination, language, concept formation, self-evaluation, problem solving, and comprehension. This area of research is experiencing great success.

Concepts learned by direct instruction and the theory of reinforcement form the basis for the **behavioural model**. Measurable goals are set for each student, behaviours are observed, and desirable behaviour is reinforced. Direct instruction is provided to accomplish goals, and progress is charted to provide data that determine the next instructional task. For example, Abbott, Walton, and Greenwood (2002) used research on **phonemic awareness** to identify skills appropriate for Kindergarten, Grade 1, and Grade 2. Students showing low performance during regular shared-book activities were given lessons several times a week, depending on their level of weakness. Performance was closely monitored and intervention intensified as needed. The Evidence-Based Practice box on page 98 provides an example of a Grade 1 lesson for teaching phonemic awareness.

Mercer (2005) recommends a program that combines features from each approach. He suggests some structure, the availability of free-choice activities, direct instruction in targeted areas, daily charting and feedback, developmental activities, and spontaneous learning experiences. McCardle, Cooper, Houle, Karp, and Paul-Brown (2001) speak to the importance of the birth-to-five period as the foundation for learning as children

FURTHER READING

Learn more about the early identification and diagnosis of specific learning disabilities by reading A.G. Harrison's article, "Recommended Best Practices for the Early Identification and Diagnosis of Children with Specific Learning Disabilities in Ontario," in volume 20 of *Canadian Journal of School Psychology*, 2005 (pp. 21–43).

Explore

Why Hasn't Someone Told Me About This Before?

Evidence-Based Instruction: Sound Blending

Phonemic awareness activities that you may see in Grade 1 classrooms:

Phoneme deletion: Children recognize the word that remains when you take away a phoneme.

Example
Teacher: What is space without the *s*?
Children: *Space* without the *s* is *pace*.

Phoneme addition: Children make a new word by adding a phoneme to a word.

Example
Teacher: What word do you have if you add *p* to the beginning of *lace*?
Children: *Place.*

Phoneme substitution: Children substitute one phoneme for another to make a new word.

Example
Teacher: The word is *rag*. Change *g* to *n*. What's the new word?
Children: *Ran.*

Teaching phonics and word recognition

The teacher …
explicitly teaches the children letter–sound relationships in a clear and useful sequence. The teacher also teaches children "irregular" words they will see and read often, but that do not follow the letter–sound relationships they are learning. These are often called *sight words*—words such as *said, is, was, are.*

The children …
learn to blend sounds to read words—first one-syllable words and, later, words with more than one syllable. They read easy books that include the letter–sound relationships they are learning as well as sight words that they have been taught. They recognize and figure out the meaning of compound words (words made of two words put together, such as *background*). They practise writing the letter–sound relationships in words, sentences, messages, and in their own stories.

From *A Child Becomes a Reader* (p. 33), National Institute for Literacy.

acquire knowledge and develop abilities—particularly in the area of reading. They, like others, speak against the "wait to fail" approach, where children are not identified as struggling readers until Grade 3 or 4. These researchers recommend a focus on book reading, writing, and fine-motor activities such as colouring and drawing, as well as on developmental experiences that enhance vocabulary and increase language and communication skills.

These methods allow individual needs to be met in an inclusive setting without stigmatizing children. Children at this age are more likely to be falsely identified as learning disabled because of a maturational lag or lack of educational opportunities, so it is particularly important to teach them in inclusive settings if at all possible. Lyon et al. (2001) agree that the most efficient way to intervene early in reading is through general education. They and others recommend that resources be allocated for intervention instead of the expensive process of determining eligibility. Lyon et al. (2001) summarized several studies stating that when intervention is used with the bottom 18 percent of the student population and works on 70 percent of those children, the number of at-risk children requiring services drops from 18 to 5.4 percent.

Elementary Services The importance of intervention during the early elementary years is validated by Lyon et al. (2001), who suggest that over 70 percent of children with a reading disability in Grade 3 continue to demonstrate difficulties in Grade 12. Similarly, Cunningham and Stanovich (1997) found that reading ability in Grade 1 was a strong predictor of reading ability in Grade 11. As discussed in the section "Characteristics of

TEACHING TIP

To build social interaction skills, encourage preschool children to interact with peers in a variety of community settings (e.g., library story hour, swimming lessons).

CROSS REFERENCE

Read more about curricular content and instructional adaptations for elementary level students in chapter 13.

Most children with learning disabilities are identified during early elementary grades.

Students with Learning Disabilities," many of these areas of difficulty remain a problem throughout an individual's life. The intervention begun during elementary years may be equally important at the secondary level and for some adults. Intervention is important in academic and language difficulties, social-emotional problems, and cognitive and metacognitive deficits.

Children with learning disabilities may have academic and language deficits in any or all of the following areas:

- basic reading skills
- reading comprehension
- math calculation
- math reasoning
- written expression
- oral expression
- listening

These areas are usually the focus of an elementary curriculum and therefore can often be addressed in the general education classroom. Both general and special education teachers have been trained to provide instruction in these areas, so collaborative teaching is possible. Due to the uneven skill development and unique areas of strength and need in children with learning disabilities, individualized assessment is required. Informal methods, such as the curriculum-based assessment discussed in chapter 1, are usually effective for planning instruction. This assessment should include an evaluation of the student's strengths, which may indicate the most effective method for instruction.

Student strengths and areas of need are diverse; a single method of teaching may not meet the needs of all students with learning disabilities. For example, in the area of reading instruction, the general education teacher may use a reading approach based on reading literature for meaning; development in areas such as phonics is assumed to occur naturally as the reader becomes more efficient. In this method, often referred to as the **whole language method**, the teacher might note difficulty with a phonetic principle during oral reading and subsequently develop a mini-lesson using text to teach the skill. Unfortunately, many children with learning disabilities do not readily acquire the alphabet code because of limitations in processing the sounds of letters. Research has shown a dramatic reduction in reading failure when comprehensive, explicit instructions are provided in **phonemic awareness**, as seen when a **structured sequential phonics program** is used that focuses on decoding and fluent word recognition, processing text to construct meaning, vocabulary, spelling, and writing. A small number of children will need an intense, small-group or one-on-one format (Foorman & Torgesen, 2001). A survey of teaching practices used by special education teachers nominated as effective literacy teachers showed that they use the best of whole language and direct instruction. See Table 4.1 to review the practices and philosophies of these outstanding teachers.

One strength of the whole language method is its focus on the comprehension of authentic reading material; the teacher using the phonics method must purposely develop those important comprehension skills. These two reading methods are discussed further in chapter 13.

Evidence supporting teaching strategies is presented in the literature. Hammill (2004) reviewed over 450 studies of reading and concluded that educators concerned with teaching reading should focus on direct teaching of reading skills, especially programs linking reading to writing and including the following:

Simulate

Using Learning Strategies

Watch

Graphic Organizer

- print awareness and alphabet knowledge
- phonics (e.g., letter–sound correspondence), word attack, and word identification
- comprehension
- oral and silent reading fluency
- written composition, spelling, sentence punctuation, and textual composition

The activity in "Evidence-Based Instruction: Sound Blending" incorporates writing to strengthen comprehension skills and uses text to reinforce the phonics skill being taught through direct instruction.

Another way to facilitate success for students with learning disabilities in inclusive settings is to teach a **strategy** for the students to apply during the process of learning new information or skills. Lenz, Deshler, and Kissam (2004) define a strategy as an individual's approach to a task. Teaching a strategy provides a specific set of steps for thinking strategically, including how to approach difficult and new tasks, how to guide actions and thoughts, and how to finish tasks successfully and in a timely manner. Students with learning disabilities may not automatically develop strategies for learning, or the ones they develop may be inefficient. For example, using mnemonic strategies can help students with learning disabilities who are demonstrating memory problems. In order to remember $4 \times 8 = 32$, the student might associate *door* for *4*, *gate* for *8*, and a *dirty shoe* for *32*. Therefore, the association to visualize would be a door on a gate by a dirty shoe (Wood & Frank, 2000). One very simple but effective strategy for increasing reading

TEACHING TIP

Many students with learning disabilities will resist the challenge to write because of prior negative feedback. Try giving them multiple opportunities without grading, and then grade only one or two skills at a time. For example, one week you might grade punctuation, and the next, spelling. You can also give one grade for content and another for mechanics, and then average the two scores for the final grade.

Table 4.1 Philosophies, Learning Environments, and Instructional Processes and Practices Frequently Reported by Effective Special Education Teachers of Reading and Writing

General Philosophies and Learning Environments

Identification with a whole language philosophy

Use of the language experience approach

Creation of a literate environment in the classroom, including in-class library, chart stories, signs and labels, and word lists

Use of themes to organize reading and writing instruction, with these themes extending into other curricular areas

Attempts to motivate literacy, encouraging positive attitudes, providing positive feedback, reducing risks for attempting literacy activities, accepting where students are and working from that point, creating an exciting mood, encouraging personal interpretations, and conveying the importance of reading and writing in daily life

Encouragement of ownership and personal decision making

General Teaching Processes

Ability grouping for half of instruction; however, not in the form of traditional reading groups

Predominantly small-group and individualized instruction

Direct instruction of attending behaviours

Direct instruction of listening skills

Assessment of learning styles and adjustment of instruction accordingly

Parent communication and involvement—specific reading and writing activities occurring with parents at home

Monitoring of progress several times a week by both formal and informal methods

Teaching of Reading

Types of Reading and Materials

Total class and individual silent reading

Individual oral reading, including round-robin reading

Different types of materials used—materials with controlled reading level, outstanding children's literature, materials that provide practice in specific phonetic elements and patterns (about half as often as the others)

What Is Taught

Concepts of print, including punctuation, sounds associated with print, concept of words and letters, parts of a book, directionality of print; taught both in context and isolation

Alphabetic principle and alphabet recognition; taught in context, in isolation, with games and puzzles

Letter–sound associations, auditory discrimination, and visual discrimination; taught in context, in isolation, with games and puzzles

Decoding skills taught several times a day in both context and isolation, most frequently teaching sounding out words and use of context cues

Explicit teaching of phonics based on individual student needs

Explicit teaching of sight words

Development of new vocabulary, using words from stories, other reading and writing, and student-selected words

Direct teaching of comprehension strategies, most frequently teaching prediction of upcoming events, finding the main idea, and activation of prior knowledge

Explicitly attempting to develop background knowledge

Teaching text elements, including character analysis, sequence of events, theme, details, and plot

Teaching about various illustrators

Instructional Practice—Both Traditional and Whole Language

Use of worksheets and workbooks for specific instructional purposes

Use of frequent drill and repetition (for learning such things as sight words, phonic elements, spelling words, letter recognition), occurring both in the context of reading and writing and in more traditional practice methods

Tracing and copying of letters and words

Daily reading, both independent and in groups

Reading of stories to students with students "reading along"

Overt modelling of reading and writing

Asking of comprehension questions for nearly all stories read

Use of weekly literature discussions

Use of story mapping or webbing to teach text elements

Publishing of students' work

Teaching of Writing

Encouraging frequent writing (several times a week to several times a day)

Modelling of the writing process

Having students write stories, journals, and books

Using guided writing

Having students write in response to reading

Teaching planning, drafting, and revising as part of writing

Teaching punctuation, both in context of real writing and in isolation

Teaching spelling, including high-frequency words, words from spelling and reading curriculum, and words from students' writing

Accepting and encouraging invented spelling

Adapted from "Literacy in Special Education" (p. 221), by J. L. Rankin-Erickson and M. Pressley, 2000, *Learning Disabilities Research and Practice, 15*(4), 206–225.

Figure 4.5 Effective Intervention Components

From "Reading Comprehension Instruction for Secondary Students: Challenges for Struggling Students and Teachers" (p. 106), by M. A. Mastropieri, T. E. Scruggs, and J. E. Graetz, 2003, *Learning Disability Quarterly, 26*, pp. 103–116.

- Use clear objectives
- Follow specific sequence for teaching
  - State the purpose
  - Provide instruction
  - Model
  - Use guided practice
  - Use corrective feedback
  - Promote independent practice
  - Use generalization practice
- Inform the students of importance of the strategy
- Monitor performance
- Encourage questions that require students to think about strategies and text
- Encourage appropriate attributions
- Teach for generalized use of the strategy

comprehension is a questioning strategy, where students are taught how to ask and then answer the following summarization questions:

- Who or what is the paragraph about?
- What is happening to whom or what?
- Create a summary sentence using fewer than 10 words.

CROSS REFERENCE

Reading intervention and strategy instruction are discussed further in chapters 13 and 14.

 Explore

Kids in the Hall

Mastropieri, Scruggs, and Graetz (2003) put forth this strategy and the research to support it; however, they note that the set of instructional features found in Figure 4.5 is critical to successful strategy instruction. Additional strategies are discussed in chapter 13.

Students with learning disabilities in the area of mathematics have been described by Gersten, Jordan, and Flojo (2005) as lacking in "number sense." They propose that the traditional method of math instruction for students in special education, which focuses on teaching algorithms and being drilled on number facts, has led to a lack of general understanding. They described these students as being able to "do" math without "knowing" how to reason and communicate math meaning. Their work supports the use of "responsiveness to intervention" for young children who show math difficulties; such intervention should focus on teaching math combinations, counting strategies, and number sense (Gersten et al., 2005). Additional strategies proposed by Furner, Yahya, and Duffy (2005) include teaching vocabulary; demonstrating with real objects; relating vocabulary and math problems to prior knowledge and daily life experiences; using manipulatives and drawing pictures to solve problems; using the computer and co-operative learning activities with heterogeneous student groupings; connecting math to other disciplines, such as history and literature; and making cultural connections when teaching math (e.g., taking "internet field trips"). Cawley and Foley (2001) describe methods of enhancing the quality of mathematics for students with learning disabilities by teaching the big ideas in math and using instructional techniques that promote students as problem solvers rather than routine followers. These methods in turn develop the "number sense" that encourages students to think about what they "know" and are "doing." Figure 4.6 presents a list of websites for math activities and help with math anxiety.

www.mathpower.com

This website by Professor Freedman offers great resources for both teachers and students. Students can take a math anxiety test to evaluate their level of math anxiety, and they can learn math study skills and get help with basic math and algebra. The Student's Math Anxiety Bill of Rights is great for hanging in the classroom. For teachers, the website provides a plethora of information on math anxiety and ways to help students who are math anxious.

www.funbrain.com

This website, designed for teachers, parents, and students, provides great math activities and games that offer practice in a gamelike setting. The site also offers teachers tools for making tests and activity sheets, and provides a grade book. Parents will find the site wonderful for teaching and motivating their children to learn math as well as language arts, science, history, music, geography, art, technology, and physical education.

http://funschool.kaboose.com

This great site for teachers, parents, and children is like educational software but presented through the internet. It offers a wide variety of math and literacy games and activities to keep any child engaged and motivated mathematically for a long time.

http://coolmath.com

One of the most exciting websites for children, it is full of colour and offers exciting activities in math and science, including many interesting math facts and statistics. Kids can practise running a business selling lemonade while dealing with the weather and other factors, using both math and science skills in a real-life application.

Figure 4.6 Websites that Address Math Anxiety and Teach Mathematics

From "Equity for All students in the New Millenium: Disabling Math Anxiety" (p. 73), by J. M. Furner and M.L. Dubby, 2002. *Intervention in School and Clinic, 38*(2), pp. 67–74.

Written language is often difficult to master for children and adults with learning disabilities. Unfortunately, making too many adaptations in this area may result in underdeveloped skills. For example, if a student is always allowed to use another student's notes or to take tests orally in place of written exams, the short-term benefits may be helpful, but instruction and experience in note-taking and writing essay answers must be continued if growth is to occur in these areas. This is another area in which strategy instruction can be used to develop important skills. An impressive method for team-teaching a report-writing strategy in a general education classroom is described by Graham, Harris, and MacArthur (2006), in which the special education teacher takes the lead in introducing the strategy and working with the struggling writers, and the general education teacher participates in all phases of instruction. The authors point out that by explicitly teaching these strategies for planning, drafting, and revising text, the struggling writers, as well as their classmates, are given help to develop better writing skills.

Improvement in oral language may be stimulated by promoting a better self-concept, teaching the skills of language production directly, and enriching the language environment. When students speak, listen closely to their message and respond appropriately; save corrections for a later teaching moment. The respect you show for attempts at communication will increase conversation and confidence. Providing opportunities for students to share their experiences and expertise is also a nonthreatening way to promote use of oral language. Listening and praising help reinforce talking. Bos and Vaughn (2002) reviewed the research in the area of spoken language and made the following additional recommendations:

- Increase wait time to allow sufficient time for comprehension and a response.
- Model good language.

TEACHING TIP

In order to promote successful verbal interactions with peers, encourage students to take conversational turns (e.g., Student 1: "I really liked that movie we saw yesterday." Student 2: "It was pretty good. What did you like about it?")

- Take the student's words and briefly elaborate or expand on his or her ideas.
- Use parallel talk and self-talk to describe what you and others are doing and thinking.
- Use a structured language program and build in activities in a variety of settings to develop generalization.

Poor listening skills also limit individuals with learning disabilities, influencing success both in the classroom and in social interactions. It is important for teachers to analyze the amount of listening required in their classrooms; study the barriers to good listening, such as distracting noises; and teach and reinforce specific listening strategies (Swain, Friehe, & Harrington, 2004). The following is a simple strategy to cue listening behaviours, which can be modified for use with all age groups. Students follow these steps:

L　Look at the teacher.

I　Ignore the student next to you.

S　Stay in your place.

T　Try to visualize and understand the story.

E　Enjoy the story.

N　Nice job! You're a good listener.

Computers and other technology can assist in teaching individuals with learning disabilities in inclusive classrooms. Olson and Platt (1996) describe the following advantages of technology:

TEACHING TIP

The amount of software available for supporting instruction can be overwhelming, and costly mistakes can be made when ordering a program based on a catalogue description alone. Organize a plan for the teachers in your school to share the names of effective software. Preview a copy before ordering, whenever possible.

- It is self-pacing and individualized.
- It provides immediate feedback.
- It has consistent correction procedures.
- It provides repetition without pressure.
- It confirms correct responses immediately.
- It maintains a high frequency of student response.
- It builds in repeated validation of academic success.
- It is an activity respected by peers.
- It is motivating.
- It encourages increased time on task.
- It minimizes the effects of the exceptionality.

Writing is an area in which technology can be most helpful. The computer can be used effectively for curriculum support in math, language arts, social studies, science, and other areas. Various types of software provide instructional alternatives such as tutoring, drill and practice, simulation, and games. Teachers should carefully evaluate each program for ease of use and appropriateness for exceptional students.

Intervention related to social interactions and emotional maturity is critical for many students with learning disabilities. The inclusion movement provides opportunities for interactions; the question is how to best prepare both the children with exceptionalities and their typically developing peers for positive interactions. Changing a student's self-image, social ability, and social standing is difficult. Until recently, the research and literature on learning disabilities focused primarily on the efficacy of treatments for the most obvious characteristic—academic difficulties. The importance of social skills is now being recognized and given the attention it deserves.

Intervention in the area of social standing and interaction can take two courses: changing the child or changing the environment. Optimally, both receive attention. Good teaching techniques can lead to academic achievement and eventually to higher self-esteem. Teachers can create a positive learning environment by incorporating praise and encouragement for specific accomplishments (e.g., making positive comments about themselves and others). Teachers should also set goals and be very explicit about expectations for academic work and behaviour in class. Teachers should monitor progress closely, and provide frequent feedback (Polloway et al., 2001).

Improvement in low academic self-concept has also been made by correcting maladaptive *attributional styles* or teaching students to take credit for their successes. Students with higher academic self-concepts have been found to work harder to achieve (Tabassam & Grainger, 2002). It is important to model prosocial skills and provide natural opportunities for conversation and conflict resolution. Positive self-talk is important. A forum during group time can be used to pose potential problems and generate discussions to brainstorm possible solutions before the situations occur (Morris, 2002). Role-playing successful co-operation, followed by experience in collaborative group projects, can also provide positive social experiences if the teacher monitors the activity closely. Figure 4.7 provides a lesson plan in which the goal is to provide direct instruction to teach students to interact with other individuals.

CONSIDER THIS

Describe some situations you have observed in which a child displayed inappropriate social skills or responses in the classroom. How could you, as the classroom teacher, respond in these situations to promote more appropriate behaviours?

Nonverbal Behaviour
1. Face the student.
2. Maintain eye contact.
3. Maintain a neutral or pleasant facial expression.

Paraverbal Behaviour
4. Maintain a neutral tone of voice.
5. Speak at a moderate volume.

Verbal Teaching Behaviour
6. Begin with a compliment related to the student's efforts and achievements.
7. Introduce the social skill and define what the social skill means.
8. Give a rationale for learning the skill and for using the skill with others.
9. Share an experience when you used the social skill or could have used the social skill.
10. Specify each behaviour (e.g., nonverbal and verbal behaviour) to be considered when exhibiting the skill.
11. Demonstrate or model the use of the skill.
12. Have the student rehearse the social skill. (Observe the student's behaviour.)
13. Provide positive corrective feedback. State what the student did correctly.
14. Practise the social skill with the student. (Make sure you do not prompt.)
15. Continue to provide corrective feedback to practise until the student masters (100 percent) the social skill in a novel situation.
16. Plan, with the student, when and where to use the social skill.

Figure 4.7 Teaching Interaction

Remember: Make sure the student participates throughout the lesson. To do so, ask questions and let the student share ideas and thoughts. Always praise the student for participating and rehearsing the social skill.

From *Strategies for Teaching Learners with Special Needs* (p. 212), by E. A. Polloway, J. R. Patton, and L. Serna, 2001, Upper Saddle River, NJ: Merrill.

Figure 4.8 Examples of Social Skills

From "Social Skills Interventions for Individuals with Learning Disabilities" (p. 33), by K. A. Kavale and M. P. Mostert, 2004, *Learning Disability Quarterly, 27,* pp. 31–43.

Starting a conversation	Expressing your feelings	Using self-control
Asking a question	Negotiating	Keeping out of fights
Introducing yourself	Setting goals	Feeling sad
Asking for help	Working co-operatively	Responding to aggression
Learning how to listen	Dealing with frustration	Responding to failure
Apologizing	Controlling anger	Decision making

The overall goal of social programs is to teach socially appropriate behaviour and social skills that are self-generated and self-monitored. The cognitive problems of students with learning disabilities often make this type of decision making very difficult, and these skills must be directly taught. Areas potentially in need of instruction are presented in Figure 4.8. The effectiveness of social skills training has had little empirical support, but they are an important life skill, and research efforts should continue (Kavale & Mostert, 2004).

Intervention in cognitive and metacognitive skills has only recently received support from learning disabilities professionals. Powerful techniques are being studied to improve learning. Some of the ideas are relatively simple and require only common sense. First, and most important, is to make sure children are paying attention to the stimulus being presented. Students' attention might be gained by dimming the lights, calling for attention, or establishing eye contact. Then, students' attention might be maintained by having students work for short periods of time or breaking up instruction with activities. Learning will not take place without attention.

Lerner (2000) suggests that teachers present new information in well-organized, meaningful chunks. As new information is presented to be memorized, it should be linked to previously learned, meaningful information. For example, to teach subtraction, the teacher would demonstrate its relationship to addition. Students should also be encouraged to rehearse new information and be given many opportunities for practice. These and other effective learning strategies are presented throughout the text.

Secondary Services Academic and language difficulties, social and emotional problems, and differences in cognitive and metacognitive functioning continue to plague many adolescents with learning disabilities. The focus in junior and high school is on content classes; therefore, **remediation** of basic skills often is minimal. Students who continue to benefit from remediation should be provided these opportunities. For example, research-based strategies are available to teach secondary students who are struggling readers to read the all-important multi-syllable words. Several of these are described by Archer, Gleason, and Vachon (2003); the Evidence-Based Practice box demonstrates one strategy in which students are taught to decode these words by breaking them into smaller, more readable parts while the teacher introduces new content vocabulary.

The adaptations described in the next section and the learning strategies discussed in the previous section can also be used with secondary students to facilitate basic skill acquisition and to make learning and performance more effective and efficient (Chamberlain, 2006). For example, instead of trying to bring basic skills to a level high enough to read a chapter in a content area textbook written at grade level, a teacher might assist students in comprehension by reading the heading and one or two sentences in each paragraph in a chapter. Students can be taught self-questioning strategies such as, "What or who is the paragraph about?" and "What is happening to whom or what?" to increase their comprehension (Mastropieri

Part-by-Part Decoding Instruction when Pre-Teaching Content Area Words

Overt Strategy

1. Circle the word parts (prefixes) at the beginning of the word.
2. Circle the word parts (suffixes) at the end of the word.
3. Underline the letters representing vowel sounds in the rest of the word.
4. Say the parts of the word.
5. Say the parts fast.
6. Make it a real word.

Example

re con struction

Covert Strategy

1. Look for word parts at the beginning and end of the word, and vowel sounds in the rest of the word.
2. Say the parts of the word.
3. Say the parts fast.
4. Make it a real word.

From "Decoding and Fluency: Foundation Skills for Struggling Readers," by A. L. Archer, M. C. Gleason, and V. L. Vachon, 2003, *Learning Disability Quarterly 26*, 89–103.

et al., 2003). Strategies can enable a student to handle the increased amount of content information, but it is equally important to be sure that the student's cognitive level is sufficient to handle the strategy (see Figure 4.9). Don Deshler, credited with validating the learning strategies model, warns that other elements also important to content learning include teaching critical vocabulary skills, building prior knowledge to connect to new information, and teaching an understanding of the structure of text (Chamberlain, 2006).

The teacher can also make an impact on student learning and performance by accounting for individual differences when developing lesson plans. Many students fail not because of an inability to perform but because they do not understand directions, cannot remember all the information, or cannot process verbal information fast enough. Most adults and older children automatically lower the language they use when speaking to younger children or individuals with obvious exceptionalities. Unfortunately, they do not typically do so when speaking to school-age children and adults with learning disabilities—even though the latter may have language-based learning disabilities. Johnson (1999) suggests the following strategies to meet the needs of students with language difficulties in an inclusive classroom setting:

- Be conscious of the level of language used, including rate of presentation, complexity of vocabulary, and sentence structure.

- Prepare a list of relevant terms prior to instruction; pre-test students to determine their level of understanding.

CONSIDER THIS

Review the strategies described in Figure 4.9. Discuss situations in which each one would be helpful for students.

Self-Questioning

Students quietly ask themselves questions about the material. This process is also referred to as *verbal mediation*. The internal language, or covert speech, helps organize material and behaviour. Camp and Bash (1981) suggest the following types of questions:

What is the problem? (or) What am I supposed to do?
What is my plan? (or) How can I do it?
Am I using my plan?
How did I do?

Verbal Rehearsal and Review

Students practise and review what they have learned. This self-rehearsal helps students remember. People forget when the brain trace, which is a physical record of memory, fades away. Recitation and review of material to be learned help the student remember.

Students observe the instructor's modelling of verbalization of a problem.
Students instruct themselves by verbalizing aloud or in a whisper.
Students verbalize silently.

Organization

To aid in recall, students figure out the main idea of the lesson and the supporting facts. The organization of the material has a great deal to do with how fast we can learn it and how well we can remember it. Already-existing memory units are called *chunks*, and through *chunking*, new material is reorganized into already-existing memory units. The more students can relate to what they already know, the better they will remember the new material.

Using Prior Knowledge

New material is linked to already-existing memory units. The more students can relate what they are learning to what they already know, the better they will remember.

Memory Strategies

If new material is anchored to old knowledge, students are more likely to remember it. For example, one student remembered the word *look* because it had two eyes in the middle. Some pupils can alphabetize only if they sing the "ABC" song. Some adults can remember people's names by using a mnemonic device that associates the name with a particular attribute of that individual—for example, "blond Bill" or "green-sweater Gertrude."

Predicting and Monitoring

Students guess what they will learn in the lesson and then check on whether their guesses were correct.

Advance Organizers

This technique establishes a mindset for the learner, relating new material to previously learned material. Students are told in advance what they are going to learn. This sets the stage for learning and improves comprehension and the ability to recall what has been learned.

Cognitive Behaviour Modification

This behavioural approach teaches students self-instruction, self-monitoring, and self-evaluation techniques (Meichenbaum, 1977). There are several steps:

The teacher models a behaviour while giving an explanation.
The student performs the task while the teacher describes it.
The student, out loud, talks through the task.
The student whispers the task to himself or herself.
The student performs the task with nonverbal self-cues.

Modelling

The teacher provides an example of appropriate cognitive behaviour and problem-solving strategies. The teacher can talk through the cognitive processes being used.

Self-Monitoring

Students learn to monitor their own mistakes. They learn to check their own responses and become conscious of errors or answers that do not make sense. To reach this stage requires active involvement in the learning process in order to recognize incongruities.

Figure 4.9 Learning Strategies

From *Learning Disabilities: Theories, Diagnosis, and Teaching Strategies* (6th ed.) (pp. 207–208), by J. W. Lerner, 1993, Houghton Mifflin Company. Used with permission.

- Adjust the level of language until students have basic concepts.
- Use demonstrations as needed.
- Repeat instructions individually to students if necessary.
- Select a method of testing knowledge to match the student's best method of communication. For example, a student may be able to select the correct answer from options given but not be able to answer open-ended questions. (p. 6)

As we discussed earlier, a major problem for secondary students with learning disabilities is low self-concept and social and emotional problems that often stem from years of school failure. In response, school environments must be structured to create successful experiences. One method involves **self-determination**, or making students more active participants in designing their educational experiences and monitoring their own success; this can be done by teaching self-awareness and self-advocacy skills. Students should use these skills as active participants in their IEP meetings. Participation in IEP meetings is particularly important when a student is deciding whether to continue post-secondary education or obtain employment after high school (Pocock et al., 2002).

Giving students more power and responsibility for determining their life outcome is very important at the secondary level; it is also important to maintain communication with parents and involve them in this process (Jayanthi et al., 1999). Parents can promote responsibility in their children by setting clear expectations and consequences in regard to school achievement. Teachers can help by doing the following:

- Giving parents and students information on course assignments for the semester, available adaptations, and policies.

- Providing progress reports, including descriptive comments on the quality of homework.

- Putting assignment calendars on brightly coloured paper to prevent misplacement.

- Collaborating with other teachers to prevent homework overload.

- Communicating with parents regarding the amount of time students spend completing homework and adjusting the workload correspondingly.

- Understanding that homework may be a low priority in some families where other stressors, such as family illness or school attendance, may be a priority.

CROSS REFERENCE

Read more about facilitating student success at the secondary level in chapter 14.

Adolescents should be active participants in meetings concerning them.

High school students with learning disabilities especially need to acquire transition skills (e.g., abilities that will help them be successful after high school in employment and independent living). For students in inclusive settings, teachers can find ways to integrate transition topics into the regular curriculum. For example, when an English teacher assigns letter writing or term papers, students might focus their work on exploring different career opportunities. Math teachers can bring in income tax and budget forms to connect them to a variety of math skills. When planning any lesson, ask yourself, "Is there any way I can make this meaningful to my students' lives after high school?" (See Table 4.2.)

CROSS REFERENCE

Read more about transition planning at the secondary level in chapter 14.

Adults The instruction provided in high school classes can have a powerful impact on the outcome for adults with learning disabilities. The life skills applications of various school activities and lessons are described in chapter 14. Relevant lessons in the general education curriculum can help adults be more successful in many aspects of independent living. Individuals with learning disabilities are deficient in choosing and carrying out strategies, and they do not automatically generalize previously learned information to new challenges.

An important study by Raskind, Goldberg, Higgins, and Herman (2002) identified characteristics of highly successful adults with learning disabilities. Teachers and other individuals can encourage development of many of these factors, although some seem to be innate personality traits of the individuals themselves (e.g., emotional stability). One of the strongest predictors for success was the desire and willingness to persist and work extremely hard. Understanding one's strengths and areas of need, identifying appropriate goals, and working proactively to meet them were also important. The successful adults developed a plan and then worked hard to accomplish their goals. They also developed and used support groups. These characteristics were more powerful predictors of success than were academic achievement, IQ, life stressors, socio-economic status, or race.

Unfortunately, many adults leave high school without the skills and confidence necessary to find employment to help them realize their maximum potential and live independently. According to Madaus (2006), 72 percent of workers with learning disabilities reported that their learning disabilities did impact work at least occasionally. The biggest problems noted were writing skills, rate of processing information, reading comprehension, organizational skills, math computation, and time management.

These skills can be taught and should be addressed in a secondary curriculum. For adults with learning disabilities, the Learning Disabilities Association of Canada (LDAC) offers a number of resources as well as access to a specific group of adults with learning disabilities that advises the Association. (See "Resources" at the end of the chapter.)

Controversial Approaches

Some interventions, often presented to the public through television or newsstand magazines, are controversial and have not been validated as effective for students with learning disabilities. Educators may be asked for an opinion on these therapies by parents who are attempting to find solutions to their children's frustrating problems. Traditional, evidence-based interventions, which have been shown to be successful, often take time, sometimes years. And even then, progress may not be at the desired level. Parents are understandably drawn to promises of a "quick cure," even if the treatment carries a big

Table 4.2 Examples of Study Skill Functions In and Out of the Classroom

Study Skill	School Examples	Life Skills Applications
Reading Rate	Reviewing an assigned reading for a test	Reviewing an automobile insurance policy
	Looking for an explanation of a concept discussed in class	Reading the newspaper
Listening	Understanding instructions about a field trip	Understanding how a newly purchased appliance works
	Attending to morning announcements	Comprehending a radio traffic report
Note Taking/ Outlining	Capturing information given by a teacher on how to dissect a frog	Writing directions to a party
	Framing the structure of a paper	Planning a summer vacation
Report Writing	Developing a book report	Completing the personal goals section on a job application
	Completing a science project on a specific marine organism	Writing a complaint letter
Oral Presentations	Delivering a personal opinion on a current issue for a social studies class	Describing car problems to a mechanic
	Describing the results of a lab experiment	Asking a supervisor/boss for time off work
Graphic Aids	Setting up the equipment of a chemistry experiment based on a diagram	Utilizing the weather map in the newspaper
	Locating the most densely populated regions of the world on a map	Deciphering the store map in a mall
Test Taking	Developing tactics for retrieving information for a closed-book test	Preparing for a driver's licence renewal test
	Comparing notes with textbook content	Participating in television self-tests
Library Usage	Using picture files	Obtaining travel resources (books, videos)
	Searching a computerized catalogue	Viewing current periodicals
Reference Materials	Accessing CD-ROM encyclopedias	Using the yellow pages to locate a repair service
	Using a thesaurus to write a paper	Ordering from a mail-order catalogue
Time Management	Allocating a set time for homework	Maintaining a daily "to do" list
	Organizing a file system for writing a paper	Keeping organized records for tax purposes
Self-Management	Ensuring that homework is signed by parents	Regulating a daily exercise program
	Rewarding oneself for controlling temper	Evaluating the quality of a home repair

From *Teaching Students with Learning Problems to Use Study Skills: A Teacher's Guide* (p. 7), by J. J. Hoover & J. R. Patton, 1995, Austin, TX: Pro-Ed. Reprinted by permission.

price tag. Educators and parents must be armed with techniques to study these controversial therapies as they appear.

Dr. Larry Silver (2003) is helping to distinguish between those treatments that are backed by research and those that have no scientific basis. Caution should be used when contemplating therapies that are presented with a broad claim and offer a cure, and that imply research but do not present it (Silver, 2003).

One controversial therapy involves the prescription of **tinted glasses** as a cure for dyslexia. In this approach, light sensitivity, proposed to interfere with learning, is treated by identifying a coloured lens to reduce sensitivity. Another treatment provides **orthomolecular therapy**, involving vitamins, minerals, and diet. Proponents of this treatment claim that large doses of vitamins and minerals straighten out the biochemistry of the brain to reduce hyperactivity and to increase learning. Hair analysis and blood studies are used to determine the doses needed.

Research on the efficacy of these diet-related interventions usually consists of clinical studies without control groups. The inclusion of control groups in experimental research "enables the researcher to determine whether the treatment has had an effect or whether one treatment is more effective than another" (Fraenkel & Wallen, 2000, p. 284). When control groups are used, the diets do not substantiate the claims made for them. Only a small percentage of children benefit from such diets.

Vision therapy or training is another controversial treatment for individuals with a learning disability. It is based on the theory that learning disabilities are the result of visual defects that occur when the eyes do not work together and that these deficits can be cured by visual training. This widespread practice has been supported primarily by groups of optometrists. The American Academy of Ophthalmology (1984) issued a statement clearly stating that "no credible evidence exists to show that visual training, muscle exercises, perceptual, or hand/eye co-ordination exercises significantly affect a child's Specific Learning Disabilities" (p. 3).

Silver (2003) and the International Dyslexia Association (2001) have issued a warning against one of the latest proposals, which purports that learning disabilities are due to cerebellar developmental delay, whereby the brain cannot process information quickly enough. Centres offer children exercises to stimulate the underdeveloped cerebellum, claiming the brain will then function faster with improved cognitive and motor skills. In studying the information on this approach at the website of the Dore Achievement Centres, Silver found reference to "a major research program to measure the possible effectiveness of the novel treatment," but no published data. In responding to the claims of the centres using this treatment approach, the International Dyslexia Association (IDA, 2001) expressed concern over the exorbitant cost of this treatment for families and, more important, the human cost incurred by postponing research-based intervention and reading instruction that is sequential, systematic, and phonetically based.

CLASSROOM ADAPTATIONS FOR STUDENTS WITH LEARNING DISABILITIES

One important consideration for individuals of all ages with exceptionalities, including learning disabilities, is the appropriate use of adaptations during testing. Using adaptations helps ensure that common characteristics of learning disabilities, such as poor reading, distractibility, or slow work rate, do not lower the results of an assessment of the child's learning. Care must be taken when implementing these adaptations, because, while disallowing fair adaptations prevents a student from demonstrating his or her knowledge, overly permissive adaptations will inflate scores. Inflated scores may give students an overestimate of their abilities and may lead to unrealistic post-secondary goals. Inflated scores also may reduce pressure on schools to maintain high expectations and to offer students a challenging program with intense instruction (Fuchs & Fuchs, 2001). The researchers note, however, that when students may be penalized for low test scores (as is the case for "high stakes" assessment, which is the gateway to promotion or graduation), a more liberal allowance of adaptations should be made.

When you are developing classroom adaptations, remember the wide range of behaviours identified earlier that might characterize individuals with learning disabilities. The heterogeneity in this population is sometimes baffling. No child with a learning disability is going to be exactly like any other, so teachers must provide a wide range of adaptations to meet individual needs. In the following sections, adaptations are discussed for each of the areas described earlier: academic and language deficits, social-emotional problems, and other differences, such as attention, memory, cognition, metacognition, perception, and motor skills.

FURTHER READING

Read N.L. Heath and T. Glen's article investigating overestimates of performance by students with learning disabilities in volume 34, issue 2 of the *Journal of Clinical Child and Adolescent Psychology*, 2005 (pp. 272–281).

Academic and Language Problems

Students with learning disabilities may manifest problems in the academic areas of reading skill, reading comprehension, math calculation, math applications, listening, speaking, and written language. Chapters 13 and 14 provide extensive adaptations and modifications for students with learning disabilities at the elementary and secondary levels. The following are some general guidelines written by a high school student with learning problems and AD/HD. His teachers helped him write the guidelines (Biddulph, Hess, & Humes, 2006):

- Provide copies of notes and overheads for students so they won't have to worry about getting all the information down; this can help the student pay attention and improve his/her concentration.

- Read tests to students so they can process the information better by hearing it as they read it.

- Let a student sit close to the front of the class and not by a window. This helps the student focus on the important information and not be distracted by other students or things happening outside.

- Let a student sit with another student he or she is comfortable with and whom he or she can ask for help.

- Provide a decreased amount of homework—for example, fewer math problems—or let the student have extra time to complete homework.

- Have math formulas posted for quick reference.

- Have books on tape available to help with focus and comprehension (see Figure 4.10 for textbook modification suggestions).

- Provide examples on how to complete homework.

- Make sure the student has everything needed to complete homework and understands the assignment.

Figure 4.10 Guidelines for Adapting Content Area Textbooks

Adapted from "Guidelines for Adapting Content Area Textbooks: Keeping Teachers and Students Content," by J.S. Schumm and K. Strickler, 1991, *Intervention in School and Clinic,* 27(2), pp. 79–84.

Determine "goodness of fit" by comparing the text's readability level and the student's reading ability. If accommodations are needed, consider the following:

1. **Substitute textbook reading by**
   - Supplying an audiotape of the text
   - Pairing students to learn text material together
   - Substituting the text with direct experiences or videos
   - Holding tutorial sessions to teach content to a small group

2. **Simplify text by**
   - Developing abridged versions (volunteers may be helpful)
   - Developing chapter outlines or summaries
   - Finding a text with similar content written at a lower level

3. **Highlight key concepts by**
   - Establishing the purpose for reading
   - Overviewing the assignment before reading
   - Reviewing charts, graphs, vocabulary, and key concepts before reading
   - Reducing amount of work by targeting the most important information or slowing down pace of assignments

FURTHER READING

Read Busch, Pederson, Espin, and Weissenburger's article investigating a first-year teacher's perceptions of teaching students with learning disabilities in volume 35, issue 2 of the *Journal of Special Education,* 2001 (pp. 92–99).

TEACHING TIP

Each word-processing program has unique features. Try to have several programs available so students can experiment and find the one that works best for them.

- Have students use an organized binder with dividers and colour coding; have a different folder for each class.
- Let students take tests in a quiet place.
- Create study guides for tests.

For students with learning difficulties in writing, a word processor can be invaluable. It allows students to see their work in a more legible format and simplifies proofreading and revising.

A variety of software programs meet the needs of students with learning disabilities. In addition to those that help students to work around or accommodate their difficulties, there are programs that provide fun and interesting drill and skill-building activities for younger children. The programs that provide accommodations for students with learning disabilities include the common spell checkers, grammar checkers, thesaurus options, and less common voice word processors. Voice word processors allow students with learning disabilities to dictate their written work and then listen to the computer read it back to them. As a student dictates, the words appear on the screen, where they can be reviewed. Drill and skill-building programs consist of a variety of game-format drills in areas such as basic math facts, word attack, other reading skills, and spelling. Other skill-building programs that are appropriate for both younger and older students teach geography, history, science, and problem solving. A few of the best-established, award-winning programs are listed below; however, because new innovations occur constantly in the field, contact your local computer software outlet to obtain information on the newest software to fit your needs.

- *Magic School Bus series by Microsoft*: Software programs explore a variety of science activities in an interactive manner. Ages 6 to 10.

- *Early Learning House series by Edmark Corporation*: The series teaches a variety of math, reading, and science concepts. It includes Sammy's Science House, Millie's Math House, and Bailey's Book House. Ages 3 to 6.

- *Reader Rabbits by the Learning Company*: This program builds basic reading skills. Ages 3 to 8.

- *Blaster series by Knowledge Adventure*: Reading Blaster, Math Blaster, and Spelling Blaster software programs build basic skills through fun drills. Ages 5 and up.

- *Carmen Sandiego series by the Learning Company*: Where in the World Is Carmen Sandiego? and Where in Time is Carmen Sandiego? teach geography and history, respectively, using an interactive game format. Ages 8 and up.

In summary, software distributors that have consistently earned high ratings by educators are Knowledge Adventure (www.knowledgeadventure.com/school/contact.aspx), the Learning Company (www.learningcompany.com), and Edmark/Riverdeep (http://riverdeep.net). Children and adolescents with learning disabilities benefit enormously from computer software that allows them to control their own learning.

Social-Emotional Problems

As discussed earlier, the social and emotional problems of individuals with learning disabilities may be closely tied to academic failure. Many of the academic adaptations and accommodations already described will encourage success in the classroom, which, ultimately, leads to a better self-concept, increased emotional stability, and greater confidence in approaching new academic tasks. A student who has weak or limited social skills may need previously described training. However, some adaptations and accommodations may still be needed even as the training begins to show results. Students may need to work in an isolated setting in the classroom during particularly challenging times. Distractions caused by peers may interfere with meeting academic challenges successfully. However, making the student with learning disabilities sit in a segregated portion of the room all the time sends a bad message—to the student and to others. Including students with exceptionalities in group activities, such as co-operative learning, provides them with models of appropriate interactions and social skills. Teachers should identify the students in the classroom who seem to work best with individuals with a learning disability, and give them opportunities to interact. When conflicts arise, teachers should provide good modelling by verbalizing the bad choices that were made and the good choices that could have been made instead.

Students with learning disabilities may have difficulty responding appropriately to verbal and nonverbal cues, so teachers should avoid sarcasm and use simple, concrete language when giving directions and when teaching. If a student has difficulty accepting new tasks without complaint, consider providing a written assignment that the student can refer to for direction. When a student frequently upsets or irritates others in the classroom, you might agree on a contract to reduce the inappropriate behaviour and reinforce positive peer interaction. Periodically review the rules for the classroom, and keep them posted as a quick reference. In order to assist students who have difficulty making and keeping friends, you can subtly point out the strengths of the individual with the learning

FURTHER READING

Read about teachers' perceptions of learning disabilities in Ferri, Keefe, and Gregg's article, "Teachers with Learning Disabilities: A View from Both Sides of the Desk," in volume 34, issue 1, of *Journal of Learning Disabilities,* 2001 (pp. 22–32).

FURTHER READING

Tips for accommodating a variety of behaviours associated with learning disabilities and attention deficit can be found in a book by R.A. Barkley, *Taking Charge of ADHD: The Complete, Authoritative Guide for Parents* (rev. ed.), published in 2000 by Guilford Press.

disability to encourage the other students to want to be his or her friend. Allowing a student to demonstrate his or her expertise in an area or to share a hobby may stimulate conversations that can eventually lead to friendships.

Many students with learning disabilities cannot predict the consequences of negative behaviour. Therefore, teachers need to explain the consequences of rule breaking and other inappropriate actions. Though you can implement many behaviour management techniques to reinforce positive behaviour, it is important to train the student in methods of **self-monitoring** and **self-regulation**. The ultimate goal is for the student to be able to identify socially inappropriate behaviour and get back on track.

Cognitive Differences

Cognitive problems described earlier include deficits in attention, perception, motor abilities, problem solving, and metacognition. Adaptations and accommodations for individuals exhibiting problems in attention will be described more fully in chapter 5. Adaptations and accommodations can also help individuals with difficulties or preferences in the area of perception. For some students, presenting information visually through an overhead projector, reading material, videos, and graphics will be most effective. Other individuals will respond better by hearing the information. Teachers can accommodate these individual differences by identifying the preferred style of learning and ensuring that instruction and directions are provided by teaching in a multisensory fashion that stimulates both auditory and visual perception. Combining seeing, saying, writing, and doing provides multiple opportunities for presenting new information and helps children remember important information.

Difficulties in the area of motor abilities might manifest as poor handwriting skills or difficulty with other fine motor activities. Accommodations might include overlooking the difficulties in handwriting and providing a grade based not on the appearance of the handwriting but on the content of the material. You might allow students with such difficulties to provide other evidence of their learning, such as oral reports or special projects, or allow students to use a word processor or speech-activated software when completing assignments. Let students select physical fitness activities that focus on their areas of strength rather than their areas of need.

Students with difficulties in problem solving require careful direction and programming. Their difficulties in reasoning skills make them especially prone to academic failures. The instructional strategies described earlier will remedy problems in this area; frequent practice and modelling of problem-solving strategies will also strengthen developing skills.

Students with problems in the area of metacognition need to keep an assignment notebook or a monthly calendar to project the time needed to complete tasks or to prepare for tests. Students should be taught to organize their notebooks and their desks so that materials can be retrieved efficiently. If students have difficulty following or developing a plan, assist them in setting long-range goals and breaking down those goals into realistic steps. Prompt them with questions such as, "What do you need to be able to do this?" Help students set clear time frames in which to accomplish each step. Assist them in prioritizing activities and assignments, and provide them with models they can refer to often.

 Explore

Sorry, I Got the Wrong Day, Again!

TEACHING TIP

When giving students a series of directions (e.g., giving an assignment), pair oral directions with written directions. This will give students a visual representation of your directions to reference.

Encourage students to ask for help when needed and to use self-checking methods to evaluate their work on an ongoing basis. Reinforce all signs of appropriate self-monitoring and self-regulation in the classroom. These behaviours will facilitate success after high school.

Adaptations and accommodations for attention deficits and hyperactivity are addressed in chapter 5.

PROMOTING A SENSE OF COMMUNITY AND SOCIAL ACCEPTANCE

After identifying an appropriate educational plan for individuals with learning disabilities and determining the adaptations and accommodations that should lead to a successful educational program, the next challenge is to ensure that the children in the general education classroom and the child with the learning disability understand the exceptionality and the need for special education. Primarily, children should be made aware that all people are different.

Teaching tips for general educators are offered in chapters 13 and 14, which focus on behaviour management and adaptations and accommodations for elementary and secondary classrooms. The following list of recommended guidelines for teaching children and adolescents with learning disabilities has been compiled from work by Mercer (1997), Deiner (1993), and Bender (2001):

1. Be consistent in class rules and daily schedules of activities.

2. State rules and expectations clearly. Tell children what to do—not what *not* to do. For example, instead of saying, "Don't run in the halls," say, "Walk in the halls."

3. Give advance organizers to prepare children for any changes in the day's events and to highlight the important points to be covered during instructional time.

4. Eliminate or reduce visual and auditory distractions when children need to concentrate. Help children focus on the important aspects of the task.

5. Give directions in clear, simple words. A long series of directions may need to be broken down and given one at time. Reinforcement may be needed as each step is completed.

6. Begin with simple activities focused on a single concept and build to more abstract ideas as the child appears ready. If problems occur, check for the presence of the prerequisite skills or knowledge of the vocabulary being used.

7. Use concrete objects or demonstrations when teaching a new concept. Relate new information to previously known concepts.

8. Teach the children strategies for remembering.

9. Present information visually, auditorially, and through demonstrations to address each child's preferred learning style.

10. Use a variety of activities and experiences to teach or reinforce the same concept. Repetition can be provided without inducing boredom.

11. Use activities that are short or that encourage movement. Some children may need to work standing up!

12. Incorporate problem-solving activities or other projects that involve the children. Use both higher level and lower level questions.

13. Always gain the student's attention before presenting important information.

14. Use co-operative instructional groupings and peer tutoring to vary modes of instruction.

15. Plan for success!

SUMMARY

- A learning disability is frequently misunderstood because it is not visible. It may be mistaken for purposely unco-operative behaviour.

- The study of learning disabilities is a relatively young field, and basic definitions, etiology, and criteria for special education eligibility remain controversial.

- The most widely used criterion for identifying a learning disability is a severe discrepancy between ability and achievement that cannot be explained by another disabling condition or by lack of learning opportunity.

- School personnel must determine that the primary cause of a student's learning difficulties is not cultural or linguistic diversity.

- Cultural and linguistic differences need to be taken into account when any assessment of a student's skills occurs so that the student is not mistakenly referred to a special education setting.

- Characteristics of learning disabilities manifest across the lifespan.

- Learning disabilities manifest in seven areas of academics and language: reading skills, reading comprehension, mathematical calculations, mathematical reasoning, written expression, oral expression, and listening comprehension.

- Other common characteristics of learning disabilities include social-emotional problems and difficulties with attention and hyperactivity, memory, cognition, metacognition, motor skills, and perceptual abilities.

- Teaching strategies for preschool children with learning disabilities include developmental, cognitive, and behavioural models.

- Interventions for elementary children with learning disabilities address academic and language deficits, social-emotional problems, and cognitive and metacognitive problems.

- Secondary students with learning disabilities continue to need remediation of basic skills, but they also benefit from strategies that will make them more efficient learners.

- A secondary curriculum that includes application of life skills can produce successful outcomes for adults with learning disabilities.

- Successful adults with learning disabilities are goal-directed, work hard to accomplish their goals, understand and accept their strengths and limitations, and advocate for themselves.

- Adaptations and accommodations in the general education classroom can address the academic, social-emotional, and cognitive, metacognitive, and attentional differences of students with learning disabilities.

- The role of the classroom teacher includes using effective teaching strategies and accommodations to address the challenges of students with learning disabilities, as well as helping a child with a learning disability and other children in the general class understand and accept a learning disability.

- Students need to be aware that all people are different; this awareness will promote a positive, accepting atmosphere in the general education classroom.

Weblinks

Learning Disabilities Association of Ontario (LDAO)
www.ldao.ca
LDAO's site, one of the few specifically Canadian sites on learning disabilities, provides a number of resources and suggests books and videos, as well as other related links.

LD Online
www.ldonline.org
This site provides information on research, links, articles, and more. It is recommended by the Learning Disabilities Association of Canada.

Division for Learning Disabilities (DLD)
www.dldcec.org
One of 17 divisions of the Council for Exceptional Children, DLD provides mainly American links, but there is information that is applicable to all individuals with LD.

Council for Learning Disabilities (CLD)
www.cldinternational.org
The CLD site provides services to professionals who work with individuals with learning disabilities. Information focuses on interventions for teachers working with individuals with LD. Journal and conference information is available.

National Center for Learning Disabilities (NCLD)
www.ncld.org
As this site reflects, the NCLD develops training and educational materials for parents and practitioners.

Learning Disabilities Association of America (LDA)
www.ldanatl.org
Visit this website to see the range of resources available through the Learning Disabilities Association of America. The LDA national office has a resource centre with more than 500 publications for sale; it also operates a film rental service.

Departments of Education Across Canada
www.edu.gov.on.ca/eng/relsites/oth_prov.html
In order to explore the learning resources produced by the departments of education in each of Canada's provinces and territories, use this link above to explore their websites.

Chapter 5

Teaching Students with Attention Deficit/Hyperactivity Disorder

Chapter Objectives

After reading this chapter, you should be able to

- discuss the basis for providing services to students with attention deficit/hyperactivity disorder (AD/HD)

- describe the characteristics and identification process for students with AD/HD, including the impact of cultural diversity

- discuss educational, technological, and medical intervention
- discuss strategies to enhance instruction and classroom adaptations and accommodations
- discuss methods for promoting a sense of community and social acceptance

Bobby has always been an active child. When he turned four years old, his parents enrolled him in a structured preschool. In his preschool class, Bobby was the child whose voice was always louder than all of the other children's. He was the child who never finished an art project because he had spent the designated time getting in and out of his chair to sharpen his pencil or to check on what the other kids were doing. He spent playtime moving from activity to activity, never spending more than a few minutes on each task. When Bobby started Kindergarten, this pattern continued. Bobby's Kindergarten teacher, Ms. Kozak, found it difficult to keep him focused on a task. She was constantly trying to direct him back to the activity the rest of the class was working on, and this started to take time away from the other children. When Ms. Kozak reviewed student progress at the midpoint of the school year, she found Bobby had missed out on acquiring a lot of the pre-reading and pre-math skills the class had focused on. Ms. Kozak met with Bobby's parents to discuss her concerns. During their conversation, they decided to make some adaptations to the way activities and directions were being presented, both in the classroom and at home, to improve Bobby's abilities to attend to tasks. These adaptations included breaking up larger tasks into a series of smaller tasks, repeating information given verbally, and incorporating opportunities for Bobby to get up and move around during the course of activities.

Ms. Kozak met again with Bobby's parents a month later to review Bobby's progress. Although the adaptations had effected some improvement, Ms. Kozak and Bobby's parents recognized that Bobby's attention skills had improved only slightly over the past month. They decided it would be beneficial to have a psycho-educational assessment completed to investigate Bobby's areas of difficulty. Bobby's parents would take him to their family physician to have a complete physical examination, while Ms. Kozak initiated a referral to the school psychologist. Ms. Kozak would also meet with the school's special education teacher to discuss how they could all work together to improve Bobby's pre-reading and pre-math skills and his ability to focus for longer periods of time and follow directions.

Questions to Consider

1. While waiting for the psycho-educational assessment to be completed, what other adaptations would you suggest Ms. Kozak use in the classroom to improve Bobby's time on task?

2. Are there any other professionals who should be consulted when planning classroom interventions to address Bobby's areas of difficulty?

INTRODUCTION

Attention deficit/hyperactivity disorder (AD/HD) is a complex condition that has been a major concern in public education for several years. It is a complicated but intriguing topic and a real challenge for classroom teachers. This condition remains controversial because professional perspectives and personal opinions vary regarding the nature of AD/HD and effective intervention techniques. In the past few years, awareness of this exceptionality has significantly increased, along with successful intervention plans for students who struggle with it. The National Institutes of Health (NIH) in the United States released a consensus statement that, despite the controversy, there is enough scientific evidence to conclude that AD/HD is a valid disorder (National Institutes of Health, 2000). It is a lifelong condition, and it has a negative impact on an individual's social, educational, and occupational life (Weyandt, 2001).

✳ Explore

Attention Deficit Disorder

In Canada, provincial educational jurisdictions do not list AD/HD as a distinct category of exceptionality. In general, the policy in most Canadian provinces is that children with AD/HD may qualify for services under other categories such as "behavioural disorders" and "learning disabilities." The identification of a student with AD/HD requires a physician's input, and although it has significant impact in the school setting, it is not primarily an educational diagnosis.

In the United States, the *Individuals with Disabilities Education Act* (IDEA) ensures services to children with exceptionalities throughout the country (IDEA, 2004). This Act governs how states and public agencies provide services (i.e., early intervention, special education) to infants, toddlers, children, and youth with exceptionalities. Students with attention deficit disorder (ADD) who need special education or related services can qualify for those services under existing special education categories (e.g., specific learning disabilities). For students whose primary exceptionality is AD/HD, however, the category "other health impaired" is recommended as the appropriate classification (U.S. Department of Education, 1991). This category includes "any chronic and acute condition that results in limited alertness and adversely affects educational performance" (U.S. Department of Education, 1991). Regulations for implementing amendments in 1999 to the IDEA actually added both ADD and AD/HD to the list of conditions that could render a child eligible under "other health impaired." The IDEA definition explains that a child with ADD or AD/HD has a heightened awareness of or sensitivity to environmental stimuli, which results in a limited alertness to the educational environment (U.S. Department of Education, 1999). In other words, the child is so busy paying attention to everything going on around him or her that attention is directed away from important educational stimuli, and school performance therefore is negatively affected.

Teachers must understand AD/HD in order to recognize its characteristics and to implement effective intervention strategies and accommodations to facilitate success for these students in their classrooms.

CONSIDER THIS

Although you have not yet studied behavioural disorders or intellectual disabilities, can you predict how they differ from learning disabilities? How would AD/HD overlap with these other exceptionalities?

FURTHER READING

The *DSM-IV-TR* is a diagnostic guide and classification system for mental disorders. Survey a copy to see the range of disorders included. Select a disorder, such as conduct disorder or oppositional defiant disorder, and compare the criteria for identification to that of AD/HD.

BASIC CONCEPTS ABOUT ATTENTION DEFICIT/HYPERACTIVITY DISORDER

Attention deficit/hyperactivity disorder is an invisible disability in that no unique physical characteristics differentiate children with the disorder from others. However, AD/HD is *not* hard to spot in the classroom. In some children, inattention is the clue: they don't seem to listen, their thoughts appear to be elsewhere, they turn in messy work with careless errors, they may not finish their work, or they may finish their work but never turn it in. Work may be found months later crammed into a cluttered desk. These children may have trouble organizing and may start one task and shift to another before completing the first. They are not defiant or oppositional; they simply do not perform as expected based on their ability. Other children can be spotted even more quickly: they are squirming, talking excessively, jumping out of their seat, or interrupting the teacher at inappropriate times. They may be referred to as the *class clown*.

Unfortunately, the disabling behaviours associated with AD/HD may be misunderstood and misinterpreted as being lazy, disorganized, and even disrespectful. The condition can be recognized only through specific behavioural manifestations that may occur during academic and nonacademic activities such as those found in social and employment settings. In fact, the greatest limitation for someone with AD/HD is difficulty in areas of self-sufficiency and what can be referred to as "street smarts" (Schuck & Crinella, 2005). As a **developmental disability**, AD/HD becomes apparent before the age of seven; however, as many as 75 percent of children will continue to demonstrate symptoms into adolescence and about one half of the adolescents will continue to have serious problems into adulthood (Hammerness, 2009). AD/HD occurs at a fairly consistent rate in various countries throughout the world and across all cultural, racial, and socioeconomic groups. It can affect children and adults with all levels of intelligence (Hammerness, 2009).

Attention Deficit/Hyperactivity Disorder Defined

Although a variety of terms have been used over the years to describe this disorder, currently the term *attention deficit/hyperactivity disorder*, used in the *Diagnostic and Statistical Manual of Mental Disorders*, Fourth Edition, Text Revision (*DSM-IV-TR*, 2000), is most common. On a global level, the *International Classification of Diseases* (10th ed.; *ICD-10*, 1992) is used to describe this disorder, which refers to conditions related to problems in attention and hyperactivity as **hyperkinetic disorders**.

AD/HD primarily refers to deficits in attention and to behaviours characterized by impulsivity and hyperactivity. The *DSM-IV-TR* (American Psychiatric Association, 2000) classifies AD/HD as a disruptive disorder expressed in persistent patterns of inappropriate degrees of attention or hyperactivity-impulsivity. A distinction must be made between AD/HD and other disorders, such as conduct disorder (e.g., physical fighting) and oppositional defiant disorder (e.g., recurrent patterns of disobedience). The *DSM-IV-TR* has been widely adopted as a guide for the diagnosis of AD/HD (Zentall, 2006). According to this document, AD/HD encompasses four types of exceptionalities: attention deficit/hyperactivity disorder, predominantly inattentive type; attention deficit/hyperactivity disorder, predominantly hyperactive-impulsive type; attention deficit/hyperactivity disorder, combined type; and attention deficit/hyperactivity disorder not otherwise specified. The identification of the specific type of AD/HD depends on the number and type of symptoms that can be ascribed to the child.

Students identified as hyperactive-impulsive will seem to be always on the go; they have trouble sitting still and may talk constantly. Adolescents and adults will often not be as visibly active but would describe their thoughts as racing and will report internal feelings of restlessness. Students who are impulsive may blurt out answers before questions are complete, interrupt others, and fail to think before acting or speaking. Teens and adults may show impulsivity in the same way, but they may also be impulsive drivers, changing lanes frequently and ignoring caution and stop signs. These behaviors result in more speeding and traffic tickets and more traffic accidents (Hammerness, 2009), and of course, more driving disasters. Students who are inattentive are less likely to be considered trouble in the classroom but may be unsuccessful due to a short attention span or lack of concentration or focus on the critical learning activity. They may also have trouble beginning a task and difficulty finishing an assignment or meeting expected timelines. The teacher is often the first to bring the AD/HD–like behaviours to the attention of the parents. When parents initiate contact with the school to find help, they will be best served by teachers who are already well informed about this condition and the special education assessment process.

Prevalence and Causes of Attention Deficit/Hyperactivity Disorder

AD/HD is one of the most common child behavioural disorders. Estimates of the prevalence of attention deficit/hyperactivity disorder in school-age children range from a conservative figure of less than 2 percent to a more liberal figure of 30 percent; however, the United States Centers for Disease Control and Prevention (2005) report that 7.8 percent of children between ages 4 and 17 have been diagnosed at some point in their lives with AD/HD; 11 percent of boys and 4.4 percent of girls are affected (U.S. Department of Education, 2005). Similarly, according to the Canadian Pediatric Society, the prevalence of attention deficit/hyperactivity disorder in school-age children in Canada ranges from 3 to 5 percent. The extreme differences found in prevalence figures reflect the lack of agreement on a definition and the difficulty and variance in identification procedures. Regardless of the exact prevalence, most students with this condition attend general education classes.

The majority of children will demonstrate the combined AD/HD, in which symptoms of inattention and hyperactivity-impulsivity are present. The second most prevalent type of AD/HD in the classroom is the inattentive type, and the least common is the hyperactive-impulsive type, in which students have typical characteristics of focusing and listening but are abnormally active, talkative, and impulsive. Boys are more often diagnosed than girls, possibly due to higher rates of other behavioural problems like fighting, defiance, and stealing that may put them under more scrutiny by school officials and doctors (Hammerness, 2009). Several individuals have noted that the prevalence of AD/HD is increasing; however, researchers generally feel that this perception is due to increased media attention, which alerts parents and teachers to the disorder's existence, and to better training of clinicians and physicians

Although the exact cause of AD/HD is unknown, several theories have been proposed, and rigorous research is ongoing. Hammerness (2009) suggests that an increased risk for AD/HD can result from influences of the environment or gene pool. The influence of genes is evidenced by a higher prevalence rate in some families. Studies have shown that biological parents, siblings, and other family members of individuals with the disorder have higher rates of AD/HD than expected in the general population. The fact that adopted children are less likely to have AD/HD suggests that genetics is more likely a causative factor than simply living in a disorganized environment and passing that disorganization down through the family. Rosemary Tannock of the Brain and Behaviour Program at Toronto's Hospital for Sick Children has also worked on a number of research projects looking at the role genetics plays in AD/HD (e.g., Feng et al., 2005; Makkar et al., 2007).

Barkley (2006) notes that environmental factors such as alcohol and drug consumption and smoking may influence the presence of AD/HD during the pre-natal period by limiting the delivery of nutrients, blood, and oxygen while the brain of the fetus is developing. Premature birth is also associated with AD/HD; other factors include complications during pregnancy and delivery, exposure to toxins through contaminated foods, brain injury, and lead poisoning. It is known that some children's brains are slow to develop and as a result these children may never reach the ability to function as a "healthy" child. Other research has shown that the differences measured in the attention area of brains are not permanent, and AD/HD symptoms can improve as the brain develops. Most likely, a combination of gene and environmental influences offers the best explanation as to cause (Hammerness, 2009). While many theories of cause have been

There are many different theories regarding the cause of AD/HD.

put forth, some have little or no evidence to support them, including aspects of the physical environment such as fluorescent lighting, soaps, disinfectants, yeast, preservatives, food colouring, aspartame, certain fruits and vegetables, sugar, social factors, and poor parental management (Weyandt, 2001).

For most students, the precise cause of the disorder may never be understood. Although many parents want to understand why their children have a developmental disability, its cause is not relevant to educational strategies or medical treatment. These can succeed without pinpointing the root of the problem.

Characteristics of Students with Attention Deficit/Hyperactivity Disorder

The characteristics of AD/HD manifest in many different ways in the classroom. Recognizing these characteristics and identifying adaptations and accommodations to lessen their impact constitute a significant challenge for teachers. The characteristics listed in the *DSM-IV-TR* criteria (APA, 2000) highlight the observable behaviours. Barkley (2006) groups these characteristics into the following three most common areas of difficulty:

1. *Limited sustained attention or persistence of attention to tasks*: Particularly during tedious, long-term tasks, students become rapidly bored and frequently shift from one uncompleted activity to another. They may lose concentration during long work periods and fail to complete routine work unless closely supervised. The problem is not due to inability to comprehend instructions, to memory impairment, or to defiance. The instructions simply do not regulate behaviour or stimulate the desired response. One study found limitations in sustained attention characterized most of the children, while deficits in selective attention, executive attention, and orienting attention were characteristic of over half (Tsal, Shalev, & Mevorach, 2005).

2. *Reduced impulse control or limited delay of gratification*: This feature is often manifests in an individual's difficulty in waiting for his or her turn while talking to others or playing. Students may not stop and think before acting or speaking. They may have difficulty working toward long-term goals and long-term rewards, preferring to work on shorter tasks that promise immediate reinforcement.

3. *Excessive task-irrelevant activity or activity poorly regulated to match situational demands*: Individuals with AD/HD are often extremely fidgety and restless. Their movement seems excessive and often not directly related to the task—for example, tapping pencils, rocking, or shifting positions frequently. They also have trouble sitting still and inhibiting their movements when the situation demands it.

Other areas of difficulty in psychological functioning include working memory, or remembering to do things; sensing time, or using time as efficiently as their peers; and using internal language to talk to themselves in order to think about events and purposefully direct their own behaviour. Students with AD/HD have problems inhibiting their reaction to events, often appearing more emotional or hotheaded and less emotionally mature. They are easily frustrated and seem to lack willpower or self-discipline. They may have difficulty following instructions or rules or even their own "to-do" lists. They demonstrate considerable variation in the quantity, quality, and speed with which they perform their assigned tasks. Their relatively high performance on some occasions, coupled with low levels of accuracy on others, can be baffling. Low levels of performance often occur with repetitive or tedious tasks.

CONSIDER THIS

Refer to the opening vignette in this chapter. Identify which of Bobby's characteristics would lead a teacher or parent to suspect AD/HD.

Symptoms are likely to change from one situation to another. More AD/HD symptoms may be present in group settings, during boring work, when students are without supervision, and when work has to be done later in the day. Individuals behave better when there is immediate payoff for doing the right thing, when they enjoy what they are doing or find it interesting, when they are in one-on-one situations, and when they can work earlier in the day (Barkley, 2006). One researcher reported the following as the AD/HD motto; it seems to summarize the challenge of AD/HD in the classroom: "It's got to be fun! If it is not fun, it's got to be moving! If its [sic] not moving and I'm not moving, maybe I can make it mad!" (Zentall, 2006).

The characteristics of AD/HD may also be present in adulthood; an estimated 50 to 60 percent of children with AD/HD will be impaired during their adult lives as they continue to experience severe symptoms (Barker, 2010). For some individuals, the condition causes problems and limitations at work as well as in other life activities. For example, the symptoms of inattention and poor organization can lead to problems in relationships and finances (Hammerness, 2009). Figure 5.1 provides a summary of common characteristics

Figure 5.1 Common Characteristics of Individuals with AD/HD

From *An AD/HD Primer* (p. 17) by L.L. Weyandt, 2001, Boston: Allyn & Bacon.

Early Childhood
Excessive activity level
Incessant talking
Difficulty paying attention
Difficulty playing quietly
Impulsiveness and easily distracted
Academic underachievement

Middle Childhood
Excessive fidgeting
Difficulty remaining seated
Messy and careless work
Failure to follow instructions
Failure to follow through on tasks
Academic underachievement

Adolescence
Feelings of restlessness
Difficulty engaging in quiet sedentary activities
Forgetful and inattentive
Impatience
Engagement in potentially dangerous activities
Academic underachievement

Adulthood
Feelings of restlessness
Difficulty engaging in quiet sedentary activities
Frequent shifts from one uncompleted activity to another
Frequent interruption of or intrusion on others
Avoidance of tasks that allow for little spontaneous movement
Relationship difficulties
Anger management difficulties
Frequent changes in employment

for varying age groups, including adults. Barkley (2010) reports that adults with AD/HD are more likely to be fired, typically change jobs three times more often than adults without the disorder in a 10-year period, are more likely to divorce, and typically have more traffic citations and accidents. On the positive side, the outcome is much brighter for individuals with AD/HD who receive treatment, such as medication, behaviour management, and social skills training. Many adults with AD/HD are very successful; Zentall (2006) proposes three possible reasons for this:

■ Some professions have built-in support personnel, such as computer operators, administrative assistants, and accountants.

■ Some jobs have built-in accommodations, including frequent travel or a stimulating work setting such as a hospital or a high-volume sales floor.

■ Some jobs require the personal qualities frequently found in individuals with AD/HD, such as extroversion, spontaneity, humour, energy, risk taking, multitasking, and entrepreneurship.

In any case, AD/HD and its treatment can have a significant impact on adult outcomes. A large part of a successful outcome for any person with an exceptionality is self-determination and persistence. However, successful outcomes greatly depend on the support of others. Teachers who can identify and plan meaningful interventions for students with AD/HD can have a powerful impact on their success during the school years as well as on their quality of life as adults.

Identification, Assessment, and Eligibility

Although in the United States the assessment of an AD/HD is the responsibility of public education personnel, in Canada its identification ultimately requires the involvement of a physician or psychiatrist. However, the identification of AD/HD in a student frequently begins in the school, through a teacher or parent referral to the school psychologist or school team. There is a large overlap between attention deficits and other recognized exceptionalities such as learning disabilities and behavioural disorders; therefore, the school assessment of the student with suspected AD/HD is essential. Teachers should be familiar with the specific behaviours and the commonly used assessment techniques associated with attention deficit disorders, since they are an integral part of the assessment process. Formal assessment for AD/HD should require the teacher to complete measures assessing the student's behaviour at school and documenting behaviour over a period of time and in different settings, and to conduct ongoing monitoring of the child's behaviour in response to medication.

As soon as the school suspects that a child is experiencing attention problems, the parents should be notified and invited to meet with the school team. Often, the parents, the teacher, the principal, and the school special education teacher will come together for the initial meeting. During this meeting, parents should be asked to respond to the observations of the school personnel and describe their own experiences with attention problems outside the school setting. If the team agrees that additional testing is needed, a referral is made to the school psychologist, who will direct the assessment process. The psychologist must understand the impact of AD/HD on the family; the bias that might occur during the assessment process because of cultural, socio-economic, language, and

TEACHING TIP

As another technique for recording a student's behaviour, observe a child for three to five minutes every hour during a school day, and document whether the child is on or off task. Record what the child is supposed to be doing, what he or she is actually doing, and the consequences of that behaviour (e.g., praise, ignoring). Figure out the percentage of on- and off-task behaviour.

◉┤**Watch**

ADHD

Figure 5.2

Sample Form for
Documenting Classroom
Manifestations
of AD/HD–like
Behaviours

| Teacher: _____ | School: _____ | |
| Child: _____ | Grade: _____ | Age: _____ |

Class Activity	Child's Behaviour	Date/Time

ethnic factors; and other conditions that may present as AD/HD, thereby preventing an accurate diagnosis.

Initially, a teacher who has been trained in identifying the symptoms of attention deficit/hyperactivity disorder may begin to observe that a particular student manifests these behaviours in the classroom to a greater degree than do peers. At this point, the teacher should begin to keep a log to document the child's AD/HD–like behaviours, noting the times at which behaviours appear to be more intense, more frequent, or of a longer duration. Figure 5.2 provides a simple format for this observational log. For example, a teacher might document behaviour such as constantly interrupting, talking excessively, not following directions, leaving a designated area, not finishing assignments, or not turning in homework.

Although schools are not required to use a specific set of criteria to identify attention deficit/hyperactivity disorder, the *DSM-IV-TR* criteria described earlier are highly recommended (Weyandt, 2001; Zentall, 2006).

A variety of methods and assessment procedures will be needed to gather information to evaluate the presence of AD/HD in a child. The school system will most likely interview the child, parents, and teachers; obtain a developmental and medical history; review school records; review or evaluate intellectual and academic performance; administer rating scales to the child, parents, teachers, and possible peers; and document the impact of the behaviour through direct observation. Figure 5.3 presents a rating form that can be used at home or at school to document activity. This form is especially helpful as it is configured to allow comparison of data for a child not suspected of having AD/HD.

After the necessary observations have been made, the interview process can begin. According to Weyandt (2001), an interview with parents might include the following topics:

- the student's medical, social-emotional, and developmental history
- family history
- parental concerns and perception of the problem
- the student's behaviour at home
- academic history and previous testing

1. Activity—off chair/up and down, talk/noisemaking
2. Inattention—changes in the focus of play or free-time activities, visual off task, verbal off task (e.g., off the subject)
3. Social impulsivity—disrupt, interrupt
4. Social negativity
   - *Verbal*—disagree/argue/command/verbal statement
   - *Physical*—negative physical contact with another or noncompliance or nonperformance of a request or an assigned task (Zentall, 1985a)

This behaviour has been converted to a data collection procedure (see below)

Coding Time Intervals

Child A	1	2	3	4	5	6	7	8	9	10	11	12	13	14	15
Up/down, noise															
Change focus															
Disrupt/interrupt															
Social negative															
Child B	1	2	3	4	5	6	7	8	9	10	11	12	13	14	15
Up/down, noise															
Change focus															
Disrupt/interrupt															
Social negative															

	Totals	
	Child A	Child B
Up/down, noise/activity	Activity /15	/15
Change focus/inattention	Inattention /15	/15
Disrupt/interrupt/impulsivity	Social impulsivity /15	/15
Social negative	Social negative/15	/15
	Child A	Child B
	/60	/60

Figure 5.3 Home and Classroom Activity Indicators

The intervals are defined as 1 to15. The observer needs to select time units of 1 to 4 minutes per interval. (If 4 minutes, then total time observed = 1 hour; if 2 minutes, then total time = 30 minutes; and if 1 minute, then total time = 15 minutes.)

From *AD/HD and Education Foundations, Characteristics, Methods, and Collaboration* (p. 25), by S.S. Zentall, 2006, Upper Saddle River, NJ: Pearson.

An interview with the child is appropriate in many cases to determine the child's perception of the reports by the teacher, his or her attitude toward school and family, and his or her perception of relationships with peers. Although the child's responses will be slanted by personal feelings, they are still an important source of information.

The assessment of achievement and intelligence can document the effect the condition is having on the individual's success at school and is essential to determine if the child can qualify for services in categories of learning disabilities or intellectual disabilities. Also, knowing the levels of intelligence and achievement will help in eventually developing an intervention plan.

Rating scales that measure the presence of AD/HD symptoms are widely used to quantify the severity of the behaviours. They offer a way to measure the extent of the problem objectively. Several informants who know the child in a variety of settings should complete rating scales and the results should be compared to responses from interviews and the results of observations. Some rating scales are limited to an assessment of the primary symptoms contained in the *DSM-IV-TR* criteria; other assessment instruments are multidimensional and might address social-emotional status, communication, memory, reasoning and problem solving, and cognitive skills, such as planning and self-evaluation.

When the school team reconvenes to review the data, the *DSM-IV-TR* (APA, 2000) criteria should be considered. The school team should look for consistency across reports from the assessment instruments and the informants to validate the existence of AD/HD. If AD/HD is confirmed, the team must determine if the disorder has caused an adverse effect on school performance and if a special educational plan is needed.

Following the assessment, a meeting should be called for all participants to discuss the findings and recommendations. This meeting might be very emotional and overwhelming for parents, or it might generate relief and hope that the services can truly assist the child. The team must be sensitive to the parents' feelings and take adequate time to describe the results of the testing. If the parents are emotionally upset, it may help to wait a week before developing the intervention plan for school services.

After the educational plan has been developed, the parents and school personnel should monitor the child's progress closely to ensure success. Adjustments may be needed occasionally to maintain progress. For example, reinforcement for good behaviour may eventually lose its novelty and need to be changed. The ultimate goal is to remove accommodations and support as the child becomes capable of regulating his or her behaviour. As the setting and school personnel change each year, re-evaluating the type of special services needed will yield benefits. As the student becomes more efficient in learning and demonstrates better social skills, new, less restrictive plans must be designed to complement this growth.

Cultural and Linguistic Diversity

When AD/HD coexists with cultural and linguistic diversity, it presents a special set of challenges to the educator. Failure to address the special needs of these children can be detrimental to their academic success. Issues related to assessment and cultural diversity have been discussed previously; the same concerns exist in the identification and treatment of students with AD/HD. In order to address the needs of multicultural students with AD/HD, teachers must become familiar with their unique values, views, customs, interests, and behaviours.

Teachers must learn to recognize the cultural differences of each child in the classroom. The majority of teachers (in both special and general education) in Canada generally lack training related to meeting the individual needs of culturally diverse children. During the identification process, the team must recognize cultural differences and

TEACHING TIP

Begin a parent conference by relaying the student's strengths. Give parents time to respond to the limitations observed in the school setting by reporting examples of behaviour from home and other environments.

influences for what they are, rather than labelling them as a symptom of attention deficit/hyperactivity disorder. Gay (2003) proposes that the frequent mismatch between the cultures of teachers and their students in regard to language, culture, and socio-economic background causes many students to display behaviours that may be misinterpreted as AD/HD. For example, students learning English will likely have difficulty concentrating and attending to large amounts of information presented in their new language (Salend & Rohena, 2002). They may be observed as fidgety, distracted, or seeming not to listen, much like students with AD/HD.

Barkley (2006) raises the issue that a chaotic home environment exacerbates the problems of children with AD/HD. Although the homes of many children with AD/HD may seem disorganized and the parenting characterized by inconsistencies or lack of structure, teachers and schools should seriously question such judgments. Individuals being interviewed during the assessment process should be asked to describe how the student's behaviour might be affected by his or her culture, language, or experiential background (Duhaney, 2000).

Adaptations and accommodations can be important in both assessing and teaching children with racial, cultural, and linguistic diversity. Gestures, demonstrations, visuals, and simulations may help provide a context that promotes learning (Salend & Rohena, 2002). Teachers can also integrate personal and community experiences into teaching an academic concept to help make it relevant. The literature tells us that when teachers carefully organize and structure instruction, these students benefit. These and other strategies and accommodations appropriate for all students with AD/HD, including the culturally diverse, are described more fully in the following sections. The Personal Spotlight on page 138 provides a glimpse of one professional's thoughts on the importance of considering a child's background experiences when addressing his or her areas of need in the classroom.

THE ROLE OF MEDICATION

Since many students with AD/HD will be prescribed medication by their physicians (Connor, 2006), teachers need to understand the types of medications often used, their potential side effects, and the way they work. Pharmacological therapy can be defined as treatment by chemical substances that prevent or reduce inappropriate behaviours, thus promoting academic and social gains for children with learning and behaviour problems. Studies have shown that different outcomes occur for different children. In approximately 76 percent of cases, children with AD/HD (ages six and older) respond in a positive manner to stimulant medication such as methylphenidate (Ritalin or Concerta) or amphetamines (Dexedrine or Adderal) (Hammerness, 2009). The desired outcomes include increased concentration, more on-task behaviour, completion of assigned tasks, improved social relations with peers and teachers, increased appropriate behaviours, and reduction of inappropriate, disruptive behaviours such as talking out, getting out of classroom seats, and breaking rules. These changes frequently lead to improved academic and social achievement as well as increased self-esteem.

For some children, the desired effects do not occur. In these situations, the medication has no negative effect but simply does not lead to the hoped-for results. However, parents and teachers often give up too soon, prematurely concluding that medication did not help. It is important to contact the physician when no effect is noticed, because the

Most children with AD/HD are in general education classrooms.

dosage may need to be adjusted or a different type of medication may be called for. Barkley (2006) reports that when individuals continue to try different stimulants after one fails, the success rate rises to 90 percent.

Side effects—i.e., changes that are not desired—are another possible response to medication. The most common side effect, loss of appetite, occurs more than 50 percent of the time; however, it has not been found to affect adult stature (Barkley, 2006). When this happens, individuals may take the medication during or after a meal or add high calorie snacks to their diet. Other possible side effects include anxiety or irritability, headaches, dry mouth, dizziness, or nausea (Barkley, 2010). Figure 5.4 lists the most common side effects of the medications used for AD/HD. The checklist may be used by parents and teachers when communicating with physicians. Teachers should be constantly on the lookout for signs of side effects and report any concerns to parents or the child's physician.

The most commonly prescribed medications for AD/HD are **psychostimulants**, such as Ritalin and Concerta (methylphenidate), Adderall (amphetamine salts), and Cylert (dextroamphetamine) (Austin, 2003). Studies have shown that Ritalin accounts for 90 percent of the market in stimulants prescribed (Weyandt, 2001). This medication is considered a mild central nervous system stimulant; it is effective for approximately four hours and is at its peak after one-and-a-half to two-and-a-half hours. The dosage should be increased until the optimal response is obtained with the fewest side effects. The medication is thought to stimulate the underaroused central nervous system of individuals with AD/HD, increasing the amount or efficiency of the neurotransmitters needed for attention, concentration, and planning (Weyandt, 2001). Students who are described as anxious or tense, have tics, or have a family history or diagnosis of **Tourette syndrome** are generally not given Ritalin. Adderall is gaining in usage partly because it is effective for up to 15 hours and because a second dose does not have to be taken at school. The specific

CONSIDER THIS

Adolescents often refuse to take medication prescribed for AD/HD. What happens during this developmental period that might account for this behaviour?

Figure 5.4 Stimulant Side Effects Checklist

From *AD/HD Project Facilitate: An In-Service Education Program for Educators and Parents* (p. 55), by R. Elliott, L.A. Worthington, and D. Patterson, Tuscaloosa, AL: University of Alabama. Used with permission.

Side Effects Checklist: Stimulants

Child _____ Date Checked _____

Person Completing Form _____ Relationship to Child _____

I. SIDE EFFECTS

Directions: Please check any of the behaviours which this child exhibits while receiving his or her stimulant medication. If a child exhibits one or more of the behaviours below, please rate the extent to which you perceive the behaviour to be a problem using the scale below (1 = Mild to 7 = Severe).

	Mild						Severe
1. Loss of appetite	1	2	3	4	5	6	7
2. Stomachaches	1	2	3	4	5	6	7
3. Headaches	1	2	3	4	5	6	7
4. Tics (vocal or motor)	1	2	3	4	5	6	7
5. Extreme mood changes	1	2	3	4	5	6	7
6. Cognitively sluggish/disoriented	1	2	3	4	5	6	7
7. Excessive irritability	1	2	3	4	5	6	7
8. Excessive nervousness	1	2	3	4	5	6	7
9. Decreased social interactions	1	2	3	4	5	6	7
10. Unusual or bizarre behaviour	1	2	3	4	5	6	7
11. Excessive activity level	1	2	3	4	5	6	7
12. Light picking of fingertips	1	2	3	4	5	6	7
13. Lip licking	1	2	3	4	5	6	7

II. PSYCHOSOCIAL CONCERNS

Please address any concerns you have about this child's adjustment to medication (e.g., physical, social, emotional changes; attitudes toward the medication, etc.).

III. OTHER CONCERNS

If you have any other concerns about this child's medication (e.g., administration problems, dosage concerns), please comment below.

IV. PARENT CONCERNS (FOR PARENTS ONLY)

Using the same scale above, please check any behaviours which this child exhibits while at home.

	Mild						Severe
1. Insomnia; sleeplessness	1	2	3	4	5	6	7
2. Possible rebound effects (excessive hyperactivity, impulsivity, inattention)	1	2	3	4	5	6	7

dose of medicine must be determined individually. Generally, greater side effects come from higher dosages, but some students may need a high dosage to experience the medication's positive effects. No clear guidelines exist as to how long a child should take medication, and both adolescents and adults respond positively to these stimulants. Constant monitoring, preferably through behavioural rating scales completed by parents and teachers, is essential.

Antidepressants are also used to manage AD/HD. They are prescribed less frequently than psychostimulants and might include Tofranil (imipramine), Norpramin (desipramine), and Elavil (amytriptaline). These medications are generally used when

FURTHER READING

For more information on the role of medication in the treatment of AD/HD, read the Canadian Pediatric Society's position paper in volume 7, issue 10 of *Paediatric Child Health*, 2002 (pp. 693 and 696).

negative side effects have occurred with stimulants, when the stimulants have not been effective, or when an individual is also depressed. The long-term use of antidepressants has not been well studied. Again, frequent monitoring is necessary for responsible management. Other medications that are used much less frequently include antipsychotics, such as Mellaril (thioridazine), Thorazine (chlorpromazine), Catapres (clonidine), Eskalith (lithium), and Tegretol (carbamazepine) (Austin, 2003). Whatever medication is prescribed by the child's physician, teachers should ask for a thorough description of the possible positive and negative outcomes for that medication.

Remember, not all children diagnosed with attention deficit/hyperactivity disorder need medication. The decision to intervene medically should come only after a great deal of thought about the possibility of a variety of interventions. Children whose impairments are minimal are certainly less likely to need medication than those whose severe impairments result in major disruptions. Answers to the following questions should be determined by the team before making the final decision to use medication (Austin, 2003):

- Is the child younger than six years? (Methylphenidate has not been approved for preschool children [Leo, 2002].)
- Have other interventions been tried, and, if so, why were they ineffective?
- How severe are the child's current symptoms?
- Can the family afford the costs associated with pharmacological intervention?
- Can family members adequately supervise the use of medication and prevent abuse?
- What are the attitudes and cultural perspectives of family members toward medication?
- Is there a substance-abusing family member in the home?
- Does the child have concomitant disorders, such as tics or mental illness?
- Is the child overly concerned about the effects of the medication?
- Does the physician seem committed to appropriate follow-up monitoring?
- Is the child or adolescent involved in competitive sports or planning to enter the military? (The medication will be detected as a "controlled substance" in the course of urinalysis [Kollins et al., 2001].)

FURTHER READING

For more information on alternative therapies in the treatment of AD/HD, read the Canadian Pediatric Society's position paper in volume 7, issue 10 of *Paediatric Child Health*, 2002 (pp. 710–718).

Although teachers and other school personnel are important members of a therapeutic team engaged in exploring, implementing, and evaluating diverse treatment methods, the decision to try medication is primarily the responsibility of the parents and the physician. Teachers are generally cautioned by their school systems not to specifically recommend medication because the school may be held responsible for any charges incurred. Educators, therefore, find themselves in a dilemma when they feel strongly that medication is needed to address the symptoms of the AD/HD. However, teachers must also realize that medication alone is insufficient. The use of medication to control behaviour is controversial, since studies are not conclusive. Individual parents may prefer not to use medication. School personnel must respect the opinion of many that these medications are being prescribed for far too many children (Scheffler, Hinshaw, Modrek, & Levine, 2007). Students with AD/HD need a multimodal approach, including the cognitive and behavioural strategies addressed in the following section.

Occasionally, teachers and parents will hear of alternative treatment therapies that seem to offer a "quick fix." These are often advertised in newspapers and popular magazines or seen on television, but they seldom appear in professional literature. Alternative approaches that have been used include the use of megavitamins, diet restrictions (e.g., sugar or additives), caffeine, massage therapy, chiropractic skull manipulations, biofeedback, play therapy, and herbs. Critics caution that if an approach were that amazing, everyone would use it. Evidence supporting any treatment should be fully documented before submitting children to the treatment and investing resources.

STRATEGIES FOR INSTRUCTION AND CLASSROOM ADAPTATIONS AND ACCOMMODATIONS

Since no two children with attention deficit/hyperactivity disorder are exactly alike, a wide variety of interventions and service options must be used to meet their needs. Success for these students depends on the teacher's qualifications, effective strategies for instruction, and classroom adaptations and accommodations.

Classroom Adaptations and Accommodations

Since attention deficit/hyperactivity disorder describes a set of characteristics that affect learning, most interventions take place in the school setting. Any approach to addressing the needs of students with AD/HD must be comprehensive. Figure 5.5 depicts a model of educational intervention built on four intervention areas: environmental management, instructional accommodations, student-regulated strategies, and medical management. Medical management was described previously. This section identifies specific strategies for addressing the challenges of AD/HD in the classroom.

Managing the Classroom Environment A classroom with even one or two students with AD/HD can be difficult to manage. Teachers, therefore, need to be skilled in

CROSS REFERENCE

Teachers should develop a list of procedures to make the classroom run smoothly. For example, how should students request help? How should they respond during a fire drill? For more tips, refer to chapter 12.

Figure 5.5 Model for AD/HD Intervention

From *Attention-Deficit/Hyperactivity Disorder in the Classroom: A Practical Guide for Teachers*, by C.A. Dowdy, J.R. Patton, E.A. Polloway, & T.E.C. Smith, 1997, Austin, TX: Pro-Ed.

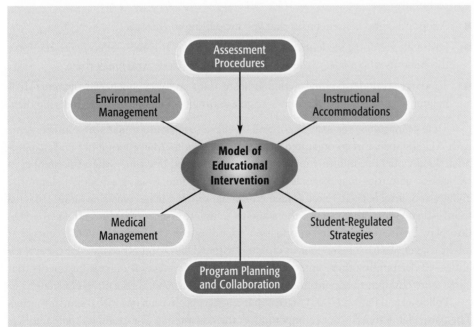

classroom management. Rather than reacting spontaneously—and often inconsistently—to disruptive situations, teachers should have a management system to help avoid crises. Good classroom management is beneficial for all students, including those with AD/HD. Techniques include group management, physical management, and behaviour management.

Group Management   Group management techniques benefit all members of a classroom, but they are critical in managing the behaviour of individual students with AD/HD. One of the most basic and effective techniques is to establish classroom rules and consequences for breaking those rules. Children with AD/HD need to understand these rules and school procedures in order to be successful. Polloway, Patton, and Serna (2005) suggest that students feel more committed to following rules when they have contributed to developing them. The rules should be displayed prominently in the room and reviewed periodically, if students with AD/HD are to retain and follow them. It is important for teachers to apply the rules consistently, even though students can sometimes frustrate teachers and make them want to "give in." Teachers may start the process of rule development by offering one or two rules of their own and then letting the children pick up with their own ideas. The following is a list of recommendations for developing rules:

■   State rules positively and clearly. A rule should tell students what to do instead of what not to do!

■   Rules should be stated in simple terms so students can easily understand them. For young students, rules can be depicted with drawings and figures.

■   The number of rules should be no more than five or six.

■   Rules should be displayed conspicuously in the room.

■   Rules should be practised and discussed at the beginning of the year and periodically throughout the year.

■   For students with AD/HD, role playing how to carry out the rules is an effective technique.

■   Adopt rules and consequences that you are willing to enforce.

■   Positively reinforce students who abide by the rules. It is more effective to reinforce the students who abide by the rules than to punish those who break them.

■   To avoid misunderstandings, communicate rules and consequences to parents. It is helpful to have parents and students sign a contract documenting their understanding.

CONSIDER THIS

What are some appropriate activities to begin and end the day or class period for elementary and secondary students?

Time management is also important in effective classroom management. Students with AD/HD thrive in an organized, structured classroom. Many acting-out and inappropriate behaviours occur during unscheduled, unstructured free time, when the number of choices of activities may become overwhelming. If free time is scheduled, limit the choices and provide positive reinforcement for appropriate behaviour. Encourage students to investigate topics that interest them and to complete projects that bring their strengths into play. Figure 5.6 provides information regarding the types of classroom events that might trigger negative behaviour in children with AD/HD and other types of exceptionalities. Understanding these antecedent events can help teachers make adjustments that allow more children to benefit from their education in a general education classroom.

Polloway and Patton (2005) suggest that teachers begin each day with a similar routine. The particular activity is not as important as the consistency. For example, some teachers

Students with AD/HD

Behaviour difficulties will increase when:

■ the task is effortful in its length, repetitiveness, and nonmeaningfulness

■ little opportunity exists for movement or choice

■ few opportunities exist for active involvement in learning

■ many students and only one teacher are present, and learning is large-group teacher directed

■ little supervision, feedback, or positive reinforcement takes place

■ periods of transition exist with little structure (for a review, see Zentall, 1993; 1995)

Students with AD/HD Plus Aggression

Aggression occurs primarily:

■ when entering new groups

■ when resources are scarce or information is needed

■ during low structure

■ during difficult tasks

■ when little flexibility exists

■ when few adults and much activity are present

■ when no apparent way to escape tasks or social demands is available

■ when a peer group values "toughness"

Students with AD/HD Plus Learning Disabilities

Task avoidance behaviour, such as off-task behaviour, occurs primarily when:

■ presented with a task that is within the student's area of specific learning disability (e.g., with reading requirements, mathematical calculations)

■ presented with any kind of auditory input, such as listening tasks, group discussion, social interactions (in these contexts the child may be more likely to actively refuse, avoid, or act disruptively)

■ presented with complex visual input, such as copying from the board or from dictionary to paper, art tasks using collage (with such tasks, the child may take a long time to produce work)

■ asked to respond in certain ways (e.g., fine motor handwriting or talking) (with such response requirements, the child may avoid or become negative and noncompliant)

Students with AD/HD and Giftedness

Off-task or disruptive behaviour is observed primarily when:

■ tasks are too easy

■ teachers believe that if the child can't do the easy work, he or she can't do the challenging work

■ tasks involve a lot of rote lower-level skills

Students with AD/HD and Developmental Disabilities

Disruptive behaviour and poor performance occur primarily:

■ during difficult, complex, higher-level tasks that require problem solving, analysis, synthesis, or reasoning abilities

(continued)

Figure 5.6 Antecedents That Often Trigger Negative Behaviours for Children with Different Exceptionalities

Students with AD/HD and Anxiety

Avoidance, inflexible, or repetitive behaviour occurs:

- when entering new groups
- in the presence of a lot of activity and confusion
- during difficult or unstructured (ambiguous) tasks
- when it is noisy
- when unpredictable activities that have not been scheduled are provided or changes in a schedule have been made

From *AD/HD and Education: Foundations, Characteristics, Methods, and Collaboration* (pp. 73–74), by S.S. Zentall, 2006, Upper Saddle River, NJ: Pearson.

Figure 5.6 Continued

like to start the day with quiet reading, whereas others might begin with singing, recognizing birthdays, or talking about special events that are coming up. This routine will set the stage for a calm, orderly day, and students will know what to expect from the teacher. Secondary teachers need to advise students of scheduling changes (e.g., assembly, pep rally) and provide a brief overview of the topics and activities to be expected during the class period.

Just as at the beginning of the day, closure of the day's or the class period's activities is important for secondary students. Reviewing the important events of the day and describing the next day's activities help students with AD/HD. Take the time to provide rewards for students who have maintained appropriate behaviour. If parents are involved in a contract, discuss the transmitted notes and review homework that might have been assigned.

Personal Spotlight

Alternate Education Teacher Heather Merasty

Heather Merasty has taken on a number of different roles in her teaching career (classroom teacher, special education coordinator, and alternate education teacher). In the northern communities where she has worked, Heather has found it challenging to work with students who have been diagnosed with attention deficit/hyperactivity disorder (AD/HD).

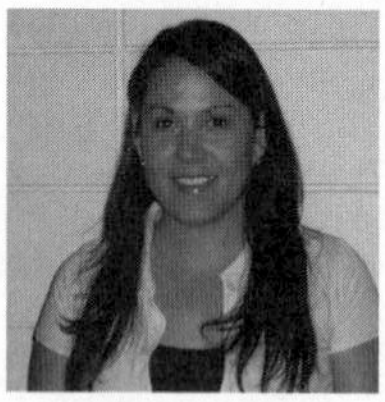

Heather has found that often, classroom teachers are left to fend for themselves when working with AD/HD students. However, establishing working relationships with other teachers and "surrounding students with a team of professionals that includes the student and student's family works to better support the needs of the AD/HD student." Networking with other teachers within the school and the school division and with other professionals in the community (mental health professionals, community health nurses) helps her to better meet the needs of her students.

A key tool Heather uses to establish appropriate interventions for her students with AD/HD is to spend time building a working relationship with students. "Children tend to behave well for teachers they have an emotional bond with—it is crucial to develop meaningful, trusting relationships with the student and the family. When students feel safe and secure in their environment, they are more likely to become involved in their educational program." Building a relationship enables a teacher to talk openly with students about their areas of ability and need, and gain their insights as to what works best for them. Heather also finds it helpful to let this relationship develop over time and not to force it. "It's important to be patient . . . give students a chance to become more involved in their education. Teaching to their strengths and interests helps. Don't get caught up in what they can't do; focus on what they *can* do."

Teachers may want to offer incentives to individual students and groups to reward outstanding work. For example, you might place a marble in a jar each time students are "caught being good." When the jar is filled the class receives an award, such as a picnic or a skating party. Another technique involves adding a piece to a puzzle whenever the teacher recognizes that the class is working especially hard. When the puzzle is complete, the class is rewarded. These group incentives can be very effective; however, some students will need an individual behaviour management plan to aid in directing their behaviour. Babkie (2006) offers the following additional tips for proactive classroom management:

- Make boundaries clear for students' appropriate interactions with you and with peers. Remember, you are not your students' friend—you are their teacher. Be sympathetic and supportive but reinforce the boundaries.

- Cue students when activities are about to change, and teach transitioning skills.

- Teach cognitive strategies to facilitate success in academic and social environments.

- Pace lessons and alter the workload based on student needs and responses instead of punishing students for not "keeping up."

- Give learning a purpose by providing real-world uses for new skills.

- Use activity-based work that is not always a paper-and-pencil task or test.

- At all times, be respectful toward students. Consider how you would want to be treated. Ensure that students are comfortable in the classroom and feel like successful, contributing members.

Physical Management   The physical environment of a classroom can also have an impact on the behaviours of students with AD/HD. The arrangement of the room is most important. The classroom needs to be large enough for students to have space between themselves and others, so they will be less likely to impose themselves on one another. Each student needs some personal space.

Desk arrangement is also important. The student with AD/HD may need to be near the teacher in order to focus attention on the information being presented in the classroom. However, students should never be placed near the teacher as a punitive measure. A seat near the front may help a student who is distracted by someone's new hairstyle or flashy jewellery. There should also be various places in the room where quiet activities can take place, small groups can work together, sustained attention for difficult tasks can be maintained, and a relaxed and comfortable environment can be enjoyed for a change of pace. At one time, classrooms with lots of visual stimulation were considered inappropriate for students with AD/HD, leading to the creation of sterile environments with colourless walls and no bulletin boards. This is no longer considered necessary, but order is needed in the classroom. Materials should be consistently kept in the same place, and bulletin boards should be well organized. Set aside places where students can work in a carrel or other private space with minimal visual and auditory stimuli, and have a place for a child who seems under-aroused to be able to move around and get rejuvenated (Carbone, 2001).

Behavioural Support   Behavioural support techniques can enhance the education of students with AD/HD, especially those that reward desired behaviour. For example, when students with AD/HD are attending to their tasks, following classroom rules, or

CONSIDER THIS

These ideas are effective with elementary-age students. Generate some reinforcers that would be more effective in secondary settings.

participating appropriately in a co-operative learning activity, their behaviours should be positively reinforced. Unfortunately, teachers often ignore appropriate behaviour and call attention only to what is inappropriate. When students receive attention for actions that are disruptive or inconsiderate, the negative behaviours can be reinforced and may thus increase in frequency.

Positive reinforcement tends to increase appropriate behaviour. Teachers should consider which rewards appeal most to the individuals who will receive them. Common ones include small toys, free time, time to listen to music, time in the gym, opportunities to do things for the teacher, having lunch with the teacher, and praise. A reward that acts as a reinforcer for one student may not work for another; therefore, teachers might generate a menu of rewards and allow students to select their own. Rewards do not have to be expensive; in fact, simply allowing students to take a break, get a drink of water, or sharpen a pencil may be just as effective as providing expensive toys and games.

CONSIDER THIS

What is an example of how the Premack principle can be applied for elementary, junior, and high school students?

Another helpful idea in working with children with AD/HD is called the Premack principle. Also known as "grandma's law," it is based on the traditional comment, "If you eat your vegetables, then you can have your dessert" (Polloway, Patton, & Serna, 2001, p. 74). The teacher announces that a reward or highly desired activity will be awarded to students after they complete a required or desired activity. For example, students might be required to sit in their seats and complete work for 15 minutes, then a snack or free time will follow. This simple technique can be very effective for students with AD/HD.

Negative reinforcement (removing an aversive stimulus) is also effective in increasing desired behaviour. For example, students might be told that those who complete 15 of the assigned 25 math questions in the remaining 20 minutes of class time will not have to complete the task as homework. Removal of homework (the aversive stimulus) will motivate "on-task" behaviour. This technique is also often effective for students with AD/HD.

Often, students will need an individual plan that focuses on their particular needs. Sometimes this plan involves the creation of a "contract." Together, student and teacher develop goals to improve behaviour and then put these goals in writing. They also stipulate consequences for not following the contract and reinforcement for completing it. This instrument provides structure and forms an explicit way to communicate with children with AD/HD and their parents. Downing (2002) offers the following guidelines for making and using such contracts:

- Determine the most critical area(s) of concern.
- Consider when the behaviour usually occurs, the events that trigger it, and why you think the behaviour is occurring.
- Specify the desired behaviour in measurable terms, using clear, simple words.
- Specify the reinforcers that will be used and the consequences that will follow if the contract is not fulfilled.
- See that both teacher and student (and the parents, when appropriate) sign the contract.
- Keep a record of the student's behaviour.
- Provide the agreed-upon consequences or reinforcements in a timely fashion.
- When the goal is reached, celebrate, and write a new contract!

A sample contract is provided in Figure 5.7.

I, Bobby, agree to:

▶ Follow the classroom rules and teacher's directions.

▶ Handle conflict situations appropriately, using the strategies I have learned rather than running away.

▶ Express my negative feelings in a calm, quiet voice without making threats and/or refusing to do what I am told.

For this effort, I will earn:

▶ Fifteen minutes of free time at the end of each successful day to play *The Magic School Bus Explores the Rainforest* computer game.

▶ A visit from Billy the Boa Constrictor at the end of every week if I am successful for at least 4 out of 5 days.

Date:

Student Signature:

Teacher Signature:

Figure 5.7 An Example of a Contingency Contract

From "Individualized Behavior Contracts" (p. 170), by J.A. Downing, 2002, *Intervention in School and Clinic, 37*(3).

Be cautious with the use of contracts. As an agreement between the student and the teacher, and sometimes the parents, a contract must not be coercive. It is essential that the student be able to do the things listed in the contract. In other words, the student must be able to achieve success.

Another behaviour management technique is cueing or signalling students with AD/HD when they are on the verge of inappropriate behaviour. First, student and teacher sit down privately and discuss the inappropriate behaviour that has been creating problems in the classroom. The teacher offers to provide a cue when the behaviour begins to be noticed. Teachers and students can have fun working together on the signal, which might involve flipping the light switch, tapping the desk lightly, or making simple eye contact. These cueing techniques help establish a collegial relationship between the teacher and the student that says, "We are working on this together; we have a problem, but we also have a plan" (Wood, 2006).

Making Instructional Adaptations and Accommodations

Children with AD/HD usually don't have a problem with skills, they have problems with performance. However, these students are often misunderstood and labelled as lazy or unmotivated, as if they are choosing not to perform at their maximum potential. Teacher comments such as, "I know you can do this work because you did it yesterday" or "You can do better; you just aren't trying" probably suggest a lack of understanding of the inconsistent

 Watch

ADHD

Cueing or signalling students is one method that teachers can use to help get their attention.

performance characteristic of this disability. Instead, teachers need to find ways to cope with the frustration and stress that are sometimes involved in working with students with AD/HD, while modifying their teaching style, their curriculum, and possibly their expectations in order to engineer academic success.

Modifying Teacher Behaviour Since students with AD/HD are not easily stimulated, they need novelty and excitement in their learning environment. Although complete and thorough directions, structure, and consistency are extremely important, students need challenging, exciting activities to keep them focused and learning (Jakobson & Kikas, 2007). One innovative strategy that addresses learning difficulties and inattention was developed by Vesely and Gryder (2009). These educators designed a word-of-the-day activity that teaches students an important, relevant, new vocabulary word daily and engages students in keeping a tally of the number of times that word was used by anyone throughout the day. Reading and speaking vocabularies increase while students improve in self-monitoring and selective attention. Professional journals and the internet offer endless ideas for "jazzing up" lesson plans or developing new ones.

The incidence of inappropriate behaviour increases during nonstimulating, repetitive activities. Teachers should vary activities, allow and encourage movement that is purposeful and not disruptive, give frequent breaks, and even let students stand as they listen, take notes, or perform other academic tasks. "Legal movement," such as pencil sharpening or a hall pass for walking to the restroom or getting water, might be pre-approved for a student's restless times. Here are some recommendations from Zentall (2006) for best practice in teaching strategies:

- Don't try to accomplish so much in one time period.
- Give frequent breaks or shorter assignments.
- Increase novelty—use treasure hunts, games, group projects. For example, play the game "What's My Verb?" where one team acts out a verb for the other team to guess and use the word in a sentence.
- Use technology.
- Incorporate student interests.
- Use "real-world" projects. For example, "If we have $100 for a party, what could we afford for refreshments and entertainment?"
- Alternate high-interest and low-interest tasks.
- Increase opportunities for motor responses during or after a task. For example, use flash cards, games, and timed drills.
- Do not take away recess or other special classes. One young man said that he learned to dawdle more because he never got recess anyway.

- Give unique topics and assignments.
- Allow students to "play" with objects during lectures or longer tasks.

During a long lecture period, teachers might list main ideas or important questions on the chalkboard or use the overhead projector to help students focus on the most important information. When a student's attention does wander, a small, unobtrusive signal, such as a gentle pat on his or her shoulder, can cue the student to return to the task. To perk up tiring students, try a quick game of Simon Says or purposeful physical activities such as taking a note to the office, feeding the animals in the classroom, or returning books to the library. Motivating these students can be difficult but should be a high priority. Smith, Salend, and Ryan (2001) suggest using a competency-oriented approach where students are referred to in terms of their strengths and where all students are given opportunities to assume leadership roles. Smith et al. encourage teachers to offer the students choices and ask for their preferences. Establish a rapport by talking to students about topics that interest them; attend after-school events and cultural activities. Also important is creating a positive learning atmosphere by demonstrating your love of teaching and learning (Salend, 2010)!

✱⎯Explore

Why Can't Annie Listen and Finish Her Work?

Modifying the Curriculum Although students with AD/HD are typically taught in the general education classroom, using the regular curriculum, they need a curriculum that is adapted to focusing on "doing" and that avoids long periods of sitting and listening. These adaptations can benefit all students. For example, experience-based learning, in which students might develop their own projects, perform experiments, or take field trips, can help all students grow as active learners. Resources can be found in story problems within traditional textbooks, curriculum-based experiments and projects, or lesson extensions such as writing letters to environmental groups to obtain more information than is offered in a textbook.

Teachers are also encouraged to vary their assessment techniques. Oral examinations, multiple-choice instead of essay or short-answer questions, take-home tests, open-book or open-note exams, portfolio assessment, and informal measures are alternative assessment methods that provide a different perspective on what students know. Students with AD/HD will generally be able to take the same tests as their peers; however, testing adaptations may be needed to specifically address the AD/HD characteristics. These might include extra time to take the test (usually no more than time-and-a-half), frequent breaks, taking the exam in a distraction-reduced environment, or using a computer to record responses.

Developing Student-Regulated Strategies

The previous sections on classroom environment and instructional adaptations and accommodations focused on activities that the teacher directs and implements to increase the success of children with AD/HD. This section will describe student-regulated strategies. Dowdy et al. (1998) define student-regulated strategies as interventions initially taught by the teacher that the student will eventually implement independently.

The following discussion addresses four types of student-regulated strategies: study and organizational tactics, self-management, learning strategies, and social skills.

Study and Organizational Tactics Children with AD/HD have difficulty organizing their work and implementing effective study skills in general education classrooms. Teachers may designate space for students to keep materials, establish the routine of having students write down their assignments daily in an assignment notebook, and provide notebooks in different colours for each subject to help students develop their organizational skills. Pierangelo and Giuliani (2006) suggest the following techniques to assist students with AD/HD in developing the study skills necessary for academic success:

- Teach children how to use Venn diagrams to organize new information in academic subjects.
- Teach children how to use a note-taking strategy, such as Anita Archer's Skills for School Success (Archer & Gleason, 2002).
- Provide children with checklists that identify categories of items needed at home and school for various assignments. They can remember to check those lists for themselves before departing.
- Teach children how to "unclutter" and organize their workspace for more efficient work.
- Involve children and parents in ongoing monitoring of homework.

Students should practise planning as an organizational strategy. For an assignment such as a term paper, deciding how to break the task into small parts and how to complete each part should be practised before such an assignment is made. Students should also practise estimating how much time will be needed for various activities so they can establish appropriate and realistic goals. Outlining skills can also help with organization and planning. Students may want to use a word processor to order their ideas and to help organize their work.

Self-Management The primary goal of programs that teach self-management or self-control is to "make children more consciously aware of their own thinking processes and task approach strategies, and to give them responsibility for their own reinforcement" (Reeve, 1990, p. 76). Here are some advantages of teaching self-control:

- It saves the teacher's time by decreasing the demand for direct instruction.
- It increases the effectiveness of an intervention.
- It increases the maintenance of skills over time.

Polloway and Patton (2005) cite four types of self-regulation. In *self-assessment*, the individual determines the need for change and also monitors personal behaviour. In *self-monitoring*, the student attends to specific aspects of his or her own behaviour. While learning to self-monitor, a student can be given a periodic beep or other cue to signal that it is time for him or her to evaluate "on-" or "off-" task behaviour. In *self-instruction*, the student cues himself or herself to inhibit inappropriate behaviours or to express appropriate ones. In *self-reinforcement*, the student administers self-selected reinforcement for an appropriate behaviour that has been previously specified. Figure 5.8 presents a self-management planning form that was completed to help a high school student control his anger. Figure 5.9 provides a self-monitoring sheet for the student to use to reflect on his or her use of the strategy. Eventually the student will begin to automatically self-monitor and

Figure 5.8 A Self-Management Strategy for Dealing with Anger

From "Collaborating to Teach Prosocial Skills" (p. 145), by D.H. Allsopp, K.E. Santos, & R. Linn, 2000, *Intervention in School and Clinic, 35*(3).

1. **W**ATCH for the "trigger."
   ▶ Count to 10.
   ▶ Use relaxation techniques.

2. **A**NSWER, "Why am I angry?"

3. **I**DENTIFY my options.
   ▶ Ignore the other person.
   ▶ Move away.
   ▶ Resolve the problem.
   ▶ "I feel this way when you . . ."
   ▶ Listen to the other person.
   ▶ Talk to the teacher.

4. **T**RY an appropriate option for dealing with my anger.

will begin to use the appropriate response to situations that previously triggered an inappropriate display of anger. Other behaviours commonly targeted for self-regulation include completing assignments (productivity), appropriate classroom behaviour (such as staying in one's seat), accuracy of work (such as percent correct), and staying on task.

Learning Strategies A strategy is defined by Lenz, Deshler, and Kissam (2004) as an individual's approach to a task. A strategy includes how an individual thinks and acts when planning, executing, or evaluating performance. The learning strategies approach combines what is going on in an individual's head (cognition) with what a person actually does (behaviour) to guide the performance and evaluation of a specific task. All individuals use strategies, but not all strategies are effective. Strichart and Mangrum (2010) recommend the learning strategies approach to assist students who are inefficient learners.

Babkie and Provost (2002) encourage teachers and students to create their own strategies or cues to teach a difficult concept or behaviour. For example, a key word is identified that specifies the targeted area (whatever they are working on). A short phrase

✳ Explore

He Just Needs a Little Discipline

What a Puzzle!

What was the trigger?	Why was I angry?	Did I identify my options?	What option did I choose and was it successful?
1.			
2.			
3.			
4.			
5.			

Figure 5.9 A Self-Monitoring Sheet for Dealing with Anger

From "Collaborating to Teach Prosocial Skills" (p. 146), by D.H. Allsopp, K.E. Santos, & R. Linn, 2000, *Intervention in School and Clinic, 35*(3).

Figure 5.10 A Learning Strategy for Homework

From "Select, Write, and Use Metacognitive Strategies in the Classroom" (p. 174), by A.M. Babkie and M.C. Provost, 2002, *Intervention in School and Clinic, 37*(3).

Organization: **Homework**
Have a place to work
Organize assignments according to difficulty
Make sure to follow directions
Examine the examples
Weave my way through the assignments
Observe work for errors and omissions
Return work to school
Keep up the effort!

or sentence that tells the student what to do is written for each letter in the key word. Figure 5.10 illustrates a strategy developed to cue students to organize homework.

Social Skills Students with attention deficit/hyperactivity disorder often do not exhibit good problem-solving skills and are unable to predict the consequences of their inappropriate behaviour; therefore, specific and direct instruction in social skills may be necessary. In order for students to be able to assess their own inappropriate behaviour and adjust it to acceptable standards, many may first need social skills training. For example, students who misread or totally miss social cues can benefit from role-playing situations. The problems students have encountered are re-enacted under controlled circumstances (i.e., a shoving incident in the lunchroom, a fight on the playground, inappropriately interrupting a teacher). This allows students to proactively rehearse correct responses for future social encounters. Repeated opportunities to practise appropriate social skills may be needed in order for the correct responses to be internalized (Sharpe, 2008).

PROMOTING INCLUSIVE PRACTICES FOR ATTENTION DEFICIT/HYPERACTIVITY DISORDER

The Professional Group for Attention and Related Disorders (PGARD) proposes that most children with AD/HD can be served in the general education program by trained teachers providing appropriate instruction and modifications. In addition to activities teachers can use to promote a supportive classroom environment, school-wide support should be promoted through exceptionality-awareness activities, the use of positive discipline, and the use of adult volunteers. The entire community can become involved through the establishment of business partnerships and the provision of organized activities such as scouting and other forms of sports and recreation. Of course, school administrators have to make a commitment to dedicate resources for training and to facilitate change.

The two critical features for successful inclusion of students with AD/HD are the skills and behaviours of the teachers and the understanding and acceptance of the general education peers.

Community-Building Skills for Teachers

One of the most important aspects of promoting success for children with AD/HD is the teacher. Fowler (1992) suggests that success for children with AD/HD might vary from year to year, class to class, and teacher to teacher. She reports that the most commonly cited reason for a positive or negative school experience is the teacher, and presents the following 17 characteristics of teachers as likely indicators of positive learning outcomes for students with AD/HD:

1. Positive academic expectations
2. Frequent review of student work
3. Clarity of teaching (e.g., explicit directions, rules)
4. Flexibility
5. Fairness
6. Active interaction with the students
7. Responsiveness
8. Warmth
9. Patience
10. Humour
11. Structured and predictable approach
12. Consistency
13. Firmness
14. Positive attitude toward inclusion
15. Knowledge of and willingness to work with students with exceptional needs
16. Knowledge of different types of effective interventions
17. Willingness to work collaboratively with other teachers (e.g., sharing information, requesting assistance as needed, participating in conferences involving students)

> **CONSIDER THIS**
>
> Use these characteristics of an effective teacher as a tool for self-assessment. Identify your strengths, and determine goals for improving your teaching skills.

Resources for Developing Awareness in Peers

Teachers with the traits listed in the previous section will represent a positive role model for students in how to understand and accept children with AD/HD. Teachers should confer with parents and the child with AD/HD to obtain advice on explaining the disorder to other children in the classroom. The child with AD/HD may wish to be present during the explanation or even to participate in informing his or her classmates.

The following books may help introduce this topic to children.

Jumping Johnny Get Back to Work—A Child's Guide to AD/HD/Hyperactivity
Michael Gordon, Ph.D., Author
Connecticut Association for Children and Adults with LD
25 Van Zant Street
Suite 15–5
East Norwalk, CT 06855-1719
(203) 838-5010
Email: cacld@optonline.net

Shelley, the Hyperactive Turtle
Deborah Moss, Author
Woodbine House
6510 Bells Mill Rd.
Bethesda, MD 20817
(800) 843-7323 or (301) 897-3570

Sometimes I Drive My Mom Crazy, but I Know She's Crazy about Me!
Childworks
Center for Applied Psychology, Inc.
P.O. 61586
King of Prussia, PA 19406
(800) 962–1141

You Mean I'm Not Lazy, Stupid, or Crazy?
Peggy Ramundo and Kate Kelly, Authors
Tyrell & Jerem Press
P.O. Box 20089
Cincinnati, OH 45220
(800) 622–6611

Otto Learns about His Medicine
Michael Gaivin, M.D., Author
Childworks
Center for Applied Psychology, Inc.
P.O. Box 61586
King of Prussia, PA 19406
(800) 962–1141

Eagle Eyes: A Child's View of Attention Deficit Disorder
Jeanne Gehret, M.A., Author
Childworks
Center for Applied Psychology, Inc.
P.O. Box 61586
King of Prussia, PA 19406
(800) 962–1141

Feelings about Friends
Linda Schwartz, Author
Creative Teaching Press
(800) 235–5767
Email: customerservice@creativeteaching.com

Brakes: The Interactive Newsletter for Kids with AD/HD
Magination Press
750 First Street NE
Washington, DC 20002–4242
Order Department: 1(800) 374–2721
Fax: (202) 336–5502

Collaborating with Parents of Students with Attention Deficit/Hyperactivity Disorder

Teachers can often promote success for students with AD/HD by working closely with parents to practise and reinforce desirable academic and social behaviour. Brandes (2005) stresses the importance of keeping parents involved in their child's education through meaningful communications. She offers these recommendations to promote healthy relationships based on respect:

■ Be an active listener, sit or stand beside parents, and give them your undivided attention.

■ Take notes while talking with parents and review those notes for accuracy as the parents leave; recap the meeting.

■ View a challenging parent as an opportunity to grow. Be respectful when working with an angry parent, write down his or her concerns, and do not be defensive.

■ Share specific behavioural and curricular goals early and provide their relevance.

■ Communicate regularly and often, always share some of the positive events from school, let parents know how much you appreciate their support and follow-through at home, and specify future communications.

SUMMARY

■ AD/HD is a complex condition that offers a real challenge to classroom teachers.

■ In Canada, AD/HD is not a separate category of exceptionality in provincial educational jurisdictions.

■ AD/HD is a hidden disability with no unique physical characteristics to differentiate children who have it from others in the classroom.

■ The diagnosis of AD/HD is primarily based on criteria in the *Diagnostic and Statistical Manual of Mental Disorders (DSM-IV-TR)*.

■ Many theories explain the cause of AD/HD; however, it is considered primarily a neurologically based condition.

■ AD/HD manifests across the lifespan; characteristics include limited sustained attention, reduced impulse control, excessive task-irrelevant activity, deficient rule following, and greater than normal variability during task performance.

■ The process of identifying AD/HD must be done in collaboration with a psychiatrist or a physician and at the school level. Identifying AD/HD includes a preliminary assessment, an initial meeting of the school team, a formal assessment and follow-up meeting of the school team, a collaborative meeting to develop an intervention plan, and follow-up and progress reviews.

■ Cultural and linguistic diversity complicates issues related to assessment and treatment for children with AD/HD.

■ The majority of students with AD/HD spend all or most of the school day in general education classes.

■ An individual accommodation plan is written collaboratively with parents, professionals, and, when possible, the student to identify interventions that will create success in the general education classroom.

■ Medication is frequently used to enhance the educational experience of students with AD/HD.

■ The most commonly prescribed medication is a psychostimulant, such as Ritalin, Concerta, or Adderall.

■ Both positive outcomes and negative side effects should be monitored for individual children taking medication for AD/HD.

■ Classroom adaptations include environmental management techniques, instructional adaptations, and student-regulated strategies.

■ Techniques used to manage the classroom environment include strategies for group management, physical arrangement of the room, and individual behaviour management techniques.

■ Through instructional accommodations, teachers modify their behaviour to include novel and stimulating activities, provide structure and consistency, allow physical movement as frequently as possible, include co-operative learning activities, and give both spoken and written direction.

■ The curriculum for students with AD/HD should be stimulating and should include experience-based learning and problem-solving activities.

■ Student-regulated strategies include study and organizational tactics, self-management techniques, learning strategies, and social skills training.

■ Effective teachers for students with AD/HD provide positive classroom environments, review student work frequently, and are flexible, fair, responsive, warm, patient, consistent, firm, and humorous. They develop knowledge of the strengths and needs of their students with AD/HD and know about different intervention strategies. They are willing to work collaboratively with other teachers, parents, and professionals.

Weblinks

Children and Adults with Attention Deficit/ Hyperactivity Disorder (CHADD)
www.chadd.org
This comprehensive website provides basic facts about AD/HD, current research, helpful strategies, up-to-date resources, and related links. The focus is on education, advocacy, and support for people with AD/HD, their parents, and educators.

CH.A.D.D. Canada
www.chaddcanada.org
This website describes the mission of CHADD in Canada and provides links to local chapters across the country.

Attention Deficit Disorder Association (ADDA)
www.add.org
The Association's website is especially focused on the needs of adults and young adults with ADD, but is also relevant for parents of children with ADD. It provides specific sites focused on family issues, school, and ADD, as well as a kids' area. An excellent aspect of this website is a bookstore for which the Association has selected and reviewed books and categorized them by topic (e.g., for parents, for children, for educators).

About.com
http://add.miningco.com/health/add
Fascinating to browse, this website provides a guide to a huge array of information related to AD/HD. It covers parenting, educating, medication, comorbid disorders, career issues, and more, and offers book lists, video lists, and chat rooms.

Chapter 6
Teaching Students with Emotional or Behavioural Disorders

Chapter Objectives

After reading this chapter, you should be able to

- define emotional or behavioural disorders (EBD)
- understand the complexity of defining EBD and how this complexity affects estimates of prevalence and service delivery
- describe the characteristics of children and youth with EBD
- discuss ways to identify and assess students with EBD
- identify effective interventions for students with EBD
- discuss the roles of teachers, families, and other support personnel in working together to meet the needs of students with EBD

1. What are some possible explanations for why Cameron's parents noticed his inappropriate behaviours only when he started formal schooling?

2. What are some of the positive behaviour support strategies the team may want to consider implementing to improve Cameron's behaviour?

3. What are some of the advantages and disadvantages of identifying and labelling Cameron's inappropriate behaviours as a behavioural disorder?

Cameron is an eight-year-old Grade 3 student. He has always had difficulty expressing himself verbally, following set classroom routines and rules, behaving appropriately in class, and interacting with his peers. For example, when he wants to attract his peers' attention, he is often physically aggressive. This includes kicking individuals as he walks by, purposefully bumping into others, and taking classroom supplies out of his peers' desks without asking permission. Cameron has been seeing a speech-language pathologist since he was a preschooler to improve his receptive and expressive language skills. Although his language skills have steadily improved (i.e., he is now demonstrating a mild receptive and expressive language disorder), his inappropriate behaviours have only worsened. Cameron's parents noticed his behavioural problems when he started Kindergarten. Academically, Cameron has experienced some success in math activities, but is struggling in the area of reading and writing. Mr. Grant, Cameron's new teacher, has found dealing with Cameron's inappropriate behaviours a challenge. He has tried to consistently enforce consequences for any behaviour difficulties or classroom rules that Cameron violates (e.g., when Cameron takes property that belongs to another student without permission, he must return the item and apologize). However, his behaviour improves for only a short period of time, and then he gets into trouble again. Mr. Grant recognizes that Cameron's behaviour and poor language skills are negatively impacting his academic performance. After meeting with Cameron's parents, the special education teacher, and his speech-language pathologist, it has been decided that Cameron should be referred to the school psychologist to investigate his academic and behavioural difficulties. Academically, the school psychologist has found Cameron's math skills to be within the range typically expected for a child his age, and his reading and writing skills to be mildly delayed (he is about six months behind his peers). She has also identified Cameron as having a behaviour disorder.

Cameron's parents and the team of professionals involved in Cameron's programming are now meeting to discuss where they should go from here. They have established that their first priority will be to create and implement a behaviour management program in the classroom to address Cameron's behavioural concerns. Their next course of action will be to discuss how they can continue to work on improving his language and academic skills in the home and school environments.

INTRODUCTION

Although most children and youth are disruptive from time to time, the majority do not display negative behaviours sufficient to create serious problems in school. Most comply with classroom and school rules without needing extensive interventions. However, some students' behaviours and emotions result in significant problems for themselves, their peers, and their teachers—problems that may be exacerbated by the way school personnel deal with those behaviours. A student may not respond as expected to typical interventions. Students such as Cameron whose behaviours and emotions result in significant school problems may require identification and intervention. At a minimum, they require that classroom teachers try different methods in an effort to enhance students' school success, reduce their problem behaviour, and increase their pro-social behaviours (Wagner et al., 2005).

Although emotional and behavioural problems are correlated with anxiety and mood disorders and may result in serious actions, such as suicides, most teachers have identified discipline problems—i.e., acting out and disruptive behaviours—as the primary issues they must address when dealing with students with emotional and behavioural difficulties.

Students who experience emotional or behavioural disorders receive a variety of labels. The U.S. federal government first identified this group as seriously emotionally disturbed (SED), and later as emotionally disturbed, under the IDEA. Whereas SED is the category used in most states, others classify this group of children as having behavioural disorders. The most widely accepted term by professionals in the field is emotional and behavioural disorders (EBD), because this term better describes the students who receive special education services. EBD is the term that will be used throughout this chapter.

Wagner and colleagues provided a summative statement on the challenges of working with students with EBD, noting from their research that "Children and youth with ED [emotional disturbances] are a group that has serious, multiple, and complex problems. Parents report that a wide range of disabilities affect their children, including anxiety, bi-polar disorder, depression, oppositional behaviour, and psychosis. Almost two-thirds of the students were reported to have AD/HD, and one-fourth were reported to have a learning disability in addition to ED [emotional disturbances]" (Wagner et al., 2005, p. 91). This chapter addresses these challenges and provides recommendations for successfully educating students with EBD.

CONSIDER THIS

What kinds of children do you think of when you hear the term *emotionally disturbed*? What kinds of children do you think of when you hear the term *emotionally or behaviourally disordered*? Can these terms have an impact on teachers' expectations of children?

BASIC CONCEPTS ABOUT EMOTIONAL AND BEHAVIOURAL DISORDERS

This section provides basic information about emotional and behavioural disorders. Understanding children with these problems aids teachers and other educators in developing appropriate intervention programs. Figure 6.1 illustrates a parent's perspective on intervention programs.

Emotional and Behavioural Disorders Defined

In Canada, no single definition of emotional or behavioural disorders is in use in schools, but practitioners have established certain commonalities in their understanding of what constitutes an emotional or behavioural disorder. These commonalities include the following:

■ behaviour that goes to an extreme, that is significantly different from what is normally expected

■ a behaviour problem that is chronic and does not quickly disappear

■ behaviour that is unacceptable because of social or cultural expectations

■ behaviour that affects the student's academic performance

■ behaviour that cannot be explained by health, sensory, or social difficulties

In most cases, in identifying a student as having an emotional or behavioural disorder, the school assessment team will use criteria aimed at establishing these general assumptions. There are a number of difficulties with the development of an appropriate definition for emotional and behavioural disorders. Kauffman and Landrum (2009a) contend that

Figure 6.1 A Parent's
Perspective on EBD:
Patti Childress
(Lynchburg, VA)

From:	pchildress [mailto: patti@inmind.com]
Sent:	Tuesday, June 6, 2000 11:42 PM
TO:	Polloway, Edward 'Ed'
Subject:	Re: Concerns

Dr. Polloway:

    Thanks for trying to help and please keep thinking about resources that can assist me as both a teacher and a parent.

    It bothers me tremendously when I see children with E/BD often getting a "raw deal." People seem to think that it is fine for these children to have a disorder and maybe/maybe not receive special services, but heaven forbid if they can't control themselves or if they do something that appears to be a bit irrational. At times I feel like I am jumping in front of a firing squad to protect that [child whom some seem to see as that] "bad kid that shouldn't be in school anyway." I would like to work with a group that supports parents, provides understanding and advocacy regarding disorders, and seeks support and additional resources for help, etc. What is available in this field? Much is needed.

    I have always had a huge heart for "the kid who is a little bit or a long way out there" even before I became a parent of a child with a mood disorder.

    From an educational perspective, I know that these children can be very difficult in a group; however, they seem to function much better when they feel in control, are able to make choices, and are spoken to in a calm tone.

    From a parent's perspective, I am an educated individual with a traditional home makeup: dad, mom, daughter, and son. . .and I know the difficulties of saying, "Yeah, we've got a very bright child with mood problems." We've been through every medication from ritalin to cylert and clonodone. The next stop would be lithium, weekly counselling, and psychiatric treatment to regulate the medications. I want teachers to understand that getting "meds" is not an easy task or a quick fix. It has taken us over a year of trying various medications until we have, hopefully, found the right combination for now. It requires the constant efforts of counsellor, doctor, parents, and teachers working together and exchanging information.

    Children without support have got to have advocates to help them get help. These children are very fragile and need to be treated as such. My heart goes out to such a child and the family that simply does not understand why their child is not like everybody else's. In the school environment, even when I listen to special education teachers, I do not find the same level of empathy and understanding for children with E/BD as for those with LD.

these difficulties derive from different conceptual models for understanding the nature of emotional and behavioural disorders; different purposes of definitions based on, for example, the setting to which they are being applied (e.g., public schools, the legal system, community agencies); difficulties related to the measurement of behaviour and emotions; the range and variability of normal behaviour and its relationship with deviant behaviour; and the possible transient nature of some emotional and behavioural problems. However, exactly how to apply the definition remains vague: when the definition is interpreted broadly, many more children are served. Provincial education funding protocols may not require identification but expect service to be provided as part of supporting student diversity. For example, in Saskatchewan, funding is provided to school divisions based on their total enrolment. School divisions are expected to use this funding to support students with a variety of diverse learning and behavioural needs, including those with emotional and behavioural disorders. This may help explain the variability in prevalence estimates from province to province.

In Canada's National Longitudinal Survey of Children and Youth (NLSCY), 28.6 percent of Canadian children were determined to be vulnerable to EBD (Willms, 2002, p. 66): "These children are vulnerable in the sense that unless there is a serious effort to intervene on their behalf, they are prone to experiencing problems throughout their childhood and are more likely to experience unemployment and poor physical and mental health as young adults" (p. 3). The NLSCY estimates the prevalence of children in Canada who are vulnerable due to behavioural problems to be 19.1 percent (p. 67). Comparing this information with numbers of students identified as having EBD and served throughout school divisions across Canada suggests that this population of students may be underserved.

Classification of Emotional or Behavioural Disorders

Children who experience emotional or behavioural disorders make up an extremely heterogeneous population. Professionals typically have subcategorized the group into smaller, more homogeneous subgroups so that these students can be better studied, understood, and served. Several different classification systems are used to group individuals with emotional and behavioural disorders.

One classification system focuses on clinical elements found in the field of emotional and behavioural problems. This system is detailed in the *DSM-IV-TR* (American Psychiatric Association, 2000), a manual widely used by medical and psychological professionals in both Canada and the United States, though infrequently used by educators. It categorizes emotional and behavioural problems according to several different clinical subtypes, such as developmental disorders, organic mental disorders, and schizophrenia. Educators need to be aware of the *DSM-IV-TR* classification system because of the importance of working with professionals from the field of mental health.

A second classification system was developed by Quay and Peterson (1987). They described six major subgroups of children with emotional and behavioural disorders:

1. Individuals are classified as having a **conduct disorder** if they seek attention, are disruptive, and act out. This category includes behaving aggressively toward others.

2. Students who exhibit **socialized aggression** are likely to join a "subcultural group," a group of peers who are openly disrespectful to their peers, teachers, and parents. Delinquency, truancy, and other "gang" behaviours are common among this group.

3. Individuals with **attention problems–immaturity** can be characterized as having attention deficits, being easily distractible, and having poor concentration. Many students in this group are impulsive and may act without thinking about the consequences.

4. Students classified in the **anxiety/withdrawal** group are self-conscious, reticent, and unsure of themselves. Their self-concepts are generally very low, causing them to simply "retreat" from immediate activities. They are also anxious and frequently depressed.

CONSIDER THIS

How would you, as a teacher, decide which behaviours are "significantly different" from behaviour normally expected? How would teachers' evaluations differ as a function of experience, tolerance levels, and school climate?

FURTHER READING

For more information on the American Psychiatric Association's classification of students with EBD, review the *Diagnostic and Statistical Manual (DSM-IV-TR)*, published in 2000 by the American Psychological Association.

CONSIDER THIS

Do students without exceptionalities ever exhibit these characteristics? What differentiates typical students from those classified as having EBD?

5. The subgroup of students who display **psychotic behaviour** may hallucinate, deal in a fantasy world, talk in gibberish, and display other bizarre behaviour.

6. Students with **motor excess** are hyperactive. They have difficulties sitting still, listening to another individual, and keeping their attention focused. Often these students are also hypertalkative. (See chapter 5 for more information on hyperactivity.)

It is important for the teacher to know that students can demonstrate behaviour from a number of different dimensions or categories; in other words, the categories are not mutually exclusive. For example, Ryan, a Grade 8 student who is constantly disruptive and threatens both his peers and his teachers (conduct disorder), may suffer from depression (anxiety and withdrawal).

Classification becomes less important when school personnel utilize a functional assessment/intervention model. This approach, which will be described in more detail later, emphasizes finding out which environmental stimuli result in inappropriate behaviours. Once these stimuli are identified and altered, the inappropriate behaviours may decrease or disappear (McConnell, Patton, & Polloway, 2006). In such instances, the process of classifying a student's behaviour problem becomes less relevant to the design of educational programs.

Prevalence and Causes of Emotional and Behavioural Disorders

CONSIDER THIS

What factors will likely lead to larger or smaller numbers of children being identified as having emotional or behavioural disorders?

Compared to children classified as having learning disabilities and intellectual disabilities, the category of EBD has been thought to represent a smaller number of children.

Although prevalence rates vary by province or territory in Canada, most estimates place the frequency of EBD well below that of learning disabilities. However, information provided by the NLSCY suggests that up to 19.1 percent of Canadian children are vulnerable to poor outcomes due to behavioural problems. According to the Organisation for Economic Co-operation and Development (as cited in Willms, 2002, p. 67), 29.2 percent of Canadian youth fail to graduate from secondary school at the typical age. Although not all of this percentage of students failed to graduate at a typical age due to behavioural disorders, certainly this is one example of a "poor outcome" to which Canadian children with behavioural problems are vulnerable. Kauffman and Landrum (2009a) concluded a reasonable estimate of the prevalence of emotional and behavioural disorders would be approximately 3 to 6 percent of the overall student population. Statistics like these suggest that prevalence estimates of emotional and behavioural disorders may be low. The specific number arrived at depends on the definition used and on the interpretation of the definition by individuals who classify students. It also depends on whether these students are identified, served, and "counted," or whether they are just "disciplined." However, the suggestion is that EBD may be a dramatically underserved category of disability with far more students in need of supports than the less than 1 percent currently identified.

The discrepancy between identified and actual rates of children with EBD may also be due to students with EBD being identified as having other exceptionalities, such as a learning disability. Or, if students are showing more anxious or withdrawn behaviours, they may be overlooked altogether.

Many different factors can cause students to display emotional or behavioural disorders. Kauffman and Landrum (2009a) discussed the possible causes and correlates of emotional and behavioural disorders as including factors within the: (1) biological, (2) family, (3) school, and (4) cultural domains. They further stressed that these possible factors were likely to be interactive. It is clear that determining specific causes for emotional behavioural disorders is a complex task with no easy resolution. Biological causes can include the possibility of genetic disorders, brain dysfunction or damage (such as traumatic brain injury), health-related issues, and possibly childhood temperament considerations (e.g., newborns' inborn tendency toward certain behavioural patterns). Family factors that have been explored for possible causative impact include issues related to family definition and structure (e.g., single-parent families, substitute care) and family interaction patterns (e.g., management models used by parents, possible child abuse; Kauffman & Landrum, 2009a).

When considering school-related factors, it is typically difficult to analyze whether school failure is the source of emotional and behavioural problems, or if the reverse is true. School-related factors could include the fact that students identified as having emotional and behavioural disorders generally have an overall lower IQ than students in general (average in the 90s); the common pattern of academic underachievement that frequently corresponds with behaviour problems in school; the failure to acquire appropriate social skills; and the overall impact of school failure on adjustment (Kauffman & Landrum, 2009a). Further, schools may contribute to problems by being insensitive to the individual needs of students, by setting inappropriate expectations, and by using instructional and management strategies that may exacerbate problems (e.g., inconsistent behavioural management).

Cultural influences are another possible cause or correlate of emotional and behavioural disorders. Particular areas of concern include the absence of peers who serve as positive models for children, undesirable socialization patterns with peers, the influence of neighbourhoods such as in urban areas, and the effects of poverty on child development and ultimately on learning and behaviour (Kauffman & Landrum, 2009a).

It is critical to note that many students experience emotional or behavioural disorders because of environmental factors that affect their lives. In Canadian society, potential causative elements may include variables related to family, school, and community. Thus, it is essential that a broad view of the problems experienced by students be considered. Figure 6.2, a model designed in reference to antisocial youth, outlines this interaction of factors.

There is substantial support for the fact that students identified with EBD are far more likely to come from backgrounds that are characterized as being economically disadvantaged. While this finding is not direct evidence of causation, the correlational data in this area suggest that people from lower socio-economic backgrounds are at increased risk for having mental disorders (Wagner et al., 2005). A factor that is often overlooked but is related to both economic disadvantage and school achievement is school instability (Rothstein, 2006). This phenomenon of changing schools is particularly a concern for students with EBD because they experience more school environmental instability than other students. Wagner and colleagues (2005) summarized this issue as follows:

> They change schools more often than students in other disability groups and nondisabled peers, with one-third of the elementary/middle school students and two-thirds of the secondary students attending at least four different schools. Furthermore, an

Depression is a characteristic of students with emotional or behavioural disorders.

Figure 6.2 The
Development of
Antisocial Behaviour

From "Antisocial Behaviour, Academic
Failure, and School Climate: A Critical
Review" (p. 133), by A. McEvoy &
R. Welker, 2000, *Journal of Emotional
and Behavioural Disorders, 8.*

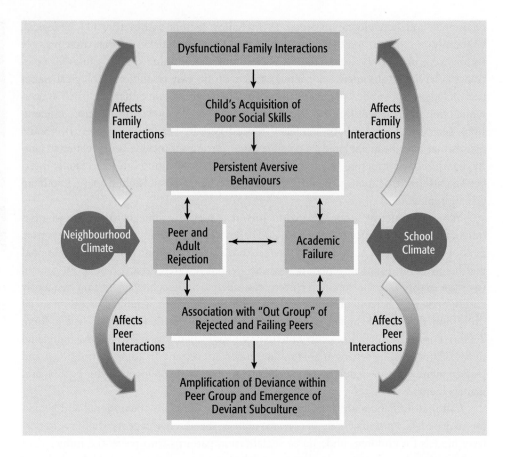

examination of the most recent move indicates that the students with [emotional distur-
bances] are reassigned to new schools by their school district at a rate much higher than
that of both their nondisabled peers and those in other disability groups. In addition,
almost half of the elementary/middle school students and three-fourths of the secondary
students have been suspended or expelled. These rates are more than four times that of
peers in other disability categories and of students in the general population. (p. 92)

Although risk factors cannot be adjudged to be causes in the typical way that causation is conceptualized, a consideration of risks does provide a broad view of the issues that
may exacerbate the functioning of students who are identified as having EBD.

Characteristics of Students with Emotional
or Behavioural Disorders

Students with emotional or behavioural problems exhibit a wide range of characteristics
that differ in type as well as intensity. They typically engage in behaviours that are rated
by teachers and parents as more challenging than those of students with learning disabilities and intellectual disabilities (Sabornie et al., 2005). Students with EBD are frequently
behaviourally disruptive and often noncompliant, aggressive, and verbally abusive (Reid
et al., 2004). The wide range of behaviours and emotions experienced by all individuals

reflects the broad variety of characteristics associated with individuals with emotional or behavioural problems.

According to the current federal definition of emotional disturbance in the United States, there are five key eligibility characteristics: inability to learn, relationship problems, inappropriate behaviour, unhappiness or depression, and physical symptoms or fears. Cullinan and Sabornie (2004) investigated these five characteristics to confirm whether students with EBD in middle and high school settings could be differentiated from their peers across these characteristics. Overall, their data confirmed that on measures for each of the five characteristics, the scores of those adolescents who are identified as having EBD did, in fact, exceed the scores of their typically achieving peers. At the same time, the researchers posed several key questions that relate to both the definition and the research on these characteristics:

■ To what extent is each characteristic related to the likelihood that a student will be referred to a multidisciplinary team for consideration or ultimately identified as [emotionally disturbed]?

■ How do these characteristics change over the course of middle school and high school, and how are such changes affected by different interventions in education environments?

■ What school-based interventions should be available to students who manifest the characteristics differently? (Cullinan & Sabornie, 2004, pp. 165–166)

Problems typically associated with children with emotional or behavioural disorders may include:

■ aggressive/acting-out behaviours
■ social deficits
■ inadequate peer relationships
■ hyperactivity/distractibility
■ lying, cheating, and stealing
■ academic deficits
■ language disorders
■ depression
■ anxiety

CONSIDER THIS

Do students without disabilities ever exhibit these characteristics? What differentiates typical students from those classified as having EBD?

Children classified as having emotional or behavioural disorders do not exhibit all of these characteristics. The ones exhibited by a particular child will depend on the nature of their emotional or behavioural problem.

A common and helpful way to conceptualize emotional and behavioural disorders is to categorize them as externalizing or internalizing behaviours. The list in Table 6.1 provides such an illustration.

One problem associated with emotional or behavioural disorders that is often overlooked is depression. Teachers should be alert to signs of depression in order to assist students in the classroom, where depression may be associated with an inability to concentrate or achieve. More dramatically, depression can be associated with suicide, estimated to be the third leading cause of death for adolescents and young adults.

Table 6.1 Categorizing Emotional and Behavioural Disorders	
Externalizing Behaviours	**Internalizing Behaviours**
■ Aggressive toward people and objects	■ Withdrawn
■ Has temper tantrums	■ Apathetic, restricted activity levels
■ Defiant	■ Fixated on certain thoughts
■ Jealous	■ Avoids social situations
■ Disobedient	■ Fearful, anxious
■ Distrustful, blames others	■ Inferiority
■ Destructive	

From *Childhood Behavioural Disorders: Applied Research and Educational Practices* (2nd ed., p. 69), by R. Algozzine, L. Serna, & J.R. Patton, 2001, Austin, TX: Pro-Ed.

FURTHER READING

For more information on the conflict resolution process for children with high and low depressive symptoms, read Rinaldi and Heath's article, "An Examination of the Conflict Resolution Strategies and Goals of Children with Depressive Symptoms" in volume 11, issue 3 of *Emotional and Behavioural Difficulties*, 2006 (pp. 187–204).

Based on a review of research on the language skills of students with EBD, Nelson, Benner, and Cheney (2005) noted the common co-occurrence of language deficits and problem behaviours. These researchers discovered that children who experience language deficits were 10 times more likely than those in the general school population to also exhibit antisocial behaviours. The relatively limited research in this area suggests that receptive and expressive language problems (particularly in the area of pragmatics) are more likely to place students at risk for inappropriate behaviour than are speech disorders, for instance. Speech-language pathologists should be involved in assessment and intervention planning for students with EBD due to the high comorbidity rate between EBD and language deficits (Benner, Nelson, & Epstein, 2002). While the focus of research on the characteristics of students with EBD is generally on social and behavioural concerns, it should not be overlooked that academic problems are also a key concern (Sabornie et al., 2005; Wagner et al., 2005). Students with EBD have routinely been described as having difficulties in academic achievement. Mihalas et al. (2009) noted that "students with EBD fail more courses in school, are retained more frequently, are more likely to be absent from school, have lower grade point averages, drop out of school more frequently, and are less likely to graduate high school compared to students without EBD" (p. 109). It should be added that these characteristics are more common in students with EBD than in students with other disabilities.

The difficulty that students with EBD experience in reading has been noted in several studies and reviews of the literature (e.g., Nelson, Benner, & Gonzalez, 2005). This difficulty is compounded because, as Nelson et al. (2005) contend, research indicates a likely poor response by the students to otherwise generally effective interventions for pre-reading and reading. Given the common findings of significant problems in reading and lack of responsiveness to some effective practices, Nelson et al. (2005) stressed the vital importance of the use of appropriate interventions for young children as a way to prevent significant subsequent problems.

While the academic performance deficits of students with EBD are often generalized across subject areas, the most common focus has been in reading and literacy. However, Reid et al. (2004) reported in their review of research that math and spelling problems were even more significant than reading problems, although the difference was not statistically significant.

For all academic areas, however, the deficits are substantial enough and wearisome enough that teachers should use research-validated interventions to enhance academic achievement.

Outcomes and Postschool Adjustment A critical concern for students with emotional and behavioural disorders is the determination of postschool outcomes. The number of individuals with EBD in the U.S. who completed high school and received a regular diploma increased gradually over a 10-year period from 33.7 percent in 1994–1995 to 38.4 percent in 2003–2004. Logically, there has been a decrease in the dropout rate from 69.3 percent in 1985–1996 to 52.3 percent in 2003–2004. Nevertheless, EBD remains the disability with the highest dropout rate (USDOE, 2009). Kortering (2009) summarized the special challenges associated with school dropout patterns. While dropouts only comprise approximately 20 percent of the general population, they are estimated to account for over 80 percent of the general prison and juvenile justice population. Student dropouts often fail to access adult and community services and, consequently, educators may represent their last opportunity to develop the necessary skills for successful adult adjustment, including employment.

Newman et al. (2009) reported that only 63.4 percent of individuals with EBD had been employed at some point in time since high school, with just 42.3 percent employed at the time of the research interview. For those working one to four years after high school, positions included skilled labour (10.1 percent), food services (17.2 percent), stocking and shipping (5.4 percent), serving as a cashier (12.9 percent), and clerical (7.5 percent). Newman et al. (2009) noted that students with emotional and behavioural disorders offered the following reasons for why they had left a previous or their most recent job: 46.5 percent had quit, 31.5 percent had a temporary job that ended, 15.5 percent had been fired, and 6.6 percent had been laid off.

One somewhat encouraging finding is that students with EBD have greater success in adult education programs. Scanlon and Melland (2002) hypothesized that the context of adult programs may contribute to this success because such programs may be "less antagonizing and more accepting of any emotional or behavioural problems" (p. 253).

A study reported by McConaughy and Wadsworth (2000) provided some guidance in predicting which individuals would fare better as adults. Based on life histories, they concluded that young adults with good outcomes tended to have more stable and quality living situations, better family relationships, more positive relationships with friends, were more goal-oriented, and experienced more successes and fewer stresses than did young adults with poor outcomes. In addition, more young adults with good outcomes held full-time jobs in the community, and fewer associated with friends who used drugs or who were in trouble with the law or violent (pp. 213–214).

Also, following up (after three years) on a group of American adolescents who participated in a statewide system of care, Pandiani, Schacht, and Banks (2001) reported that these individuals, when compared to other young people, were eight times more likely to be hospitalized for behavioural health care, and the young men in the sample were five times as likely to be incarcerated. For young women, the rate of maternity was generally similar to the general population.

Identification, Assessment, and Programming

TEACHING TIP

When you suspect a student of having an emotional or behavioural disorder, use systematic methods to collect observations of the student's behaviour (e.g., document its frequency, intensity, and duration). This information will be useful when designing interventions and determining student progress or the success of interventions.

Students with emotional or behavioural disorders are evaluated for several purposes, including identification, assessment to determine appropriate intervention strategies, and determination of appropriate special education services. The first step is for students to be identified as potentially having emotional or behavioural problems. Teachers' awareness of the characteristics of students with these problems is critical in the identification process. Behavioural checklists can be used to identify students for possible referral.

Once students are identified as possibly having emotional or behavioural problems, they are referred for formal assessment to ascertain appropriate intervention strategies and to determine their eligibility for special education supports. Kaplan (1996) lists clinical interviews, observations, rating scales, personality tests, and neurological examinations as methods for obtaining information for assessment. Table 6.2 summarizes each of these procedures.

One encouraging approach to the assessment of students with emotional and behavioural disorders is through the use of strength-based assessment. Unlike widely used deficit-oriented assessment models, strength-based assessment focuses on the student and

Table 6.2 Assessment Procedures Used for Students with Emotional and Behavioural Disorders

Clinical Interview

■ The clinical interview is the most common tool for assessment.

■ Questions are directed to the child and others regarding behaviours and any relevant relationships.

■ Some questions are planned; some are developed as the interview progresses.

■ The interview can be highly structured, using questions generated from the *DSM-IV-TR* criteria.

Observation

■ The observation can be structured with time limitations, or unstructured.

■ Observations should occur in a variety of different settings and at different times.

Rating Scales

■ A rating scale contains a listing of behaviours to note.

■ It provides for much more structure than simple observation.

■ It ensures that certain behaviours are observed or asked about.

Personality Tests

■ The two kinds of personality tests include self-completed inventories and projective tests.

■ Both kinds of personality tests can provide insightful information.

■ Interpretation of personality tests is subjective and needs to be done by a trained professional.

From *Pathways for Exceptional Children: School, Home, and Culture*, by P. Kaplan, 1996, St. Paul, MN: West Publishing.

his or her family "as individuals with unique talents, skills, and life events as well as with specific unmet needs. Strength-based assessment recognizes that even the most challenged children in stressed families have strengths, competencies, and resources that can be built on in developing a treatment approach" (Epstein, 1999, p. 258).

Strength-based assessment is based on the following principles:

1. All children have strengths.

2. Assessing a child's strengths in addition to his or her deficits may result in enhanced motivation and improved performance from the child.

3. Deficits should be viewed as opportunities to learn rather than as fixed or stable.

4. Families and children are more likely to positively engage in treatment when service plans include a focus on strengths (Harniss & Epstein, 2005, p. 126).

A current focus in intervention planning is the study of *risk* and *resiliency*. *Risk factors* are those that increase a child's likelihood to experience negative life outcomes. A combination of risk factors present in a child's life increases overall risk. *Resiliency* is the ability to thrive despite risk. *Protective factors* are those that increase the likelihood that a child will be resilient and avoid negative life outcomes. There are a number of things that schools can do to increase resilience in their students with emotional or behavioural disorders. When schools have high expectations of their students and provide the supports necessary for the students to achieve the expectations, resiliency is evident. When schools focus on recognizing and using students' strengths and avoid the use of punitive disciplinary practices, students with emotional or behavioural disorders are able to be more resilient.

Functional Behavioural Assessment

One important approach to assessment warrants separate consideration because of its clear implications for intervention efforts. **Functional behavioural assessment (FBA)** provides a consideration of specific behaviours and behavioural patterns set within an environmental context. It has been defined as "an analysis of the contingencies responsible for behavioural problems" (Malott, Whaley, & Malott, 1997, p. 433).

An FBA is a "systematic procedure . . . [to explain] why a behaviour occurs by analyzing the behaviour and generating hypotheses about its purpose or intended function. Ultimately, these hypotheses should assist school personnel in identifying interventions that change the student's undesirable behaviour" (McConnell et al., 2006, p. viii). A sample FBA is presented in Figure 6.3.

When determining appropriate intervention strategies, functional behavioural assessment provides extensive information for teachers. It helps teachers better understand disruptive behaviours, which can lead to an insightful intervention approach. Foster-Johnson and Dunlap (1993) list the following variables that influence behaviours:

1. Physiological factors
   - sickness or allergies
   - side effects of medication
   - fatigue
   - hunger or thirst
   - increased arousal due to a fight, missing the bus, a disrupted routine

FURTHER READING

To learn more about risk and protective factors, read "Preventing Antisocial Behaviour in Disabled and At-Risk Students" from Appalachia Educational Laboratory, available from LD OnLine at www.ldonline.org/article/5973.

CONSIDER THIS

How can using functional behavioural assessment help teachers focus on specific issues related to inappropriate behaviours?

The Functional Behavioural Assessment (FBA) addresses the relationship among precipitating conditions, the behaviour, its consequences, and the function of the behaviour. The FBA also reflects a consideration of all relevant data gathered, both as background information and by using specific assessment techniques. Refer to the Functional Behavioural Assessment Discussion Guide (found on page 16 of the manual) for assistance in completing this form.

Behaviour # __3__ Physical aggression/fighting

Precipitating Conditions (Setting, time, or other situations typically occurring *before* the behaviour)	**Specific Behaviour** (*Exactly* what the student does or does not do)	**Consequences** (Events that typically *follow* the behaviour)	**Function of the Behaviour** (*Hypothesized purpose[s]* the behaviour serves)
☒ unstructured time in hallways/on the bus	Casey pushes, hits, trips other students, often students who are smaller; Casey's aggression occurs more often when no adults are watching her (on bus; in halls).	☒ teacher attention	☐ escape/avoidance
☐ academic instruction in		☒ peer attention	☐ gaining attention
		☒ verbal warning/reprimand	☒ expression of anger
☐ when given a directive to		☐ loss of privilege (what kind?)	☐ frustration
			☒ vengeance
☒ when close to smaller students		☐ time out (where/how long?)	☒ seeking of power/control
			☒ intimidation
☐ when provoked by			☐ sensory stimulation
		☒ detention (how long?) after school	☐ relief of fear/anxiety
☐ when unable to		☐ removal from class	☐ other
		☒ in-school suspension (how long?) 3 days	
☒ other when unsupervised		☐ other	
☐ none observed			

Specific Assessment Techniques Used to Analyze This Behaviour

☒ Observation   ☐ Student Interview   ☒ Administrative Interview   ☒ Parent Interview
☒ Behaviour Checklist/Rating Scale   ☐ Video/Audio Taping   ☒ Teacher Interview   ☐ Other _____

Relating Information/Considerations

Academic: Low grades—homework not turned in

Family: Casey's behaviour has disrupted family life. Mother reports she is afraid of Casey.

Social/Peer: Few friends

Other:

Figure 6.3 An Example of a Functional Behavioural Assessment (FBA)

2. Classroom environment
   - high noise level
   - uncomfortable temperature
   - over- or under-stimulation
   - poor seating arrangement
   - frequent disruptions

3. Curriculum and instruction
   - few opportunities for making choices
   - lack of predictability in the schedule
   - inadequate level of assistance provided to the student
   - unclear directions provided for activity completion
   - few opportunities for the student to communicate

- activities that are too difficult
- activities that take a long time to complete
- activities that the student dislikes
- activities for which the completion criterion is unclear
- activities that might not be perceived as being relevant or useful by the student

After reviewing these variables with a particular child in mind, teachers can devise interventions that target a specific variable to alter a particular behaviour. While an evaluation of the environmental context is necessary for developing hypotheses regarding the causes of a problem behaviour, the only valid way to reach a conclusion about behavioural influence is to change the environmental setting and/or the events associated with the behaviour, and to observe whether a change in behaviour results.

STRATEGIES FOR CURRICULUM AND INSTRUCTION FOR STUDENTS WITH EMOTIONAL OR BEHAVIOURAL DISORDERS

Watch

Including Students with EBD in General Education

Students with emotional or behavioural disorders often present significant problems for teachers, especially in general education settings. Their behaviour may affect not only their own learning, but often the learning of others. Mihalas et al. (2009) hypothesized that students with EBD experience difficulty for six key reasons: (1) Many are not identified early and/or provided appropriate supports at that point in time; (2) incongruence exists between the needs of these students and instructional practices that are used with them; (3) many teachers are inadequately prepared to meet their needs; (4) services provided for these students may be fragmented and not reflect the collaboration necessary with involvement of professionals from multiple disciplines; (5) the emphasis on standards-based curriculum, high-stakes testing, and school accountability have combined to create a zero-tolerance school climate less conducive to addressing the broad needs of students with EBD; and (6) the behaviours exhibited by these students have often been associated with interventions that resulted in students being removed from school rather than being educated in a proactive fashion within schools. Overall, Mihalas et al. summarized the key concerns as the following:

> a disconnect between what students with EBD need from schools and what they are actually provided. It is evident that the overall school milieu does not support the needs of the students. When one considers the state of outcomes of student with EBD and combines it with the truth that the educational system operates in ways contrary to the students' needs, it's apparent that lack of caring for students with EBD exists. (Mihalas et al., 2009, pp. 109–110)

It is a challenge to appropriately serve students with emotional or behavioural disorders, especially when the realities of how schools respond to these students are considered. The intransigence of behavioural or emotional problems underscores the importance of preventive programs, as does the common delay between identification and services initiation (Wagner et al., 2005). Walker et al. (2005) have developed a comprehensive preventative program, discussed in the Evidence-Based Practice box.

First Step to Success: A Preventive Program for Behaviourally At-Risk Children (K–2)

First Step to Success was designed as an early intervention program to address emerging patterns of antisocial behaviour. The program includes three components:

1. A screening and early detection procedure that provides four different options for use by adopters.

2. A school intervention component that teaches an adaptive behaviour pattern to facilitate successful adjustment to the normal demands of schooling.

3. A parent training component, called HomeBase, that teaches parents how to develop their child's school success skills (e.g., co-operation, accepting limits, sharing, doing one's work).

The program is set up and operated initially in the classroom by a behavioural coach (school psychologist, counsellor, early interventionist, behavioural specialist), who invests approximately 50 to 60 hours of time during the approximately three-month implementation period.

Coaches must be school professionals who can coordinate the roles of these participants and contribute approximately 60 hours during the implementation period. Typically, coaches are trained in the First Step screening, implementation, and parental training procedures during one- and two-day training sessions for staff members. The coach conducts screening activities, identifies candidates who meet eligibility criteria, and secures parental consent for the child's participation as well as teacher co-operation. The coach explains to the child and classmates how the First Step program works and then he operates it during two brief daily sessions for the first five program days. On day six, the coach turns the program over to the general education classroom teacher, who operates it as part of his or her ongoing teaching routine, with supervision, assistance, and support provided by the coach.

After day 10, First Step is operated independently by the regular classroom teacher. The behavioural coach then contacts the target child's parents to enlist their co-operation in learning how to teach the child school success skills at home. Parents meet for approximately an hour-and-a-half weekly with the First Step coach for a six-week period. During each weekly session, parents and caregivers learn to teach one of the following school success skills: communication and sharing, co-operating, setting limits, solving problems, making friends, and developing self-confidence. The general education classroom teacher looks for, recognizes, and praises the child's display of these skills.

From "The Oregon First Step to Success Replication Initiative: Statewide Results of an Evaluation of the Program's Impact," by H. Walker et al., 2005, *Journal of Emotional and Behavioural Disorders, 13,* p. 165.

CONSIDER THIS

What role should mental health professionals play in serving students with EBD? How can educators work more co-operatively and effectively with mental health professionals?

Canadian provinces and territories are committed to the inclusion of children with EBD in the regular classroom. However, since the services for students with EBD across Canada are variable, largely because of the lack of a clear definition, eligibility for services is difficult to determine.

Emotional or Behavioural Disorders and Inclusion

The challenge of inclusion of students with emotional or behavioural disorders has given rise to a number of perspectives on the relative advantages of inclusive versus restrictive settings, which can prove helpful to teachers as they plan inclusive programs. McConnell's (2001) perspectives are presented in Table 6.3.

Most students with emotional or behavioural problems are included in general education classrooms; therefore, classroom teachers and special education teachers need to collaborate in developing and implementing intervention programs. Without this collaboration, appropriate interventions will be much less effective. Consistency in approach and in specific strategies among all teachers who work with the student is critical. If

Table 6.3 Advantages and Disadvantages of More Restrictive and Less Restrictive Placements for Students with Serious Emotional Disturbance

Placements	Advantages	Disadvantages
Less Restrictive Regular classrooms (with and without support) Resource rooms	Prevents the regular educator from giving up on the student and turning to "experts" Permits students to model appropriate behaviour of their peers; increased interaction Possibly less expensive May be able to serve more students Students do not experience problems with reintegration Students follow general curriculum more easily	Expense and time required to train general educators to work with students and special educators to work collaboratively with general educators Problems with classroom management and discipline Lack of consistent expectations for the students Time and materials required for individualization Fear and frustration of general education
More Restrictive Separate classes Separate campuses Residential facilities Hospitals	Flexibility to provide different curricula and different goals Progress can be more closely monitored Accountability of program is more clearly defined Intervention can be more consistent Student follows only one set of guidelines and expectations One team for consistent discipline	Student's opportunities for peer interactions are limited, especially when student is not at neighbourhood school with peers from neighbourhood Travel time for students can be excessive No possible modelling of appropriate peers; no opportunities for socialization with nondisabled peers Difficulties with reintegration into regular school or class

From "Placements" (p. 324), by K. McConnell, 2001, in R. Algozzine, L. Serna, & J.R. Patton (Eds.), *Childhood Behaviour Disorders: Applied Research and Educational Practices* (2nd ed.), Austin, TX: Pro-Ed.

students receive feedback from the special education teacher that significantly differs from the feedback received from the classroom teacher, confusion often results, and success is compromised.

Successful inclusive practices for students with EBD are contingent on strong teacher–student relationships. These relationships lead to a sense of caring that in turn results in the students being more connected to the classroom and to school, more likely to persist toward graduation, and more likely to be successful within school and after school. Mihalas et al. (2009) identified a series of specific strategies that can result in stronger, caring teacher–student relationships. These include teachers assuming the role of advocate for individual students, getting to know the students and understand the lives they live, inviting them to be partners in their educational experience, actively listening to what students are communicating, asking them on a regular basis for feedback on their experiences in the classroom and in school, having students write in journals about their experiences and their reflections on those experiences, finding time to meet with individual students on a consistent basis for discussions on how to solve problems, celebrating with students when they are successful (in order to counteract the fact that the students most often experience failure), and collaborating with other teachers and with professionals representing other disciplines (such as those involved in wraparound services) to ensure that the curricular, extra-curricular, and community experiences enhance the lives and learning opportunities of these students.

As more students with exceptionalities are included in general education classrooms, including students with emotional or behavioural disorders, the ability of students and teachers to effectively deal with behavioural problems is critical for success.

Effective Instruction

 Explore

Striving for Balance

Don't Ruin Good Books for the Students Who Deserve Them!

Teaching students with emotional or behavioural disorders is clearly challenging. Landrum et al. (2006) concluded from their review of research on the teacher acceptability of intervention strategies that the strategies that would be most acceptable to classroom teachers and consequently most likely be implemented as designed would include those that are "easy to implement, not time-intensive, positive, perceived to be effective by the teacher, and compatible with the context in which the intervention will be employed (e.g., resources available, teacher experiences, treatment philosophy, instructional environment)." As the researchers further noted, however, "many interventions that have proven effective for addressing the behavioural and academic needs of students with EBD do not meet these criteria . . . and therefore are not likely to be implemented with integrity, if implemented at all" (p. 20). As a consequence, it is important that general education and special education teachers work together to design effective instructional strategies. Research offers promising directions for effective instructional practices, which should include the following:

- providing appropriate structure and predictable routines
- establishing a structured and consistent classroom environment
- establishing a consistent schedule with set rules and consequences and clear expectations
- fostering positive teacher–student interaction with adequate praise and systematic responses to problem behaviours
- frequently implementing instructional sequences that promote high rates of academic engagement
- creating a classroom environment in which independent seat work is limited, and sufficient time is allotted for establishing positive social interaction (Wehby, Symons, Canale, & Go, 1998, p. 52)

An important emphasis in effective instruction for students with EBD is to use functional assessment procedures as a basis for making effective classroom adaptations. For example, Kerr, Delaney, Clarke, Dunlap, and Childs (2001) demonstrated that adaptations based on assessment data, which identified activities associated with problem behaviour and also activities not associated with such behaviour, resulted in increased task employment, decreases in challenging behaviour, and increased academic productivity— all without significant difficulties in implementation by the teacher. Further, Reid and Nelson (2002) reported that FBA provides a promising approach with research validation for planning positive behavioural interventions, which can have a significant effect on improving student behaviour. They contend that there remains a need for closer attention to the practicality of such interventions within the school setting to confirm that these methods will be acceptable to teachers.

Social Skills Instruction

In addition to the importance of implementing validated academic curricular strategies for all students, a particular area of concern for students with EBD is social skills instruction. Social skills are typically learned from observing others who display appropriate skills; however, when this does not happen, a more formal instructional effort must be made. When using a formal instructional process to teach social skills, the first step is to determine the student's level of social competence.

Assessing social skills requires eliciting informed judgments from persons who interact regularly with the student. Many different checklists are available to assist in assessing social competence. Self-monitoring charts and sociometric measures can also be used.

Following the assessment process, an instructional approach to teaching social skills must be developed. Numerous methods may be used to teach social skills and promote good social relations, including modelling, direct instruction, prompting, and positive practice. Teachers must determine the method that will work best with a particular student.

Quinn, Kavale, Mathur, Rutherford, and Forness (1999) reported a comprehensive research analysis of the use of social skills training with students with EBD. In general, they caution that only about half of students with EBD have been demonstrated to benefit from social skills training, particularly when the focus was on the broader dimensions of the social domain. Greater success was obtained when the focus was on specific social skills (e.g., social problem solving, social interaction, and co-operation; Kauffman & Landrum, 2009b). Forness (1999) and Kavale (2001) hypothesized that the reason more substantive positive effects have not been obtained from social skills training may be that the training programs used in the research studies were too limited in duration and intensity.

CLASSROOM ADAPTATIONS FOR EMOTIONAL AND BEHAVIOURAL DISORDERS

Effective classroom management is critical for teachers of students with emotional and behavioural disorders because of the interference of their behaviour with their own learning and their impact on the learning of other students.

Standard Operating Procedures

Classroom rules and procedures are a critical management tool for students with EBD. Rules should be developed with the input of students and should be posted in the room. Remember that "the process of determining rules is as important as the rules themselves" (Zabel & Zabel, 1996, p. 169). Some examples of classroom rules include:

- Be polite and helpful.
- Keep your space and materials in order.
- Take care of classroom and school property.
- Raise your hand before speaking.

TEACHING TIP

Whenever possible, teach appropriate social skills in the context in which they will be used. If they must be taught in a different context, plan for their transfer to more typical settings.

CROSS REFERENCE

Refer to chapter 3 for more information on social skill deficits and strategies for addressing social skills in classroom environments.

TEACHING TIP

In order to address behavioural issues in all aspects of a child's life, a collaborative effort between school and home is particularly important in educational programs for students with EBD.

CONSIDER THIS

How can classroom rules and procedures result in improved behaviour for children with emotional and behavioural disorders? Are they also effective with nondisabled students?

- Leave your seat only with permission.
- Only one person in the washroom at a time. (Walker & Shea, 1995, p. 252)

Teachers should establish classroom procedures to ensure an orderly environment. These include procedures for the beginning of a period or the school day, use of classroom equipment, social interaction, the completion of work and group and individual activities, and the conclusion of instructional periods and the school day.

Physical Accommodations

The accessibility of the classroom warrants special attention. The concept of **accessibility** extends beyond physical accessibility, touching on overall program accessibility for students with special needs. This means that students with exceptionalities must be able to utilize the classroom as other students do and that the room must be free of potential hazards. For students with EBD, accessibility is an issue when social isolation or time out is used for substantial periods of time. This type of treatment limits the student's access to the classroom and is therefore problematic.

The physical arrangement of the classroom has an impact on the behaviours of students with emotional and behavioural disorders. Attention to the classroom arrangement can both facilitate learning and minimize disruptions (Zabel & Zabel, 1996). The following considerations can help maintain an orderly classroom:

- arranging traffic patterns to lessen contact and disruptions
- arranging student desks to facilitate monitoring of all students at all times
- physically locating students with tendencies toward disruptive behaviours near the teacher's primary location
- locating students away from stored materials that they may find tempting
- creating spaces where students can do quiet work, such as a quiet reading area

Preventive Discipline

Explore

Encouraging Appropriate
Behaviour

Probably the most effective means of working with students who display emotional and behavioural problems is preventive in nature. If inappropriate behaviours can be prevented, then disruptions will be minimal, and the student can attend to the learning task at hand. Rather than waiting to respond to inappropriate behaviours, preventive measures remove the need for inappropriate behaviours.

Sabatino (1987) describes 10 components of a preventive discipline program:

1. Inform pupils of what is expected of them.
2. Establish a positive learning climate.
3. Provide a meaningful learning experience.
4. Avoid threats.
5. Demonstrate fairness.
6. Build and exhibit self-confidence.
7. Recognize positive student attributes.

8. Recognize student attributes at optimal times.

9. Use positive modelling.

10. Structure the curriculum and classroom environment.

Teacher behaviour can greatly facilitate preventive discipline. Teachers have to be consistent in discipline; they must not treat one student's inappropriate behaviours differently than they treat other students' misbehaviour. Teachers must also apply consequences systematically. Disciplining a student for an inappropriate behaviour one time and ignoring the same behaviour another time will only cause the student to be confused over expectations. This discussion on preventive discipline is consistent with the trend toward positive behavioural supports discussed in the next section.

General Behaviour Support Strategies

The development of **positive behaviour supports (PBS)** has been a significant achievement in the education of students with special needs and has particular relevance for students with EBD. Carr et al. (2002) describe PBS in this way:

> *Positive behaviour includes all those skills that increase the likelihood of success and personal satisfaction in . . . academic, work, social, recreational, community, and family settings. Support encompasses all those educational methods that can be used to teach, strengthen, and expand positive behaviour and . . . increase opportunities for the display of positive behaviour. The primary goal of PBS is to help an individual change his or her lifestyle in a direction that gives . . . teachers, employers, parents, friends, and the target person him- or herself the opportunity to perceive and to enjoy an improved quality of life. An important but secondary goal of PBS is to render problem behaviour irrelevant, inefficient, and ineffective by helping an individual achieve his or her goals in a socially acceptable manner. (pp. 4–5)*

Functional behavioural assessment is an important basis for the development of positive behavioural supports. PBS interventions provide an alternative to an emphasis on punitive disciplinary strategies and provide guidance to students with behavioural problems to make appropriate changes in their behavioural patterns. PBS emphasizes proactive, preventive strategies and early intervention with students deemed to be at risk. Further, programs that are organized on a school-wide basis have an increased likelihood of success (Nelson et al., 2005).

The behaviours of teachers can have great impact on effective behaviour management.

As described by Lewis and Sugai (1999), an effective positive behavioural support program for a school should include the following components:

■ specialized individual behaviour support for students with chronic behavioural problems

■ specialized group behaviour support for students with at-risk problem behaviour

■ universal group behaviour support for most students (p. 4)

The system developed by Lewis and Sugai emphasizes school-wide programs that put in place a preventive, proactive system and provide a foundation for the appropriate design of programs for individuals experiencing significant behavioural problems.

✳️ Explore

Behaviour Chart (K-2)

Numerous positive behavioural support strategies have been developed for use with students experiencing emotional or behavioural problems. Particular behavioural strategies that have merit for use with students with EBD include the good behaviour game, contingency contracting, and individual behaviour management plans. Along with additional strategies for classroom management, they will be discussed in detail in chapter 12.

Cognitive approaches are of particular importance to students with EBD. For these students, a particular focus should be on the development of behavioural self-control, whereby students are taught to use self-management strategies throughout the day.

Another technique, peer mediation, has also been used effectively with students with emotional and behavioural disorders. As Gable, Arllen, and Hendrickson (1994) noted, while most behavioural programs rely on adults to monitor and provide reinforcement for desirable behaviours, this technique instead relies on peers. After reviewing peer interaction studies, they concluded that peer behaviour modifiers could be effective among students with emotional and behavioural problems: "The generally positive results surfacing from the modest number of investigations in which EBD students have served as behaviour modifiers underscore the relevance of this procedure for those facing the daunting task of better serving students with emotional/behavioural disorders" (p. 275).

Table 6.4 provides some sample hypothesis statements and possible interventions related to functional behavioural assessment–based interventions. Such an approach does not lock teachers into specific strategies, thus allowing them to tailor interventions to specific behaviours and causes (Kauffman et al., 1995).

Table 6.4 Sample Hypothesis Statements and Possible Interventions

	Intervention	
Hypothesis Statements	**Modify Antecedents**	**Teach Alternative Behaviour**
Suzy pinches herself and others around 11:00 A.M. every day because she gets hungry.	Make sure Suzy gets breakfast. Provide a snack at about 9:30 A.M.	Teach Suzy to ask for something to eat.
Jack gets into arguments with the teacher every day during reading class when she asks him to correct his mistakes on the daily reading worksheet.	Get Jack to correct his own paper. Give Jack an easier assignment.	Teach Jack strategies to manage his frustration in a more appropriate manner. Teach Jack to ask for teacher assistance with the incorrect problems.
Tara starts pouting and refuses to work when she has to sort a box of washers because she doesn't want to do the activity.	Give Tara half of the box of washers to sort. Give Tara clear directions about how much she has to do or how long she must work.	

Table 6.4 Continued

| Hypothesis Statements | Intervention | |
	Modify Antecedents	**Teach Alternative Behaviour**
Frank kicks other children in morning circle time and usually gets to sit right by the teacher.	Give each child a clearly designated section of the floor that is his or hers.	Teach Frank how to ask the children to move over. Teach Frank how to ask the teacher to intervene with his classmates.
Harry is off task for most of math class when he is supposed to be adding two-digit numbers.	Ask Harry to add the prices of actual food items. Intersperse an easy activity with the more difficult math addition so Harry can experience some success.	Teach Harry how to ask for help. Teach Harry how to monitor his rate of problem completion, and provide reinforcement for a certain number of problems.

From "Using Functional Assessment to Develop Effective, Individualized Interventions for Challenging Behaviours" (p. 49), by L. Foster-Johnson and G. Dunlap, 1993, *Teaching Exceptional Children, 25*. Used with permission.

Behaviour Management

An important component of classroom management involves the management of specific behaviours that disrupt the learning environment. Yet the ability to control inappropriate behaviours represents only a part of a comprehensive behaviour management program. Such a plan should also include techniques for creating new behaviours or increasing desirable behaviours that are minimally existent. Moreover, a sound program must ensure that behaviours learned or changed will be maintained over time and demonstrated in different contexts, and must also teach self-control mechanisms. The Inclusion Strategies feature on page 174 describes the components of a behaviour management plan.

 Watch

Behaviour Disorders

Multicultural Considerations

Educators must always remember the multicultural issues related to classroom management. Different cultural groups expect different behaviours from their children. Methods used for disciplining children vary significantly from group to group. School expectations regarding discipline and management principles also vary from culture to culture.

As schools become increasingly more diverse, teachers and other school personnel must take the time to learn about the different cultures represented in the school district. Having a better understanding of parents' expectations of the school as well as of their children can facilitate communication between parents and school personnel and lead to more effective behaviour management programs.

Medication

Many students with emotional or behavioural problems experience difficulties in maintaining attention and controlling behaviour. Many different kinds of medication have been found to be effective with students' behavioural problems, including stimulants, tranquilizers, anticonvulsants, antidepressants, and mood-altering drugs.

The use of medication to help manage students with emotional and behavioural problems is controversial and has been investigated extensively. Findings include the following:

1. Medication can result in students' increased attention.
2. Medication can result in reduced aggressive behaviours.
3. Various side effects can result from medical interventions.
4. The use of medication for children experiencing emotional and behavioural problems should be carefully monitored. (Smith et al., 1993, p. 214)

Numerous side effects may accompany medications taken by children for emotional and behavioural problems. Ritalin is commonly prescribed to help students with attention and hyperactivity problems. Several potential side effects of Ritalin include nervousness, insomnia, anorexia, dizziness, blood pressure and pulse changes, abdominal pain, and weight loss. Teachers can monitor side effects by keeping a daily log of student behaviours that could be attributed to the medication.

CONSIDER THIS

Can general classroom teachers effectively deal with students who have emotional or behavioural disorders in their classrooms? What factors will enhance the likelihood of success?

ENHANCING INCLUSIVE CLASSROOMS FOR STUDENTS WITH EMOTIONAL OR BEHAVIOURAL DISORDERS

Classroom teachers usually make the initial referral for students with emotional or behavioural problems. Unless the problem exhibited by the student is severe, it may have gone unrecognized until the school years. In addition to referring students, classroom teachers must be directly involved in implementing the student's individualized education program (IEP), because the majority of students in this category receive at least a portion of their educational program in general education classrooms. General education classroom teachers must deal with behavioural problems much of the time because there are a large number of students who occasionally display inappropriate behaviours, although they have not been identified as having emotional or behavioural disorders.

Supports for General Education Teachers

Since most students with emotional or behavioural disorders are educated in general classrooms, classroom teachers are the key to these students' success. Too often, if these students do not achieve success, the entire classroom will be disrupted. Therefore, appropriate supports must be available to teachers, including special education personnel, psychologists and counsellors, and mental health service providers.

The level of collaboration among professionals who provide services to this group of students is critical. The involvement of mental health professionals and, in some cases, personnel from the juvenile justice system, the child welfare system, and social work agencies will be of benefit to students with EBD and to their families, as well as to school personnel. Without a close working relationship among the many groups who serve children and adolescents with EBD, services will be fragmented and disorganized.

Special educators should be available to collaborate with teachers regarding the development of behavioural as well as instructional supports. A particularly helpful way to assist classroom teachers involves modelling methods of dealing with behavioural problems. Dr. Ingrid Sladeczek of McGill University continues to study various methods of joint consultation between school psychologists and parents and teachers to manage behavioural disorders in the regular classroom. She is the first in Canada to study empirically the effectiveness of conjoint behavioural consultation (e.g., Sladeczek, Madden, Illsley, Finn, & August, 2006).

At times, it is best for students with emotional or behavioural problems to leave the general education setting and receive instruction from special educators. School psychologists and counsellors are critical in providing a comprehensive program for students with EBD. They can provide intensive counselling; they may also consult with teachers about implementing specific programs such as a student's individual behaviour management plan.

Finally, mental health personnel can provide helpful supports for teachers. Too often, mental health services are not available to schools; however, some schools are beginning to develop school-based mental health programs that serve students with emotional or behavioural disorders. These programs, jointly staffed by school personnel and mental health staff, provide supports for teachers as well as direct interventions for students. If mental health services are not available in a particular school, teachers should work with school administrators to involve mental health specialists with students who display emotional or behavioural problems.

SUMMARY

- Most children and youths are disruptive from time to time, but most do not require interventions. Some students' emotional or behavioural problems are severe enough to warrant interventions.

- Many problems complicate serving students with emotional and behavioural disorders, including inconsistent definitions of the disorder, the large number of agencies involved in defining and treating it, and limited ways to objectively measure the extent and precise parameters of the problem.

- Definitions for emotional disturbance and behavioural disorders are typically subject to alternative explanations.

- There is limited consistency in classifying persons with emotional and behavioural problems.

- Determining the eligibility of students with EBD is difficult because of problems with identification and assessment.

- Students with emotional and behavioural problems are significantly underserved in schools.

- Students with EBD are commonly included in general education classes. General education teachers and special education teachers must collaborate so that there is consistency in the development and implementation of intervention methods.

- A variety of curricular, classroom, and behavioural management strategies are available to enhance the educational programs for students with EBD.

- Social skills development is important for students with EBD.

- Interventions based on functional behavioural assessment, preventive discipline, and positive behavioural supports are important methods for reducing the impact of problems or for keeping problems from occurring.

- General education teachers must realize that the skills, attitudes, and beliefs needed to work effectively with students with EBD may vary from those that are effective for nondisabled students.

- Positive reinforcement and peer tutoring are possible tactics for preventing students with EBD from feeling isolated in the general education classroom.

- Special education teachers and mental health personnel need to be available to provide guidance for general education teachers who are implementing a student's behaviour management plan.

Weblinks

Council for Children with Behavioral Disorders (CCBD)
www.ccbd.net
The Council for Children with Behavioral Disorders (CCBD) is a division of the Council for Exceptional Children. This site has a number of recent relevant publications, suggested resources, and a list of upcoming relevant events and conferences.

B.C. Ministry of Education
www.bced.gov.bc.ca/specialed/landbdif/toc.htm
The BC Ministry of Education's resource guide on learning and behavioural difficulties appears online. In addition to providing specific classroom strategies, this website lists related resources.

Depression and Bipolar Support Alliance (DBSA)
www.dbsalliance.org
The association's website provides information about adolescent depression, including a screening list of symptoms specifically for adolescents, a list of symptoms for the use of others in the student's life, and a suicide prevention plan.

Chapter 7
Teaching Students with Intellectual Disabilities

Chapter Objectives

After reading this chapter, you should be able to

- discuss the concept of intellectual disability

- summarize key definitional and classification considerations

- identify the instructional implications of common characteristics of students with intellectual disabilities

- highlight the transitional needs of students with intellectual disabilities

Questions to Consider

1. How can Scott's curriculum include peers who are typically achieving and use the functional curriculum designed by special educators?

2. How can the curriculum balance short-term objectives with preparation for competitive employment and independent living?

3. What strategies can enhance a positive influence from peers?

4. What available community resources will aid his transition to independent living?

- apply considerations of the needs of students with intellectual disabilities to curriculum design

- present ways of enhancing the inclusion of students with intellectual disabilities

Scott is currently a Grade 11 student at Centennial High School. He has been receiving special education supports throughout his school career. Prior to Kindergarten, he was identified as "at risk" in part because of language delays and in part because of the difficult home situation in which he was raised. (His grandmother has been his guardian since his mother was incarcerated when Scott was four years old; his father has not been part of his life since he was an infant.) When Scott began elementary school, he was identified as developmentally delayed. However, when assessments were completed on Scott at age eight, he was formally identified as intellectually disabled.

Scott has progressed well in part because of his continued involvement in general education classrooms through elementary school and into high school. With in-class support and periodic remedial instruction, he has developed his reading skills to a Grade 4 level with comparable achievement in mathematics and other academic areas. Currently, the focus of his program is on building his academic skills in the inclusive environment and complementing these with a functional curriculum to prepare him for success in the community.

Scott has become an active participant in the development of his individualized education program and, more recently, his individual transition plan. His short-term objective is to obtain his driver's license, for which he is currently eligible based on chronological age. He is enrolled in both an instructional program to complete the written portion of the test and the behind-the-wheel component. A longer-term focus of his program is to prepare him for competitive employment in the community. Through a series of community-based instructional programs, he has become aware of the options that are available to him, and an apprenticeship program in maintenance at the local Wal-Mart will be available next year. Scott's success is a combination of his motivation to succeed, detailed planning by key individuals in his life, and ongoing support provided by teachers, his grandmother, his football coach, and several significant peers who are more academically able.

INTRODUCTION

The Canadian Association for Community Living (CACL) is an association that works to promote the full participation of people with intellectual disabilities in all aspects of community life. The association's membership includes individuals with intellectual disabilities as well as advocates for those individuals.

The CACL defines an intellectual disability as an impaired ability to learn that sometimes causes difficulty in coping with the demands of daily life; the CACL notes that the disability is usually present from birth and differs from mental or psychiatric illness. An intellectual disability is sometimes referred to as "mental retardation," although the CACL (n.d.) states, "We have been informed by people who have an intellectual disability that they resent being labeled by this term. For this reason, we always refer to people for who they are, rather than by what they are (i.e., the 'disabled'). Preferred terms are:

people who have an intellectual disability, people who have a mental handicap, and people who have a developmental disability."

For the purposes of our discussion, we will respect the CACL position and use the term *intellectual disability*. Bear in mind that the actual terminology is less important than respecting the preferences of students and parents.

In the field of intellectual disabilities, the past decade or so has seen momentous changes. Shifts in public attitudes toward persons with intellectual disabilities and the resulting development and provision of services and supports for them have been truly phenomenal. Consequently, the first decade of the new millennium is an exciting time to be participating in the changing perspectives on intellectual disabilities.

BASIC CONCEPTS ABOUT INTELLECTUAL DISABILITIES

The concept of intellectual disability is a broad one that includes a wide range of functioning levels, from mild exceptionalities to more severe limitations. This chapter will address the global concept of intellectual disability first, followed by a discussion of the educational implications of intellectual disabilities.

Intellectual Disabilities Defined

It has been difficult for professionals to formulate definitions of intellectual disabilities that could then be used to govern practices such as assessment and placement. Intellectual disability has been most often characterized by two dimensions: limited intellectual ability and difficulty in coping with the social demands of the environment. Thus, all individuals with intellectual disabilities must, by definition, demonstrate some degree of impaired mental abilities, most often reflected in an intelligence quotient (IQ) significantly below average, which relates to a **mental age (MA)** appreciably lower than the individual's chronological age (CA). In addition, these individuals would necessarily demonstrate less mature adaptive skills, such as social behaviour or functional academic skills, when compared to their same-age peers. For individuals with mild exceptionalities, this discrepancy can be relatively subtle and may not be readily apparent in a casual interaction outside school. These individuals may be challenged most dramatically by the school setting, and thus between the ages of 6 and 21 their inability to cope may be most evident—for example, in problems with peer relationships, difficulty in compliance with adult-initiated directions, or academic challenges.

The American Association on Intellectual and Developmental Disabilities (AAIDD) has for decades developed and revised successive definitions of mental retardation, and now intellectual disability. The organization's efforts are broadly recognized and its definitions have often been incorporated, with modifications, into state and federal statutes. Although use of their definitions in educational regulations and practice has been uneven (see Denning et al., 2000; Frankenberger & Harper, 1988; Polloway et al., 2009; Polloway, Lubin et al., 2010), the AAIDD's definitions are generally considered as the basis for diagnosis in the field. Although discussed as a comprehensive exceptionality, intellectual disability has been typically defined, and diagnosed, as reflecting limitations in three dimensions: intellectual functioning, adaptive behaviour or skills, and the developmental period. The concept of intellectual functioning is intended as a

Watch

Down Syndrome

CONSIDER THIS

What are some dangers of relating the concept of intellectual disability to a numerical index, such as IQ?

Table 7.1 Examples of Conceptual, Social, and Practical Adaptive Skills

Conceptual	Social	Practical
■ Language (receptive and expressive)	■ Interpersonal	■ Activities of daily living
■ Reading and writing	■ Responsibility	■ Eating
■ Money concepts	■ Self-esteem	■ Transfer/mobility
■ Self-direction	■ Gullibility (likelihood of being tricked or manipulated)	■ Toileting
	■ Naïveté	■ Dressing
	■ Follows rules	■ Instrumental activities of daily living
	■ Obeys laws	■ Meal preparation
	■ Avoids victimization	■ Housekeeping
		■ Transportation
		■ Taking medication
		■ Money management
		■ Telephone use
		■ Occupational skills
		■ Maintains safe environments

From *Mental Retardation: Definition, Classification, and Systems of Supports* (p. 42), by R. Luckasson et al., 2002, Washington, DC: American Association on Mental Retardation.

broad summation of cognitive abilities, such as the capacity to learn, solve problems, accumulate knowledge, adapt to new situations, and think abstractly. Operationally, however, it has often been reduced to performance on a test of intelligence, typically with a flexible upper IQ range of 70 to 75. This approximate IQ range is a relatively common component of state identification practices if an IQ cut-off score is required at all (Polloway, Lubin et al., 2010). However, low IQ scores alone are not sufficient for diagnosis, so the adaptive dimension must be considered.

An individual's adaptive behaviour represents the degree to which the individual meets "the standards of maturation, learning, personal independence, and/or social responsibility that are expected for his or her age level and cultural group" (Grossman, 1983, p. 11). Particularly important are the skills necessary to function independently in a range of situations and to maintain responsible social relationships. In contemporary practice, this dimension of the definition requires that an individual show significant deficits in overall adaptive behaviour or in conceptual, social, or practical adaptive skills (see Table 7.1).

The third definitional component is the developmental period. It has most often been defined as the period between conception and 18 years of age. Below-average intellectual functioning and disabilities in adaptive behaviour must appear during this period for an individual to be considered to have an intellectual disability.

Schalock et al. (2010) defines intellectual disability as follows:

Intellectual disability is characterized by significant limitations both in intellectual functioning and in adaptive behaviour as expressed in conceptual, social, and practical adaptive skills. This disability originates before age 18. The following five assumptions are essential to the application of the definition:

1. *Limitations in present functioning must be considered within the context of community environments typical of the individual's age peers and culture.*
2. *Valid assessment considers cultural and linguistic diversity as well as differences in communication, sensory, motor, and behavioural factors.*
3. *Within an individual, limitations often coexist with strengths.*
4. *An important purpose of describing limitations is to develop a profile of needed supports.*
5. *With appropriate personalized supports over a sustained period, the life functioning of the person generally will improve. (p. 1)*

Classification of Intellectual Disabilities

Historically, classification in this field has been done by both etiology (i.e., causes) and level of severity. Whereas the former has limited application to nonmedical practice, the latter has been used by a range of disciplines, including education and psychology. The classification system cited most often in the professional literature is one reported by Grossman (1983). This system uses the terms **mild**, **moderate**, **severe**, and **profound**, which are summative judgments based on intelligence and adaptive behaviour assessment. Often, however, the emphasis has been on the former only, so IQ scores have, unfortunately, been equated with level of functioning.

Terms such as **educable** and **trainable** reflect an alternative system that has been used in some school environments. These archaic terms remain in use today in some places, and some students with intellectual disability are referred to as EMR (educable mentally retarded) and TMR (trainable mentally retarded). However, they are inherently stereotypical and prejudicial terms; consequently (and appropriately) they have often been criticized and should no longer be used.

One alternative has been to classify intellectual disabilities according to only two levels of functioning (i.e., mild and severe) and to avoid reliance on IQ scores in considerations of level of severity. Consideration of level of adaptive skills would thus be used as a yardstick for determining level of intellectual disability, resulting in a more meaningful, broad-based system of classification.

Finally, another alternative is the revised AAIDD classification system of Luckasson et al. (2002), which has particular merit for use in inclusive settings. According to this system, classification is not derived from levels of deficit, but rather from needed levels of support. Thus, this system would classify the needs, rather than the deficits, of the individual. Individuals would be designated as needing intermittent, limited, extensive, or pervasive levels of support as related to each of the adaptive skills areas. Of course, in a given area, an individual may not need any support to function successfully. These levels of support are defined as follows:

Intermittent: Supports on an "as needed," episodic (person not always needing the support), or short-term nature (support needed during lifespan transitions—e.g., job loss or an acute medical crisis). Intermittent support may be high or low intensity when provided.

Terms such as *educable* and *trainable* have often been used to categorize students with intellectual disabilities, but are no longer acceptable.

CONSIDER THIS

What are some advantages to using a classification system based on levels of support rather than on levels of severity?

CROSS REFERENCE

Review the causes of other exceptionalities (see chapters 3–11) to determine the overlap of etiological factors.

CONSIDER THIS

Why do you think the prevalence of students identified as having an intellectual disability has declined so much over the past 20 years?

Limited: Supports are consistent over time, are time-limited but not intermittent, and may require fewer staff and less cost than more intense levels of support (e.g., employment training or transitional supports during the school-to-adult period).

Extensive: Supports characterized by regular involvement (e.g., daily) in at least some environments (e.g., school, work, or home) and not time-limited in nature (e.g., long-term support and long-term home living support).

Pervasive: Supports characterized by their constancy and high intensity; provided across environments, potentially life-sustaining in nature. Pervasive supports typically involve more staff and intrusiveness than extensive or limited supports. (Adapted from Luckasson et al., 2002, p. 152)

Prevalence, Causes, and Characteristics of Intellectual Disabilities

There are hundreds of known causes of intellectual disabilities, though numerous cases exist for which the cause is unknown. Table 7.2 outlines some causes to show the complexity of this area of concern. When all of these different causes are considered, it is estimated that about 1 million Canadians, or 3 percent of the population, have an intellectual disability (CACL, n.d.). In the United States, the 29th Annual Report to Congress (USDOE, 2009) provided a 10-year perspective on prevalence and confirmed limited annual variance in intellectual disabilities during this decade. Consistently the trend has been that slightly less than 1 percent (approximately 0.9 percent for 1995–2003; 0.84 percent in 2004) of school-age children in the U.S. are likely to be identified as having an intellectual disability.

Table 7.2 Selected Causes of Intellectual Disabilities

Cause	Nature of Problem	Considerations
Down syndrome	Trisomy 21 (3 chromosomes on this pair)	Wide variance in learning characteristics
	IQ range from severe intellectual impairment to nonimpaired	Classic physical signs
		Most common chromosomal anomaly
Environmental disadvantage	Elements of poverty environment (e.g., family constellation, resources, educational role models)	Can be related to mild disability
		Commonly associated with school failure
Fetal alcohol syndrome	Caused by drinking during pregnancy	Associated with varying degrees of disability
	Related to toxic effects of alcohol	May be accompanied by facial and other malformations and behavioural disturbances
		Among the three most common biologically based causes of intellectual impairment
Fragile X syndrome	Genetic disorder related to the gene or X chromosome	Most often transmitted from mother to son
		Frequently associated with intellectual impairment in males and learning disabilities in females (in some instances)
		May be accompanied by variant patterns of behaviour (e.g., self-stimulation), social skills difficulties, language impairment
Hydrocephalus	Multiple causes (e.g., genetic, environmental)	Previously associated with enlarged head and brain damage
	Disruption in appropriate flow of cerebrospinal fluid on the brain	Controlled by the implantation of a shunt
Phenylketonuria	Autosomal recessive genetic disorder	Associated with metabolic problems in processing high-protein foods
		Can be controlled via restrictive diets implemented at birth
Prader-Willi syndrome	Chromosomal error of the autosomal type	Associated with biological compulsion to excessive eating
		Obesity as a common secondary trait to retardation
Tay-Sachs disease	Autosomal recessive genetic disorder	Highest risk for Ashkenazic Jewish people
		Associated with severe disabilities and early mortality
		No known cure
		Prevention by means of genetic screening

Intellectual disabilities are associated with a number of challenges to learning. Table 7.3 identifies the most significant learning domains, lists representative problem areas, and notes certain instructional implications. In addition, the table focuses on related concerns for cognitive, language, and socio-behavioural development.

Table 7.3 Characteristics and Implications of Intellectual Disabilities

Domain	Representative Problem Areas	Instructional Implications
Attention	Attention span (length of time on task)	Teach students to be aware of the importance of attention.
	Focus (inhibition of distracting stimuli)	Teach students how to actively monitor their attention (i.e., self-monitoring).
	Selective attention (discrimination of important stimulus characteristics)	Highlight salient cues.
Use of mediational strategies	Production of strategies to assist learning	Teach specific strategies (rehearsal, labelling, chunking).
	Organizing new information	Involve student in active learning process (practise, apply, review).
		Stress meaningful content.
Memory	Short-term memory (i.e., over seconds, minutes)—common deficit area	Because strategy production is difficult, students need to be shown how to use specific strategies in order to proceed in an organized, well-planned manner.
	Long-term memory—usually more similar to that of persons who are nondisabled (once information has been learned)	Stress meaningful content.
Generalized learning	Applying knowledge or skills to new tasks, problems, or situations	Teach in multiple contexts.
		Reinforce generalization.
	Using previous experience to formulate rules that will help solve problems of a similar nature	Remind students to apply what they have learned.
Motivational considerations	External locus of control	Create environment focused on success opportunities.
	Outer directedness	Emphasize self-reliance.
	Lack of encouragement to achieve	Promote self-management strategies.
	Failure set (expectancy of failure)	Encourage problem-solving strategies (vs. only correct responses).
Cognitive development	Ability to engage in abstract thinking	Provide concrete examples in instruction.
	Symbolic thought, as exemplified by introspection and hypothesizing	Encourage interaction between students and the environment, being responsive to their needs so that they may learn about themselves as they relate to people and objects around them.
Language development	Delayed acquisition of vocabulary and language rules	Create environment that facilitates development and encourages verbal communication.
	Possible interaction with cultural variance and language dialects	Provide opportunities for students to interact with language.
	Speech disorders (more common than in general population)	Provide opportunities for students to use language for a variety of purposes and with different audiences.
		Encourage student speech and active participation.

(continued)

Table 7.3 Continued

Domain	Representative Problem Areas	Instructional Implications
Academic development	Delayed acquisition of reading, writing, and mathematical skills, decoding, and comprehension of text	Use learning strategies to promote effective studying.
	Problem-solving difficulties in mathematics	Teach sight words with emphases on functional applications (see Polloway, Smith & Miller, 2003).
		Teach strategies for decoding unknown words (Joseph & Seery, 2004) and place skills in context of literacy development (Katims, 2001).
		Provide strategies to promote reading comprehension and math problem solving.
		Adapt curriculum to promote success.
Socio-behavioural considerations	Social adjustment	Promote social competence through direct instruction in social skills.
	Problems in "everyday intelligence" (Greenspan, 1996)	Reinforce appropriate behaviours.
	Self-concept	Seek an understanding of reasons for inappropriate behaviour.
	Social acceptance	Involve peers as classroom role models.
	Classroom behavioural difficulties (e.g., disruptions)	Program for social acceptance.
		Use peers in reinforcing.

Identification, Assessment, and Eligibility

Procedures for the identification of intellectual disability differ from province to province. However, common requirements include evidence of significantly below-average intellectual functioning combined with impairments in adaptive functioning. Eligibility for special education services depends on the degree of intellectual impairment and its effect on the student's adaptive functioning. The degree of intellectual impairment is determined through psychological assessment carried out by registered psychologists, using an individually administered test of intellectual functioning and other measures as appropriate. The *Diagnostic and Statistical Manual of Mental Disorders*, Fourth Edition (*DSM-IV*) specifies four degrees of severity of "mental retardation":

- Mild mental retardation: IQ level 50–55 to approximately 70
- Moderate mental retardation: IQ level 35–40 to 50–55
- Severe mental retardation: IQ level 20–25 to 35–40
- Profound mental retardation: IQ level below 20 or 25. (p. 42)

The degree of impairment in adaptive functioning informs educational planning. The individual education plan reflects the student's individual needs and builds on individual strengths.

TRANSITION CONSIDERATIONS

Occupational success and community living skills are among the critical life adjustment variables that ensure successful transition into adulthood. Numerous studies and case histories confirm the successes that individuals achieve, often thanks to the supports of teachers, family, and friends. Two general and equally critical considerations are: (1) Through which means do students exit special education? (2) What opportunities and supports are available to them during adulthood?

According to CACL (n.d.), "People with intellectual disabilities face major barriers to decent jobs with living wages. When people lack access to education, volunteer and community opportunities in their childhood and youth, labour force exclusion is often the result in their adulthood. It is estimated that 65% of adults with intellectual disabilities are either unemployed or outside of the labour force."

When effective transition programs are in place, outcomes are more optimistic: "There are many innovative adult literacy, training, and employment initiatives that are helping to build the capacity of community colleges, literacy programs, employers, and community services to ensure the adult education and workplace inclusion of people with intellectual disabilities" (CACL, n.d.). Examples of the challenges of adulthood in terms of life demands are summarized in Table 7.4.

In general, the vast majority of adults with intellectual disabilities can obtain and maintain gainful employment. However, a number of critical factors influence their success. First, postschool adjustment hinges on their ability to demonstrate personal and social behaviours appropriate to the workplace. Second, the quality of the transition programming provided will predict subsequent success. Such programs recognize that programming must reflect a top-down perspective (i.e., from community considerations to school curriculum) that bases curriculum on the demands of the next environment in which the individual will live, work, socialize, and recreate.

Third, the workplace of the future poses special challenges. The increasingly complex demands of the workplace will become problematic for this group. Many of the jobs that traditionally have been available to individuals with intellectual disabilities (e.g., in the service industry) may be in shorter supply. Finally, individuals with intellectual disabilities are likely to have increased leisure time. Thus, an important component of transition planning should be preparing students to use their leisure time in rewarding and useful ways (Patton, Polloway, & Smith, 2000).

While general education teachers would be quite unlikely to have full responsibility for meeting the transitional needs of students with intellectual disabilities, this focus is one of the most critical curricular and instructional aspects of students' needs. Patton and Dunn (1998) summarized the essential features of transition, highlighting the following:

- Transition efforts must start early, and planning must be comprehensive.
- Decisions must balance what is ideal with what is possible.
- Active and meaningful student participation and family involvement are essential.
- Supports are beneficial and used by everyone.
- Community-based instructional experiences have a major impact on learning.
- The transition planning process should be viewed as a capacity-building activity.
- Transition planning is needed by all students.

Table 7.4 Major Life Demands

Domain	Subdomain	Sample Life Demands
Employment/ Education	General job skills	Seeking and securing a job
		Learning job skills
		Maintaining one's job
	General education/ training considerations	Gaining entry to post-secondary education/training settings (higher education, adult education, community education, trade/technical schools, military service)
		Finding financial support
		Utilizing academic and system survival skills (e.g., study skills, organizational skills, and time management)
	Employment setting	Recognizing job duties and responsibilities
		Exhibiting appropriate work habits/behaviour
		Getting along with employer and co-workers
Home and family	Home management	Setting up household operations (e.g., initiating utilities)
		Cleaning dwelling
		Laundering and maintaining clothes and household items
	Financial management	Creating a general financial plan (e.g., savings, investments, retirement)
		Paying bills
		Obtaining government assistance when needed (e.g., Medicare, food stamps, student loans)
	Family life	Preparing for marriage, family
		Maintaining physical/emotional health of family members
		Planning and preparing meals (menu, buying food, ordering take-out food, dining out)
Leisure pursuits	Indoor activities	Performing individual physical activities (e.g., weight training, aerobics, dance, swimming, martial arts)
		Participating in group physical activities (e.g., racquetball, basketball)
	Outdoor activities	Engaging in general recreating activities (e.g., camping, sightseeing, picnicking)

Transition planning is critical to success for students with intellectual disabilities, and therefore school districts can significantly improve their understanding of students' needs and further develop their instructional approaches from analyzing the life outcomes of their graduates.

STRATEGIES FOR CURRICULUM AND INSTRUCTION

The education of students with intellectual disabilities in inclusive settings is a challenge. Without question, however, educators must deliver quality programs; otherwise, the prognosis for young adults with intellectual disabilities will not be positive.

Challenges for General Education

The data on postschool outcomes point out areas that teachers must address when they work with students with intellectual disabilities in inclusive settings. These concerns should be kept in mind as curricula and instructional plans are developed and implemented in collaboration with special education teachers. Patton et al. (1996) identify four primary goals for individuals who have mild intellectual disabilities: productive employment, independence and self-sufficiency, life skills competence, and opportunity to participate successfully within the school and the community. These goals should guide the educational program for these students.

In terms of *employment*, teachers should build students' career awareness and help them see how academic content relates to applied situations; at the secondary level, this thrust should include training in specific job skills. This concern should be the primary focus of vocational educators.

In terms of *independence* and *self-sufficiency*, young adults with mild intellectual disabilities need to become as responsible for themselves as possible. As Miller (1995) states, the educational goal "is to develop self-directed learners who can address their own wants and concerns and can advocate for their goals and aspirations" (p. 12). Thus, successful

Personal Spotlight

Former Executive Director of Saskatoon Association for Community Living Jeanne Remenda

For over 15 years, Jeanne was the executive director of the Saskatoon Association of Community Living. "The association provides services to persons of all ages with many kinds of intellectual disabilities. The main focus is family support/advocacy in the areas of respite, school, day or work programs, and housing. Staff of the association are often asked to attend planning meetings for these programs as a support person/advocate for the parents of children and youth with intellectual disabilities." Two of the areas Jeanne believes are vital to consider when working with individuals with all types of exceptionalities are developing social skills and recognizing people as individuals.

Jeanne believes it is important to develop social skills when working with individuals with exceptionalities. "While academics are always an important part of school, it is the social component that children and youth with disabilities often find the most challenging. All children want to be accepted by their peers but this can be difficult when they are perceived as being different, particularly in the adolescent years. It is important to create a classroom that is welcoming of diversity, and equally important to provide instruction to children and youth to assist them in learning social skills (i.e., how to ask a friend to play)."

Recognizing people as individuals is a second important area to consider when working with individuals with exceptionalities. "While labels such as autism, learning disabled, etc., can be useful in terms of providing appropriate supports or designations, it is important to remember that these students are children first. Not every problem, behaviour, or physical ailment can be attributed to a particular disability. These children still go through puberty with all that entails, get the flu and stomach aches, and feel sad when teased by their classmates, just like all the other kids. Rely on your own knowledge of children when assessing behaviour. Integrated/inclusive education is still relatively new, so administrators, educators, and parents are still working through the process. There needs to be an emphasis on flexibility and student-centred planning to meet the unique needs of each child. Some of the available information focuses on the characteristics of the disability to such an extent that the child is lost in the process."

inclusion of students who have intellectual disabilities depends on the ability of teachers, peers, and the curriculum to create a climate of empowerment. One essential element of empowerment is self-determination (Smith, Polloway, Smith, & Patton, 2007). Wehmeyer (1993, p. 16) noted the following:

> *Self-determination refers to the attitudes and abilities necessary to act as the primary causal agent in one's life, and to make choices and decisions regarding one's quality of life free from undue external influence or interference.*

A series of specific behaviours constitutes self-determination. For example, Zhang (2001) included the following: "making choices, making decisions, solving problems, setting and attaining goals, being independent, evaluating our performance, self-studying, speaking up for self, having internal motivations, believing in one's own abilities, being aware of personal strengths and weaknesses, and applying strengths to overcome weaknesses" (p. 339).

A third key consideration is the inclusion of *life skills* in the curriculum, focusing on the importance of competence in everyday activities. This area includes, but is not limited to, use of community resources, home and family activities, social and interpersonal skills, health and safety skills, use of leisure time, and participation in the community as a citizen (e.g., compliance with legal and cultural standards). With increased commitment to inclusion, a particularly challenging consideration for both general and special educators will be ways to include a life skills and transitional focus within the general education curriculum beginning at the elementary school level and reflected throughout formal schooling. A critical concern is the successful blending of a standards-based curriculum with a focus on life skills and community preparation (Hoover & Patton, 2005).

A fourth consideration is successful *community involvement*, which requires that students experience inclusive environments. Students with intellectual disabilities can learn to participate in school and community by being included in general education

FURTHER READING

For more information on some of the health issues facing individuals with intellectual disabilities, read the article "Understanding Health Disparities and Inequities Faced by Individuals with Intellectual Disabilities" by H. Ouellette-Kuntz, published in 2005 in the *Journal of Applied Research in Intellectual Disabilities*, volume 18 (pp. 113–121).

A key to successful inclusion for students with intellectual disabilities is provision of appropriate supports.

FURTHER READING

For more information on best practices for promoting and supporting self-determination, read *Steps to Self-Determination: A Curriculum to Help Adolescents Learn to Achieve Their Goals,* by S. Field and A. Hoffman, published in 2005 and available from the Council for Exceptional Children (CEC) at http://canada.cec. sped. Org.

⊙ Watch

Mental Retardation

TEACHING TIP

The supports model emphasizes providing whatever supports are necessary to enable a student with intellectual disabilities to succeed in a general education setting.

classrooms. Although school inclusion is viewed by some as an end in itself, it is better viewed as a condition that can provide instruction and training for success in subsequent inclusive community activities.

Finally, consideration must be given to the perspectives of the individuals themselves about educational programs and their outcomes. To provide a picture of the views of the outcomes of interventions with persons with intellectual disabilities, Fox and Emerson (2001) solicited input from persons with intellectual disabilities, parents, clinical psychologists, nurses, program managers, and direct support workers. The focus was on two groups of individuals with intellectual disabilities who also had challenging behaviours: children and young adults living at home and young adults in group homes. The most salient outcomes for these two groups identified by stakeholders present an interesting contrast. While program managers, nurses, and psychiatrists, for example, stressed reductions in the severity of challenging behaviours for both groups of individuals, persons with intellectual disabilities from both groups identified increased friendships and relationships as their priority outcome goals.

General Considerations for Inclusion

The key to including students with intellectual disabilities in the general education classroom is providing necessary and appropriate supports. These include personal supports (e.g., self-regulation skills, academic skills), natural supports (e.g., parents, friends), support services (e.g., specialized instruction), and technical supports (e.g., assistive technology). A focus on the concept of **supported education** as a necessary complement to inclusion assumes that individuals should be educated in inclusive classroom settings to the maximum degree possible and supported in those locations in order to ensure successful learning.

There has been a tendency simply to physically place the student in the classroom. Inclusion, as supported education, should focus on welcoming and involving persons with intellectual disabilities in the general education classroom. Merely placing students in general education without social integration and active classroom participation is not the intent of inclusion and will be far less likely to result in positive gains for students. Likewise, adults with intellectual disabilities who live in the community but do not participate in community activities do not fulfill the true spirit of inclusion.

Successful inclusion, therefore, is inescapably linked to how well general education is prepared to handle students who will require differentiated strategies in terms of content, instructional materials, instruction, assignments, testing, products, setting, and management (Hoover & Patton, 2005; 2008). Wehmeyer, Lattin, and Agram (2001) developed a model related to access to the general curriculum for individuals with intellectual disabilities. Presented in Figure 7.1, the model reflects the fact that a series of key decisions needs to be made in curriculum development in order for students to succeed in the general education classroom. Particular emphases include the use of assistive technology, the development of curricular adaptations (see the next section), the augmentation of the curriculum (to include emphasis on strategy training and self-determination), and the availability of curricular alternatives (which stress a more functional emphasis often not present in the general curriculum).

As previously described, a significant concern for teaching students with intellectual disabilities is ensuring that the students are held to high expectations. In order to respond

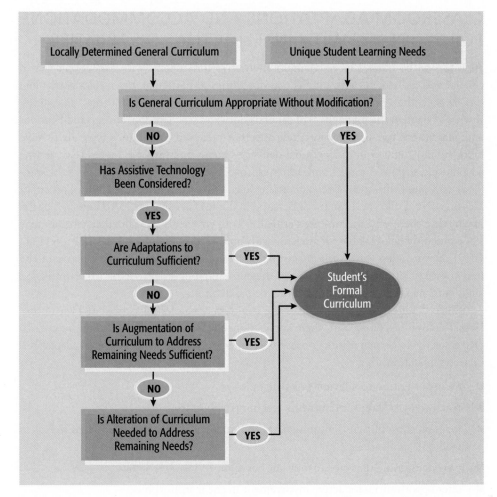

Figure 7.1 A Model to Gain Access to the General Curriculum

From "Achieving Access to the General Curriculum for Students with Mental Retardation: A Curriculum Decision-Making Model" (pp. 327–342), by M.L. Wehmeyer, D. Lattin, & M. Agram, 2001, *Education and Training in Mental Retardation and Developmental Disabilities, 36.*

to the challenges related to teacher expectations, a number of principles are available to guide educational practice. Teacher behaviours that are associated with communicating low expectancies, and thus should be avoided, include the following (McGrew & Evans, 2004):

- offering more limited opportunities to learn new material
- providing less "wait" time to answer questions
- providing answers for a student or calling on someone else
- using criticism for failure or offering insincere praise
- providing limited reinforcement and having it not be contingent on completed tasks
- engaging in differential treatment among students (e.g., less friendly or responsive, limited eye contact, fewer smiles)
- providing briefer and less useful feedback to responses
- asking lower-level cognitive questions to the exclusion of those that challenge the students' thinking

CROSS REFERENCE

See chapters 1 and 2 to review the purposes of including students with exceptionalities in general education settings.

CLASSROOM ADAPTATIONS AND ACCOMMODATIONS FOR STUDENTS WITH INTELLECTUAL DISABILITIES

As inclusion becomes a more common alternative for students with exceptionalities in general and individuals with intellectual disabilities in particular, the regular curriculum has become the "program of choice" for more students with intellectual disabilities. Review of data on the preferences of general education teachers concerning modifications and adaptations for such students indicates that preferred adaptations typically revolve more around changes in instructional delivery systems and response modes (e.g., testing adaptations, such as extended time) than in changes in the actual curriculum or the standards associated with the curricular content (e.g., Polloway, Bursuck, Jayanthi, Epstein, & Nelson, 1996; Polloway, Epstein, & Bursuck, 2002; see also chapter 13). Therefore, to the extent that these observations are verified, it is likely that a specialized curriculum may less commonly be available for students with mild intellectual disabilities (Patton et al., 2000). Nevertheless, given the preceding discussion, teachers need to be aware of the importance of a functional focus within the curriculum in order to enhance learning and adult outcomes for students with an intellectual disability.

Table 7.3 presented an outline of the common characteristics associated with intellectual disabilities, along with their implications for instruction. When they are considered collectively, certain instructional themes emerge. Teachers should focus on adaptations or accommodations that

- ensure attention to relevant task demands
- teach ways to learn content while teaching content itself
- focus on content that is meaningful to the students, to promote learning as well as to facilitate application
- provide training that crosses multiple contexts
- offer opportunities for active involvement in the learning process

One promising approach that has merit for all students and can particularly benefit students with intellectual disabilities is the use of cognitively oriented instructional methods (e.g., strategy training). Based on the premise that learning problems experienced by low-achieving students are due more to a lack of knowledge regarding the processes involved in independent learning than to any underlying deficits, these approaches incorporate learning strategies, metacognition, and cognitive behaviour modification (e.g., self-monitoring) as exciting alternatives to traditional instructional practices.

Curricular adaptations are likewise important to consider. In general, the key focus should be on relevant and meaningful curricular content that students can master and apply to their current and future lives. Teachers should focus on the subsequent environments for which students will prepare (in terms of learning, working, residing) as a basis for curriculum design. The subsequent-environments rationale has applicability across school levels as individuals prepare for successful transitions and life challenges. Most important is the assurance that the secondary school curriculum prepares students with intellectual disabilities (as well as all students) for adulthood, whether that means further education, job placement, or independent living. To make the curriculum appropriate for students with intellectual disabilities, specific adaptations can enhance learning and increase relevance.

TEACHING TIP

The use of peer supports can greatly enhance the success of students with intellectual disabilities in general education settings.

Assistive Technology: Enhancing Quality of Life

The potential for technology to contribute to "the good life" was a primary motivation behind the passage of Public Law 100–407 in the United States, the *Technology-Related Assistance for Individuals with Disabilities Act* of 1988. This legislation noted (p. 1044) that providing assistive technology devices and services to individuals with exceptionalities enables them to

■ Have greater control over their own lives

■ Participate in and contribute more fully to activities in their home, school, and work environments, and their communities

■ Interact to a greater extent with typically achieving individuals

■ Otherwise benefit from opportunities that are taken for granted by individuals who do not have exceptionalities

People with and without exceptionalities universally value these goals of self-determination, inclusion, participation in school and community, and enhanced social relationships. This desire for greater control and inclusion and the potential of technology to lead to these outcomes are, presumably, no less true for people with exceptionalities than anyone else.

What have we learned at the Beach Center [a research centre at the University of Kansas] in our research? First, we have described modifications that can improve access to technology for people with intellectual disabilities. These device modifications follow the principles of universal design. Universal design was first applied in architecture to create barrier-free buildings that were accessible to all people. Rather than adding special features to a building so people with individuals could gain access, a building could be designed to be "universally" accessible for everyone. Universal design benefits everyone. For example, most scissors are designed for people who are right-handed; people who are left-handed must purchase specially designed scissors. Scissors that have been designed for people with limited hand strength or fine motor difficulties, however, are also easily used by people who are left-handed or right-handed. They're universally designed. A number of universal design features are important if people with intellectual and developmental disabilities are to be able to use technology. These features include the simplicity of the technology, the capacity of the technology to support repetition, and the consistency of presented information. In addition, the technology must be able to provide information on how to use a device in multiple modalities, including, in particular, audio and graphic representations.

From "Assistive Technology: Fulfilling the Promise for Individuals with Disabilities," 2006, *Beach Center Newsletter, 2*, pp. 2–4.

Technological Considerations

Assistive technology can further enhance classroom adaptations. Although students with intellectual disabilities can benefit from a variety of technological applications, the key concern is that technology be used in a way that effectively enhances learning through conscious attention to the use of technology for each of the four respective stages of learning: the acquisition of new skills; the development of fluency and proficiency; the maintenance of skills over time; and the generalization to new situations. The Technology Today feature describes how assistive technology devices can affect the learning environment.

◉ Watch

Computers as an Instructional Tool

PROMOTING INCLUSIVE PRACTICES FOR STUDENTS WITH INTELLECTUAL DISABILITIES

Beyond the curricular and instructional considerations summarized previously, several other considerations are central to the successful inclusion of students with intellectual disabilities. The first concern is the creation of a sense of community in the school in general and the classroom in particular. As noted earlier, successful inclusion represents supported education—an environment where students succeed because they are welcomed, encouraged, and involved (i.e., supported) in their learning.

The challenge for teachers seeking to successfully include students with intellectual disabilities thus reaches beyond the students' acquisition of, for example, specific academic skills. Rather, it requires finding ways to provide a "belonging place" for them in the

Evidence-Based Practice

Circles of Friends in Schools

Marsha Forest came away from her Joshua Committee experiences as if she had put on a better pair of glasses. Her position as a professor of special education suddenly seemed less important to her. She spent long hours on the road helping school boards, principals, and teachers see how everybody can experience richness when someone with an exceptionality is placed in a regular classroom and the so-called regular students are encouraged to form a circle of friends around that person.

Marsha always believed in getting teachers down to meticulous detail when it came to educating persons with exceptionalities. Now, however, she saw that some of the most valuable educational steps can come *naturally* from regular classmates, if the right conditions exist in the classroom.

She also knew that parents and teachers fear peer group pressure. After all, when kids get together these days, they can give themselves quite an education—one that often shapes lives more powerfully than adults can shape them. But peer group education doesn't always lead to belligerence and destruction and drugs. It can lead to caring and nurturing and helping others do healthy things they have never done before.

This twist, however, generated fears in some teachers when it dawned on them that a circle of friends might foster better growth and development in a student than they were capable of teaching.

And so Marsha moved into regular schools and worked hard at

1. Helping boards and principals understand the circles-of-friends process

2. Finding a teacher and class willing to include a person with an exceptionality

3. Helping the regular teacher handle any initial fears about the venture

4. Letting the teacher and class call the shots as much as possible

5. Providing strong support persons who would assist only when they really were needed

6. Then finding a handful of kids willing to work at being friends with their classmate with the exceptionality

"The first placement in a school is the toughest," she said. "After that, it's usually easy to include others."

Marsha sees building a circle of friends as a person-by-person process, not an all-encompassing program. So she focuses on students with exceptionalities one at a time, and sets up a framework that enables a circle to surround that person.

Because no two settings are alike, she watches as the circle, the regular teacher, and the rest of the students develop and coordinate their own routines for helping. Then, never predicting an outcome, she waits. And when new learning takes place in the person with the exceptionality, Marsha moves in and makes all the students, the teacher, the principal—even the board members—feel simply great.

According to her, the average school can handle up to 12 of these arrangements. After that, the efficiency of the process may diminish.

She doubts that circles of friends will work in every school. "If a school is all screwed up," she said, "and if it has lost its zest and commitment for really helping kids learn—forget it. On the other hand, I'm sure that circles of friends can help make a good school—and especially the kids—better. Then coming to school takes on fresh values and meaning. Some enjoy coming to school as they never did before."

Adapted from *Circles of Friends: People with Disabilities and Their Friends Enrich the Lives of One Another* (pp. 39–40), by R. Perske, 1988, Nashville, TN: Abingdon Press.

general education classroom. Such a place can be created through friendships, a key priority outcome as expressed by persons with intellectual disabilities (Fox & Emerson, 2001).

Despite its broad support, inclusion does bring with it the potential loss of friendships present in traditional, self-contained classes. Teachers should be sensitive to this consideration and promote an environment in which the benefits of friendship can be realized.

A helpful strategy for promoting social acceptance for students (and young adults) with intellectual disabilities involves "circles of support" or "circles of friends." The Evidence-Based Practice feature on page 194 discusses an example of such a program. As teachers consider developing such systems, they should not overlook the benefits to students who are not disabled, which may include enhanced attitudes, personal growth, and a sense of civic responsibility in addition to the benefits of friendship (Hughes et al., 2001).

✳ Explore

I Want a Best Friend

FINAL THOUGHTS

As special and general education teachers jointly develop and implement educational programs for students with intellectual disabilities, they should keep in mind that these students require a comprehensive, broad-based curriculum to meet their needs. The most effective programs will provide appropriate academic instruction adapted to facilitate learning. However, the curriculum cannot solely be academic in orientation, but rather should focus on developing social and transition skills to facilitate the students' success in general education classrooms and subsequent integration into the community.

In making curricular choices, teachers will have to consider how responsive the general education classroom can be to the needs of students with intellectual disabilities. The ultimate goal is not simply school inclusion but rather community or "life" inclusion; the curriculum that achieves that purpose most effectively is the most appropriate one. The challenge of inclusion for students with intellectual disabilities is to ensure that the curriculum they pursue prepares them for their future.

TEACHING TIP

Curricular decisions for students with intellectual disabilities should always be made with the student's future needs in mind.

SUMMARY

- The concept of *intellectual disability* has variant meanings to professionals and the lay public.

- The three central dimensions of the definition are lower intellectual functioning, deficits or limitations in adaptive skills, and an onset prior to age 18.

- The 2002 American Association on Intellectual and Developmental Disabilities (AAIDD) definition (formerly the American Association on Mental Retardation, or AAMR) stresses the importance of four assumptions: cultural and linguistic diversity, an environmental context for adaptive skills, the strengths of individuals as well as their limitations, and the promise of improvement over time.

- Common practice in the field has been to speak of three general levels of intellectual disability—mild, moderate and severe—but emerging efforts in classification stress levels of needed supports rather than levels of exceptionality.

- Social competence is a critical component of instructional programs for students with intellectual disabilities. Teaching social skills can have a positive effect on successful inclusion, both in school and in the community.

- Educational programs must be outcomes-oriented and attend to transitional concerns so that students receive the appropriate training to prepare them for subsequent environments. The curriculum should thus have a top-down orientation.

■ Attention difficulties can be addressed by modifying instruction to highlight relevant stimuli and by teaching students to monitor their own attention.

■ Teachers should teach not only content but also mediation strategies that facilitate learning. Examples include rehearsal and classification.

■ Memory problems respond to mediation strategies (as above) and to an emphasis on content that is meaningful and relevant.

■ Cognitive development for students with intellectual disabilities can be enhanced by emphasizing active interaction with the environment and concrete experiences.

■ Many students with a history of failure have an external locus of control, which can be enhanced by an emphasis on successful experiences and by reinforcement for independent work.

■ To enhance language development, teachers should provide a facilitative environment, structure opportunities for communication, and encourage speech.

■ Opportunities for inclusion are essential and should focus on social benefits, such as friendship, while not neglecting curricular needs.

Weblinks

Canadian Association for Community Living (CACL)
www.cacl.ca
The CACL advocates the full inclusion of individuals with intellectual disabilities in the community. The Association's website provides information, supports, and leads on other websites focused on inclusion. Checking it out is essential if you have questions regarding Canadian law about inclusion of individuals with exceptionalities and transition to the workplace or want to reach a provincial or territorial association.

TASH: Disability Advocacy Worldwide
www.tash.org
Here is an excellent site for learning about the disability rights movement and finding links to other websites relevant to a variety of exceptionalities. *TASH* used to stand for *The Association for the Severely Handicapped.* Although the Association no longer uses the title, it has retained the acronym. TASH is an international association of people with exceptionalities, their family members, other advocates, and pro-

fessionals. TASH's mission and commitment is achieving full inclusion and participation of persons with exceptionalities in all aspects of life. Its website provides a wealth of information relevant to achieving that goal.

American Association on Intellectual and Developmental Disabilities (formerly the American Association on Mental Retardation)
www.aamr.org
The website of this Association, which has chapters in both Canada and the United States, provides information, resources, related links, and a bookstore of current books in the area of intellectual disability.

Canadian Council for Exceptional Children (CCEC)
www.cec.sped.org/am/template.cfm?section=Home
CCEC has been an active member of the International Council for Exceptional Children since it was founded in 1922. CCEC advocates for exceptional students, including those with intellectual disabilities.

Chapter 8
Teaching Students with Autism and Fetal Alcohol Spectrum Disorder

Chapter Objectives

After reading this chapter, you should be able to

- define and describe students with autism spectrum disorders (ASD) and fetal alcohol spectrum disorder (FASD)

- discuss the causes and prevalence of ASD and FASD

- describe various intervention strategies for students with ASD or FASD

- identify strategies for successful inclusion

Questions to Consider

1. Is there a preferred placement for children with autism?

2. What kinds of supports should be available for Curtis to facilitate his success in the general education classroom?

3. Is a child ever *ready* for inclusion, or does the school have to make the placement decision and provide the necessary supports to make it work?

Curtis's parents noted something different about their child when he was about two years old. Up until that time he had developed perfectly. He walked at 13 months, started babbling at about 15 months, and loved to play with adults and other children.

Then things began to change. His babbling stopped, he developed a blank stare, his early success at toilet training seemed to be reversing, and he stopped paying any attention to other children and adults. When he was about three years old, his parents took him to the provincial children's hospital, and the diagnosis was autism.

Curtis was placed in a structured preschool program and has been receiving special education services ever since. Integrated into his neighbourhood school upon entry into Kindergarten, Curtis is now seven and is enjoying being in a regular Grade 2 classroom. Curtis has very little oral language, but seems to enjoy being with his typically achieving peers, and he is able to do some of the academic work with the assistance of a paraprofessional. Although the school has worked hard to develop and provide Curtis with an appropriate educational program, the services he receives from professionals (i.e., speech-language pathologist, psychologist) are intermittent. This situation results in the classroom teacher bearing the majority of the responsibility for managing and delivering Curtis's adapted educational program, including the training and supervision of the paraprofessional who works with Curtis for most of the school day.

INTRODUCTION

This chapter provides an introduction to and a discussion of autism spectrum disorders (ASD) and fetal alcohol spectrum disorder (FASD). Given the clear trend toward increased prevalence of ASD (e.g., Fombonne, 2003a; 2003b; 2005; U.S. Department of Education, 2006) and the unique learning challenges faced by students identified as having ASD and FASD, teachers must have a clear understanding of these conditions and their implications for education. Schools and provincial departments of education provide support for educators and students with autism and fetal alcohol spectrum disorders. Teachers should not have to "go it alone." A multidisciplinary approach to meeting the needs of students with ASD and FASD is the key to successful education.

CONSIDER THIS

What are some problems that may be encountered by general classroom teachers with which specialists could provide assistance?

AUTISM SPECTRUM DISORDERS
Basic Concepts about Autism

Autism spectrum disorders are pervasive developmental disorders that primarily affect social interactions, language, and behaviour. Although autism has been glamorized by several movies, such as *Rain Man* (1988), many students with this condition do not have the incredible abilities reflected in that movie. Even for students with extraordinary skills, the presence of autism still has a significant impact on the individuals and their families. The characteristics displayed by individuals with autism vary significantly; some are able to assimilate into community settings and activities, and others have major difficulties achieving such normality (Scheuermann & Webber, 2002). Needless to say, "children and youth with autism spectrum disorders are a particularly unique group, even when compared with other children with disabilities" (Simpson, 2001, p. 68).

CONSIDER THIS

How can movies that depict persons with exceptionalities help or hurt the cause of providing appropriate educational opportunities to students with exceptionalities?

The Geneva Centre for Autism in Toronto explains what is meant by *autism spectrum disorders*:

> *Autism is often referred to as a "spectrum disorder," meaning that its symptoms and characteristics can present themselves in a variety of combinations, ranging from mild to quite severe. The phrase "autism spectrum disorders (ASD)" refers to a broad definition of autism including the classical form of the disorder [Autistic Disorder] as well as Pervasive Developmental Disorder (PDD), Rett's syndrome, Asperger syndrome, and Childhood Disintegrative Disorder. (Geneva Centre, 2004)*

The study of autism has had a confusing and controversial history since the condition was first described less than 50 years ago by Dr. Leo Kanner (Scheuermann & Webber, 2002). Some of the early controversy centred on attempts to relate the cause of autism to poor mother–child bonding. Eventually this hypothesis was disproved, but it caused a great deal of guilt, confusion, and misunderstanding. Many professionals once thought that children with autism had made a conscious decision to withdraw from their environment because of its hostile nature. During the 1980s, autism was found to be an organic disorder, eliminating much of this speculation (Eaves, 1992).

In most jurisdictions in Canada, autism is not a separate category of exceptionality. Instead, students with autism are served under such categories as intellectual disability, communication disorder, or learning disability, depending on the severity of the condition. Historically, autism has been considered a low incidence disability. However, the number of children identified over the past few years has increased dramatically (Fombonne, 2003a; 2003b; 2005; Zirkel, 2002). The Government of Canada (2009) states:

> *The prevalence of pervasive developmental disorders, including Autism, Rett syndrome and Asperger syndrome, is estimated to be between 27.5 and 70 per 10,000 children aged 1 to 14 years. Early diagnosis of these conditions may be difficult since children can experience a wide range of symptoms, from problems with verbal and nonverbal communication and poor motor skills to repetitive routines and high functioning knowledge and skills about a single object or subject. (p. 24)*

Canadian epidemiological studies in the area of autism are in their early stages (Autism Society of Canada, n.d.). According to Fombonne (2003a; 2003b; 2005), recent research has found that the prevalence of autism spectrum disorders has increased from 40 to 60 per 10 000 people, representing approximately 190 000 Canadians. It is estimated that about one in 200 children today have ASD (Fombonne, 2003a; 2003b; 2005). The Autism Society of America (ASA, n.d.) reports that an estimated 1.5 million Americans may have some form of autism, based on a prevalence estimate of 1 in 166 births. Further, the ASA estimates that by 2015, based on an increase in prevalence of 10 to 17 percent per year, as many as 4 million Americans may be affected. The U.S. Department of Education (2006) reports that the percentage of children in schools between the ages of 6 and 21 served under the category of autism is about 0.18 percent. Across individual states, the range varies from 0.43 percent (Oregon) to 0.07 percent (Colorado).

The incidence of autism varies depending on the definition used. Byrd et al. (2002) identified plausible reasons for dramatic increases in prevalence (in the state of California). These included:

- greater awareness of the condition
- general overall population increase

- definitional changes
- influx of children from out of state
- prior misdiagnosis (e.g., intellectual disabilities)
- vaccinations

Byrd et al. admitted that none of these possible reasons could be confirmed, however.

One popular theory is that the increase is primarily a result of "diagnostic substitutions" (e.g., autism versus intellectual disabilities or learning disabilities). However, Ranta (2006) noted that the ASA has challenged the validity of this theory and argued that data confirm that the prevalence of ASD has reached "epidemic proportions."

The recent increase in the number of persons identified as having autism has given rise to new societal challenges that require a response on a greater scale than would have been anticipated even in the mid-1990s. Steuernagel (2005) highlighted the policy implications as related to the need for the following:

- enhanced teacher training
- support for general education teachers to promote successful inclusion
- increased vocational rehabilitation services for adults
- increased commitment to research on etiology
- advanced understanding of effective interventions for use by parents and teachers

Autism Defined

Although many definitions of autism have been developed, no single definition has been universally accepted. However, it is important to be familiar with two definitions: the one in the U.S. *Individuals with Disabilities Education Act* (IDEA), used primarily by educators; and the one found in the *Diagnostic and Statistical Manual of Mental Disorders (DSM-IV-TR; APA, 2000)*, used by psychologists and medical professionals. The IDEA defines autism as "a developmental disability significantly affecting verbal and nonverbal communication and social interactions, generally evident before age 3, that adversely affects a child's educational performance" (34 C.F.R. §300.7[c][1](i)).

There are other definitions of autism that are popular among some groups. For example, the website for the Autism Society of Canada (ASC) provides a link to the definition established by the Autism Society of America. That definition follows (Autism Society of America, n.d.):

FURTHER READING

To learn more about the disorders that fall under the umbrella of autism spectrum disorder, read the sections in the *Diagnostic and Statistical Manual of Mental Disorders* (2000) *(DSM-IV-TR)* that deal with autism and pervasive developmental disorders (PDD).

Autism is a complex developmental disability that typically appears during the first three years of life. The result of a neurological disorder that affects the functioning of the brain, autism and its associated behaviours have been estimated to occur in as many as 1 in 500 individuals. Autism is four times more prevalent in boys than girls and knows no racial, ethnic, or social boundaries. Family income, life-style, and educational levels do not affect the chance of autism's occurrence.

Autism interferes with the normal development of the brain in the areas of social interaction and communication skills. Children and adults with autism typically have difficulties in verbal and nonverbal communication, social interactions, and leisure or play activities. The disorder makes it hard for them to communicate with others and relate to the outside world. They may exhibit repeated body movements (hand flapping, rocking), unusual responses to people or attachments to objects, and they may resist changes in routines. (p. 3)

Within this chapter, the following referents are used: *autism spectrum disorders* (ASD), to reflect broad considerations across the spectrum of the disorders; *autism*, to be broadbased unless specified as being in specific reference to the autistic subtype under ASD; and *Asperger syndrome* (AS), to reflect only this specific subtype. Three of the conditions falling under the autism spectrum disorders umbrella will now be considered in more detail.

Asperger Syndrome As outlined by Safran, the DSM diagnostic criteria that define **Asperger syndrome** (AS) are as follows:

✷ Explore

Change Is So Hard!

A. *Qualitative impairment in social interaction, as manifested by at least two of the following:*
   1. *Marked impairment in the use of multiple nonverbal behaviors such as eye-to-eye gaze, facial expression, body postures, and gestures to regulate social interaction.*
   2. *Failure to develop peer relationships appropriate to developmental level.*
   3. *A lack of spontaneous seeking to share enjoyment, interests, or achievements with other people. . . .*
   4. *Lack of social or emotional reciprocity.*

B. *Restricted repetitive and stereotyped patterns of behavior, interests, and activities as manifested by at least one of the following:*
   1. *Encompassing preoccupation with one or more stereotyped and restricted patterns of interest that is abnormal either in intensity or focus.*
   2. *Apparently inflexible adherence to specific, nonfunctional routines or rituals.*
   3. *Stereotyped and repetitive motor mannerisms (e.g., hand or finger flapping or twisting, or complex whole-body movements).*
   4. *Persistent preoccupation with parts of objects.*

C. *The disturbance causes clinically significant impairment in social, occupational, or other important areas of functioning.*

D. *There is no clinically significant general delay in language (e.g., single words used by age 2 years, communicative phrases used by age 3 years).*

E. *There is no clinically significant delay in cognitive development or in the development of age-appropriate self-help skills, adaptive behavior (other than social interaction), and curiosity about the environment in childhood. (2005, p. 45)*

Rett Syndrome Another condition under the ASD umbrella is named for Dr. Andreas Rett, who first described it in 1966. **Rett syndrome** is present in 1 in 10 000–15 000 female births, representing a genetic disorder on the X chromosome. Young girls develop typically until sometime between 6 and 18 months. At that point, key characteristics emerge that include loss of speech and motor skills, repetitive hand movements, seizures, and motor control problems (e.g., in walking and balance).

Barbour (2004) identified the four developmental stages associated with Rett syndrome:

- *Early onset*: Begins at 6–18 months; reduced eye contact and interest in toys; hand wringing

- *Rapid destructive*: Begins at age 1–4, can last weeks or months; hand skills and spoken language may be lost; initiating motor movement is difficult

- *Plateau*: Between ages 2–10; can last for years; motor problems and seizures prominent; behaviour may improve along with communication and attention span

- *Late motor deterioration*: Can last for decades; reduced mobility, muscle weakness, rigidity; generally no decline in cognition, communication

The key intervention foci for Rett syndrome are on symptomatic treatment associated with the characteristics discussed above (e.g., medication for seizures). Occupational and physical therapy also remain key considerations in intervention programs.

Childhood Disintegrative Disorder Childhood disintegrative disorder (CDD) is characterized by "a marked regression in multiple areas of functioning following a period of at least two years of apparently normal development" (Government of Newfoundland and Labrador, 2003, p. 9). Specifically, after the age of two and prior to the age of 10, "the child has a clinically significant loss of previously acquired skills in at least two of the following areas: expressive or receptive language, social skills or adaptive behaviour, bowel or bladder control, play, or motor skills" (Government of Newfoundland and Labrador, 2003, p. 9).

Identification of Children with Autism

Just as autism is difficult to define, children with autism are difficult to identify. Problems related to the identification of these children include the following:

- Children with autism display many characteristics exhibited by individuals with other disabilities, such as speech and language disorders.

- Many children with autism, because they exhibit disorders across multiple domains, are mistakenly classified as having multiple disabilities.

- No stable classification system is used among educators and other professionals who encounter children with autism. (Eaves, 1992)

Another problem in identifying children with autism is the large, diverse group of professionals responsible for the evaluation and diagnosis. In diagnosing some exceptionalities, educators function as the lead professionals; in the area of autism, pediatricians, speech-language pathologists, psychologists, audiologists, and social workers are typically involved as well. Working with such a large group of individuals can cause logistical problems. Diverse definitions and eligibility criteria, different funding agencies, multicultural considerations (e.g., how parents from different cultural backgrounds adapt to the challenges their child presents), and varying services complicate the process of identifying and serving these children and adults (see Diversity Forum feature on page 207).

The process of identification is further complicated by professional and parental disagreement as to whether ASD reflects a continuum of disorders or several discrete categories. Volkmar (2004) referred to "clumpers" (i.e., those who include Asperger syndrome under ASD because all have social deficits) and "splitters" (e.g., those who keep Asperger on its own because of advanced language and higher cognitive functioning). Addressing the question of an autism continuum versus discrete categories, Tryon, Mayes, Rhodes, and Waldo (2006) presented data on 22 children who had been identified as having Asperger syndrome. They found that 20 met the *DSM-IV-TR* criteria for autism and that none met the criteria for Asperger. They cited their data as

> consistent with the mounting empirical evidence that Asperger's disorder is high-functioning autism [and thus encouraged that] Asperger's disorder be deleted from the next version of the DSM. High- and low-functioning autism would continue to be indicated, as before, by an Axis I diagnosis of autism with an Axis II diagnosis of mental retardation for low-functioning autism, and no Axis II diagnosis of mental retardation for high-functioning autism. According to the DSM-IV-TR, a child can still have autism even without language or cognitive delays, and a diagnosis of autism takes precedence over Asperger's disorder. If a child meets DSM-IV-TR autism criteria, the child cannot have Asperger's disorder. (p. 4)

Early Identification A critical concern in the field of ASD is early identification. The common challenge has been to determine how early autism can be detected. Goin and Myers (2004) indicated that although there were better detection rates during a child's second year, some developmental anomalies may be noticed in year one. They stressed the value of multiple sources of assessment information, including home videos, early screening devices, and parental reports. The key characteristics identified in the literature (e.g., Goin & Myers, 2004; Gomez & Baird, 2005; Zwaigenbaum et al., 2005) for earliest detection include lack of eye contact and limited social skills; differences in postural and motoric characteristics; a lack of responsiveness to others and to one's own name; a pattern of solitary or unusual play; marked passivity; fixation on objects in the environment; delayed expressive and receptive language, including gestural communication; and difficulties in self-regulation that may be reflected in, for example, impulsivity, irritability, and interference with the formation of attachments.

Causes of Autism

There is no single specific cause of autism. Although organic factors, such as brain damage, genetic links, and complications during pregnancy, may cause this condition, in most cases, no cause can be confirmed. In general, autism occurs across all segments of society. The study of causation reflects a continued focus on efforts to unravel the complexity of autism. Most accepted models suggest a combination of a genetic base influenced by environmental events. The genetic role is presumed to put in place a predisposition for ASD. However, genes alone cannot explain the recent rapid increases in prevalence.

The common assumption is that autism is related to abnormalities in brain structure or function. According to the Autism Society of America (2006),

> brain scans show differences in the shape and structure of the brain [for children who are autistic]. . . . While no one gene has been identified as causing autism, in many families there appears to be a pattern of autism or related disabilities, further supporting a genetic basis to the disorder . . . it also appears that some children are born with a higher susceptibility to autism, but researchers have not yet identified a single "trigger" that causes autism to develop. (p. 4)

Environmental factors that have been hypothesized include toxins, heavy metals, and infections. One area of debate has related to the measles-mumps-rubella (MMR) vaccine (e.g., Fombonne, Zakarian, Bennett, Meng, & McLean-Haywood, 2006). The argument of such a link was first presented in post-hoc case studies based on the presence of Thimerosal (a mercury preservative) in the MMR vaccine and the possibility that millions of children were exposed to mercury levels above U.S. Environmental Protection Agency (EPA) guidelines. The Institute of Medicine concluded, however, that while the theory is "biologically plausible," no causal relationship has been established (Immunization Safety Review Committee of the Institute of Medicine, 2004).

Characteristics of Individuals with Autism

A wide variety of characteristics are associated with autism. The Autism Treatment Services of Canada (ATSC) states that children with autism have difficulty relating to other people, avoid eye contact, and have significant impairments in communication. ATSC (February 2006) noted, "If a person were to walk into a room full of people with autism, they would likely be struck more by the differences than the similarities." Some of the more common characteristics of autism include verbal and nonverbal communication impairments (Chan, Cheung, Leung, Cheung, & Cheung, 2005; Dyches, 1998), auditory-based sensory impairments (Orr, Myles, & Carlson, 1998), and problems relating to other individuals (Autism Society of America, 2006). Some individuals with disorders on the autism spectrum engage in self-stimulation to the exclusion of academic and social learning (Kauffman, 2005). Scheuermann and Webber (2002) describe the characteristics of autism using two major groups: behavioural deficits and behavioural excesses:

1. *Behavioural deficits*
   - inability to relate to others
   - lack of functional language
   - sensory processing deficits
   - cognitive deficits
2. *Behavioural excesses*
   - self-stimulation
   - resistance to change
   - bizarre and challenging behaviours
   - self-injurious behaviours

CROSS REFERENCE

Review the section in chapter 6 on children with serious emotional disturbance (SED). Compare the characteristics of children with autism and those with SED. How are these children similar? How are they different?

Specific to Asperger syndrome (AS), Myles and Simpson (2002) noted that in the social domain, individuals are "typically thought to be socially stiff, socially awkward, emotionally blunted, self-centered, deficient at understanding nonverbal social cues, and inflexible. . . . Although they are well known for their lack of social awareness, many students with AS are aware enough to sense that they are different from their peers. Thus, self-esteem problems and self-concept difficulties are common" (p. 133).

Table 8.1 outlines some of the common characteristics of individuals diagnosed with autism spectrum disorders. Although most of these characteristics are negative, some children with autism present some positive—and unexpected—characteristics.

Table 8.1 Common Characteristics: Autism Spectrum Disorders

- Insistence on sameness; resistance to change
- Difficulty in expressing needs, using gestures or pointing instead of words
- Repeating words or phrases in place of normal, responsive language
- Laughing (and/or crying) for no apparent reason; showing distress for reasons not apparent to others
- Preference to being alone; aloof manner
- Tantrums
- Difficulty in mixing with others
- Not wanting to cuddle or be cuddled
- Little or no eye contact
- Unresponsive to normal teaching methods
- Sustained odd play
- Spinning objects
- Obsessive attachment to objects
- Apparent oversensitivity or undersensitivity to pain
- No real fears of danger
- Noticeable physical overactivity or extreme underactivity
- Uneven gross/fine motor skills
- Nonresponsive to verbal cues; acts as if deaf, although hearing tests in normal range

From "What is autism?" Autism Society of America, 2005, Retrieved April 10, 2006, from www.autism-society.org/site/PageServer?pagename=about_whatis_characteristics.

In some cases, children with autism display unique **splinter skills**, or islands of precocity where they display areas of giftedness: "Common splinter skills include (1) calendar abilities, such as being able to give the day of the week for any date you might provide (e.g., May 12, 1896); (2) the ability to count visual things quickly, such as telling how many toothpicks are on the floor when a box is dropped; (3) artistic ability, such as the ability to design machinery; and (4) musical ability, such as playing a piano" (Scheuermann & Webber, 2002, p. 9).

For students with Asperger syndrome, areas of strength include oral expression and reading recognition, while difficulties may include oral comprehension, written expression, and mathematics, particularly in the area of problem solving. Myles and Simpson (2002) caution that "these students often give the impression that they understand more than they do. . . . Their pedantic style, seemingly advanced vocabularies, parrot-like responses, and ability to word call may actually mask the deficits in higher order thinking and comprehension of some students with AS" (p. 135).

According to Barnhill (2006), students with Asperger syndrome often exhibit potential strengths in the areas of grammar, vocabulary, rote memory, absorbing facts, and honesty (often to a fault). At the same time, certain characteristics may have a negative impact on academic performance. These characteristics include insistence on sameness, impairment in social interaction, a restricted range of interests, poor concentration, poor motor coordination, academic difficulties, and emotional vulnerability (Roy, 2004;

CONSIDER THIS

How might splinter skills confuse family members about the abilities and capabilities of a child with autism?

FURTHER READING

For more information on differentiating Asperger syndrome and giftedness, read "Which is it? Asperger's syndrome or giftedness? Defining the differences," in volume 25, issue 1 of *Gifted Child Today*, 2002, pp. 58–63.

Table 8.2 Behavioural Comparison of Asperger Syndrome and Autism

	Asperger Syndrome	Autistic Syndrome
1. Intelligence measures		
Standardized scores	Average to high average range	Borderline through average range
2. Language development	Normal development	Delayed onset, deficits
Pragmatic language		
a. Verbal	Deficits can be observed	Delayed and disordered
b. Nonverbal	Deficits (e.g., odd eye gaze)	Deficits can be severe
3. Communication		
Expressive	Within normal limits	Deficits can be observed
Receptive	Within normal limits	Deficits can be observed
4. Social responsiveness		
Attachment		
a. Parents	Observed responsiveness	Lack responsiveness
b. Caregivers	Observed responsiveness	Lack responsiveness
c. Peers	Observed responsiveness	Lack responsiveness
Interactions		
a. Initiations to peers	Frequent, poor quality	Minimal frequency
b. Positive responses to peers	Frequent, awkward, and pertains to self-interests	Minimal frequency
c. Symbolic play	No impaired symbolic play	Absence of symbolic play
d. Reciprocal play	Observed but awkward	Minimal frequency
e. Coping	Deficits observed in quality	
f. Friendships	Minimal frequency	Minimal frequency
g. Requests for assistance	Observed but awkward	Minimal frequency
Emotional self-regulation		
a. Emotional empathy	Observed but awkward	Deficits can be observed
b. Emotional responsiveness	Observed but could be extreme	Aloof, indifferent
5. Physical/motor		
a. Gross motor	Observed deficits—controversial	No observed deficits
b. Repetitive behaviour	Observed	Observed

From "Asperger Syndrome and Autism: A Literature Review and Meta-analysis" (p. 237), by E. McLaughlin-Cheng, 1998, *Focus on Autism and Other Developmental Disabilities, 13*. Used with permission.

Safran, 2002; Williams, 1995). Table 8.2 presents the similarities and differences of the behavioural characteristics of children with Asperger syndrome and children with autism.

Interventions for Students with Autism

Formerly, the prognosis for individuals with autism was pessimistic: Most children with autism would grow into adulthood with severe impairments. However, intensive intervention programs have been somewhat effective with this group. No single method is successful with all children with autism, partly because they display widely variable characteristics.

TEACHING TIP

Peer buddies can be very useful to a student with autism in a general education classroom. Peers can serve as excellent role models and can provide supports for these students.

ASD and Multiculturalism

Alicia, a three-year-old child, has recently been referred for possible early childhood special education services. Her parents have indicated concerns about her developmental progress; her communication skills, behaviour, and social interactions are reflective of possible autism. Alicia's family (whose native language is Spanish) had been reluctant to seek assistance until her developmental delays caused serious concern among friends and other family members.

The importance of multicultural considerations in autism spectrum disorders is highlighted in the work of Dyches, Wilder, Sudweeks, Obiakor, and Algozzine (2004). The premise of these researchers was that "students with multicultural backgrounds and autism are challenged on at least four dimensions: communication, social skills, behavioural repertoires, and culture. The professional literature continues to address the first; it is imperative to now consider the fourth 'multicultural issues'" (p. 221). In their discussion of multicultural issues in autism, Dyches and her colleagues explore two major concerns: the prevalence of autism across ethnic groups; and the ways in which families of different cultures adapt to the challenges of raising children with autism. With regard to prevalence, they stressed the methodological challenges in this area, particularly when research has focused on immigrant and non-immigrant status. The most readily accessible data set comes from the annual U.S. Department of Education reports on the implementation of IDEA. Using these data as a basis, Dyches et al. noted that the prevalence rates were higher for children who were Black or Asian-Pacific Islander (twice the rate) than for students who were American Indian-Alaskan or Hispanic. Caucasian children were between these two groups in terms of prevalence level (approximately 0.09 percent over two years). The identification rates for the two ethnic groups that had the highest prevalence ranged, over several years, between 0.10 and 0.14 percent while the two ethnic groups with the lowest percentages were at approximately 0.06 percent.

In terms of family adaptations, Dyches and colleagues provide a detailed discussion of family responses that may be seen as more common within specific ethnic groups. For example, they discussed the possibility of negative appraisals occurring because some cultures may still see autism and other developmental disabilities as the fault of the parents. Some parents, however, may view their child's appraisal as positive: i.e., they may see a child with an exceptionality as a blessing or gift from God (e.g., by Latino mothers); or they may consider that all children are important within the family (e.g., by African-American families); or some parents may have such a spiritual orientation toward life that they view the appraisal as positive (e.g., Native Hawaiian parents); some may believe that children's functional abilities, even if limited, are important (e.g., within some Native American cultures).

These authors also discussed the issue of the supports necessary to raise a child with developmental disabilities in general and with autism in particular. Of significant concern is the strong familial support that is needed in such instances; for many ethnic groups, commitment to familial cohesion is critical for the provision of supports. At the same time, there may be differential reactions to access to organizational support, such as educational and social services. Across ethnic groups, variables that can influence a commitment to accessing such support can include awareness of programs; fear of the stigma of labels; preferences for one particular label over another that may be seen as more stigmatizing (e.g., *autism* over *intellectual impairment*); and alternative support by agencies other than governmental organizations (e.g., church support).

Questions

1. What special challenges do families face in raising a child with autism? How might these challenges be influenced by cultural background?

2. How can teachers be sensitive to cultural differences in offering to assist with the provision of family supports?

From "Multicultural Issues in Autism," by T.T. Dyches, L.K. Wilder, R.R. Sudweeks, F.E. Obiakor, and B. Algozzine, 2004, *Journal of Autism and Developmental Disabilities, 34*, pp. 211–222.

Growing evidence shows that placing children with autism with their typically achieving peers in general education settings, with appropriate supports, can make a significant difference in their behaviours. Appropriate role models appear to be very important. Recent research also indicates that behavioural treatment of children with autism, especially young children, may result in significant long-term gains in intellectual and adaptive behaviour areas. Social skills training has also been shown to be effective.

Regardless of the specific intervention used, professionals developing programs for children with autism should ask the following questions (Heflin & Simpson, 1998):

1. What are the anticipated outcomes of the programming option?
2. What are the potential risks?
3. How will the option be evaluated?
4. What proof is available that the option is effective?
5. What other options would be excluded if this option were chosen?

Since there is no single best method for teaching students with autism, school personnel must have available a variety of intervention strategies. Ruble and Dalrymple (2002) suggest a variety of environmental supports that can facilitate the success of students with autism. These are listed in Table 8.3.

Table 8.3 Environmental Supports for Children with Autism

Communicating to the person (receptive language supports)

- Slow down the pace.
- State positively what to do (e.g., "Let's walk" instead of "Stop running").
- Provide more information in visual format.

Encouraging communication from the person (expressive language supports)

- Pause, listen, and wait.
- Encourage input and choice when possible.
- Provide alternative means, such as written words or pictures, to aid communication.
- Encourage and respond to words and appropriate attempts, rather than to behaviour.

Social supports

- Build in time to watch, encourage watching and proximity.
- Practise specific skills through natural activities with one peer.
- Structure activities with set interaction patterns and roles.
- Provide co-operative learning activities with facilitation.
- Facilitate recruitment of sociable peers to be buddies and advocates.
- Provide opportunity for shared experiences using interests and strengths.

Expanding repertoires of interests and activities

- Capitalize on strengths and individual learning styles.
- Over time, minimize specific fears and frustrations.
- Use rehearsal with visuals.

From "COMPASS: A Parent-Teacher Collaborative Model for Students with Autism" (p. 76), by L.A. Ruble & N.J. Dalrymple, 2002, *Focus on Autism and Other Developmental Disabilities, 17.* Used with permission.

Self-management is a promising intervention strategy for children with autism.

Children with autism grow up to be adults with autism; the condition cannot be cured. As a result, educational programs should help them deal with the daily needs that will extend throughout their lives. To help educators focus more on the functionality of curriculum choices, they should ask themselves the following questions:

1. Does the program teach skills that are immediately useful?

2. Will the materials used be available in the student's daily environment?

3. Will learning certain skills increase the likelihood that the student will be able to do the task independently in the future?

If the answer to any of these questions is no, then the instructional program should be changed.

Programs for students with autism should also be age appropriate and **developmentally appropriate**. That is, the level of instruction should meet the developmental level of the individual. The individual's chronological age and developmental status must be considered together. These two realms are sometimes incongruent, making program planning a challenge. In this case, developmentally appropriate materials must be modified to make them as age appropriate as possible. Remember to keep chronological and developmental status in mind when developing and implementing individualized education programs and when implementing classroom adaptations.

Educational Interventions Forness, Walker, and Kavale (2003) identified four key educational goals for students with ASD:

- to develop basic language and social skills

- to provide academic instruction consistent with cognitive level

- to teach functional skills for postschool success

- to tie instruction to parental education, such as to encompass behavioural interventions to enhance social and functional skills

CONSIDER THIS

How should the curriculum for students with autism be balanced between academic skills and functional life skills? Should skills from both areas be taught to all students with autism?

CROSS REFERENCE

Review program recommendations in chapter 7 for students with intellectual disabilities. How are programs for these two groups of students similar? How are they different?

◉─Watch

Language and Social Skills

Individual Instruction on
Academic IEP Goals: Mary Ann

Another key educational goal is to implement effective early intervention programs. Hume, Bellini, and Pratt (2005) stress the importance of effective early intervention practices for students with autism. As they have noted, these practices "appear to reduce the debilitating impact of autism [and] young children with autism may make gains more quickly than young children with other severe neuro-developmental disorders. The results of a retrospective study corroborated the belief that children with autism have significantly better outcomes when an intervention begins before age 5" (p. 195).

A number of effective, broad-based educational practices were identified by Iovannone, Dunlap, Hubert, and Kincaid (2003). These include:

1. Individualized services and supports for both the family and the child
2. The systematic instruction of meaningful skills
3. Reliance on data-based decision making in educational programs
4. The creation of structured learning environments
5. The implementation of specialized curriculum for language and social skills
6. The application of a functional approach to understanding problem behaviour

The Evidence-Based Practice box provides an analysis of each of these core elements of effective interventions, which provide overall guidance for program development.

Evidence-Based Practice

Appropriate Adaptations for Students with ASD

Yell, Drasgow, and Lowrey (2005) provided a contextual discussion of autism spectrum disorders. Drawing on the research review of Iovannone and colleagues (2003), they outlined the six core elements of effective practices in education for those with autism:

1. **Individualized supports and services**: Must be tailored to meet the unique individual needs and family characteristics of each student. Individualized programming includes: (a) considering family preferences when selecting curriculum; (b) developing programming that reflects a student's preferences and interests; and (c) determining the appropriate intensity and level of instruction on the basis of the student's strengths and weaknesses.

2. **Systematic instruction**: Teaching based on identifying desirable learning outcomes, developing specific and focused teaching strategies to achieve these outcomes, consistently implementing the teaching strategies, and using information about student performance to guide daily instructional decisions.

3. **Comprehensible and structured learning environments**: Allow students to predict their daily routines and respond appropriately to behavioural expectations during different activities.

4. **Specific curriculum content**: Must include and emphasize language and social interaction because these are the primary challenges for students with ASD.

5. **Functional approach to problem behaviour**: Represents a movement away from punishment-based approaches that emphasize obedience and compliance and toward instruction that emphasizes useful skill development.

6. **Family involvement**: Improves programming because family members know their child best, spend the most time with him or her, and have an immense influence on their child. It is crucial that they are active participants in developing and implementing their child's educational programming.

From "No Child Left Behind and Students with Autism Spectrum Disorders," by M.L. Yell, E. Drasgow, and K.A. Lowrey, 2005, *Focus on Autism and Other Developmental Disabilities, 20,* pp. 130–139.

The increase in attention to students with ASD has led to the identification of more specific evidence-based interventions. Odom et al. (2003) described proposed interventions that are worthy of consideration as falling into one of the following categories:

- *Well-established*: Adult-directed intervention (prompting, scaffolding); differential reinforcement strategies

- *Emerging and effective*: Peer-mediated interventions; visual supports (graphic/photographic activity schedules; Picture Exchange Communication Systems); self-monitoring; involving families

- *Probably efficacious*: Positive behaviour support; videotaped modelling of apt behaviours; moderating task characteristics (e.g., child's choice of activities)

No single method is effective with all children who have autism, partly because, as mentioned, these children display widely variable characteristics. However, several different approaches have shown positive results. For example, one relatively recent intervention is the use of social stories. Sansosti et al. (2004) noted that social stories were initially developed to help children understand game rules but that later they were further developed to address more subtle social rules that may prove problematic for students with autism. Their goal was to clarify social expectations and provide a guide to students for their conduct while promoting self-management in specific life situations. See the Evidence-Based Practice box "Teaching Self-Management Skills" on page 213 for further information on self-management.

According to Sansosti et al. (2004), social stories identify steps in social situations and facilitate learning because students with ASD often have difficulty reading environmental, social, and behavioural cues. To do so, social stories typically

- target a specific problematic social situation
- identify salient features of context and setting
- share this information with the child and others

There is limited empirical support to date on social stories and, consequently, interventions cannot be labelled "evidence-based" as yet. However, the approach has merit because it is based on strategies that have already proven effective (e.g., social modelling, task analysis, visual aids, practice with corrective feedback, and priming to provide a preview of behaviours before entering a social situation to practise) (Sansosti et al., 2004).

Medical Interventions Another approach to treatment involves drug therapies. For students with ASD, Broun and Umbarger (2005, p. 1) noted the following behaviours that impact quality of life, and thus may warrant medical interventions:

- aggression that has moved beyond what can be tolerated or has become significantly less manageable
- self-injurious behaviour that poses a threat to the child's health and safety and/or significantly interferes with the activities of daily living
- obsessions/compulsions that significantly interfere with the child's participation in the activities of daily living or safety
- ongoing, unsafe impulsivity that may include running, climbing, mouthing, or eating inappropriate objects

Explore

A Look Inside: A Student Teacher's Dilemma

CROSS REFERENCE

Refer to chapter 3 for more information on social skill deficits and strategies for addressing social skills in classroom environments.

Hendren and Martin (2005, p. 75) aptly describe the current state of affairs with regard to psychotropic medication as follows:

> Psychotropic medications can be an important part of an effective treatment plan for individuals with ASD. Generally, a comprehensive treatment plan involves behavioural interventions, education for the family, special education services, and sometimes speech, occupational therapy, and other services as well. Improvement in symptoms as a result of these interventions plus pharmacotherapy can result in . . . better responses from the environment, leading to additional gains for the youngster with ASD. However, although psychiatric medications are widely used in the ASD population, they have not been systematically studied in great detail. Careful monitoring of their use by experienced practitioners and further research are warranted.

There are no specific drugs recommended for the direct treatment of core symptoms associated with ASD (Forness et al., 2003). Consequently, medical interventions are most often used for secondary symptoms, such as aggression or self-injurious behaviour (SIB). The process recommended to address specific symptoms with psychotropic medication is to test one drug at a time and to evaluate a drug's effects by following accepted nondrug practices (e.g., the use of applied behaviour analysis [ABA] methodology). Kalachnik et al. (1998, adapted from Schall, 2002, p. 230) recommended that the use of psychotropic drugs (i.e., any substance prescribed to improve or stabilize mood, mental status, or behaviour) should follow the following principles:

- Use a multidisciplinary plan and team to coordinate treatment and care.
- Use only in response to a specific hypothesis regarding how the medication will change behaviour.
- Obtain informed consent and develop alliances with the person and his or her parents.
- Track outcomes by collecting data on behavioural disorders and quality of life.
- Observe for the presence or absence of side effects.
- Conduct ongoing reviews of the person's clinical status, behaviour, and quality of life.
- Strive for administration of the lowest dose possible.

On the other hand, these same authors identified the following "don'ts" related to the use of psychotropic medication:

- Don't use psychotropic drugs in lieu of educational and other services.
- Don't use drugs in quantities that result in a decreased quality of life.
- Don't change drugs and doses frequently.
- Don't use multiple drugs that come from the same pharmaceutical category.
- Don't prescribe medications that are associated with addiction and/or serious side effects.
- Don't prescribe drugs without a regular schedule, and eschew the use of drugs on an "as needed" basis.

Controversial Interventions Simpson (2004) noted that "both parents & professionals can be expected to consider using various unproven interventions &

treatments. . . . Indeed, one of the most well-defined characteristics of programs and interventions (in ASD) has been the never-ending search for factors or strategies, proven or not, that purportedly restore individuals w/[sic] autism to normalcy. Of course, who would expect them to not consider approaches that might promise to reclaim children to a typical state!" (p. 140). The appropriate approach is to continue to identify and use those methods that are based on evidence. Research, therefore, is a critical component of the continued development of the field of autism spectrum disorders. Parents and teachers need to pay particular attention to the outcomes that are anticipated with a particular methodology, the potential risks that may be associated with this approach, and the ongoing commitment to evaluate the effectiveness of approaches that are being used.

Autism is a significant disability. Characterized by language deficiencies (particularly in the area of pragmatics or social language), the condition results in lifelong problems for the person with autism and his or her family. As more research into autism is completed, better methods of managing and teaching children with autism will be developed.

The dramatic increase in the prevalence of autism spectrum disorders along with the complexity of causes and the professional debate about effective treatments have all received considerable attention in the field of education in recent years. Fetal alcohol spectrum disorder is also receiving increased attention.

CONSIDER THIS

How can the use of invalidated procedures harm students? Why do some ideas become popular with some educators and family members before they are proved effective?

FURTHER READING

For more information on treatments parents report accessing for their children with autism, read the article "Internet survey of treatments used by parents of children with autism," found in volume 27 of *Research in Developmental Disabilities*, 2006, pp. 70–84.

Evidenced-Based Practice

Teaching Self-Management Skills

Teaching students with autism to increase their self-management skills is appropriate for many of these students. Following are examples of self-management goals along with supports that could help students achieve them:

Goal 1: To independently transition from one activity to another using a picture/word schedule

Supports

- Imitate peers
- Learn by observing
- Provide visual supports, including schedule for the day, steps in each activity, completion of activity, and time to move
- Train peers in how to use schedule
- Peer models

Goal 2: To stay in bounds at recess

Supports

- Imitate skills
- Learn by observing

- Teach and practise skills
- Use flags to show playground boundaries
- Use peers to model staying within boundaries
- Reinforce appropriate behaviours

Goal 3: To work quietly during individual work time

Supports

- Imitation skills
- Academic ability
- Motivation to do what other students are doing
- Peer models
- Visual reminders about being quiet
- Social story for quiet work
- Positive reinforcement for appropriate behaviours

Adapted from "COMPASS: A Parent-Teacher Collaboration Model for Students with Autism," by L.A. Ruble and M.J. Dalrymple, 2002, *Focus on Autism and Other Developmental Disabilities, 17*, pp. 76–83.

FETAL ALCOHOL SPECTRUM DISORDER

Basic Concepts about Fetal Alcohol Spectrum Disorder

FURTHER READING

For more information on FASD and Canadian government initiatives related to this disorders, visit the Public Health Agency of Canada's website at www.phac-aspc.gc.ca/fasd-etcaf/index-eng.php.

Maternal consumption of alcohol during pregnancy can result in damage to a woman's unborn child. **Fetal alcohol spectrum disorder** (FASD) is

> *an umbrella term [not a diagnostic term] used to refer to the damage or range of disabilities caused by alcohol consumption during pregnancy. These disabilities are lifelong conditions that affect not only the individual, but also the family and the community. The disabilities caused by prenatal alcohol exposure are often described as hidden or invisible because the physical characteristics can be subtle and may go unrecognized. (Saskatchewan Learning, 2004, p. 1.3)*

Disorders that may be included under the umbrella term of FASD include **fetal alcohol syndrome** (FAS), partial fetal alcohol syndrome (pFAS), alcohol-related birth defects (ARBD), and alcohol-related neurodevelopmental disorder (ARND) (Saskatchewan Learning, 2004). In the United States, the prevalence of FASD "has been reported as 1–3 per 1000 live births and the rate of FASD as 9.1 per 1000 live births" (Sokol, Delaney-Black, & Nordstrom, 2003, p. 2998). This is a rough estimate, since diagnoses of disorders falling under the FASD umbrella may be delayed or missed entirely (Sokol et al., 2003). In Canada, "there are no national statistics on the rates of FASD" (Chudley, Conry, Cook, Loock, Rosales, & LeBlanc, 2005, p. S1). However, the Government of Canada (2009) states:

> *Approximately 1% of all babies in Canada (more than 3,000 per year) are born with FASD. This estimate is thought to be low since the signs and symptoms associated with FASD are often hard to detect and may very well go unnoticed until later on in life. (p. 37)*

Some Canadian studies have estimated the prevalence of FASD in small populations. For example, when investigating the incidence of fetal alcohol syndrome in northeastern Manitoba, researchers roughly estimated the occurrence of FAS to be 7.2 per 1000 live births (Williams, Odaibo, & McGee, 1999). Large-scale studies investigating the incidence and prevalence of FASD in the Canadian population need to be undertaken in order for educators and medical professionals to better understand the potential impact of prenatal exposure to alcohol on the health and education of Canadian children.

Fetal Alcohol Spectrum Disorder Defined

Fetal alcohol syndrome is diagnosed "by a medical practitioner when there is known, significant prenatal exposure to alcohol and the child exhibits three main characteristics: evidence of growth retardation; evidence of central nervous system damage; and evidence of facial abnormalities" (Manitoba Education, Training, and Youth, 2001, p. 1.4). When maternal alcohol exposure can be confirmed and an individual "exhibits some, but not all, of the physical signs of FAS, and also has learning and behavioural difficulties which imply central nervous system damage" (Alberta Learning, 2004, p. 4), a diagnosis of partial fetal alcohol syndrome (pFAS) can be made. An individual with alcohol-related birth defects (ARBD) "displays specific physical anomalies resulting from confirmed prenatal alcohol exposure. These may include heart, skeletal, vision, hearing, and fine/gross motor problems" (Manitoba Education, Training, and Youth, 2001, p. 1.4). An individual with alcohol-related neurodevelopmental disorder (ARND) "exhibits central nervous system damage resulting from a confirmed history of prenatal alcohol exposure. This may be demonstrated as learning difficulties, poor impulse control, poor social skills, and problems with memory, attention and judgement" (Alberta Learning, 2004, p. 4). Definitions of FASD vary among provinces and territories. Refer to provincial or territorial government websites for the definitions of FASD that are followed in specific geographic areas.

Identification of Children with Fetal Alcohol Spectrum Disorder

The identification of FASD involves "screening, referral and diagnosis of newborns, children, adolescents or adults affected by prenatal substance use" (Roberts & Nanson, 2001, p. 3). Children who may have been affected by prenatal exposure to alcohol are identified by individuals working in a variety of settings (i.e., caregivers, community health nurses, educators) and referred for diagnosis (Chudley et al., 2005). Once referred, a comprehensive, multidisciplinary assessment is recommended in making a diagnosis. Although a team of professionals may be involved in the assessment of an individual suspected of presenting with a disorder related to prenatal alcohol exposure, the diagnosis of these disorders must be made by a medical doctor (Saskatchewan Learning, 2004). Typical team members include a physician specifically trained in FASD diagnosis, an occupational therapist, a speech-language pathologist, and a psychologist, as well as caregivers, counsellors, and nurses, to name a few (Chudley et al., 2005). "Assessment may occur prior to or following diagnosis and in either case, elaborates on the person's abilities and attributes beyond that provided by the diagnosis" (Roberts & Nanson, 2001, p. 3).

As with definitions of FASD, the diagnostic criteria used to identify individuals with FASD vary among provinces and territories. A subcommittee of the Public Health Agency of Canada's National Advisory Committee on FASD has been working on developing a standard approach to diagnosing FASD (Chudley et al., 2005; Health Canada, 2006).

A standard national approach to diagnosing FASD would "allow for collection of Canadian data for estimating incidence and prevalence of FASD . . . [which] is essential to identify the need for and the development of appropriate prevention and intervention programs and services" (Chudley et al., 2005, p. S2).

Causes of Fetal Alcohol Spectrum Disorder

The effects of prenatal exposure to alcohol on an unborn child are influenced by the pattern of alcohol exposure (i.e., threshold amounts of alcohol in the blood, timing of exposure during the pregnancy). However, "other factors, such as maternal health and nutrition, genetic susceptibility, and use of other psychoactive substances" may also affect an unborn child (Roberts & Nanson, 2001, p. 4). For example, if a woman with a substance use problem abused more than one substance while pregnant (i.e., alcohol and cocaine), it would be difficult to determine the unique contribution of each substance (Roberts & Nanson, 2001). Issues such as these make identifying specific causes of FASD and their effects on an individual a more complicated endeavour.

FURTHER READING

For more information on how diagnostic practices have evolved, read the article "A review of the evolution of diagnostic practices for fetal alcohol spectrum disorders," found in volume 32, issue 2 of the *Developmental Disabilities Bulletin*, 2004.

FURTHER READING

For more information on the guidelines and recommended approaches for diagnosing FASD in Canada, read the article "Fetal alcohol spectrum disorder: Canadian guidelines for diagnosis," found in volume 172.5 supplement of the *Canadian Medical Association Journal*, 2005.

Characteristics of Individuals with Fetal Alcohol Spectrum Disorder

Although students with FASD demonstrate diverse physical, health, academic, and learning characteristics, certain patterns or common characteristics that can be associated with these disorders are described as primary and secondary disabilities (Alberta Learning, 2004; Manitoba Education, Training, and Youth, 2001; Saskatchewan Learning, 2004). **Primary disabilities** "are those that a child was born with, and are a result of the damage done to the brain by alcohol. They reflect differences in brain structure and function" (Manitoba Education, Training, and Youth, 2001, p. 1.6). Primary disabilities of individuals affected by FASD typically include physical and health conditions (i.e., visual and/or hearing impairments, cardiac and/or respiratory problems); delays in reaching developmental milestones; difficulties with memory, impulse control, processing abstract information, and generalizing information from situation to situation; inconsistent performance; and an inability to understand the consequences of their actions (Saskatchewan Learning, 2004).

Secondary disabilities "are disabilities that develop over time when there is a mismatch between the person and his or her environment. They are disabilities that the individual was not born with, and which may be ameliorated through better understanding and appropriate early interventions" (Manitoba Education, Training, and Youth, 2001, p. 1.7). Examples of secondary disabilities experienced by individuals with FASD include alcohol- and drug-related problems; mental health problems; aggression; fatigue; frustration; anxiety; fearfulness; rigid, resistant, and argumentative behaviour; family and/or school problems; employment difficulties; and inappropriate sexual behaviour (Manitoba Education, Training, and Youth, 2001; Saskatchewan Learning, 2004).

Due to the variability among individuals diagnosed with FASD, the unique strengths and areas of need of each individual must be considered when planning and implementing interventions.

Interventions for Students with Fetal Alcohol Spectrum Disorder

Individuals with fetal alcohol spectrum disorder have varying strengths and areas of need. Therefore, this section will focus on general strategies that may not only benefit students with fetal alcohol spectrum disorder in the classroom, but other students as well. These strategies include structuring the learning environment, developing effective routines, teaching social and adaptive skills, and helping students generalize new skills and concepts (Alberta Learning, 2004; Manitoba Education, Training, and Youth, 2001; Saskatchewan Learning, 2004). The Personal Spotlight in this chapter on page 218 provides a glimpse of one parent educator's thoughts on the importance of meeting the individual needs of children with fetal alcohol spectrum disorder.

Structuring the Learning Environment Individuals with neurological impairments may react in an atypical manner to their physical environments. For example, an individual with poor sensory processing skills may be overwhelmed by loud noise levels in the classroom environment and react by hiding under the desk or running from the room (Alberta Learning, 2004). "Planning a safe, calm, flexible, efficient instructional setting will make instruction and learning more effective . . . students with FASD benefit from a structured, supportive approach to creating and modifying the learning environment"

FURTHER READING

For more information on addressing student needs, read the article "Teaching students with developmental disabilities: Tips from teens and young adults with fetal alcohol spectrum disorders," found in volume 39, issue 2 of *Teaching Exceptional Children*, 2006.

(Alberta Learning, 2004, p. 27). A calm, quiet environment can be created by reducing ambient noise in the classroom (i.e., carpeting on the floors, rubber bottoms on the legs of chairs and desks). In addition, students' organizational skills and independent work habits can be developed by teaching them to use a daybook to keep track of assignments and school events (Manitoba Education, Training, & Youth, 2001).

Developing Effective Routines Establishing classroom routines can also assist in organizing the classroom environment. As outlined by Alberta Learning (2004), educators can help students develop expectations relating to

> coming into class; interacting with others; requesting teacher attention, permission or assistance; accessing supplies or equipment; maintaining time on task; completing assignments; using unstructured time; requesting choices or alternatives; requesting time to talk to the teacher about something personal; [and] knowing what to do in emergencies. (Alberta Learning, 2004, p. 31).

Examples of strategies that can be used to develop these skills include teaching students to use a checklist to keep track of the steps involved in a routine or teaching students to manage their time (Manitoba Education, Training, & Youth, 2001; Saskatchewan Learning, 2004).

Teaching Social and Adaptive Skills Social skills are any number of skills that facilitate an individual's successful participation in a group, such as conversational turn taking, initiating and closing conversations, and successfully interacting with peers in a variety of settings. An **adaptive behaviour** is a way of conduct that meets the standards of personal independence and social responsibility expected from that cultural and chronological age group. "Students experiencing difficulties with adaptive behaviours and social skills may

- act younger than their chronological age
- have no friends their own age
- play with younger children
- have problems in gym class because they don't follow game rules
- have problems with time management
- be unable to manage their money in age-appropriate ways
- come to school dirty and unkempt
- be naive and gullible
- say inappropriate things or act in ways that disturb others" (Alberta Learning, 2004, p. 83).

Examples of practical strategies for addressing adaptive and social skill deficits include providing supervision and support throughout the school day, preparing students for changes in classroom routine (i.e., giving advance notice of transitions), teaching social skills (i.e., using role plays and social stories), and teaching functional life skills (Alberta Learning, 2004; Manitoba Education, Training, & Youth, 2001).

Generalizing New Skills and Concepts Individuals with neurological impairments may also demonstrate difficulties generalizing new skills and concepts to a variety of settings. Alberta Learning (2004) recommends that educators

> select individual program goals that can be taught across learning situations. Consider all the times throughout the day and the different ways students may be required

FURTHER READING

For more information on effective practices for students with fetal alcohol spectrum disorder, read the document "Planning for students with fetal alcohol spectrum disorders: A guide for Educators" (2004), found on the Saskatchewan Learning website at www.sasked.gov.sk.ca.

✳ Explore

When the Usual Approaches Don't Work

to carry out specific tasks. Give students opportunities to use the same skills and strategies in different settings, and with different teachers and peers. (Alberta Learning, 2004, p. 46)

Educators can enhance a student's ability to generalize new skills and concepts by selecting skills for generalization that are likely to increase a student's independence, to be reinforced in the natural environment, and to be used frequently in a variety of settings (Alberta Learning, 2004; Manitoba Education, Training, & Youth, 2001).

Personal Spotlight

Parent Education Facilitator Sue McCart

As a parent educator, Sue McCart's main duty is providing information, support, and encouragement to parents and guardians of children who are vulnerable. One of the programs Sue facilitates in this capacity is an FASD support group. "I've worked extensively with children with FASD. Many of the parents I work with have also been affected to some degree by prenatal exposure to alcohol. We cannot necessarily assume parents are able to understand, or retain, the information provided them. In the same fashion we accommodate learning differences in children, we must also accommodate differences in parental abilities."

One of the challenges of running a support group for parents and guardians is the diverse areas of strength and need each individual diagnosed with FASD demonstrates. "Students with FASD face challenges in all domains—social, academic, and emotional. Differences in the structural development of the brain mean that students with FASD may have difficulty reaching developmental milestones. They may have memory deficits, they may seem more immature than their peers, and they may have difficulty generalizing learning from one context to another. These are all things we expect of schoolchildren, and they are all things with which children with FASD may have difficulty. One of my pet peeves is people referring to children with FASD as 'bad,' 'unwilling to listen and learn,' or 'obstinate.' If they *could* succeed, they would choose to do so. It is a rare child who wants to be in trouble, to be reprimanded frequently, and to fail in all they attempt. Children with FASD are unable to meet social and educational expectations. As is commonly said by those who work with children with FASD, we (as educators and parents) need to

be able to make the distinction between 'can't' and 'won't.' The child is not choosing to be unsuccessful at school and at home. The alcohol damage to the brain structures means there is no choice involved. They simply cannot do as their more typically achieving peers do."

It is important that educators and other professionals providing support to parents and guardians of children diagnosed with FASD help them find effective ways of working with their children. "Repetition, repetition, repetition—but gently. When we get angry, punish, or criticize the child with FASD, we do not encourage learning. Punishment and criticism will do nothing to heal the damaged brain. By focusing on failures we may, in fact, encourage resistance to learning. By drawing attention to and encouraging what we want, we reinforce desired learning. In order to learn successfully the child may need concrete external reminders (i.e., signs in the classroom or home, timers to signal transitions, a peer-buddy to help them with classroom demands). Children with FASD are often unable to remember instructions of more than a few steps. They are better able to succeed if provided instructions one or two steps at a time. For a typically achieving child it may make sense to repeat requests or instructions only once. For the child with FASD, it makes more sense to patiently repeat expectations or instructions over and over. They learn differently—we must teach differently."

Individuals diagnosed with FASD have unique strengths and areas of need. Therefore, educators will need to tailor intervention strategies to the abilities of the individual students with whom they work.

SUMMARY

- Autism is a pervasive developmental disability that primarily affects social interactions, language, and behaviour.

- Although originally thought to be caused by environmental factors, autism is now considered to be caused by organic factors, including brain damage and complications during pregnancy.

- A dramatic increase in the number of students with ASD has occurred in the past decade.

- Although many of the behavioural characteristics displayed by children with Asperger syndrome are similar to those displayed by children with autism, the former generally have higher cognitive development and more typical communication skills.

- A number of specific interventions have been developed for students with ASD.

- Because the field of ASD has witnessed a number of "miracle cures," it is particularly important that evidence-based interventions be utilized.

- Growing evidence suggests that placing students with autism in general education classrooms results in positive gains.

- Fetal alcohol syndrome (FAS), partial fetal alcohol syndrome (pFAS), alcohol-related birth defects (ARBD), and alcohol-related neurodevelopmental disorder (ARND) are all disorders that may be included under the umbrella term of fetal alcohol spectrum disorder (FASD).

- Definitions of FASD vary among provinces and territories.

- A comprehensive, multidisciplinary assessment is recommended when diagnosing fetal alcohol spectrum disorders.

- Certain patterns or common characteristics that can be associated with FASD are described as primary and secondary disabilities.

Weblinks

Society for Treatment of Autism
www.autism.ca
Autism Treatment Services of Canada, a national affiliation of organizations, provides treatment, education, management, and consultative services to people with autism and related disorders across Canada. Their website provides excellent information about all aspects of autism as well as related resources.

Canadian Autism Intervention Research Network (CAIRN)
www.cairn-site.com
Organization dedicated to generating and disseminating research in the area of autism and to promoting effective and evidenced-based services for Canadian children with autism spectrum disorders.

Canadian Centre on Substance Abuse
http://www.ccsa.ca/Pages/Splash.htm
Site detailing the latest events and information relating to FASD.

Public Health Agency of Canada: Fetal Alcohol Spectrum Disorder
www.phac-aspc.gc.ca/fasd-etcaf/index.html
Portfolio of basic information relating to FASD, what the organization is doing relating to FASD, and resources.

Chapter 9

Teaching Students with Sensory Impairments, Traumatic Brain Injury, and Other Low-Incidence Disabilities

Chapter Objectives

After reading this chapter, you should be able to

- define and describe students with sensory impairments
- define and describe students with traumatic brain injury
- define and describe students with health problems and physical disabilities
- describe various intervention strategies for students with sensory impairments, traumatic brain injury, and other low-incidence disabilities

It was only the end of September, but Ana was already beginning to fall behind most of her Grade 2 peers. Although she had been promoted at the end of Grade 1, she had not acquired most of the skills necessary for success in Grade 2.

For the first half of Grade 1, Ana tried very hard. She wanted to learn to read like her classmates, but seemed always to miss out on sounding letters and words correctly. According to her teacher, Ms. Pryor, Ana also appeared to daydream a lot.

Ms. Pryor frequently had to go to Ana's desk to get her attention when giving directions and assignments. By the middle of Grade 1, Ana seemed to be giving up. Her efforts always fell short. Her spelling was poor, and her reading skills were not improving. She began having behaviour problems, which Ms. Pryor attributed to the influence of her older brother, who was always getting into trouble. Ana's parents were interested but did not have any answers. They said that Ana was in her own world at home and often did not respond to what was happening around her. In addition to Ana's poor academic skills and behaviour problems, she also had difficulties with her peers. She was not very popular, and some of the other students made fun of her poor articulation of certain words.

Ms. James, Ana's new Grade 2 teacher, decided to refer Ana for vision and hearing screening. Sure enough, Ana was found to have a hearing loss in both ears. Although the loss was not significant enough to warrant specialized placement, it did suggest that a hearing aid might be useful.

Thanks to Ms. James's awareness, Ana's hearing loss was detected before she experienced more failure. Unfortunately, she had missed much of what she should have learned during Grade 1 and Kindergarten, probably because of the hearing impairment.

Questions to Consider

1. Should schools routinely screen Kindergarten and Grade 1 students for hearing and vision problems? Why or why not?

2. What can Ana's Grade 2 teacher do to help her overcome the problems created by the late identification of her hearing impairment?

INTRODUCTION

The previous chapter dealt with students with autism and fetal alcohol spectrum disorders, typically considered low-incidence exceptionalities. In addition to these two categories of exceptionality, many other conditions that occur relatively rarely in children can result in significant challenges for students, their families, school personnel, and other professionals. These conditions include hearing impairments, visual impairments, traumatic brain injury (TBI), and a host of physical and health problems that may be present in school-age children, such as cerebral palsy, spina bifida, AIDS, cystic fibrosis, epilepsy, and diabetes.

Many general education classroom teachers teach their entire careers without encountering children with these problems. However, because students with these kinds of conditions may be included in their future classrooms, all teachers need to generally understand the conditions and how to support these students in the classroom. Often, schools provide support personnel for teachers who have students with these types of conditions. Therefore, teachers should not have to "go it alone" when working with students with these exceptionalities. Behavioural specialists, psychologists, physical therapists, occupational therapists, and other health personnel are often available to provide services to students and supports to their teachers. The fact that many different professionals provide services for some of these children may have repercussions for students of certain

CONSIDER THIS

What are some problems that may be encountered by general classroom teachers with which specialists could provide assistance?

cultural backgrounds. Individuals from some cultures, for example, prefer to interact with only one person at a time, rather than with a team of individuals. Professionals providing services must be sensitive to the cultural traits that characterize different families and should consider the unique characteristics of each student's cultural background.

It is impossible to describe every single condition experienced by children with low-incidence disabilities. Though this chapter will discuss the more well-known conditions and some that are unique and interesting, the conditions described here do not form an exhaustive list. Rather, they cover only a small range of the problems experienced within these groups. In addition, the classroom suggestions discussed in this chapter are general suggestions. Teachers will need to consider individuals' unique areas of strength and need as they adapt these strategies for use in their classrooms.

SENSORY IMPAIRMENTS

The category of sensory impairments includes hearing impairments and visual impairments. Students with sensory impairments may be at a distinct disadvantage in academic settings because of the extent to which both hearing and vision are used in teaching and learning. Stop and think about the things you do in class; nearly all of them include visual or auditory activities. Having limitations in these areas can cause substantial difficulties in the teaching and learning process.

As with all students with special needs, there remains some debate regarding the best setting in which to provide services to students with visual and hearing impairments. Whereas many students with sensory impairments were historically served in residential settings, today most of these students are placed in general education settings. While most of them are capable of handling the academic and social demands of these settings, a variety of adaptations and accommodations may be needed, ranging from minor seating adjustments to the use of sophisticated equipment for communicating, listening, or navigating in order for them to be successful (Freiberg, 2005). Students with these impairments may also need the support of additional personnel (e.g., a sign language interpreter or Braille instructor).

In order to provide appropriate adaptations and accommodations, teachers must have accurate information about how to modify their classrooms and adapt instruction to meet students' needs. In addition, they need to understand the psychosocial aspects of these types of exceptionalities. For some students with severe sensory problems, special consultants may be needed to assist general education teachers. Ultimately, teachers must feel comfortable and confident that they can address the range of needs these students present.

Sensory impairments are considered low-incidence exceptionalities since there are not large numbers of students with these conditions in the school population. The number of students (aged 6 to 21) with hearing or visual impairments who were officially identified and provided with special education or related services in the United States for the school year 2001–2002 was only 97 067. This is a small number, considering the total number of students in this age range. Furthermore, these groups represent a tiny percentage of all students who have exceptionalities. However, having a student with a sensory impairment in a classroom may seem overwhelming, as this student may require a variety of modifications in classroom management and in certain instructional practices. Students who have both vision and hearing losses present significant challenges for educators.

Basic Concepts about Hearing Impairment

Hearing impairment is a hidden disability—an observer typically cannot tell from looking at physical features alone that a person's hearing is impaired. However, in any context where communicative skills are needed, hearing limitations become evident.

Students with a hearing impairment pose a variety of challenges to the general classroom teacher. When students with profound hearing loss are placed in general education classes, they may need a variety of accommodations, including a sign language interpreter and technological supports (i.e., a classroom amplification system).

Students who have some degree of hearing loss (i.e., mild to severe) can function in general education settings more easily when certain adaptations and accommodations are provided. In order to achieve this success, it is critical for teachers to understand the nature of hearing impairments and to know how to address the needs associated with these conditions. Other students may have a minimal hearing loss; in other words, hearing loss that is not severe enough to make them eligible for special education services, but that puts them at a distinct disadvantage in the general education classroom if the teacher does not recognize their problem (Kaderavek & Pakulski, 2002). Students who have cochlear implants may also be included in the regular classroom.

The importance of language acquisition and usage to the development of cognitive abilities and achievement in academic subject areas is unassailable (Polloway, Miller, & Smith, 2003). While the greatest effect of a hearing impairment is on a student's ability to hear someone speak, "its impact on communication development dramatically alters social and academic skill acquisition" (Brackett, 1997, p. 355). Language is a dominant consideration when discussing appropriate education for students with hearing losses (Mayer, Akamatsu, & Stewart, 2002).

The following sections provide basic information on hearing impairments. Teachers who build a solid working knowledge in this area can teach more effectively and can communicate more clearly with families of, and other professionals working with, students with varying degrees of hearing loss.

Hearing Impairment Defined The fact that a number of different terms are associated with hearing loss often causes confusion. Three terms in particular are frequently encountered in print and professional conversation: **hearing impairment**, **deafness**, and **hard of hearing**.

1. *Hearing impairment* is the generic term that has frequently been used to cover the entire range of hearing loss.

2. *Deafness* describes hearing loss that is so severe that speech cannot be understood through the ear alone, with or without aids.

3. *Hard of hearing* describes individuals who have a hearing loss that makes it difficult, but not impossible, to understand speech through the ear alone, with or without a hearing aid. (Moores, 2001)

More detailed definitions of the terms *deaf* and *hard of hearing* are provided by the American Speech-Language-Hearing Association (ASHA). ASHA defines *deaf* as "a hearing disorder that limits an individual's aural/oral communication performance to the extent that the primary sensory input for communication may be other than the auditory channel," whereas the term *hard of hearing* is defined as "a hearing disorder, whether fluctuating or permanent, which adversely affects an individual's ability to communicate. The hard-of-hearing individual relies on the auditory channel as the primary sensory input for communication" (ASHA, 1993). ASHA's (1993) definition of *deaf* is supported by the Canadian Association of the Deaf (CAD), whose position is that "deafness is medically defined by the extent of loss of functional hearing and by dependence upon visual communication" (CAD, 2002).

Hearing loss is often measured in decibel (dB) loss. Individuals with losses from 25 to 90 dB are considered hard of hearing, whereas those with losses greater than 90 dB are classified as profoundly hearing impaired. Minimal hearing loss, which can also cause problems for students, is defined as a loss between 16 and 25 dB (Kaderavek & Pakulski, 2002).

Classification of Hearing Impairment Hearing loss can be categorized in several different ways. Typically, a hearing loss is described by three attributes: the type of hearing loss, the degree of the hearing loss (e.g., minimal to profound), and the configuration of the hearing loss (e.g., flat, sloping, reverse, bilateral or unilateral, fluctuating or stable) (ASHA, 2004b). When describing hearing loss in terms of the part of the auditory system that is damaged, there are three types: conductive hearing loss, sensorineural hearing loss, and mixed hearing loss (Northern & Downs, 2002). Table 9.1 summarizes the audiological, communicational, and educational implications for each type of loss. **Conductive hearing loss**

> *occurs when sound is not conducted efficiently through the outer and middle ears, including the ear canal, eardrum, and the tiny bones, or ossicles, of the middle ear. Conductive hearing loss usually involves a reduction in sound level, or the ability to hear faint sounds. This type of hearing loss can often be corrected through medicine or surgery.* (ASHA, 2004b)

For example, conductive loss may be the result of impacted ear wax (**cerumen**), a buildup of fluid in the middle ear, or ear infections. The most common type of hearing loss in children is **otitis media** (ASHA, 2004b). "Otitis media is an inflammation of the middle ear (the area behind the ear drum) that is usually associated with the build up of fluid. The fluid may or may not be infected. Symptoms, severity, frequency, and length of the condition vary" (ASHA, 2004b). A buildup of fluid in the middle ear, whether infected or not, typically results in **fluctuating hearing loss.** This type of loss may adversely impact speech and language development in young children, since children would be missing out on speech and language models and experiences (e.g., missing fragments of what was said by a speaker). Fluctuating hearing loss may also severely impact academic achievement in school-age children. For example, students may not always hear verbal exchanges taking place during teacher and peer interactions, and may therefore receive only part of the information that was presented or discussed in the classroom.

A second type of hearing loss is **sensorineural hearing loss**. Sensorineural hearing loss

> *occurs when there is damage to the inner ear (**cochlea**).... Sensorineural hearing loss involves a reduction in sound level, or ability to hear faint sounds, but also affects speech understanding or ability to hear clearly. . . . Sensorineural hearing loss cannot be corrected medically or surgically. It is a permanent loss.* (ASHA, 2004b)

For example, sensorineural hearing loss may be the result of an injury sustained at birth or due to genetic syndromes, viruses, head trauma, aging, exposure to noise, or tumours

Table 9.1 Symptoms Associated with Conductive Hearing Loss; Unilateral Hearing Loss; Mild Bilateral Sensorineural Hearing Loss; and Moderate-to-Severe Bilateral Sensorineural Hearing Loss

	Audiological	Communicative	Educational
Conductive Hearing Loss	■ Hearing loss 30 dB (range 10–50 dB) ■ Poor auditory reception ■ Degraded and inconsistent speech signal ■ Difficulty understanding under adverse listening conditions ■ Impaired speech discrimination ■ Hearing loss overlays developmental requirement for greater stimulus intensity before infants can respond to and discriminate between speech ■ Inability to organize auditory information consistently	■ Difficulty forming linguistic categories (plurals, tense) ■ Difficulty in differentiating word boundaries, phoneme boundaries ■ Receptive language delay ■ Expressive language delay ■ Cognitive delay	■ Lower achievement test scores ■ Lower verbal IQ ■ Poorer reading and spelling performance ■ Higher frequency of enrolment in special support classes in school ■ Lower measures of social maturity
Unilateral Hearing Loss	■ Hearing loss moderate to profound ■ Impaired auditory localization ■ Difficulty understanding speech in presence of competing noise ■ Loss of binaural advantage: binaural summation, binaural release from masking	■ Tasks involving language concepts may be depressed	■ Lags in academic achievement: reading, spelling, arithmetic ■ Verbally based learning difficulties ■ High rate of grade repetition ■ Self-described: embarrassment, annoyance, confusion, helplessness ■ Less independence in the classroom
Mild Bilateral Sensorineural Hearing Loss	■ Hearing loss 15–20 dB ■ Speech recognition depressed ■ Auditory discrimination depressed ■ Amplification considered: FM systems, classroom amplification	■ Potential problems in articulation ■ Problems in auditory attention ■ Problems in auditory memory ■ Problems in auditory comprehension ■ Possible delays in expressive oral language ■ Impact on syntax and semantics	■ Impact on vocabulary development ■ Lowered academic achievement: arithmetic problem solving, math concepts, vocabulary, reading comprehension ■ Educational delays progress systematically with age

(continued)

Table 9.1 Continued

	Audiological	Communicative	Educational
Moderate-to-Severe Bilateral Sensorineural Hearing Loss	■ Hearing loss 41–90 dB ■ Noise and reverberation significantly affect listening and understanding ■ Audiologic management: essentials, amplification recommendations, monitor hearing for: –otitis media –sudden changes in hearing –progressive hearing loss	■ Deficits in speech perception ■ Deficits in speech production (mild-to-moderate articulation problems) ■ Language deficits from slight to significant: syntax, morphology, semantics, pragmatics ■ Vocabulary deficits	■ Slight to significant deficits in literacy (reading and writing) ■ Deficits in academic achievement ■ High rate of academic failure ■ Immaturity ■ Feelings of isolation and exclusion ■ Special education supports needed

From "Hearing Loss and Its Effect," by A. O. Diefendorf. In *Hearing Care for Children*, edited by F. N. Martin and J. G. Clark, 1996, p. 5. Boston: Allyn & Bacon. Used with permission.

(ASHA, 2004b). As with conductive hearing loss, sensorineural hearing loss can adversely impact a child's speech and language development and academic achievement.

A third type of hearing loss is **mixed hearing loss**. Mixed hearing loss occurs when both conductive and sensorineural hearing loss are present (Northern & Downs, 2002).

A disorder that is associated with hearing loss but that is typically present in individuals without a hearing impairment is **auditory processing disorder** (APD). Auditory processing disorder (APD)

> *may be broadly defined as a deficit in the processing of information that is specific to the auditory modality. The problem may be exacerbated in unfavourable acoustic environments. It may be associated with difficulties in listening, speech understanding, language development, and learning. In its pure form, however, it is conceptualized as a deficit in the processing of auditory input.* (Abel, S., cited in Jerger & Musiek, 2000, p. 468)

FURTHER READING

To learn more about the similarities between auditory processing disorders and attention deficit/hyperactivity disorders (ADD and AD/HD), refer to the document "Introduction to Auditory Processing Disorders" on the Minnesota Department of Education's website, http://www.education.state.mn.us/mdeprod/groups/SpecialEd/documents/Instruction/001567.pdf.

For example, an auditory processing disorder may be the result of head trauma, stroke, or congenital brain damage "that can cause problems understanding what is being said, even though sensorineural and conductive hearing is normal" (Flexer, 1999, p. 69). A child with an auditory processing disorder may have difficulty understanding speech or directions (especially in environments in which there is excessive activity and noise), decoding letters, or sound blending or spelling, or may seem to "mishear" and substitute similar-sounding words (Minnesota Department of Education, 2003). Although auditory processing disorders and attention deficit/hyperactivity disorders are two separate disorders, they possess similar characteristics (e.g., inattentive, distracted). It is important to note that the two can occur independently or can co-exist (Keller & Tillery, 2002).

Prevalence and Causes of Hearing Impairment In Canada, "the prevalence of permanent childhood hearing impairment is about 1 per 1 000 live births in infancy for impairment greater than 40 dBHL in the better ear. In infants with documented risk factors such as extreme prematurity, congenital facial auricular defects or severe jaundice, this rate is up to 10 per 1 000" (Public Health Agency of Canada, 2005, p. xii). Only about 0.14 percent of school-age children are served in special education programs for students with hearing impairments. Hearing impairments become more prevalent as individuals get older, so the number of people experiencing hearing loss in the total population is higher than the number found in schools. It is estimated that between 2 and 5 percent of the total population has some degree of hearing loss.

In the United States, significant hearing impairments affect approximately 3–4 of every 1000 births (Hear-It.org, 2006). Approximately 71 200 students are served in special education programs for students with hearing impairments. This figure represents only about 0.11 percent of the total U.S. school population (U.S. Department of Education, 2003).

Many different factors can lead to hearing impairments. These include genetic causes (Hear-It.org, 2006); developmental anomalies (Clark & Jaindl, 1996); toxic reaction to drugs, infections, prematurity, and Rh incompatibility (Moores, 2001); birth trauma (Chase, Hall, & Werkhaven, 1996); allergies (Lang, 1998); and noise-induced hearing loss (Haller & Montgomery, 2004). Knowing the specific cause of a hearing impairment is usually not important for school personnel, since the cause rarely affects interventions needed by students.

Characteristics of Students with Hearing Impairment The characteristics of students with hearing impairment vary greatly. Table 9.1 lists characteristics associated with types and degrees of hearing losses. Four categories of characteristics are especially meaningful to the classroom setting: (1) psychological, (2) communicational, (3) social-emotional, and (4) academic. Specific characteristics that fall into each of these general categories are presented in Table 9.2.

Identification, Assessment, and Eligibility The ease of identifying students with hearing impairment is related to the degree of hearing loss. Students with severe losses are more easily recognized, while those with mild losses may go unrecognized for many years or even their entire school career (Kaderavek & Pakulski, 2002). Teachers should be aware of certain indicators of possible hearing loss and refer students who show these signs for a comprehensive assessment (e.g., turns head to position an ear in the direction of the speaker; asks for information to be repeated frequently; uses a loud voice when speaking; pulls or presses on ear; has frequent colds, earaches, or infections) (Kaderavek & Pakulski, 2002; Moores, 2001; Stewart & Kluwin, 2001).

CONSIDER THIS

Is it important for teachers to know the type of hearing loss experienced by a student? Why or why not?

CROSS REFERENCE

Review the etiological sections of chapters 3 through 9 and compare the causes of hearing impairments and other exceptionalities. There are many common factors.

TEACHING TIP

Teachers should keep records of students who display these types of behaviours to determine if there is a pattern that might call for a referral.

Individuals identified with multisensory impairments present a variety of characteristics.

Table 9.2 Possible Characteristics of Students with Hearing Impairments

Area of Functioning	Possible Effects
Psychological	■ Intellectual ability range similar to hearing peers ■ Problems with certain conceptualizations
Communicational	■ Poor speech production (e.g., unintelligibility) ■ Tested vocabulary limited ■ Problems with language usage and comprehension, particularly abstract topics ■ Voice quality problems
Social–Emotional	■ Less socially mature ■ Difficulty making friends ■ Withdrawn behaviour—feelings of being an outsider ■ Possible maladjustment problems ■ May resent having to wear a hearing aid or use other amplification devices ■ May be dependent on teacher assistance
Academic	■ Achievement levels significantly below those of their hearing peers ■ Reading ability most significantly affected ■ Spelling problems ■ Limited written language production ■ Discrepancy between capabilities and performance in many academic areas

FURTHER READING

Health Canada has developed guidelines for hearing detection and intervention in Canada. To review the document "Early Hearing and Communication Development: Canadian Working Group on Childhood Hearing (CWGCH) Resource Document" (2005), visit the Public Health Agency of Canada's website at http://publications.gc.ca/site/eng/270385/publication.html.

A teacher's careful observations and referral can spare a student months or years of struggle and frustration. While all students referred will not be found to have a significant hearing loss, they should be referred nonetheless so that an assessment can be made to determine which students need additional supports.

Formal Assessment   The assessment of hearing ability requires an **audiologist** to use various audiological techniques (i.e., **pure-tone audiometry**, bone conduction testing, and tympanometry screening). An audiologist is a professional who assesses hearing difficulties, selects and fits hearing aids, designs and implements rehabilitation strategies for hearing-impaired clients, and consults regarding hearing conservation and noise exposure (CASLPA, 2004).

Informal Assessment   In addition to the formal assessment conducted by audiologists, teachers and other school personnel should engage in informal assessment of students, especially those suspected of having a hearing impairment. Informal assessment focuses on observing students for signs that might indicate a hearing loss. Tables 9.1 and 9.2 list indicators that, if recorded over a period of time, demonstrate that a student may need formal assessment.

Eligibility The eligibility of students for special education and related services is determined by provincial and territorial guidelines, which are based on certain levels of decibel loss. Teachers should not be concerned about specific eligibility criteria, but should refer students who display characteristics suggesting the presence of hearing loss to an audiologist for evaluation.

Strategies for Curriculum and Instruction for Students with Hearing Impairments

Students with hearing impairments may present a significant challenge for general education teachers. Language is such an important component of instruction that students who have problems processing language because of hearing loss make it difficult for teachers to use standard instructional methods effectively. Teachers have to rely on the supports provided by special education staff and specialists in hearing impairments to assist them in meeting the needs of these students.

Realities of the General Education Classroom Students with hearing impairments vary greatly in their need for supports in the general education classroom. Students with mild losses, generally classified as hard of hearing, typically need minimal supports if amplification can enable them to hear clearly.

Students with severe hearing impairments—i.e., those classified as deaf—present unique challenges to teachers. Specialized instructional techniques usually involve alternative communication methods; the use of interpreters is typically a necessity for these students (see Figure 9.1). Therefore, general education teachers may need to know how to utilize the services of an interpreter to facilitate the success of students with significant hearing losses. They must remember, however, that interpreters are providers of a related service; they are typically not teachers (Heath, 2006).

Continuum of Placement Options Students with hearing impairments are educated in the complete continuum of placement options, depending on their individual needs. These options range from general education classrooms to residential schools for the deaf. The topic of educational placement for students with hearing impairments has been the most controversial aspect of educating this group of students. As with all students with exceptionalities, there is no single educational setting that is best for all students with hearing impairments. The placement decision for students with hearing impairments should be based on the unique needs of the individual student. Figure 9.2 describes the types of supports that students with hearing impairments will need in inclusive settings.

Classroom Adaptations and Accommodations for Students with Hearing Impairments

As mentioned earlier, the general education setting is appropriate for most students who are hard of hearing and for many students who are deaf. However, this statement is true only if the specific needs of these students are taken into consideration. For example, seating is the major consideration related to the physical setup of the classroom. Teachers need to ensure that students are seated to maximize the use of their **residual hearing** or to have an unobstructed view of an interpreter. Information presented visually is extremely helpful to these students; they need to be positioned to take advantage of all visual cues.

TEACHING TIP

Children will have limited benefit from language-learning experiences if they are experiencing hearing difficulties. Refer any child you suspect of having hearing problems to an audiologist for a complete assessment.

FURTHER READING

Refer to the ASHA website (www.asha.org) and the **Canadian Association of Speech-Language Pathology and Audiology (CASLPA)** website (www.caslpa.ca) for more information on hearing loss and its impact on speech and language development.

CONSIDER THIS

How do educational needs differ for a student with a mild hearing loss who can effectively use a hearing aid and a typically achieving student?

◉ Watch

Hearing Impairment

CROSS REFERENCE

Review the discussion of the continuum of placement options for students with all exceptionalities in chapter 2.

CONSIDER THIS

What are some obvious advantages and disadvantages to the different placement options for students with hearing impairments?

Figure 9.1 Interpreters in Educational Settings

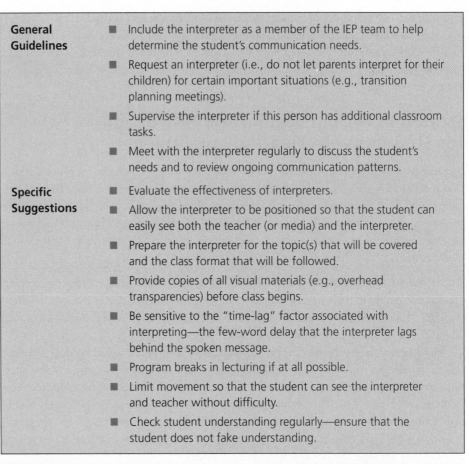

General Guidelines	■ Include the interpreter as a member of the IEP team to help determine the student's communication needs.
	■ Request an interpreter (i.e., do not let parents interpret for their children) for certain important situations (e.g., transition planning meetings).
	■ Supervise the interpreter if this person has additional classroom tasks.
	■ Meet with the interpreter regularly to discuss the student's needs and to review ongoing communication patterns.
Specific Suggestions	■ Evaluate the effectiveness of interpreters.
	■ Allow the interpreter to be positioned so that the student can easily see both the teacher (or media) and the interpreter.
	■ Prepare the interpreter for the topic(s) that will be covered and the class format that will be followed.
	■ Provide copies of all visual materials (e.g., overhead transparencies) before class begins.
	■ Be sensitive to the "time-lag" factor associated with interpreting—the few-word delay that the interpreter lags behind the spoken message.
	■ Program breaks in lecturing if at all possible.
	■ Limit movement so that the student can see the interpreter and teacher without difficulty.
	■ Check student understanding regularly—ensure that the student does not fake understanding.

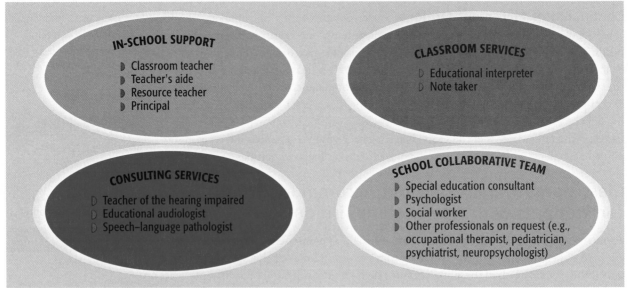

Figure 9.2 Types of Supports for Students with Hearing Impairments in Inclusive Settings

From "Educational Management of Children with Hearing Loss," (p. 306) by C. Edwards. In *Hearing Care for Children*, edited by F.N. Martin and J.G. Clark, 1996, Boston: Allyn & Bacon. Used with permission.

Teaching Science to Students Who Are Hearing Impaired

The following are several suggestions on how to give better individual attention in teaching science to students who are hearing impaired:

1. Individualize assignments so that students progress at their own rate and at the end of the period hand in what they have accomplished. This may be a laboratory or written assignment.

2. Extend special recognition to a student who goes beyond minimum acceptance level for doing and formulating a laboratory investigation.

3. Use multiple resources, including texts, in class. If a student has difficulty reading one text, endeavour to find another or attempt to help him or her learn the material in ways other than through books.

4. Offer special activities for the academically talented. Let them assist you in preparing solutions and materials for laboratory work. They should gain experiences that are educationally desirable.

5. Encourage students to do research. They should consult with a scientist or engineer in the community on their research problem. Local industries, museums, zoos, botanical gardens, and hospitals have resource people who will often help.

6. Have students from the upper grades go to some of the lower grades and demonstrate a scientific principle or explain a science project. This approach has the advantage of giving recognition to the older students while motivating the younger students to greater achievement.

7. Encourage parents to obtain books and to take trips advantageous to science students. Parents often welcome a suggestion from the teacher about books and types of trips to help enrich their children's science education.

Teachers must also carefully plan ahead to deliver instruction in a way that will benefit students with hearing impairments. For example: allow students to move about the classroom to position themselves for participation in ongoing events, ensure that adequate lighting is available to maximize students' view of facial and body cues (e.g., peers, teacher, interpreter), and use co-operative learning arrangements to facilitate student involvement with hearing peers. Teaching secondary-level content classes to students with hearing impairments is uniquely challenging. The Inclusion Strategies feature provides suggestions for teaching science to students who are hearing impaired. Specific suggestions related to grouping, lesson planning, materials acquisition and adaptation, and homework systems can be found in chapter 14.

Technology   Technology has been beneficial for individuals with hearing impairments (Stewart & Kluwin, 2001). Simple strategies, such as using closed-captioned movies, are important (Wurst, Jones, & Luckner, 2005). Students with hearing impairments placed in general education classrooms often use devices to help them to maximize their communicational abilities, and they need a supportive environment in which to use them. Teachers need a working knowledge of these devices so that they can ensure that students benefit from the equipment.

Assistive Listening Devices   Assistive listening devices (ALDs) include hearing aids and other devices that amplify voices and sounds, communicate messages visually, or alert users to environmental sounds (Marschark, Lang, & Albertini, 2002). Hearing aids are the predominant ALDs found in schools. These devices pick up sound with a microphone, amplify and filter it, and then convey that sound into the ear canal through a loudspeaker, also called a receiver (Marschark et al., 2002). They work very well with students who experience

FURTHER READING

Read more about the oral and sign language education debate in James MacDougall's article "Irreconcilable Differences: The Education of Deaf Children in Canada," in volume 44, issue 1 of *Education Canada*, 2004.

FURTHER READING

In order to learn more about cochlear implants, refer to Moore and Teagle's article "An Introduction to Cochlear Implant Technology, Activation, and Programming," in volume 33 of *Language, Speech, and Hearing Services in Schools*, 2002 (pp. 153–161).

mild-to-severe hearing loss. Increasingly, some profoundly hearing impaired students are receiving cochlear implants: "Cochlear implants are electronic devices that contain a current source and an electrode array that is implanted into the cochlea; [an] electrical current is then used to stimulate the surviving auditory nerve fibres" (ASHA, 2004c, p. 1).

This information should provide teachers with a beginning understanding of how to meet the needs of students with hearing loss. We strongly recommend that teachers consult with hearing specialists (e.g., an audiologist, hearing consultant, or teacher of the deaf) to determine the best possible adaptations or accommodations to provide an appropriate educational environment for students with hearing problems.

Supports for the General Education Teacher Students with hearing impairments often create major challenges for general classroom teachers, primarily because of the language barrier that hearing loss often creates. Therefore, teachers must rely on support personnel, such as educational consultants who specialize in the area of hearing impairment; interpreters; audiologists; speech-language pathologists; interpreters; and medical personnel to assist them in their efforts to provide appropriate educational programs (Hanks & Velaski, 2003).

Basic Concepts about Visual Impairment

Students with visual impairments also pose unique challenges to teachers in general education classrooms. Although the number of students whose vision creates learning-related problems is not large, having even one such student in a classroom may require a host of adaptations and accommodations.

Vision plays a critical role in the development of concepts, the understanding of spatial relations, and the use of printed material. In fact, "vision is intimately involved with 70% to 80% of all tasks that occur in our educational programs" (Li, 2004, p. 39). Thus, children with visual problems have unique educational needs. For students whose vision is limited, teachers have to use alternative teaching strategies, modified materials, and technology (Downing & Chen, 2003). Teachers may be able to use their usual instructional techniques with some modifications with students who have some functional vision, but for students who have very little or no vision, alternative techniques will need to be implemented to provide effective educational programs.

General education classes are appropriate settings for many students with visual impairments. However, teachers working with these students need to understand the nature of a particular student's vision problem to be able to choose appropriate adaptive or accommodative tactics. They need basic information related to four categories: (1) fundamental concepts of vision and visual impairment, (2) signs of possible visual problems, (3) typical characteristics of students with visual problems, and (4) specific adaptive and accommodative techniques for meeting student needs.

Visual Impairments Defined A number of different terms are associated with the concept of visual impairment; confusion regarding the exact meaning of visual terminology is often a problem. These are the most frequently used terms and their definitions:

1. *Visual impairment* is a generic term that includes a wide range of visual problems.
2. **Blindness** has different meanings depending upon context, resulting in some confusion. *Legal blindness* refers to a person's visual acuity and field of vision. It is defined as

a visual acuity of 20/200 or less in the person's better eye after correction, or a field of vision of 20 degrees or less. An educational definition of blindness implies that a student must use **Braille** (a system of raised dots that the student reads tactilely) or aural methods in order to receive instruction (Freiberg, 2005).

3. *Low vision* indicates that some functional vision exists to be used for gaining information through written means with or without the assistance of optical, nonoptical, or electronic devices (Freiberg, 2005).

Students with low vision are capable of handling the demands of most classroom settings, but will need some modifications to perform successfully. Students who are blind (i.e., have very little or no vision) will need major adaptations or accommodations to be successful in general education settings.

Classification of Visual Impairments Visual problems can be categorized in a number of ways. One typical method organizes them as refractive errors (e.g., farsightedness, nearsightedness, and astigmatism); retinal disorders; disorders of the cornea, iris, and lens; and optic nerve problems. In addition to common refractive problems, which usually can be improved with corrective lenses, other visual problems include the following:

- *strabismus*—improper alignment of the eyes
- *nystagmus*—rapid involuntary movements of the eye
- *glaucoma*—fluid pressure buildup in the eye
- *cataract*—cloudy film over the lens of the eye
- *diabetic retinopathy*—changes in the blood vessels of the eye caused by diabetes
- *macular degeneration*—damage to the central portion of the retina, causing central vision loss
- *retinitis pigmentosa*—genetic eye disease leading to total blindness. (Smith 2007)

Tunnel vision denotes a condition caused by deterioration of parts of the retina, which leaves the person with central vision only. Individuals who have tunnel vision can see as if they are looking through a long tube; they have little or no peripheral vision.

Regardless of the cause of the visual problem, educators primarily have to deal with its functional result. Educators focus on "what experiences a child needs in order to be able to learn" (Freiberg, 2005, p. 133). Whether the student has usable residual vision is an important issue, as is the time at which the vision problem developed. Students who are born with significant visual loss may have a much more difficult time understanding some concepts and developing basic skills than students who lose their vision after they have established certain concepts.

Prevalence and Causes of Visual Impairments Vision problems are common in our society. Fortunately, corrective lenses allow most individuals to see very efficiently. However, many individuals have vision problems that cannot be corrected this way. As with hearing impairments, the number of people with visual impairments increases with age. In the school-age population, approximately 0.06 percent of students are classified as visually impaired. In Canada, only approximately 9.2 percent of children 0 to 14 years of age identified with an exceptionality have vision difficulties (Statistics Canada, 2002). According to the Canadian National Institute for the Blind (CNIB, 1999), the prevalence rates vary by region, with First Nations peoples at increased risk of visual impairments both in youth and with age due to premature birth, trauma, and diabetes. Dr. Farrell, a member of the board of directors of the CNIB, states, "The risk of vision loss is three to four times greater in First Nations Peoples than it is in the general population."

Etiological factors associated with visual impairments include genetic causes, physical trauma, infections, premature birth, anoxia, and retinal degeneration. *Retrolental fibroplasia* (RLF) was a common cause of blindness in the early 1950s, resulting when premature infants were exposed to too much oxygen in incubators. Once the cause of this problem was understood, it became nearly nonexistent. However, this cause of blindness is reasserting itself as medical science faces the challenge of providing care to infants born more and more prematurely. Blindness sometimes accompanies very premature birth.

Characteristics of Students with Visual Impairments The most educationally relevant characteristic of students who have visual impairments is the extent of their visual efficiency. More specific characteristics can be categorized as psychological, communicational, academic, and social-emotional, as presented in Table 9.3. In a recent study of the physical activity level of students with visual impairments, it was determined that this group has low levels of physical activity for a variety of reasons (Ayvazoglu, Oh, & Kozub, 2006).

Identification, Assessment, and Eligibility Students with visual impairments can be easily identified if their visual loss is severe. However, many students have milder losses that are much more difficult to identify and may go several years without being recognized. Teachers must be aware of behaviours that could indicate a vision problem. Figure 9.3 summarizes possible symptoms.

FURTHER READING

Refer to the CNIB's website for more information on visual impairments and the products and services that are available for individuals who are visually impaired (www.cnib.ca).

Table 9.3 Possible Characteristics of Students with Visual Impairments

Area of Functioning	Possible Effects
Psychological	▪ Intellectual abilities similar to those of sighted peers
	▪ Concept development can depend on tactile experiences (i.e., synthetic and analytic touch)
	▪ Unable to use sight to assist in the development of integrated concepts
	▪ Unable to use visual imagery
Communicational	▪ Relatively unimpaired in language abilities
Social/Emotional/ Behavioural	▪ May display repetitive, stereotyped movements (e.g., rocking or rubbing eyes)
	▪ Socially immature
	▪ Withdrawn
	▪ Dependent
	▪ Unable to use nonverbal cues
Mobility	▪ Distinct disadvantage in using spatial information
	▪ Visual imagery and memory problems with functional implications
Academic	▪ Generally behind sighted peers

Behaviour	■ Rubs eyes excessively
	■ Shuts or covers one eye, tilts head, or thrusts head forward
	■ Has difficulty in reading or in other work requiring close use of the eyes
	■ Blinks more than usual or is irritable when doing close work
	■ Holds books close to eyes
	■ Is unable to see distant things clearly
	■ Squints eyelids together or frowns
Appearance	■ Crossed eyes
	■ Red-rimmed, encrusted, or swollen eyelids
	■ Inflamed or watery eyes
	■ Recurring sties
Complaints	■ Eyes that itch, burn, or feel scratchy
	■ Cannot see well
	■ Dizziness, headaches, or nausea following close eye work
	■ Blurred or double vision

Figure 9.3 Symptoms of Possible Vision Problems

From *Exceptional Learners: Introduction to Special Education* (9th ed., p. 343), by D.P. Hallahan and J M. Kauffman, 2003, Boston: Allyn & Bacon. Used with permission.

Formal Assessment   Students are screened for vision problems in schools, and when problems are suspected, a more in-depth evaluation is conducted. The typical eye examination assesses two dimensions: visual acuity and field of vision. Visual acuity is most often evaluated by the use of a **Snellen chart**. As Salvia and Ysseldyke (2004) note, two versions of this chart are available: the traditional version, using alphabetic letters of different sizes, and a version that uses the letter *E* presented in different spatial arrangements and sizes. While these charts can effectively determine the likelihood of children having vision problems, they might not detect near vision problems.

Once students are identified as having possible vision problems, they should be referred for more extensive evaluations. **Ophthalmologists**, medical doctors, and **optometrists** (who specialize in evaluating vision and prescribing glasses) are typically involved in this more extensive evaluation. These specialists determine the specific nature and extent of any vision problem.

Still other formal assessments of vision focus on the ability of students to use their vision. Examples of these types of assessments include functional-vision assessment and learning-media assessment. The learning-media assessment determines: (1) the efficiency with which students gather information from sensory modalities, (2) the types of learning media used by students, and (3) the media used for reading and writing (Salvia & Ysseldyke, 2004).

Informal Assessment   A great deal of informal assessment should be completed by school personnel. As with students with hearing impairments, the informal assessment of students with visual impairments focuses on observation. Teachers and other school personnel note behaviours that might indicate a vision loss or change in the child's vision. Once students are identified as having a problem, school personnel must be alert to any changes in the student's visual abilities.

TEACHING TIP

For students who are not doing well in their academic work and who display some of these symptoms, conduct a functional visual screening to determine if the child should be referred for more formal screening (see Figure 9.3).

Eligibility In Canada, students with a 20/200 acuity or worse in the better eye with best correction are identified as blind, whereas those with a visual acuity of 20/70 to 20/200 are considered to have low vision.

Strategies for Curriculum and Instruction for Students with Visual Impairments

Even though students with visual impairments learn similarly to their sighted peers (Bosman, Gompel, Vervloed, & van Bon, 2006), their inability to process information efficiently visually results in their needing specific curricular and instructional adaptations or accommodations. For students with low vision, these modifications may simply mean enlarging printed materials to sufficient size so that the student can see them. For students with little or no vision, modifications must be more extensive.

Realities of the General Education Classroom Students with visual impairments present a range of needs. Those who are capable of reading print, with provided support, often require minimal curricular changes; those who must read using Braille require significant changes. Teachers should remember that even students who are capable of reading print may need adaptations and accommodations in many day-to-day activities. These may be as simple as ensuring appropriate contrast in printed materials and having students sit in a place that will optimize their vision.

Continuum of Placement Options As with students with hearing impairments, students with visual problems may be placed anywhere on the full continuum of placement options, ranging from general education classrooms to residential schools for students with visual impairments. Although some blind students function very well in general education settings, many are placed in residential schools where they receive more extensive services.

Classroom Adaptations for Students with Visual Impairments

Certain classroom adaptations and accommodations will enhance the quality of programs for students with visual problems. This section recommends ways to address the needs of these students, organized according to five categories: general considerations, management considerations, curricular and instructional adaptations and accommodations, social-emotional interventions, and technology.

General Considerations When teachers are educating students with visual impairments, the unique needs of each student must be considered. However, some general practices apply for most, if not all, students with these problems. These practices include the following:

- Ask the student if assistance is needed.
- Do not assume that certain tasks and activities cannot be accomplished without adaptations, accommodations, or modifications.
- Include students with visual impairments in all activities that occur in the class.
- Use seating arrangements to take advantage of any vision the child can use.
- Encourage the use of residual vision.

FURTHER READING

Numerous resources are available for individuals who are deaf or blind across Canada (e.g., schools, support groups). Review The National Directory of Deaf-Blind Resources in Canada (2005), available at www.ioo.ca/docs/DeafblindResources.pdf.

CROSS REFERENCE

Review chapter 12 for information on rules and procedures appropriate for *all* students with exceptionalities—and even students without exceptionalities.

Physical Activity of Children with Visual Impairments

Research shows that individuals with visual impairments become less physically active with age. Physical activity among all individuals is linked to a variety of physical and mental health benefits. Ayvazoglu and colleagues (2006) identified the following ways to increase physical health among children with visual impairments:

- Promote peer involvement in physical activity.
- Ensure safety provisions are in place for family members.
- Provide children with visual impairments with the necessary skills to engage in physical activities.

- Involve family members in the physical activities of children.
- Provide school programs that are supportive of home activities.
- Focus school programs on fitness as well as recreational activities.

From "Explaining Physical Activity in Children with Visual Impairments: A Family Systems Approach," by N.R. Ayvazoglu, Hyun-Kyoung Oh, and Francis M. Kozub, 2006, *Exceptional Children, 72,* pp. 235–248.

Remember that many characteristics of students with visual impairments (i.e., intelligence, health) may not be negatively affected by their vision problem.

Children with visual impairments often have low levels of physical activity, so school personnel should work to increase activity levels. (See the Evidence-Based Practice box for suggestions for improving activity levels.) The activity level of children with visual impairments has been shown to be related to that of parents. School personnel should therefore collaborate with parents to increase students' activity levels (Ayvazoglu et al., 2006)

Management Considerations A variety of classroom management tactics can be helpful to students who have vision problems. Classroom management is discussed in detail in chapter 12. When students with vision problems are present, attention needs to be given to standard operating procedures, physical considerations, and preinstructional considerations.

CROSS REFERENCE

Classroom management is discussed in chapter 12.

Standard Operating Procedures The same standards of expected behaviour should be applied to all students, including those who have visual problems. However, students with visual limitations may need special freedom to move around the classroom in order to find the place where they can best see demonstrations or participate in activities.

Physical Considerations Students with visual problems need to know the physical layout of the classroom so that they can navigate through it without harming themselves. Teachers have to orient these students to the setting by taking them around the classroom and noting certain features, such as the location of desks, tables, and materials. A clock orientation approach is useful—for example, the front of the class is twelve o'clock, at three o'clock is the teacher's desk, at six o'clock is the reading table, and at nine o'clock is the area for students' coats and backpacks. Appropriate seating is extremely important for students who are able to use their existing vision. Placement of their desks, lighting, glare, and distractions should be considered when situating such students in the classroom. As well, teachers should guarantee that the classroom is free of hazards (e.g., low-hanging mobiles or plants) that could injure students who have a visual impairment; teachers should also label storage areas and other parts of the classroom for students with visual impairment using raised lettering or Braille.

Preinstructional Considerations   Teachers should plan ahead to adapt instruction to the needs of students with visual impairments. Class schedules must allow extra time for students who use large-print or Braille materials, as they take longer to use. Test-taking procedures may need to be adapted; for example, by preparing an enlarged version of the test, allowing extra time, or arranging for someone to read the test to the student.

Some students may need special instruction in study skills such as note taking, organizational skills, time management, and keyboarding. These become increasingly important as students move to middle school and high school. Examples of some specific adaptation and accommodation suggestions include assigning a peer helper to a classmate who may need help with mobility in an emergency situation, telling students with visual problems that you are entering or leaving a room so that they are aware of your presence or absence, orienting students to the physical layout and other distinguishing features of the classroom, and maintaining consistency in the placement of furniture, equipment, and instructional materials—removing all dangerous obstacles.

Curricular and Instructional Considerations

Teacher-Related Activities   As the principal agents in delivering instruction, teachers should use techniques that will ensure success for students who have visual problems. A special challenge involves conveying primarily visual material to those who cannot see well. For example, it will require some creativity on the part of the teacher to make a graphic depiction of the circulatory system in a life science book (a two-dimensional illustration) accessible to a student who can see little or not at all. Three-dimensional models or illustrations with raised features might address this need. Teachers have to decide what should be emphasized in the curriculum when students with visual impairments are in their classes.

Watch

Assistive Technology for Students with Visual Impairments

Materials and Equipment   Special materials and equipment can enhance the education of students who have visual impairments. Some materials (e.g., large-print resources) are not appropriate for all and must be considered in light of individual needs. Vision specialists can help teachers select appropriate materials and equipment.

Teachers need to use tactile strategies when teaching students with visual impairments. This may require making tactile adaptations of materials used. Some considerations for developing tactile adaptations include the following (Downing & Chen, 2003):

1.   Identify the objective of the lesson or the instructional concept.

2.   Select the materials to convey this concept.

3.   Close your eyes and examine the material with your hands.

4.   Take a tactile perspective, not visual, when deciding how and what to present.

5.   If the entire concept (e.g., house) is too complicated to represent through a tactile adaptation, then select one aspect of the concept (e.g., key) for the tactile representation.

6.   Consider the student's previous tactile experiences. What items has he or she examined? How does the student examine materials through the sense of touch?

7.   Decide how the item will be introduced to the student.

8. Identify what supports the student needs to tactilely examine the item.

9. Decide what language input (descriptive words) will be used to convey the student's experience of the material. (p. 59)

Many materials found in general education classrooms may pose difficulties for students who have problems with their vision. The size and contrast of print materials have a real effect on students with visual problems. For instance, low-contrast materials (in which information does not stand out well on a page) and books that are printed on glossy paper can be difficult for some students to use. Print size can generally be taken care of with magnification devices; however, little can be done to enhance the poor contrast often found on photocopies. Consider these points when using photocopies:

- Avoid using both sides of the paper (ink often bleeds through, making it difficult to see either side).

- Avoid old or light work sheet masters.

- Avoid work sheet masters with missing parts or creases.

- Give the darkest copies of handouts to students with visual problems.

- Do not give a student with a visual impairment a poor copy and say, "Do the best you can with this."

- Copy over lines that are light with a dark marker.

- Make new originals when photocopies become difficult to read.

- Avoid the use of coloured inks that may produce limited contrast.

- Do not use coloured paper—it limits contrast.

Teachers also may want to use concrete materials (i.e., *realia*—realistic representations of actual items). However, concrete representations of large real-life objects may not be helpful for young students, who may not understand the abstract notion of one thing representing another. Teachers must carefully ensure that all instructional materials for students with visual impairments are presented in the appropriate medium for the particular student.

Various optical, nonoptical, and electronic devices are also available for classroom use. These devices help students by enlarging existing printed images. If these devices are recommended for certain students, teachers will need to learn about them to ensure that they are used properly and to recognize when there is a problem. Teachers should practise using optical and electronic devices with students after consulting a vision specialist.

Some students with more severe visual limitations may use Braille as the primary means of working with written material. They may use instructional materials that are printed in Braille and may also take notes using it. Through the use of computers, a student can write in Braille and have the text converted to standard print. The reverse process is available as well. If a student uses this system of communication, the teacher should consult with a vision specialist to understand how it works.

Social-Emotional Considerations Although the literature is mixed on whether students with visual impairments are less well adjusted than their sighted peers (Hallahan & Kauffman, 2000), there is evidence that some students with visual problems experience social isolation (Huurre, Komulainen, & Aro, 1999). As a result, many students with

Watch
Visual Impairment

visual problems will benefit from attention to their social and emotional development. Social skills instruction may be particularly useful. However, because social skills are typically learned through observing others and imitating their behaviours, it is difficult to teach these skills to students who are not able to see.

Concern about emotional development is warranted for all students, including those with visual problems. Teachers should make it clear that they are available to talk about a student's concerns. A system can be developed whereby a student who has a visual impairment can signal the need to chat with the teacher. It is extremely important that teachers are accessible and that they let students know that someone is concerned about their social and emotional needs.

Technology As with students with hearing impairments, students with visual problems often use technological devices to assist them in their academic work and daily living skills. Low-vision aids enlarge print and other materials and include magnifiers, closed-circuit televisions, and **monoculars**. While access to the internet is relatively easy for students without visual problems, many students with visual impairments may have difficulty; however, certain technological devices can make the internet available to these students, including Braille printers and speech input/output devices. Access and computer training can give students with visual impairments a vast resource that can have a profound and positive impact on their education.

Promoting Inclusive Practices for Students with Visual Impairments

Students with visual impairments, like those with hearing impairments, need to be part of the school community. Many students can be included without special supports. However, for others, teachers may need to consider the following (Amerson, 1999; Desrochers, 1999; Torres & Corn, 1990):

1. Remember that the student with a visual impairment is but one of many students in the classroom with individual needs and characteristics.

2. Use words such as *see*, *look*, and *watch* naturally.

3. Introduce students with visual impairments the same way you would introduce any other student.

4. Include students with visual impairments in all classroom activities, including physical education, home economics, and so on.

5. Encourage students with visual problems to seek leadership and high-visibility roles in the classroom.

6. Use the same disciplinary procedures for all students.

7. Encourage students with visual problems to move about the room just like other students.

8. Use verbal cues as often as necessary to cue the student with a visual impairment about something that is happening.

9. Provide additional space for students with visual impairments to store materials.

10. Allow students with visual impairments to learn about and discuss with other class-mates special topics related to visual loss.

11. Model acceptance of visually impaired students as an example to other students.

12. Encourage students with visual impairments to use their specialized equipment, such as a Braille writer.

13. Discuss with specialists the special needs of the child with a visual impairment, as necessary.

14. Always tell a person with a visual impairment who you are as you approach.

15. Help students with visual impairments avoid inappropriate mannerisms associated with visual impairments.

16. Expect the same level of work from students with visual impairments as you do from other students.

17. Encourage students with visual impairments to be as independent as possible.

18. Treat children with visual impairments as you treat other students in the classroom.

19. Provide physical supports for students with concomitant motor problems.

20. Include students with visual impairments in outdoor activities and team sports.

In your efforts to promote a sense of community, consider that some students with visual impairments may have different cultural backgrounds than the majority of students in the school. School personnel must be sensitive to cultural patterns. In order to communicate clearly with a family that speaks a different language, you may need to use a language interpreter. Being sensitive to the culture and family background of students with visual impairments facilitates the delivery of appropriate services.

Supports for the General Education Teacher As noted earlier, with appropriate supports, general education teachers can effectively instruct most students with visual impairments. For example, a vision specialist may need to work with students on specific skills, such as Braille; an orientation and mobility instructor can teach students how to travel independently; an adaptive physical education instructor can help modify physical activities for the student with visual impairment. Counsellors, school health personnel, and vocational specialists may also provide support services for general education teachers. School personnel should never forget to include parents in helping develop and implement educational supports for students with visual impairments. Other ways to enhance the education of students with visual impairments include the following:

■ Get help from others. Teach other students to assist in social as well as academic settings. Call parents and ask questions when you don't understand terminology, equipment, or reasons for prescribed practices.

■ Learn how to adapt and modify materials and instruction.

■ Learn as much as you can, and encourage the professionals you work with to do the same. Find out about training that may be available and ask to go.

Suggest that others become informed, especially students. Use your local library and bookstores to find print material you can read and share.

◄●┤**Simulate**

Instructional Accommodations
Focus on the Playbook

TRAUMATIC BRAIN INJURY

Basic Concepts about Traumatic Brain Injury

FURTHER READING

Traumatic brain injuries are largely preventable (e.g., preventing injuries in motor vehicle accidents by wearing appropriate safety restraints). For more information on the prevention of traumatic brain injuries and classroom resources to address this issue, refer to the Safe Kids Canada website (www.safekidscanada.ca).

Traumatic brain injury (TBI) is defined by the American Speech-Language-Hearing Association as "an injury to the head [that] may cause interference with normal brain functions" (ASHA, 2004d). These types of injuries could be the result of a foreign object, such as a bullet, entering the brain and causing damage to specific areas (a penetrating injury), or the result of a blow to the head, such as an injury sustained in a car accident (a closed head injury) (ASHA, 2004d). Traumatic brain injuries can affect psychological and cognitive abilities, speech and language, physical functioning, and personal and social behaviours.

Traumatic brain injury can result from a wide variety of causes, including falls, vehicle accidents, and even abuse. It can also be caused by lack of oxygen to the brain, infections, tumours, and strokes. Information about the severity of a traumatic brain injury is important for teachers as it can provide a sense of the expected long-term outcomes for a student.

The social-emotional and cognitive deficits caused by the injury may persist long after physical capabilities recover. Students with TBI can experience a host of confusing and frustrating symptoms, including cognitive changes, sensory problems, coordination problems, attention problems, emotional lability, aggressiveness, and depression (Best, 2005). Teachers must guard against minimizing an injury because it presents no visible evidence and because many children exhibit typical behaviours. The prognosis for recovery depends on many variables, including the severity, location, and extent of the injury; the immediacy of treatment; the chronological age of the individual, and the extent of time in a coma (Best, 2005).

Later, recovery will be influenced by the nature of rehabilitative and educational intervention. Some students with TBI will experience academic success, while others will have long-term lingering effects (e.g., fatigue, hearing problems, memory problems, language comprehension and expression difficulties, problem-solving difficulties).

Watch

Traumatic Brain Injury

Classroom Adaptations for Students with Traumatic Brain Injury

CONSIDER THIS

What can school personnel do to facilitate the transition of children with TBI from hospital and residential settings to the public school? What kind of relationship should school personnel and hospital personnel maintain with each other after the transition is completed?

The transition of students with TBI from rehabilitation facilities to school settings needs to be coordinated among a number of people; intervention involves the efforts of professionals from many different disciplines, including teachers. In addition to the injury itself and its implications for functioning and potential learning, students are likely to have missed a significant amount of schooling. All of these factors can have a significant impact on educational performance. An effective educational program creates a positive attitude about the student's prognosis that reaches beyond just speaking positively. Teachers communicate a positive attitude by the type of programming they present and by the level of expectations they establish. A positive attitude will show the students that programs and instruction are designed to support them and not just to give them a grade. They will respond better when programs do not seem punitive.

Students identified with a traumatic brain injury will likely have an individualized education plan (IEP) put in place to address their educational needs. Teachers will need to

Table 9.4 Recommended Instructional Strategies for Children with TBI

Use a multimodal approach (overheads, videos, hands-on activities) when presenting material and instructions for assignments.

Teach compensatory strategies to students and structure choices.

Begin class with review and overview of topics to be covered.

Provide the student with an outline of the material to be presented, to assist in comprehension.

Emphasize main points and key ideas frequently.

Incorporate repetition into instruction.

Provide specific, frequent feedback on student performance and behaviour.

Encourage questions.

Break down large assignments into smaller components.

Use task analyses to determine skill acquisition and maintenance.

Ask the student how he or she could improve learning.

Use a variety of open-ended and multiple-choice questions to encourage independent thinking.

Present difficult material in a simplified fashion, using illustrations or diagrams if possible.

Provide the student with cues when appropriate.

From "Enhancing the Schooling of Students with Traumatic Brain Injury" (p. 65), by L. Keyser-Marcus, L. Briel, P. Sherron-Targett, S. Yasuda, S. Johnson, & P. Wehman, 2002, *Teaching Exceptional Children, 34.* Used with permission.

attend to the specific areas that have been identified as problematic for the individual. Table 9.4 gives ideas for helping students with problems that may result from TBI.

A well-planned program of instruction should focus on "retaining impaired cognitive processes, developing new skills or procedures to compensate for residual deficits, creating an environment that permits effective performance, identifying effective instructional procedures, and improving metacognitive awareness" (Ylvisaker, Szekeres, Hartwick, & Tworek, 1994, p. 17). The impact of the injury may require that the student learn compensatory strategies to make up for deficits. Such strategies can address problems with attending, language comprehension, memory, sequencing, and thought organization.

The following suggestions will help provide a positive learning program and environment for students with TBI:

- Prepare classmates for the re-entry of a fellow student who has sustained a traumatic brain injury—it is important to discuss any changes in physical functioning and personality.

- Modify the classroom to ensure safety and to address any specific needs of the student.

- Minimize visual and auditory distractions that may interfere with attention to task.

- Be familiar with any special equipment that might be needed (e.g., augmentative communication devices).

- Be familiar with the effects and administration procedures of prescribed medications.

TEACHING TIP

Develop and implement intervention programs based on the student's specific needs. TBI results in a wide variety of deficits, producing a great diversity of needs.

✳ Explore

A Different Child

She Doesn't Know Herself

- Consider special seating, depending on needs.

- Ensure that the student is attending to instructional activities—teach him or her to monitor their own attention behaviour.

- Help the student with memory problems by teaching mnemonic strategies.

- Assist students who are having difficulty with organization.

- Break down learning tasks into substeps.

- Create many opportunities for the student to use problem-solving skills.

- Allow extra time for the student to respond to questions, take tests, complete assignments, and move from one setting to another.

- Teach social skills appropriate for the student's age and needs.

- Implement behaviour-reduction techniques to eliminate inappropriate and undesirable behaviours.

- Help the student to understand the nature of their injury.

- Provide information about academic, social, and psychomotor progress to families on a regular basis. Describe the nature of the educational program.

LOW-INCIDENCE HEALTH PROBLEMS AND PHYSICAL DISABILITIES

👁 Watch

Physical Disabilities

Fifth Graders Discuss Different Abilities

As noted in the beginning of this chapter, many health and **physical disabilities** that result in a need for special education and related services may be present in children. The remainder of this chapter will provide a quick guide to some of these exceptionalities and some considerations for educators. Teachers who work with children with one of these conditions should refer to a more thorough reference work to learn more about it.

Asthma

In Canada, 5 to 10 percent of Canadians, and as many as 20 percent of children, have asthma. According to the Asthma Society of Canada, asthma is the most common chronic childhood disease, the number-one cause of emergency room visits in pediatric centres, and the number-one cause of school absenteeism.

Asthma is the result of the body's antibodies reacting to antigens and causing swelling, mucus secretion, and muscle tightening in the lungs (Best, 2005). This can cause repetitive episodes of coughing, shortness of breath, and wheezing. Dust, cigarette smoke, and animal dander are examples of substances that can trigger an asthma episode. While some asthma is mild and can be controlled by simply inhaling medication, severe attacks can be very dangerous and should be taken seriously by school personnel. Specific suggestions for teachers include the following:

- Know the signs and symptoms of respiratory distress.

- Ensure that students have proper medications and that they are taken at the appropriate times.

- Allow students to rest when needed, as they often tire easily.

- Eliminate any known **allergens** from the classroom.

- Determine what types of physical limitations might have to be set (e.g., restriction of a certain physical activity that can induce attacks), but otherwise encourage students to play games and participate in activities.
- Recognize the side effects of prescribed medication.
- Remain calm if an attack occurs.
- Allow the student to participate in a nonstressful activity until an episode subsides.
- Introduce a vapourizer or dehumidifier to the classroom when recommended by the student's physician.
- Work on building up the student's self-image.
- Sensitize other students in the class to the nature of allergic reactions.
- Develop an effective system for helping the student keep up with schoolwork, as frequent absences may occur.

Educators can ask the following questions to determine whether a school is prepared to deal with students with asthma (National Heart, Lung, and Blood Institute, 1998):

1. Is the school free of tobacco smoke all of the time, including during school-sponsored events?
2. Does the school maintain good indoor air quality?
3. Is a school nurse in the school all day, every day?
4. Can children take medicines at school as recommended by their doctor and parents?
5. Does the school have an emergency plan for taking care of a child with a severe asthma attack?
6. Does someone teach school staff about asthma, asthma management plans, and asthma medicines?
7. Do students with asthma have good options for fully and safely participating in physical education class and recess? (p. 168)

Childhood Cancer

Childhood cancer can take several different forms, including **leukemia**, lymphoma, tumours of the central nervous system, bone tumours, tumours affecting the eyes, and tumours affecting various organs. Treatment of cancer includes chemotherapy, radiation, surgery, and bone marrow transplantation. Whether schools provide appropriate help to students with cancer is dependent on their understanding of the condition (Spinelli, 2004). Suggestions for teachers who have children with cancer include the following:

- Express your concern about a student's condition to the parents and family.
- Learn about a student's illness from hospital personnel and parents.
- Inquire about the type of treatment and anticipated side effects.
- Refer the student for any needed special education services.
- Prepare for a student's terminal illness and possible death.

CONSIDER THIS

What are some ways that teachers can maintain contact with students with cancer during their extended absences from the classroom? How can the teacher facilitate contact between other students and the student with cancer?

Explore

My Learning Problems Won't Quit

- Encourage discussion and consideration of future events.
- Allow for exceptions to classroom rules and procedures when indicated (e.g., wearing a baseball cap to disguise hair loss from chemotherapy).
- Be available to talk with a student when the need arises.
- Share information about the student's condition and ongoing status with teachers of the student's siblings.
- Be prepared to deal with issues concerning death and dying with students.
- Provide information to school staff and parents, as needed.
- Facilitate the student's re-entry into school after an extended absence.

Cerebral Palsy

Cerebral palsy (CP) is "a group of chronic conditions affecting body movement and muscle coordination" (United Cerebral Palsy, 2006); it is caused by brain damage. Cerebral palsy is neither progressive nor communicable; it is also not "curable" in the usual sense of the word, although education, therapy, and applied technology can help persons with cerebral palsy lead productive lives. Every year in the United States, approximately 5000 babies are born with cerebral palsy and another 1200 to 1500 young children develop the condition (Best & Bigge, 2006). There are several different ways to classify individuals with cerebral palsy; most frequently, by location of the disorder and how it affects movement (Best & Bigge, 2006). Table 9.5 describes the different types of cerebral palsy according to two classification systems.

Table 9.5 Classification of Cerebral Palsy	
Topographical Classification System	**Classification System by Motor Symptoms (Physiological)**
A. *Monoplegia:* one limb	A. Spastic
B. *Paraplegia:* legs only	B. Athetoid
C. *Hemiplegia:* one-half of body	1. Tension
D. *Triplegia:* three limbs (usually two legs and one arm)	2. Nontension
	3. Dystonic
E. *Quadriplegia:* all four limbs	4. Tremor
F. *Diplegia:* more affected in the legs than the arms	C. Rigidity
	D. Ataxia
G. *Double hemiplegia:* arms more involved than the legs	E. Tremor
	F. Atonic (rare)
	G. Mixed
	H. Unclassified

From *Understanding Physical, Sensory, and Health Impairments* (p. 95), by K.W. Heller, P.A. Alberto, P.E. Forney, and M.N. Schwartzman, 1996, Pacific Grove, CA: Brooks/Cole. Used with permission.

Teachers who have students with cancer should learn about the child's illness from medical personnel.

The primary intervention approach for children with cerebral palsy focuses on their physical needs. Physical therapy, occupational therapy, and even surgery often play a part. Specific suggestions for teachers include the following:

- Create a supportive classroom environment that encourages participation in every facet of the school day.

- Allow extra time for students to move from one location to another.

- Ask students to repeat verbalizations that may be hard to understand because of their speech patterns.

- Provide many real-life activities.

- Learn the correct way for the student to sit upright in a chair or wheelchair and the methods of using adaptive equipment (e.g., prone standers).

- Understand the functions and components of a wheelchair and any special adaptive pieces that may accompany it.

- Consider using various augmentative communication techniques with students who have severe cerebral palsy.

- Encourage students to use computers that are equipped with expanded keyboards if necessary or other portable writing aids for taking notes or generating written products.

- Consult physical and occupational therapists to understand correct positioning, posture, and other motor function areas.

Cystic Fibrosis

Cystic fibrosis is an inherited, fatal disease that results in an abnormal amount of mucus throughout the body, most often affecting the lungs and digestive tract, which results in the blockage of air sacs in the lungs. This blockage causes air to be trapped in the lungs,

TEACHING TIP

Develop some simulation activities for typically achieving students that will help them understand mobility problems. Trying out wheelchairs and restricting the use of arms or hands will help them understand the problems experienced by some students with cerebral palsy.

✳ Explore

Where Do I Draw the Line Between My Responsibility and Her Privacy?

and causes the lungs to overinflate and then collapse (Best, 2005). Cystic fibrosis occurs in approximately 1 in 3500 live births (Cystic Fibrosis Foundation, 2006). While life expectancy for children with cystic fibrosis at one time was only the teens, the current median age of individuals with this condition is 35.1 years (CF Foundation, 2006). Teachers must make sure that children with cystic fibrosis take special medication before they eat. As the disease progresses, it greatly affects stamina and the student's physical condition. Here are some specific suggestions for dealing with students with this disease:

- Prepare students in class for the realities of this disease (e.g., coughing, noncontagious sputum, gas).
- Learn how to clear a student's lungs and air passages, as such assistance may be needed after certain activities.
- Know the medications a student must take and be able to administer them (e.g., enzymes, vitamins).
- Consider restricting certain physical activities.
- Inquire about the therapies being used with the student.
- Support the implementation of special diets if needed.
- Provide opportunities for students to talk about their concerns, fears, and feelings.
- Ensure that the student is included in all class activities to whatever extent is possible.
- Prepare students for the eventual outcome of the disease by discussing death and dying.

Multisensory Impairments

Students who have visual impairments or auditory impairments create unique problems for educators. When students present deficits in both sensory areas, their needs become extremely complex.

Students who have multisensory impairments may be blind or deaf, or they may have degrees of visual and auditory impairments that do not classify as blindness or deafness. Obviously, individuals identified with multisensory impairments present a variety of characteristics, representing those exhibited by students who have only a visual or a hearing impairment, the overlap of the two exceptionalities results in significant educational needs.

Wolfe (1997) suggests the following educational techniques for teachers to use when working with students with multisensory impairments:

- Use an ecological approach to assessment and skill selection to emphasize functional needs of students.
- Use a variety of prompts, cues, and reinforcement strategies in a systematic instructional pattern.
- Use time-delay prompting, where time between prompts is increased.
- Use groups and co-operative learning strategies.
- Implement environmental adaptations, such as enlarging materials, using contrasting materials, altering seating arrangements, and reducing extraneous noises to maximize residual hearing and vision of the student.

Diabetes (Juvenile Diabetes)

Diabetes is a metabolic disorder in which the pancreas cannot produce sufficient insulin to process food (Holcomb et al., 1998). Teachers should be alert to possible symptoms of diabetes, including increased thirst, appetite, and urination; weight loss; fatigue; and irritability. (See Table 9.6.) Children with type I (insulin-dependent) diabetes must take daily injections of insulin. School personnel must have knowledge of the special dietary needs of these children and understand their need for a daily activity regimen. Actions for teachers who have students with diabetes in their classroom include the following (U.S. Department of Health and Human Services, 2003):

- participating in the school health team meetings
- working with the school health team to implement written care plans
- recognizing that a change in the student's behaviour could be a symptom of blood glucose changes
- being prepared to recognize and respond to the signs and symptoms of hypoglycemia and hyperglycemia
- providing a supportive environment for the student
- providing classroom accommodations for the student with diabetes
- providing instruction to the student if the student misses class
- notifying parents in advance of changes in school schedule
- providing information for substitute teachers
- communicating with the school nurse, trained diabetes personnel, or parents regarding any concerns about the student
- attending diabetes management training
- learning about diabetes
- treating the student with diabetes the same as other students
- respecting the student's confidentiality and right to privacy
- understanding the distinction between having too much insulin in the body and not having enough. Table 9.7 describes both of these conditions and actions to address them. (p. 40)

Table 9.6 Indicators of Diabetes (Juvenile Diabetes)
Increased thirst
Increased appetite
Weight loss
Fatigue
Irritability
Increased urination

TEACHING TIP

Before an emergency develops, be prepared to deal with students with diabetes in your classroom. Keep a list of symptoms to watch for and things to do if a student has too much or too little insulin.

Epilepsy

Epilepsy is a neurological disorder that results in individuals having seizures, which are "a change in sensation, awareness, or behavior brought about by a brief electrical disturbance in the brain" (Epilepsy Foundation, 2006, p. 1). There are several different types of epilepsy, determined by the impact of abnormal brain activity. Table 9.8 details four types. In Canada, up to 2 percent of the population has been diagnosed with epilepsy. The Epilepsy Foundation of America (2006) notes the following significant signs of the disorder: (1) staring spells, (2) tic-like movements, (3) rhythmic movements of the head, (4) purposeless sounds and body movements, (5) head drooping, (6) lack of response, (7) eyes rolling upward, and (8) chewing and swallowing movements. Medical intervention is the primary recourse for individuals with epilepsy. Most people with epilepsy are able to control their seizures with the proper regimen of medical therapy.

TEACHING TIP

Turn a student's seizure into an educational opportunity for other students. Ensure that students know that they cannot "catch" epilepsy from someone.

Table 9.7 Hyperglycemia and Hypoglycemia

Category	Possible Symptoms	Cause	Treatment
Ketoacidosis; hyperglycemia (too much sugar)	Symptoms occur gradually (over hours or days): polyuria; polyphagia; polydipsia; fatigue; abdominal pain; nausea; vomiting; fruity odour on breath; rapid, deep breathing; unconsciousness	Did not take insulin; did not comply with diet	Give insulin; follow plan of action
Insulin reaction; hypoglycemia (too little sugar)	Symptoms occur quickly (in minutes): headache; dullness; irritability; shaking; sweating; lightheadedness; behaviour change; paleness; weakness; moist skin; slurred speech; confusion; shallow breathing; unconsciousness	Delayed eating; participated in strenuous exercise; took too much insulin	Give sugar; follow plan of action

From *Understanding Physical, Sensory, and Health Impairments* (p. 302), by K.W. Heller, P.A. Alberto, P.E. Forney, and M.N. Schwartzman, 1996, Pacific Grove, CA: Brooks/Cole. Used with permission.

Table 9.8 Four Types of Seizures

Generalized (grand mal)
- Sudden cry, fall, rigidity, followed by muscle jerks
- Shallow breathing, or temporarily suspended breathing, bluish skin
- Possible loss of bladder or bowel control
- Usually lasts 2–3 minutes

Absence (petit mal)
- Blank stare, beginning and ending abruptly
- Lasting only a few seconds
- Most common in children
- May be accompanied by blinking, chewing movement
- Individual is unaware of the seizure

Simple Partial
- Jerking may begin in one area of body, arm, leg, or face
- Cannot be stopped but individual is aware
- Jerking may proceed from one area to another area

Complex Partial
- Starts with blank stares, followed by chewing and random activity
- Individual may seem unaware or dazed
- Unresponsiveness
- Clumsy actions
- May run, pick up objects, take clothes off, or other activity
- Lasts a few minutes
- No memory of what occurred

From *Understanding Physical, Sensory, and Health Impairments* (p. 78), by K.W. Heller, P.A. Alberto, P.E. Forney, and M.N. Schwartzman, 1996, Pacific Grove, CA: Brooks/Cole. Used by permission.

During a generalized tonic-clonic seizure (grand mal), the person suddenly falls to the ground and has a convulsive seizure. It is essential to protect him or her from injury. Cradle the head or place something soft under it, a towel or your hand, for example. Remove all dangerous objects. A bystander can do nothing to prevent or terminate an attack. At the end of the seizure, make sure the mouth is cleared of food and saliva by turning the person on his or her side to provide an open airway and allow fluids to drain. If the person assisting remains calm, the person having the seizure will be reassured when he or she regains consciousness.

Breathing almost always resumes spontaneously after a convulsive seizure. Failure to resume breathing signals a complication of the seizure, such as a blocked airway, heart attack, or severe head or neck injury. In these unusual circumstances, CPR must start immediately. If repeated seizures occur, or if a single seizure lasts longer than five minutes, the person should be taken to a medical facility immediately. Prolonged or repeated seizures may suggest status epilepticus (nonstop seizures), which requires emergency medical treatment.

When providing seizure first aid for generalized tonic-clonic seizures, these are the key things to remember:

- Keep calm and reassure other people who may be nearby.
- Don't hold the person down or try to stop his or her movements.
- Time the seizure with your watch.
- Clear the area around the person of anything hard or sharp.
- Loosen ties or anything around the neck that may make breathing difficult.
- Put something flat and soft, like a folded jacket, under the head.
- Turn him or her gently onto one side. This will help keep the airway clear. Do not try to force the mouth open with any hard implement or with fingers. It is not true that a person having a seizure can swallow his or her tongue. Efforts to hold the tongue down can injure teeth or jaw.
- Don't attempt artificial respiration except in the unlikely event that a person does not start breathing again after the seizure has stopped.
- Stay with the person until the seizure ends naturally.
- Be friendly and reassuring as consciousness returns.
- Offer to call a taxi, friend, or relative to help the person get home if he or she seems confused or unable to get home by himself or herself.

From "First Aid for Generalized Tonic Clonic (Grand Mal) Seizures," Epilepsy Foundation website: www.epilepsyfoundation.org/answerplace/Medical/seizures/types/genConvulsive/seizuretonic.cfm. Used with permission.

Figure 9.4 Steps to Take When Dealing with a Seizure

Even persons who respond very well to medication have occasional seizures. Therefore, teachers and other school personnel must know what actions to take should a person experience a generalized seizure. Figure 9.4 summarizes the steps that should be taken when a child has a seizure. Teachers, parents, or others need to record behaviours that occur before, during, and after the seizure because they may be important to treatment.

HIV and AIDS

Human immunodeficiency virus (HIV) infection occurs when the virus attacks the body's immune system, leaving an individual vulnerable to infections or cancers. In its later stages, HIV infection becomes **acquired immunodeficiency syndrome (AIDS)**. HIV/AIDS is transmitted only through the exchange of blood or semen. Two of the fastest-growing groups contracting HIV are infants and teenagers (Johnson, Johnson, &

CONSIDER THIS

"Students with HIV and AIDS should not be allowed to attend school because of their potential ability to infect other students." Do you agree with this statement? Why or why not?

The U.S. Centers for Disease Control and the Food and Drug Administration (1988) published guidelines designed to protect health care workers and to ensure the confidentiality of patients with HIV infection. These guidelines include the following information, which is useful for classroom teachers:

■ Blood should always be handled with latex or nonpermeable disposable gloves. The use of gloves is not necessary for feces, nasal secretions, sputum, sweat, saliva, tears, urine, and vomitus unless they are visibly tinged with blood. Handwashing is sufficient after handling material not containing blood.

■ In all settings in which blood or bloody material is handled, gloves and a suitable receptacle that closes tightly and is child-proof should be available. Although HIV does not survive well outside the body, all spillage of secretions should be cleaned up immediately with disinfectants. This is particularly important for cleaning up after a bloody nose or a large cut. Household bleach at a dilution of 1:10 should be used. Only objects that have come into contact with blood need to be cleaned with bleach.

■ When intact skin is exposed to contaminated fluids, particularly blood, it should be washed with soap and water. Handwashing is sufficient for such activities as diaper change; toilet training; and clean-up of nasal secretions, stool, saliva, tears, or vomitus. If an open lesion or a mucous membrane appears to have been contaminated, AZT therapy should be considered.

From *AIDS Surveillance Report* (p. 7), Centers for Disease Control, 1988, Atlanta, GA: Author. Used with permission.

Figure 9.5 Universal Precautions for Prevention of HIV, Hepatitis B, and Other Blood-Borne Pathogens

Jefferson-Aker, 2001). Students with HIV/AIDS may display a variety of academic, behavioural, and social-emotional problems. Teachers need to take precautions when dealing with children with HIV/AIDS, hepatitis B, or any other blood-borne pathogen. See Figure 9.5 for specific precautions. Some specific suggestions for teachers include the following:

■ Follow the guidelines (universal precautions) developed by the U.S. Centers for Disease Control and the U.S. Food and Drug Administration for working with HIV-infected individuals (see Figure 9.5).

■ Ask the student's parents or physician if there are any special procedures that must be followed.

■ Discuss HIV/AIDS with the entire class, providing accurate information, dispelling myths, and answering questions.

■ Discuss with students in the class that a student's skills and abilities will change over time if he or she is infected with HIV/AIDS.

■ Prepare for the fact that the student will die, especially if AIDS is present.

■ Ensure that the student with HIV/AIDS is included in all aspects of classroom activities.

■ Be sensitive to the stress that the student's family is undergoing.

Muscular Dystrophy

Muscular dystrophy is an umbrella term used to describe several different inherited disorders that result in progressive muscular weakness. The most common and most serious form of muscular dystrophy is **Duchenne dystrophy**. In this type of muscular dystrophy, fat cells and connective tissue replace muscle tissue. Individuals with

Duchenne dystrophy ultimately lose their ability to walk, typically by age 12. Symptoms first appear between the ages of two and six years and progress at varying rates. Functional use of arms and hands will also be affected. Muscle weakness will result in respiratory complications. The condition is genetically transmitted and affects approximately one in every 3500 male births. Females carry the gene but are not affected (Best, 2005). Teachers must adapt their classrooms to accommodate the physical needs of students. Most individuals with this form of muscular dystrophy die during young adulthood. Specific suggestions for teachers include the following:

■ Be prepared to help the student deal with the loss of various functions.

■ Involve the student in as many classroom activities as possible.

■ Use assistive techniques that do not hurt the individual: i.e., help the student as needed in climbing stairs or in getting up from the floor.

■ Understand the functions and components of wheelchairs.

■ Monitor the administration of required medications.

■ Monitor the amount of time the student is allowed to stand during the day.

■ Be familiar with different types of braces (short leg, moulded ankle-foot) students might use.

■ Prepare other students in class for the realities of the disease.

Prader-Willi Syndrome

Prader-Willi syndrome is a condition characterized by compulsive eating, obesity, and intellectual disability. Other characteristics include hypotonia (deficient muscle tone), slow metabolic rate, small or underdeveloped testes and penis, excessive sleeping, round face with almond-shaped eyes, nervous picking of skin, and stubbornness (Davies & Joughin, 1993; Silverthorn & Hornak, 1993; Smith & Hendricks, 1995). The only effective treatment for persons with Prader-Willi syndrome is weight management through diet and exercise.

Spina Bifida

Spina bifida is a neural tube defect characterized by bones in the spinal column (vertebrae) not connecting properly. There are three different types of spina bifida: spina bifida occulta, meningocele, and myelomeningocele (Best, 2006b). The least serious form is spina bifida occulta. In this type, the vertebral column fails to close properly, leaving a hole in the bony vertebrae that protect the delicate spinal column. Generally, all that is required to treat this form of spina bifida is surgery to close the opening to protect the spinal column. This does not result in any problems. **Meningocele** is similar to spina bifida occulta in that the vertebral column fails to close properly, leaving a hole in the bony vertebrae. Skin pouches out in the area where the vertebral column is not closed. In meningocele, the outpouching does not contain any nerve tissue. Surgically removing the outpouching and closing the opening usually result in a positive prognosis without any problems. **Myelomeningocele** is the most common and most severe form of spina bifida. Similar to meningocele, it has one major difference: nerve tissue is present in the outpouching. Due to the presence of nerve tissue, this form of spina bifida generally results in

CONSIDER THIS

Should students who require extensive physical accommodations be placed in the same school, so that all schools and classrooms do not have to be accessible? Defend your response.

TEACHING TIP

Get in a wheelchair and try to move about your classroom to see if it is fully accessible; often, areas look accessible but are not.

CROSS REFERENCE

Review intervention approaches for students with intellectual disabilities found in chapter 7, and determine which ones would be appropriate for a student with an intellectual disability and Prader-Willi syndrome.

Children in wheelchairs need opportunities for social interactions.

permanent paralysis and loss of sensation. Incontinence is also a possible result (Best, 2006b). School personnel must ensure appropriate use of wheelchairs (see the Technology Today feature) and accommodations for limited use of arms and hands. Following are recommendations for teachers working with a child with spina bifida:

- Inquire about any acute medical needs the student may have.
- Learn about the various adaptive equipment a student may be using.

Technology Today

Pushing a Wheelchair

1. *Over rough terrain or a raised area:*

    a. Tilt the wheelchair by stepping down on tipping lever with foot as you pull down and back on hand grips.

    b. Continue to tilt chair back until it requires little or no effort to stabilize it.

    c. When the wheelchair is at the balance point, it can then be pushed over obstacles or terrain.

    d. Reverse the procedure and lower slowly. Make sure the wheelchair does not slam down or drop the last few inches.

2. *Over curbs and steps:*

    a. As you approach the curb or step, pause and tilt the wheelchair back to the balance point.

    b. When the wheelchair is stabilized, move toward the curb until casters are on the curb and rear wheels come in contact with it.

    c. Move in close to the chair and lift it up by the handles. Roll the wheelchair up over the curb and push it forward.

    d. To go down, reverse the steps—back the wheelchair down off the curb without allowing it to drop down. Once rear wheels are down, step down on tipping lever and slowly lower casters.

3. *Down a steep incline:*

    a. Take the wheelchair down backward.

    b. The wheelchair can pick up speed too easily, and you can lose control if the wheelchair goes down first.

    c. Turn the chair around until your back is in the direction you plan to go.

    d. Walk backward, and move slowly down the ramp.

    e. Look backward occasionally to make sure you are staying on track and to avoid collisions.

- Maintain an environment that assists a student who is using crutches by keeping floors from getting wet and removing loose floor coverings.

- Understand the use of a wheelchair as well as its major parts.

- Learn how to position students to develop strength and to avoid sores from developing in parts of their bodies that bear their weight or that receive pressure from orthotic devices they are using. Individuals with spina bifida do not have sensation, so they may not notice the sores themselves. Healing is complicated by poor circulation.

- Understand the process of **clean intermittent bladder catheterization (CIC),** as some students will be performing this process to become continent and avoid urinary tract infections. The process involves insertion of a clean catheter through the urethra and into the bladder four times a day and can be done independently by most children by age six.

- Be ready to deal with the occasional incontinence of students. Assure the student with spina bifida that this is not a problem and discuss this situation with other class members.

- Learn how to deal with the special circumstances associated with students who use wheelchairs and have seizures.

- Ensure the full participation of the student in all classroom activities.

- Help the student with spina bifida develop a healthy, positive self-concept.

- Notify parents if there are unusual changes in the student's behaviour or personality or if the student has various physical complaints such as headaches or double vision—this may indicate a problem with increased pressure on the brain.

Tourette Syndrome

Tourette syndrome is a neurological disorder that results in multiple motor and verbal tics. The condition is genetically transmitted, with parents having a 50 percent chance of passing the gene to offspring. Tourette syndrome develops before the age of 18 (Facts about Tourette Syndrome, 2006). Characteristics include various motor tics; inappropriate laughing; rapid eye movements; winks and grimaces; aggressive behaviours; in infrequent cases, intellectual disabilities; mild to moderate incoordination; and peculiar verbalizations. The condition manifests several characteristics that negatively impact educational success (Prestia, 2003):

- incomplete work
- illegible or poor quality of written work
- inattentive and/or distractible in class
- disorganization of work and work space
- difficulty obtaining and understanding verbal instruction (p. 68)

Most important, school personnel should be understanding with children who have Tourette syndrome. Monitoring medication and participating as a member of the interdisciplinary team are important roles for teachers and other school personnel. See the Evidence-Based Practice box on page 256 for suggestions for other interventions.

CONSIDER THIS

How should students with Tourette syndrome be dealt with when they shout obscenities and display other inappropriate behaviours that disrupt the classroom?

Evidence-Based Practice

Interventions for Students with Tourette Syndrome

Research has identified best practices for working with students with Tourette syndrome:

- Break down assignments to avoid overwhelming the student.
- Allow students to use computers to eliminate frustrations and to focus on the content of the work.
- Allow preferential seating.
- Use grid paper to assist students with vertical alignment.
- Use multisensory interventions and instruction.
- Ensure students have ample time to complete work without increasing frustration levels.
- Test in quiet rooms with minimal distractions.
- Ensure a predictable routine for the school day or class period.
- Provide direct teaching of social skills.

From "Tourette's Syndrome; Characteristics and Interventions," by K. Prestia, 2003, *Intervention in School and Clinic, 39*, pp. 67–71.

SUMMARY

- Many students with sensory deficits are educated in general education classrooms.

- For students with sensory impairments to receive an appropriate education, various adaptations and accommodations must be made.

- Students with hearing and visual problems represent a heterogeneous group.

- Most students with hearing problems have some residual hearing ability.

- The term *hearing impairment* includes individuals with deafness and those who are hard of hearing.

- Vision plays a critical role in the development of concepts such as understanding the spatial relations of the environment.

- Teachers must use a variety of adaptations and accommodations for students with visual disabilities.

- Most students with visual disabilities have residual or low vision.

- Refractive errors are the most common form of visual disability.

- Visual problems may be congenital or occur later in life.

- Physical and health impairments constitute low-incidence disabilities.

- The severity, visibility, and age of acquisition affect the needs of children with physical and health impairments.

- Children with traumatic brain injury (TBI) exhibit a wide variety of characteristics, including emotional, learning, and behaviour problems.

- Asthma affects many children; teachers primarily need to be aware of medications to control asthma, side effects of medication, and the limitations of students with asthma.

- The survival rates for children with cancer have increased dramatically over the past 20 years. Teachers need to be prepared to deal with the emotional issues surrounding childhood cancer, including death. Children with cancer may miss a good deal of school; the school should make appropriate arrangements in these situations.

- Cerebral palsy is a condition that affects muscles and posture; it can be described by the way it affects movement or by which limb is involved.

- Physical therapy is a critical component of treatment for children with cerebral palsy. Accessibility, communication, and social-emotional concerns are the primary areas that general educators must attend to.

- Cystic fibrosis is an inherited fatal disease that affects the mucous membranes of the lungs.

- Juvenile diabetes results in affected children having to take insulin injections daily. Diet and exercise can help manage diabetes.

- Epilepsy is caused by abnormal activity in the brain that is the result of some brain damage or insult. Teachers must know specific steps to take in case children have a generalized tonic-clonic seizure in the classroom.

- Infants and teenagers are two of the fastest-growing groups to contract HIV. Teachers need to keep up to date with developments in HIV/AIDS prevention and treatment approaches.

- Muscular dystrophy is a term used to describe several different inherited disorders that result in progressive muscular weakness and that may cause death.

- Prader-Willi syndrome, a condition caused by a defect in the number 15 chromosome pair, is characterized by excessive overeating and mild intellectual disabilities.

- Spina bifida is caused by a failure of the spinal column to close properly; this condition may result in paralysis of the lower extremities.

- Tourette syndrome is a neurological disorder that results in multiple motor and verbal tics, inappropriate laughter, rapid eye movements, winks and grimaces, and aggressive behaviours.

Weblinks

Asthma Society of Canada
www.asthma.ca
This website will help teachers work with students with asthma. It has a whole section on managing asthma at school for teachers, who often misunderstand the problem. In a class of 30 students, an average of 4 will have asthma; it is one of the most common health impairments in the classroom. The Asthma Society of Canada, a national organization, is devoted to enhancing the quality of life of people living with asthma.

Epilepsy International
www.epilepsy-international.com
At this website, there are forums where teachers can pose questions about epilepsy and receive informed answers. Any teacher of a student with epilepsy should find this site a useful resource.

Spina Bifida and Hydrocephalus Association of Canada
www.sbhac.ca
This website is an excellent starting point for any parent or teacher of a child with spina bifida (SB). In addition to providing a fact sheet, it lists links to related sites and educational information on students with SB, especially about common learning disabilities associated with the problem.

National Resource Centre for Traumatic Brain Injury
www.neuro.pmr.vcu.edu
This U.S. website provides practical information on traumatic brain injury for professionals, persons with brain injury, and family members.

Muscular Dystrophy Canada
www.muscle.ca
This website provides information on all types of muscular dystrophy and related resources as well as a forum where you can pose questions to a qualified expert. This site is very useful for teachers who may be working with a student with muscular dystrophy.

Chapter 10

Teaching Students with Special Gifts and Talents

Chapter Objectives

After reading this chapter, you should be able to

- define *giftedness*
- describe the characteristics of students with gifts and talents

- describe ways to identify and evaluate students with gifts and talents
- describe appropriate instructional methods for students with gifts and talents
- identify ways to enhance curriculum and instruction within the general education setting

Carmen is truly an amazing young woman whose story provides a glimpse of what gifted-ness might look like in a student. However, not all students who are gifted display the breadth of exceptionality that Carmen does. She was a student in classes for gifted/talented/creative students for six years, from Grades 1 to 6. Learning came very easily for Carmen, and she excelled in all subjects. However, mathematics was her personal favourite. When she was in Grade 5, she successfully completed pre-algebra, and when she was in Grade 6, Carmen attended a Grade 7/Grade 8 gifted mathematics class, where she received the highest grades in algebra. Carmen's writing skills are also well developed. Several of her essays and poems have already been published. After completing her first year of junior high school, Carmen was awarded two out of five academic awards given to seventh grade students at her school for outstanding achievement in science and mathematics.

Carmen is also musically talented. When she was in Grade 2, a music specialist who came to school on a weekly basis informed her teacher that Carmen should be encouraged to continue with piano lessons because she demonstrated concert pianist abilities. When she entered junior high school, Carmen took up playing the clarinet in the band. At the end-of-the-year banquet, she received the top honour after being in the band for only one year. Additionally, Carmen is psychomotorically talented: she is an accomplished gymnast, dancer, and competitive ice skater, and she played soccer for two years on champion soccer teams and was a walk-on for her junior high's cross-country track team.

Carmen also has artistic strengths, demonstrates leadership abilities, and has good social skills. Carmen's career goals have remained consistent for a long time. She wants to be either a dentist or an astronaut; she can probably be either.

Questions to Consider

1. What kinds of challenges can students like Carmen create, not only for themselves but for their teachers?
2. How do individuals like Carmen, who are highly gifted, differ from other students who are gifted?
3. Should children like Carmen be included in general education classrooms all the time, be separated from time to time, or be provided with a completely different curriculum?

INTRODUCTION

Children and youth such as Carmen, who perform or have the potential to perform at levels significantly above those of other students, have special needs as great as those of students whose areas of need demonstrably limit their performance. These needs are notable because most of these students are likely to spend much of their school day in general education settings. As a result, teaching students with gifts and talents provides challenges to general education teachers that are equal to, if not greater than, those associated with meeting the needs of students with other special needs. In order for classroom teachers to feel confident working with students who are gifted and talented, they should have basic information about giftedness and be able to implement some useful techniques for maximizing the students' educational experiences.

Although there is no general agreement on the best way to educate students who are gifted and talented, many professionals argue that such students benefit from a curricular focus different from that provided in general education. Although some point out that gifted classes and special schools are more effective settings for students who are highly gifted (Clarkson, 2003), the vast majority of students who are gifted and talented spend a considerable amount of time in the general education classroom, offering teachers the challenges and rewards of working with them.

The purpose of this chapter is twofold: (1) to provide basic information about children and youth who are gifted or talented; and (2) to suggest practices for working with these students in inclusive settings. This chapter is a primer only; confidence and competence in teaching students who are gifted and talented come with study and experience. More in-depth information about teaching students who are gifted can be found by referencing additional sources (Clark, 2006; Colangelo & Davis, 2003; Coleman & Cross, 2001; Davis & Rimm, 1998; Heller et al., 2000).

BASIC CONCEPTS ABOUT STUDENTS WHO ARE GIFTED AND TALENTED

CONSIDER THIS

Should there be provincial or territorial legislation to provide appropriate educational programs for students who are gifted and talented?

Students with exceptional abilities continue to be an underidentified, underserved, and often inappropriately served group. In some provinces and territories, special services are available, but others do not identify or provide services for students who are gifted or talented. Moreover, local school boards vary greatly in the type and quality of services provided—if they are provided at all.

Students who could benefit from special programming are often not identified because of several factors. Teachers in general education may not be aware of the characteristics that suggest giftedness, as only a few students are "highly" or "exceptionally" gifted and thus are fairly recognizable. This oversight is particularly common for students who differ from the general student populations because of culture, gender, or exceptionality. Historically, ineffective assessment practices have not identified students who are gifted or talented who come from diverse backgrounds.

For students who are identified as gifted or talented, a common problem is a mismatch between their academic, social, and emotional needs and the programming they receive. In many schools, a limited amount of instructional time is devoted to special activities. Furthermore, some of the gifted programming that exists today is geared toward students who are gifted in the linguistic and mathematical areas. In too many instances, students who are gifted or talented do not receive the type of education they need in the general education classroom.

Services to students who are gifted and talented remain controversial, partly because the general public and many school personnel hold misconceptions about these students. Hallahan and Kauffman (2006) highlight some misguided beliefs:

CONSIDER THIS

Why do you think these misconceptions developed about children and adults who are gifted and talented?

■ People with special intellectual gifts are physically weak, socially inept, narrow in interests, and prone to emotional instability or early decline. *Fact:* There are wide individual variations, and most gifted individuals are healthy, well adjusted, socially attractive, and morally responsible.

■ Children with special gifts or talents are usually bored with school and antagonistic toward those who are responsible for their education. *Fact:* Most children with special gifts like school and adjust well to their peers and teachers, although some do not like school and have social or emotional problems.

■ Students who have a true gift or talent will excel without special education. They need only the incentives and instruction that are appropriate for all students.

Fact: Some children with gifts or talents will perform at a remarkably high level without special education of any kind, and some will make outstanding contributions even in the face of great obstacles to their achievement. But most will not come close to achieving at a level commensurate with their potential unless their talents are deliberately fostered by instruction that is appropriate for their advanced abilities. (p. 455)

The portrayal in movies of individuals who are gifted is noteworthy. As Coleman and Cross (2001) describe, too often the portrayal has negative connotations. They cite the features of key characters in a number of movies: For example, in the movie *Little Man Tate* (1991), the main character—a gifted boy—was portrayed as dysfunctional. The problem with negative portrayals of individuals who are gifted is that they lead to inaccurate perceptions and attitudes, ultimately resulting in unfair, and often discriminatory, practices.

Another example of stereotyping that occurs is the use of various terms to describe children, adolescents, and even adults who are gifted or talented. Historically, terms such as *nerd* and *geek* have been used to refer disparagingly to this group of students. What might be an encouraging trend is that these terms may not carry the same virulence that they once did (Cross, 2005). This is most likely due to the prominence of some very successful and public individuals who might be associated with such terms (e.g., Bill Gates).

Many professionals in the field of gifted education find current services unacceptable and are frustrated by the lack of specialized programming for these students. Undoubtedly, the programming provided in inclusive settings to students who are gifted should be improved. Students who are gifted or talented should be provided with curriculum opportunities that allow them to attain optimum levels of learning, and that are carefully planned, implemented, and evaluated.

Gifted Defined

Our understanding of giftedness has changed over time, and the terminology used to describe it has also varied. The term **gifted** is often used to refer to the heterogeneous spectrum of students with exceptional abilities, although in Canada the term *developmentally advanced* is also recognized. Other terms, such as **talented** and **creative**, are used to differentiate subgroups of people who are gifted.

Across Canada, definitions of giftedness vary. In British Columbia, the definition is as follows:

> *A student is considered gifted when she/he possesses demonstrated or potential abilities that give evidence of exceptionally high capability with respect to intellect, creativity, or the skills associated with specific disciplines. Students who are gifted often demonstrate outstanding abilities in more than one area. They may demonstrate extraordinary intensity of focus in their particular areas of talent or interest. However, they may also have accompanying disabilities and should not be expected to have strengths in all areas of intellectual functioning.* (B.C. Ministry of Education, 2002)

In contrast, Yukon defines intellectual exceptionality in this way: "[i]ntellectual abilities are two or more standard deviations above the mean on a standardized, individually administered test of cognitive abilities in conjunction with superior performance in one or more academic subjects as measured by standardized achievement tests or classroom performance."

FURTHER READING

For more information on the history of services to children who are gifted and talented, read chapter 1 in the *Handbook of Gifted Education*, edited by N. Colangelo and G.A. Davis, published in 2003 by Allyn & Bacon.

CONSIDER THIS

Review the definitions of other categories of exceptionalities discussed in previous chapters to compare components of definitions.

FURTHER READING

For more information on multiple intelligences, read chapter 8 in the *Handbook of Gifted Education*, edited by N. Colangelo and G.A. Davis, published in 2003 by Allyn & Bacon.

These two definitions illustrate two different approaches. While Yukon's emphasis on standardized test scores significantly above the mean is the more traditional approach to giftedness, the broader definition offered by British Columbia is more indicative of current thought in the field of giftedness. Of special interest in this type of definition is the reference to "potential abilities"—students do not have to have already produced significant accomplishments to be considered gifted. Also, the statement that the students should not be expected to have strengths in all areas should be noted, since many teachers believe that a student who is gifted must perform extremely well in all aspects of school.

Many different ways to understand gifts and talents have been presented in the professional literature. Three of the more popular conceptualizations are Renzulli's three-ring conception of giftedness, Sternberg's triarchic theory of intelligence, and Gardner's Theory of Multiple Intelligences.

One way to conceptualize giftedness is to consider the interaction of three interlocking clusters of traits (Renzulli, 1979; Renzulli & Reis, 1991) as essential elements associated with outstanding accomplishments. The three clusters are as follows:

- high ability—including high intelligence
- high creativity—the ability to formulate new ideas and apply them to the solution of problems
- high task commitment—a high level of motivation and the ability to see a project through to its completion

These criteria are found in the two types of people who are truly gifted: those who produce and those who perform (Tannenbaum, 1997).

A popular theory of intellectual giftedness has been developed by Sternberg (1991). His theory includes three types of abilities: analytic giftedness (i.e., ability to dissect a problem and understand its parts); synthetic giftedness (i.e., insight, intuitive creativity, or skill at coping with relatively novel situations); and practical giftedness (i.e., ability to apply aspects of analytical and synthetic strengths to everyday situations). All individuals demonstrate some blend of these three abilities, but individuals who are gifted show high ability in one or more of these areas.

FURTHER READING

Another interesting perspective on the development of talents, the Differentiated Model of Giftedness and Talent (DMGT), was proposed by Francoys Gagné, an honourary professor (retired) at the University of Quebec in Montreal. In order to learn more about this model, read his article "Transforming Gifts into Talents: The DMGT as a Developmental Theory" in *High Ability Studies*, volume 15 (pp. 119–147).

Another perspective, constituting a broad theory of intelligence, has important applications for conceptualizing giftedness and for programming. Gardner and Hatch (Gardner, 1983; Gardner & Hatch, 1989) have developed a very popular model that proposes the idea of **multiple intelligences**. The model, which originally comprised only seven areas, has been expanded to include an eighth area (naturalistic). Gardner has considered three other intelligences, but they are not yet part of his model: spiritual intelligence, existential intelligence, and moral intelligence (Smith, 2002). Table 10.1 describes the features of each type of intelligence along with examples of roles that might be characteristic of a person with a high degree of a given intelligence.

If Gardner's ideas were followed closely, students would be assessed in all areas of intelligence and, if found to have strengths in an area, would be provided opportunities to expand their interests, skills, and abilities accordingly. The attractiveness of this concept is that: (1) It acknowledges some ability areas that are frequently overlooked, and (2) it recognizes the importance of different types of intelligences and puts them all on equal footing.

Table 10.1 Multiple Intelligences

Intelligence	End States	Core Components
Logical–Mathematical	Scientist Mathematician	Sensitivity to and capacity to discern logical or numerical patterns; ability to handle long chains of reasoning
Linguistic	Poet Journalist	Sensitivity to the sounds, rhythms, and meanings of words; sensitivity to the different functions of language
Musical	Composer Violinist	Abilities to produce and appreciate rhythm, pitch, and timbre; appreciation of the forms of musical expressiveness
Spatial	Navigator Sculptor	Capacities to perceive the visual–spatial world accurately and to transform one's initial perceptions
Bodily–Kinesthetic	Dancer Athlete	Abilities to control one's body movements and to handle objects skillfully
Interpersonal	Therapist Salesperson	Capacities to discern and respond appropriately to the moods, temperaments, motivations, and desires of other people
Intrapersonal	Person with detailed, accurate self-knowledge	Access to one's own feelings and the ability to discriminate among them and draw upon them to guide behaviour; knowledge of one's own strengths, weaknesses, desires, and intelligences
Naturalistic	Naturalist Park ranger	Affinity and appreciation for the wonders of nature

From "Multiple Intelligences Go to School: Educational Implications of the Theory of Multiple Intelligences," by H. Gardner and T. Hatch, 1989, *Educational Researcher, 18*(8), p. 6. Copyright © 1989 by the American Educational Research Association. Reprinted with permission of the publisher.

Concept of Creativity

Creativity is a major part of Renzulli's three-ring model, as illustrated in Figure 10.1. The concept is difficult to pinpoint, yet its importance as it relates to individuals who are gifted makes it a current topic for debate and discussion. As Coleman and Cross (2001) note, this topic has been part of the ongoing discussion of individuals who are gifted ever since the publication in 1959 of Guilford's seminal work on the subject.

As indicated previously, the concept is somewhat elusive, and no one definition explaining creativity is definitive. The concept might best be characterized by the phrase, "You know it when you see it." Coleman and Cross (2001) describe the difficulties in defining creativity:

> A single accepted definition of creativity does not exist. In fact, neither is there universal agreement about what relevant attributes are needed to define an act as creative. The difficulty of selecting relevant attributes illustrates the problem of defining creativity. The terms originality and novelty pervade the literature on creativity. They express a quantitative and a qualitative standard, but they fail to say to what criterion a person is being compared. (p. 240)

The concept of creativity continues to receive wide attention, and efforts to better understand it and be able to apply it in meaningful ways within the context of education are warranted.

Figure 10.1 Renzulli's Three-Ring Conception of Giftedness

From *What Makes Giftedness?* (Brief #6, p. 10), by J. Renzulli, 1979, Los Angeles: National/State Leadership Training Institute. Reprinted with permission.

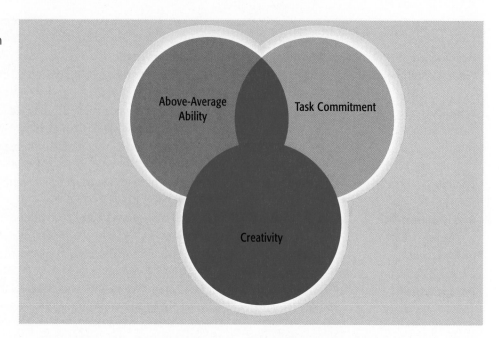

Prevalence and Origins of Giftedness

The number of students who display exceptional abilities is uncertain. It is, of course, influenced by how *giftedness* is defined and how it is measured. That is, the type of definition used to identify giftedness or talent, and the selection, both critically impact prevalence (Bélanger, & Gagné, 2006). The critical reader should note the distinction between the number of students served and the number of students who might be gifted. Only certain types of students who are gifted may be served because of the methods used for identification. Such figures generally underestimate the number of students who are gifted who are ethnically or culturally different, female, or who have been identified with an exceptionality (e.g., a learning disability). These subgroups are underrepresented in programs for students with exceptional abilities.

Much professional discussion has focused on what contributes to giftedness. Most researchers suggest that it results from the interaction between biology and environment, and research has shown that behaviour is greatly affected by genetics. Although this notion is sometimes overemphasized, genetic factors do play a role in giftedness. Other biological factors, such as nutrition, also have an impact on an individual's development.

The environment in which a child is raised also affects later performance and intellectual abilities. Homes in which significant amounts of stimulation and opportunity to explore and interact with the environment exist, accompanied by high expectations, tend to produce children more likely to be successful scholastically and socially.

Characteristics of Students Who Are Gifted

Students who are gifted demonstrate a wide range of specific aptitudes, abilities, and skills. Though they should not be overgeneralized or considered stereotypical, certain characteristics distinguish these students. A comprehensive list depicting the characteristics of students who are gifted has been developed by Clark (2002); a summary is presented in Table 10.2.

CONSIDER THIS

How can the way *gifted* and *talented* are defined influence the prevalence of children classified as such?

Table 10.2 Differentiating Characteristics of the Gifted

Domain	Characteristic
The Cognitive Function	■ Extraordinary quantity of information; unusual retentiveness
	■ Advanced comprehension
	■ Unusual varied interests and curiosity
	■ High level of language development
	■ High level of verbal ability
	■ Unusual capacity for processing information
	■ Accelerated pace of thought processes
	■ Flexible thought processes
	■ Comprehensive synthesis
	■ Early ability to delay closure
	■ Heightened capacity for seeing unusual and diverse relationships, integration of ideas, and disciplines
	■ Ability to generate original ideas and solutions
	■ Early differential patterns for thought processing (e.g., thinking in alternatives; abstract terms; sensing consequences; making generalizations; visual thinking; use of metaphors and analogies)
	■ Early ability to use and form conceptual frameworks
	■ An evaluative approach toward oneself and others
	■ Unusual intensity; persistent goal-directed behaviour
The Affective Function	■ Large accumulation of information about emotions that have not been brought to awareness
	■ Unusual sensitivity to the expectations and feelings of others
	■ Keen sense of humour—may be gentle or hostile
	■ Heightened self-awareness, accompanied by feelings of being different
	■ Idealism and a sense of justice, which appear at an early age
	■ Earlier development of an inner locus of control and satisfaction
	■ Unusual emotional depth and intensity
	■ High expectations of self and others, often leading to high levels of frustration with self, others, and situations; perfectionism
	■ Strong need for consistency between abstract values and personal actions
	■ Advanced levels of moral judgment
	■ Strongly motivated by self-actualization needs
	■ Advanced cognitive and affective capacity for conceptualizing and solving societal problems
	■ Leadership ability
	■ Solutions to social and environmental problems
	■ Involvement with the "meta-needs" of society (e.g., injustice, beauty, truth)

(continued)

Table 10.2 Continued	
Domain	**Characteristic**
The Physical/Sensing Function	■ Unusual quantity of input from the environment through a heightened sensory awareness
	■ Unusual discrepancy between physical and intellectual development
	■ Low tolerance for the lag between their standards and their athletic skills
	■ Cartesian split—can include neglect of physical well-being and avoidance of physical activity
The Intuitive Function	■ Early involvement and concern for intuitive knowing and metaphysical ideas and phenomena
	■ Open to experiences in this area; will experiment with psychic and metaphysical phenomena
	■ Creative approach in all areas of endeavour
	■ Ability to predict; interest in future

From *Growing Up Gifted* (6th Ed.) by Barbara Clark. Copyright 2002 by Merrill/Prentice Hall. Reprinted by permission.

An interesting phenomenon is the paradoxical negative effect of certain positive behaviours displayed by students who are gifted. For instance, students' sincere, excited curiosity about a topic being covered in class can sometimes be interpreted as annoying or disruptive by a teacher or fellow students. Their quick answers or certainty that they are right may be misconstrued as well, in that such desirable behaviour can be misperceived as problem behaviour.

Some characteristics can outright be problematic for students who are gifted. For instance, traits such as uneven precocity, interpersonal difficulties (possibly due to cognitive differences), underachievement, nonconformity, perfectionism, and frustration and anger may indeed be negative.

Clark (2002) also points out that different levels of ability and performance exist within the ranks of those who are gifted. She distinguishes among students who might be considered typical or moderately gifted, those who are highly gifted, and those who are exceptionally gifted. Carmen, who was introduced at the beginning of the chapter, represents an individual who could be considered highly gifted. According to Clark, students who are highly gifted "tend to evidence more energy than gifted individuals; they think faster and are more intent and focused on their interests and they exhibit a higher degree of ability in most of the traits . . . identified with giftedness" (2002, p. 63). Clark describes individuals who are exceptionally gifted as those who "seem to have different value structures . . . tend to be more isolated by choice and more invested in concerns of a meta-nature (e.g., universal problems) . . . seldom seek popularity or social acclaim" (2002, p. 63). Both students who are highly gifted and students who are exceptionally gifted pose significant challenges to educators in meeting their needs within the general education classroom. Most of the discussion in this chapter is directed toward the typical student who is gifted.

An interesting characteristic that has important classroom implications is the gifted student's expenditure of minimum effort while still earning high grades. Many students who are gifted are able to handle the general education curriculum with ease. However, the long-term effect of being able to excel without working hard may be a lack of the work habits needed for challenging programs at a later point in time (i.e., advanced placement classes in high school or university).

Identification, Assessment, and Eligibility

General education teachers need to know about the assessment process used to confirm the existence of exceptional abilities. Teachers play a crucial role in the initial stages of the process, for they are typically the first to recognize that a student might be gifted.

The assessment process includes a sequence of steps, beginning with an initial referral (i.e., nomination) and culminating with the validation of the decision. General education teachers are largely responsible for identifying students who are gifted. Although many children displaying exceptional abilities may be spotted very early (i.e., preschool years), many are not recognized until they are in school. For this reason, teachers need to be aware of classroom behaviours typically displayed by students who are gifted. A listing of such behaviours is provided in Table 10.3.

Teachers who recognize such behaviours should determine whether a student should be evaluated more comprehensively. This usually involves nominating the student for gifted services. Oakland and Rossen (2005) suggest that a nomination that "first informs, then educates, and then encourages teachers, parents, and students to become engaged" (p. 61) is most likely to identify a diverse range of students who might have gifts or talents. Teachers can take part in the next step in the assessment process as well. After a student has been nominated or referred, teachers can assemble information to help determine whether the student should receive special services. The following sources of information can contribute to understanding a student's demonstrated or potential ability: formal tests; informal assessments; interviews with teachers, parents, and peers; and actual student products.

A helpful technique used in many school systems to determine the performance capabilities of students is **portfolio assessment**. Portfolios contain a collection of student-generated products, reflecting the quality of a student's work. They may also contain permanent products, such as artwork, poetry, or video recordings of student performance (e.g., theatrical production, music recital).

Students who are culturally different and come from socially and economically disadvantaged backgrounds may be overlooked in the process of identifying students for gifted programs. For the most part, this problem results from entry requirements that stress performance on standardized tests. When students obtain low test scores on standardized instruments that may be biased against them, exclusion results. Oakland and Rossen (2005) recommend the use of local norms over national norms as a way to avert this problem.

It has also been difficult to identify and serve students who are gifted and also have identified exceptionalities. For instance, the problems that characterize a learning disability (e.g., problems in language-related areas) often mask high levels of accomplishment in other areas, such as drama, art, or music. Special services or activities are warranted for these students.

TEACHING TIP

Classroom teachers need to be alert to students who may be gifted or talented and refer these students to appropriate professionals for testing and services.

◉—|Watch

Portfolios and Self-Assessments

Standardized Tests

Too few students from minority cultural groups are identified as gifted and talented.

Table 10.3 Classroom Behaviours of Gifted Students

Does the child

- Ask a lot of questions?
- Show a lot of interest in progress?
- Have lots of information on many things?
- Want to know why or how something is so?
- Become unusually upset at injustices?
- Seem interested and concerned about social or political problems?
- Often have a better reason than you do for not doing what you want done?
- Refuse to drill on spelling, math, facts, flash cards, or handwriting?
- Criticize others for dumb ideas?
- Become impatient if work is not "perfect"?
- Seem to be a loner?
- Seem bored and often have nothing to do?
- Complete only part of an assignment or project and then take off in a new direction?
- Stick to a subject long after the class has gone on to other things?
- Seem restless, out of seat often?
- Daydream?
- Seem to understand easily?
- Like solving puzzles and problems?
- Have his or her own idea about how something should be done? And stay with it?
- Talk a lot?
- Love metaphors and abstract ideas?
- Love debating issues?

This child may be showing giftedness cognitively.

Does the child

- Show unusual ability in some area? Maybe reading or math?
- Show fascination with one field of interest? And manage to include this interest in all discussion topics?
- Enjoy meeting or talking with experts in this field?

- Get math answers correct, but find it difficult to tell you how?
- Enjoy graphing everything? Seem obsessed with probabilities?
- Invent new obscure systems and codes?

This child may be showing giftedness academically.

Does the child

- Try to do things in different, unusual, imaginative ways?
- Have a really zany sense of humour?
- Enjoy new routines or spontaneous activities?
- Love variety and novelty?
- Create problems with no apparent solutions? And enjoy asking you to solve them?
- Love controversial and unusual questions?
- Have a vivid imagination?
- Seem never to proceed sequentially?

This child may be showing giftedness creatively.

Does the child

- Organize and lead group activities? Sometimes take over?
- Enjoy taking risks?
- Seem cocky, self-assured?
- Enjoy decision making? Stay with that decision?
- Synthesize ideas and information from a lot of different sources?

This child may be showing giftedness through leadership ability.

Does the child

- Seem to pick up skills in the arts—music, dance, drama, painting, etc.—without instruction?
- Invent new techniques? Experiment?
- See minute detail in products or performances?
- Have high sensory sensitivity?

This child may be showing giftedness through visual or performing arts ability.

From *Growing Up Gifted* (3rd ed., p. 332) by B. Clark, 2002, Upper Saddle River, NJ: Merrill/Prentice Hall. Copyright 2002 by Pearson Education. Reprinted by permission.

Diversity Forum

Observational Checklist for Identifying Strengths of Culturally Diverse Children

1. Ability to express feeling and emotions
2. Ability to improvise with commonplace materials and objects
3. Articulateness in role playing, sociodrama, and story-telling
4. Enjoyment of and ability in visual arts, such as drawing, painting, and sculpture
5. Enjoyment of and ability in creative movement, dance, drama, etc.
6. Enjoyment of and ability in music and rhythm
7. Use of expressive speech
8. Fluency and flexibility in figural media
9. Enjoyment of and skills in group or team activities
10. Responsiveness to the concrete
11. Responsiveness to the kinesthetic
12. Expressiveness of gestures, body language, etc., and ability to interpret body language
13. Humour
14. Richness of imagery in informal language
15. Originality of ideas in problem solving
16. Problem-centredness or persistence in problem solving
17. Emotional responsiveness
18. Quickness of warmup

From "Identifying and Capitalizing on the Strengths of Culturally Different Children," by E.P. Torrance. In *The Handbook of School Psychology,* edited by C.R. Reynolds and J.B. Gulkin, 1982, pp. 451–500. New York: Wiley. Copyright 1982 by John Wiley & Sons. Reprinted by permission.

After a student has been identified as gifted or talented and begins to participate in special activities, ongoing assessment should become part of his or her educational program. Practical needs, such as progress in academic areas and realization of potential, and personal needs, such as feeling accepted and developing confidence, should be monitored regularly.

Multicultural Issues

As pointed out earlier, cultural diversity remains an area of concern in the education of students who are gifted. Too few students who are culturally different from the majority of their peers are identified and served through programs for students who are gifted.

Teachers should look for certain behaviours associated with giftedness in children who are culturally different. An example of an observational checklist for accomplishing this task is presented in the Diversity Forum feature.

Even when students from culturally diverse backgrounds have been identified as having gifts or talents, programming is often not sensitive to their needs. For example, programs may not have the resources (i.e., personnel, materials) available to tap the interests and strengths of these students. Often, the general education teacher needs such supports to address these students' educational needs in inclusive settings. The twofold challenge for teachers is to (1) respect racial, ethnic, and cultural differences of students from diverse backgrounds, and (2) integrate diverse cultural topics into the curriculum.

STRATEGIES FOR CURRICULUM AND INSTRUCTION FOR STUDENTS WHO ARE GIFTED

The literature on providing effective services for students with exceptional abilities consistently stresses the need for **differentiated programming**. This means that learning opportunities provided to these students must differ according to a student's needs and

CONSIDER THIS

How can teachers take into consideration multicultural issues when identifying children who are gifted?

FURTHER READING

For more information on students with disabilities who are gifted and talented, read the article "Inclusive Education for Gifted Students with Disabilities," by C. Yewchuk and J. Lupart, in *International Handbook of Giftedness and Talent* (2nd edition), edited by K.A. Heller et al., 2000 (pp. 659–672).

Goals for Curricula of Children Who Are Gifted

- Include more elaborate, complex, and in-depth study of major ideas, problems, and themes—those that integrate knowledge with and across systems of thought.

- Allow for the development and application of productive thinking skills that enable students to reconceptualize existing knowledge or generate new knowledge.

- Enable students to explore constantly changing knowledge and information, and to develop the attitude that knowledge is worth pursuing in an open world.

- Encourage exposure to, selection of, and use of appropriate and specialized resources.

- Promote self-initiated and self-directed learning and growth.

- Provide for the development of self-understanding and the understanding of one's relationship to persons, societal institutions, nature, and culture.

- Evaluate students with stress placed on their ability to perform at a level of excellence that demonstrates creativity and higher-level thinking skills.

From *Diverse Populations of Gifted Children* (pp. 15–16), by S. Cline and D. Schwartz, 1999, Columbus, OH: Merrill.

✱ Explore

Always Challenging

FURTHER READING

For further information and suggestions, read the document "The Journey: A Handbook for Parents and Children Who Are Gifted and Talented" (2004) from Alberta Learning (available at http://education.alberta.ca/admin/special/resources/journey.aspx).

CROSS REFERENCE

Review chapters 3–9, and compare curriculum and instruction adaptations and accommodations suggested for students with other special needs.

abilities. Differentiation includes the content of what students learn, the processes used in learning situations, and the final products that students develop (see the Evidence-Based Practice box for some suggested curricular goals for children who are gifted).

Many professionals in the field of gifted education argue that the preferred setting for students who are gifted, particularly for highly and exceptionally gifted students, is not general education; they recommend differentiated programs delivered in separate classes for the greater part, if not all, of the school day. However, students who are gifted are more likely to spend nearly all day in general education classrooms, possibly receiving some differentiated opportunities in a pull-out program.

Realities of the General Education Classroom

In general education settings, students who are gifted or talented are sometimes subject to conditions that hinder the possibility for having their individual needs met. Concerns related to educating students who are gifted in general education settings may include:

- *Elementary level*
  - The general education curriculum does not challenge students who are gifted.
  - Most students who are academically talented have already mastered up to one-half of the required curriculum offered to them in elementary school.
  - Classroom teachers do little to accommodate the different learning needs of children who are gifted.
  - Most specialized programs are available for only a few hours a week.
  - Students talented in the arts are offered few challenging opportunities.
- *Secondary level*
  - Appropriate opportunities in junior high schools are scattered and uncoordinated.
  - High school schedules do not meet the needs of talented students (i.e., pacing of coverage of content).

- The university preparatory curriculum generally does not require hard work from able students.
- Small-town and rural schools often have limited resources and are unable to offer advanced classes and special learning opportunities.
- Specialized schools, magnet schools, and intensive summer programs serve only a fraction of the secondary students who might benefit from them.
- Dual enrolment in secondary school and university is uncommon.

Other more specific practices that can be problematic for students who are gifted include the following:

- When involved in group activities, students who are gifted may end up doing all of the work.
- They are often subjected to more stringent grading criteria.
- When they finish assignments early, they are given more of the same type of work or assigned more of the same types of tasks at the outset.
- They are overused as co-teachers to help students who need more assistance.
- Vocabulary use in the average classroom is inappropriate for advanced learners.
- Advanced levels of critical thinking are not typically incorporated into lessons.
- Instructional materials in general education classrooms are frequently limited in range and complexity.

Unfortunately, most general education teachers are not provided with the necessary understanding, skills, and resources to deal appropriately with this population. This situation is exacerbated by the fact that teachers have to deal with a wide range of abilities and needs in their classrooms. The composition of the general education classroom in many of today's public schools requires an array of accommodative knowledge and skills.

In addition, some teachers feel uncomfortable working with students who have exceptional abilities. Figure 10.2 highlights this situation by way of a personal experience. Teachers are also concerned about being asked questions they are unprepared to answer or

Figure 10.2 A Personal Experience

From *Exceptional Children in Focus* (p. 216), by J.R. Patton, J. Blackburn, and K. Fad, 1996, Columbus, OH: Merrill. Used with permission.

Not long ago, I was invited to go on a "reef walk" with a class of gifted third- and fourth-graders. It was a very educational experience.

While we were wading in shallow water, we came upon a familiar marine organism commonly called a feather duster (tube worm). Forgetting that these students had vocabularies well advanced of their nongifted age peers, I was ready to say something like, "Look how that thing hangs on the rock."

Before I could get my highly descriptive statement out, Eddie, who always amazes us with his comments, offered the following: "Notice how securely anchored the organism is to the stationary coral?"

All I could reply was "Yes. I did."

challenged on points they may not know well. These are reasonable fears; however, they can be minimized by using these opportunities as a way of increasing everyone's knowledge and by understanding how to address the needs of students who are gifted within the general classroom setting.

Differentiated programming for students with exceptional abilities, wherever it occurs, must address individual needs and interests in the context of preparing the students for a world characterized by change and complexity.

Continuum of Placement Options

A variety of ways exist for providing educational programs to students who are gifted and talented. The value of a particular option reflects the extent to which it meets an individual's needs. A continuum of potential settings for providing programs to students who are gifted is shown in Figure 10.3. As Clark (2002) points out, all of the options have some advantages; none address the needs of all students with exceptional abilities. For this reason, she feels that school systems should provide a range of programming alternatives.

Students who are gifted who are in general education classrooms for the entire instructional day can have their needs met through a variety of special provisions, such as **enrichment**, acceleration, or special grouping and clustering. The challenge for teachers is to coordinate these provisions with those required for other students in the classroom.

FURTHER READING

For more information on programs for students who are gifted and talented in Canada, read J.A. Leroux's article "A Study of Education for High Ability Students in Canada: Policy, Programs, and Student Needs," in *International Handbook of Giftedness and Talent* (2nd edition), edited by K.A. Heller et al., 2000 (pp. 695–702).

Figure 10.3 Placement Options for Gifted Students

From *Growing Up Gifted* (3rd ed., p. 256) by B. Clark, 2002, Upper Saddle River, NJ: Merrill/Prentice Hall. Copyright 2002 by Pearson Education. Reprinted with permission.

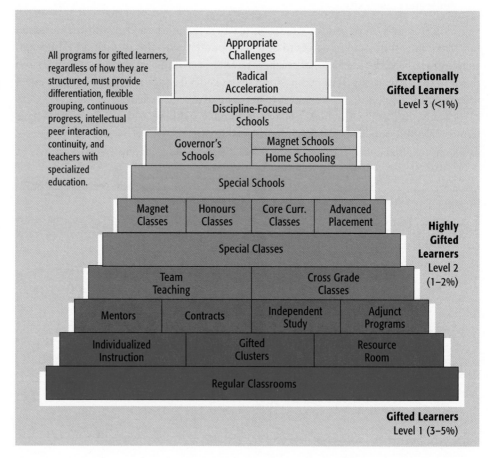

All programs for gifted learners, regardless of how they are structured, must provide differentiation, flexible grouping, continuous progress, intellectual peer interaction, continuity, and teachers with specialized education.

Appropriate Challenges

Radical Acceleration

Discipline-Focused Schools

Governor's Schools — Magnet Schools — Home Schooling

Special Schools

Magnet Classes — Honours Classes — Core Curr. Classes — Advanced Placement

Special Classes

Team Teaching — Cross Grade Classes

Mentors — Contracts — Independent Study — Adjunct Programs

Individualized Instruction — Gifted Clusters — Resource Room

Regular Classrooms

Exceptionally Gifted Learners Level 3 (<1%)

Highly Gifted Learners Level 2 (1–2%)

Gifted Learners Level 1 (3–5%)

In some schools, students who have been identified as gifted are pulled out for a specified period of time each day to attend a special class. When they are in the general education setting, it may be possible for them to participate in an individualized program of study, apart from the regular curriculum.

Students who are gifted may also participate in various adjunct programs, such as mentorships, internships, special tutorials, independent study, and resource rooms—many of which occur outside the regular classroom. For students at the secondary level, spending time in special programming for part of the day, in addition to attending heterogeneous classes, is another possibility.

These programming options affect the role and responsibilities of the general education teacher. In some situations, the general education teacher will be the primary source of instruction for these students. In others, he or she may serve as a manager, coordinating the services provided by others. It is probable that most teachers will be responsible for providing some level of instruction to students who are gifted.

Approaches to Programming

Three general practices are used in designing programs for students who have exceptional abilities: acceleration, enrichment, and special grouping. All three have merit and can be used in general education settings.

Acceleration refers to practices that introduce content, concepts, and educational experiences to students who are gifted sooner than for other students. According to Coleman and Cross (2001), accelerations can be thought of as a way "in which the learner completes a course of study in less time than ordinarily expected" (p. 298). This approach presents students who are gifted with more advanced materials appropriate to their ability and interests. There are many types of accelerative practices, as reflected in the array of options provided in the Inclusion Strategies feature on page 274.

All of the accelerative options described by Southern and Jones (1991) still have relevance for students who are gifted in general education classrooms. The techniques that have the most direct application in the general education classroom are **continuous progress**, **self-paced instruction**, **subject-matter acceleration**, combined classes, **curriculum compacting**, and **curriculum telescoping**. If these practices are to be used, teachers must plan and implement instructional activities.

Other accelerative practices have a more indirect impact on ongoing activities in the general education classroom. Nevertheless, teachers should be aware of them. They include early entrance to school, grade skipping, mentorships, extracurricular programs, concurrent enrolment, advanced placement, and credit by examination. Research relating to the effects of acceleration does not clearly indicate a trend of either positive or negative effectives (Callahan, 2003; Van Tassel-Baska, 2000).

Enrichment refers to techniques that provide topics, skill development, materials, or experiences that extend the depth of coverage beyond the typical curriculum. Coleman and Cross (2001) explain enrichment in the following way: "In its broadest interpretation, enrichment encompasses a number of modifications in standard educational practices. In its narrowest interpretation, enrichment means providing interesting and stimulating tributaries to the mainstream of school" (p. 298).

This practice is commonly used in general education classes to address the needs of students who move through content quickly. Many teachers' manuals and guides provide

Watch

Challenging Gifted Students

FURTHER READING

For more information on schoolwide enrichment, read chapter 14 in the *Handbook of Gifted Education*, edited by N. Colangelo and G.A. Davis, published in 2003 by Allyn & Bacon.

Range and Types of Accelerative Options

1. Early entrance to Kindergarten or Grade 1	The student is admitted to school prior to the age specified by the district for normal entry to first grade.
2. Grade skipping	The student is moved ahead of normal grade placement. This may be done during an academic year (placing a Grade 3 student directly into Grade 4), or at year end (promoting a Grade 3 student to Grade 5).
3. Continuous	The student is given material deemed appropriate for current achievement progress as the student becomes ready.
4. Self-paced instruction	The student is presented with materials that allow him or her to proceed at a self-selected pace. Responsibility for selection of pacing is the student's.
5. Subject-matter acceleration	The student is placed for a part of a day with students at more advanced grade levels for one or more subjects without being assigned to a higher grade (e.g., a Grade 5 student going to Grade 6 for science instruction).
6. Combined classes	The student is placed in classes where two or more grade levels are combined (e.g., Grades 3 and 4 split rooms). The arrangement can be used to allow younger children to interact with older ones academically and socially.
7. Curriculum compacting	The student is given reduced amounts of introductory activities, drill review, and so on. The time saved may be used to move faster through the curriculum.
8. Telescoping curriculum	The student spends less time than normal in a course of study (e.g., completing a one-year course in one semester, or finishing junior high school in two years rather than three).
9. Mentorships	The student is exposed to a mentor, who provides advanced training and experiences in a content area.
10. Extracurricular programs	The student is enrolled in course work or summer programs that confer advanced instruction and/or credit for study (e.g., fast-paced language or math courses offered by universities).
11. Concurrent enrolment	The student is taking a course at one level and receiving credit for successful completion of a parallel course at a higher level (e.g., taking algebra at the junior high level and receiving credit for high school algebra as well as junior high math credits upon successful completion).
12. Advanced placement	The student takes a course in high school that prepares him or her for taking an examination that can confer [university] credit for satisfactory performances.
13. Credit by examination	The student receives credit (at high school [or university] level) upon successful completion of an examination.
14. Correspondence	The student takes high school or college courses by mail (or, more recently, courses through video and audio presentations).
15. Early entrance into junior high, high school [or university]	The student is admitted with full standing to an advanced level of instruction (at least one year early).

ideas on how to deliver enriching activities to students who finish their work quickly. Comprehensive lesson plans should include a section on "early finishers," which will often include students who are gifted, so that enriching activities are available for those who complete assignments before the rest of the class.

Some enrichment activities ultimately involve acceleration. For instance, whenever topics of an advanced nature are introduced, a form of acceleration is actually being employed. There is, however, a distinction between materials or activities that are accelerated and possess a dimension of difficulty or conceptual complexity and materials or activities that provide variety but do not require advanced skills or understanding.

Special grouping refers to the practice whereby students who are gifted and who have similar ability levels or interests are grouped together for at least part of the instructional day. One commonly cited technique is the use of cluster grouping. This practice allows for interaction with peers who share a similar enthusiasm, bring different perspectives to topics, and stimulate the cognitive and creative thinking of others in the group.

CLASSROOM ADAPTATIONS AND ACCOMMODATIONS FOR STUDENTS WHO ARE GIFTED

This section highlights techniques for addressing the needs of students with exceptional abilities. Teachers who will be working closely with these students are encouraged to consult resources that thoroughly discuss teaching students who are gifted in general education settings—e.g., see Winebrenner, 2000).

First and foremost, teachers should strive to create classroom settings that foster conditions in which students who are gifted feel comfortable and are able to realize their potential. They need a comprehensive long-term plan of education and must enjoy learning experiences that reflect this plan.

Although special opportunities for enrichment, acceleration, and the use of higher-level skills are particularly beneficial to students who are gifted, these opportunities can also be extended to other students when appropriate. Many students in general education settings will find practices such as integrated programming (combining different subject matter) to be exciting, motivating, and meaningful.

Management Considerations

It is essential to organize and systematically manage the classroom environment. The learning environment should be safe, accepting, and supportive. It is also useful to design instructional activities that allow for extensive social interactions among all students in the class.

Grouping students who are gifted is useful and can be done in a variety of ways— for example, co-operative cluster grouping on the basis of similar abilities or interests, dyads, or seminar-type formats. Students who are gifted should be afforded an opportunity to spend time with other students who are gifted, just as competitive tennis players must play opponents with similar or more advanced ability in order to maintain their skills.

CONSIDER THIS

How can special opportunities for children who are gifted or talented benefit other students, including those with other special needs?

TEACHING TIP

Pairing a student who is gifted with students who are not gifted can make an excellent co-operative learning situation for all students, but it should not be used to the exclusion of similar ability grouping.

Teachers must create a psychological classroom climate that is conducive to a variety of ideas and viewpoints.

Even though the merits of co-operative learning in classroom settings have been established, heterogeneous co-operative learning arrangements involving students who are gifted must be managed carefully. In such arrangements, teachers must guarantee that most of the work does not always fall on students who are gifted. Co-operative learning arrangements should be encouraged but continually monitored to ensure effectiveness and fairness.

Teachers should develop comprehensive record-keeping systems that monitor the progress of all students, including students who are gifted who may be taking part in a mix of enrichment and accelerated activities. A differentiated report card may be useful for conveying to parents more information about the performance of a student who is gifted. An example of such a report is shown in Figure 10.4. Qualitative information about student performance can be communicated through this document.

The following are some specific suggestions for dealing with students who are gifted:

- Get to know students who are gifted early in the school year through interviews, portfolios of previous work, child-created portfolios, and dynamic assessment (test-teach-retest).

- Enlist parents as colleagues early in the school year by soliciting information and materials.

- Require students who are gifted to follow classroom rules and procedures while allowing them to explore and pursue their curiosity when appropriate.

- Include students who are gifted in the development of class procedures that emerge during the course of a school year (e.g., introduction of animals in the room).

- Explain the logic and rationale for certain rules and procedures.

- Use cluster seating arrangements rather than strict rows.

Differentiated–Integrated Curriculum Report

Student: _____
Teacher: _____
Semester/Year: _____

DISCIPLINES

CONTENT

Area of Study	Broad-Based Theme	Language Arts Enrichment/Acceleration				Math/Science Enrichment		Social Science	Arts	Individual Extension Activities
		Reading	Written Expression	Oral Expression	Spelling	Math	Science	Social Studies/ Social Issues	Music/ Visual Arts/ Performance Arts	

PROCESSES

Basic Skills

Research Skills

- Reading for general information
- Creating hypothesis
- Taking notes
- Making an outline
- Reading for supportive evidence
- Writing the thesis
- Using various sources
- Writing bibliography
- Making appendices

- Brainstorm
- Observe
- Classify
- Interpret
- Analyze
- Evaluate
- Judge

Productive Thinking/Critical Thinking Skills

- Compare
- Categorize
- Synthesize
- Exhibit fluency
- Display flexibility
- Demonstrate originality
- Problem solve

- Elaborate
- Hypothesize
- Exhibit awareness
- Appreciate
- Create
- Redesign
- Prove

PRODUCTS

a variety of ways to communicate and express selves ▲ the opportunity to share information with an audience

☐ Proposed
☐ Completed
} in-depth study of student's choice:

Figure 10.4 Differentiated–Integrated Curriculum Report

Adapted from Sandra N. Kaplan by Joy Kataoka, revised 1990. Copyright © ASSETS 1996.

- Identify a portion of the room where special events and activities take place and where stimulating materials are kept.

- Develop lesson plan formats that include instructional ideas for students who are gifted.

- Consult teacher guides of textbook series for ideas for enrichment activities.

- Let students who are working in independent arrangements plan their own learning activities.

- Use contracts with students who are involved in elaborate independent study projects to maximize communication between teacher and students.

- Involve students in their own record keeping, which assists the teacher and helps develop responsibility.

- Use periodic progress reports, daily logs, and teacher conferences to monitor and evaluate students who are in independent study arrangements.

Curricular and Instructional Considerations

CONSIDER THIS

How can differentiated programming be used effectively with students with a variety of different learning needs?

Many professionals interested in gifted education promote the use of differentiated programming. Keeping this in mind, general education teachers should develop instructional lessons that consider a range of abilities and interests. For students who are gifted, instructional activities should be qualitatively different from those assigned to the class in general—or completely different if certain accelerative options are being used.

The notion of differentiated instruction, particularly to professionals who have worked in the field of special education for any length of time, is not a new idea. However, the attention that has been given to it in recent years is welcome in that the underlying constructs have important implications for addressing a range of needs in today's classrooms.

Guiding Questions When designing instructional activities for the entire class, teachers can use the following series of questions offered by Kitano (1993) to guide planning for students who are gifted:

- Do the activities include provisions for several ability levels?

- Do the activities include ways to accommodate a variety of interest areas?

- Does the design of activities encourage development of sophisticated products?

- Do the activities provide for the integration of thinking processes with concept development?

- Are the concepts consistent with the comprehensive curriculum plan? (p. 280)

Selecting Programming Ideas An accelerative technique that can be used effectively with students who are gifted and talented in general education classes is **curriculum compacting**, which allows students to cover assigned material in ways that are faster or different. Teachers first assess what students know and the skills they possess, identify ways of covering the curriculum, and suggest enrichment and accelerative options (see Figure 10.5).

Figure 10.5 Curriculum Compacting Form

From *The Revolving Door Identification Model* (p. 79), by J. Renzulli, S. Reis, and L. Smith, 1981, Mansfield Center, CT: Creative Learning Press. Reprinted with permission from Creative Learning Press, copyright © 1981.

Individual Educational Programming Guide
The Compactor

Name _____   Age _____   Teacher(s) _____   Individual conference dates and persons participating in planning of IEP

School _____   Grade _____   Parent(s) _____

Curriculum areas to be considered for compacting. Provide a brief description of basic material to be covered during this marking period and the assessment information or evidence that suggests the need for compacting.	*Procedures for compacting basic material.* Describe activities that will be used to guarantee proficiency in basic curricular areas.	*Acceleration and/or enrichment activities.* Describe activities that will be used to provide advanced-level learning experiences in each of the regular curricula.

Many viable ways exist to address the needs of students who are gifted within the context of a general education lesson. An example of such practice is provided in Figure 10.6, which illustrates how the play *Romeo and Juliet* can be taught, keeping in mind the needs of the regular students and students who are gifted. This example developed by Shanley (1993) shows how the content of the play and the activities used by the teacher can be adapted.

The following are more specific suggestions related to areas such as questioning strategies and product differentiation:

- Balance coverage of basic disciplines and the arts.
- Consult teacher/instructor guides of textbook series for ideas for enrichment activities.
- Incorporate internet-based activities into lessons.
- Acquire an array of different learning-related materials for use with students who are gifted—these can include textbooks, magazines, artifacts, software, CD-ROM disks, and other media.

 Explore

Having Someone Explain Things to You Is Important

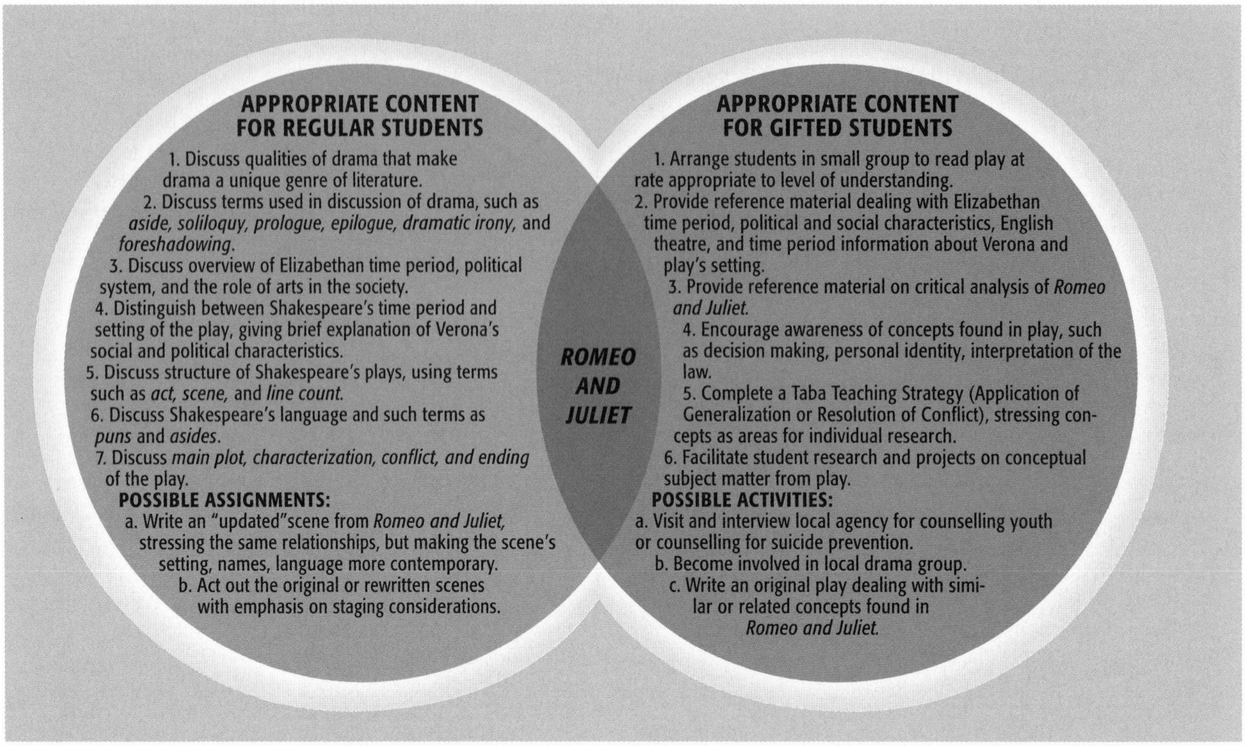

Figure 10.6 Adapting Curricular Content for Teaching *Romeo and Juliet*

From "Becoming Content with Content," by R. Shanley. In *Critical Issues in Gifted Education: Vol. 1. Defensible Programs for the Gifted*, edited by C.J. Minaker, 1993, pp. 43–89. Austin, TX: Pro-Ed. Used by permission.

- Include time for independent study; use independent study contracts.

- Teach research skills (data-gathering and investigative techniques) to students who are gifted to develop their independent study abilities.

- Use integrated themes for interrelating ideas within and across domains of inquiry. This type of curricular orientation can be used for all students in the general education setting, with special activities designed for students who are gifted. An example of an integrated unit on the topic of change is provided in Figure 10.7.

- Include higher-order thinking skills in lessons (Johnson, 2001)—for example, in-class discussions include questions that are open-ended and of varying conceptual levels.

- Allocate time for students to have contact with adults who can provide special experiences and information to students who are gifted (e.g., mentors).

- Avoid assigning regular class work missed when students who are gifted spend time in special programs.

- Manage classroom discussions so that all students have an equal opportunity to contribute, feel comfortable doing so, and understand the nature of the discussion.

- Use standard textbooks and materials carefully, as students who are gifted will typically be able to move through them rapidly and may find them boring.

DISCIPLINES

CONTENT

Area of Study	Terminal Objective Broad-Based Issue/Problem/Theme	Language Arts Enrichment/Acceleration — Reading	Written Expression	Oral Expression	Spelling	Math Enrichment — Math	Science	Social Science — Social Studies/Social Issues	Arts — Music/Visual Arts/Performance Arts
Geological Evolution Civil Rights	**Change**	Research to locate answers in various sources Teacher-made handouts specific to area of study/issue Poetry and/or short stories related to issues Literature Jr. Great Books	Reports Essays Poetry cinquains acrostics narrative poems Short stories Creation legends Personal reaction papers	Oral presentation of each procedure outlined under written expression Discussions Inquiry discussions	Functional spelling Dictionary skills New vocabulary words Word search Crossword puzzles	Graphing reading designing Problem solving Logic	Geology (elements of change in geology) Metamorphosis Archaeology Astronomy beliefs seasons/tides	Historical and contemporary issues that have influenced change in our society Civil rights	Redesigned lyrics Team skits 3-D posters Illustrations Improvisation Role playing/role reversals simulations
Evolution of Humanity's Beliefs Mythology → Scientific Fact → Literature		Research to gain/locate information on individual topics Mythology Literature (poetry on topic)	Note taking Outlining Referencing Writing/editing Final draft of integrated paper	Oral reports Oral discussions Demonstration of scientific project	Functional spelling Dictionary/thesaurus skills New vocabulary words Word search	Graphs Charts Diagrams Time lines where applicable	Research on scientific facts Process diagram Working model Demonstration	How humanity's beliefs/ideas and knowledge evolved Progress or dissension? Compare/contrast with contemporary issues	Process diagram Illustrations 3-D diagram Simulations
Hawaiiana		Research to locate information from various sources Teacher-made handouts specific to discussion topics Legends of old Hawaii	Legends Creation myth Migration letter Evolution of plant life, birds, insects Lava poetry Reports on selected topics Script for skit	Daily oral discussions Oral presentations Skits	Functional spelling Dictionary/thesaurus skills New vocabulary words Vocabulary board Word search	Averaging age of islands Graphing Problem solving Logic	Geology and geography Volcanism Continental drift Revegetation after eruption How plants/animals got to Hawaii Evolution of plant life, birds, insects	Study of ancient Hawaiian civilization and factors that influenced change: *Migration:* reasons for beginning a new society *Social Issues:* compare and contrast problems in ancient Hawaii to contemporary Hawaiian/world issues	Skit Vocabulary board Illustrations Role playing/role reversals simulations Creative dramatics

Figure 10.7 A Differentiated–Integrated Curriculum

- Make sure students who are gifted have access to the latest developments in microcomputers, including simulation software, interactive technologies, CD-ROM databases, and telecommunications (internet access). See the Technology Today box for some websites that contain curriculum-appropriate suggestions for students and teachers.

- Provide a range of options for demonstrating student mastery of curricular/instructional objectives—for instance, for final product development—see Figure 10.8 for a list of examples.

Career Development Students who are gifted and talented need to learn about possible career choices that await them. They may need to do so at an earlier time than other students because they may participate in accelerated programs that necessitate early decisions about career direction. Students should learn about various career options, the dynamics of different disciplines, and the training required to work in a given discipline.

Teachers can select different ways to address students' career needs. One way is to ensure that students who are gifted have access to mentor programs, spending time with adults who are engaged in professional activities that interest them. Another method is to integrate the study of careers into the existing curriculum by discussing various vocations when appropriate and by requiring students to engage in some activities associated with different careers.

Career counselling and guidance are also recommended. If students demonstrate multiple exceptional abilities and a wide range of interests, they may have a difficult time making career choices or narrowing down mentorship possibilities. These students should spend some time with counsellors or teachers who can help them make these choices and other important post-secondary decisions.

Social-Emotional Considerations

Students who are gifted have the same physiological and psychological needs as their peers. In general, high-ability students seem to be as well adjusted as their peers in school (Neihart et al., 2002). In other words, most students with special gifts and talents do not experience more social and emotional problems than other students. They may be dealing with perplexing concepts that are well ahead of the concerns of their peers, however. For

LITERARY

- Literary magazine (prose or poetry)
- Newspaper for school or class
- Class reporter for school newspaper
- Collections of local folklore (*Foxfire*)
- Book reviews of children's books for children, by children
- Storytelling
- Puppeteers
- Student editorials on a series of topics
- Kids' page in a city newspaper
- Series of books or stories
- Classbook or yearbook
- Calendar book
- Greeting cards (including original poetry)
- Original play and production
- Poetry readings
- Study of foreign languages
- Organizer of story hour in local or school library
- Comic book or comic book series
- Organization of debate society
- Monologue, sound track, or script

MATHEMATICAL

- Contributor of math puzzles, quizzes, games for children's sections in newspapers, magazines
- Editor/founder of computer magazine or newsletter
- Math consultant for school
- Editor of math magazine, newsletter
- Organizer of metrics conversion movement
- Original computer programming
- Programming book
- Graphics (original use of) films

MEDIA

- Children's television show
- Children's radio show
- Children's reviews (books, movie) on local news shows
- Photo exhibit (talking)
- Pictorial tour
- Photo essay
- Designing advertisement (literary magazine)
- Slide/tape show on self-selected topic

ARTISTIC

- Displays, exhibits
- Greeting cards
- Sculpture
- Illustrated books
- Animation
- Cartooning

MUSICAL, DANCE

- Books on life of famous composer
- Original music, lyrics
- Electronic music (original)
- Musical instrument construction
- Historical investigation of folk songs
- Movement–history of dance, costumes

HISTORICAL AND SOCIAL SCIENCES

- Roving historian series in newspaper
- "Remember when" column in newspaper
- Establishment of historical society
- Establishment of an oral history tape library
- Published collection of local folklore and historical highlight stories
- Published history (written, taped, pictorial)
- Historical walking tour of a city
- Film on historical topic
- Historical monologue
- Historical play based on theme
- Historical board game
- Presentation of historical research topic (World War II, etc.)
- Slide/tape presentation of historical research
- Starting your own business
- Investigation of local elections
- Electronic light board explaining historical battle, etc.
- Talking time line of a decade (specific time period)
- Tour of local historical homes
- Investigate a vacant lot
- Create a "hall" of local historical figures
- Archaeological dig
- Anthropological study (comparison of/within groups)

SCIENTIFIC

- Science journal
- Daily meteorologist posting weather conditions
- Science column in newspaper
- Science "slot" in kids' television show
- Organizer at a natural museum
- Science consultant for school
- "Science Wizard" (experimenters)
- Science fair
- Establishment of a nature walk
- Animal behaviour study
- Any prolonged experimentation involving manipulation of variables
- Microscopic study involving slides
- Classification guide to natural habitats
- Acid rain study
- Future study of natural conditions
- Book on pond life
- Aquarium study/study of different ecosystems
- Science article submitted to national magazines
- Plan a trip to national parks (travelogue)
- Working model of a heart
- Working model of a solar home
- Working model of a windmill

Figure 10.8 Outlet Vehicles for Differentiated Student Products

From "Differentiating Products for the Gifted and Talented: The Encouragement of Independent Learning," by S.M. Reis and G.D. Schack. In Critical Issues in Gifted Education: Vol. 3. Programs for the Gifted in Regular Classrooms, edited by C.J. Maker, 1993, pp. 161–186. Austin, TX: Pro-Ed. Used with permission.

instance, a girl in Grade 4 who was gifted asked her teacher questions related to abortion—a topic with which she was already dealing conceptually. In addition, students who are gifted may be dealing with some issues that are different from their typically achieving peers, such as stress, hypersensitivity, control, perfectionism, underachievement/lack of motivation, coping mechanisms, introversion, peer relationships, need for empathy, self-understanding, and self-acceptance.

Perhaps the most important recommendation is for teachers to develop relationships with students in order that students feel comfortable discussing their concerns and questions. Teachers can become important resources to students who are gifted, not only for advice, but also for information. Regularly scheduled individual time with a teacher can have important paybacks for the student and the teacher.

Teachers may also find it beneficial to schedule weekly room meetings or class councils to identify and address social, procedural, or learning-related problems that arise in the classroom. The group discussion might include the articulation of a problem, brainstorming and discussion of possible solutions, the selection of a plan of action, and implementation, evaluation, and reintroduction of the problem if the plan of action is not effective.

The following are specific suggestions for dealing with the social-emotional needs of students who are gifted:

- Know when to refer students to professionals trained to deal with certain types of emotional problems.

- Create a classroom atmosphere that encourages students to take academic risks and allows them to make mistakes without fear of ridicule or harsh negative critique.

- Provide time on a weekly basis, if at all possible, for individual sessions with students so that they can share their interests, ongoing events in their lives, or concerns.

Methods that are effective with gifted students are also useful for typically achieving students.

- Encourage the involvement of volunteers (e.g., parents, college practicum students) to assist in addressing the needs of students who are gifted.

- Provide opinions for developing differentiated products as outcomes of various projects or lessons—see Figure 10.8 for a list of examples.

- Have students consider intended audiences when selecting potential final products of their endeavours.

- Maintain regular, ongoing communication with the families of students who are gifted, notifying them of the goals, activities, products, and expectations you have for their children.

- Require, and teach if necessary, appropriate social skills (e.g., appropriate interactions) to students who display problems in these areas.

- Work with parents on the personal development of students.

- Use different types of activities (e.g., social issues) to develop self-understanding and decision-making and problem-solving skills.

Personal Spotlight

Parents of Two Gifted Children: Chad Coller and Danielle Gaudet

Danielle and Chad have two daughters who have been identified as gifted. As parents, they have two main concerns related to the focus and structure of their children's educational program.

Danielle has always focused on the academic aspect of their children's education. "My daughters are two separate individuals, with very different needs in a classroom. I think that it's important to understand that. Even though two children may be identified as gifted, their needs are going to vary as widely as though you were to compare any two children side by side." While Danielle and Chad both agree their daughters are socially and emotionally well adjusted, Chad believes that often the social and emotional well-being of students who are gifted and talented are not always balanced with their academics. "While academic achievement and providing challenge and motivation are particularly important, ensuring the social and emotional development of gifted students should also be given high significance. Academics are often focused on to the exclusion of other areas of development when dealing with gifted students."

Along with the issue of balancing the academic and social-emotional needs of students who are gifted and

talented, the inclusion of Danielle and Chad's children in the regular classroom has raised concerns. "A typical classroom is often overloaded, and teachers don't have the time or expertise to effectively challenge gifted students. It's far easier to use a gifted student as a peer tutor, or to allow the student to self-teach and to monitor that progress. It seems as though the main guiding principles in schools these days are to deal with the outwardly problematic kids first (e.g., those with emotional or behavioural problems). The kids that can sit in a corner and teach themselves, or can teach other students, will always be left in that corner, and will always be a peer tutor (both of which I've experienced with my daughters). The main problem with this principle is that, while the students will be 'fine,' they won't have been challenged, and they won't have had a good experience at school," says Danielle. As parents, their preference is to have their children work with a teacher and a group of peers who are at a similar academic level for at least part of the day. Danielle and Chad want their children to be engaged in an educational program that specifically addresses their individual needs, allows them to explore their interests, and challenges them to expand on their existing abilities.

- Teach students who are gifted how to deal with their "uniqueness."
- Recognize that students who are gifted may experience higher levels of social pressure and anxiety—for example, peer pressure not to achieve at a high level, or lofty expectations originating internally or from others.

ENHANCING INCLUSIVE CLASSROOMS FOR STUDENTS WHO ARE GIFTED

Addressing the needs of students with exceptional abilities in the context of the general education classroom is a monumental challenge. Current realities and probable trends in programming for students who are gifted and talented suggest that general education will continue to be the typical setting in which they receive instruction. Thus, it is important that we do all that we can to enrich the educational experiences of this population in these settings. To do so requires the following: (1) creating classrooms where students who are gifted feel wanted and supported, in addition to having their instructional needs met by appropriate programming; (2) providing the necessary supports to general education teachers to achieve desired outcomes for this group of students; (3) offering supports to parents and families; and (4) preparing classroom teachers to ensure attention is given to the topic of giftedness.

Promoting a Sense of Community and Social Acceptance

The climate of any classroom is determined by the interaction between the teacher and the students; in particular, the teacher plays a leading role in establishing the parameters by which a classroom operates and the foundation for classroom dynamics. The degree to which a classroom becomes a community in which students care for one another and strive to improve the daily experience for everyone will depend on each class's unique dynamics. When a healthy and nurturing classroom context is established, students who are gifted can be important members of the classroom community. In such an environment, their abilities are recognized as assets to the class rather than something to be jealous of, envied, or despised.

In order to promote acceptance of students who are gifted, teachers should strive to dispel prevailing stereotypes. They should discuss the uniqueness of these students in terms of the diversity of the classroom, recognizing that everyone is different. The notion that we all have strengths and weaknesses is also useful. It is particularly important to support students who are gifted who come from underserved groups, such as students with disabilities, those who are economically disadvantaged, and those from different racial or ethnic groups. Special attention should be given to the needs of females who are gifted; some suggestions for nurturing giftedness in females are discussed in Reis's (2001) article (see Further Reading).

Instructionally, many of the strategies suggested for students who are gifted can also be used successfully with typically achieving students. By doing this, teachers can accommodate the needs of these students without drawing undue attention to the special programming they are receiving.

CROSS REFERENCE

Review chapters 3–9 and 11 to determine if methods of enhancing an inclusive classroom for students with other special needs will be effective with students who are gifted or talented.

TEACHING TIP

Assigning students who are gifted or talented to be peer tutors can both enhance their acceptance in the classroom and give them opportunities for leadership. It should be done in moderation, however.

FURTHER READING

Find out more about nurturing giftedness in females in S.M. Reis's article "External Barriers Experienced by Gifted and Talented Girls," in volume 24, issue 4 of *Gifted Child Today*, 2001 (pp. 33–34).

SUPPORTS FOR THE GENERAL EDUCATION TEACHER

The responsibility to deliver a quality education to students who are gifted in general education settings rests on the shoulders of the instructional staff, especially general education teachers. As discussed earlier in the text, for an inclusion model to work successfully, the following features must be in place:

- Classroom teachers need to be well trained in dealing with the many and varied needs of students who are gifted.

- Teachers need to be provided with resource personnel (specialists who assist the general education teacher by helping in the classroom or providing classroom teachers with strategies and materials).

- Teachers need adequate planning time. (Goree, 1996, p. 22)

Teacher training programs may not have adequately prepared teachers to address the academic, social, and emotional needs of students with gifts or talents (Matthews & Foster, 2005). Therefore, regular classroom teachers may need training and support to better meet the needs of diverse learners identified with gifts and talents.

Using school-based supports, such as teacher assistance teams, can also assist with addressing the needs of students who are gifted. When staffed properly, these teams become a rich resource of experience and ideas for dealing with myriad student needs. Parents also play an important, and often indirect, role in the school-based programs of their children. The Personal Spotlight on page 285 in this chapter outlines the perspective of the two parents on the challenges of raising two girls who are gifted.

If appropriate training and supports are provided to general education teachers, we will do a great service to students with exceptional abilities.

CONSIDER THIS

What kind of supports would be ideal to help general education teachers meet the needs of gifted and talented students in their classes?

SUMMARY

- Definitions of *gifted* and services to students who are gifted vary across Canada.

- Professionals do not agree on the best way to provide educational programs for children who are gifted and talented.

- Children with exceptional abilities continue to be an underidentified, underserved, and often inappropriately served group.

- Controversy and confusion characterize the delivery of services to students who are gifted.

- There are many misconceptions about students who are gifted and talented.

- The understanding of giftedness has changed over time.

- Remarkable potential to achieve is a key component of many definitions of giftedness.

- The concept of multiple intelligences suggests that there are different kinds of intelligence.

- The generally accepted prevalence rate of giftedness is 2 percent in schools.

- Students who are gifted demonstrate a wide range of aptitudes, abilities, and skills.

- Identification of students who are gifted and talented is a complex and multifaceted process.

- Students who are gifted and who have diverse cultural backgrounds and exceptionalities are underidentified.

- Differentiated programming is necessary to meet the needs of students who are gifted and talented.

- Enrichment, acceleration, and grouping are ways to address the educational programs of students who are gifted and talented.

- Many general educators are not provided with the necessary understanding, skills, and resources to deal effectively with students who have gifts and talents.

- There are numerous ways to accelerate programs for students who are gifted and talented.

- Special methods used for students who are gifted are often very effective for other students.

- Students who are gifted should be encouraged to develop career interests early in their educational programs.

- Teachers need to address the social-emotional needs of students who are gifted.

- Teachers can do a great deal to promote a sense of community and social acceptance in their classrooms.

- General classroom teachers need to have a variety of supports in order to effectively meet the needs of students who are gifted and talented.

- Comprehensive gifted programs must be committed to identifying and serving underrepresented groups of students who are gifted. These include students who are female, culturally and ethnically different, economically disadvantaged, or have been identified with an exceptionality.

Weblinks

Gifted Canada
www3.telus.net/giftedcanada
Gifted Canada provides a variety of resources, information, and related links in the area of giftedness and lists provincial and territorial chapters. It covers organizations, research, and teaching strategies useful for teachers and parents. An excellent collection of teaching resources is presented.

The Association for the Gifted (TAG)
www.cectag.org
This U.S.-based association is a division of the Council for Exceptional Children. Its website provides a number of publications that are relevant for teachers of gifted students.

National Association for Gifted Children (NAGC)
www.nagc.org
This U.S.-based association's website provides excellent resources relevant to all teachers of gifted students. Look especially for NAGC publications for teachers: these are useful, practical, and very affordable.

Chapter 11
Teaching Students Who Are at Risk

Chapter Objectives

After reading this chapter, you should be able to

- define students who are considered to be at risk
- describe the different types of children who are considered at risk for developing learning and behaviour problems
- discuss general considerations for teaching at-risk students
- describe specific methods for teaching at-risk students effectively

1. What types of interventions does Kayla need? What services would you recommend?

2. Should Kayla be considered for special education support?

3. What can teachers do with Kayla and students like her to help prevent failure?

Kayla is a nine-year-old with blond hair and blue eyes. She is currently in Grade 3, having spent two years in Kindergarten. Mr. Tate, her teacher, does not know how to help her. He referred Kayla for special education. Assessment revealed that she has average intelligence. Kayla is shy and very insecure.

Kayla has significant problems in reading and math. Although she seems sharp at times, she is achieving below even her own expected level. Her eyes fill with tears of frustration as she sits at her desk and struggles with her work.

Kayla frequently cries if Mr. Tate leaves the classroom; she is very dependent on her teacher. She should have a cluster of good friends, but she is a social outcast. Even though on rare occasions a few of the other girls in the classroom will include her, she is typically teased, ridiculed, and harassed by her peers. She has been unable to establish and maintain meaningful relationships with either her classmates or with adults. Kayla's attempts to win friends are usually couched in a variety of undesirable behaviours, yet she craves attention and friendship. She just does not demonstrate the appropriate social skills requisite of someone her age.

Kayla lives with her mother and one younger brother in a small apartment. Her mother has been divorced twice and works as a waitress at a local restaurant. Her mother's income barely covers rent, utilities, groceries, and other daily expenses. Occasionally, when Kayla's mother gets the chance to work extra hours at the restaurant, she will do so, leaving Kayla in charge of her brother. Although Kayla's mother appears interested in Kayla's schoolwork, she has been unable to get to a teacher's meeting with Mr. Tate, even though several have been scheduled. Kayla's mother's interest in helping her daughter with her homework is limited by the fact that she did not complete school herself and does not have a great command of the content that Kayla is studying.

Mr. Tate recognizes that Kayla could benefit from some assistance, particularly in reading and in social and affective areas.

INTRODUCTION

The movement to include students with special needs in general education has made substantial progress over the past several years. One beneficial result has been the recognition that many students who are not officially eligible for special education services still need them. Although they do not manifest problems severe enough to result in a disability classification, these students are **at risk** of developing achievement and behaviour problems that could limit their success in school and as young adults.

Kayla, the student in the vignette, is a good example of a child who is already experiencing some issues that are limiting her ability to succeed, and she is at risk for developing major academic and behaviour problems. In the current system, children like Kayla cannot be provided with special education and related services from provincial or territorial programs. The result too often is that Kayla and children like her drop out of school and experience major problems as adults.

The term *at risk* can be defined in many different ways. It is often used to describe children who have personal characteristics, or who live in families that display characteristics, that are associated with problems in school. Using education as a frame of reference, children and youth who are at risk are defined as those who are in situations that can lead to academic, personal, and behavioural problems that could limit their success in school and later in life. Students identified as being at risk generally have difficulty learning basic academic skills, exhibit unacceptable social behaviours, and/or cannot keep up with their peers. They represent a heterogeneous group. The term **vulnerable** has also been used, referring to

> children who are experiencing an episode of poor developmental outcomes. . . . These children are vulnerable in the sense that unless there is a serious effort to intervene on their behalf, they are prone to experiencing problems throughout their childhood and are more likely to experience unemployment and poor physical and mental health as young adults. (Willms, 2002, pp. 3–4)

The term *vulnerable children* is used by the team that reports findings from Canada's National Longitudinal Survey of Children and Youth (2002) because their "focus is on outcomes rather than on factors that predict outcomes" (Willms, 2002, p. 45). As Willms (2002) stated, "[o]ne can estimate the prevalence of children at risk of experiencing certain outcomes, but it is impossible to estimate the prevalence of children at risk in a general sense" (p. 45).

Unlike students with exceptionalities, who have historically been segregated full-time or part-time from their chronological-age peers, students considered at risk have been fully included in educational programs. Unfortunately, rather than receiving appropriate interventions, they have been neglected in the classroom and consigned to failure. Although not eligible for special education and related services, students who are at risk need special interventions. Without them, many will be retained year after year, will develop behaviour problems, will develop drug or alcohol abuse problems, will drop out of school, will fail as adults, or will possibly even commit suicide (Huff, 1999). School personnel need to recognize students who are at risk of failure and develop appropriate programs to facilitate their success in school and in society.

Although certain factors can increase the vulnerability of students becoming at risk as we have defined the term, it is important to recognize that this phenomenon is not only associated with students who are poor or educationally disadvantaged in some other way. Barr and Parrett (2001) underscored this point:

> . . . any young person may become at risk . . . the risks now facing our youths have become a matter of life and death. It is now clear that students who are at risk are not limited to any single group. They cut across all social classes and occur in every ethnic group. (p. 2)

TYPES OF STUDENTS WHO ARE AT RISK

Many factors place students at risk of developing school problems. These include poverty, homelessness, single-parent homes, death of a significant person, abusive situations, substance abuse, teen pregnancy, sexual identity issues, delinquency, and unrecognized disabilities. Although the presence of these factors often makes failure more likely, it is important not to label every child who is poor or who lives with a single parent as an at-risk student. Many students are resilient even when faced with some difficult life situations. The concept of resilience is further described later in the chapter.

CONSIDER THIS

Should students at risk of failure be identified as exceptional and be served in special education programs? Why or why not?

FURTHER READING

For more information on vulnerable children in Canada, read *Vulnerable Children: Findings from Canada's National Longitudinal Survey of Children and Youth*, edited by J.D. Willms, published by The University of Alberta Press in 2002.

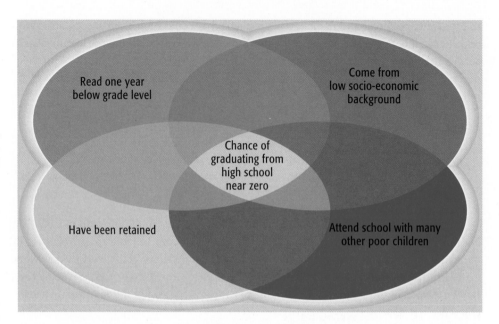

Figure 11.1 Research on Grade 3 Students

From *Policy Perspectives Increasing Achievement of At-Risk Students at Each Grade Level*, by J.M. McPartland and R.E. Slavin, 1990, Washington, D.C.: U.S. Department of Education. Cited in *Hope at Last for At-Risk Youth* (p. 10), by R.D. Barr and W.H. Parrett, 1995, Boston: Allyn & Bacon. Used with permission.

Although overly simplistic conclusions should not be drawn about students at risk, research identifies certain factors as having a clear correlation with school problems. Figure 11.1 depicts the relationship between these four strong predictors of school failure.

Particular risk factors (or correlates) include absence of significant parental guidance and mediation, maternal educational level, inadequate housing, and poor school attendance. At the same time, poverty environments may be associated with a cluster of variables that may include inadequate prenatal care, lead exposure, nutritional deficiencies, and substance abuse during pregnancy (Polloway, Patton, & Nelson, 2010). However, the relative effects of poverty in these figures are hard to determine.

Even when children are strongly indicated as being at risk, school personnel must be cautious about predicting their actual abilities and potential for achievement. Similarly, before teachers refer students who appear to be at risk and who represent culturally or linguistically different backgrounds, they should consider the characteristics included in the Diversity Forum feature. Addressing these issues will decrease the likelihood of referring students for special education programs when in-class interventions might be effective.

Students Who Grow Up in Poverty

Poverty is a social condition associated with many different kinds of problems. It has been related to crime, physical abuse, learning problems, behaviour problems, and emotional problems. Professionals in the field of learning disabilities have begun to realize that poverty can be a significant factor in their etiology (Young & Gerber, 1998). The Government of Canada (2009) states:

> *Children living in families with low SES [socio-economic standing] are less likely to have their basic needs met (sufficient family income, adequate food and shelter) and are more likely to experience ill health. In Canada, 12% of children under the age of 12 live in poverty—a level that has declined over time but remains higher than in*

Issues to Consider before Referring Students from Culturally Diverse Backgrounds for Special Education Programs

■ *Stage of language development:* At what stage of language proficiency, oral and written, is the student in L1 (student's first language) and L2 (student's second language)? What impact have past educational experiences had on language development? Will the environment facilitate further development?

■ *Language skills:* What are the particular strengths and weaknesses of the student in oral and written L1 and L2 skills? What curriculum materials and instructional expertise are available to meet the student's needs? What skills are the parents able to work on at home?

■ *Exceptionality/at-risk status:* What impact does the student's specific exceptionality or at-risk circumstances have on the acquisition of language skills in L1 and L2 and on other academic skills? Does the teacher have an adequate knowledge base to provide effective services? Does the school have access to community supports?

■ *Age:* What impact does the student's age have on the ability to acquire L1 and L2 and to achieve in content areas? Is there a discrepancy between a child's age and emotional maturity? Is the curriculum developmentally appropriate?

■ *Needs of the student:* What are the short-term and long-term needs of the student in academic, vocational, and community life? What are the needs of the student in relation to other students in the environment?

■ *Amount of integration:* How much time will be spent in L1 and L2 environments? Will the student be able to interact with students who have various levels of ability?

■ *Personal qualities:* How might the student's personality, learning style, and interests influence the acquisition of L1 and L2, achievement in content areas, and social-emotional growth? How might personal qualities of the student's peers and teacher influence learning?

From *Assessment and Instruction of Culturally and Linguistically Diverse Students with or at Risk of Learning Problems* (pp. 221–222), by V. Gonzalez, R. Brusca-Vega, and T. Yawkey, 1997, Boston: Allyn & Bacon. Used with permission.

---

some other countries. In addition, 10% of families with children report experiencing higher rates of income-related food insecurity and 13% of all Canadian households report being unable to access acceptable housing. These rates are higher among some populations; in particular Aboriginal households. (p. 2)

Poverty is associated with a range of learning, behavioural, and emotional problems (Adelman & Taylor, 2002) as well as different kinds of exceptionalities, including intellectual disabilities (Beirne-Smith et al., 2006), learning disabilities (Smith, Dowdy, Polloway, & Blalock, 1997; Young & Gerber, 1998), and various health problems. Poverty is also associated with poor prenatal care, poor parenting, hunger, limited health care, single-parent households, and poor housing conditions. Evertson, Emmer, and Worsham (2006) caution that students who live in extreme poverty may lack the basic "going to school" skills that contribute to successful school outcomes. These researchers note that "a key to success for these children is a strong, trusting relationship with the teacher in an environment in which they can feel safe, not threatened or stressed" (p. 215).

CROSS REFERENCE

Review chapters 4 and 7 to read more about how poverty relates to incidence of intellectual disabilities and learning disabilities.

Hunger Although many people in this country have a difficult time believing it, thousands of children go to bed hungry every night. Hunger leads to malnutrition, which in turn can result in damage to a developing neurological system. Children who are hungry have a difficult time concentrating on schoolwork and frequently display behaviour problems in the classroom. Although free school breakfast programs have been instituted in

CONSIDER THIS

What kinds of actions can society take to reduce poverty? What are some barriers to doing these things?

past years as a result of nutrition budgets from ministries of education, hunger among schoolchildren remains a significant problem. Now that education budgets have been cut, many of the nutrition programs have been decreased. Frequently, local home and school associations have worked in the schools to provide this essential service. These parent-run organizations are prominent in many Canadian schools.

School Personnel and Poverty Unfortunately, there is not a great deal teachers and other school personnel can do to alleviate the poverty that students experience. However, teachers can reduce the impact of poverty on achievement and behaviour in the following ways:

1. Recognize the impact that poverty can have on students.

2. Make all students in the classroom feel important.

3. Avoid placing students in situations in which limited family finances become obvious to other students.

4. Coordinate with school social workers or other school personnel who can work with family members to secure social services.

5. Realize that students may not have supplies and other equipment required for certain class activities. Contingency funds or other means to help pay for these items should be available.

Students Who Are Homeless

The growing number of homeless people in society represents a tragedy. The problems of homeless people have only recently become commonly known. Whereas "the homeless" historically were aging adults, often with mental illness or alcohol abuse, today as many as 39 percent of all homeless persons are children—with 42 percent of these children under the age of five (National Coalition for the Homeless, 2006). Hall (2007) noted that "despite the fact that obtaining solid data on the number of homeless is a challenge, substantial evidence supports the theory that the number of children who are homeless the United States has dramatically increased in recent years. By some accounts, the number has more than doubled in recent decades. And contrary to popular belief, the homeless population is not necessarily concentrated in urban areas" (p. 10).

Poverty is directly associated with homelessness, so the problems of poverty also affect this group of children (Elders, 2002); the added impact of not having a home greatly compounds problems of poverty, however. Children and youth who are homeless are usually very embarrassed by the fact that they do not have a place to live. Although some are lucky enough to stay in a shelter, many live on the streets or in cars with their parents.

School personnel can do little to find homes for these children. Probably the best advice is to avoid putting students in situations in which their homelessness will result in embarrassment. For example, going around the room after Christmas and having everyone tell what gifts they received would be very uncomfortable for students who do not have a home to go to after school. If you insist on a home visit, families may avoid interaction with you to escape an embarrassing situation.

A key consideration for school personnel is to ensure that students have access to critical resources inclusive of adequate food, sufficient clothing, medical care, and emergency shelter as needed (Hall, 2007). In addition, another important consideration is to monitor attendance so that patterns of absences are understood and can be appropriately responded to. Hall (2007) listed specific strategies that teachers could employ within the classroom setting, including providing a home-like environment within the classroom by striving for consistency in the arrangement of furniture, including elements (student photographs, classroom pet, plans) that can provide a stable and warm environment for students; and establishing a predictable daily routine.

In order to work with parents who are homeless, teachers and other school personnel should consider the following:

- Realize that a large percentage of students who are homeless will not attend school on a regular basis.

- Be vigilant and sensitive to students who may be homeless—the students may need services, but their families may fear that to get needed services, discovery is required and the forced breakup of the family may follow.

- Monitor behaviour and progress in the classroom, paying particular attention to physical, health, emotional, and social manifestations.

- Become a safe resource for students and their parents.

- Arrange to meet parents at their place of work or at school.

- Offer to assist family members in securing services from available social service agencies.

- Do not require excessive school supplies that many families cannot afford.

- Do not expect homework of the same quality as that of children who have homes.

Students in Single-Parent Homes

"In 2006, 17% of children under the age of 12 in Canada lived in single-parent households, representing a 0.3% increase since 1991" (Government of Canada, 2009, p. 17). The academic achievement of both boys and girls has been shown to be affected, with lower achievement correlating to a limited presence of the father.

Although not nearly as prevalent as single-parent homes headed by mothers, the number of single-parent homes headed by fathers has increased significantly over the past decade. The effects of growing up in a single-parent home headed by a father vary from child to child. Some study findings indicate that single-parent fathers are more likely than single-parent mothers to use other adults in their support networks, and children seem to fare better with a large adult support network than with a limited one.

Role of Schools with Children in Single-Parent Families Children who find themselves in single-parent families, due to divorce, death, illness, or incarceration, require a great deal of support. And, as has been previously stated, being raised in a single-parent family does not imply that these families' situations are not healthy, nurturing, and encouraging. The reality is that when single parents are living at poverty level or have other complications (e.g., substance abuse) in their lives, children and youth are placed at risk. For many of these children, school may be their most stable environment. Growing up in restricting conditions interferes with a child's opportunity to develop and mature. The consequences of not having a stimulating environment must be diminished through intervention (Polloway, Smith, & Antoine, 2010).

School personnel must develop supports to prevent negative outcomes, such as school failure, manifestation of emotional problems, or the development of behaviour problems. An interview conducted with children residing in single-parent homes resulted in the following conclusions on the positive role schools can play:

1. Schools are a place of security and safety for students from single-parent homes.

2. Students who lose parents due to death are often treated differently by school personnel than when the loss is from divorce. Unfortunately, the child's needs are similar in both situations.

3. Teachers are the most important people in the school for children who are in single-parent homes because of their tremendous influence on self-esteem.

4. Students want to be considered just as they were before they were from a single-parent home.

5. Trust in peers and teachers is the most important factor for students from single-parent homes.

6. School personnel often seem oblivious to the new financial situation of families with only one parent.

7. Keeping a log or diary is considered an excellent method to explore feelings and create opportunities for meaningful discussions. (Lewis, 1992)

There are many things schools should and should not do when dealing with students from single-parent homes. Figure 11.2 summarizes some of these "dos and don'ts."

Figure 11.2 Some Dos and Don'ts When Working with Children with Single Parents

Adapted from "Meeting the Needs of Single-Parent Children: School and Parent Views Differ," by C.L. Wanat, 1992, *NAASP Bulletin*, 76, pp. 43–48. Used with permission.

Some DOs
- Collect information about students' families.
- Analyze information about students' families to determine specific needs.
- Create programs and practices that address areas of need unique to particular schools.
- Include curricular areas that help students achieve success, such as study skills.
- Provide nonacademic programs such as child care and family counselling.
- Involve parents in determining appropriate roles for school and family.
- Take the initiative early in the year to establish a communication link with parents.
- Enlist the support of both parents, when possible.
- Provide a stable, consistent environment for children during the school day.

Some DON'Ts
- Don't treat single parents differently than other parents.
- Don't call attention to the fact that a child lives with only one parent.
- Limit activities such as "father/son" night or other events that highlight the differences in a single-parent home.
- Don't have "room mothers," have "room parents."
- Don't overlook the limitations of single-parent homes in areas such as helping with projects, helping with homework, and so forth.

For children whose parents are divorced, schools must consider the involvement of the noncustodial parent. Unfortunately, many schools do not even include spaces for information on forms for students' noncustodial parents. In order to ensure that noncustodial parents are afforded their rights regarding their children, and to actively solicit their involvement, school personnel should do the following:

1. Establish policies that encourage the involvement of noncustodial parents.

2. Maintain records of information about the noncustodial parent.

3. Distribute information about school activities to noncustodial parents.

4. Insist that noncustodial parents be involved in teacher conferences.

5. Structure parent conferences to facilitate the development of a shared relationship between the custodial and noncustodial parent.

More than 14 percent of children live with a single parent, usually a mother.

6. Conduct surveys to determine the level of involvement desired by noncustodial parents. (Austin, 1992)

Students Who Experience Significant Losses

Although the continued absence of one or both parents through separation or divorce is considered a loss, the death of a parent can result in significantly more problems for children. Unlike children living in the early twentieth century, when extended families often lived together and children observed death close at hand, often in the home environment with grandparents, children today are generally insulated from death. Therefore, when death does occur, especially that of a significant person in a child's life, the result can be devastating and often results in major problems in school.

Death of a Parent When a child's parent dies, external events impinge on the child's personality. For example, the child may have to learn to deal with the death itself, with resulting changes in the family, and with the absence of the deceased parent.

Children respond in many different ways to a parent's death. Some responses are guilt, regression, denial, bodily distress, hostile reactions to the deceased, eating disorders, enuresis (incontinence), sleep disturbances, withdrawal, anxiety, panic, learning difficulties, and aggression. It is also not unusual for sibling rivalry to become very intense and disruptive. Often, extreme family turmoil results from the death of a parent, especially when the parent who dies was the controlling person in the family (Van Eerdewegh et al., 1982).

TEACHING TIP

Involve the school counsellor and other support personnel when providing information on death and dying; invite these persons into the class when a student is experiencing a death in the family or of a friend.

✱ Explore

Don't Push Me! I Can't Take It!

Death of a Sibling A sibling plays an important and significant part in family dynamics, so the death of a sibling can initiate a psychological crisis for a child. Sometimes the grief of the parents renders them unable to maintain a healthy parental relationship with the remaining child or children, significantly changing a child's life situation.

When coping with the death of a sibling, children frequently fear that they themselves will die. When an older sibling dies, the younger child may revert to childish behaviours in hopes of not getting older, thereby averting dying. Older children often react with extreme fear and anxiety if they are ignored by parents during the grieving period.

For the most part, the best advice for teachers is to be aware of how the student who experiences loss is doing when in school. Equally important is knowing when to contact the school counsellor, if he or she is not already involved in some ongoing work with the student. Some of the issues that may arise require intervention that is outside the training and expertise of most teachers. Therefore, it is valuable to know about other school-based and outside resources.

CONSIDER THIS

Think about how being abused would affect you at this point in your life. Then consider these feelings from the perspective of a young child. How might they affect a child's school activities?

Students Who Are Abused and Neglected

The Government of Canada (2009) states:

> In 2003, there were more than 75,000 substantiated cases of maltreatment among Canadian children aged 0 to 11 years—equivalent to 22 cases per 1,000 population for that age group. The majority involved exposure to domestic violence and neglect as the primary form of abuse, and in almost all cases the perpetrator (or at least one, if there was more than one perpetrator) was a relative of the child. (p. 32)

Growing up in an abusive or neglectful family places children at significant risk of problems. Child abuse and neglect occur in families from every socio-economic status, race, religion, and ethnic background in society. Family members, acquaintances, or strangers may be the source of the abuse. Although there is no single cause, there are many factors that add to the likelihood of abuse and neglect. These include poverty, large family size, low maternal involvement with children, low maternal self-esteem, low father involvement, and a stepfather in the household (Brown, Cohen, Johnson, & Salzinger, 1998).

Children can be abused in several different ways that place them at risk of problems in school. A variety of taxonomies exists for categorizing abuse and neglect. The following discussion, organized around the two major concepts of abuse and neglect, uses the following system:

- *Abuse*: emotional, physical, and sexual
- *Neglect*: physical, educational, emotional, and medical

There are three major types of abuse: (1) **emotional abuse,** (2) **physical abuse**, and (3) **sexual abuse**. Emotional abuse, which accompanies all other forms of child abuse, can involve unreasonable demands placed on children by parents, siblings, peers, or teachers, or the failure of parents to provide the emotional support necessary for children to grow and develop (American Humane, 2003).

Research has revealed that verbal abuse by itself can result in lowered self-esteem and school achievement (Solomon & Serres, 1999). Although difficult to identify, several characteristics may be exhibited by children who are being emotionally abused. These include the following:

- absence of a positive self-image
- behavioural extremes
- depression
- psychosomatic complaints
- attempted suicide
- impulsive, defiant, and antisocial behaviour
- age-inappropriate behaviours
- inappropriate habits and tics
- enuresis
- inhibited intellectual or emotional development
- difficulty in establishing and maintaining peer relationships
- extreme fear, vigilance
- sleep and eating disorders
- self-destructive tendencies
- rigidly compulsive behaviours (Gargiulo, 1990, p. 22)

Physical abuse is more easily identified than emotional abuse and is defined as "nonaccidental trauma or physical injury caused by punching, beating, kicking, biting, burning, or otherwise harming a child" (American Humane, 2003). It has also been defined as "any physical injury that has been caused by other than accidental means, including any injury which appears to be at variance with the explanation of the injury" (*At Risk Youth in Crisis*, 1991, p. 9). In Canada, "according to 122 police services, in 2003, children and youth under the age of 18 accounted for 21% of victims of physical assault and 61% of victims of sexual assault, while representing 21% of the population" (Statistics Canada, 2005, p. 11). In the United States, Prevent Child Abuse America reported that over 3 million children were referred for child protective service agencies in 1997; more than 1 million children were confirmed as victims of abuse. The number of child abuse cases increased 41 percent between 1988 and 1997. Statistics from 2004 indicate that the prevalence of physical abuse is 2.1 out of every 1000 U.S. children (U.S. Department of Health and Human Services, 2006).

Children who are physically abused are two to three times more likely than nonabused children to experience failing grades and to develop discipline problems. They have difficulty with peer relationships, show physically aggressive behaviours, and are frequent substance abusers (Emery, 1989). Studies also show that children who suffer from physical abuse are likely to exhibit social-skill deficits, including shyness, inhibited social interactions, and limited problem-solving skills. Deficits in cognitive functioning are also found in greater numbers in students who are abused than in their nonabused peers (Weston, Ludolph, Misle, Ruffins, & Block, 1990).

FURTHER READING

For more information on long-term effects of abuse, read the article "The Long-Term Sequelae of Children and Adolescent Abuse: A Longitudinal Community Study," by R.B. Silverman, H.Z. Reinherz, and R.M. Giaconia, published in 1996 in volume 20 of *Child Abuse & Neglect* (pp. 709–723).

Sexual abuse is another form of abuse that puts children and youth at risk for school failure. Children may be sexually abused by their own families as well as by strangers. Sexual abuse can be differentiated into three areas: "touching" sexual offenses (e.g., fondling, intercourse), "nontouching" sexual offenses (e.g., indecent exposure, exposing children to pornographic material), and "sexual exploitation" (e.g., prostitution, participating in the creation of pornographic material) (American Humane, 2003). Children who are sexually abused are not only at risk of developing problems during their school years, but will typically manifest problems throughout adulthood (Silverman, Reinherz, & Giaconia, 1996).

School personnel should be aware of typical physical and behavioural symptoms of sexual abuse:

- physical injuries to the genital area
- sexually transmitted diseases
- difficulty in urinating
- discharges from the penis or vagina
- pregnancy
- aggressive behaviour toward adults, especially a child's own parents
- sexual self-consciousness
- sexual promiscuity and acting out
- inability to establish appropriate relationships with peers
- running away, stealing, and abusing substances
- using the school as a sanctuary, coming early, and not wanting to go home

Neglect refers to situations where a child is exposed to a substantial risk of harm. Neglect is much more difficult to recognize, as no visible physical signs are evident—unless, of course, physical harm occurs. Signs of neglect are reflected through behaviours. Examples of neglect could include placing a child in an unsupervised situation that could result in bodily injury, failing to seek and obtain proper medical care for a child, or failing to provide adequate food, clothing, or shelter. As mentioned earlier, it is this last element that casts fear into the minds of parents who are homeless. The four major types of neglect, as defined by American Humane (2003), are:

- *Physical neglect*: generally involves the parent or caregiver not providing the child with the basic necessities (e.g., adequate food, clothing, shelter)
- *Educational neglect*: failure of a parent or caregiver to enrol a child of mandatory school age in school or provide appropriate home schooling or needed special education training, thus allowing the child or youth to engage in chronic truancy
- *Emotional neglect*: includes actions such as engaging in chronic or extreme spousal abuse in the child's presence, allowing a child to use drugs or alcohol, refusing or failing to provide needed psychological care, constantly belittling the child, and withholding affection
- *Medical neglect*: failure to provide appropriate health care for a child (although financially able to do so), thus placing the child at risk of being seriously disabled or disfigured or dying (pp. 1–2)

The first thing that school personnel should be prepared to do when dealing with children who might be abused is to report any incident to the appropriate agencies. School personnel have a moral and legal obligation to report suspected child abuse. If you suspect a student is being abused, you should follow your school district's procedures for reporting the problem. If you are uncertain about those procedures, contact your principal. School personnel need to understand their responsibility in reporting suspected abuse and know the specific procedures to follow when making such a report.

CROSS REFERENCE

Review chapter 6 for more information on emotional and behavioural disorders, and consider the impact of child abuse on emotional and behavioural functioning.

Students Who Abuse Substances

Substance abuse among children and adolescents results in major problems and places students significantly more at risk for school failure (Vaughn & Long, 1999). Students who are abusing substances have a much more difficult time than their peers with succeeding in school. While most people consider substance abuse to relate to the improper use of alcohol and drugs, it can also refer to the use of tobacco, as many health issues are related to tobacco.

While no factors are always associated with drug use in children and youth, some appear to increase the likelihood of such use. Parental factors, such as (1) drug use by parents, (2) parents' attitudes about drug use, (3) family management styles, and (4) parent–child communication patterns, have an impact on children's drug use. Additional cross-pressures such as the perception of friends' approval or disapproval of drug use, peer pressure to use drugs, and the assessment of individual risk also play a role.

Although a great deal of attention has been paid to the impact of marijuana, cocaine, and alcohol abuse on children and youth, only recently has attention been focused on **inhalants**. Inhalant use increased for every grade level from 1991 to 1995 in the United States (*The Condition of Education*, 1998). One of the problems with inhalants is the wide number of readily available ones that can be used by students, such as cleaning solvents, gasoline, room deodorizers, glue, perfume, wax, and spray paint.

School personnel must be alert to the symptoms of substance abuse, whether the substance is alcohol, marijuana, inhalants, or something else. The following characteristics might indicate possible substance abuse:

- inability to concentrate
- chronic absenteeism
- poor grades or neglect of homework
- poor scores on standardized tests not related to IQ or learning disabilities
- uncooperative and quarrelsome behaviour
- sudden behaviour changes
- shy and withdrawn behaviour
- compulsive behaviours
- chronic health problems
- signs of neglect and abuse
- low self-esteem
- anger, anxiety, and depression
- poor coping skills

- unreasonable fears
- difficulty adjusting to changes

Once a student is identified as having a substance abuse problem and has been referred to the appropriate agency, a supportive classroom environment must be provided. This includes a structured program to build self-esteem and create opportunities for students to be successful. Research has shown that substance-abusing adolescents do not respond positively to lecturing. Rather, successes appear to be related to the development of self-esteem and to interventions that are supportive. School personnel involved with students who are substance abusers should consider establishing connections with Alcoholics Anonymous and Narcotics Anonymous to help provide support (Vaughn & Long, 1999).

Students Who Become Pregnant

Breault and Trail (2005) reviewed the research on teenage pregnancy and identified a group of characteristics that are associated with a greater likelihood that a young woman may become pregnant. These factors include external locus of control, self-efficacy, age at onset of sexual experience, socio-economic status, level of education, mother's level of education, and the teenager's mother's ethnicity, race, locale, and family history.

There are many unfortunate outcomes from teenage pregnancies, and one of the most significant is the increased risk that young girls and boys who find themselves involved in a pregnancy will drop out of school (Trad, 1999). In an era of extensive sex education and fear of HIV/AIDS, the continued high levels of teenage pregnancy are surprising. Despite all the information available for adolescents about sex and sexually transmitted diseases (STDs), it appears that many continue to engage in unprotected sexual activity (Weinbender & Rossignol, 1996).

School personnel should deal with teenage pregnancy issues before pregnancy occurs. Sex education, information about HIV/AIDS, and the consequences of unprotected sex should be a curricular focus. Unfortunately, sex education and practices such as distributing free condoms are controversial, and many schools refuse to enter the fray of such emotion-laden issues.

In addition to having a pregnancy-prevention program, school personnel can do the following to intervene in teenage pregnancy situations:

- Provide counselling and parent-skills training for girls who become pregnant and boys who are fathers.
- Develop programs that encourage girls who are pregnant to remain in school—these programs need to include the availability of a school-based child-care program.
- Do not discriminate against students who become pregnant, have children, or are married.
- Work with families of girls who are pregnant to ensure that family support is present.

Students Who Are Gay, Lesbian, Bisexual, or Transgendered

One of the most vulnerable and overlooked groups who might be at risk comprises those students whose sexual identity differs from those around them. Currently referred to in general as *GLBT* or *LGBT* youth, this group includes students who are gay, lesbian, bisexual, or

> **TEACHING TIP**
>
> Work with school health personnel to obtain useful and appropriate teaching materials and suggestions for HIV/AIDS education.

transgendered. Statistics reflect the fact that these students experience some uncomfortable situations at school. A study conducted by the Gay, Lesbian, and Straight Education Network (GLSEN) (2005) in the United States found that GLBT youth had experienced the following:

- 75.4 percent had heard derogatory remarks frequently at school.
- 37.8 percent had been physically harassed.
- 17.6 percent had been physically assaulted (beaten, punched, kicked).
- GLBT students skipped school five times more often than the general population of students.
- The overall grade averages for students who were physically harassed were half a grade lower than those of GLBT students who experienced less harassment.

The home environment for this population may also be unsafe. This is especially true in cases where parents have a difficult time accepting a child who "comes out" or who tells family members about this difference. Many GLBT youth experience physical violence at home.

Youth who are GLBT come to school feeling that few, if any, school-based staff understand their situation. To a great extent, they are correct. Most school personnel lack understanding of their needs and the daily dynamics of their lives at school. Most of the time, this lack of understanding is unintentional; sometimes it is not. This group of students in general is prone to being absent more frequently than their classmates and to dropping out of school more often as a result of their discomfort and lack of safety at school. Positive outcomes are achieved when schools have a staff that is supportive and understanding (GLSEN, 2005).

Students whose sexual identity differs from those around them often remain unidentified as at risk.

On a personal level, GLBT youth are at greater risk for depression and attempting suicide; they often feel alienated and isolated. As Peebles-Wilkins (2006) noted, "for youth between ages 15 and 24, suicide is more likely than any other reason to be the cause of death" (p. 195). A number of specific risk factors are associated with suicide, including "biological predisposition, depression, substance abuse, sexual-orientation-related factors, poor coping and interpersonal skills, stressful life events, and suicide in the family history" (Peebles-Wilkins, 2006, p. 195).

Substance abuse is greater with this group. Furthermore, these students find themselves homeless more often than their straight peers, as they are sometimes thrown out of their homes by parents. It should be noted, however, that some GLBT students report very positive and productive school experiences.

A number of actions can be taken to improve the climate of acceptance for GLBT youth. Some district- and school-level suggestions include the following:

- Include sexual orientation in all anti-harassment and antidiscrimination policies.
- Educate all school-based personnel regarding GLBT issues.
- Commit resources to this issue.
- Have diversity days that include GLBT youth.
- Establish a clear anti-slur policy.
- Develop and disseminate positive images and resources. (American Civil Liberties Union Freedom Network, n.d.)

Teachers, as mentioned earlier, play a key role. The following suggestions can be helpful to teachers and to students who are GLBT:

- Recognize your own attitudes about this topic.
- Refer GLBT youth who are experiencing personal problems to personnel who are more comfortable with this issue, if you are not.
- Recognize your obligations to act on behalf of GLBT youth when their rights are violated or policies are disregarded (e.g., harassment).
- Create and maintain a safe classroom environment.
- Let students know if you are a "safe" person with whom they can consult if they need to do so.
- Create and maintain a classroom environment where diversity is respected and different points of view are welcomed.
- Use language in the classroom that is sexual-orientation neutral.
- Include GLBT topics in the curriculum if at all possible.

Students Who Are Delinquents

Students who get into trouble with legal authorities are frequently labelled *juvenile delinquents*. Morrison (1997) defines *delinquency* as "behaviour that violates the rules and regulations of the society" (p. 189). **Juvenile delinquency** frequently results in school failure; students who take part in illegal activities often do not focus on school activities. Juvenile delinquency must be considered in light of other factors related to at-risk students, though the relationship of these factors may be difficult to discern. Juvenile delinquency is, for example, highly correlated with substance abuse and may be found in higher rates among poor children than among children who are raised in adequate income environments. It is also more prevalent in single-parent homes (Morgan, 1994b).

Juvenile delinquency is frequently related to gang activity. Gangs currently represent a major problem for adolescents, especially in large urban areas. Morgan (1994b) cites numerous studies showing that adolescents raised in single-parent homes or in homes that sustain a great deal of conflict often join gangs and exhibit other delinquent behaviours. Again, although no single factor leads children to delinquent behaviours, certain elements can indicate high risk. Delinquent behaviours often disrupt school success. School personnel need to work with legal and social service agencies to reduce delinquency and academic failure.

STRATEGIES FOR CURRICULUM AND INSTRUCTION FOR STUDENTS WHO ARE AT RISK

As educators, we want to promote **resilience** in students who are at risk or vulnerable. Resilience can be defined as:

> *a dynamic process encompassing positive adaptation within the context of significant adversity. Implicit within this notion are two critical conditions: (1) exposure to significant threat or severe adversity; and (2) the achievement of positive adaptation despite major assaults on the developmental process. (Luthar, Cicchetti, & Becker, 2000, p. 543)*

In other words, we want to promote "good outcomes in spite of serious threats to adaptation or development" (Masten, 2001, p. 228).

There are four primary approaches to dealing with students who are at risk of failure in schools: compensatory education, prevention programs, intervention programs, and transition programs. Figure 11.3 depicts these approaches. Compensatory education programs "are designed to compensate or make up for existing or past risk factors and their effects in students' lives" (Morrison, 1997, p. 192).

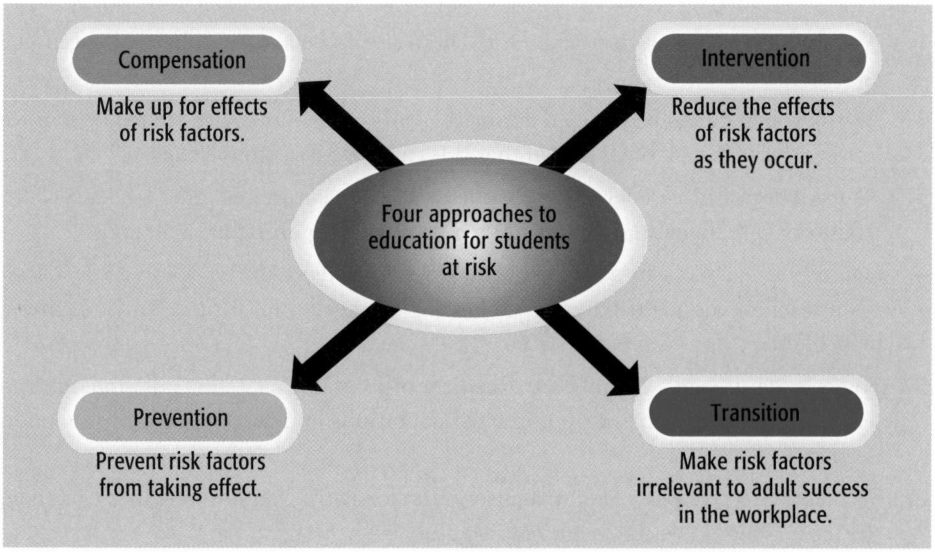

FURTHER READING

For more information on resilience, read the article "Ordinary Magic: Resilience Processes in Development," by A. Masten, published in 2001 in volume 56 of the *American Psychologist* (pp. 227–238).

Figure 11.3 Four Approaches to Education for Students at Risk

From *Teaching in America* (p. 193), by G.S. Morrison, 1997, Boston: Allyn & Bacon. Used with permission.

Compensation
Make up for effects of risk factors.

Intervention
Reduce the effects of risk factors as they occur.

Four approaches to education for students at risk

Prevention
Prevent risk factors from taking effect.

Transition
Make risk factors irrelevant to adult success in the workplace.

Prevention programs focus on developing appropriate skills and behaviours that lead to success and that, if used, are incompatible with other undesirable behaviours. Prevention programs focus on keeping certain negative factors from having an impact on students. Drug prevention programs, antismoking educational efforts, and sex education programs are examples of efforts designed to keep students from developing problem behaviours. Intervention programs focus on eliminating risk factors. They include teaching teenagers how to be good parents and helping at-risk preschool children (Sexton et al., 1996). Finally, transition programs are designed to help students see the relationship between what they learn in school and how it will be used in the real world. School-to-work programs, which help students move from school to work, are effective transition programs (Morrison, 1997).

After-school programs, along with involvement with various school-sponsored extracurricular activities, provide an opportunity for schools to implement many strategies that are effective with at-risk students. Many students who are at risk for problems face extreme challenges in the afternoon hours following school:

> *School-age children and teens who are unsupervised during the hours after school are far more likely to use alcohol, drugs, and tobacco, engage in criminal and other high-risk behaviours, receive poor grades, and drop out of school than those children who have the opportunity to benefit from constructive activities supervised by responsible adults. (U.S. Department of Education, 1998, p. 5)*

After-school programs combine prevention, intervention, and compensatory elements.

Schools must use a variety of programs to prevent problems from developing and to address problems that do develop. The use of technology often proves beneficial.

Characteristics of Effective Programs

Watch

The Challenges of Cultural Biases

Effective programs are those that see through the myths that have evolved in relation to at-risk students and have become barriers to successful efforts. Barr and Parrett (2001) identified seven myths that must be overcome:

1. At-risk youth need slow learning. *Fact:* They need to be academically challenged like all students.

2. At-risk youth should be retained during the early grades until they are ready to move forward. *Fact:* Research has shown that this can have disastrous effects.

3. At-risk youth can be educated with the same expenditures as other students. *Fact:* Additional programming that might be needed will require additional funds.

4. Classroom teachers can adequately address the needs of at-risk youth. *Fact:* Classroom teachers can contribute, but addressing the needs of at-risk students requires a team effort.

5. Some students can't learn. *Fact:* Reaffirmation of the fact that all students *can* learn, if provided with the appropriate adaptations and accommodations, is often needed.

6. The most effective way to improve instruction for at-risk youth is to reduce classroom size. *Fact:* This is a desirable but not necessary element.

Table 11.1 Essential Components of Effective Programs

Positive School Climate

Choice, commitment, and voluntary participation

Small, safe, supportive learning environment

Shared vision, co-operative governance, and local autonomy

Flexible organization

Community partnerships and coordination of services

Customized Curriculum and Instructional Program

Caring, demanding, and well-prepared teachers

Comprehensive and continuing programs

Challenging and relevant curricula

High academic standards and continuing assessment of student progress

Individualized instruction: personal, diverse, accelerated, and flexible

Successful transitions

Personal, Social, and Emotional Growth

Promoting personal growth and responsibility

Developing personal resiliency

Developing emotional maturity through service

Promoting emotional growth

Promoting social growth

From *Hope Fulfilled for At-Risk and Violent Youth: K–12 Programs That Work* (p. 73) by R. D. Barr and W. H. Parrett, 2001, Boston: Allyn & Bacon. Copyright 2001 by Allyn & Bacon. Reprinted with permission.

7. Students who are having learning difficulties need special education. *Fact:* A tendency to refer to special education must be balanced with the idea of addressing the needs of at-risk students within the general education classroom with necessary assistance and supports.

Table 11.1 provides a list of factors, culled from research over the past 25 years, that have been found to be essential to school programs where at-risk students are learning effectively.

The movement to include students with exceptionalities in general education classrooms provides an opportunity to meet the needs of at-risk students. In an inclusive classroom, students should be educated based on their needs rather than on their clinical labels. In fact, inclusion, rather than separate programming, is supported by the lack of evidence that different teaching techniques are required by students in different exceptionality groups. Techniques developed for a specific population often benefit everyone. By removing labels from students and providing programs based on individual needs, students who are at risk can benefit from the strategies and activities supplied for students with various exceptionalities (Wang, Reynolds, & Walberg, 1994–1995).

Specific Strategies for Students at Risk

In addition to the general principles cited earlier, specific programs can prove effective with these students. These include an emphasis on teaching every child to read, **accelerated schools**, **alternative schools**, one-on-one tutoring, extended day programs, co-operative learning activities, **magnet schools**, teen-parent programs, vocational-technical programs, mentoring, and school-to-work programs (Barr & Parrett, 2001). Table 11.2 provides a brief description of each of these approaches.

Table 11.2 Strategies for Teaching Students at Risk

Strategy	Description
Reading emphasis	■ Recognizes the importance of reading
	■ Emphasizes teaching reading early to each child
Accelerated schools	■ Use the same approaches as with gifted and talented children
	■ Use an extended school day with emphasis on language and problem solving
	■ Stress acceleration rather than remediation
Alternative schools	■ Have a separate focus that may meet the needs of at-risk students better than regular schools
	■ *Example*: Montessori schools, back-to-basics schools, nongraded schools, and open schools
One-on-one tutoring	■ Provides concentrated time for direct instruction
	■ Uses volunteers from the community, peers, or older students as tutors
	■ *Example*: Reading Recovery, a one-on-one program (using a certified teacher) showing major success
Extended school day	■ Provides after-school programs as an opportunity for extra tutoring time
	■ Is staffed with regular teachers or volunteers
Co-operative learning	■ Provides opportunities for learning from other students in small groups
	■ Is shown by research to be a very successful model for at-risk students
Magnet schools	■ Focus on specific areas, such as the arts or international studies
	■ Give students an opportunity to focus on their strengths and interests
Teen-parent programs	■ Provide opportunities for students to learn parenting techniques
	■ Help students with young children stay in school
Vocational-technical programs	■ Enable students to develop skills that are specific to jobs
	■ Help with transition from school to postschool environments
	■ Enable students who do poorly in academic areas to perform well in other areas
Mentoring	■ Provides role models for students
	■ Creates opportunities for tutoring and social skills development
School-to-work programs	■ Give students the opportunity to begin work early
	■ Provide training for students in real jobs

From R. D. Barr and W. H. Parrett, *Hope Fulfilled for At Risk and Violent Youth* © 2001. Published by Allyn & Bacon, Boston, MA. Copyright © 2000 by Pearson Education. Reprinted with permission of the publisher.

Mentor programs provide opportunities for at-risk students to meet with adults in the community and develop positive personal relationships.

One program described in Table 11.2 has been used effectively in many schools: a **mentor program** (Slicker & Palmer, 1993). Elementary, middle, and high schools design such programs to provide students with a positive personal relationship with an adult—something that many children and youth lack (Barr & Parrett, 2001). A mentor can be any person of any background who is committed to serve as a support person for a child or youth.

Mentor programs range in scope from national programs, such as Big Brothers/Big Sisters, to programs developed by and for specific schools, such as a program wherein adults employed in the community have lunch with students. Programs large and small have proven effective for many children. It is important to ensure that a positive match is made between the mentor and the child. Other features of successful mentor programs are listed in the Evidence-Based Practice feature.

CROSS REFERENCE

Review some of the teaching strategies included in chapters 3–10, and determine whether any of these methods would be effective with children who are at risk.

Evidence-Based Practice

Components of Effective Mentoring Programs for At-Risk Students

- *Program compatibility:* The program should be compatible with the organization's policies and goals. In a program for students in a community group, for example, program organizers should work closely with school personnel to ensure that the mentoring they provide complements the student's education.

- *Administrative commitment:* The program must be supported from the top as well as at a grassroots level. In a school-based program, all school and district administrators, teachers, and staff must provide input

and assistance. For a sponsoring business, the president or chief executive officer must view the program as important and worthy of the employees' time and attention.

- *Proactive:* Ideally, the programs should be proactive—that is, not a quick-fix reaction to a crisis. Successful mentoring programs for youth work because they are well-thought-out, they have specific goals and objectives, and they exist within a larger realm of programs and policies that function together.

(continued)

- *Participant oriented:* The program should be based on the goals and needs of the participants. These goals will determine the program's focus, recruitment, and training. For example, if the primary aim of a mentoring program is career awareness, students should be matched with successful businesspeople in the youth's area of interest. Activities and workshops should be job-related.

- *Pilot program:* The first step should be a pilot program of 6 to 12 months, with 10 to 40 participants, in order to work out any problems before expanding to a larger audience. Trying to start out with a large-scale plan that includes more than this number can prove unwieldy and disastrous. In the words of Oregon's guide to mentorship programs, "Think big but start small."

- *Orientation:* An orientation should be provided for prospective participants. It will help determine interest and enthusiasm, as well as give prospective mentors and students an idea of what to expect. In addition, it will provide them with opportunities to help design the program.

- *Selection and matching:* Mentors and their protegés should be carefully selected and matched. Questionnaires are helpful in determining needs, areas of interest, and strengths.

- *Training:* Training must be provided for all participants, including support people, throughout the program. Assuming that because a person is knowledgeable, caring, and enthusiastic he or she will make a good mentor is a mistake. Training must be geared to the specific problems experienced by at-risk youth as well as different styles of communication.

- *Monitoring progress:* The program should be periodically monitored for progress and results to resolve emerging conflicts and problems.

- *Evaluation and revision:* The program should be evaluated with respect to how well goals and objectives are achieved. This can be done using questionnaires, interviews, etc.

From *Mentoring Programs for At-Risk Youth* (pp. 5–6), by National Dropout Prevention Center, 1990, Clemson, SC: Clemson University.

The population of at-risk children and youth is incredibly diverse. Many different professionals need to get involved in developing and implementing programs for this group of students. Nevertheless, teachers will continue to play a major role in the lives of students who are at risk. Teachers and students will spend a considerable amount of time together during the week, so the teacher–student relationship is critical.

Personal Spotlight

Public Librarian Kim Hebig

As a librarian, Kim Hebig encounters children from all cultural, linguistic, and socio-economic demographics when working in the community. One group of children with whom she diligently works to build literacy skills are children who may be vulnerable or at risk for a variety of reasons. "From my perspective as a librarian, I feel it is very important to meet the academic, social, and emotional needs of these students. These needs can be met in different ways within the library." Some children have little interest in books or literacy activities in general. Finding materials that are at a child's reading level yet are interesting to read is one way to engage children in reading. "There are high interest /low vocabulary books that may be especially useful. These books are written for older students, using ideas, settings,

plots that would be interesting to an older student, but they are written using simpler language."

Creating opportunities in their neighbourhoods for kids to listen to a story being read or singing songs may also spark an interest in literature (e.g., storytime in the park). "This is especially beneficial in urban areas where children would not otherwise get to a library. For many children this may be one of their first experiences with a library, having a story read to them, or even acting out stories or singing silly songs. The kids begin to look for the 'library people' and the rapport that is built with these kids can last. Take advantage of what your public library and/or school library has to offer. There are resources out there that would be beneficial to children and youth who may be at risk."

SUMMARY

- Students who are at risk may not be eligible for special education programs.

- At-risk students include those who are in danger of developing significant learning and behaviour problems.

- Poverty is a leading cause of academic failure.

- Poverty among children is increasing in this country.

- Poverty is associated with homelessness, poor health care, hunger, and single-parent households.

- Hunger is a major problem in Canada.

- Students in single-parent homes face major problems in school.

- More than 14 percent of all children live in single-parent homes.

- Schools must take into consideration the rights of the noncustodial parent.

- The death of a parent, sibling, or friend can have a major impact on a child and on school success.

- Reports from 122 police services in Canada found children under the age of 18 accounted for 21 percent of victims of physical assault and for 61 percent of victims of sexual assault.

- Child abuse is a major problem in this country and causes children to experience much emotional trauma.

- School personnel are required by law to report suspected child abuse.

- Teenage pregnancy continues to be a problem, despite the fear of HIV/AIDS and the presence of sex education programs.

- Numerous programs and interventions have proved effective in working with at-risk students.

Weblinks

Canadian Centre on Substance Abuse
www.ccsa.ca
As part of the Centre's work to minimize the harm associated with the use of alcohol, tobacco, and other drugs, this site provides information and resources on a variety of issues related to at-risk youth, including prevention and education.

The Internet Public Library on Substance Abuse
www.ipl.org
As an internet library, this site provides a catalogue of websites that pertain to teen substance abuse, including information, clubs, and support groups.

Child Welfare Information Gateway
www.childwelfare.gov
This website provides online information about the prevention of child abuse and neglect and outlines how educators can help to both prevent and treat the problem. It lists the different levels of prevention, the individuals at risk, the ways to evaluate risk, and how to work together with the community for prevention. A lot of information and some related resources are offered, but the funding information is not relevant because this site is American-based; no equivalent Canadian site was found.

Chapter 12
Classroom Organization and Management

Chapter Objectives

After reading this chapter, you should be able to

- identify the key components of classroom management
- describe the roles of students, teachers, peers, and family members in promoting a positive classroom climate
- describe ways to increase desirable classroom behaviours, decrease undesirable behaviours, and maintain behaviours over time
- identify self-regulatory approaches and procedures
- identify possible strategies to enhance classroom and personal organization

This year has been particularly challenging for Laurie Sturby. She has been teaching Grade 5 for 10 years, but she cannot recall any year in which her students' needs were more diverse and the tasks of managing the classroom and motivating her students were more challenging.

While many of her students present unique needs, 11-year-old Sam clearly stands out as the most difficult student in the class. Sam is too frequently out of his seat and often yells to other students across the room. He has great difficulty staying on task during instructional periods and at times spreads a contagion of misbehaviour in the classroom.

During large-group language arts lessons, Sam is inattentive and frequently unco-operative. Laurie is beginning to believe that his high level of inattentive behaviour may make it virtually impossible for him to progress and achieve in the general education classroom, although at the same time, Laurie does not see him as a candidate for a special class or other pull-out program. Further, his inattentive behaviour is gradually resulting in his falling far behind academically. Although it is only November, Laurie seriously wonders whether this will be a productive year for Sam.

Sam currently receives no special education supports or services. However, Laurie has referred Sam to the student support team, and they are pondering suggestions that may be effective in Laurie's classroom as well as considering a request for a more comprehensive assessment that may elucidate instructional or curricular alternatives.

Questions to Consider

1. What recommendations would you give Laurie for focusing on Sam's behaviour and its consequences?

2. Which procedures can Laurie use to significantly increase Sam's attention to attention-to-task behaviours?

3. How can Sam's peers be involved in a comprehensive behaviour management program?

4. How can co-operative teaching facilitate successful intervention in the inclusive classroom?

INTRODUCTION

A teacher's ability to manage his or her classroom effectively and efficiently can greatly enhance the quality of the educational experience for all students. Well-organized and well-managed classrooms allow more time for productive instruction for all students, including those with special needs. As Marzano (2003) points out, "Teachers play various roles in a typical classroom, but surely one of the most important is that of classroom manager. Effective teaching and learning cannot take place in a poorly managed classroom" (p. 13).

The overriding theme of this chapter relates to the notion of creating a classroom community. The absence of heavy-handed adult-directed management systems is characteristic of classrooms where students are valued and solid relationships between teachers and students are established (Bender, 2003). When attention is given to preventive action rather than reactive intervention, classrooms run smoothly and without notice. Smith (2004) has referred to this notion as "invisible management" and suggests that, when effective management is operant, it is hard to discern, unless you know what to look for.

This chapter presents a model for thinking about the major dimensions of *classroom management*, a discussion of these dimensions, and specific suggested pedagogical practices for creating an effective learning environment. Sound organizational and management tactics promote learning for all students and are particularly relevant to the successful inclusion of students with special learning needs. When management and organizational tactics are devised by general and special educators working collaboratively, the likelihood of establishing an effective learning setting is further enhanced.

CONSIDER THIS

Does the inclusion of students with exceptionalities result in greater need for good classroom management? If so, why?

FURTHER READING

For an in-depth discussion on the principles of classroom management, read the book *Principles of Classroom Management: A Professional Decision-Making Model (Canadian Edition)*, written by James Levin, James Nolan, James Kerr, and Anne Elliott, published in 2005 by Pearson Education.

BASIC CONCEPTS ABOUT CLASSROOM MANAGEMENT AND ORGANIZATION

The importance of good classroom management and organization techniques has been affirmed numerous times by professionals in the field of education. Although much attention is given to curricular and instructional aspects of students' educational programs, organizational and management dimensions are typically underemphasized, despite their importance as prerequisites to instruction (Evertson & Weinstein, 2006). This area is consistently identified as most problematic by first-year teachers (Jones, 2006). Further, the smooth functioning of the general education classroom often represents a challenge for teachers as classrooms become more diverse. Jones and Jones (2007) describe the profile of a typical Grade 1 class as being composed of a vast array of students with specific needs that might include any combination or all of the following: a range of disabilities, English language learners, in-school and out-of-school counselling, abusive situations and other unsafe home lives, homelessness, and frequent relocation. Students with any of these features in their lives require special attention in school. Evertson, Emmer, and Worsham (2003) accurately articulate the relationship between the diversity found in today's schools and the need for well-run classrooms:

> Students entering [North American] schools come with such widely diverse backgrounds, capabilities, interests, and skills that meeting their needs and finding appropriate learning activities requires a great deal of care and skill. Because one of the first and most basic tasks for the teacher is to develop a smoothly running classroom community where students are highly involved in worthwhile activities that support learning, establishing an effective management system is a first priority. (p. ix)

This topic is too important to be overlooked, as attention to the elements described within this chapter can benefit a wide range of students with exceptionalities in the general education classroom. Although reading about classroom management cannot take the place of practice and experience, this chapter offers a variety of management strategies to assist both new and experienced educators.

Most definitions describe **classroom management** as a systematic designing of the classroom environment to create conditions in which effective teaching and learning can occur. This chapter broadly defines the concept as all activities that support the efficient operations of the classroom and that help establish optimal conditions for learning (i.e., creating an effective learning environment). A key feature of well-managed classrooms is student choice, empowerment, and growth.

Model of Classroom Management

Every classroom environment involves a number of elements that have a profound impact on the effectiveness of instruction and learning (Doyle, 1986). Six of these are described briefly here:

1. *Multidimensionality* refers to the wide variety of activities that occur in a classroom within the course of an instructional day.

2. *Simultaneity* refers to the fact that many different events occur at the same time.

3. *Immediacy* refers to the rapid pace at which events occur in classrooms.

4. *Unpredictability* refers to the reality that some events occur unexpectedly and cannot consistently be anticipated, but require attention nonetheless.

5. *Publicness* refers to the fact that classroom events are witnessed by a significant number of students who are very likely to take note of how teachers deal with these ongoing events.

6. *History* refers to the reality that, over the course of the school year, various events (experiences, routines, and rules) will shape the evolving dynamics of classroom behaviour.

Considering these elements reaffirms the complexity of teaching large numbers of students who have diverse learning needs in our schools today. To address these classroom dynamics, teachers need to identify ways to organize and manage their classrooms to maximize the potential opportunities for learning. Figure 12.1 depicts a model of classroom organization and management that highlights the multifaceted dimensions of this topic. It evolved from a model designed by Polloway, Patton, and Serna (2008) that reflects an adaptation of what they identify as "precursors to teaching" and stresses the comprehensiveness feature by identifying six key areas that need to be considered.

The effective and efficient management of a classroom is based on numerous considerations. To create a positive, supportive, and nurturing environment conducive to learning, teachers must pay attention to psychosocial, procedural, physical, behavioural, instructional, and organizational variables that have a critical impact on learning and behaviour. Teachers need to consider much of the content of the dimensional model (see Figure 12.1) discussed in this chapter, *before* the beginning of the school year to prevent

TEACHING TIP

Teachers need to have a comprehensive behaviour management plan that not only includes consequences for actions by students (reactive elements) but, more important, focuses on rules, procedures, and overall classroom organization (proactive elements).

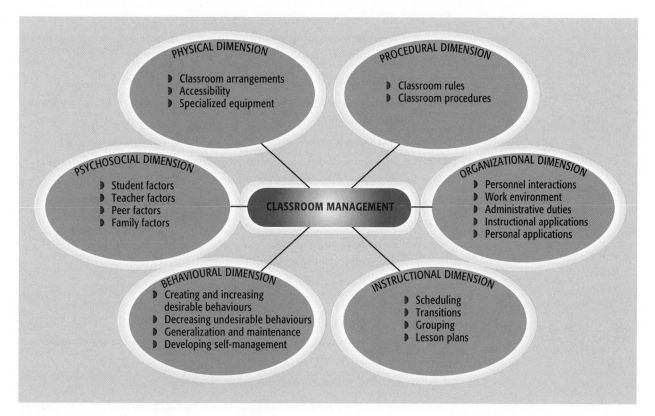

Figure 12.1 Dimensions of Classroom Organization and Management

classroom-related issues from developing. Prevention will likely be more effective than crisis intervention, which might be needed after issues have become significant disciplinary problems. Prevention takes work, however, and classroom time at the beginning of the year must be dedicated to this task. McEwan (2006) stresses the importance of prevention in her "3 + 3 = 33" rule: "[T]he more consistently you teach your students the routines, rubrics, and rules (3Rs) of your classroom at the beginning of the school year (three weeks), the more productive the rest of your year (thirty-three weeks) will be" (p. 2).

◄●┤ **Simulate**

Creating Behavioural
Classroom Expectations

Guiding Principles

The idea that classroom management needs to be comprehensive is endorsed by others as well. Jones and Jones (2007) suggest that teachers must demonstrate competence (i.e., knowledge and skills) in four areas if they are to implement comprehensive classroom management effectively. To these authors, classroom management:

- should be based on a solid understanding of current research and theory of classroom management and of students' personal and psychological needs
- depends on creating a positive classroom climate and a community of support
- involves using instructional methods that facilitate optimal learning by responding to the academic needs of individual students and the classroom group
- involves the ability to use a wide range of counselling and behavioural methods that involve students in examining and correcting their inappropriate behaviour. (Jones & Jones, 2007, pp. 24–25)

In addition, 11 overarching principles guide the development and implementation of appropriate classroom organization and management procedures:

1. All students must be valued.
2. Meaningful relationships between teachers and students need to be developed and cultivated (Bender, 2003).
3. Successful management derives from a positive classroom climate.
4. Teachers have control over a number of critical factors that have a major impact on student learning and behaviour (Jones & Jones, 2007).
5. Good classroom organization and management must be planned ahead of time.
6. Affording students choices contributes to effective classroom dynamics.
7. Teachers and students in effective classrooms are considerate of individual differences, including cultural and familial differences.
8. Proactive management is preferable to reactive approaches.
9. Consistency is the key to establishing an effective management program.
10. Teachers should not feel that they are alone—resources, such as other teachers, administrators, and parents, can contribute to the successful implementation of a classroom management system.
11. Effective classroom management is "invisible" (Smith, 2004).

Although sound classroom management practices are useful in working with all students, the recommendations in this chapter are particularly helpful for students who have special needs and who require individualized consideration. Without question, these students struggle to learn in environments that are not well organized and effectively managed.

Cultural Considerations

When developing and implementing a comprehensive classroom management system, teachers must be mindful of the diverse range of students in their classrooms. One of the most overlooked areas of diversity is cultural diversity. Levin (2003) noted two very important points that have to be acknowledged and addressed in regard to students who come from cultural backgrounds different than those of their teachers: (1) Schools and classrooms are not culturally neutral or culture free, and (2) because of cultural differences, many children from underrepresented groups experience cultural dissonance or lack of cultural synchronization in school (i.e., teacher and student expectations of appropriate behaviour may differ).

Weinstein, Tomlinson-Clarke, and Curran (2004) identified five components that should be part of a *culturally responsive* classroom management system:

- recognition of one's own ethnocentrism and biases
- knowledge of students' cultural backgrounds
- understanding of the broader social, economic, and political context of the . . . educational system
- ability and willingness to use culturally appropriate classroom management strategies
- commitment to building caring classroom communities. (p. 27)

COMPONENTS OF EFFECTIVE CLASSROOM ORGANIZATION AND MANAGEMENT

This section of the chapter discusses the major elements and subcomponents of **classroom organization** management as highlighted in the multidimensional model in Figure 12.1.

Psychosocial Dimension

This dimension refers to the psychological and social dynamics of the classroom. Its primary focus is on **classroom climate**, the classroom atmosphere in which students must function.

The dynamics of classrooms are influenced by certain *student factors*. Factors that can have a remarkable impact on how students behave and react to organizational and management demands are those students' attitudes about school as well as their relationships with teachers, other authority figures, and classmates. Fries and Cochran-Smith (2006) note the following factors that also impact students' attitudes about school and teachers:

- home life
- cultural heritage
- individual temperament
- language resources
- social and interpersonal skills (p. 945)

The dynamics of a classroom are determined by many different student factors.

Other factors that shape student attitudes include the nature of previous educational experiences, how students feel about themselves, and their own expectations concerning their scholastic futures (i.e., potential for success or failure). Teachers need to be mindful that all these factors are subject to cultural and familial variations.

The psychological atmosphere of any classroom depends in great part on certain *teacher factors*, including disposition, competencies and skills, and behaviours. A teacher's attitudes toward students with exceptionalities can dramatically affect the quality of education that a student will receive during the time he or she is in that teacher's classroom. Personal philosophies about education, management and discipline, and curriculum weigh heavily as well. The type of expectations a teacher holds for students can significantly influence learning outcomes.

One particular set of skills that has bearing on the psychological aspects of the classroom is teacher communication skills. Evertson and colleagues (2006) note that the ability to communicate clearly and effectively with students influences the nature of ongoing dynamics in the classroom. They stress that to become an effective communicator, teachers need to display three related skills: constructive assertiveness (e.g., describing concerns clearly), empathic responding (e.g., listening to the student's perspective), and problem solving (e.g., ability to reach mutually satisfactory resolutions to problems).

Peers are also key players in forming the psychological and social atmosphere of a classroom, especially among middle and high school students. Teachers must understand peer values, pressures, and needs and use this knowledge to benefit students with exceptionalities. Valuable co-operative learning opportunities can evolve based on successful peer involvement strategies.

The final component involves a variety of *family-related factors*. Three major issues, all of which have cultural implications, include family attitudes toward education, level of family support and involvement in the student's education, and amount of pressure placed on a child by the family. Extremes can be problematic—for example, a family that burdens a student (e.g., a gifted child) with overwhelming pressure to succeed can cause as many difficulties as one that takes limited interest in a child's education.

Because of the importance of family-related factors on classroom dynamics, teachers should make efforts to establish relationships with parents and guardians. At the very least, a letter (with correct grammar, punctuation, and spelling) should be sent to each family describing the nature of the classroom management system and asking for feedback. This is particularly important if no other means exists for conveying this information, such as some type of orientation or information session. A benefit of developing a relationship with parents is that the teacher can determine a family's status on the dimensions mentioned in the previous paragraph.

The following recommendations should help create a positive, nurturing environment that contributes to positive outcomes for all students:

- Let students know that you are sensitive to their needs and concerns.
- Convey enthusiasm about learning and the school experience.
- Create a supportive, safe environment in which students who are different can learn without fear of being ridiculed or threatened.
- Teach students what fairness is, and model this by treating all students fairly.
- Acknowledge all students in some personal way each day to affirm that they are valued in the room.
- Create a learning environment that is built on success and minimizes failure experiences common to the learning histories of students with exceptionalities.
- Understand the family and cultural contexts from which students come.
- Establish that each student in the classroom has rights (e.g., not to be interrupted when working or responding to a teacher inquiry) and that you expect everyone to respect those rights.
- Instill in students the understanding that they are responsible for their own behaviour through the choices they make.
- Convey to students that every student's thoughts and ideas are important.
- Encourage risk taking, and nurture all students (i.e., gifted, average, and disabled) to take on scholastic challenges.

Procedural Dimension

As noted in Figure 12.1, the procedural dimension refers to the rules and procedures that are part of the operating program of a classroom. The guidelines discussed provide direction to school staff and students as to what is expected of all. The teacher must identify all guiding principles, rules, procedures, and other regulations before the school year begins and should plan to *teach* them to students during the first days of the year.

Equally important is preparation for dealing with violations of rules. Immediate and consistent consequences are needed. Various disciplinary techniques can be implemented to ensure that inappropriate behaviour is handled effectively. (These will be covered in a subsequent section of the chapter.)

CONSIDER THIS

Why are classroom rules such an important component of classroom management? Describe the likely climate of classrooms with effective rules and those without effective rules.

Students with exceptional needs will benefit from being taught systematically the administrative and social rules operative in a classroom (social skills). The suggestions provided in this section focus on classroom rules and in-class procedures.

Most individuals respond best when they know what is expected of them. Guiding principles provide standards that are in place at all times in the classroom. They can be thought of as "guidelines for life at school" and should include very general statements that can be invoked in many different situations. The following are representative examples of guiding principles that are adapted from Smith (2004): treat each other fairly; show respect and responsibility; school is a safe place to learn; our classroom is our community; students have the right to learn and teachers have the right to teach; be safe, kind, and productive.

Classroom rules provide a general sense of what is expected of students. They should be essential to classroom functioning and should help create a positive learning environment. Reasonable classroom rules, presented appropriately, will be particularly beneficial to students with exceptionalities who are in general education settings because this process assists in clarifying expectations. Evertson and colleagues (2006) offer four general rules that cover many classroom behaviours: respect and be polite to all people, be prompt and prepared, listen quietly when others are speaking, and obey all school rules. Rubrics can be developed for these rules to assist students in recognizing the continuum of levels at which a rule can be performed along with the acceptable levels for the classroom. Some specific suggestions related to classroom rules are presented in Table 12.1.

An area of classroom management that may be overlooked is the development of logical *classroom procedures*. Classroom procedures refer to the specific way in which various classroom activities will be performed or the way certain situations will be handled. For example, depending on age, procedures may need to be established for using the pencil sharpener, using the washroom, and entering and leaving the classroom. Evertson and

Table 12.1 Recommendations for Classroom Rules

- Develop no more than seven rules for the classroom.
- Consider involving the students in rule development.
- Keep the rules brief, and state them clearly.
- State the rules in a positive way—avoid statements that are worded in negatively, such as "not allowed."
- Teach the rules through modelling and practice, and verify that all have been learned.
- Post the rules in a location that all students can see.
- Discuss exceptions in advance so that students understand them.
- Discuss specific consequences if rules are violated.
- Review the rules on a regular basis and when new students join the class.
- Use reminders of rules as a preventive measure for times when possible disruptions are anticipated.
- Use positive reinforcement to encourage rule compliance.

colleagues (2006) have identified five general areas in which specific procedures should be developed:

- *Room use*: teacher's desk, student desks, storage, drinking fountains, sink, pencil sharpener, centres, computer stations, board.

- *Individual work and teacher-led activities*: attention during presentations, participation, talk among students, obtaining help, when work has been completed.

- *Transitions into and out of the room*: beginning of the day, leaving the room, returning to the room, ending the day.

- *Procedures during teacher-led, small-group instruction*: getting the class ready, student movement, expected behaviour of the students in the group, expected behaviour out of the group, materials and supplies.

- *General procedures*: distributing materials, classroom helpers, interruptions or delays, washrooms, library use, office visits, cafeteria, playground, fire and disaster drills. (pp. 38–39)

Again, clearly defined procedures are of particular importance, especially for some students with exceptionalities who may have difficulty attending to details or following instructions. This is one area where adequate consideration of these activities can prevent the development of many behaviour-related problems.

Failing to address procedural issues in the classroom can cause distress for teachers if not attended to at the beginning of the school year. Teachers are often surprised by the complexity and detail associated with many seemingly trivial areas. The procedures for these areas combine to form the mosaic of one's management system. Here are some suggestions:

- Identify all situations for which a procedure will be needed.

- Develop the procedures collaboratively with the students.

- Explain (describe and demonstrate) each procedure thoroughly.

- *Teach* each procedure through modelling, guided practice, independent practice, and feedback, allowing every student to have an opportunity to practise the procedure and demonstrate learning on an appropriate level.

- Introduce classroom procedures during the first week of school, scheduling priority procedures for the first day and covering others on subsequent days—remember the "3 + 3 = 33" rule (McEwan, 2006).

- Avoid introducing too many procedures at once.

- Incorporate any school regulations of importance and relevance into classroom procedures instruction (e.g., hall passes, washroom use).

Physical Dimension

The physical dimension includes the aspects of the physical environment that teachers can manipulate to enhance the conditions for learning. As Doyle (2006) notes, "[t]he data on classroom design and furniture arrangements indicate that different patterns of spatial organization have little effect on achievement but some effect on attitudes and conduct" (p. 106). The physical environment of the classroom does in fact have an impact on behaviour and attitudes (McEwan, 2006). For students with certain exceptionalities,

Explore

Effective Room Management

Table 12.2 Seating Arrangements
Seat students with behaviour problems first so that they are in close proximity to the teacher for as much of the time as possible.
After these students demonstrate more self-control, more distant seating arrangements are possible and desirable.
Locate students for whom visual distractions can interfere with attention to tasks (e.g., learning and attention problems, hearing impairments, behaviour problems) so that these distractions are minimized.
Establish clear lines of vision (a) for students so that they can attend to instruction and (b) for the teacher so that students can be monitored throughout the class period (Rosenberg et al., 1991).
Ensure that students with sensory impairments are seated so that they can maximize their residual vision and hearing.
Consider alternative arrangements of desks (e.g., table clusters) as options to traditional rows.

some features of the physical setting may need to be specially arranged to ensure that individual needs are met.

Classroom arrangements refer to physical facets of the classroom, including classroom layout (i.e., geography of the room), arrangement of desks, storage, wall space, and signage. Teachers are encouraged to consider carefully the *seating arrangement* for students who have problems with controlling their behaviours, those who experience attention deficit, and those with sensory impairments. Table 12.2 provides recommendations. The judicious use of seating arrangements can minimize problems as well as create better learning opportunities for students. Carbone (2001) provides a host of suggestions for arranging the physical dimensions of a general education classroom for addressing the needs of students with AD/HD.

Other suggestions for classroom arrangement are as follows:

■ Consider establishing areas of the classroom for certain types of activities (e.g., discovery or inquiry learning, independent reading).

■ Clearly establish which areas of the classroom, such as the teacher's desk, are off limits—this recommendation is also a procedural one.

■ Be sure students can be seen easily by the teacher and that the teacher, or other presenters, can be seen easily by students (Evertson et al., 2006).

■ Begin the year with a more structured environment, moving to more flexibility after rules and procedures have been established.

■ Notify students with visual impairments of changes made to the physical environment.

■ Arrange furniture so that the teacher and students can move easily around the classroom.

■ Direct students' attention to the information to be learned from bulletin boards, if they are used for instructional purposes.

■ Establish patterns of moving around the classroom that minimize disruption—keep high-traffic areas free of congestion (Evertson et al., 2006).

■ Keep frequently used teaching materials and student supplies readily accessible (Evertson et al., 2006).

- Secure materials and equipment that are potentially harmful if used without proper supervision, such as certain art supplies, chemicals, and science equipment.

- Avoid creating open spaces that have no clear purpose, as they often can become staging areas for problem behaviours.

- Provide labels and signs for areas of the room to assist younger or more delayed students in better understanding what and where things are.

The concept of **accessibility** extends beyond physical accessibility, touching on overall program accessibility for students with exceptionalities. Students who are identified with exceptionalities, as well as students qualifying as having substantial limitations in a major life function such as walking or learning, are able to benefit from needed accommodations.

Students with exceptionalities must be able to use the classroom like other students, and the room must be free of potential hazards. Most of the time, making a classroom physically accessible is neither difficult nor costly. Specific suggestions for creating an accessible classroom include the following:

- Ensure that the classroom is accessible to students who use wheelchairs, braces, crutches, or other forms of mobility assistance—this involves doorways, space to move within the classroom, floor coverings, learning centres, microcomputers, chalkboards or dry-erase boards, bookshelves, sinks, tables, desks, and any other areas or physical objects that students use.

- Guarantee that the classroom is free of hazards (e.g., low-hanging mobiles or plants) that could injure students who have a visual impairment.

- Label storage areas and other parts of the classroom for students with visual impairments by using raised lettering or Braille.

- Pay special attention to signs identifying hazards by providing nonverbal cautions for nonreaders.

Some students with exceptionalities require the use of *specialized equipment*, such as wheelchairs, hearing aids and other types of amplification systems, communication devices, adaptive desks and trays, prone standers (i.e., stand-up desks), and medical equipment. This equipment allows programmatic accessibility and, in many instances, access to the general education curriculum. These types of assistive devices were introduced earlier in the book so that teachers may understand how the equipment works, how it should be used, and what adaptations will need to be made to the classroom environment to accommodate the student using it. The other students in the classroom should be introduced to the special equipment as well. Instructional lessons on specific pieces of equipment will not only be helpful in creating an inclusive environment, but may also provide a basis for curricular tie-ins in areas including health and science. Suggestions include the following:

CROSS REFERENCE

Review the sections in chapter 9 on students with low-incidence exceptionalities and those with sensory impairments, and consider the implications of equipment needed by these groups of students.

- Identify the special equipment that will be used in the classroom prior to the arrival of the student who needs it.

- Learn how special equipment and devices work and how to identify problems or malfunctions.

- Find out how long students need to use time-specified equipment or devices.

- Structure learning activities in which the student with a disability (perhaps paired with a peer) demonstrates appropriate usage of the specialized equipment.

Behavioural Dimension

◄●─ Simulate

Who's in Charge?

The ability to manage inappropriate behaviours that may disrupt the learning environment is an important component of classroom management. Yet this ability is only a part of a comprehensive behaviour management program. To be most effective, such a plan should also include techniques for developing new behaviours or increasing desirable behaviours within the students' repertoire. Moreover, a sound program must ensure that behaviours learned or changed will be maintained over time and generalized (e.g., demonstrated in different contexts). Such a program must teach self-control and self-regulatory mechanisms.

Recently, more attention is being given to behaviour that goes beyond the typical emphasis on external behavioural tactics. Bender (2003) promotes the concept of "relational discipline":

> Relational discipline focuses squarely on the relationship between the teacher and the student, and various tactics and strategies are implemented within that broader context. It is this relationship, rather than the specific disciplinary tactics that are used, that forms the basis for appropriate classroom behaviour and that eventually develops into self-discipline. (p. 3)

TEACHING TIP

Students should be involved in selecting positive reinforcers to make sure they are attractive to them.

Related to the notion that relationship is important, Bender (2003) points out that "behavioural interventions practices" (i.e., disciplinary tactics) must be understood from a developmental perspective. Differential techniques must be considered in terms of age-related needs and predominant influences operative at a given age. Bender notes that few disciplinary systems have, to any reasonable extent, built on the influence of peer groups with older students.

An Ontario-based program that teaches secondary students how to develop healthy relationship skills is in the process of being adopted nationally. Table 12.3 highlights the guiding principles of The Fourth R Project.

Table 12.3 The Fourth R: Promoting Positive Youth Relationships

Guiding Principles of The Fourth R

- Relationship skills are just as important for students to learn as reading, writing, and arithmetic. If students do not feel safe and connected to their schools, other learning can be impeded.
- Relationship skills can be taught, like athletic skills, through skill development and practice.
- Education following the principles of harm reduction and health promotion is effective for reducing teen risk behaviour.
- The harm reduction approach assumes that most teens are likely to engage in some risk behaviours, or find themselves in unsafe situations. Practice using life skills can help them prevent or deal with these situations.
- Prevention of high-risk teen behaviours can be approached through holistic strategies involving healthy, nonviolent teen relationships at the core.
- Our relationship-based, health-promotion approach goes beyond harm reduction in attempting to develop healthy relationship skills.

The Fourth R is supported in part by grants from the U.S. National Institute of Alcohol Abuse and Alcoholism (NIAAA), the Ontario Mental Health Foundation, the National Crime Prevention Centre's Community Mobilization Program (Canadian Department of Justice), the Canadian Institutes of Health, and a donation from the Royal Lepage Shelter Foundation.

The Fourth R Project Team: David A. Wolfe, Ph.D.; Peter Jaffe, Ph.D.; Claire Crooks, Ph.D.; Ray Hughes, M.Ed.

Reprinted with permission from The Fourth R Project, in partnership with the Centre for Research on Violence Against Women & Children, the University of Western Ontario, the Thames Valley District School Board, and the CAMH Centre for Prevention.

Given the importance of the behavioural dimension, most general educators will probably work regularly with special educators to develop effective programs for students with exceptionalities and with behavioural problems. To provide a flavour of the areas for possible emphasis, Etscheidt and Bartlett (1999) identified the following sample factors:

■ *Skills training*: Could the student be involved in social skills instruction? Does the student need counselling?

■ *Behaviour management plan*: Does the student need a behaviour management plan that describes a reinforcement system, supportive signals, and corrective options?

■ *Self-management*: Could the student use self-monitoring of target behaviours?

■ *Peer support*: Could peers help monitor or redirect behaviour? Could peers take notes, help prepare for exams, etc.?

■ *Class-wide systems*: Could the teacher implement an interdependent group contingency for the class? Could a "circle of friends" be initiated? (p. 171)

Because research confirms the effectiveness of behavioural techniques for promoting learning in students with exceptionalities, such interventions should clearly be key components of a teacher's repertoire. Today, professionals in the area of behaviour have been stressing the need to implement positive behavioural interventions and supports. This emphasis has been accompanied by a de-emphasis on the use of more negative and punitive tactics.

Not all facets of behaviour management can be covered in sufficient detail in this chapter. However, the following sections provide recommendations that should guide practice in increasing desirable behaviours, decreasing undesirable behaviours, promoting generalization and maintenance, and enhancing self-management.

Creating and Increasing Desirable Behaviours Effecting desired new behaviours, whether academic, personal, behavioural, social, or vocational, is a classroom goal. A new desired behaviour can be affirmed with **reinforcement**—any event that rewards, and thus strengthens and increases the frequency of, the behaviour it follows. **Positive reinforcement** presents a desirable consequence for performance of an appropriate behaviour. Positive reinforcers can take different forms; however, what serves as reinforcement for one individual may not hold true for another. Reinforcers can consist of praise, physical contact, tangible items, activities, or privileges. The use of reinforcement is the most socially acceptable and instructionally sound tactic for increasing desired behaviours. The goal of most behavioural regimens is to internalize the nature of reinforcement (i.e., self-reinforcement).

Three basic principles must be followed for positive reinforcement to be most effective: it must be meaningful to the student, contingent upon the proper performance of a desired behaviour, and presented immediately. In other words, for positive reinforcement to work, students must find the reinforcement desirable in some fashion, understand that it is being given as a result of the behaviour demonstrated, and receive it soon after they do what was asked. It must also happen more frequently than correction, so that the student feels encouraged to attempt the rewarding behaviour. Principles for the use of positive reinforcement are presented in Table 12.4. Generally, attention to the systematic nature of the reinforcement program should parallel the severity of a student's intellectual, learning, or behavioural problem. Too often, teachers do not pay close enough attention to the principles we have noted,

✳ Explore

Back To Square One

⬅⊙ Simulate

Developing Behaviour Change Plans

Table 12.4 Implementing Positive Reinforcement Techniques

Determine what reinforcements will work for particular students:

1. Ask the child by using direct formal or informal questioning or by administering an interest inventory or reinforcement survey.

2. Ask those who are knowledgeable about the student (e.g., parents, friends, or past teachers).

3. Observe the student in the natural environment as well as in a structured observation (e.g., arranging reinforcement alternatives from which the student may select).

Select meaningful reinforcements that are easy and practical to deliver in classroom settings (Idol, 1993).

"Catch" students behaving appropriately, and provide them with the subsequent appropriate reinforcement (referred to as the differential reinforcement of behaviour incompatible with problem behaviour). Begin this technique early so that students experience the effects of positive reinforcement.

Use the Premack (1959) principle "Grandma's law" regularly (e.g., "Yes, you can have dessert, as soon as you finish your vegetables").

Use reinforcement techniques as the student makes gradual progress in developing a desired behaviour that requires the mastery of numerous substeps (reinforce each successive approximation). This concept is called shaping.

Demonstrate to a student that certain behaviours will result in positive outcomes by reinforcing nearby peers, or by prompting.

CONSIDER THIS

Some people say that contracts, as well as other forms of positive reinforcement, amount to little more than bribery. Do you agree or disagree, and why?

and, as a result, do not implement techniques with any power. Another potential problem is that some powerful positive behavioural interventions cannot be implemented because of such factors as cost or complexity (Bender, 2003).

The first illustrative application of the principle of positive reinforcement is **contingency contracting**, a concept introduced by Homme (1969). With this method, the teacher develops contracts with students that state (1) what behaviours (e.g., academic work, social behaviours) students are to complete or perform and (2) what consequences (e.g., reinforcement) the instructor will provide. These contracts are presented as binding agreements between student and teacher. To be most effective, contracts should (1) initially reward imperfect approximations of the target behaviour, (2) provide frequent reinforcement, (3) reward accomplishment rather than obedience, and (4) be fair, clear, and positive. Figure 12.2 shows an example of a contract for a secondary school student.

Group contingencies, which are set up for groups of students rather than individuals, provide excellent alternatives for managing behaviour and actively including students with exceptionalities in the general education classroom. There are three types:

1. *Dependent contingencies*: All group members share in the reinforcement if one individual achieves a goal (i.e., the "hero" strategy).

2. *Interdependent contingencies*: All group members are reinforced if all collectively (or all individually) achieve the stated goal.

3. *Independent contingencies*: Individuals within the group are reinforced for individual achievement toward a goal.

Whereas independent contingencies are commonly used, the other two forms are less widely seen in the classroom. The dependent strategy is sometimes referred to as a "hero approach" because it singles out one student's performance for attention. Although it can be abused, such an approach may be particularly attractive for a student who responds well

Figure 12.2 Sample Contract between Student and Teacher

From *Behaviour Management: Applications for Teachers and Parents* (p. 189) by T. Zirpoli and G. Melloy, 1993, Columbus, OH: Merrill. Used with permission.

Contract

_____ will demonstrate the following appropriate behaviours
(Student's name)

in the classroom:

1. Come to school on time.
2. Come to school with homework completed.
3. Complete all assigned work in school without prompting.
4. Ask for help when necessary by raising hand and getting teacher's attention.

_____ will provide the following reinforcement:
(Teacher's name)

1. Ten tokens for the completion of each of the above four objectives. Tokens for the first two objectives will be provided at the beginning of class after all homework assignments have been checked. Tokens for objectives 3 and 4 will be provided at the end of the school day.
2. Tokens may be exchanged for activities on the Classroom Reinforcement Menu at noon on Fridays.

_____   _____
Student's signature   Teacher's signature

                                          _____
                                          Date

to peer attention. A student with special needs may feel more meaningfully included in class when his or her talents are recognized in this way.

Others may feel reinforced and accepted as part of a group when interdependent contingencies are used: the most common is the "good behaviour game." Because it is most often used as a behavioural reduction intervention, it is discussed later in the chapter.

The benefits of group-oriented contingencies (or peer-mediated strategies, as they are often called) include the involvement of peers, the ability of teachers to enhance motivation, and increased efficiency for the teacher. In some instances, students will raise questions of fairness concerning group contingency programs. Those who typically behave appropriately may feel that they are being penalized for the actions of others if reinforcement occurs only when the whole group evidences a desired behaviour. You can assure them that ultimately, they and everyone else will benefit from group success with particular guidelines or goals. Two resources, one for young students—*Practical Ideas That Really Work with Students Who Are Disruptive, Defiant, and Difficult: Preschool Through Grade 4* (McConnell, Ryser, & Patton, 2002a)—and the other for older students—*Practical Ideas That Really Work with Students Who Are Disruptive, Defiant, and Difficult: Grades 5–12* (McConnell, Ryser, & Patton, 2002b)—include many practical ideas for using individual and group contingencies.

Decreasing Undesirable Behaviours Every teacher will face situations involving undesirable behaviours that require behaviour reduction techniques. Teachers can select from a range of techniques; however, it is best to begin with the least intrusive and more neutrally oriented interventions. A recommended sequence of reduction strategies is

Figure 12.3

Recommended Sequence of Selected Behaviour Reduction Techniques

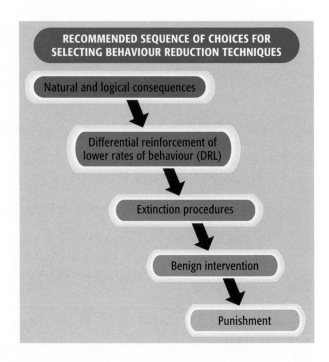

illustrated in Figure 12.3. As teachers consider reductive strategies, they are cautioned to keep records, develop plans of action, and follow school and division guidelines.

The use of *natural* and *logical consequences* can help children and adolescents learn to be more responsible for their behaviours. These principles are particularly important for students with exceptionalities who often have difficulty seeing the link between their behaviour and the resulting consequences.

With **natural consequences**, the situation itself provides the contingencies for a particular behaviour. For example, if a student forgets to return a permission slip to attend an off-campus event, the natural consequence is that the student is not allowed to go and must remain at school. Thus, rather than intervening in a given situation, the teacher allows the situation to teach the students. Natural consequences can be an effective means to teach common sense and responsibility.

In **logical consequences**, there is a logical connection between inappropriate behaviour and the consequences that follow. If a student forgets lunch money, a logical consequence might be that money must be borrowed from someone else. The uncomfortable consequence is the hassle or embarrassment of requesting financial assistance. These tactics can help students recognize that their own behaviour has created the discomfort and not something the teacher has done to them. When using this approach, teachers should clarify to students that they are responsible for their own choices. Logical consequences relate the disciplinary response directly to the inappropriate behaviour.

As noted earlier in the chapter, an important recently developed approach to behavioural reduction is the use of positive behavioural supports. As Horner (2000) notes, "Positive behaviour support involves the assessment and reengineering of environments so people with problem behaviours experience reductions in (these behaviours) and increased social [and] personal quality in their lives . . . . It is an approach that blends values about the rights of people with disabilities with the practical science about how learning and behaviour change occur" (p. 181).

The essential element of positive behaviour support is the emphasis on fixing environments rather than focusing just on changing the behaviour of individuals. Thus, the key element is to design schools and curricula to prevent problem behaviours from occurring and thus make them "irrelevant, inefficient, and ineffective" (Horner, 2000, p. 182). As discussed in chapter 6, the basis for effective positive behaviour support programs is the use of functional behavioural assessment, which identifies classroom events that serve to predict the occurrence of problem behaviours and function to maintain positive behaviours (Horner, 2000). Thus, the reader is encouraged to consider the remaining behavioural reduction strategies discussed in this chapter in light of the need to balance the focus on the individual with the more significant focus on designing a curriculum and operating a classroom in ways that minimize behavioural disturbances and encourage acceptance of students with exceptionalities as members of the classroom.

The next option on the continuum is the use of *differential reinforcement of lower (DRL) rates of behaviour*. This technique uses positive reinforcement strategies as a behaviour reduction tool. A teacher using this procedure provides appropriate reinforcement to students for displaying lower rates of a certain behaviour that has been targeted for reduction. It is important to remember that the goal should be to decrease the frequency or duration of the unwanted behaviour.

An example of this technique used with groups of students is the "good behaviour game" (originally developed by Barrish, Saunders, & Wolf, 1969), in which student teams receive reinforcement if the number of occurrences of inappropriate behaviours remains under a preset criterion.

A modification of this game that de-emphasizes competition would have all students playing the game on the same team, and working to reach a frequency goal to win the game.

Here are additional considerations:

- Understand that undesirable behaviours will still occur and must be tolerated until target levels are reached.

- Reduce the criterion level after students have demonstrated stability at the present level.

- Avoid making too great a jump between respective criterion levels to ensure that students are able to meet the new demands.

The next reduction option involves **extinction** procedures. In this technique, the teacher withholds reinforcement for a behaviour. Over time, such action, in combination with the positive reinforcement of related desirable behaviours, should extinguish the inappropriate behaviour. One example is for the teacher to cease responding to student misbehaviour. For some situations, it will be necessary to involve a student's peers in the extinction process to eliminate a behaviour because the peers' actions are controlling the relevant reinforcers. The following are additional suggestions:

- Analyze what is reinforcing the undesirable behaviour, and isolate the reinforcer(s) before initiating this procedure.

- Understand that the extinction technique is desirable because it does not involve punishment, but it will take time to be effective.

CONSIDER THIS

What are some advantages of using a DRL approach when working on a complex behaviour, rather than simply reinforcing the student only after a targeted behaviour has completely disappeared?

TEACHING TIP

Being physically close to students who often display behaviour problems is a powerful method of reducing inappropriate behaviours. It is sometimes referred to as *proximity management*.

TEACHING TIP

When attempting to reduce an inappropriate behaviour by ignoring it, teachers must remember to positively reinforce alternate desired behaviours.

- Do not use this technique with behaviours that require immediate intervention (e.g., fighting).

- Recognize that the withholding of reinforcement (1) is likely to induce an increase ("spiking" effect) in the occurrence of the undesirable behaviour, as students intensify their efforts to receive the reinforcement they are used to getting, and (2) may produce an initial aggressive response.

- Provide reinforcement to students who demonstrate appropriate incompatible behaviours (e.g., taking turns versus interrupting).

The fourth option in selected behaviour reduction is the use of techniques that border on being punishment but are so unobtrusive that they can be considered *benign tactics*. These suggestions are consistent with a concept developed by Cummings (1983) called the "law of least intervention" and that of Evertson and colleagues (2006) called "minor interventions." The main idea is to eliminate disruptive behaviours quickly with a minimum of disruption to the classroom or instructional routine. The following suggestions can be organized into physical, gestural, visual, and verbal prompts:

- Position yourself physically near students who are likely to create problems (proximity).

- Redirect behaviour in unobtrusive ways (i.e., not embarrassing to an individual student) directed to the whole class or through the use of humour.

- Touch a student's shoulder gently to convey your awareness that the student is behaving in some inappropriate (albeit previously identified) way.

- Use subtle and not-so-subtle gestures to stop undesirable behaviours (e.g., pointing, head shaking, finger spelling).

- Establish eye contact and maintain it for a while with a student who is behaving inappropriately. This results in no disruption to the instructional routine.

- Stop talking for a noticeable length of time to redirect student attention.

- Call on students who are not attending, but ask them questions that they can answer successfully.

- Give the student a choice.

- Use an "I-message" (e.g., "I felt disrespected when you were speaking when I was giving directions").

- Minimize "dead" time.

- Avoid sarcasm and confrontation.

The last option in this reduction hierarchy and the one that is most intrusive is the use of **punishment**. It is the least preferable option because it involves the presentation of something unpleasant or the removal of something pleasant as a consequence of the performance of an undesirable behaviour. This option should be considered only as a last resort. However, in situations in which a more immediate cessation of undesirable behaviours is required, punishment may be necessary. Because of their potency, punishment strategies should be weighed carefully; they can interfere with the learning process if not used sparingly and appropriately. Given that all teachers are likely to use punishment at some point, the key is to ensure that it is used appropriately.

Positioning yourself near a student who is disruptive can be a powerful management technique.

Three punishment techniques are commonly used in classrooms: **reprimands**, **time out**, and **response cost**. For these forms of punishment to work, it is critical that they be applied immediately after the occurrence of the undesirable behaviour and that the students understand why they are being applied.

A *reprimand* represents a type of punishment in which an unpleasant condition (verbal reprimand from the teacher) is presented to the student. The following are some specific suggestions:

- Do not let this type of interchange dominate your interactions with students.
- Look at the student and speak in a composed way.
- Do not verbally reprimand a student from across the room. Get close to the student, maintain a degree of privacy, and minimize embarrassment.
- Let the student know exactly why you are concerned.
- Convey to the student that it is the behaviour that is the problem and not him or her.

With *time out*, a student is removed from a situation in which he or she typically receives positive reinforcement, thus being prevented from enjoying something pleasurable. Different ways are available to remove a student from a reinforcing setting: (1) students are allowed to observe the situation from which they have been removed (contingent observation); (2) students are excluded from the ongoing proceedings entirely (exclusion time out); and (3) students are secluded in a separate room (seclusion time out). The first two versions are most likely to be considered for use in general education classrooms. The following suggestions are extremely important if time out is to succeed:

- Confirm that the ongoing situation from which a student is to be removed is indeed reinforcing; if not, this technique will not serve as a punisher and, rather, may be a form of positive reinforcement.
- Ensure that the time-out area is devoid of reinforcing elements. If it is not a neutral setting, this procedure will fail.
- Do not keep students in time out for long periods of time (i.e., more than 10 minutes) or use it frequently (e.g., daily), as students will miss significant amounts of instructional time.
- As a rule of thumb with younger children, never allow time-out periods to extend beyond one minute for every year of the child's age (up to a maximum of 10 minutes).
- Use a timer to ensure accuracy in the length of time out.
- Incorporate this procedure as one of the classroom procedures explained and taught at the beginning of the school year.
- Consider using a time-out system in which students are given one warning before being removed.
- Signal to the student when it is appropriate to return.
- Do not use this technique with certain sensitive students.
- Keep records on frequency, reason for using, and amount of time placed when using seclusion time-out procedures.

TEACHING TIP

To ensure proper compliance, teachers must always be aware of division or school policies and practices when using time out for reducing student behaviour.

Simulate

You're in Charge!

Response cost involves the loss of something the student values, such as privileges or points. It is a system in which a penalty or fine is levied for occurrences of inappropriate behaviour. The following are some specific suggestions:

- Explain clearly to students how the system works and how much they will be fined for a given offence.
- Make sure all penalties are presented in a nonpersonal manner.
- Confirm that privileges that are lost are indeed reinforcing to students.
- Make sure that all privileges are not lost quickly, resulting in a situation in which a student may have little or no incentive to behave appropriately.
- Tie this procedure in with positive reinforcement at all times.

Generalization and Maintenance After behaviours have been established at acceptable levels, the next stages involve transferring what has been learned to new contexts and maintaining established levels of performance. Teachers often succeed in teaching students certain behaviours but fail to help them apply the skills to new situations or to retain them over time. Teaching appropriate behaviours and then hoping that students will be able to use various skills at some later time is detrimental to many students with exceptionalities because a core difficulty they experience is performing independently in the classroom.

Teachers need to program for generalization—the wider application of a behaviour skill—by giving students opportunities to use new skills in different settings, with different people, and at different times. Students often need help in identifying the cues that should trigger the performance of an acquired behaviour, action, or skill.

Students also need to practise what they have learned previously in order to maintain their skills. Instructional planning should allow time for students to determine how well they have retained what they have learned. This time can usually be provided during seatwork activities or other arrangements.

Suggestions for generalization and maintenance include the following:

- Create opportunities for students to practise in different situations what they have learned.
- Work with other teachers to provide additional opportunities.
- Place students in settings that simulate situations they will encounter in the near and distant future, both in school and in other areas of life.
- Show students how these skills or behaviours will be useful to them in the future.
- Prompt students to use recently acquired skills in a variety of contexts.
- Maintain previously taught skills by providing ongoing practice or review.

As noted previously, the use of positive behaviour supports has become more popular in working with students with exceptionalities, particularly because of its effectiveness and its emphasis on the environment rather than the individual. A key to behavioural generalization and maintenance, therefore, is to focus beyond the student and ensure that the learning environment is designed in such a way that students can use their newly acquired skills effectively to become accepted and active members of the classroom while enhancing their learning opportunities. In addition, key elements of generalization and maintenance relate to self-management strategies, which become essential in work with adolescents.

Self-Management Ultimately, we want all students to be able to manage their own behaviours without external direction because this ability is a requirement of functioning independently in life. Special attention needs to be given to those who do not display independent behavioural control and thus must develop *student-regulated strategies*—interventions that, though initially taught by the teacher, are intended to be implemented independently by the student. Bender (2003) refers to this end state as the "self-discipline" phase.

The concept is an outgrowth of cognitive behaviour modification, a type of educational intervention for students with disabilities in use since the 1980s, and stresses active thinking about behaviour. Shapiro, DuPaul, and Bradley-Klug (1998) provide a good overview of self-management. They state:

> It is helpful to conceptualize self-management interventions as existing on a continuum. At one end, the intervention is completely controlled by the teacher . . . this individual provides feedback regarding whether the student's behaviour met the desired criteria and administers the appropriate consequences for the behaviour. At the other end, the student engages in evaluating his or her own behaviour against the criteria for performance, without benefit of teacher . . . input. The student also self-administers the appropriate consequences. In working with students with behaviour problems, the objective should be to move a student as far toward the self-management side of the continuum as possible. Although some of these students may not be capable of reaching levels of independent self-management, most are certainly capable of approximating this goal. (p. 545)

Fiore, Becker, and Nerro (1993) state the rationale for such interventions: "Cognitive-behavioural [intervention] is . . . intuitively appealing because it combines behavioural techniques with cognitive strategies designed to directly address core problems of impulse control, higher order problem solving, and self-regulation" (p. 166). Whereas traditional behavioural interventions most often stress the importance of teacher monitoring of student behaviour, extrinsic reinforcement, and teacher-directed learning, cognitive interventions instead focus on teaching students to monitor their own behaviour, to engage in self-reinforcement, and to direct their own learning in strategic fashion.

Such approaches have become particularly popular with students with learning and attention difficulties because they offer the promise of

- increasing focus on selective attention
- modifying impulsive responding
- providing verbal mediators to assist in academic and social problem-solving situations
- teaching effective self-instructional statements to enable students to "talk through" tasks and problems
- providing strategies that may lead to improvement in peer relations

Why is it so important to teach students to manage their own behaviours without external guidance from teachers? How can self-management assist students with exceptionalities in their inclusion in the community?

Classroom Organization and Management **333**

Figure 12.4
Components of Self-Management

From *Guide to Attention Deficits in the Classroom* (p. 162) by C.A. Dowdy, J.R. Patton, E.A. Polloway, and T.E.C. Smith, 1998, Austin, TX: Pro-Ed. Used with permission.

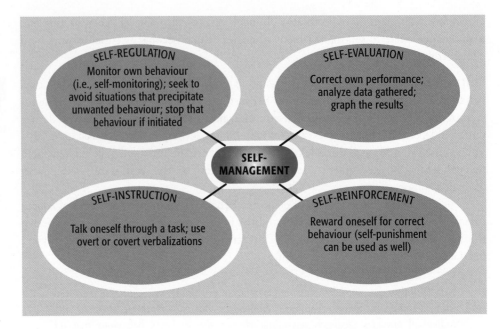

SELF-REGULATION
Monitor own behaviour (i.e., self-monitoring); seek to avoid situations that precipitate unwanted behaviour; stop that behaviour if initiated

SELF-EVALUATION
Correct own performance; analyze data gathered; graph the results

SELF-MANAGEMENT

SELF-INSTRUCTION
Talk oneself through a task; use overt or covert verbalizations

SELF-REINFORCEMENT
Reward oneself for correct behaviour (self-punishment can be used as well)

CONSIDER THIS

Do you engage in any self-monitoring techniques? If so, how do you use them, and how effective are they?

CROSS REFERENCE

Review chapter 4 on learning disabilities; consider how self-monitoring and self-instructional techniques could be used with students with learning disabilities.

While studies of using self-management strategies with students with exceptionalities in inclusive settings has been far more limited than studies of using them in pull-out programs, the moderate to strong positive outcomes reported in research are encouraging.

Student-regulated strategies form the essence of self-management. Although variations exist in how these are defined and described, the components listed in Figure 12.4 represent the central aspects of self-management.

Two components with particular utility for general education teachers are self-monitoring and self-instruction. **Self-monitoring**, a technique in which students observe and record their own behaviour, has been commonly used with students with learning problems. Self-monitoring of behaviour, such as attention, is a relatively simple technique that has been validated with children who have learning disabilities, intellectual disabilities, multiple disabilities, attention deficits, and behavioural disorders; it has also been profitable for typically achieving students. Increased attention, beneficial to academic achievement, has been reported as a result.

A common mechanism for self-monitoring was developed by Hallahan, Lloyd, and Stoller (1982). It involves using a tape-recorded tone, which sounds at random intervals (e.g., every 45 seconds), and a self-recording sheet. Each time the tone sounds, children ask themselves whether they are paying attention and then mark the *yes* or the *no* box on the tally sheet. While students are often not accurate in their recording, positive changes in behaviour have nevertheless been observed in many research studies. While self-monitoring procedures may prove problematic for one teacher to implement alone, a collaborative approach within a co-operative teaching arrangement offers much promise.

Teachers should consider ways to creatively use self-monitoring in their classrooms as an adjunct to other ongoing management strategies.

Self-instruction represents another useful intervention. Pfiffner and Barkley (1991) describe components of a self-instruction program as follows:

> Self-instructions include defining and understanding the task or problem, planning a general strategy to approach the problem, focusing attention on the task, selecting an answer or solution, and evaluating performance. In the case of successful performance, self-reinforcement (usually in the form of a positive self-statement, such as "I really did a good job") is provided. In the case of an unsuccessful performance, a coping statement is made (e.g., "Next time I'll do better if I slow down"), and errors are corrected. At first, an adult trainer typically models the self-instructions while performing a task. The child then performs the same task while the trainer provides the self-instructions. Next, the child performs the task while self-instructing aloud. These overt verbalizations are then faded to covert self-instructions. (p. 525)

Clear, simple self-instruction strategies form an appropriate beginning for interventions with students with learning or attention difficulties in the general education classroom. Such approaches are likely to enhance success. Detailed and systematic procedures have been developed for implementing self-management strategies. Some basic recommendations follow:

■ Allocate sufficient instructional time to teach self-management to students who need it.

■ Establish a sequence of activities that move by degrees from teacher direction to student direction and self-control.

■ Include objectives relevant to improved behaviour and enhanced learning (e.g., increased attention yields reading achievement gains).

■ Provide strategies and assistive materials (e.g., self-recording forms) for students to use.

■ Model how effective self-managers operate. Point out actual applications of the elements of self-management (as highlighted in Figure 12.4), and give students opportunities to practise these techniques with your guidance.

■ Provide for the maintenance of learned strategies and for generalization to other settings in and out of school.

This section has outlined management strategies to use with a variety of students. Table 12.5 highlights strategies especially helpful to older students.

✳ Explore

Encouraging Appropriate Behaviour

Hang in There

Eric's Last Stand

Table 12.5 Considerations for Working with Adolescents

Anticipate the likely consequences of any intervention strategy being considered.

Emphasize self-management strategies.

Stress the application of natural and logical consequences.

Use group-oriented contingencies to involve peers in a comprehensive plan for change.

Select only age-appropriate reinforcements.

Avoid response cost procedures that are likely to result in confrontation.

Collaborate with other professionals and parents in designing effective programs.

Select strategies that will not exacerbate problem situations.

◀⊙ Simulate

Addressing Disruptive and Noncompliant Behaviours (Part 1)

Addressing Disruptive and Noncompliant Behaviours (Part 2)

Instructional Dimension

In general, teachers need to provide instruction that fulfills the objectives set by school standards and that matches the needs of their students. Levin and Nolan (2003) recommend that "students need to be assigned tasks that are moderately challenging but within their capability" (p. 16). Carter and Doyle (2006) suggest that students do better with familiar tasks—that is, "tasks that are typical or recognizable, have a clearly defined product and explicit grading criteria, and have been routinized in class" (p. 383)—than they do with novel work.

All of the dimensions of classroom organization and management discussed in this chapter relate to the broad concern for instructional outcomes. However, certain aspects of instruction are closely related to sound organizational and management practices, such as scheduling, transitions, grouping, lesson planning, and technology, and can have a significant impact on quality of instruction.

Scheduling involves the general temporal arrangement of events for both (1) the entire day (i.e., master schedule) and (2) a specific class period. This section focuses on the latter. The importance of a carefully planned schedule cannot be overemphasized. This is particularly true in classrooms that include students with exceptionalities.

The thoughtful scheduling of a class period can contribute greatly to the amount of time that students can spend actively engaged in learning. It can also add to the quality of what is learned. For instance, a science lesson might include the following components:

- transitional activities (into the classroom)
- attention-getting and motivating techniques
- data-gathering techniques
- data-processing techniques
- closure activities
- transitional activities (to the next class period)

All components support the instructional goal for the day. Reminders or cues from the teacher can augment such a system. The following are some specific suggestions:

- Provide time reminders (visual and audible) for students during the class period so that they know how much time is available.
- Plan for transitions (see following discussion of *transition*).
- Require students to complete one activity or task before moving on to the next.
- Vary the nature of class activities to keep students engaged and to create a stimulating instructional tempo and pace.
- Minimize noninstructional time when students are not academically engaged.

Scheduling involves planning for class period *transitions*. Efficient transitions can minimize disruptions, maximize the amount of time allocated to instructional tasks, and maintain desired conditions of learning. Structured approaches to transitions will be particularly helpful to students with exceptionalities. Several ways to ease transitions follow:

- Model appropriate transitions between activities.
- Let students practise appropriate transition skills.
- Use specific cues (e.g., blinking lights, a buzzer, teacher signal) to signal students that it is time to change instructional routine.

Table 12.6 Potential Transition Problems and Suggested Solutions

Transition Problem	Suggested Solution
Students talk loudly at the beginning of the day. The teacher is interrupted while checking attendance, and the start of content activities is delayed.	Establish a beginning-of-day routine, and clearly state your expectations for student behaviour at the beginning of the day.
Students talk too much during transitions, especially after a seatwork assignment has been given but before they have begun working on it. Many students do not start their seatwork activity for several minutes.	Be sure students know what the assignment is; post it where they can easily see it. Work as a whole class on the first several seatwork exercises so that all students begin the lesson successfully and at the same time. Watch what students do during the transition, and urge them along when needed.
Students who go for supplemental instruction stop work early and leave the room noisily while rest of the class is working. When these students return to the room, they disturb others as they come in and take their seats. They interrupt others by asking for directions for assignments.	Have a designated signal that tells these students when they are to get ready to leave, such as a special time on the clock. Have them practise leaving and returning to the room quietly. Reward appropriate behaviour. Leave special instructions for what they are to do, when they return, in a folder, on the chalkboard, or on a special sheet at their desks. Or for younger students, establish a special place and activity (e.g., the reading rug) for returning students to wait until you can give them personal attention.
During the late afternoon activity, students quit working well before the end; they then begin playing around and leave the room in a mess.	Establish an end-of-day routine so that students continue their work until the teacher gives a signal to begin preparations to leave; then instruct students to help straighten up the room.
Whenever the teacher attempts to move the students from one activity into another, a number of students don't make the transition, but continue working on the preceding activity. This delays the start of the next activity or results in confusion.	Give students a few minutes' notice before an activity is scheduled to end. At the end of the activity students should put all the materials from it away and get out any needed materials for the next activity. Monitor the transition to make sure that all students complete it; do not start the next activity until students are ready.

From *Classroom Management for Elementary Teachers* (2nd ed., pp. 127–128) by C.M. Evertson, E.T. Emmer, B.J. Clements, J.P. Sanford, and M.E. Worsham, 1989, Englewood Cliffs, NJ: Prentice-Hall. Used with permission.

Several other examples of strategies for transitions are listed in Table 12.6.

Grouping refers to how students are organized for instructional purposes. The need to place students into smaller groups depends on the nature of the curricular area or the goal of a specific lesson. Evertson and colleagues (2006) discuss seven ways to group students for instruction: whole group, small teacher-led group, small co-operative group, small noncompetitive group, student pairs, individualized instruction, and centres or stations. Each of these formats has advantages and disadvantages for students and teachers.

For students with exceptionalities, the main concern within a group setting is attention to individual needs. Using innovative grouping arrangements and providing different co-operative learning opportunities allow for variety in the instructional routine for students with exceptionalities. Some specific suggestions follow:

- Give careful consideration to the makeup of groups.
- Make sure that group composition is not constant. Vary membership as a function of having different reasons for grouping students.

- Use different grouping arrangements that are based on interest or for research purposes.

- Use co-operative learning arrangements on a regular basis, as this approach, if structured properly, facilitates successful learning and socialization.

- Determine the size of groups based on ability levels: the lower the ability, the smaller the size of the group.

- Use mixed-ability groups when co-operative learning strategies are implemented to promote the active involvement of all students.

Lesson plans help teachers prepare for instruction. Many teachers start out writing very detailed lesson plans and eventually move to less comprehensive formats. However, some teachers continue to use detailed plans throughout their teaching careers, as they find the detail helpful in providing effective instruction. Detailed planning is frequently needed for lessons that must be modified to be appropriate for gifted students or students with exceptionalities. Six research-based components of lessons include: lesson introduction, clarity, coached practice, closure, solitary practice, and review (Levin & Nolan, 2003). Other key elements of lesson planning that should be considered are options for early finishers, specific accommodations that some students may require, and techniques for evaluation. Suggestions for developing lesson plans follow:

- Create interest in and clarify the purpose of lessons. This concern is particularly important for students with exceptionalities.

- Consider the importance of direct instruction to help students acquire an initial grasp of new material.

- Assign independent practice, some of which can be accomplished in class and some of which should be done as homework.

- Plan activities for students who finish early. Such planning might be particularly useful for gifted students.

- Anticipate problems that might arise during the course of the lesson, and identify techniques for dealing with them.

The application of *technology* to curriculum and instruction is widespread. From a management perspective, teachers must consider a number of variables when deciding to use technology. While more software choices are available commercially in recent years, the selection of software that is appropriate for students and that relates to instructional objectives requires effort and knowledge. Some suggestions follow:

- Consider accessibility needs of students with exceptionalities.

- Obtain necessary input and output devices for students who require such hardware.

- Determine whether websites are considerate of students with exceptionalities.

- Make sure that websites are appropriate for usage.

- Consider the use of internet filters.

- Design lessons that utilize computers in ways that are engaging.

- Teach students "dos and don'ts" of using email and the internet (e.g., not giving out private information).

Lesson planning helps teachers prepare for instruction and aids in managing classrooms.

Organizational Dimension

The increased diversity in today's general education classrooms has created numerous new challenges for the teacher. Some have likened the current classroom to a "one-room schoolhouse," in which the classroom teacher must respond to the unique needs of many students. This section acknowledges how time management in the areas of personnel interactions, the work environment, administrative duties, instructional applications, and personal applications can promote success.

In the typical education classroom, teachers regularly interact with special education teachers, other classroom teachers, professional support staff (e.g., speech-language pathologists, psychologists), paraeducators or educational assistants, student-teachers, volunteers, and peer tutors. To enhance *personnel interactions*, teachers should consider these recommendations:

CONSIDER THIS

What are some of the key issues associated with having educational assistants (i.e., paraeducators) working with students with exceptionalities in general education classrooms?

- Establish good initial working relationships with support personnel.
- Clarify the supports that professional personnel are providing to students in your class.
- Clarify the roles of these persons and the classroom teacher as collaborators for instructional and behavioural interventions.
- Establish the roles and responsibilities of educational assistants, volunteers, and student teachers.
- Determine the level of expertise of educational assistants, and discuss with them specific activities they can perform and supports they can provide to students.
- Delegate noninstructional (and, as appropriate, instructional) duties to educational assistants when these assistants are available.
- In cases in which an educational assistant accompanies a child with an exceptionality in the general education classroom, develop a comprehensive plan with the special education teacher for involving this assistant appropriately.

The *work environment* refers to the immediate work area used by teachers—usually a desk and files. Teachers must consider how to utilize and organize work areas. For instance, a teacher's desk may be designated as off-limits to all students or may be used for storage only or as a work area. Suggestions for establishing a work environment are as follows:

- Keep the teacher's desk organized and free of stacks of papers.
- Organize files so that documents and information can be retrieved easily and quickly.
- Use colour-coded systems for filing, if possible.

Along with instructional duties, teaching includes numerous *administrative duties*. Two of the most time-demanding activities are participating in meetings and handling paperwork, including various forms of correspondence. The presence of students with exceptionalities will increase such demands. The following are some strategies for handling paperwork:

- Prepare form letters for all necessary events (e.g., permissions, notifications, status reports, memo formats, reimbursement requests).
- Prepare master copies of various forms that are used regularly (e.g., certificates and awards, record sheets, phone conversation sheets).

- Keep notes of all school-related phone conversations with parents, teachers, support staff, administrators, or any other person.
- Handle most paperwork only once.
- Make the most of meetings—request an agenda and ask that meetings be time-limited and be scheduled at times that are convenient.

Some additional *instructional applications* of time-management techniques are provided here, focusing on materials and technology that can make the job of teaching easier. The most attractive piece of equipment available to teachers is the computer. With the appropriate software, teachers can greatly reduce the amount of time spent on test generation, graphic organizers, IEP development, and so on. The following are some specific suggestions:

- Use self-correcting materials with students to reduce the amount of time required to correct student work.
- Use grade-book programs for recording student scores and determining grades.
- Use computers to generate a variety of instructionally related materials (tests, graphic organizers, puzzles).
- Give students computer-generated calendars that include important dates.

As was pointed out earlier in the chapter, communication with parents or guardians is essential. Establishing a home–school communication system prior to the start of the school year and making it operational as soon as school begins is highly recommended. Many of the following suggestions are taken from ideas identified by Jones and Jones (2007):

- Obtain parental agreement for student support and positive classroom behaviours via an introductory letter, a phone call, a home visit, or a "back-to-school" night.
- Maintain teacher–parent communication throughout the year via Friday envelopes (work completed during the week), newsletters, and progress reports.
- Create a website that provides various types of information—be sure to include homework assignments and important dates (e.g., when projects are due, when quizzes and tests are scheduled).

Since it is impossible to completely divorce the management of one's personal time from management of professional time, it is worthwhile considering various time-management tactics that have a more *personal application* but can affect one's efficiency and effectiveness in the classroom as well. Some basic recommendations are:

- Use a daily to-do list.
- Break down major tasks into smaller pieces and work on them.
- Avoid getting overcommitted.
- Work during work time. This might mean avoiding situations at school in which long social conversations will cut into on-task time.
- Avoid dealing with trivial activities if important ones must be addressed.
- Use idle time (e.g., waiting in lines) well. Always be prepared for these situations by having reading material or other portable work available.

The efficient management of one's professional and personal time can pay off in making day-to-day demands less overwhelming. Thus, efforts to become a better time manager are certainly worthwhile.

SUMMARY

- Classroom management includes all teacher-directed activities that support the efficient operations of the classroom and establish optimal conditions for learning.

- Effective management of a classroom requires consideration of psychosocial, procedural, physical, behavioural, instructional, and organizational variables.

- The key elements of the classroom environment that have a significant effect on instruction and learning include multidimensionality, simultaneity, immediacy, unpredictability, publicness, and history, while the key principles of successful management are careful planning, proactive strategies, consistency, awareness, and overlapping.

- Teachers need to take students' cultures into consideration when dealing with management issues.

- Classroom rules provide a general sense of what is expected of students.

- Rules should be essential for classroom functioning and for the development of a positive learning environment.

- Classroom procedures should include the specific ways in which certain activities or situations will be performed.

- Effective physical management includes classroom arrangement, seating, accessibility, and the use of specialized equipment.

- Desirable behaviours are increased through the use of positive reinforcement.

- Undesirable behaviours can be reduced through a variety of reduction strategies.

- Hierarchy of options would include (from least to most restrictive) natural and logical consequences, differential reinforcement, extinction, benign tactics, reprimands, time out, and response costs.

- Successful educational programs help students develop self-management strategies.

- Instructional management includes careful attention to scheduling, transitions, grouping, and lesson plans.

- Successful teachers are organized and engage in the careful management of time. Technology can assist teachers with this task.

Weblinks

Canadian Education Association (CEA)
www.cea-ace.ca
The Canadian Education Association is a bilingual, federally incorporated nonprofit organization with charitable tax status, actively linking students, parents, educators, researchers, writers, business, government, school administrators—and everyone who values education as fundamental to our society.

Chapter 13
Teaching Students with Special Needs in Elementary Schools

Chapter Objectives

After reading this chapter, you should be able to

- describe the impact of the inclusion movement on the placement of elementary students with exceptionalities

- define the concept of *comprehensive curriculum* for students at the elementary level

- identify curricular content considerations for academic instruction, social skills instruction, and transitional instruction

- identify appropriate instructional adaptations and accommodations for students with exceptionalities in elementary schools

Julie Bennington was told by one of her university professors that elementary classrooms were becoming increasingly similar to the old "one-room schoolhouses," encompassing a diversity of learning needs that had never been greater. Julie was excited by this challenge and, in her first year of teaching, often reflected on this comment.

Julie is teaching a class of Grade 3 students in a self-contained arrangement. She has full responsibility for 25 eager students in all subjects except art, music, and physical education. She has found their diversity to be both exciting and somewhat overwhelming.

Naturally, one of her greatest concerns is in the area of language arts. After doing some informal evaluation and reading the records of her students, she realized during the second week of the academic year that the ability levels of her students ranged greatly: two students were virtual nonreaders, and five pupils were significantly above grade level.

It has become apparent to Julie that these students do not all learn in the same way, but she continues to struggle to find approaches that will meet the needs of her diverse classroom. She is fortunate to be working two hours a day during her language arts block with Alisa Rinaldi, a special education teacher who is certified in learning disabilities.

Questions to Consider

1. How can Julie and Alisa develop effective co-operative teaching strategies that will take advantage of their own talents and meet the needs of their students?

2. How can they resolve the ongoing questions about the effectiveness of holistic versus decoding approaches for beginning reading instruction for those with learning difficulties?

3. What adaptations in the curriculum can be made to more effectively meet the needs of students with special needs in this classroom?

INTRODUCTION

As the opening vignette illustrates, elementary school presents both unique challenges and unique opportunities for young students with exceptionalities and other special needs to be included in general education. Although the learning needs of these students are frequently quite diverse and challenging, the degree of curricular differentiation (i.e., the need for alternative curricular focuses) tends to be more limited than it is at the secondary level. In elementary school, the necessity for similarity of educational content for all students is at its greatest. Thus, in terms of curricular content, there is an excellent opportunity for students with special needs to prosper in general education with the support of special education professionals.

Elementary school offers an important beginning for students with exceptionalities to profit from positive interactions with their typically achieving peers. Preparation for successful lives beyond the school setting requires the ability to learn, live, and work with a diversity of individuals. Thus, inclusion offers benefits both to students who are exceptional and to their peers. There is clearly no better time for school interaction to take place than in early childhood and throughout the primary and elementary grades.

The trend toward inclusion is demonstrated in Table 13.1. This analysis from Hoover and Patton (2005) reflects the changes in professional perspectives that have occurred over the past several decades, and it highlights the core rationales for inclusive classrooms.

The advent of the inclusion movement has increased the likelihood that many students with exceptionalities will receive a significant portion, or all, of their instruction in the general education classroom. Beginning at the elementary level, careful attention must be given to these students' educational needs.

The two critical questions in education are "What?"—the question of curriculum— and "How?"—the question of instruction. Effective school programs, then, begin by

CONSIDER THIS

Inclusive classrooms are more common at the elementary than secondary level. Why do you think this is the case?

Table 13.1 Trends in Educational Placements of Special Education Students in Elementary and Secondary Schools

Predominant Theme	Primary Placement(s)	Prevailing Thought toward Education	Predominant View toward Curriculum
Separate special education is needed.	Self-contained classroom	Students who cannot benefit from general education would be best served in special classrooms.	Specialized curriculum and techniques are needed to effectively educate individuals with disabilities.
Effectiveness of separate special classrooms is questioned.	Self-contained classroom	Educators are questioning the practice and effects of educating students with disabilities in separate special classes.	The need for special curriculum and techniques for many students with disabilities is being questioned.
Education for many students with special needs does not occur in separate classroom.	Resource rooms with some education in general education classrooms	Many learners may benefit from education in general education classrooms, requiring only some education in a special classroom.	Selected aspects of the general education curriculum are appropriate for learners with special needs.
Students with special needs may be educated appropriately in general education classrooms.	General education classrooms with some education in resource rooms	The least restrictive environment for many students termed "disabled" is education in the general education classroom.	Many students may benefit from the general education curriculum if proper adaptations and modifications are provided.
Students with disabilities should achieve full inclusion into general education.	Full integration into general education classrooms	The education of all students with disabilities is best achieved in the general education setting.	Continued expansion of integrated programs and curricula can be implemented in inclusive education settings.
Many diverse needs are to be met in inclusive settings.	Reaffirmation of full inclusion and full integration for students with special needs	The inclusive education setting is responsible for meeting an ever-increasing range of diverse needs.	Curriculum and instruction must be differentiated in collaborative ways to meet all diverse needs in the classroom.

Adapted from *Curriculum Adaptations for Students with Learning and Behavior Problems: Principles and Practices for Differentiating Instruction* (p. 29), by J.J. Hoover and J.R. Patton, 2005. Austin, TX: Pro-Ed.

considering *what* information students need to learn and *how* they can best learn that information. This chapter provides an overview of curricular and instructional accommodations and adaptations for elementary-age students with special needs in inclusive settings. The initial section outlines core curriculum considerations. The discussion that follows emphasizes instructional accommodations and adaptations that provide the means for achieving curricular goals.

GENERAL CURRICULAR CONSIDERATIONS

Simulate

Content Standards

Evaluating Reading Progress

Four general considerations provide a foundation for curriculum development. These include emphases on the general education (standards-based) curriculum, the need for a multitiered model of curriculum, universal design for learning, and the importance of a comprehensive curriculum.

The curriculum for virtually all elementary students with special needs is based on the *standards of learning*. The core of the standards-based reform movement in recent years has been its focus on *content and performance standards*. As Pemberton, Rademacher, Tyler-Wood, and Cereijo (2006) note, "[c]ontent standards define the knowledge and skills of students or what students should know and be able to accomplish as a result of their educational experiences. Performance standards define how well students should demonstrate the knowledge and skills" (pp. 283–284).

Providing further clarification, Wehmeyer (2006) referenced the work of the Committee on Goals 2000 and the Inclusion of Students with Disabilities (1997) in the United States in noting several ways in which standards could be made defensible for use with students with exceptionalities. Wehmeyer contends that content standards must reflect those skills that are critical to the success of students after leaving school, that these standards should be appropriate based on the age of the students, and that the standards-based curriculum should be taught to students with special needs while not effectively impacting on their opportunity to be taught, and to acquire, functional behaviours and skills that are critical for community success.

The emphases in standards-based curriculum and the need for students with special needs to have access to the general curriculum have provided the impetus for the second general consideration for curriculum development—*multitiered models for curriculum development*. The model developed by Hoover and Patton (2006) defines the three tiers as follows:

1. *High-quality core instruction*: This tier refers to empirically validated and systematic instruction that is embedded in a challenging curriculum in the general education classroom. Universal design for learning and differentiated instruction, for example, provide guidelines for successful implementation of tier-one interventions. For most elementary students, this is the core curriculum they will follow.

2. *High-quality, targeted supplemental instruction*: The focus of the second tier is to provide supplemental supports in addition to the core program. Such instruction could be provided in the general education classroom or through a variety of pull-out programs, such as resource rooms. Specific examples of such programs are those that are identified as general education supports programs. For many elementary students with special needs, this tier will provide the instructional supports they require. The discussion on adaptations later in the chapter provides numerous such examples.

3. *High-quality intensive intervention*: The third tier is more consistent with the traditional concept of special education as modified to reflect scientifically validated instructional programs to teach relevant curricular content. Such programs are typically offered to students with more significant exceptionalities and may more often be delivered in specialized settings. Examples include certain remedial programs. However, many of these curricular goals can be achieved in general education as well.

The third key emphasis in curriculum development is the importance of *universal design* for learning. It is important to note here how this design relates to standards for learning. A number of practices are consistent with this concept and are relatively straightforward and intuitive (Acrey, Johnstone, & Milligan, 2005). As a consequence, teachers are encouraged to design the learning environment using basic original principles for universal design and architecture as a model (e.g., considering ways to make lessons more accessible to all in the same way that buildings can be made so). In order to meet the needs of all students, including those with special needs, a curriculum that is based on universal design principles should be open-ended rather than close-ended. As Wehmeyer (2006) notes, "Close-ended standards are specific and require narrowly defined outcomes or performance indicators. Open-ended standards do not restrict the ways in which students exhibit knowledge with skills and focus more on the expectations that students will interact with the content, ask questions, manipulate materials, make observations, and then communicate their knowledge in a variety of ways."

For all students, any consideration of curriculum should include an *outcomes orientation*. Therefore, our concept of curriculum, even at the elementary level, must embrace consideration for the preparation for life after the completion of K–12 schooling. As a result, it is important to consider the *comprehensive curriculum*. It takes into account the reality that students are enrolled in school on a time-limited basis. Educators must consider what will happen to their students in the future and the environments that students will need to adapt to in order to function successfully. Thus, curriculum design should be predicated on a focus on these subsequent environments (e.g., middle school, high school, university, community). The degree to which this subsequent-environments attitude permeates general education will significantly affect the ultimate success of students with exceptionalities taught in such settings (Polloway, Patton, & Serna, 2008).

An elementary-level comprehensive curriculum, then, should respond to the needs of the individual at the current time, reflect the importance of achieving maximum interaction with peers while addressing critical curricular needs, and attend to relevant forthcoming transitional needs (e.g., transition from elementary to middle school) (Polloway et al., 2008).

CURRICULAR CONTENT
Academic Instruction

Elementary students in general, and certainly most students with exceptionalities, primarily need sound instruction in reading, writing, and mathematics to maximize their academic achievement. These needs can typically be met by a developmental approach to instruction, supplemented as needed by a remedial focus for students who experience difficulty. In addition, students with special needs will benefit from a curriculum that addresses social skills and transitional needs. In the sections that follow, an overview of principles and practices is provided.

Reading Instruction Reading problems are a foremost concern for all elementary teachers working in inclusive classrooms. Young students with special needs commonly experience difficulties in both the decoding processes inherent in word recognition as well as in reading comprehension. In a general sense, educators have responded to the need for quality instruction by selecting one (or a combination) of the three common approaches in elementary-level reading and language arts programs: (1) **basal series**, (2) **direct instruction**, and (3) **whole language**.

Basal Series Basal series, or class graded-reading texts, are the most typical means of teaching reading—and, for that matter, other curricular domains, including spelling and

CONSIDER THIS

Although general educators can rarely offer a truly "comprehensive curriculum," collaborative efforts with special educators can effect a more broad-based program. How does this work?

 Simulate

The Reading Blues

Watch

Blending Individual Sounds

Segmenting Individual Sounds

Pre-Alphabetic (Part 1)

Pre-Alphabetic (Part 2)

Pre-Alphabetic: K (Part 3)

Pre-Alphabetic: 1 (Part 4)

Post-Alphabetic Multisyllable Regular Words

math—in elementary school. Most reading basals are intended to meet developmental needs in reading. However, there is a multiplicity of programs, and it would be impossible to typify the focus of all basal series. Although basals are routinely criticized, Polloway, Miller, and Smith (2003) indicate that they have both advantages and disadvantages. On the positive side, basals contain inherent structure and sequence, a controlled vocabulary, a wide variety of teaching activities, and materials that provide preparation for the teacher. Weaknesses, on the other hand, include inappropriate pacing for an individual child, a common concern for certain skills to the exclusion of others, and encouragement of group instructional orientation.

Direct Instruction

Direct instruction (i.e., the directive teaching of reading skills) has often been associated with a remedial perspective, although it clearly has played a significant preventive role as well. Often, direct instruction has been tied to a focus on basic skills, which has typically constituted the core of most elementary special education curricula. In the area of reading, direct instruction programs are often associated with an emphasis on skills-based decoding (i.e., phonetic analysis).

Basic skills programs are typically built on the development of phonological awareness (i.e., sensitivity to the sounds inherent in our language system) and subsequent phonetic analysis instruction. Research on beginning reading emphasizes the critical importance of children's developing sound–symbol correspondences as a basis for subsequent reading success.

Basic skills programs typically have a long-term orientation based on the assumption that such skills ultimately will increase students' academic achievement and enable all to reach at least a minimal level of functional literacy. Not all basic skills programs are equally effective; those that incorporate effective instructional practice have most often empirically demonstrated substantial gains in achievement. The characteristic features of successful direct instruction include high levels of academic engaged time, signals for attention, ongoing feedback to learners, group-based instruction, fast pacing, and error-free learning.

Whole Language

Whole language approaches at the primary and elementary levels dramatically increased in popularity in the 1990s. Emphasizing meaning in the beginning of the reading process, they embrace a more holistic view of learning than direct instruction, which tends to be oriented to specific skills acquisition. Whole language programs attempt to break down barriers within the language arts between reading, writing, and speaking, as well as barriers between reading and other curricular areas, by stressing an integrated approach to learning.

Polloway et al. (2008) provide a series of examples of whole language instruction:

- orally sharing stories by the teacher
- sustained silent reading
- silent reading time segments in which students write responses to what they are reading and share this with other students or with the teacher in individual conferences
- language experience activities in which children write stories in a group or individually to be used for future reading experiences
- time set aside for large-group writing instruction followed by students' writing, revising, editing, and sharing their own writing
- reading and writing activities that involve a content area theme, such as science or social studies (pp. 16–17)

CONSIDER THIS

Basal programs vary significantly in terms of emphasis. How does this affect students with special needs?

Watch

Sound Writing

First Reading—Sounding Out Loud

Second Reading—Subvocal

Third Reading—The Fast Way

Individual Turns with Comprehension

FURTHER READING

The principles of direct instruction are based on the classic work in the mid-1960s by Carl Bereiter and Siegfried Engelmann with at-risk children. See *Teaching Disadvantaged Children in the Preschool,* published in 1966 by Prentice-Hall.

CONSIDER THIS

The emphasis on meaning and the integration of the language arts make whole language approaches particularly attractive for use with students with special needs. Why do you think this is effective?

FURTHER READING

For a summary of the most effective instructional strategies, read the U.S. National Reading Panel's report "Teaching Children To Read" (2000), available at www.nationalreadingpanel. org/publications/summary. htm.

The following two Evidence-Based Practice boxes list effective practices for reading instruction in general, and for reading comprehension in particular.

Writing Elementary-age children with special needs commonly experience problems with writing, especially with written expression. It is essential that they be given ample opportunities to write and that appropriate attention be given to handwriting and spelling (see Polloway, Miller, & Smith, 2003, for a discussion of writing instruction).

In a recent research review, Vaughn, Gersten, and Chard (2000) summarized findings in research with students in Grades 3 through 9. They concluded that best practices in expressive writing instruction included the following:

- *Explicit teaching of the critical steps in the writing process.* This was often supported by a "think sheet," prompt card, or mnemonic. However, the teacher invariably modelled how to use these steps by writing several samples.

- *Explicit teaching of the conventions of a writing genre.* These "text structures" provided a guide for undertaking the writing task at hand, whether it was a persuasive essay, a personal narrative, or an essay comparing and contrasting two phenomena.

- *Guided feedback.* Teachers or peers provided frequent feedback to students on the quality of their work, elements missing from their work, and the strengths of their work. (p. 103)

Evidence-Based Practice

Teaching Reading with Emphasis on Word Recognition

- Develop balanced programs that emphasize both decoding skills and comprehension skills.

- Determine whether students have sufficient phonological awareness skills to be able to use phonetic analysis as a decoding strategy.

- Develop phonological awareness skills by enhancing students' ability to differentiate, analyze, and blend sounds, and to tie this effort to word study.

- Teach word meanings directly, and complement students' ability to recognize words with the ability to understand their meaning.

- Teach phonetic analysis conventions that have high levels of utility (i.e., have applicability to multiple words, such as the "silent e" rule and the "two vowels together" format).

- Teach students word structures by providing opportunities for them to take advantage of structural analyses skills to focus on prefixes, suffixes, contractions, and compound words.

- Teach students to use context to enhance word recognition and comprehension. However, use caution in placing significant weight on contextual analysis because of the difficulties presented as students engage in reading with more difficult vocabulary. As this occurs, phonetic cues are likely to be more effective than context cues.

- Teach students to use a strategy for attacking unknown words in print so they can determine if it is important that they be able to say the word accurately (such as may not be the case with a proper noun), to use phonetic analysis skills, and to use structural analysis, for example.

- Ensure that students have ample opportunity to read and encounter words, concepts, and knowledge through print.

- Provide motivational strategies for struggling readers that can relate to extrinsic strategies, such as the use of reinforcement, and intrinsic strategies related to student interest and self-management.

- Ensure that skills instruction is explicit, intensive, and ongoing to result in the acquisition, maintenance, and generalization of skills.

Teaching Reading Comprehension

- **Comprehension monitoring**: Readers learn how to be conscious of their understanding during reading and learn procedures to deal with problems in understanding as they arise.
- **Co-operative learning**: Readers work together to learn strategies in the context of reading.
- **Graphic and semantic organizers**: Readers learn to present graphically the meanings and relationships of the ideas that underlie the words in the text.
- **Story structure**: Readers learn to ask and answer "who, what, where, when, and why" questions about the plot and to map out the timeline, characters, and events in stories.

- **Question answering**: Readers answer questions posed by the teacher and are given feedback on the correctness of their answers.
- **Question generation**: Readers ask "what, when, were, why, what will happen, how, and who" questions.
- **Summarization**: Readers attempt to identify and write the main idea that integrates the other meanings of the text into a coherent whole.
- **Multiple-strategy teaching**: Readers use several of these procedures and interact with the teacher over the text.

Adapted from The National Reading Panel, 2000, pp. 4–6.

A key concern is to provide sufficient opportunities to write that are seen as meaningful tasks (e.g., writing for an authentic audience, or choosing a topic that is important or interesting to the student). The Evidence-Based Practice box provides a list of practices associated with effective writing instruction.

Teaching Writing Skills

- Establish a writing environment where students understand that there is an audience for their work that includes teachers, other students, and individuals beyond the classroom.
- Encourage legible handwriting styles as alternatives to formal styles that may otherwise be taught to young children but abandoned by middle school. A helpful approach is to encourage a mixed script with cursive and manuscript forms blended together.
- After legibility has been achieved, focus instruction on maintenance through attention to continued legible work.
- Relate spelling instruction to emphases within the reading curriculum to take advantage of, for example, words that have significant personal interest, words from linguistic families, and words that are important for all writing efforts (i.e., high-frequency words).
- Beyond initial instruction, emphasize handwriting and spelling as tool subjects that can be improved in conjunction with writing skills.

- Avoid having students monitor errors only while writing, and emphasize the importance of expressing ideas and monitoring errors during the postwriting stage.
- Teach writing through a process approach in which students learn the importance of, and strategies related to, prewriting, drafting, and postwriting (i.e., editing, revising) stages.
- Use learning strategies to promote student independence, such as in areas inclusive of error monitoring and sentence, paragraph, and composition generation.
- Provide text structures, such as graphic organizers, to provide a model for students to follow in writing.
- Use student–teacher conferences to review student work and make recommendations for changes as related to both the craft (structure, mechanics) and the content (ideas, themes) of written work.
- Have students write often so that they have an opportunity to develop skills and to reinforce interest.

Group A: Geometry (8 students)	Group B: Fractions (10 students)	Group C: Addition (5 students)
Manipulate/Manipulate*	**Display/Write**	**Write/Write**
Input:	*Input:*	*Input:*
Teacher walks the perimeter of a geometric shape.	Write the fraction that names the shaded part.	$\begin{array}{r} 3 \\ +\ 2 \\ \hline \end{array}$
		Write the answer.
Output:	*Output:*	*Output:*
Learner does the same.	Learner writes $\frac{1}{2}$	Learner writes 5
Display/Identify	**Manipulate/Say***	**Display/Write**
Input:	*Input:*	*Input:*
From the choices, mark the shape that is the same as the first shape.	Teacher removes portion of shape and asks learner to name the part.	Write the number there is in all.
Output:	*Output:*	*Output:*
Learner marks	Learner says, "One fourth"	Learner writes 5
Write/Identify	**Write/Write**	**Say/Say***
Input:	*Input:*	*Input:*
Circle	one half	Teacher says, "I am going to say some addition items. Six plus six. Tell me the answer."
Mark the shape that shows the word.	Write this word statement as a numeral.	
Output:	*Output:*	*Output:*
Learner marks	Learner writes $\frac{1}{2}$	Learner says, "Twelve"

Figure 13.1 Interactive Unit Model

*Teacher present in group

From *Developmental Teaching of Mathematics for the Learning Disabled* (p. 246), by J.F. Cawley (Ed.), 1984, Austin, TX: Pro-Ed. Copyright 1984 by Pro-Ed Inc. Reprinted with permission.

Mathematics Mathematics represents another challenging academic area for students with exceptionalities. Development of both computational skills and problem-solving abilities forms the foundation of successful math instruction and learning.

Computation In the area of computation, teachers should focus first on students' conceptual understanding of a particular skill and then on the achievement of automaticity (automatic responses to math facts) with that skill. Cawley's (1984) interactive unit and Miller, Mercer, and Dillon's (1992) concrete/semiconcrete/abstract systems afford excellent options for the teacher (see Figure 13.1). The interactive unit gives teachers 16 options for teaching math skills based on four teacher input variables and four student output variables. The resulting 4 × 4 matrix provides a variety of instructional approaches that can be customized to assist learners who experience difficulties. The interactive unit also reflects a logical process that begins with the important emphasis on the concrete instructional activities (manipulate/manipulate) to build mathematical concepts, moves to a semiconcrete focus (display/identify) to enhance concept development, and arrives at the abstract (say/say, write/write), which focuses on achieving automaticity. These emphases offer two proven benefits in the general education classroom: they have been used successfully with students with exceptionalities, and they offer alternative teaching strategies for all learners—a particularly significant advantage, given that math is the most common area of failure in schools.

Problem Solving Problem solving can be particularly difficult for students with exceptionalities and thus warrants special attention. For learners with special needs, and for many other students as well, instruction in specific problem-solving strategies can greatly enhance math understanding. A given strategy's steps should be taught and followed systematically so that students learn to reason through problems and understand problem-solving processes. One such example is the SOLVE-IT strategy (see Figure 13.2). The use of learning strategies and their value for students with and without exceptionalities are discussed further in chapter 14. The next Evidence-Based Practice box provides a list of recommendations for effective practice.

The potential benefits of including students with special needs in general education classrooms to study core academic areas (i.e., basic skills) also extend to other academic areas. Subjects such as science, social studies, health and family life, and the arts offer excellent opportunities for social integration, while effective instructional strategies can

FURTHER READING

John Cawley's research in mathematics over the past 30 years has been very influential in the development of effective programs for students with disabilities. See his article "Connecting Math and Science for All Students" in volume 34, issue 4 of *Teaching Exceptional Children*, 2002 (pp. 14–19).

S	**SAY**	the problem to yourself (repeat).
O	**OMIT**	any unnecessary information from the problem.
L	**LISTEN**	for key vocabulary indicators.
V	**VOCABULARY**	Change vocabulary to math concepts.
E	**EQUATION**	Translate problem into a math equation.
I	**INDICATE**	the answer.
T	**TRANSLATE**	the answer back into the context of the word problem.

Figure 13.2
Problem-Solving Strategy for Mathematics

From *Strategies for Teaching Learners with Special Needs* (7th ed., p. 328), by E.A. Polloway, J.R. Patton, and L. Serna, 2001. Columbus, OH: Merrill. Reprinted with permission.

Teaching Mathematics

- Base instruction on a concrete/semiconcrete/abstract model in which initial instruction of a new skill is grounded in an understanding that comes through concrete representation and in which students learn to use visual representations (semiconcrete) to enhance skills and more abstract math to facilitate automaticity inclusive of accuracy and speed (e.g., through reliance on numerals and mathematical symbols).

- Ensure that prerequisite skills have been achieved in sequential fashion in mathematics (i.e., students should have 1-to-1 correspondence before counting and should have effective counting skills before addition).

- Use math attack strategies to learn, recall, and apply basic skills related to specific math operations (such as through the use of mnemonics to recall ways to perform multiplication, long division, and algebraic equations).

- Teach problem-solving strategies that enable students to attack word problems and reach solutions (see, for example, Figure 13.2).

- Place word problems in the context of real-life settings in which students are not directly cued as to the correct algorithm (operation) to be used but rather are challenged to think about the task.

- Present word problems that include distracters or extraneous information to teach students how to focus on relevant aspects for problem solutions.

- Develop graduated word problems, such as through a matrix approach that enables students to enhance their skills in terms of the language structure of problems, the computational challenges, and the presence or absence of distracters, for example.

lead to academic achievement. These subjects also lend themselves well to integrated curricular approaches (discussed later in the chapter). **Co-operative teaching** presents an excellent instructional alternative in these areas because it combines the expertise and resources of the classroom teacher with the talents of the special education teacher, rather than requiring them each to develop separate curricula in these areas.

Social Skills Instruction

Virtually all students identified as having an intellectual disability or an emotional or behavioural disorder, and many with learning disabilities, have difficulties related to the development of **social skills**. The challenge for classroom teachers is to find ways to incorporate this focus in their classes. Seeking assistance from a speech-language pathologist is a good idea. Speech-language pathologists—professionals who specialize in helping individuals of all ages communicate more effectively—have extensive understanding and expertise in social skill development. The development of social skills should not be neglected, since performance in the social domain is often predictive of success or failure in inclusive settings. All educators agree about the importance of social competence, but concern remains about the modest effects that social skills instruction has demonstrated in research (Kavale, 2001). The Evidence-Based Practice box on the following page presents a series of recommendations for practice.

A second consideration in social skills instruction involves selecting a social adjustment program that promotes both social skills and *social competence*. Whereas social skills facilitate individual interpersonal interactions, **social competence** involves the broader ability to use skills at the right times and places, showing social perception, cognition, and judgment of how to act in different situations. A focus limited to specific skill training may make it difficult for the child to maintain the specific social skills or transfer them to various settings.

Teaching Social Skills

- Emphasize social competence as the key focus of instruction.
- Use social skills curricula with caution, and evaluate success on an ongoing basis because of the limited efficacy data on most programs.
- Determine the specific social skills that will enhance performance both within and beyond the school setting, and focus instruction on these areas.
- Develop targeted behaviours and skills that are important for all students to learn.
- Place priority on skills that are most needed for immediate interactions in the classroom in order to enhance the likelihood of successful inclusion. These may include skills such as taking turns, asking for assistance, following directions, and interacting positively with adults and peers.

- Emphasize self-management or self-control strategies that are cognitively based and require students to think about their actions.
- Collect data on student behaviour to determine the effectiveness of instructional, teacher management, and student self-management interventions, and make modifications as needed.
- Develop positive behavioural support programs that are applicable across individuals within the classroom and, if possible, throughout the school.
- Develop a collaborative plan that includes involvement of general education teachers, special education teachers, speech-language pathologists, school counsellors, and school psychologists as needed.

Third, a decision must be made as to who will teach social skills. Often, initial instruction occurs in pull-out programs (e.g, resource rooms) with generalization plans developed for transfer to the general education classroom. For inclusive classrooms, a useful strategy is the use of co-operative teaching (e.g., a speech-language pathologist working with the classroom teacher in the classroom environment).

Transitional Needs

In addition to the academic and social components of the curriculum, career education and transition form an important emphasis even for younger children. For all elementary students, career awareness and a focus on facilitating movement between levels of schooling (i.e., vertical transitions) are curricular essentials.

Transition from Preschool to Primary School Research on students moving from preschool programs into school settings has identified variables that predict success in school. Four such variables include academic readiness skills, social skills, responsiveness to instructional style, and responsiveness to the structure of the school environment. Analyzing the new school environment can help a teacher determine the skills a student will need to make this crucial adjustment.

Academic readiness skills have traditionally been cited as good predictors of success at the primary school level. Examples include the ability to recognize and to write numbers and letters, to grasp a writing utensil, and to count to 10. Yet a clear delineation between academic readiness and academic skills is not warranted. Rather, to use reading as an example, it is much more productive to consider readiness as inclusive of examples of early reading skills, or what has been termed emergent literacy. Programming in this area should focus on academic activities that advance the processes of learning to read, write, or calculate.

Watch

Early Intervention

TEACHING TIP

Teachers should accept responsibility to prepare students for their next school-life challenge or transition (e.g., preschool to elementary school, elementary school to secondary school).

Social skills consistent with the developmental attributes of other five- and six-year-olds are clearly important to success in elementary school. It is particularly critical that students be able to function in a group. Thus, introducing small group instructional activities in preschool programs prepares students to function in future school situations.

Developing *responsiveness to a new instructional style* is another challenge for the young child. Providing instructional experiences that the student can generalize to the new school setting will be helpful, since the instructional arrangement in the preschool program may vary significantly from that of the school program; some learning activities in the preschool class should approximate those of Kindergarten. For example, a child entering an immersion program should have basic terms and phrases in the future language of instruction introduced in preschool.

Responsiveness to the daily learning environment is a fourth concern. Changes may include new transportation arrangements, extended instructional time, increased expectations of individual independence, and increased class size resulting in a reduction in individual attention. Teachers may set up opportunities for preschoolers to visit Kindergarten classes to familiarize them with the future environment.

FURTHER READING

For a discussion of the use of co-teaching to facilitate life skills learning in the inclusive classroom, read Ellen Fennick's article "Coteaching: An Inclusive Curriculum for Transition" in volume 33, issue 6 of *Teaching Exceptional Children*, 2001 (pp. 60–66).

TEACHING TIP

Integrated curricular approaches can enable students who are gifted to extend their learning beyond the curriculum.

Elementary Curricular Considerations Career education in general, and **life skills** education in particular, have become major emphases among secondary school teachers, especially among those who work with students who have exceptionalities. Yet life skills concepts should also be incorporated into elementary and middle school programs. Table 13.2 provides a matrix of topics that may be incorporated into an elementary-level life skills curriculum. Even programs for young children should be designed to encourage positive long-term outcomes for all students.

Concepts and topics related to life skills should be integrated into existing subject areas, thus broadening the curriculum without creating a "new subject." This can be done in three ways. The first approach, *augmentation*, uses career education–oriented materials to supplement the existing curriculum. The second approach *infuses* relevant career education topics into the lessons laid out in the existing curriculum. A third approach employs an *integrated curriculum*, similar to the unit approach traditionally used in many education programs. An integrated curriculum addresses a topic by drawing together content related to it from various academic areas, enabling students to apply academic skills across these areas. Life skills related to the broad topic can be woven into the curriculum. This curriculum can help primary- and elementary-age students understand that different academic subjects have important interrelationships.

Transition to Middle School Students with exceptionalities in elementary school need to be prepared for movement to middle school or junior high school. In order to make this vertical transition successful, students need an organized approach to their work, time management and study skills, note-taking strategies, homework strategies, and the ability to use lockers.

A variety of instructional strategies may assist in the transition process: having junior high school faculty visit elementary classes to discuss programs and expectations, viewing video recorded junior high school classes, and taking field trips to the

Table 13.2 Life Skills in the Elementary School Curriculum

	Consumer Economics	Occupational Knowledge	Health	Community Resources	Government and Law
Reading	Look for ads in the newspaper for toys.	Read books from the library on various occupations.	Read the school lunch menu.	Find television listing in the *TV Guide*.	Read road signs and understand what they mean.
Writing	Write prices of items to be purchased.	Write the specific tasks involved in performing one of the classroom jobs.	Keep a diary of food you eat in each food group each day.	Complete an application to play on a Little League team.	Write a letter to the mayor inviting him/her to visit your school.
Speaking, Writing, Viewing	Listen to bank official talk about savings accounts.	Call newspaper in town to inquire about delivering papers in your neighbourhood.	View a film on brushing teeth.	Practise the use of the 9-1-1 emergency number.	Discuss park playground improvements with the mayor.
Problem Solving	Decide if you have enough coins to make a purchase from a vending machine.	Decide which job in the classroom you do best.	Role play what you should do if you have a stomach ache.	Role play the times you would use the 9-1-1 emergency number.	Find the city hall on the map. Decide whether you will walk or drive to it.
Interpersonal Relations	Ask for help finding items in a grocery store.	Ask a student in the class to assist you with a classroom job.	Ask the school nurse how to take care of mosquito bites.	Call the movie theatre and ask the show times of a movie.	Role play being lost and asking a police officer for help.
Computation	Compute the cost of a box of cereal with a discount coupon.	Calculate how much you would make on a paper route at $3 per hour for 5 hours per week.	Compute the price of one tube of toothpaste if they are on sale at 3 for $1.	Compute the complete cost of going to the movie (admission, food, transportation).	Compute tax on a candy bar.

From "Curricular Considerations: A Life Skills Orientation," by J.R. Patton, M.E. Cronin, E.A. Polloway, D.R. Hutchison, and G.A. Robinson. In *Best Practices in Mild Mental Retardation*, edited by G.A. Robinson, J.R. Patton, E.A. Polloway, and L. Sargent, 1989, p. 31. Reston, VA: CEC-MR. Used with permission.

junior high school to get a sense of the physical layout, the changing of classes, and environmental and pedagogical factors. Co-operative planning and follow-up between general and special education teachers at the two school levels will smooth the transition.

Community-Based Instruction In developing life skills and facilitating transition, community-based instruction can benefit all students but is particularly effective for students with exceptionalities, as it addresses common problems in applying academic learning to life outside the classroom. Field trips to stores to make purchases, to observe work patterns, and to learn about advertising and marketing techniques can be supplemented by bringing community members into the classroom to speak about careers or to demonstrate life skills. Curriculum guides can assist teachers in integrating community resources into instructional programming.

Science class offers an excellent opportunity for social integration of students with special needs.

Diversity Considerations

Watch

Teaching Bilingual Students

Educators need to consider issues related to cultural diversity when working with elementary-age students with special needs. Students who come from different language backgrounds and whose families reflect values that differ from those of the majority culture must be treated with sensitivity and respect. Thus, teachers should often make adaptations to instruction so that it reflects effective responses to multicultural considerations.

Considerations of linguistic and cultural diversity must inform all aspects of curriculum design and should be reflected in instructional practices. Students with exceptionalities benefit from direct, hands-on approaches to such topics. Teachers should introduce specific activities that promote cultural awareness and sensitivity to develop students' appreciation of diversity at the elementary level, and then lay the foundation for subsequent programming at the middle and secondary level.

Teachers need to incorporate material that is relevant to the cultures of students in their classroom. Due to the country's enormous diversity, the Canadian education system will never provide prepackaged relevant curricula. In Northern Quebec, for example, a classroom will have a large proportion of First Nations peoples; in Vancouver, a significant number of students are of Asian heritage; in many rural areas across Canada, students of European and East European descent may predominate, although, in this instance, diversity will be less apparent—families may have been here for three or more generations. Therefore, the responsibility almost always remains with individual teachers to adapt their curricula to reflect the diversity in their classrooms.

An excellent source for building a multicultural focus in the curriculum is through the use of the internet. The Technology Today box presents an innovative approach to web use.

Virtual Technology in the Special Education Classroom

Smedley and Higgins (2005) advocate the use of virtual technology to bring the world to students with exceptionalities. One of their examples is through the use of "virtual field trips." Through this approach, teachers can take advantage of the various benefits of such trips without the concerns of preparation time, scheduling, funding, transportation, and liability. Some examples from their list of online virtual field trips to selected locations are provided below:

Expedition online: Students may take virtual field trips to caves, volcanoes, and glaciers around the world (e.g., http://nationalgeographic.com)

Virtual field trips: During these virtual experiences, a class may pair up with another class in a different location, with one group serving as the host (e.g., www.rite.ed.qut.edu.au/oz-teachernet/projects/virtual-field-trips/index.htm).

CTI: Students tour art galleries and museums as well as visit Europe, Asia, America, and Antarctica (e.g., www.field-trips.org).

Hidden New York: This website highlights 12 little-known areas around New York City (e.g., www.pbs.org/wnet/newyork/hidden/index.html).

Since virtual field trips and other types of simulations are generally delivered using several modalities, students with and without exceptionalities can use diverse learning approaches while participating in these activities. In addition, a computer-delivered course of instruction allows students to work at their own pace. Such virtual excursions also encourage students to focus on the most pertinent topics or details prior to an in-class lesson or an actual field trip.

While the application of technology obviously offers students many additional opportunities to learn and interact with the world around them, teachers should be aware that technology use presents challenges as well. One potential challenge is that both teachers and students will require additional training in the appropriate use of each simulation or software program. Despite such challenges, virtual programs and other forms of computer technology continue to offer all students an opportunity to learn using multiple modalities and to demonstrate their unique strengths.

From "Virtual Technology: Bringing the World into the Special Education Classroom," by T.M. Smedley and K. Higgins, 2005, *Intervention in School and Clinic, 41*, pp. 114–119.

INSTRUCTIONAL ADAPTATIONS AND ACCOMMODATIONS

In general, students with exceptionalities profit directly from the same types of teaching strategies that benefit all students. However, in particular, certain research-validated interventions are associated with successful learning outcomes for students with learning disabilities and other special needs. Vaughn et al. (2000) identified three instructional features that stand out as producing the most significant impact on learning:

- control of task difficulty (i.e., sequencing examples and problems to maintain high levels of student success)

- teaching students in small interactive groups of six or fewer students

- directed response questioning (i.e., involves the use of procedures . . . that promote "thinking aloud" about text being read, mathematical problems to be solved, or about the process of composing a written essay or story). (p. 101)

Clinical and Educational Audiologist Cassandra Grabowski

Cassandra has worked as an audiologist in a variety of settings including, hospitals, community clinics, schools. In the school environment, auditory difficulties can significantly influence a child's development. "Even a mild or temporary hearing loss can significantly impact speech and language development, learning, and socialization. In a social setting, a student with a hearing impairment may perceive themselves as different, particularly if they wear hearing aids and have difficulty communicating. Teachers must take an active role in developing activities that promote inclusion with their typically hearing peers. Therefore, it is critical to address all areas of the student's life whether that may be academic and/or social. As an audiologist, I strive to provide a support system for the teacher and family. Providing strategies for academic and social success at school, and at home, are key elements when working with a student with a hearing impairment."

Each individual's hearing loss will vary in severity. Each individuals will also have unique strengths and areas of need. However, there are some general suggestions that teachers and families can use when interacting with an individual with a hearing loss. "Always check to make sure that the individual with a hearing impairment has heard and understood what was said. The student often may not realize that they misunderstood a message. Repetition is key! Always make sure that the student's hearing aids and FM system are actually working. It is of utmost importance to complete a daily check of the hearing aids and FM system. This daily check should include a visual inspection, a listening check, and a battery check. This applies to both school and home. Make home and school listener-friendly by monitoring internal and external noises on an ongoing basis, and look for adjustments to improve the acoustics (i.e., placing carpet on hard-surfaced floors to dampen the noise)."

It is important for a child with a hearing loss to be surrounded by a team of professionals (i.e., audiologist, speech-language pathologist, classroom teacher, educational assistant) and their parents when planning interventions to meet their needs. "Regular classroom teachers have been given minimal training/coursework about the students with hearing impairments. They are faced with large class sizes and students with a variety of other special needs. Consequently, the teacher has limited time to spend with a student with a hearing impairment. Therefore, we must pool our resources and work as a team to develop an appropriate educational plan."

Vaughn et al. (2000) further noted that *all students* benefit when best practices for students with learning disabilities such as these are used.

These basic principles, reflected in the adaptations or accommodations made to instructional programs in the general education classroom, form the keys to successful inclusion. (See Figure 13.3, in which multilevel instruction is identified as one of several effective inclusive practices.) As the adage goes, special education is not necessarily special, it is just *good teaching*. "Good teaching" often means making appropriate adaptations or accommodations. Assuming the curricular content is appropriate for individual students who have exceptionalities, the challenge is to adapt it to facilitate learning.

In inclusive elementary school environments, instruction must be based on the realities of that environment. Successful programs thus reflect collaborative practices—both between teachers and among students. These concerns are discussed below. Following these sections on professional collaboration and co-operative learning, the succeeding sections address curricular and instructional adaptations—necessary considerations in the elementary classroom.

Figure 13.3 Effective Inclusive Practices

Adapted from "National Survey Identifies Inclusive Educational Practices," Appalachian Educational Laboratory, 1995, *The Link, 14* (1), Spring/Summer 1995, p. 8.

The following practices have been identified by the U.S. National Center on Educational Restructuring and Inclusion as supporting inclusive education:

■ **Multilevel instruction** allows for different kinds of learning within the same curriculum. Here the focus is on key concepts to be taught, alternatives in presentation methods, acceptance of varying types of student activities and multiple outcomes, different ways in which students can express their learning, and diverse evaluation procedures.

■ **Co-operative learning** involves heterogeneous groupings of students, allowing for students with a wide variety of skills and traits to work together. Models of co-operative learning differ in the amount of emphasis given to the process of the group's work and to the assessment of outcomes for individual members as well as for the team as a whole.

■ **Activity-based learning** emphasizes learning in natural settings, the production of actual work products, and performance assessment. It moves learning from being solely classroom-based to preparing students to learn in community settings.

■ **Mastery learning** specifies what a student needs to learn and then provides sufficient practice opportunities to gain mastery.

■ **Technology** is often mentioned as being a support for students and teachers. Uses include record keeping, assistive devices such as reading machines and braille-to-print typewriters, and drill and instructional programs.

■ **Peer support and tutoring programs** have multiple advantages. Placing students in instructional roles enhances the teaching resources of the school. It recognizes that some students learn by teaching others.

Professional Collaboration

The successful elementary classroom is a model of collaboration. Both teachers and students benefit from support from their peers. Professional collaboration is a key component of effective elementary schools and a necessity for successful inclusion. Collaboration can occur in IEP meetings, through co-operative teaching, and within the pre-referral (or child study) process. Co-operative teaching can potentially help prevent or correct all students' learning problems while remediating identified deficits for students with exceptionalities. Co-operative teaching, perhaps the best vehicle for attaining successful inclusive classrooms, truly provides **supported education**, the school-based equivalent of supported work, in which students are placed in the least-restrictive environment and provided with the necessary support (e.g., by the special educator) to be successful.

Co-operative Learning

Co-operative learning has been promoted as a means of facilitating the inclusion of students with exceptionalities in general education classrooms. It is categorized by classroom techniques that involve students in group-learning activities in which recognition and reinforcement are based on group, rather than individual, performance. Heterogeneous small groups work together to achieve a group goal, and an individual student's success directly affects the success of other students.

A variety of formats can be used to implement co-operative learning. These include peer tutoring and group projects of various types.

Watch

Classwide Peer Tutoring

Peer Tutoring Peer teaching, or **peer tutoring**, is a relatively easy-to-manage system of co-operative learning. It can benefit both the student being tutored and the tutor. Specific activities that lend themselves to peer tutoring include reviewing task directions, doing drill and practice, recording material dictated by a peer, modelling acceptable or appropriate responses, and providing pre-test practice (such as in spelling).

A research-based approach for using students as instructors is *classwide peer tutoring (CWPT)*, using instructional strategies that involve students being taught by peers who were previously trained and then supervised by teachers. Maheady, Harper, and Mallette (2003) identified the four primary components of *classwide peer tutoring (CWPT)* as follows:

> *competing teams; a highly structured tutoring procedure; daily point earning and public posting of people performance; and direct practice in the implementation of instructional activities. In using CWPT, the teacher's role changes from primary "deliverer" of instruction to facilitator and monitor of peer-teaching activities. (p. 1)*

CWPT is intended to be a reciprocal tutoring approach. That is, students assume roles as both tutor and tutee during individual instructional sessions. Further, the sessions are highly structured by the teacher to ensure that students are on task and focused on key instructional content. As summarized by Seeley (1995), this system involves the following arrangements:

- Classes are divided into two teams, which engage in competitions of one to two weeks' duration.

- Students work in pairs, both tutoring and being tutored on the same material in a given instructional session.

- Partners reverse roles after 15 minutes.

- Typical subjects tutored include math, spelling, vocabulary, science, and social studies.

- The teacher breaks down the curriculum into manageable subunits.

- Students accumulate points for their team by giving correct answers and by using correct procedures, and they receive partial credit for corrected answers.

- Individual scores on master tests are then added to the team's total.

CWPT has been positively evaluated in terms of enhancing content learning, promoting diversity and integration, and freeing teachers to prepare for other instructional activities (Maheady et al., 2003).

Another example of a successful peer tutoring approach is Peer Assisted Learning Strategies (PALS), described by Mathes and Torgesen (1998). In PALS, beginning readers are assisted in learning through paired instruction in which each member of the pair takes turns serving as a coach and a reader. The first coach is the reader who is at a higher achievement level, who listens to, comments on, and reinforces the other student before the roles are reversed. These researchers found that the use of this approach enhanced students' reading by promoting careful attention to saying and hearing sounds, sounding out words, and reading stories. They recommended using the approach three times a week for approximately 16 weeks, with each session lasting 35 minutes. The PALS program complements general education instruction by enhancing the academic engaged time of each student. This strategy can also be effectively used in other subject areas such as mathematics (see Kroeger & Kouche, 2006).

Co-operative Projects *Group projects* allow students to pool their knowledge and skills to complete an assignment. The task is assigned to the entire group, and the goal is to develop a single product reflecting the contributions of all members. For example, in art, creating a collage is a good example of a group project. In social studies, a report on one of the provinces or territories might involve making individual students responsible for particular tasks: drawing a map, sketching an outline of a province or territory's history, collecting photos of scenic attractions, and developing a display of products from that province or territory. The benefits of groups are enhanced when they include high, average, and low achievers.

The Jigsaw Technique The jigsaw format involves giving all students in a group individual tasks to be completed before the group can reach its goal. Each individual studies a portion of the material and then shares it with other members of the team. For example, Salend (1990) discussed an assignment related to the life of Dr. Martin Luther King, Jr., in which each student was given a segment of his life to research. The students then had to teach others in their group the information from the segment they had mastered.

Student-Team Achievement Divisions The concept of student-team achievement divisions (STAD) involves assigning students to diversely constituted teams (typically four to a group), which then meet to review specific teacher-generated lessons. This technique typically focuses on learning objectives that relate to one correct answer (e.g., facts). The teams work together toward content mastery, comparing answers, discussing differences, and questioning one another. Subsequently all students take individual quizzes, without assisting one another. The combined scores of the group determine how well the team succeeds. STAD embraces three concepts central to successful team learning methods: team rewards, individual accountability, and equal opportunities for success. Team rewards derive from content learning by members, who are then assessed by team scores produced by pooled individual scores. Individual accountability is essential because all must learn the content for the team to be successful. Equal opportunities for success come by focusing on degree of individual improvement.

Co-operative learning strategies offer much promise as inclusive practices. The various approaches can be used successfully with low, average, and high achievers to promote academic and social skills and to enhance independence. The fact that co-operative learning appears to be effective in general education and special education classrooms seems to support the benefits of its use with heterogeneous populations (McMaster & Fuchs, 2002).

Co-operative learning can enhance the social adjustment of students with special needs and help create natural support networks of which typically achieving peers are a part. However, co-operative learning strategies should be used for only part of the curriculum, not exclusively.

Specific adaptations and accommodations for students with exceptionalities in elementary classes are discussed next. They vary in nature and in terms of treatment acceptability. The authors do not mean that all suggestions will be appropriate or desirable in a given situation. Teachers should determine how far to go in making specific adaptations. Many of the suggested adaptations will prove beneficial to all students, not only those with special needs.

Enhancing Content Learning through Listening

Many children will not listen carefully just because they are told to do so. Rather, they often need oral presentations provided in ways that promote successful listening. Students who

FURTHER READING

For more information on co-operative learning, see R.E. Slavin's article "Cooperative Learning in Middle and Secondary Schools" in volume 69, issue 4 of *The Clearing House*, 1996 (pp. 200–204).

struggle with selective attention (i.e., focus) or sustained attention (i.e., attention maintained over a period of time) respond more easily to speaking that supports the listener. Wallace, Cohen, and Polloway (1987) note that listeners attend more when the following occur:

- Content is [emphasized] through repetition, vocal emphasis, and cueing.
- The message is meaningful, logical, and well organized.
- Messages are given in short units.
- The speaker can be clearly heard and understood.
- The speaker allows for listener participation in the form of clarification, feedback, or responding.
- The speaker has focused attention by stating how the message will be of importance to the listener.
- Reinforcement for attending is given in the form of participation, praise, or increased ability to perform.
- Oral presentations are accompanied by visual aids that emphasize important points.
- The listener knows there will be an opportunity to reflect upon and integrate the message before having to formulate a response. (p. 75)

Adapting Oral Presentations

In order to facilitate learning, teachers must consider effective vehicles for presenting content. Adaptations and accommodations in this area typically prove beneficial to all students. Some specific considerations follow:

- When mastery of prior content is uncertain, use concrete concepts before teaching abstractions (e.g., teach the concept of human rights by discussing specific rights that the students are entitled to).
- Relate information to students' prior experiences.
- Provide students with an overview before beginning.
- Reduce the number of concepts introduced at a given time.
- Encourage children to detect errors in messages and report what they could not understand.
- Monitor and adapt presentation language to make sure that students understand you. Adjust vocabulary level and complexity of sentence structures accordingly. Avoid puns, idiomatic speech, and metaphors unless clear explanations are provided.
- Review lessons before additional content is introduced.
- Lessen distractions, such as visual and auditory ones, within the environment.
- Adjust pace as needed.
- Keep oral directions short and direct, and supplement them with written directions as needed.
- Provide repetition, review, and additional examples.
- Provide further guided practice by requiring more responses, lengthening practice sessions, or scheduling extra sessions.

■ Clarify directions for follow-up activities so that tasks can be completed successfully. (Adapted from Chalmers, 1991; Cheney, 1989; Dowdy, 1990; McDevitt, 1990.)

The Personal Spotlight in this chapter provides a glimpse of one professional's thoughts on the importance of meeting the needs of students with auditory difficulties in the classroom.

Facilitating Note Taking Learning from classroom presentations is obviously critical to academic achievement. For students in the primary grades, instruction is generally not delivered through lengthy oral presentation. However, as lecturing begins to become more common in the upper elementary grades and in junior high school, students will need to develop note-taking skills. Special education teachers may teach note taking; it is important to focus on how content is presented. The following pointers are adapted from Beirne-Smith (1989a, 1989b); they overlap somewhat with the ideas for listening and adapting presentations discussed earlier.

1. Organize your lecture.
2. Use key words and phrases, such as *first* or *the main theme*.
3. Summarize ideas.
4. Repeat important statements for emphasis.
5. Pause occasionally to allow students time to fill in blank spaces or catch up to the previous statement.
6. Provide advance organizers (e.g., topic outlines, partially completed notes) to assist the student in organizing and recording information.
7. Write important points on the board.
8. Simplify overhead transparencies. Too much information is confusing and less likely to be recorded.
9. Encourage students to record all visually presented material exactly as displayed and to leave space between main sections for questions about the material.
10. Use humour or anecdotes to illustrate important points.
11. Model note-taking skills (e.g., with the overhead projector).

Adapting Reading Tasks

In many instances, instructional tasks, assignments, or materials may be relevant and appropriate for students with exceptionalities, but may present problematic reading demands. Teachers should consider options for adapting the task or the materials. The following suggestions address problems that may arise in processing reading content:

■ Clearly establish a given assignment's purpose and importance.

■ Highlight key words, phrases (e.g., colour-coding text) and concepts (e.g., providing outlines and study guides).

■ Encourage periodic feedback from students to check their understanding.

■ Preview reading material with students to assist them in establishing purpose, activating prior knowledge, budgeting time, and focusing attention.

- Create vocabulary lists, and teach these words to ensure that students can use them rather than simply recognize them.

- Provide page numbers where specific answers can be found in a reading comprehension or content assignment.

- Use brief individual conferences with students to verify their comprehension.

- Locate lower-level content material on the same topic to adapt tasks for students with reading difficulties.

- Tape a reading of a text, or have it read orally to a student. Consider using peers, volunteers, and paraprofessionals in this process.

- Rewrite material (or solicit volunteers to do so) to simplify its reading level, or provide chapter outlines or summaries.

- Use advance organizers and visual aids (e.g., charts, graphs) to provide an orientation to reading tasks or to supplement them.

- Demonstrate how new content relates to content previously learned.

- Encourage students to facilitate their comprehension by raising questions about a text's content.

CROSS REFERENCE

Ultimately, students will need to learn to adapt reading tasks themselves, through the use of learning strategies, in order to become independent learners. See chapter 14 for how this plays out at the secondary level.

- Teach students to consider K-W-L as a technique to focus attention. *K* represents prior knowledge, *W* what the student wants to know, and *L* what has been learned as a result.

- Teach the use of active comprehension strategies in which students periodically pause to ask themselves questions about what they have read.

- Use reciprocal teaching. Have students take turns leading discussions that raise questions about the content read, summarize the most important information, clarify concepts that are unclear, and predict what will occur next. (Adapted from Chalmers, 1991; Cheney, 1989; Dowdy, 1990; Gartland, 1994; Hoover, 1990; Reynolds & Salend, 1990; Schumm & Strickler, 1991.)

Another key element to successful reading is the strategies acquired by students to promote independence. Students need to develop approaches that enable them to engage in the following:

- *Comprehension monitoring* (i.e., teaching students to monitor their comprehension and use "repair strategies" when they begin to lose understanding of the text)

- *Text structuring* (i.e., providing students with ways to ask themselves questions about what they read) (Vaughn et al., 2000, p. 104)

Enhancing Written Responses

The adaptations noted here may assist students who may have difficulty with responding in written form. These suggestions relate not to the presentation of material but rather to the responses implicit in the task or assignment. The suggestions will enhance children's ability to meet the written language demands of the inclusive classroom.

- Avoid assigning excessive amounts of written class work and homework.

- When appropriate, allow children to select the most comfortable method of writing, whether it be cursive, manuscript, or typing.

- Change the response mode to oral when appropriate.
- Set realistic, mutually agreed upon expectations for neatness.
- Allow children to circle or underline responses.
- Let students record answers instead of giving them in writing.
- Fasten materials to the desk to alleviate coordination problems.
- Provide the student with a copy of lecture notes produced by the teacher or a peer.
- Reduce amounts of board copying or text copying; provide the written information itself or an outline of the main content.
- Allow sufficient space for answering problems.
- Allow group-written responses (via projects or reports; see the section on involving peers earlier in the chapter). (Adapted from Chalmers, 1991; Cheney, 1989; Dowdy, 1990.)

In addition to enhancing written responses, teachers should work to improve students' writing ability. Provide sufficient opportunities to write relative to meaningful tasks (e.g., for an authentic audience, or on a topic important or interesting to the student). Graham (1992, p. 137) suggests the following ideas for providing frequent and meaningful writing opportunities:

- Assist students in thinking about what they will write.
- Ask students to establish goals for what they hope to achieve.
- Arrange the writing environment so that the teacher is not the sole audience for students' writing.
- Provide opportunities for students to work on the same project across days or even weeks.
- Incorporate writing as part of a larger, interesting activity.

Portfolios also represent a positive approach to enhancing writing development. They involve students in the evaluation of their own writing samples by selecting work to be kept and by comparing changes in their writing over time.

Promoting Following Instructions and Completing Assignments

Another key area is enhancing children's ability to follow instructions and complete work assignments. The following suggestions are adapted from *CEC Today* (1997, p. 15):

- Get the student's attention before giving directions.
- Use alerting cues.
- Give one direction at a time.
- Quietly repeat the directions to the student after giving them to the entire class.
- Check for understanding by having the student repeat the directions.
- Break up tasks into workable and obtainable steps, and include due dates.
- Provide examples and specific steps to accomplish the task.
- List or post requirements necessary to complete each assignment.

FURTHER READING

The key consideration for all students is to provide frequent opportunities to write. The work of Donald Graves has been particularly influential in encouraging teachers to increase chances for true writing. See Graves, Tuyay, and Green's article "What I've Learned from Teachers of Writing" in volume 82, issue 2 of *Language Arts*, 2004 (pp. 88–94).

- Check assignments frequently.
- Arrange for the student to have a study buddy.

Adapting the Classroom Environment

Two key considerations of adapting the classroom environment are time and physical arrangement. Time is a critical element and can be associated with special challenges for students with exceptionalities. Thus, adapting deadlines and other requirements can help promote success. When handled properly, these adaptations need not impinge on the integrity of the assignments or place undue burdens on the classroom teacher. Other examples include:

CROSS REFERENCE

See also the discussion on classroom arrangement in chapter 12.

- reviewing with students to reinforce routines
- providing each student with a copy of the schedule
- increasing the amount of time allowed to complete assignments or tests
- teaching time-management skills (use of timelines and checklists, and prioritization of time and assignments)

Changes in classroom arrangement can also help in accommodating students with special needs. Some specific examples include establishing a climate that fosters positive social interactions among students, using study carrels, and establishing high and low frequency areas for class work (thus using the Premack principle to allow students to move to "fun" areas contingent on work completion in more academically rigorous areas).

CONSIDER THIS

The importance of homework adaptations to the successful inclusion of students with special needs has been confirmed in numerous recent research studies. How important do you think homework adaptations are?

Teachers should avoid assigning excessive amounts of written classroom and homework to some students with special needs.

Developing Effective Homework Programs

Homework has always been an essential element of education, but recently its use by teachers in elementary education has increased. Traditional research on the effectiveness of homework as an instructional tool suggests that it leads to increased school achievement

Figure 13.4 Homework Communication Problems Noted by Elementary Teachers

From "Homework Communication Problems: Perspectives of General Education Teachers" by M.H. Epstein, E.A. Polloway, G.H. Buck, W.D. Bursuck, L.M. Wissinger, F. Whitehouse, and M. Jayanthi, 1997. In *Learning Disabilities Research and Practice, 12,* pp. 221–227. Used with permission.

Note: Items were ranked by general education teachers from *most* to *least* serious.

1. Do not know enough about the abilities of students with disabilities who are mainstreamed in their classes.
2. Do not know how to use special education support services or teachers to assist students with disabilities about homework.
3. Lack knowledge about the adaptations that can be made to homework.
4. Are not clear about their responsibility to communicate with special education teachers about the homework of students with disabilities.
5. Are not aware of their responsibility to communicate with parents of students with disabilities about homework.

for students in general, with particular benefits in the area of habit formation for elementary students.

Homework for students with exceptionalities presents several dilemmas for general education teachers. Epstein et al. (1996) recognized that communication concerning homework is often negatively affected by the inadequate knowledge base of general education teachers. Figure 13.4 presents typical problems (ordered from most to least serious by teachers) in this area.

Table 13.3 summarizes these responses; each column reflects teachers' ratings from most to least helpful. Patton and colleagues (2001) reviewed the research on collaboration concerning homework and identified recommended practices that are respectively school-based, teacher-directed, parent-initiated, and student-regulated. These are listed in Table 13.4.

Developing Responsive Grading Practices

The assignment of grades is an integral aspect of education. Grading serves multiple purposes in contemporary education (Salend & Duhaney, 2002). For example, grading can be used to indicate progress effort, and to provide feedback to students and their families (Salend & Duhaney, 2002). Thus, grading practices have been subject to frequent evaluation and review, generating a number of problematic issues.

A related issue is the feasibility of specific adaptations in general education.

Questions of fairness influence the discussion on grading (e.g., Are adaptations in grading made only for students with exceptionalities really fair to other students?) Bursuck et al. (1996) report that only 25 percent of general education teachers think such adaptations are fair. Those studied who believed they were fair noted that students should "not be punished" for an inherent problem, such as a disability; that adaptations for effort are appropriate because the students are "fighting uphill battles"; and that adaptations allow students to "be successful like other kids."

Those teachers who thought adaptations were unfair indicated that other students experience significant learning problems even though they have not been formally identified, that some students have extenuating circumstances (e.g., divorce, illness) that necessitate adaptations, and that all students are unique and deserve individual consideration

CROSS REFERENCE

Parental involvement in homework is discussed at length in chapter 15.

FURTHER READING

For a discussion of effective grading practices and policies for meeting individual student needs, read Salend and Duhaney's article "Grading Students in Inclusive Settings," in volume 34 of *Teaching Exceptional Children*, 2002 (pp. 8–15).

CROSS REFERENCE

Grading issues become more problematic at the secondary level; see chapter 14 for more information.

Table 13.3 Teachers' Ratings of Helpfulness of Homework Adaptations and Practices

Types of Homework	Teacher-Directed Activities	Consequences		Adaptations
		Failure to Complete	Complete Assignments	
Practice of skills already taught	Communicate clear consequences about successfully completing homework.	Assist students in completing the assignment.	Give praise for completion.	Provide additional teacher assistance.
Preparation for tests	Begin assignment in class, and check for understanding.	Make adaptations in assignment.	Provide corrective feedback in class.	Check more frequently with student about assignments and expectations.
Unfinished class work	Communicate clear expectations about the quality of homework completion.	Talk to them about why the assignment was not completed.	Give rewards for completion.	Allow alternative response formats (e.g., oral or other than written).
Make-up work due to absences	Use a homework assignment sheet or notebook.	Require corrections and resubmission.	Monitor students by charting performance.	Adjust length of assignment.
Enrichment activities	Communicate clear consequences about failure to complete homework.	Call students' parents.	Record performance in grade book.	Provide a peer tutor for assistance.
Preparation for future class work	Give assignments that are completed entirely at school.	Keep students in at recess to complete the assignment.	Call students' parents.	Provide auxiliary learning aids (e.g., calculator, computer).
	Begin assignment in class without checking for understanding.	Keep students after school to complete the assignment.		Assign work that student can do independently.
		Lower their grade.		Provide a study group.
		Put students' names on board.		Provide extra credit opportunities.
				Adjust (i.e., lower) evaluation standards.
				Adjust due dates.
				Give fewer assignments.

Note: Arranged from most helpful to least helpful.

From "A National Survey of Homework Practices of General Education Teachers" (p. 504) by E.A. Polloway, M.H. Epstein, W. Bursuck, M. Jayanthi, and C. Cumblad, 1994, *Journal of Learning Disabilities, 27.* Used with permission.

(i.e., students with and without exceptionalities may need specific adaptations). Such attitudes seem to indicate jointly developed adaptations. A significant minority of general educators believe that classes have standards to uphold; thus, all students need to meet those standards without adaptations.

Table 13.4 Recommended Homework Practices

School-based

- Require frequent written communication from teachers to parents.
- Schedule parent–teacher meetings in the evening.
- Provide release time for teachers to communicate with parents.
- Establish telephone hotlines.
- Establish after-school sessions to provide extra help.
- Institute peer tutoring programs.

Teacher-directed

- Require and teach students to use homework assignment books.
- Assess students' skills related to homework completion.
- Involve parents and students in the homework process from the beginning of the school year.
- Establish an ongoing communication system with parents to convey information related to homework assignments.
- Coordinate homework assignments with other teachers.
- Present assignments clearly and provide timely feedback.
- Teach students techniques for managing their time more effectively.

Parent-initiated

- Discuss homework assignments with their children daily.
- Attend parent–teacher conferences.
- Communicate views, concerns, and observations about homework to teacher(s) or other school personnel.
- Provide support to their child when doing homework by creating and maintaining an appropriate homework environment.

Student-regulated

- Demonstrate a range of self-advocacy skills, including the ability to ask for help when needed.
- Become an interdependent learner.
- Manage time more effectively.

From "Home–School Collaboration about Homework: What Do We Know and What Should We Do?" by J.R. Patton, M. Jayanthi, and E.A. Polloway, 2001, *Reading & Writing Quarterly, 17*, p. 233.

Polloway et al. (2008) suggest these overall considerations about grading:

- Plan for special and general education teachers to meet regularly to discuss student progress.

- Emphasize acquiring new skills as a basis for grades assigned, thus providing a perspective on the student's relative gains.

- Investigate alternatives for evaluating content that has been learned (e.g., oral examinations for poor readers in a science class).

- Engage in co-operative grading agreements (e.g., grades for language arts might reflect performance both in the classroom and in the resource room).

- Use narrative reports as a key portion of, or adjunct to, the report card. These reports can include comments on specific objectives within the student's IEP.

- Develop personalized grading plans for students (see Munk & Bursuck, 2001).

The Evidence-Based Practice box on effective grading provides additional perspectives.

Effective Grading Practices

Grading is a critical element of successful inclusion. Salend and Duhaney (2002) provide a series of recommendations, which include the following:

- **Communicating expectations and grading guidelines**. Student performance is enhanced when teachers clearly communicate their expectations to students and families and share their grading guidelines and criteria with them.

- **Informing students and families about grading progress on a regular basis**. Providing students and their families with ongoing information about current performance and grades helps all involved parties understand the grading guidelines. Ongoing sharing of students' grading progress facilitates the modification of instructional programs so that students and families are not surprised by the grades received at the end of the grading period. It also prompts students to examine their effort, motivation, and attitudes and their impact on performance and grades.

- **Using a range of assignments that address students' varied learning needs, strengths, and styles**. Rather than assigning grades based solely on test performance or a limited number of assignments, many teachers determine students' grades by weighing a variety of student assignments (e.g., tests, homework, projects, extra credit, class participation, attendance, behaviour, and other factors).

- **Employing classroom-based assessment alternatives to traditional testing**. Whereas grades are frequently determined by students' performance on tests, they also can be based on classroom-based assessment techniques, such as performance assessment, portfolio assessment, and curriculum-based measurement. By using performance assessment, teachers grade students on authentic products (e.g., creating and making things, solving problems, responding to stimulations) that demonstrate their skills, problem-solving abilities, knowledge, and understanding of the learning standards. Similarly, student portfolios and curriculum-based measurements that are linked to the learning standards serve as tools for grading students and guiding the teaching and learning process.

- **Providing feedback on assignments and grading students after they have learned something rather than while they are learning it**. Before grading students on an assignment or a test, teachers should provide a range of appropriate learning activities and give nongraded assignments that help students practise and develop their skills. As students work on these assignments, teachers should give them feedback and additional instructional experiences to improve their learning of the material, which is then assessed when they have completed the learning cycle.

- **Avoiding competition and promoting collaboration**. While grading on a curve results in a consistent grade distribution, it hinders the teaching and learning process by promoting competition among students. Therefore, educators minimize competition by grading students in reference to specific learning criteria and refraining from posting grades. Teachers also promote collaboration among students by structuring learning and assessment activities so that students work together and are graded co-operatively.

- **Designing valid tests and providing students with appropriate testing accommodations**. Teachers enhance the value of their tests and promote student performance by developing valid tests and providing students with appropriate testing accommodations. In designing valid tests, teachers select the content of the test so that it relates to the learning standards, the manner in which the content was taught, and the amount of class time devoted to the topics on the test. Teachers also carefully examine the format and readability of their tests, and provide students with the testing accommodations outlined on their IEPs.

- **Teaching test taking to students**. Instruction in test-taking skills helps students perform at their optimal levels by reducing testing anxiety and assisting them in feeling comfortable with the format of the test.

Adapted from "Grading Students in Inclusive Settings" (pp. 13–14) by S. Salend & L.M.G. Duhaney, 2002, *Teaching Exceptional Children, 34* (3).

SUMMARY

- The curriculum for elementary students with exceptionalities should meet their current and long-term needs, facilitate their interactions with typically achieving peers, and facilitate their transition into junior high school.

- Reading instruction should reflect emphases on both decoding skills and whole language to provide a comprehensive, balanced program.

- Math instruction should provide students with concrete and abstract learning opportunities and should stress the development of problem-solving skills.

- Teachers should select programs and strategies that focus on the social skills most needed by students in their classrooms.

- Life skills instruction should be a part of the elementary curriculum through the use of augmentation, infusion, or an integrated curriculum.

- Instructional adaptations should be evaluated against their "treatment acceptability"—that is, their feasibility, desirability, helpfulness, and fairness.

- Listening is a skill that requires conscious effort on the part of students and planned intervention strategies on the part of teachers.

- Reading tasks can be adapted through a variety of instructional strategies, such as clarifying intent, highlighting content, modifying difficulty level, and using visual aids.

- Written responses can be facilitated by modifying the response requirement.

- Co-operative learning affords teachers a unique opportunity to involve students with disabilities in classroom activities, but should not be used exclusively.

- Adaptations to class schedules or classroom arrangements should be considered in order to enhance the learning of students with exceptionalities.

- Motivation to learn cannot be taken for granted, and educational programs should be designed to reflect its importance.

- Homework creates significant challenges for students with special needs; these should be addressed by using intervention strategies.

- Classroom grading practices should be flexible enough to facilitate inclusion.

Weblinks

The Education Planet—The Education Web Guide
http://educationplanet.com
This search engine covers all education-relevant sites. If you want to find specifically Canadian material, you can limit searches to Canadian sources. This highly interesting and rewarding resource provides access to lesson plans, videos, manuals, curriculum materials, and much more.

Teachers.net
http://teachers.net
As a huge U.S. website, Teachers.net covers a variety of topics of interest to teachers, including curriculum suggestions, resources, and chat

rooms with different education issues. It has subject-specific listings of chat boards, where ideas, such as teaching secondary school math in innovative ways, are shared. Many resources are available through this website for elementary and secondary teachers.

Canadian.Teachers.net
http://canadian.teachers.net
This uniquely Canadian offshoot of Teachers.net provides a specifically Canadian forum with chat rooms, job postings, catalogues, information, professional development with guest speakers, and listings of related sites.

Chapter 14

Teaching Students with Special Needs in Secondary Schools

Chapter Objectives

After reading this chapter, you should be able to

- define the concept of a comprehensive curriculum, and discuss curricular alternatives for students with exceptionalities

- discuss ways to determine the curricular needs of secondary school students

- discuss the transition planning process for students with exceptionalities

- identify and describe the key elements of effective instruction

- discuss the roles of general education and special education teachers in ensuring successful secondary school programs for students with special needs

- identify accommodations and adaptations that can facilitate learning for secondary school students

- identify and give examples of study skills and learning strategies that can enhance school performance for adolescent learners
- define *transition* and describe how school personnel should implement transition planning and services

Questions to Consider

1. What adolescent characteristics is Jim displaying?
2. What role did Jim's parents play in developing Jim's problems and solutions?
3. What could parents and teachers have done throughout Jim's school years to help him to understand and address his transition challenges effectively?

When Jim turned 17, he seemed extremely happy about reaching this milestone in his life, but his personality began to change. He gradually went from an easygoing Grade 11 student to one who was more oppositional, lashing out occasionally at his fellow students and teachers. Although he had always been close to his parents, they were having similar problems at home. He wanted to stay in his room most of the time and was unusually resistant to helping around the house or talking about what was going on at school. He sat for hours, pretending to do homework without making much progress, and his grades began to drop. In the past, Jim had welcomed his parents' assistance in reading difficult content material, but now when they tried to help, he became agitated and refused the assistance. During a teacher–parent conference, it was decided that Jim needed counselling. After a bit of cajoling, an appointment was scheduled; several sessions later, the counsellor was able to get Jim to express his feelings. He was becoming overwhelmed by all of the "unknowns" in his life. His driving test was coming up, and he was afraid he would not be able to pass the written test, especially the part where he had to read a map. And would he pass the academic courses he needed to graduate? Would he go to university? What college should he enter? Would someone be available to help in university, as his teachers and parents had helped in high school? At least now the IEP team—and Jim—had identified the concerns. What could be done to help?

In a family session, Jim agreed to continue meeting with the counsellor to explore these feelings, and a midyear IEP meeting was scheduled that included the counsellor, the general and special education teachers, Jim's parents, and Jim. His teachers agreed to teach Jim skills in self-advocacy so he could access agencies and develop a network of support in his upcoming life after high school. The counsellor agreed to send Jim for a vocational assessment to determine his strengths, interests, and challenges. She also suggested that, during the school breaks for the remaining year-and-a-half, Jim job-shadow adults whose jobs held an interest for him. His parents promised to work more with Jim on driving to obtain his permanent license, and the school assigned a driving instructor to add support and to assist Jim in requesting accommodations for taking the written driving test. Insightful counsellors, teachers, and parents, and a "relieved" student, turned this story around, with a positive ending.

INTRODUCTION

Secondary school can be a stressful setting for students with and without exceptionalities. Important differences exist between elementary and secondary settings in terms of organizational structure, curricula, and learner variables. These differences create special challenges for successful inclusion. Certainly, one concern is the gap between the demands of the classroom setting and the ability of many students with exceptionalities. Academically, this gap widens in secondary school; many students with exceptionalities exhibit limited basic skills, study skills, and strategies, and therefore experience difficulty in performing higher-level cognitive tasks.

CONSIDER THIS

Do special education support staff need different skills at the secondary level than they need in elementary schools? If so, what are some of the differences?

A second concern is that teachers are often trained primarily as content specialists yet are expected to present complex material in such a way that a diverse group of students can master the information (Masters, Mori, & Mori, 1999). Secondary teachers are more likely to focus on teaching content than on individualizing instruction to meet each student's unique needs. Further, because there may be reluctance to change grading systems or to make other accommodations, it may become difficult for students with exceptionalities to experience success in general education settings.

A third challenge is the general nature of adolescence, which is a difficult and trying time for all young people. And for students with exceptionalities, the developmental period is even more challenging. Problems such as a lack of motivation associated with adolescence are exacerbated by the presence of an exceptionality (Masters et al., 1999).

Regardless of the difficulties associated with placing adolescents with special needs in general education programs, more students with exceptionalities are going to depend on classroom teachers to help develop and provide appropriate educational programs. Therefore, classroom teachers in secondary schools must be prepared to offer specialized instruction and modified curricula to facilitate success for students with exceptionalities.

SECONDARY SCHOOL CURRICULA

More curricular differentiation has been advocated at the secondary level to accommodate the individual needs and interests of the wide variety of students attending high school. At the same time, most high schools have a general curriculum that all students must complete. This curriculum, typically prescribed by the provincial education ministry, includes science, math, social studies, English, and French. Often, provinces and local education boards add to the required general curriculum such areas as education on sexuality, drug education, and third languages.

Although the specific curricula offered in different secondary schools vary, they generally follow provincial guidelines. Individual schools, however, offer unique curricular options that appeal to particular students. The curricular focus that students choose should be an important consideration, since this decision could have long-term implications after high school.

Special Education Curriculum in Secondary Schools

The curriculum for students with exceptionalities is the most critical programming consideration in secondary schools. Even if students have excellent teachers, if the curriculum is inappropriate to meet their needs, then the teaching may be ineffective. The high school curriculum for students with exceptionalities must be comprehensive—that is, it must:

- be responsive to the needs of individual students;
- facilitate maximum integration with typically achieving peers;
- facilitate socialization; and
- focus on students' transition to post-secondary settings.

Determining Students' Curricular Needs

As noted in chapter 13, the adoption of a curriculum for any student should be based on an appraisal of desired long-term outcomes and an assessment of current needs. At the elementary level, consideration of the future demands of middle/junior and high school suggests a primary focus on the development and refinement of basic academic and social skills, as well as a beginning emphasis on career awareness and life skills.

Polloway and Patton (1997) suggest that elementary students be taught specific skills that will facilitate success in high school, such as self-management, study skills, note taking, and homework skills. Still other nonacademic abilities, such as resisting peer pressure, negotiating, accepting negative feedback, and asking questions, should be addressed in the elementary curriculum to facilitate the success of students in secondary settings. Although some schools in the process of restructuring are providing learning opportunities in these areas, many continue to focus on academics.

Regardless of the seemingly "common" areas that should be included in an elementary curriculum, curricular variation is common. The result is that students arrive in secondary settings with a wide range of academic preparation and varying, often limited, degrees of exposure to transitional subjects such as life skills, career awareness, study skills, and self-management. Curricular considerations and decisions are critically important since high school represents a final chance for public education personnel to prepare students for their postschool futures. Data on school exit patterns and follow-up studies of students with exceptionalities have, for the most part, suggested that schools need to improve programs that prepare students with exceptionalities for life after high school. As many as 50 percent of students with learning disabilities drop out of high school.

CONSIDER THIS

What are some things that schools could do to increase the number of students with exceptionalities who stay in school and graduate?

PROGRAMS FOR STUDENTS IN SECONDARY SCHOOLS

Most secondary students with exceptionalities are included in general education classrooms for at least a portion of each school day. Therefore, the responsibility for these students becomes a joint effort between general education classroom teachers and special education personnel (Walther-Thomas et al., 2000). Unfortunately, many of these students do not experience success in the general classroom setting. They frequently fail classes, become frustrated and act out, and may even drop out of school because they are not prepared to meet the demands placed on them by secondary teachers. There are numerous reasons why many students with exceptionalities fail in secondary classes, including the following:

- lack of communication between special education personnel and classroom teachers
- discrepancies between the expectations of classroom teachers and the abilities of students
- students' lack of understanding about the demands of the classroom
- classroom teachers' lack of understanding and knowledge about students with exceptionalities
- special education personnel's lack of knowledge in working with classroom teachers

Regardless of why some students with exceptionalities do not achieve success in general education settings, the fact remains that the majority will be taught in inclusive settings, so educators—both classroom teachers and special education personnel—must

TEACHING TIP

Teachers and other school personnel must include students with exceptionalities and their family members in planning for the future.

CONSIDER THIS

The roles of general educators and special educators must change for effective inclusion to occur. What are some likely barriers to these changes, and how can they be overcome?

Figure 14.1
Instructional
Conditions and
Essential Services
for Students with
Learning Problems

From *Teaching Students with Learning Problems* (6th ed., p. 532), by
C.D. Mercer and A.R. Mercer, 2001,
Upper Saddle River, NJ: Merrill.

INSTRUCTIONAL CONDITIONS	ESSENTIAL SERVICES
Learning Characteristics	**Learning Strategies**
▶ Academic deficits	▶ Techniques, principles, or rules that enable students to learn, to solve problems, and to complete tasks independently
▶ Learning strategy deficits	
▶ Study skill deficits	
▶ Thinking deficits	
▶ Social interaction problems	
▶ Motivation problems	
	Content Enhancements
Academic Demands	▶ Devices and teaching routines that help teachers present content in a learner-friendly manner to help students identify, organize, comprehend, and recall critical information
▶ Acquire information written at secondary level	
▶ Gain information through lectures	
▶ Demonstrate knowledge through tests	
▶ Express information in writing	
▶ Use problem-solving strategies	
▶ Work independently	**Study Skills Techniques**
▶ Be motivated to learn	▶ Specific techniques and devices to help students acquire, retain, and express knowledge
Setting Realities	
▶ Coverage of large amounts of content	
▶ Use of difficult texts	
▶ Limited opportunities for academic interactions	
▶ Classes of diverse learners	
▶ Emphasis on achieving students	
▶ Limited planning and teaching time	

General education teachers
are primarily responsible for
students with special needs
in their classrooms.

work together to increase the chances of success. Figure 14.1 displays the frequent mismatch between the characteristics of students with exceptionalities and the academic and setting demands of high school, as well as the need for instructional interventions, which will be described later in the chapter.

Roles of Personnel

As noted, the responsibility for educating students with exceptionalities in public schools is shared by general classroom teachers and special education personnel. Educators must improve their skills at working together to help students with various learning and behaviour problems.

General Education Teachers The primary role of general classroom teachers is to assume the responsibility for students with exceptionalities in particular classes or subject areas. Most classroom teachers present information using one general technique, but they will probably have to expand their instructional activities when dealing with students with exceptionalities. Various accommodations, adaptations, and modifications in instructional techniques and materials will be discussed later in the chapter (also see Table 14.1)

Table 14.1 Examples of Adaptations, Accommodations, and Modifications

Characteristic	Accommodations and Modifications
Difficulty completing assignments	■ List or post (and say) all steps necessary to complete each assignment. ■ Break the assignment into manageable sections with specific due dates. ■ Make frequent checks for work/assignment completion. ■ Arrange for the student to have a "study buddy," with phone number, in each subject area.
Difficulty with tasks that require memory	■ Combine seeing, saying, writing, and doing; student may need to subvocalize to remember. ■ Teach memory techniques as a study strategy (e.g., mnemonics, visualization, oral rehearsal, numerous repetitions).
Difficulty with test taking	■ Allow extra time for testing; teach test-taking skills and strategies; allow student to be tested orally. ■ Use clear, readable, and uncluttered test forms. Use test format that the student is most comfortable with. Allow ample space for student response. Consider having lined answer spaces for essay and short-answer tests.
Confusion from nonverbal cues (misreads body language, etc.)	■ Directly teach (tell the student) what nonverbal cues mean. Model them, and have student practise reading cues in a safe setting.
Confusion from written material (difficulty finding main idea from a paragraph; attributes greater importance to minor details)	■ Provide an outline of important points from reading material. ■ Teach outlining, main idea versus details, concepts. ■ Provide tape of text.
Confusion from spoken material, lectures, and audio-visual material (difficulty finding main idea, attributes greater importance to minor details)	■ Provide student with a copy of presentation notes. ■ Allow peers to share carbon-copy notes from presentation (have student compare own notes with copy of peer's notes). ■ Provide framed outlines of presentations (introducing visual and auditory cues to important information). ■ Encourage use of tape recorder. ■ Teach and emphasize key words (the following . . . , the most important . . . , etc.)

Classroom teachers have general responsibilities for *all* of the students in their classes. These responsibilities include managing the classroom environment, providing instruction at an appropriate level and pace, using an appropriate curriculum, evaluating student success, and modifying instruction as appropriate. (Table 14.2 shows a list of steps with questions that can be used by teachers for self-evaluation following a lesson.) For students with exceptionalities, general classroom teachers have the added responsibility of participating on an interdisciplinary team.

In addition, teachers should ensure that all students have an opportunity to answer questions and a good chance at achieving at least moderate success in classroom activities.

Table 14.2 Steps in an Effective Lesson and Corresponding Evaluation Questions

Steps	Questions
1. Reviews previous lesson	Was my transition smooth and meaningful?
2. Uses advanced organizer to introduce new lesson	Were my objectives clear? Did I have the right number of objectives?
3. Obtains student attention and commitment to learn	Was my motivational or attention-getting technique effective? Did I make the lesson relevant to the student?
4. Provides direct instruction (includes modelling, demonstration, manipulation)	Was my subject matter background okay? Did I use overhead, chalkboard, graphics, models, etc.? Was there a balance between student and teacher talk?
5. Uses a variety of tasks, activities, and questions to maintain interest and generate student responses	Were my questions effective? Did my class ask questions? Did I wait for replies to my questions? Did I involve all students?
6. Provides guided practice (board work, simple worksheets, small group games with teacher)	Did I transform students from "passive listeners" to "active participants"? Was teacher activity balanced with student activity? Did I provide timely feedback?
7. Provides independent practice for generalization (workbooks, textbooks, computer, games)	Did I include appropriate homework? Did I use materials that require generalization?
8. Asks students to evaluate learning, uses informal tests (rapid-fire questioning, brief written assessment)	If I didn't know something, did I promise to look it up? Did I ask them what they had learned to teach self-evaluation? Was my assessment directly related to my objective?
9. Closes with summary and transition to next lesson	Did I have a smooth closing and transition to the next activity?
10. Provides student feedback as appropriate	Did I identify students who needed an individual behaviour change plan?
11. Documents observations: students and self	Was my behaviour management technique effective? Was learning effective and fun?

FURTHER READING

For more information on specific techniques to use with students with exceptionalities in general education classrooms, read *Teaching Adolescents with Learning Disabilities,* by D. Deshler, E. Ellis, and K. Lenz, published in 1996 by Love Publishing.

This is not a call for teachers to "give" students with exceptionalities passing grades, only a request that students with exceptionalities receive an equal chance at being successful.

Classroom teachers should do all they can to work effectively with special education professionals. Open communication and dialogue between classroom teachers and special education personnel is crucial if inclusion is to be successful. Communication among all individuals providing services to students with exceptionalities is the most important factor related to the success of inclusion (Walther-Thomas et al., 2000).

Collaborative Role of the Special Education Teacher The special education teacher plays an important role in the successful inclusion of students with exceptionalities in secondary schools. In addition to collaborating with general educators, the special education teacher must prepare students for the challenges that occur daily in the general education environment and equip them for future challenges in independent living and employment. Above all, special education teachers play a major support role for general classroom teachers. They should communicate regularly with classroom teachers and provide assistance through consultation or through direct instruction.

The specific roles of the special education teacher include counselling students for the personal crises that may occur daily and preparing students for content classes, high school exams, post-secondary training, independent living, and, ultimately, employment.

Special education teachers play a major support role for general classroom teachers.

Special education teachers, general teachers, and individuals from other agencies often collaborate in performing these roles.

Counselling for Daily Crises Adolescence is a difficult time of change for all children; for children with exceptionalities, the period is even more challenging as they carry the joy and sorrow of adolescence as well as the stigma of an exceptionality (Sabornie & deBettencourt, 2004). In our society, students are constantly trying to grasp the subtle changes in roles for males and females. They experience more exposure to drugs and alcohol, and pregnancy and HIV/AIDS are common issues. The increased tension, frustration, and depression can lead to a variety of behavioural and emotional problems, or to suicide, the third leading cause of death in university students (Aseltine & DeMartino, 2004).

Special education teachers need to collaborate with general educators to help students deal with these problems. One innovative program that tries to increase access to the general education program and provide a support system for students with moderate or severe exceptionalities is the peer support program (Copeland et al., 2004). A student with an exceptionality and a student without are partnered for shared activities that might be academic (e.g., tutoring functional academics and life skills) or nonacademic (e.g., "hanging out" between classes and attending sporting events). Typically achieving peers report that the experience improved their knowledge of exceptionalities and allowed them to develop a friendship rather than simply offering help. It also gave them experience in advocating for someone else, gave them feelings of accomplishment, and was fun. The effect for students with exceptionalities is a decrease in alienation, a common problem for adolescents, especially those with exceptionalities (Brown, Higgins, & Paulsen, 2003). It is important for teachers to develop a nonthreatening classroom atmosphere where anxiety about learning is reduced and open lines of communication are maintained (Schloss, Schloss, & Schloss, 2007).

TEACHING TIP

Perform self-monitoring (or monitor teachers you may be observing) to determine the amount of time spent teaching. What are some ways to increase the amount of teaching?

TEACHING TIP

Evaluation of student performance must be continual in order to provide teachers with feedback to determine the effectiveness of the instructional program and to inform necessary changes.

FURTHER READING

For more information on collaborative activities of special educators, read Sharon Cramer's book *Collaboration: A Success Strategy for Special Educators,* published by Allyn & Bacon in 1997.

University Professor Dr. Julie Corkett

As a former high school teacher, and in her current position as an assistant professor at Nipissing University, Julie believes that two of the most important issues to address in the classroom are a student's self-regulation and self-efficacy skills.

"Self-regulation has a broad and dramatic impact on students' academic, emotional, and behavioural performance. Regardless of the students' knowledge and skills, if they do not know how to apply that knowledge or even what to do with that knowledge it will lead to academic failure. For example, while the student may be able to read and understand an assignment, the student may lack the skills for understanding what is required to accomplish the task. By incorporating learning and study strategies into your lesson plans it will enable students to develop the ability to handle new and challenging tasks." In order to develop these skills in the classroom, Julie says you can "incorporate mini-lessons into your lesson plans that address the self-regulatory strategies (e.g., goal setting, learning strategies, study strategies, etc.) that they require to accomplish a task. And remember, just because you have addressed a skill in a mini-lesson does not mean that you won't need to re-address it the next time the skill is needed.

"As a teacher you also need to take the time to address your students' self-efficacy. This can be as simple as acknowledging specifically what the student has done correctly. Remember, students have a tendency to just look at their final mark. They don't take the time to reflect on their performance to see what they are capable of accomplishing. They only see the failure (remember, failure doesn't necessarily equate to a failing grade, but to the inability to meet personal expectations). Failure will dominate their memories to a higher degree than successes. Portfolios are one method of enabling students to bear witness to their successes and improvements. Have the students write a reflection on what they did right and what they need to improve upon. Have the students begin each assignment by identifying their goals and how they are going to accomplish their goals. Then they will be able to direct their effort and motivation toward meeting those goals. If you do journal writing, you can have each student write about themselves as learners or assign each student a classmate to write about why they are good students." Having students engage in these reflective activities may help them to see their strengths and abilities through another person's eyes, since "often others will see strengths that we do not see in ourselves."

CROSS REFERENCE

Review materials in chapters 3 through 11, and reflect on how different exceptionalities have an impact on preparation for high school content courses.

Preparing for High School Content Classes The special education teacher should be aware of classroom teacher expectations, teaching styles, and the demands of the learning environment. One way special education teachers can help students deal with the "general education world" is to teach them how to self-advocate. In order to do this, students need to understand their specific learning problems. Therefore, special education teachers may need to have a discussion with their students about the nature of specific exceptionalities.

When working with students with exceptionalities in general education classrooms, the role of the special educator expands. It includes informing the general educator as to the unique abilities and challenges presented by each student, providing ongoing support and **collaboration** for the student and teacher, and doing frequent monitoring to ensure that the arrangement is satisfactory for both the student and the teacher.

Lenz and Deshler (2004) propose that effective teaching is based on making meaningful connections between teachers and students, students and students, and students and the content they need to learn. They challenge teachers to understand what their students already know as a result of prior learning as well as their life experiences, and to select content that is based on the general education standards but is relevant to their future life goals. Finally, they recommend compensating for students' learning problems by using evidence-based teaching methods to enhance instruction and by explicitly teaching students how to use and develop learning strategies so they learn how to learn. These strategies have been highlighted throughout the text and will be addressed again later in this chapter. An example of an effective strategy to help students perform at their maximum level in class is presented in Figure 14.2.

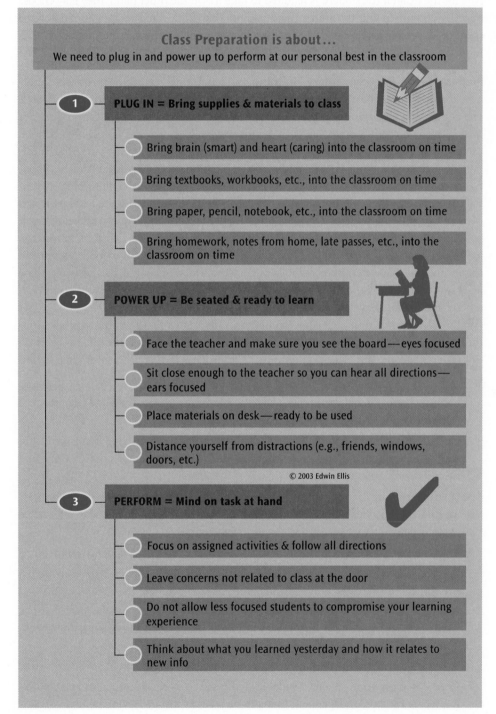

Figure 14.2 Sample Hierarchic Flowchart Used to Teach Class Preparation

From "Graphic Organizers: Tools to Build Behavioral Literacy and Foster Emotional Competency," by M.L. Rock, 2004, *Intervention in School and Clinic, 40*(1), p. 24.

Class Preparation is about...
We need to plug in and power up to perform at our personal best in the classroom

1   PLUG IN = Bring supplies & materials to class

- Bring brain (smart) and heart (caring) into the classroom on time
- Bring textbooks, workbooks, etc., into the classroom on time
- Bring paper, pencil, notebook, etc., into the classroom on time
- Bring homework, notes from home, late passes, etc., into the classroom on time

2   POWER UP = Be seated & ready to learn

- Face the teacher and make sure you see the board—eyes focused
- Sit close enough to the teacher so you can hear all directions—ears focused
- Place materials on desk—ready to be used
- Distance yourself from distractions (e.g., friends, windows, doors, etc.)

© 2003 Edwin Ellis

3   PERFORM = Mind on task at hand

- Focus on assigned activities & follow all directions
- Leave concerns not related to class at the door
- Do not allow less focused students to compromise your learning experience
- Think about what you learned yesterday and how it relates to new info

Preparing for High School Exams The requirements regarding final high school credit exams vary across Canada. These exams are monitored by the appropriate ministry of education and are aimed at maintaining a province- or territory-wide standard of performance.

Special education teachers, in conjunction with classroom teachers, have two roles regarding high school exams. On the one hand, they are obligated to help the student prepare for the exam if the student is required to take it. On the other hand, they may choose to focus on convincing the student and parents that time could more appropriately be spent on developing living skills rather than on preparing for exams. Information on testing is discussed later in the chapter.

TEACHING TIP

For students with exceptionalities planning to attend university, consult the National Educational Association of Disabled Students for information. Phone: (613) 526–8008; website: www.neads.ca.

Explore

Preparing Students and Families for Post-School Transition

Preparing for Post-Secondary Training Students with exceptionalities absolutely should aim for post-secondary education if they have the ability and motivation. This is one component of a transition program for students. Post-secondary education does not have to mean attending a university. A community college, vocational-technical school, trade school, or some other form of post-secondary education and training are other possibilities. Teachers, in both general and special education, need to inform students about future employment trends and help them select realistic careers with employment potential. Reports regarding the importance of education in the future for students with and without exceptionalities have concluded that higher levels of academic achievement will be required and that very few jobs will be available for individuals deficient in reading, writing, and math. Technology will also play an increasing role for all individuals. For Jim in our opening vignette, the possibility of going to a new school at the post-secondary level was terrifying. His parents had been instrumental in getting services set up in high school, and suddenly everyone was talking to him about self-advocacy.

Luckily, the IEP team picked up on his concerns and wrote the training needed into the Jim's program (e.g., developing his self-advocacy skills and preparing him for his transition to post-secondary education/training). Other ideas that are helpful in preparation for post-secondary education are summarized by Schloss and colleagues (2007):

1. Identify the match between the student's academic and career goals and the programs available at universities and technical programs.

2. Consider the entrance requirements carefully. Some schools have open admission with a high school diploma, and others require a minimum grade point average and specific scores on entrance exams.

3. Consider the size of the campus. Navigating smaller campuses may be easier, and they may be able to offer more individualized services. A larger campus may offer more extracurricular activities and a wider variety of courses.

4. Examine the cost and help the student and parents to identify financial resources.

5. Encourage families to meet with the head of the unit that assists students with special needs to discuss services, policies, and procedures to document the exceptionality and request appropriate adaptations and/or accommodations. Students must also be taught self-advocacy skills so they can self-identify with their professors (Madaus & Shaw, 2004).

6. Arrange for the student to shadow currently enrolled students.

7. Consider living arrangements available, and begin to work with students and families to prepare for more independent living if the student will be leaving home.

Preparing for Independent Living Independent living is a realistic goal for the vast majority of individuals with exceptionalities; however, to live successfully in today's complex, automated world, direct instruction in certain independent living skills may be required. This type of instruction is also important in a student's transition program. The following areas may be problematic for persons with exceptionalities:

- sexuality
- managing personal finances
- developing and maintaining social networks
- maintaining a home
- managing food
- employment
- transportation
- self-confidence and self-esteem
- organization
- time management

CONSIDER THIS

In what ways can self-advocacy and self-determination affect young adults with exceptionalities? Should schools help teach self-advocacy skills to adolescents with exceptionalities? Why or why not?

Preparing for Employment One important goal of education is the employment of graduates at their maximum vocational potential. Teachers need to help students prepare for employment by teaching them the necessary skills for vocational success.

Inclusive vocational and technical programs present a unique opportunity to offer students both a functional curriculum as well as integration with typically achieving peers. These programs can provide appropriate entry into work-study programs, business apprenticeships, and technical and trade school programs.

Teachers must be sure that students with exceptionalities can communicate their strengths and limitations to persons in post-secondary and future employment settings. Self-advocacy skills will empower individuals to seek employment and independent living opportunities on their own. In best practice, encouragement and development of self-determination or self-advocacy skills begin in elementary school. Table 14.3 provides a list of activities that can promote these skills. Many can be carried out with parents or teachers in multiple contexts (Test et al., 2005). The Personal Spotlight in this chapter provides a glimpse of one special education professional's thoughts on the importance of developing a student's self-regulation and self-efficacy skills.

METHODS TO FACILITATE STUDENTS' SUCCESS IN GENERAL EDUCATION CLASSES

Students with exceptionalities traditionally have been placed in general education classrooms for instruction when they were determined to have the requisite academic ability necessary for success. With the advent of the inclusion movement, however, students with exceptionalities are often placed in such classes for other reasons. For most of these students, success can be engineered by teachers using evidence-based teaching practices and developing contingency strategies for giving assistance to students who still need it

TEACHING TIP

For students with intellectual disabilities, consult the local branch of the Canadian Association for Community Living about transition issues; contact information can be found on their website: www.cacl.ca.

Table 14.3 Items of the Survey Instruments by Grade Level

Level	Items
Elementary	1. Provide opportunities to choose from several different strategies for a task.
	2. Ask the child to reconsider choices made in the recent past, in light of those choices' subsequent consequences.
	3. Encourage the child to "think aloud" with you, saying the steps the child is taking to complete a task or solve a problem.
	4. Provide opportunities for the student to talk about how he or she learns and help him or her test out his or her answer.
	5. Provide opportunities for the child to systematically evaluate his or her work.
	6. Help the child set simple goals and check to see whether he or she is reaching the goals.
Secondary	1. Provide opportunities for the student to make decisions that have an important impact on his or her academic goals, such as what program and what courses the student wants to take.
	2. Provide opportunities for the student to make decisions that have an important impact on his or her career, such as what the student wants to do after finishing high school.
	3. Provide opportunities for the student to make decisions that have an important impact on his or her schedule.
	4. Make it easy for the student to see the link between the goals he or she sets for himself or herself and the daily decisions he or she makes.
	5. Provide guidance in breaking the student's long-term goals into a number of objectives.
	6. Lead the student through planning activities to determine the steps to take to progress toward goals.
	7. Assist the student in realistically recognizing and accepting weaknesses in key skills.
	8. Assist the student in requesting academic and social supports from teachers.

From "A conceptual framework of self-advocacy for students with disabilities," by D.W. Test et al., 2005, *Remedial and Special Education*, p. 59. Austin, TX: Pro-Ed.

(see the Evidence-Based Teaching Strategies box). Some students will require accommodations or adaptations; others can achieve success when taught to use effective study skills and learning strategies.

✱ Explore

A Report to My Teachers

General Guidelines for Teaching Algebra

Accommodations and Adaptations

In most instances, general education teachers are responsible for making accommodations and adaptations to help students with exceptionalities achieve in secondary school.

Evidence-Based Teaching Strategies

The evidence-based teaching strategies that have been shared throughout this text are critical for students with exceptionalities to benefit from their educational placement. Even if the IEP goals and general education curricular standards are a perfect match, an ineffective teacher can stop progress. Of particular importance are the behavioural support techniques and comprehensive lesson plans that include components backed by research. Figure 14.3 provides the format for a written lesson plan for secondary students. These plans should be written out in long form until the process becomes second nature. Figure 14.4 demonstrates a written lesson plan with the contingency plans that could be used to address learning needs at several levels.

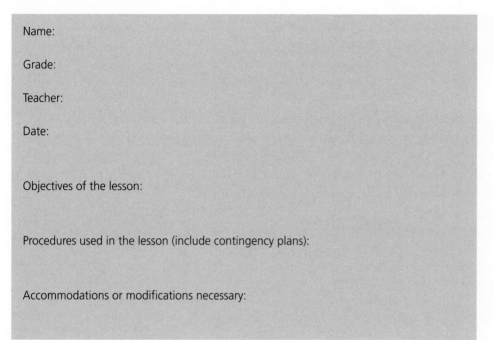

Figure 14.3 Format for Lesson Plan for Secondary Students

Name:

Grade:

Teacher:

Date:

Objectives of the lesson:

Procedures used in the lesson (include contingency plans):

Accommodations or modifications necessary:

Unfortunately, even though most general education teachers view adaptations as desirable and reasonable, they often do not implement them. In Table 14.4, Lenz and Deshler (2004) provide adaptations, accommodations, and modifications that can be made during the major components of a lesson plan. Figure 14.5 provides a checklist teachers can use for further ideas, documentation, and evaluation of options that can be implemented to accommodate learning needs.

Recall from chapter 2 that the term *accommodation* is used in this text to refer to the "specialized support and services that are provided to enable students with diverse needs to achieve learning expectations. This may include technological equipment, support staff, and informal supports" (Saskatchewan Learning, 2000, p. 145). The term *adaptation* is used to refer to the "adjustments to curriculum content, instructional practices, materials or technology, assessment strategies, and the learning environment made in accordance with the strengths, needs, and interests of the learner" (Saskatchewan Learning, 2000, p. 145). Finally, the term *modification* is used to refer to changes in policy that will support students with exceptionalities in their learning (e.g., altering school curriculum or attendance policy). Adaptations are usually simple actions that make success for individual students much more likely. For example, allowing visually impaired students to read using Braille is universally accepted. Altering teaching methods or materials for students with other problems is a conceptually similar process.

Accommodations and adaptations should be designed to offer the *least* amount of alteration of the regular programming that will still allow the student to benefit from instruction. This approach provides students with exceptionalities with a realistic sense of their abilities and limitations. If too many accommodations or adaptations are made, some students may be set up for failure in a university or other academically demanding environment. Students with too many accommodations or adaptations may also begin to feel

CROSS REFERENCE

Review chapters 3 through 11 to determine specific accommodations and adaptations suggested for students with different exceptionalities.

CONSIDER THIS

Should teachers who refuse to make accommodations or adaptations for students with different learning needs in their classes be required to do so? What are the consequences for students included in classrooms where teachers refuse to make accommodations or adaptations?

Objective

Given 10 word problems involving addition and subtraction, the student will use a calculator to compute the answer with 100 percent accuracy.

Procedures

1. Review previous work, describe today's activity, and emphasize how this skill will be useful to students.
2. Read a sample problem with the class. Determine the correct operation. Turn on the calculator. Show how to enter the first number, the operation sign, the second number, and the equal sign. Identify and record the answer.
3. Repeat with another problem requiring a different operation.
4. Show the class a third problem using a transparency on the overhead projector.
   a. Call on a student to read the problem out loud.
      Contingency: For a student unable to read parts of the problem, read it for him or her; then have the student repeat it.
   b. Determine the correct operation.
      Contingency: Students unable to determine the operation will be provided a list of key words and phrases that provide hints. For example, "How much more?" indicates subtraction.
   c. Turn on the calculator.
      Contingency: Use a red marker to highlight the "on" button for students unable to locate it.
   d. Enter the first digit of the first number.
      Contingency 1: Students unable to determine which number should be entered first will be assisted in setting up the problem on paper first.
      Contingency 2: Students unable to determine which digit of a number should be entered first will be told to enter the digits as they are softly repeated out loud.
   e. Enter the operation sign.
      Contingency: Students unable to locate the operation sign will be referred to a sample problem on the board and asked to match the sign written on the board with the button on the calculator.
   f. Enter the equal sign.
      Contingency: Use a blue marker to highlight the "[=]" button for students unable to locate it.
   g. Record the answer.
5. Repeat with another problem presented to the entire group.
6. Provide a worksheet with 10 word problems to those who needed no assistance during the teacher-directed activity.
   Contingency: Continue to work in a small group with those who experienced difficulty.
7. If time permits, allow students who have mastered the skill to go "Christmas shopping" using a catalogue from a department store. Tell them they have $200 to spend. They must keep track of their expenses.
   Contingency: Have students previously engaged in small group instruction complete the worksheet containing 10 problems.
   Be available to provide assistance.

From *Instructional Methods for Secondary Students with Learning and Behavior Problems* (4th ed., p. 85), by P.I. Schloss, M.A. Schloss, and C.N. Schloss, 2007. Boston: Allyn & Bacon.

Figure 14.4 Contingency Plans Included in a Written Lesson Plan

that they bring very little to the class; this assessment can further damage an already fragile self-concept. Accommodations and adaptations used in settings or classes designed to prepare an individual for a future job or post-secondary training program should reflect real conditions present in these future environments.

Table 14.4 Curriculum or Instruction Adaptations

Stage of Instruction	Accommodations (Examples)	Modifications (Examples)
Initial Instruction	■ Clear overheads/graphic organizer ■ Partners repeat or read to each other ■ Teacher uses signals ■ Study guide/guided notes ■ Highlighted text ■ Teacher position/proximity to particular students	■ Different study guide (partially filled out) ■ Different text ■ Introduce different but related skill
Guided Practice	■ Notated/highlighted/more structured assignment or activity ■ Teacher/student model ■ Partners do/check ■ Frequent checks by teacher ■ Alter pace	■ Different assignment or activity on same skill or content ■ Different assignment or activity on related skill or content ■ Physical guidance by teacher/paraeducator/peer
Independent Practice	■ Slower transition from guided practice ■ More structure	■ Do less of same task ■ Different task ■ Teach parent/sibling to coach ■ Do with a partner
Evaluation	■ Test under different conditions (more time, different location, test read to student) ■ Same rubric or standard but different tasks ■ Portfolio ■ Mastery standard, but vary time allowed to mastery ■ Evaluation based on more than curriculum mastery	■ Evaluation of different objectives/different outcomes

From *Teaching Content to All: Evidence-Based Inclusive Practices in Middle and Secondary Schools* (p. 315), by B.K. Lenz and D.D. Deshler, 2004. Boston: Allyn & Bacon.

Homework, Grading, and Testing

Homework, grading, and testing stand out as important considerations in students' success in secondary school classrooms. They have become more significant in light of trends toward making academic standards more rigorous and toward accountability in general education classrooms. Higher expectations for student performance in general education classes affect testing and grading. This section explores these problem areas, focusing on adaptations to facilitate student success.

Homework Problems in **homework** often become more pronounced at the secondary level. Given that students typically have four to six teachers, assignments represent a significant hurdle for junior and high school students with exceptionalities. While the amount of homework assigned provides a challenge, the unique difficulties of students with exceptionalities are underscored by the types of problems they are likely to have. Just as the characteristics

TEACHING TIP

Accommodations and adaptations are helpful for all students, including those without exceptionalities who do not need specialized instruction. Many accommodations and adaptations simply reflect good teaching.

Student _____ Teacher _____ Date(s) _____

[Circle accommodations attempted; mark successful accommodations with plus (+), unsuccessful with minus (–)]

Classroom
Design constructive learning environment.

Preferential seating (specify): _____

Group size:	___ 1–1 w/teacher	___ 1–1 w/peer	___ Small group	___ Large group
Need for movement:	___ Little	___ Average	___ High	
Distraction management:	___ Carrels	___ Headsets	___ Seating	___ Other
Noise:	___ None	___ Quiet	___ Moderate	
Lighting:	___ Dim	___ Average	___ Bright	
Temperature:	___ Warm	___ Average	___ Cool	

Other (specify): _____

Schedule
Arrange productive learning schedule.

Peak time:	___ Early morning	___ Late morning	___ Midday	___ Afternoon
Lesson length:	___ 5–10 min.	___ 15–20 min.	___ 25–30 min.	___ 30+ min.
Variation needed:	___ Little	___ Some	___ Average	___ Much
Extra time needed:	___ Little	___ Some	___ Average	___ Much

Other (specify): _____

Lessons
Use best stimulus/response format.

Stimulus Format

Visual:	___ Observe	___ Read
Auditory:	___ Oral	___ Discuss
Touch:	___ Hold	___ Feel
Model:	___ Coach	___ Demonstrate
Multisensory:	___ Combination	

Response Format

Choose:	___ Point	___ Mark
Tell:	___ Restate	___ Explain
Write:	___ Short answer	___ Essay
Word process:	___ Some	___ All
Show:	___ Demonstrate	___ Make

Other (specify): _____

Materials
Make constructive material adjustments.

___ Vary stimulus/response	___ Vary directions	___ Vary sequence
___ Highlight essential content	___ Use partial content	___ Add steps
___ Expand practice	___ Add self-checking	___ Add supplements
___ Segment	___ State key concepts in margins	(see below)

Other (specify): _____

Supplements
Provide supplementary aids to facilitate learning.

Instructional Strategies	Materials	Assignments	Human Resources
___ Advance organizers	___ Adaptive/assistive device	___ Adapted testing	___ Co-teacher
___ Charted progress	___ Audiotapes of text	___ Advance assignment	___ Co-operative group
___ Checklist of steps	___ Calculator	___ Alternate assignments	___ Instructional coach
___ Computer activities	___ Captioned films	___ Extended time	___ Interpreter
___ Evaluation checklists	___ Coded text	___ Extra practice	___ Peer advocate
___ Graphic organizers	___ Computer programs	___ Outlined tasks	___ Peer note taker
___ Modelling	___ Games for practice	___ Partial outlines	___ Peer prompter
___ Mnemonic guides	___ Highlighted text	___ Question guides	___ Peer tutor
___ Multisensory techniques	___ Key term definitions	___ Reference access	___ Personal attendant
___ Organization charts	___ Large print texts	___ Scripted practice	___ Study buddy
___ Repeated readings	___ Manipulatives	___ Segmented tasks	___ Volunteer tutor
___ Scripted demonstrations	___ Math number charts	___ Shortened assignments	
___ Self-questioning	___ Multiple text	___ Simplified directions	*Management Strategies*
___ Strategy posters	___ Parallel text	___ Simplified tasks	___ Charted performance
___ Verbal rehearsal	___ Simplified text	___ Structured notes	___ Checklists
___ Video modelling	___ Summaries	___ Study guides	___ Contracts
___ Visual imagery	___ Video enactments	___ Timed practice	___ Extra reinforcement
___ Other	___ Other	___ Other	___ Other

_____ _____ _____ _____

_____ _____ _____ _____

Figure 14.5 Checklist of Options for Accommodating Learning Needs

From *Successful inclusive teaching: Proven ways to detect and correct special needs* (3rd ed., p. 38), by J.S. Choate, 2002, Boston: Allyn & Bacon.

of each exceptionality, described in previous chapters, can have a negative impact on classroom performance, they create additional challenges as students attempt to complete work without the guidance of a teacher, the modelling of a peer, or the structure of a classroom.

Polloway and colleagues (2005) suggest that although homework can pose a special challenge for students with exceptionalities and their families, effective intervention techniques have been identified. Teachers and parents can work together to implement these procedures, which can increase students' success with homework and ultimately have a positive effect on school achievement. Following is a list of homework practices that are organized as management, assignment, student considerations, and parent involvement.

Management considerations

- Assess a student's homework skills to identify potential problems.
- Assign homework early in the year and on a regular basis.
- Present clear instructions: state the purpose, give directions, identify the format and materials to be used, give an estimate of how long the assignment should take, and clarify how the assignment will be graded.
- Use an incentive program. (Figure 14.6 shows a homework pass that can be given for turning in homework. When the specified number is collected, a homework assignment can be skipped.)
- Use assignment notebooks, and have parents sign off on work.

Assignment considerations

- Give the purpose of each assignment and establish relevance.
- Select activities appropriate for independent work.
- Use homework adaptations, such as shorter assignments that cover the same content, extended due dates, and grades based on effort not accuracy or only one component of the assignment, or assign group homework.

Student considerations

- Teach study skills, such as time management and dictionary skills.
- Consider student preferences on homework assignments.
- Help students develop self-management behaviours.

FURTHER READING

For more information on homework and students with exceptionalities, read "Improving Homework Completion and Academic Performance: Lessons from Special Education," by T. Bryan and K. Burstein, published in 2004 in volume 43 of *Theory into Practice* (pp. 213–219).

CONSIDER THIS

Should school policies on homework be altered to increase the likelihood of success for students with exceptionalities, or should these students be required to follow a rigid policy set for all students? Why or why not?

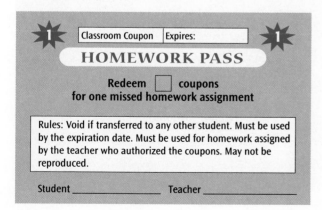

Figure 14.6 Example of a Homework Pass Used for Reinforcement

From *Successful Inclusive Teaching* (3rd ed., p. 389), by J.S. Choate, 2000. Boston: Allyn & Bacon.

Parental involvement

- Support and reinforce skills learned at school.
- Create an environment for homework that occurs at the same time daily in a distraction-reduced setting with all needed materials available.
- Provide ongoing encouragement and support.

Grading The challenges of inclusion of adolescents with exceptionalities are perhaps most clearly reflected in the area of grading. Schools should develop a diverse committee to study the best practices in grading that support mastery of academic standards and meet legal guidelines to develop a policy for the entire system (Salend & Duhaney, 2002). Figure 14.7 provides optional grading systems that might be adopted for different purposes.

Numeric/Letter Grades: Teachers assign numeric or letter grades based on students' performance on tests or specific learning activities.

Checklists/Rating Scales: Teachers develop checklists and rating scales that delineate the benchmarks associated with their courses and evaluate each student according to mastery of these benchmarks. Some school districts have revised their grading systems by creating rating scales for different grade levels. Teachers rate students on each skill, using a scale that includes "not yet evident," "beginning," "developing," and "independent."

Anecdotal/Descriptive and Portfolio Grading: Teachers write descriptive comments regarding students' skills, learning styles, effort, attitudes, and growth, and strategies to improve student performance. These comments can be included with examples of students' work as part of portfolio grading.

Pass/Fail Systems: Minimum course competencies are specified and students who demonstrate mastery receive a "P" grade, while those who fail to meet the minimum standards are given an "F" grade. Some schools have modified the traditional pass/fail grading system to include such distinctions as honours (HonourP), high pass (HP), pass (P), and low pass (LP).

Mastery Level/Criterion Systems: Students and teachers meet to divide the material into a hierarchy of skills and activities, based on an assessment of individual needs and abilities. After completing the learning activities, students take a post-test or perform an activity to demonstrate mastery of the content. When students demonstrate mastery, they receive credit for that accomplishment and repeat the process with the next skill to be mastered.

Progressive Improvement Grading: Students take exams and engage in learning activities, and receive feedback and instruction based on their performance throughout the grading period. Only performance on cumulative tests and learning activities during the final weeks of the grading period, however, are used to determine students' grades.

Multiple Grading: Teachers grade students in the areas of ability, effort, and achievement. Students' report cards can then include a listing of the three grades for each content area, or grades can be computed by weighting the three areas.

Level Grading: Teachers use a numeric subscript to indicate the level of difficulty at which the students' grades are based. For example, a grade of B6 can be used to note that a student is working in the B range at the sixth-grade level. Subscript systems can also be devised to indicate whether students are working at grade level, above grade level, or below grade level.

Contract Grading: Teachers and students agree on a contract outlining the learning objectives; the amount, nature, and quality of the products students must complete; and the procedures for evaluating student products and assigning a grade.

Individualized Education Program (IEP) Grading: Teachers assign grades that acknowledge students' progress in meeting the students' IEP goals and performance criteria.

Figure 14.7 Grading Systems

From "Grading Students in Inclusive Settings," by S.J. Salend & L.G. Duhaney, 2002, *Teaching Exceptional Children*, January/February, p. 11.

Munk and Bursuck (2001) and Salend and Duhaney (2002) propose the following 11 purposes for grades (cited in Schloss et al., 2007):

1. Document achievement of curricular goals and specific skills.
2. Measure progress over time.
3. Measure effort put into learning.
4. Make comparisons among students.
5. Determine program effectiveness.
6. Motivate students to succeed and learn.
7. Identify student strengths and weaknesses for planning instruction.
8. Communicate and provide feedback to families.
9. Factor in educational and career planning.
10. Determine eligibility for programs, graduation, awards, and promotions.
11. Provide accountability to the community, legislators, employers, and educational policy-makers.

Testing The inclusion movement has raised concerns regarding how students with special needs will be assessed. Simple adaptations can make the difference between taking a test successfully or poorly. For example, reading a test to a student who is a very poor reader gives the student a chance to display knowledge or skills. If such students have to read the questions themselves, test results will reflect students' poor reading skills and fail to assess knowledge of a particular content area. Teachers can address this situation in the following ways:

- Have another student, teacher, or aide read the test to the student.
- Use technology to scan and read text.
- Give the student additional time to complete the test. The extra time gives the student a chance to read the material first to identify the words and then read it again for better comprehension.
- Reword the test to include only words that are within the student's reading vocabulary.

A full consideration of adaptations in **testing**, however, extends beyond the consideration of reading ability. Other ways that teachers can make tests more accessible to students is to use the COLA checklist (Figure 14.8), a strategy developed by Rotter (2006) to guide the development of written material presented to students. The following examples are additional techniques that can be used to adapt measurement instruments and assessment procedures:

- Use information about performance outside of school in making evaluations.
- Administer frequent short quizzes throughout the course, rather than a few long tests.
- Divide tests or tasks into smaller, simpler sections or steps.
- Develop practice items or pre-test trials using the same response format as the test (teaching students how to respond), which may help reduce a student's fear of evaluation.
- Consider the appropriateness of the instrument or procedure in terms of age or maturity.
- Give open-book or open-note tests.

CONSIDER THIS

If alternative grading requirements are used with students with exceptionalities, should these students be eligible for the honour roll and honours programs? Why or why not?

CROSS REFERENCE

Review chapters 3 through 11, and determine specific testing adaptations that might be necessary for students with different types of exceptionalities.

Figure 14.8 The COLA Checklist

From "Creating Instructional Materials for All Pupils: Try Cola", (p. 281) by K. Rotter, 2006, *Intervention in School and Clinic, 4115*, pp. 273–282.

C	Contrast	There is plenty of white space around important information and answer spaces.
		Colour of the text is in clear contrast from background (this includes avoiding the use of pencil or lightly printed dittos).
		Colour, underlining, dark borders, and/or highlights are used to point out critical information, such as directions.
		Bold font is used infrequently, for highlighting important information only.
O	Orientation	Important information, such as directions, is in the top-left position.
		All information reads from left to right, top to bottom.
		Material is aligned to the left.
L	Lettering	Material is printed, not handwritten.
		The same clear font is used throughout.
		The font is big enough to read easily at the typical viewing distance.
		The material uses upper- and lowercase letters as they would typically appear in print. (No use of all caps or small caps fonts.)
		Italicized fonts are not used.
A	Artwork	Artword is used only to support information and not to make the paper "pretty."
		The page is not too "busy," and pictures are not distracting.
		Artwork is culturally sensitive.

- Reduce the number of test items or remove items that require more abstract reasoning or have high levels of difficulty.
- Use different levels of questions for different students (i.e., test items for low-functioning children should be more concrete).
- Have a student develop a product or packet of materials that shows knowledge and understanding of the content of a unit (portfolio assessment).
- Provide alternative projects or assignments.
- Video record a student performing a task and then play it back to him or her to show skills learned and areas needing improvement.
- Use a panel of students to evaluate each other on task performance.
- Allow students to type answers.
- Allow students to use a computer during testing.
- Allow small groups to work together on a task to be evaluated (such as a project or test).
- Use short written or verbal measures on a daily or weekly basis to provide more feedback on student progress.

- Increase the amount of time allowed to complete the test to compensate for slower reading, writing, or comprehension.

- Alter the types of responses to match a student's strengths (written, oral, short-answer, or simple marking).

- Have a student review the course or unit content verbally so that he or she is not limited to test item recall.

- Limit the number of formal tests by using checklists to observe and record learning.

- Assess participation in discussions as an indicator of mastery of content.

- Give extra credit for correction of mistakes.

A survey of middle school students' opinions found that preferred adaptations were open-note or open-book tests, practice questions for study, and multiple-choice instead of essay. Their least preferred adaptations were having the teacher read the test, tests with fewer questions, and tests covering less material (Nelson et al., 2000).

Bolt and Thurlow (2004) offer several suggestions for identifying the most appropriate adaptations that will have the greatest impact on student performance:

1. Be sure that the adaptation does not compromise the purpose of the test. For example, a math or science test could be read to a student but a test of reading comprehension could not.

2. Choose the least intrusive options. For example, if a poor reader can function with extra time, he or she should not be assigned an individual who will read the material to him or her.

3. Let students get used to the adaptation before using it during a "high stakes" assessment.

4. Individuals providing the adaptations should be trained; for example, no prompts or cues should be given unless specified.

5. Monitor the effectiveness of the adaptation. One student was given extended time on a test, but the extra time was during the loud break time of the other 100 students taking the test!

For students to perform successfully on tests, they will need to learn individual test-taking and organizational strategies, which are often difficult for students with exceptionalities. Such strategies are typically subsumed within the area of study skills, discussed in the next section.

Study Skills and Learning Strategies

Teachers' accommodations and adaptations are insufficient to guarantee that students with special needs will be successful. Students must develop their own skills and strategies to help them overcome, or compensate for, an exceptionality. Understanding how to use study skills will greatly enhance their chances for being successful in future academic, vocational, or social activities. Classroom teachers can encourage students by helping them acquire a repertoire of study skills.

Study skills can be defined as the tools students can use to assist them with their learning. Many students have an innate ability in these areas. For example, some are good readers, adept at comprehension and able to read quickly; others find it easy to memorize facts. These students may not need instruction in study skills. For other students, however, study skills represent an "invisible curriculum" that must be taught directly to be successful. For example,

CROSS REFERENCE

Refer to chapter 13 for information on treatment acceptability.

the study skill of listening is critical in most educational settings because teachers provide so much information verbally. If students are not able to attend to auditory information, they will miss a great deal of content. Following is a list of ways to help secondary students prepare to study and follow up after studying, developed by Lambert and Nowacek (2006):

Preparing to study

- Explain that it's easier to study during the daytime, especially in study halls and during time provided in class.
- Assist students in deciding on a routine time and a distraction-reduced, well-lit area at home for study.
- Help students identify needed materials for study (e.g., study guides, texts, notes, planners, pencils).
- Teach students to develop a study agenda, beginning with the hardest items as soon as they are assigned.
- Help students learn to break difficult and long-term assignments into shorter parts with timelines identified that can be checked off as they are completed.
- Remind students to use positive self-talk, reminding themselves that they "can do" instead of "can't do."

Studying the content areas

- Show students how to prioritize and focus, not jump from one subject to another without completion.
- Encourage them to study for 50 minutes (using a timer) and then take a 10 minute break.
- Teach chapter previewing skills, looking first at the title, subheads, graphics, and questions to be answered.
- Teach the paraphrasing strategy, where the main ideas are developed for each subhead.
- Teach students to use graphic organizers to summarize information and show relationships.
- Teach students to identify what they do not understand and find a solution (e.g. search web, look in reference book, or ask a student or teacher).
- Remind them to keep up the positive self-talk (e.g., "This is working! I am really making progress.").

Following up after studying

- Help students keep in organized notebooks or separate folders material that will be needed later.
- Have students establish the habits of writing three questions about what they've read or studied—to discuss in class—and putting homework in notebooks and backpacks.
- Encourage students to reflect on what they have learned and to relate the new information to what they already knew.
- Teach students to reward themselves with a favourite activity after working.

Closely related to study skills are *learning strategies*—specific steps to use to guide learning before, during, and after active learning to acquire and use new information and solve problems ("learning to learn"). Teachers should be alert to ways to teach content and ways students can learn and use that content. Reading comprehension, error monitoring in writing, problem solving in math, and test preparation are also important skills that can be developed and strengthened through strategy training. A comprehensive source on numerous strategies for learning (and their use) is provided by Lenz and Deshler (2004). Examples of learning strategies include the following:

■ **SCROL** (Grant, 1993) is a strategy that helps students learn how to use textbook headings to improve comprehension. There are five steps in the strategy (Scholes, 1998):

1. *Survey* the heading. Read each heading and subheading and answer the following questions: What do I already know about this topic? What do I expect the author to include in this section?

2. *Connect* the parts of the reading. How are the headings related to each other? Write down words from the headings that provide connections between them.

3. *Read* the text. As you read, look for words or phrases that provide important information about the headings. Stop to make sure you understand the major ideas and supporting details at the end of each section. Reread if you don't understand.

4. *Outline* major ideas and supporting details in the section. Try to do this without looking back.

5. *Look back* at the text to check the accuracy of your outline. Correct your outline as needed. (p. 111)

■ *The* **COPS** *strategy* (Schumaker et al., 1981) is an error-monitoring strategy for writing. The acronym stands for four tasks:

1. Capitalization.

2. Overall appearance (e.g., neatness, appropriate margins).

3. Punctuation.

4. Spelling. (p. 11)

CONSIDER THIS

What would it be like if all students were provided with instructional strategies that made them more effective learners? How would this affect the number and types of children needing special education?

Students with special needs often require instruction in study skills.

Efforts to validate the use of specific strategies in inclusive classrooms have been ongoing for many years and cover a variety of purposes. Although many are used to make content learning more efficient, teachers have been able to develop their own strategies to assist their students in a variety of areas. The range of uses of learning strategies is limited only by one's creativity. An exciting aspect of instruction in strategies is the potential to benefit students with and without exceptionalities in inclusive settings (Keith & Lenz, 2004).

SUMMARY

- Important differences exist between elementary and secondary settings in terms of organizational structure, curriculum, and learner characteristics.

- From a curricular perspective, integrating students with exceptionalities into general classes is more challenging at the secondary level than at the elementary level.

- The period of adolescence adds to the problems experienced by students with exceptionalities.

- Curricular options for students at the secondary level with particular relevance for students with exceptionalities include basic skills, social skills, tutoring, learning strategies, vocational skills, and life skills.

- Future-based assessment offers one method for developing programs for adolescents with exceptionalities.

- Classroom teachers and special education teachers must collaborate to ensure effective secondary school programs.

- Special education teachers must help prepare students for academic content classes.

- Transition to the secondary level is a major endeavour for students with exceptionalities.

- Accommodations, adaptations, and modifications are changes that teachers can make to facilitate the success of students with exceptionalities.

- Specific challenges for successful inclusion occur in the areas of homework, grading, and testing.

- Study skills are skills that students with exceptionalities can use to help them achieve success in general and special education classes.

- Learning strategies enable students to achieve independence as they "learn how to learn."

Weblinks

The Education Planet—The Education Web Guide
http://educationplanet.com
A highly interesting and rewarding resource, this search engine covers all education-relevant sites, providing access to lesson plans, videos, manuals, curriculum materials, and much more. If you want to find specifically Canadian material, you can limit searches to Canadian sources.

Teachers.net
http://teachers.net
As a huge U.S. website, Teachers.net covers a variety of topics of interest to teachers, providing curriculum suggestions, resources, and chat rooms about different education issues. It also has subject-specific listings of chat boards where ideas are posted and shared. Many resources are available through this website for elementary and secondary teachers.

Canadian.Teachers.net
http://canadian.teachers.net
Derived from Teachers.net, this site provides a specifically Canadian forum with chat rooms, job postings, catalogues, information, professional development with guest speakers, and listings of related sites.

Chapter 15

Working with Families of Students with Exceptionalities

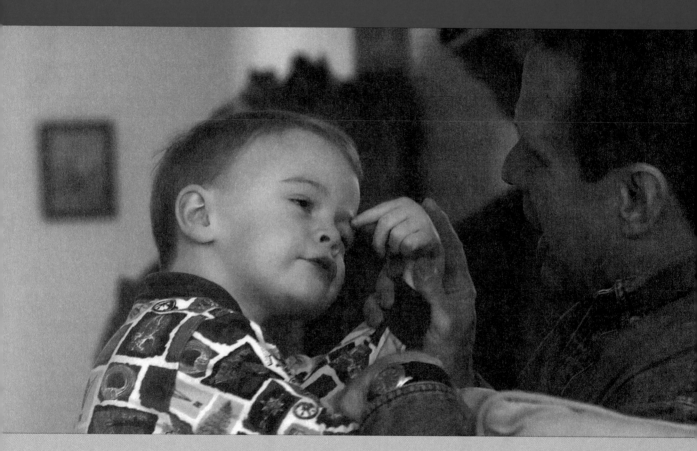

Chapter Objectives

After reading this chapter, you should be able to

- identify changes in the Canadian family structure that have implications for public schools in the first decades of the new millennium

- discuss the particular challenges experienced by parents of individuals with exceptionalities

- discuss effective ways to involve the family in education programs

- list principles of effective communication with parents

- delineate support roles that parents and family members can play

1. Analyze George and Judy's potential feelings and possible reactions upon learning that Patrick has an exceptionality.

2. What advice, recommendations, and help would you provide for these parents?

3. What would you tell them about the advantages and challenges of inclusive preschool programs?

4. What influence could Patrick's condition have on George and Judy's marriage?

5. How could other parents with children like Patrick help George and Judy deal with their child's diagnosis?

People always said what wonderful parents George and Judy were to their son Patrick. They shared in child-rearing activities and seemed to love every moment when they were with him. Patrick was healthy and appeared to be developing exactly on time, if not a little ahead of those infamous developmental milestones associated with rolling over, sitting, standing up, walking, smiling, and cooing. When Patrick was about 24 months old, he began doing some odd things. He stopped smiling, would withdraw from adults and other children, and seemed to be perfectly content "doing his own thing." He began waking up multiple times during the night, wanting to get up to play. He began to focus on particular objects, one being a toy car that he had played with for several months. Rather than playing with the car in an appropriate way, he would only spin the wheels, over and over and over. He would pick up objects, such as crumpled paper, and not want to have them taken away from him.

Soon after Patrick's change in development, George and Judy took him to their pediatrician for a general checkup. They noted that Patrick had begun to coo and make word sounds at about 18 months but then stopped. Patrick was not interested in toilet training, playing with other children, or doing just about anything you would expect a two-year-old to do. Dr. Johnson, the pediatrician, thought that Patrick was okay and that he would get back on track soon; however, at the request of George and Judy he referred Patrick to the university's Child Study Centre. After two days of extensive assessments, George and Judy were told that their son had autism. They were shattered. About the only thing they knew about autism was that it was a lifelong, debilitating disorder. Their hopes and dreams for Patrick went out the window. The next two years were very difficult on the family. George and Judy took Patrick to several doctors and clinics, hoping for a different diagnosis, which never came. George and Judy's relationship suffered. It seemed as if they were always getting up in the middle of the night or constantly on vigil when Patrick was awake to ensure that he did not do something that could be dangerous. George and Judy's lives were changed forever.

INTRODUCTION

Since the 1980s, there has been a significant change in the provision of educational services to students with exceptionalities: the increased involvement of parents and family. In the past, schools frequently did not encourage parents to participate in the education of their children. As a result, parents were often left out of the decision-making process leading to interventions. Often, they were not even informed of the programs that the school was implementing for their children. Some school personnel made significant efforts to include parents in the education of their children; others did little or nothing to promote this. Given the numerous concerns parents may have and the value of parental involvement in schools, the move to encourage it is welcome.

CROSS REFERENCE

See chapter 7 to review how family supports have been established in the field of intellectual disabilities.

Legislation and parental advocacy have established the current high level of parental involvement in the education of students with exceptionalities. Virtually all school personnel now acknowledge the merit of having parents actively participate in the educational process, including identification, referral, assessment, program planning, and program implementation. Comprehensive programs of family involvement begin when children are young and continue until transition into adulthood.

The challenge for educators is to consider diverse, effective ways to involve families in the education of children with exceptionalities.

Some families become more involved in the education of their children than others. School personnel need to encourage those parents who are active in their children's education to maintain their commitment while developing strategies to increase the active role of other parents.

Family participation can and should occur in many areas. These include assessment and IEP development, parent groups, observation of the student in the school setting, and communication with educators. Of these areas, participation in developing the IEP process occurs most frequently.

Schools meet the letter of the law by simply inviting parental participation. However, school personnel should develop strategies to facilitate more parental involvement or, more appropriately, family involvement. Although some parents create challenges for schools because of their intense level of involvement, for the most part educational programs are greatly strengthened by parental support. This chapter provides perspectives on the family and identifies strategies for enhancing family participation.

Families are playing a bigger part in special programs for their children. Some families are learning more about special education programs and particular types of exceptionalities through technology. The internet offers a wide variety of information about exceptionalities, educational programs, and how to provide supports for individuals at home. The Technology Today feature provides information on websites families can access to learn more about a variety of exceptionalities.

CONSIDER THIS

Not unexpectedly, the degree of parental participation in the IEP process is correlated with socio-economic level. Why do you think this is the case?

Technology Today

Websites for Families of Children with Exceptionalities

The Alliance	www.taalliance.org
National Federation of Families for Children's Mental Health	www.ffcmh.org
The Center for Law and Education	www.cleweb.org
Family Voices	www.familyvoices.org
National Down Syndrome Congress	www.ndsccenter.org
National Council on Independent Living	www.ncil.org
National Indian Child Welfare Association	www.nicwa.org
National Coalition for Parent Involvement in Education	www.ncpie.org
Fiesta Educativa	www.fiestaeducativa.org
National Association for Parents of Children with Visual Impairments	www.spedex.com/napvi
The Arc of the United States	www.thearc.org
Autism Society of America	www.autism-society.org
Brain Injury Association of America	www.biausa.org
Epilepsy Foundation of America	www.efa.org
Learning Disabilities Association of America	www.ldanatl.org
Spina Bifida Association	www.sbaa.org

THE FAMILY

The viewpoint of what constitutes a **family** has changed dramatically in recent decades. Traditionally, the family has been described as a group of individuals who live together that includes a mother, a father, and one or more children. However, this picture has been challenged by the reality that many—perhaps most—families do not resemble this model. The **nuclear family** with a stay-at-home mother and wage-earner father is no longer the typical family structure. The family of today, unlike the family of the early twentieth century, can more simply be described as a group of individuals who live together and care for one another's needs.

Currently, numerous family constellations exist. For example, more couples are not having children, or those with children are choosing not to get married and instead live in common-law relationships. In 2001, married or common-law couples living with children (24 years of age or younger) accounted for 44 percent of all families in Canada, while 41 percent of all families were accounted for by couples who had no children living at home (Statistics Canada, 2001b). Some single-parent families are headed by a father, and, in some cases, children live with one or more of their grandparents, without either mother or father present. Other families consist of a husband and wife without children. And, although not as common as they once were, some families constitute extended family units, with a grandmother or grandfather living with the parents and children. Some children live in foster homes, in which the foster parents fill all legal roles as birth parents would. School personnel must also be able to interact with families composed of parents living in gay or lesbian relationships.

The realities of the early twenty-first century pose further challenges to the family: an increase in both younger and older parents, an increase of families living below the poverty line, the realities of substance abuse, new considerations with regard to HIV/AIDs within the family, the permeation of violence throughout society, and a move away from residential care for children who require serious support. There may never have been a time when family changes and challenges have more clearly called for understanding and support.

Simulate

Teachers at the Loom

Although undergoing major changes in structure, the family remains the basic unit of our society. It is a dynamic, evolving social force, and a key ingredient in a child's life. Teachers must be sensitive to the background of the family. Montgomery (2001) notes that culturally responsive classrooms acknowledge diversity in students and help find connections between these students and others in the classroom. Often, teachers do not fully understand different cultures, so a self-assessment of culture should be carried out to help teachers understand the diversity that is present in their classroom and how to respond to it. One of the primary actions that teachers can take is to establish a classroom atmosphere that is respectful of all. Montgomery (2001) states that teachers should (1) pay attention to their bulletin boards, (2) maintain reading books that deal with cultural diversity, (3) engage in cross-cultural literature discussions with students, and (4) use language arts and social studies programs to promote opportunities to learn about other cultures.

In addition, it is critical that school personnel remember that parents—or grandparents, in some cases—should take part in educational programs regardless of the specific composition of the family. School personnel must put aside any personal feelings they may have about various lifestyles and work with families to develop and implement the best possible programs for students. School personnel must include the family in all key decisions affecting children—both those with special needs and those without (Wehmeyer et al., 1999). See Table 15.1 for the major categories of family support principles.

Table 15.1 Major Categories and Examples of Family Support Principles

Category/Characteristic	Examples of Principles
1. *Enhancing a sense of community* Promoting the coming together of people around shared values and common needs in ways that create mutually beneficial interdependencies	■ Interventions should focus on the building of interdependencies between members of the community and the family unit. ■ Interventions should emphasize the common needs and supports of all people and base intervention actions on those commonalities.
2. *Mobilizing resources and supports* Building support systems that enhance the flow of resources in ways that assist families with parenting responsibilities	■ Interventions should focus on building and strengthening informal support networks for families rather than depending solely on professionals' support systems. ■ Resources and supports should be made available to families in ways that are flexible, individualized, and responsive to the needs of the entire family unit.
3. *Shared responsibility and collaboration* Sharing of ideas and skills by parents and professionals in ways that build and strengthen collaborative arrangements	■ Interventions should use partnerships between parents and professionals as a primary mechanism for supporting and strengthening family functioning. ■ Resources and support mobilization interactions between families and service providers should be based on mutual respect and sharing of unbiased information.
4. *Protecting family integrity* Respecting the family's beliefs and values and protecting the family from intrusion upon its beliefs by outsiders	■ Resources and supports should be provided to families in ways that encourage, develop, and maintain healthy, stable relationships among all family members. ■ Interventions should be conducted in ways that accept, value, and protect a family's personal and cultural values and beliefs.
5. *Strengthening family functioning* Promoting the capabilities and competencies of families necessary to mobilize resources and perform parenting responsibilities in ways that have empowering consequences	■ Interventions should build on family strengths rather than correct weaknesses or deficits as a primary way of supporting and strengthening family functioning. ■ Resources and supports should be made available to families in ways that maximize the family's control over, and decision-making power regarding, services they receive.
6. *Proactive human service practices* Adoption of consumer-driven human service delivery models and practices that support and strengthen family functioning	■ Service-delivery programs should use promotion rather than treatment approaches as the framework for strengthening family functioning. ■ Resource and support mobilization should be consumer-driven rather than service provider–driven or professionally prescribed.

From "Family-Oriented Early Intervention Policies and Practices: Family-Centered or Not?" by C.J. Dunst, C. Johanson, C.M. Trivette, and D. Hamby, 1991, *Exceptional Children, 58*, p. 117. Copyright 1991 by the Council for Exceptional Children. Reprinted with permission.

CONSIDER THIS

What are some problems faced by families following the birth of, or identification of, a child with an exceptionality?

FURTHER READING

For stories by and about families with children with exceptionalities, visit the Lanark County Chapter of the Ontario Association for Families of Children with Communication Disorders website at www.oafccd.com.

CROSS REFERENCE

Review chapters 3–11, which discuss specific exceptionalities that can affect children. Then reflect on how different types of problems can cause different reactions.

Families and Children with Exceptionalities

The arrival of any child results in changes in family structure and dynamics. Obviously, a first child changes the lives of the mother and father, but subsequent births also affect the dynamics of the family unit, including finances, the amount and quality of time parents can devote to specific children, the relationship between the husband and wife, and future family goals. The birth of a child with an exceptionality exacerbates the challenges of such changes. For example, the almost immediate financial and emotional impact can create major problems for all family members, including parents and siblings.

When a child with an exceptionality becomes a member of the family, whether through birth, adoption, or later onset of the disability, the entire family must make adjustments. Families with children with exceptionalities have unique experiences and challenges (Hutton & Caron, 2005).

In addition to these problems, a primary difficulty is accepting and understanding the child and the exceptionality. Understanding a diagnosis and its implications is critical to a family's acceptance of the child. Parents with a limited understanding of a diagnosis will probably have difficulty in developing realistic expectations of the child, possibly creating major problems between the child and other family members. For example, parents might not understand the nature of a learning disability and therefore accuse the child of being lazy and not trying. Parents who may overlook the potential of a child with an intellectual disability might develop low expectations that will limit the child's success. For example, parents of adolescents might not support a school work program for their son or daughter because they believe that adults with intellectual disabilities are not capable of holding a job.

Families who discover that a child has an exceptionality obviously undergo a wide variety of feelings and reactions. Some of these may include the following (Smith et al., 2006):

■ grief

■ loss

■ denial

■ guilt

■ bargaining

■ anger

■ depression

■ acceptance

■ stress

Although it cannot be assumed that all or even most parents experience these particular reactions, many must deal with complicated emotions. Some parents and other family members experience all these different reactions; others may experience only some of them. Regardless, family members typically experience negative reactions upon learning that a child has an exceptionality. Sileo, Sileo, and Prater (1996) refer to the "shattering of dreams" that underlies many of the feelings. School personnel, including teachers, social workers, counsellors, and administrators, need to be aware of these dynamics and be prepared to deal with family members who are experiencing various feelings. For example, when parents say that they feel guilt after learning that their child has a disability, school

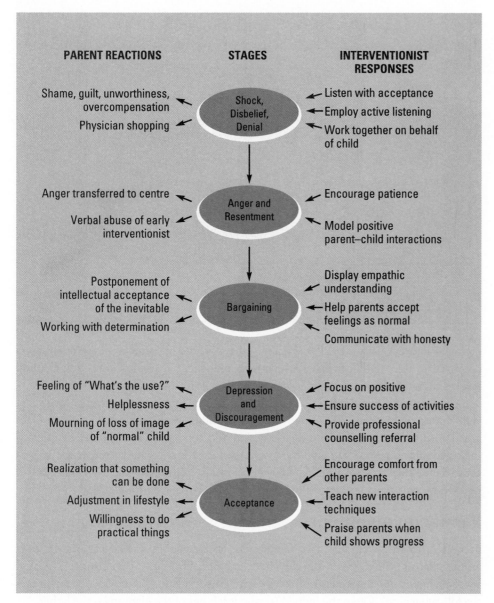

Figure 15.1 Parent Reactions and Possible Interventions

Ruth E. Cook, Diane M. Klein, Annette Tessier, *Adapting Early Childhood Curricula for Children in Inclusive Settings*, Sixth Edition, © 2000, p. 24. Reprinted by permission of Pearson Education, Inc., Upper Saddle River, NJ.

personnel should listen with acceptance and help the parents understand the nature of the disability and the fact that they are not responsible for it. Figure 15.1 lists possible parental reactions and interventions that schools can use to help family members.

School personnel need to be aware of family members' acceptance level of children with exceptionalities and make appropriate efforts to support this acceptance. This effort begins with assisting parents to understand their child's exceptionality; at the same time, the educator or administrator should listen to the parents in order to better understand the child from their perspective. Further, teachers must be sensitive to the fact that many parents do not see the school as a welcoming place for various reasons (e.g., problems the parents experienced as students themselves, negative responses communicated to them as advocates for their child). Professionals must understand that their actions can have a

Many parents of students with special needs require assistance in accepting their child's exceptionalities.

CONSIDER THIS

As a teacher, how could you deal with families experiencing various reactions to a child with an exceptionality? What role, if any, should a teacher play in helping parents work through their reactions?

TEACHING TIP

Teachers need to be aware of the different reactions that parents may experience and know some specific strategies for dealing with these reactions.

FURTHER READING

For more information on fostering inclusive views, read S.J. Salend's article "Fostering Inclusive Views in Children: What Families Can Do," in volume 37, issue 1 of *Teaching Exceptional Children*, 2004 (pp. 64–69).

profound impact on families. For example, "the way in which diagnostic information is conveyed to the family can have a long-term influence on parents' attitudes, families' level of stress and acceptance, and coping strategies" (Hutton & Caron, 2005, p. 180).

Families of children with exceptionalities cope in many ways, some good and some bad. Hutton and Caron (2005) interviewed 21 families of children who had been diagnosed with autism to determine their reaction and coping mechanisms. Their findings indicated that 43 percent felt grief and loss, 29 percent felt shock and surprise, and 10 percent blamed themselves. Of the families in the study, 52 percent said the diagnosis had resulted in some relief in terms of knowing what was wrong with their child.

Family Involvement

Too often, when people hear that families are taking part in a child's education, they assume that the "family" is really the child's mother. This view is unfortunate, because involvement of the entire family is the goal (see the Evidence-Based Practice feature on the following page). Often the individual who is left out of the planning is the father.

In addition to the adults in a family, siblings are also important in developing and implementing appropriate educational programs. Approximately 10 percent of the school population is identified as having a disability; therefore, the number of children with siblings identified with an exceptionality must be significant—a working estimate of 20 percent or more seems realistic. Although not all siblings experience adjustment problems, some will doubtlessly have significant difficulties responding to the exceptionality. Hutton and Caron (2005) found that 38 percent of siblings in their survey reacted with resentment or jealousy, 12 percent with fear, and 12 percent with sadness. The survey found that an additional 12 percent were accepting of their sibling, while 6 percent felt awkward having a sibling with an exceptionality. Regardless of the reactions of siblings, the presence of a child with an exceptionality in a family presents a unique opportunity to learn about the diversity of individual needs.

Parent-Delivered Interventions

The involvement of parents and other family members in intervention strategies has been described a great deal in the literature. In fact, as the role of families in the lives of individuals with exceptionalities increases, parent-delivered interventions will likely increase. DiPipi-Hoy and Jitendra (2004) identify six general rules for parent-delivered interventions related to teaching purchasing skills to young adults with exceptionalities outside the home setting:

1. Review the target skill prior to leaving the house.

2. Refrain from jumping in to help too quickly.

3. Do not complete the entire step when providing assistance.

4. Allow for self-correction of errors prior to intervening.

5. Direct a store clerk's attention to the student when the clerk attempts to communicate with the parent.

6. Discuss the routine, provide praise for appropriate behaviours, and address areas that need improvement with the student on the way home.

From DiPipi-Hoy, C., & Jitendra, A. (2004). "A parent-delivered intervention to teach purchasing skills to young adults with disabilities." *The Journal of Special Education*, 38 (3), 144–157. DiPipi-Hoy & Jitendra, 2004, p. 145.

Meyer (2001) summarized the literature and noted these areas of concern expressed by siblings:

- a lifelong and ever-changing need for information about the disability or illness

- feelings of isolation when siblings are excluded from information available to other family members, ignored by service providers, or denied access to peers who share their often ambivalent feelings about their siblings

- feelings of guilt about having caused the illness or disability, or being spared having the condition

- feelings of resentment when the child with special needs becomes the focus of the family's attention or when the child with special needs is indulged, overprotected, or permitted to engage in behaviours unacceptable by other family members

- a perceived pressure to achieve in academics, sports, or behaviour

- increased care-giving demands, especially for older sisters

- concerns about their role in their sibling's future (p. 30)

Siblings of children with exceptionalities need support from family members as well as other adults. Teachers and other adults should be aware of the stress and other impacts a sibling with an exceptionality can have (Smith et al., 2006). Following are some suggestions for adults dealing with children who have siblings with exceptionalities:

- Express love for the sibling.

- Provide siblings with information about the exceptionality.

- Keep the sibling informed about changes and stress on the family.

- Include the sibling in family and school meetings.

- Work for equity within the family duties and responsibilities.

- Prevent siblings from becoming second parents in the areas of care and discipline.

- Be aware that the needs of all the children will change through the family life cycle. (Smith et al., 2006, p. 61)

CONSIDER THIS

The recent emphasis on family (rather than parental) involvement reflects the importance of siblings and others in supporting the child. Is it a good idea to include siblings in the education of a brother or sister with an exceptionality? Why or why not?

Figure 15.2
Recommendations
for Siblings

Adapted from "Meeting the Unique
Concerns of Brothers and Sisters of
Children with Special Needs" by D.
Meyer, 2001, *Insight, 51*(4), p. 31.

- Parents and service providers have an obligation to proactively provide brothers and sisters with helpful, age-appropriate information.
- Provide siblings with opportunities to meet other siblings of children with special needs. For most parents, "going it alone" without the benefit of knowing another parent in a similar situation is unthinkable. Yet this happens routinely to brothers and sisters. Sibshops (workshops for siblings) and similar efforts offer siblings the same common-sense support that parents value.
- Encourage good communication with typically developing children. Good communication between parent and child is especially important in families where there is a child with special needs.
- Encourage parents to set aside special time to spend with the typically developing children. Children need to know from their parents' deeds and words that their parents care about them as individuals.
- Parents and service providers need to learn more about siblings' experiences. Sibling panels, books, newsletters, and videos are all excellent means of learning more about sibling issues.

Building on his analysis of the challenges, concerns, and opportunities for siblings of a child with an exceptionality, Meyer (2001) provided a series of recommendations to alleviate concerns and to enhance opportunities; these are presented in Figure 15.2.

Parent Education

Many educators believe parents of children with exceptionalities benefit tremendously from attending parent education classes. One reason is that parents too frequently attribute normal and predictable misbehaviour to a child's exceptionality rather than to the age and stage of a child. Seeing that all parents face similar challenges with their children can be both comforting and empowering to parents (West, 2002). Some helpful hints parents learn through parent education include the following (from West, 2002):

1. Never compare children.
2. Notice the improvements and accomplishments of each child in the family, and always reinforce the positive.
3. Hold family meetings that allow children a weekly opportunity to voice their concerns, accept chores, and plan enjoyable family nights and outings.
4. Learn to help children become responsible by the use of logical and natural consequences rather than using punishment or becoming permissive.
5. Spend special time alone with each child in the family. Be sure that no child feels lost or left out because others require more attention.
6. Plan family events that allow children to enjoy being together.
7. Reduce criticism and increase encouragement.
8. Be sensitive to the possibility that children functioning at a higher academic level in the family may be finding their place through perfectionism and a need to excel at all costs.
9. Invest time in your marriage. A strong marriage is important to your children's sense of well-being.

10. All families experience stress. The more that stress is encountered, the more time they need together to share their feelings, plan ahead, solve problems mutually, and plan time to enrich relationships.

Family and School Collaboration

School personnel and families of students with problems need to collaborate in order to maximize educational efforts. All school personnel, classroom teachers, special education teachers, administrators, and support workers need to be actively involved with families to improve the education of children with exceptionalities.

Parents of children with exceptionalities and school personnel are partners in providing appropriate educational services. Parents should actually be seen as the "senior partners," because they are responsible for the children every day until they reach adulthood.

Family involvement can only enhance educational programs. School personnel need to be actively involved with families to meet the needs of the child. "Parents who are supported in their initial attempts to participate in decision making will likely continue these efforts later in their child's school career" (Dabkowski, 2004, p. 38). Unfortunately, too often partnerships between families and school personnel fall short. These shortcomings can result for several reasons, including the following (Summers et al., 2005):

- professionals feeling unprepared to work with families
- professionals feeling that they do not have administrative support
- communication difficulties
- failure to recognize and adapt to cultural differences
- disagreement on appropriate services for the child

In working with parents of students with special needs, educators find that parents vary tremendously in knowledge and expertise about exceptionalities. Some parents may be well-versed in special education practices and may have informed opinions that must be considered in effective instructional planning. Other parents may be limited in their knowledge and their understanding of special education. In this case, educators are responsible to inform parents so that they can become effective advocates for their child and partners in educational programming. The Personal Spotlight in this chapter provides a glimpse of one special education professional's thoughts on the importance of collaboration when working with families of children with special needs.

In Canada, parental rights for involvement in the assessment, programming (IEP/IPP), and monitoring of children's school performance vary across the country. In the majority of jurisdictions, however, parents have the right to help make assessment and programming decisions. In all jurisdictions, attempts are made to include parents wherever possible.

SPECIFIC COLLABORATION ACTIVITIES

There are numerous ways parents and other family members can become involved with the education of a child with an exceptionality or one who is at risk for developing problems. The following suggestions focus on areas in which general education teachers can have a positive effect.

TEACHING TIP

Teachers and other school personnel must keep in mind that parents are not only equal partners in the education of their children, but are the senior partners and should be involved in all major decisions.

Watch

Working with Parents and Families

Collaboration and Communication with Teachers and Parents

Special Education Teacher Cordell Osmond

As a special education teacher with more than 14 years of experience, Cordell Osmond has worked in schools in Eastern and Western Canada. In his most recent position, his duties included assisting in the development of individualized education plans, assessing student achievement, and implementing appropriate pullout and inclusive interventions. These activities involved a great deal of collaboration with students, other professionals (e.g., speech-language pathologists, educational psychologists), and parents. "I believe it is important to address every aspect of an individual's development within a specialized population. A differently abled person's needs go far beyond academic achievement. Often, every facet of their lives is affected: emotionally, spiritually, socially, and physically. If we are to truly care for their needs, we must be open to the possibility that it will involve more than an academic-focused, unidimensional approach."

Parents and the family of a child with an exceptionality play a vital role in meeting that student's overall needs. "Collaboration is paramount. Collaboration puts the developing strengths of the student first, and ensures that those involved in the planning and implementation of a personalized program hold each other accountable to a common goal." When working with school personnel and parents, Cordell encourages the team to develop sensitivity to each student's needs, abilities, culture, and unique set of circumstances. "Be aware of your own biases and limitations in working with people within any population so that anything you have to contribute will not negatively impact the process. And it is vital to collaborate. I can't stress the importance of this enough."

Communicating with Parents

A critical element in any collaboration between school personnel and parents is communication. Many parents observe that too little communication flows between themselves and the school. Perhaps this is to be expected—approximately 50 percent of both general and special education teachers indicate that they have received no training in this area and, consequently, rate themselves as only moderately skilled (e.g., Buck et al., 1996; Epstein et al., 1996). This situation is particularly unfortunate, since problems between parents and school personnel can often be avoided by proper communication. School professionals should make a conscious effort to begin the year with a discussion of roles and responsibilities in terms of communication (Munk et al., 2001). Parents need to have information in order for parent–professional communication to be effective. For example, sharing assessment information with parents will foster collaboration (Pemberton, 2003). Parents of children with exceptionalities want access to their child's teachers (Nelson et al., 2004).

True family involvement in the education of a child cannot occur without good communication. Brandes (2005) makes the following recommendations for teachers to enhance communication between schools and parents:

- Give parents your undivided attention, and be an active listener.
- Stand or sit alongside parents when communicating.
- Take notes openly while conversing with parents.
- When first meeting parents, engage them in conversation and pay close attention to what they choose to discuss.

- View parents who are challenging as an opportunity for you to grow.

- When working with angry parents, maintain a respectful demeanour and take notes rather than defend your actions at the time of the accusations.

- Allow parents to regard you as one of the experts in their child's education.

- Share the relevance of the curriculum to the student's goals.

- Share specific behavioural expectations early and regularly.

- Explain that you will try to resolve any conflict their child may have at school before you engage the parents.

- Model respect for the student by frequently acknowledging his or her efforts and achievements.

- Share some of the student's positive events that happen at school, such as successfully serving on a committee.

- Set up regular and frequent positive communication avenues, such as a weekly newsletter that is sent home each Thursday.

- Be specific about when you will return phone calls, emails, and notes.

- Communicate often.

- Let parents know you appreciate their support and their follow-through at home.

- Encourage parents to make child-care provisions for the children who do not need to be at a meeting.

- Try to have both parents present when "major" topics are discussed.

- Start every meeting with a welcome, introductions, and review; clarification of the purpose of the current meeting and the ending time; and a recap of the meeting before everyone leaves.

- Never assume parents know how to help with homework. (pp. 52–54).

Effective communication must be regular and useful. Communicating with parents only once or twice per year, such as with IEP conferences, or communicating regularly but with information that is not useful, will not facilitate meeting educational goals.

One good way to communicate with parents is though a home-to-school notebook. The home-to-school notebook is simply a notebook that the child takes daily from school to home and back to school; it contains notes from the teacher and parents about the child's activities. This communication device serves three functions. First, it can encourage problem solving; second, the notebook helps parents and school personnel analyze information; and finally, it provides documentation of program implementation (Hall, Wolfe, & Bollig, 2003). Table 15.2 provides procedural recommendations for parents and school personnel in using a home-to-school notebook. Without both parties engaged in the day-to-day activities of the notebook, however, it will not likely be a successful communication tool.

Communication between school personnel and parents can take many forms. It does not have to be formal written communication; effective communication can be informal—for example, telephone calls, written notes, or newsletters. When communicating with parents, school personnel should be aware of how they convey messages. For example, they should never "talk down" to parents, and they should choose their words thoughtfully. Some words convey very negative meanings, whereas others transmit a message effectively in a more positive manner. Table 15.3 lists words that should be

Table 15.2 Procedural Recommendations for Using a Home-to-School Notebook

Procedural Recommendations for School

- Entry to classroom, collect journals.
- Morning routine to discuss with student what parent wrote.
- Keep journals in one place during day.
- Respect confidentiality.
- Structure journal writing during daytime routine, versus at the end of a busy day.
- Get input from specialists/teachers and others working with student (personal care aide).
- If student is included in a general education setting for a substantial part of day, the journal should travel to that setting and that teacher should make an entry.
- Analyze the journal; look for patterns of behaviour.
- Establish a routine to return journal home.
- Avoid educational jargon.

Procedural Recommendations for Parents

- Establish routine to review journal with student.
- Keep journal available.
- Include information from specialists (e.g., medical personnel, occupational and physical therapists).
- Obtain input from family members to include in journal entry (e.g., siblings).
- Establish a consistent, quiet time to write in journal.
- Review journal entries, analyze data, look for patterns of behaviour.
- Review journal: Are your questions being addressed?

From "The Home-to-School Notebook," by T.E. Hall, P.S. Wolfe, and A.A. Bollig, 2003, *Teaching Exceptional Children, 36*, p. 72. Used with permission.

Table 15.3 Making Positive Word Choices

Avoid	Use Instead
Must	Should
Lazy	Can do more with effort
Culturally deprived	Culturally different, diverse
Troublemaker	Disturbs class
Uncooperative	Should learn to work with others
Below average	Works at his (her) own level
Truant	Absent without permission
Impertinent	Discourteous
Steals	Takes things without permission
Dirty	Has poor grooming habits
Disinterested	Complacent, not challenged
Stubborn	Insists on having his (her) own way
Wastes time	Could make better use of time
Sloppy	Could be neater
Mean	Has difficulty getting along with others
Time and time again	Usually, repeatedly
Poor grade or work	Works below his (her) usual standard

Adapted from *Parents and Teachers of Children with Exceptionalities: A Handbook for Collaboration* (2nd ed., p. 82), by T.M. Shea and A.M. Bauer, 1991, Boston: Allyn & Bacon. Used with permission.

Teachers must communi-
cate regularly with parents
to keep them informed
about their child's progress
and needs.

avoided, along with preferred alternatives. When communicating with parents, school personnel should also be aware of cultural and language differences. Taking these factors into consideration will enhance the quality of communication with family members. School personnel must remember that the use of professional jargon can be just as much of a barrier as communicating with parents whose primary language is not English (Dabkowski, 2004).

The following discussion focuses on types of effective communication.

Informal Exchanges Informal exchanges can take place without preparation. Teachers may see a parent in the community and stop and talk momentarily about that parent's child. Teachers should always be prepared to talk to parents about their children, regardless of the setting, but should avoid talking about confidential information in the presence of individuals who do not need to know about it. If the conversation becomes too involved, the teacher should request that it be continued later, in a more appropriate setting.

Parent Observations Parents should be encouraged to visit the school to observe their child in the educational setting. Although the parents' presence could cause some disruption in the daily routine, school personnel need to keep in mind that parents have a critical stake in the success of the educational efforts. Therefore, parents should always feel welcome to observe the student in the educational setting. If the teacher feels that one time would be better than another, this information should be conveyed to the parent.

Telephone Calls Many teachers use telephone calls frequently and effectively to communicate with parents. Parents feel that teachers are interested in their child if the teacher takes the time to call and discuss the child's progress. When using the telephone for communication purposes, teachers should remember to call when there is good news about the child as well as to report problems the child is experiencing. It makes parents feel good to get a call from a teacher who says that the child is doing well and is not having problems. Again, understanding the language and culture of the home is important. Giving parents your home telephone number is an option that may prove reassuring to parents.

Written Notes Written communication to parents is also an effective method of communicating about a child's progress. When using written communication, teachers should consider the parents' literacy level and use words and phrases that will be readily understandable. They should also be aware of the primary language of the home. Written communications that are not understood can be very intimidating for parents. When using written communication, teachers should provide an opportunity for parents to respond, either in writing or through a telephone call. Increasingly, email offers opportunities for ongoing communication. However, as Patton, Jayanthi, and Polloway (2001) noted, "Although the use of new technologies [is] attractive in terms of their immediacy and efficiency, such use poses a dilemma, as a significant number of families may not have access to technology" (p. 228).

Home Visits There is no better way to get an understanding of the family than by making a home visit. When possible, school personnel should consider making the extra effort required to arrange and make home visits. When visiting homes, school personnel need to follow certain procedures, including the following:

- Have specific information to deliver or obtain.
- If you desire to meet with parents alone, find out if it is possible to have the child elsewhere during the scheduled visit.
- Keep visits to an hour or less.
- Arrive at the scheduled time.
- Dress appropriately, but be sensitive to cultural variance (e.g., formal, professional dress may distance yourself from the family in some homes).
- Plan visits with another school system resource person.
- Be sure to do as much listening as talking.
- Leave on a positive note. (Adapted from Westling & Koorland, 1988.)

Although we list home visits as an option, we are also cognizant of the low "treatment acceptability" of this practice. General education teachers report that they consider home visits the least effective (and perhaps least desirable) alternative available to them in terms of home–school collaboration (Polloway et al., 1996). Among other possible concerns, home visits may simply be unrealistic for a potentially large number of children.

Other Forms of Communication Another way for school personnel to convey helpful information to parents is to consider these options:

- newsletters
- parent or family support groups
- open houses

School personnel should use every available means to communicate with parents. Both general and special education teachers have this responsibility. Teachers should never assume that other school personnel will take care of communicating with parents. Effective communication involves many different people.

Parent–Teacher Conferences

Parent–teacher conferences are another excellent method of communication. They can be formal, such as IEP meetings, or informal, arranged when parents call a teacher and request a meeting with one or more teachers about a particular problem. Most schools have twice yearly or more regular parent–teacher meetings for all children. Regardless of the purpose or formality of the meeting, school personnel should focus attention on the topics at hand. They should send advance information home to parents and make the parents feel at ease about participating in the meeting.

When preparing to meet with parents to discuss children who are experiencing problems, school personnel need to anticipate the components of the discussion. They should gather information about the questions that parents may ask and know what information to address with the parents. Figure 15.3 provides typical questions raised at such conferences. By anticipating the questions in advance, school personnel will be in a better position to have a successful meeting.

IEP Meetings Parents should be involved in the development of students' individualized education programs for two reasons. First, most provincial and territorial jurisdictions require parental participation. The more important reason for involvement, however, is to gain parents' input. In most regards, parents know more about their children than school personnel do. They have interacted with the child longer, and beyond the hours of a school day. Schools need to take advantage of this knowledge about the child when developing an IEP. Too often, for a variety of reasons, parents do not fully participate in IEP meetings. They are present, but often feel intimidated or unworthy of contributing to the discussion. School personnel can facilitate the active involvement of parents at these meetings. In reflecting on how professionals encourage parental participation, Dabkowski (2004) suggests asking the following questions:

1. Are parents equal partners with you in the education of students with exceptionalities?

2. Do you actively invite parents, accommodate their schedules, and welcome their differing cultural contributions?

3. Are you aware of cultural and linguistic team processes or environments that might make parents uncomfortable?

4. Are you wondering how to improve parent participation in your decision-making processes? (p. 34)

By asking these questions, it is hoped that professionals will have a better understanding not only of how involved parents are in the process but also how to increase the level of involvement.

Questions Parents May Ask Teachers	Questions Teachers Should Ask Parents
■ What is normal for a child this age?	■ What activities at home could you provide as a reward?
■ What is the most important subject or area for my child to learn?	■ What particular skill areas concern you most for inclusion on the IEP?
■ What can I work on at home?	
■ How can I manage her behaviour?	■ What behaviour at home do you feel needs to improve?
■ Should I spank?	■ Would you be interested in coming to a parent group with other parents of my students?
■ When will my child be ready for community living?	
■ Should I plan on her learning to drive?	■ When is a good time to call at home?
■ Will you just listen to what my child did the other day and tell me what you think?	■ May I call you at work? What is the best time?
	■ Is there someone at home who can pick up the child during the day if necessary?
■ What is a learning disability?	
■ My child has emotional problems; is it my fault?	■ Would you be interested in volunteering in our school?
■ The doctor said my child will grow out of this. What do you think?	■ What is the most difficult problem you face in rearing your child?
■ Will physical therapy make a big difference in my child's control of his hands and arms?	■ What are your expectations for your child?
	■ How can I help you the most?
■ Have you become harder on our child? Her behaviour has changed at home.	■ What is your home routine in the evenings? Is there a quiet place for your child to study?
■ Can I call you at home if I have a question?	■ Can you or your spouse do some special activity with your child if he or she earns it at school?
■ What is the difference between delayed, retarded, and learning disabled?	
■ What kind of after-school activities can I get my child involved in?	■ Can you spend some time tutoring your child in the evening?
■ Can my child live on his own?	■ Would you like to have a conference with your child participating?
■ What should I do about sexual activity?	■ When is the best time to meet?
■ What's he going to be like in five years?	
■ Will she have a job?	
■ Who takes care of him when I can no longer care for him?	
■ What happens if she doesn't make her IEP goals?	

Figure 15.3 Common Questions Asked by Parents and Teachers

Adapted from *The Special Educator's Handbook* (pp. 208–209), by D.L. Westling and M.A. Koorland, 1988, Boston: Allyn & Bacon. Used with permission.

Consider having a parent advocate assigned to attend the IEP conference with the parents in order to increase parental participation. The advocate, a member of the school staff, can facilitate participation by introducing the parents to the other team members, verbally reinforcing parental input, directing questions to the parents, and summarizing the discussion at the end of the conference.

HOME-BASED INTERVENTION

Families can become involved with the education of a family member with an exceptionality through home-based intervention. For preschool children, home-based services are fairly common; however, parents less frequently provide instruction at home for older students. Still, many reports have noted that such instruction can be very beneficial to students with exceptionalities. Parents can be helpful in numerous ways.

Parents and other family members can further the student's educational program by providing reinforcement and direct instructional support at home, and by supporting homework efforts.

Providing Reinforcement

Most students with exceptionalities experience a great deal of failure and frustration. Frequently, the more they attend school, the more they fail. This failure cycle becomes difficult to break, especially after it becomes established over several years. Reinforcing success can help break the cycle. Parents need to work with school personnel to provide positive reinforcement for all levels of success. If students are not capable of achieving full success in an area, then they need to be rewarded for their positive efforts in the appropriate direction.

Parents are in an excellent position to provide reinforcement. They spend more time with their child than school personnel do and are involved in all aspects of the child's life. As a result, parents can provide reinforcement in areas where a child most desires rewards, such as time with friends, money, toys, or trips. For many students, simply allowing them to have a friend over or to stay up late at night on a weekend may prove reinforcing. School personnel do not have this range of reinforcers available to them; therefore, parents should take advantage of their repertoire of rewards to reinforce students' positive efforts.

A special example of reinforcement in the home is *home–school contingencies*, which typically involve providing reinforcement contingencies in the home that are based on the documentation of learning or behavioural reports from school. The basic mechanisms for home–school contingencies are written reports that highlight a student's behaviour relative to particular targets or objectives. Two popular forms are daily report cards and passports.

Daily report cards give feedback on schoolwork, homework, and behaviour. They range in complexity from forms calling for responses and simple rating scales to more precisely designed behavioural instruments with direct, daily behavioural measures. *Passports* typically take the form of notebooks, which students bring to each class and then take home daily. Individual teachers (or all of a student's teachers) and parents can make regular notations. Reinforcement is based both on carrying the passport and on meeting the specific target behaviours that are indicated on it.

Providing Direct Instructional Support

For many students with exceptionalities, direct involvement of family members in instruction can be critical to success. Unfortunately, many family members provide less

CONSIDER THIS

Parents generally know more about their children than school personnel do. In what ways can this knowledge be used to develop programs that meet the needs of children?

CROSS REFERENCE

A full description of the principles of reinforcement is presented in chapter 6.

TEACHING TIP

Regardless of the format, the key element in home–school contingencies is ongoing, effective communication between school personnel and parents.

direct instruction as the child gets older, assuming that the student is capable of doing the work alone. Too often, the reverse is true: students may need more assistance at home as they progress through the grades. Parents are generally with the child more than school personnel are, so it is logical to involve them in selected instructional activities. Advocates for expanding the role of parents in educating their children adhere to the following assumptions:

- Parents are the first and most important teachers of their children.
- The home is the child's first schoolhouse.
- Children will learn more during the early years than at any other time in life.
- All parents want to be good parents and care about their child's development. (Ehlers & Ruffin, 1990, p. 1)

Although the final assumption may not always be reflected in practice, it provides a positive foundation for building home programs. Devlin and Harber (2004) described a program where parents and professionals collaborated with discrete trial training in the treatment of a child with autism. The program used collaboration among family members, special education teachers, the resource room teacher, and the speech-language pathologist to achieve various goals and objectives for the child. The end result was that after 28 weeks of intervention, significant progress was made toward goals and objectives. The study concluded that such an intervention program, using family members as part of the intervention team, could result in significant gains by the child. In another study, Skoto and colleagues (2004) concluded that parental involvement with reading stories could result in positive gains by young girls with Rett syndrome.

Parents can also be involved in interventions that promote self-determination. Lee and colleagues (2006) describe a model for parent–teacher collaboration that focuses on improving self-determination. Using the program, called Self-Determined Learning Model of Support (SDLMS), parents are able to influence the self-determination of children with and without exceptionalities. Using such a program at home facilitates partnerships between schools and families (Lee et al., 2006).

Providing Homework Support

Homework may be the most problematic area of discussion for successful home–school collaboration. Teachers and parents indicate concerns about failures to initiate communication (in terms of informing the other of a student's learning and behaviour characteristics as well as the delineation of roles and responsibilities) and to provide follow-up communication, especially early on, when problems first become evident. It is believed that several variables influence the severity of these problems (e.g., lack of time, student-to-teacher ratio, student interference, not knowing whom to contact). Munk et al.'s (2001) survey research on 348 parents confirmed this pattern of findings.

Teachers should be sensitive to over-involved parents and, when appropriate, encourage them to "not do for children what [they] can do for themselves."

CROSS REFERENCE

School-based aspects of homework are discussed in chapters 13 and 14.

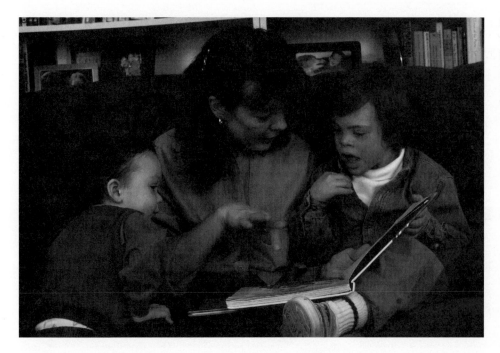

Lack of clear communication from teachers about homework expectations can lead parents to be either underinvolved or overinvolved.

Despite the numerous problems associated with homework, solutions can be found. Based on their study, Bursuck et al. (1999) found that special education teachers indicate the following recommendations:

- General educators and parents need to take an active and daily role in monitoring and communicating with students about homework.

- Schools should find ways to provide teachers with the time to engage in regular communication with parents and should provide students with increased opportunities to complete homework after school.

- Teachers need assistance in taking advantage of technological innovations (e.g., homework hotlines, computerized student progress records).

- Students need to be held responsible for keeping up with their homework.

- Special educators need to share with general educators more information about the needs of students with exceptionalities and appropriate instructional accommodations or adaptations.

Examples of strategies ranked most effective in resolving homework dilemmas by general education teachers are provided in Figure 15.4. Note that many of these strategies have validity for all students, not only those with special needs.

As Patton et al. (2001, p. 240) noted, "Even conscientious parents who understand the significance of homework in their children's lives and the importance of their own role in supporting, nurturing, and helping their children have successful homework experiences sometimes simply fail at their daily responsibilities of checking the assignment book or asking 'What homework did you get today?' and 'Have you completed it?'" Thus, teachers should be understanding when communicating with parents for whom homework may be a lower priority when compared with other issues

Parents' Efforts to Communicate

Parents should

- check with their child about homework daily.
- regularly attend parent–teacher conferences.
- sign their child's assignment book daily.

Adopting Policies to Facilitate Communication

Schools should

- provide release time for teachers to communicate with parents on a regular basis.
- require frequent written communication from teachers to parents about homework (e.g., monthly progress reports).
- schedule conferences in the evenings for working parents.

General Education Teachers' Roles

Teachers should

- require that students keep a daily assignment book.
- provide parents at the start of school with a list of suggestions on how parents can assist with homework.
- remind students of due dates on a regular basis.

Technologies to Enhance Communication

Schools should

- establish telephone hotlines so that parents can call when questions or problems arise.
- regularly provide computerized student progress reports for parents.
- establish systems that enable teachers to place homework assignments on audiotapes so that parents can gain access by telephone or voice mail.

Figure 15.4 Effective Strategies Relative to Homework

From "Strategies for Improving Home–School Communication Problems about Homework for Students with Disabilities," by M.H. Epstein, D.D. Munk, W.D. Bursuck, E.A. Polloway, and M.M. Jayanthi, 1999, *Journal of Special Education, 33,* pp. 166–176.

(e.g., school attendance, family illness); teachers should respond accordingly by helping to address these other issues first.

FINAL THOUGHTS

It is a safe assumption that establishing good working relationships with parents and families enhances the school experience of children. Thus, an important objective for schools should be to achieve and maintain such relationships. Most professionals acknowledge the importance of parent and family involvement in the schooling of their children, and this importance can be especially critical for students with exceptionalities. However, programs that promote home–school collaboration must aim for more than students' classroom success. Often, parental involvement is focused on children's goals (i.e., student progress), with less attention given to parental outcomes (i.e., their particular needs). Teachers, parents, and other family members can all gain from co-operative relationships that truly flow in both directions and that are concerned with success in home and school settings. General and special education teachers need to help family members understand the importance of their involvement, give them suggestions on how to take part, and empower them with the skills and confidence they will need. Students with exceptionalities, and those at risk of developing problems, require assistance from all parties in order to maximize success. Family members are critical components of the educational team.

SUMMARY

- The past two decades have seen a major change in provision of educational services to students with special needs—the active involvement of families.

- Encouraging parents to participate in school decisions may be difficult but is nevertheless essential.

- Schools need to take proactive steps to ensure the involvement of families of students with exceptionalities.

- Unlike families of the past, today's families vary considerably in their composition.

- School personnel must involve all family members of a student with special needs, regardless of the type of family.

- Family members must make adjustments when a child with an exceptionality becomes a family member.

- Siblings of students with exceptionalities may also experience special problems and challenges.

- Families and schools must collaborate to ensure appropriate educational programs for students with exceptionalities.

- Most provincial and territorial policies require that schools involve families in educational decisions for students with exceptionalities.

- A critical component in any collaboration between school personnel and family members is effective communication.

- All types of communication between schools and families are important.

- School personnel should encourage parents and other family members to participate during school conferences.

- Family members should be encouraged and taught how to become involved in the educational programs implemented in the school.

- A variety of strategies are available to facilitate successful home intervention programs (e.g., reinforcement, instruction, homework support).

Weblinks

CanadianParents.com
www.canadianparents.com
A wonderful resource for parents, Canadian Parents Online provides information on all aspects of parenting, with supports, resources, and questions and answers from lawyers, nutritionists, and physicians. It is also a resource for teachers to share with parents and to read for suggestions about schooling, homework, health, and behaviour.

Child and Family Canada
www.cccf-fcsge.ca
The Child and Family Canada website provides information on all aspects of the family. There is some excellent information on parenting children with special needs, as well as information on child abuse, family supports, and much more. The site is invaluable for teachers who have questions about family issues.

Parentbooks
www.parentbookstore.com
Parentbooks, a Toronto-based bookstore, offers a huge selection of resources, including books, videos, and manuals in the area of parenting, families, and education. The store has numerous resources specifically for teachers and in the area of special needs.

National Parent Network on Disabilities (NPND)
www.npnd.org
This U.S. association provides advocacy information for parents of individuals with disabilities. Although much material is specific to the United States, there is some extremely useful information on resources, related websites, different disabilities, planning for aging, and much more.

Mobility Resource
www.disabilityresource.com
The Mobility Resource site provides resources and other weblinks to parents and professionals working with children with disabilities. If you have any questions about a disability or its management, this site will direct you to a wealth of information.

Family Education Network
www.familyeducation.com
Although the material on this website is intended to be shared primarily with families and parents, it is also useful to the classroom teacher. There are suggestions for educational activities and resources, and tips on managing different special needs concerns.

Glossary

Accelerated schools Schools that provide optional programming for students considered at risk of failure.

Acceleration A form of programming for students who are classified as gifted or talented, where the students move through the curriculum at a more rapid pace than their chronological-age peers.

Accessibility The ability of a person with an exceptionality to make use of a physical location or program.

Accommodations The specialized support and services provided to students with diverse needs to assist them in achieving learning expectations (e.g., technological equipment, support staff, etc.).

Acquired immuno deficiency syndrome (AIDS) A disease transmitted by body-fluid contact that results in a depressed immune system.

Adaptation The changes made to instructional practices, materials or technology, assessment strategies, curriculum content, and the learning environment in order to meet the strengths, needs, and interests of individual students.

Adaptive behaviour A way of conduct that meets the standards of personal independence and social responsibility expected from a particular cultural and chronological age group.

Allergens Substances that individuals are allergic to, such as dust, certain foods, or animal dander.

Alternative communication Any system of conveying ideas that is used in lieu of human speech.

Alternative schools Schools designed to provide alternative environments for students with behavioural and emotional disorders.

American Speech-Language-Hearing Association (ASHA) The major American professional organization for speech-language and hearing professionals.

Annual goals Goals for the year that are developed for each student served in special education and made a part of the student's individualized education program (IEP).

Antidepressants Medications that can be used for managing attention deficit/hyperactivity disorder.

Anxiety/withdrawal A form of emotional-behavioural disorder where children are very anxious and do not interact with their peers.

Articulation disorder The most common speech disorder, this problem centres around word and sound pronunciations.

Asperger syndrome First listed in 1994 in the fourth edition of the *Diagnostic and Statistical Manual of Mental Disorders* as one of five pervasive developmental disorders. There is significant impairment in social functioning, but otherwise no cognitive delay.

Assessment The process of collecting information about a particular student to determine eligibility for special services and strengths and areas of need for programming purposes.

Assistive technology Devices that allow students, especially those with specific needs, to participate fully, or even partially, in ongoing classroom activities.

Asthma A disease that affects breathing that is due to narrowing of the small air passages in the lungs caused by irritation of the bronchial tubes by allergic reactions.

Astigmatism The distortion or blurring of vision for objects at any distance due to the cornea curving more in one direction than the other.

At-risk students Students who are likely to develop learning or behaviour problems because of a variety of environmental factors.

Attention deficit/hyperactivity disorder (AD/HD) A problem associated with short attention spans and excessive motor movements.

Attention problems–immaturity A form of behaviour problem associated with attention deficits.

Audiologist A professional who assesses hearing difficulties, selects and fits hearing aids, designs and implements rehabilitation strategies for hearing-impaired clients, and consults regarding hearing conservation and noise exposure.

Auditory processing disorder A deficit in the processing of information specific to the auditory modality.

Augmentative communication Methods used to facilitate communication in individuals, including communication boards, computers, and sign language.

Authentic assessment A method of evaluating students in which students are asked to perform real-world tasks that demonstrate meaningful application of essential knowledge and skills.

Autism A severe disorder that affects the language and behaviour of children, caused by neurological problems.

Basal series The type of reading programs traditionally used in most elementary schools in general education classrooms.

Behaviour management Systematic use of behavioural techniques, such as behaviour modification, to manage ways of conduct.

Behavioural approach An intervention model based on behaviourism that is often used with children with emotional problems.

Behavioural model A curriculum model in which concepts are learned by direct instruction and the theory of reinforcement.

Blindness A category of disabilities characterized by severe visual impairment that usually results in an inability to read printed material.

Braille A system of writing for the visually impaired that uses characters made up of raised dots.

Canadian Association of Speech-Language Pathologists and Audiologists (CASLPA) The major Canadian professional organization for speech-language and hearing professionals.

Canadian Charter of Rights and Freedoms A part of Canada's *Constitution Act* that guarantees, among other rights, the rights of all individuals with exceptionalities.

Career education A curricular model that focuses on the future vocational opportunities for students.

Cerebral palsy A disorder affecting balance and voluntary muscles that is caused by brain damage.

Childhood cancer Any form of cancer that affects children; generally leukemia, bone cancer, or lymphoma.

Childhood disintegrative disorder A disorder marked by regression in multiple areas of functioning. Typically after the age of two and before the age of 10 the child demonstrates a significant loss of previously acquired skills (i.e., expressive or receptive language skills, motor skills, bowel or bladder control).

Chronic health problem A physical condition that is persistent and results in school problems for the child.

Circle of friends A peer support network for an individual student fostered by the classroom teacher.

Classroom climate The nature of the learning environment, including teacher rules, expectations, discipline standards, and openness of the teacher.

Classroom management A combination of techniques used by teachers in classrooms to manage the environment, including behaviour modification.

Classroom organization Methods used by teachers to manage the learning environment through physical organization of the classroom, classroom rules, and use of other structure.

Clean intermittent bladder catheterization (CIC) A medical process where a tube is inserted into the catheter to allow urinary waste to leave the body.

Cochlea The part of the inner ear containing fluid and nerve cells that processes information to the brain.

Cochlear implant A technological device inserted in place of the cochlea that enables some individuals to hear sounds.

Cognitive-behavioural intervention Instructional strategies that use internal control methods, such as self-talk and self-monitoring, in ways that help students learn how to control their own behaviour.

Cognitive deficiency A deficiency in the intelligence processes, including thinking, memory, and problem solving.

Cognitive model (or constructionist model) A curriculum model, based on the work of Jean Piaget, with a primary focus on stimulating the child's cognitive or thinking abilities.

Collaboration The process of interactions between teachers, special education teachers, and/or other professionals to provide instruction to an inclusive classroom.

Communication board An augmentative communication device that includes letters or symbols that enables a person to communicate either manually or through computer technology.

Community-based instruction (CBI) A model in which instruction is provided in a community setting where skills that are learned will actually be used.

Conduct disorder A type of behaviour problem that is characterized by negative and hostile behaviours, generally toward authority figures.

Conductive hearing loss A form of hearing impairment caused by problems with the outer or middle ear that impede sound travelling to the inner ear.

Contingency contracting Developing behavioural contracts with students based on their completing specific tasks or meeting certain behavioural expectations in return for positive reinforcements.

Continuous progress A form of educational programming that allows students to move through a curriculum at their own pace.

Continuum of services A model that provides placement and programming options for students with exceptionalities along a continuum of least-to-most restrictiveness.

Co-operative learning An instructional and learning process that uses teams of children to teach each other and work together on various learning activities.

Creative A form of intelligence characterized by advanced divergent thinking skills and the development of original ideas and responses.

Criterion-referenced assessment Tests that compare a child to a particular mastery level rather than to a normative group.

Curriculum compacting An approach used with gifted and talented students, where less time is spent on general curriculum activities and more time on enrichment activities.

Curriculum telescoping An approach used with students who are achieving well academically that enables them to move through a curriculum at a more rapid pace than is typical.

Curriculum-based assessment A form of criterion-referenced assessment that uses the actual curriculum as the standard.

Cystic fibrosis A health disorder that is characterized by fluid and mucus buildup in the respiratory system, resulting in death.

Deaf A severe level of hearing impairment that generally results in the inability to use residual sound for communication purposes.

Developmental disability A disability that has a direct impact on a person's mental or physical development.

Developmental model A curriculum model stressing the provision of an enriched environment, in which the child is given numerous experiences and opportunities for learning.

Developmentally appropriate A level of instruction that meets the developmental level of children being taught.

Diabetes A health condition where the pancreas does not produce sufficient levels of insulin to metabolize various substances, including glucose.

Diagnostic and Statistical Manual of Mental Disorders (DSM-IV-TR) The diagnostic manual used by medical and psychological professionals.

Differential reinforcement of lower rates of behaviour (DRL) A model that provides reinforcement for behaviours that are moving the student in the desired direction.

Differentiated programming An instructional approach that requires various curricula or programs for different students in the same classroom.

Direct instruction A technique where the teacher instructs students on a particular topic.

Distortions Speech production problems characterized by altering the sound(s) of letters and words.

Dual education system The education model that supports separate programs for students with exceptionalities and those in general education.

Duchenne dystrophy A very severe form of muscular dystrophy that results in fat replacing muscle tissue.

Dysarthria A disorder characterized by muscles that are weak, slowly moving, or do not move at all (e.g., muscles of the mouth, face, and respiratory system) as the result of a stroke or other brain injury.

Dyscalculia A disability in which a person has difficulty understanding math concepts and solving arithmetic problems.

Dysgraphia A disability in which a person finds it difficult to form letters or write within a defined space.

Dyslexia A specific learning disability in which a person typically experiences difficulties in accurately and/or fluently recognizing, spelling, and decoding words.

Ecological assessment Evaluating individuals in the context of their environments and taking into consideration all environmental factors.

Educable mentally retarded (EMR) A term traditionally used to describe students with an intelligence quotient (IQ) in the 50–70 range.

Emotional abuse A form of child abuse that centres around emotionally abusing a child, such as ridiculing the child in public or always making a child feel like a failure.

Enrichment A variety of methods that are used to facilitate appropriate education for students classified as gifted and/or talented, enabling students to progress beyond the typical curriculum.

Epilepsy A disability that is caused by random, erratic electric impulses in the brain, which results in seizures.

Exceptionalities Special physical and/or intellectual needs that require special services for the students that have them.

Expressive language Language that is spoken, written, or communicated visually (e.g., sign language); language that is expressed in some way.

Extinction The removal of reinforcement from an individual that will result in a particular behaviour being terminated.

Facilitated communication A controversial method of dealing with children with autism in which an individual provides limited resistance to a child's arm, which then uses a communication board to communicate.

Family A unit of individuals who are related or who are together through legal means, providing support for each other.

Family support A model to provide services for individuals with exceptionalities by providing a wide array of supports for families.

Farsightedness (hyperopia) The ability to clearly see objects at a distance, but not up close.

Fetal alcohol spectrum disorder An umbrella term (not a diagnostic term) used to refer to the damage or range of disabilities caused by alcohol consumption during pregnancy.

Fetal alcohol syndrome A combination of physical and central nervous system abnormalities caused by maternal consumption of alcohol during pregnancy.

Fluctuating hearing loss Hearing loss that improves and/or gets worse over time (e.g., hearing loss due to otitis media).

Fluency The smoothness and rapidity in various skills, such as speech, oral language, reading, and other skills associated with thinking.

Form The rule systems of language: phonology, morphology, and syntax.

Full inclusion The movement or trend to fully include all students with exceptionalities, regardless of the severity, into all general education programs.

Functional behavioural assessment (FBA) An analysis of the specific behaviours and behavioural patterns demonstrated by an individual within varied environmental contexts.

Gifted A term used to describe students who perform significantly above average in a variety of areas, including academic, social, motor, and leadership.

Gifted and/or talented (GT) A term frequently used to describe high-achieving students as well as students who excel in other areas, such as the arts.

Hard of hearing A disability category that refers to individuals who have a hearing loss but who can benefit from their residual hearing abilities.

Hearing impairment A disability that affects an individual's sense of hearing. The term applies to any level of hearing loss, including being hard of hearing (residual hearing) or deaf.

Homework A form of individual practice that generally occurs in the home environment after school hours.

Human immunodeficiency virus (HIV) A major fatal disease that is currently impacting all areas of our society, including children in public schools.

Hyperkinetic disorders Another label to describe individuals who are hyperactive.

IEP Individualized education program. An IEP is required by most educational jurisdictions for every child receiving special education services. Other terms used to describe this type of program include individualized program plan (IPP) and personal program plan (PPP).

Inclusion A practice based on the belief that students with exceptionalities belong in general education settings, with support services provided in the general classroom by specialists.

Inhalants A group of drugs and substances that can cause hallucinations and other reactions; examples include fingernail polish, paint thinner, and glue.

Integration A term that has been used to describe the placement of students with exceptionalities in general education classrooms, at least for a portion of each school day; otherwise known as mainstreaming.

Intellectual disability An impaired ability to learn that may cause difficulty in coping with the demands of daily life; usually present from birth.

Intelligence quotient (IQ) A number used to express the apparent relative intelligence of a person, as determined by a standardized intelligence test.

Intelligence tests Tests that are designed to determine an individual's intelligence level, which is usually reported as an intelligence quotient (IQ).

Juvenile delinquency A legal term used to describe youth who have broken the law.

Language A formal method of human communication that uses signs and symbols to represent ideas and thoughts, and the rules that apply to standardize the system.

Language disabilities Any number of impairments that interfere with an individual's ability to communicate with others, such as voice disorders, expressive language skills, and receptive language abilities.

Language disorders Impairments of comprehension or use of language.

Learning disabilities (LD) The disability category that is characterized by students not achieving commensurate with their ability levels.

Least restrictive environment (LRE) The placement of students with exceptionalities alongside their typically achieving peers as much as possible.

Leukemia A form of cancer that attacks the blood cells; frequently found in children.

Life skills A curricular orientation that emphasizes teaching those abilities that will be required for a student to function as an adult in a community setting.

Logical consequences Expected repercussions after a particular behaviour.

Low vision Students who have a visual impairment but who also have functional use of some residual vision; these students can read print.

Magnet schools Schools that offer an alternative curriculum to attract students.

Mainstreaming The term originally used to describe placing students with exceptionalities in general education classroom settings.

Meningocele A form of spina bifida where an outpouching occurs along the spinal cord, which has not been closed; there is no paralysis associated with this form of spina bifida.

Mental age A measure used in psychological testing that expresses a person's mental attainment in terms of the number of years it takes an average child to reach the same level.

Mental retardation The term previously used for a disability related to deficiencies in cognitive abilities that occurs before the age of 18 and is associated with deficits in adapted behaviour; this classification generally requires the individual to have an IQ score of about 70 or below; preferred term is now *intellectual disability*.

Mentor program Program in schools where adults serve as mentors to children, especially children at risk of failure.

Metacognition Thinking about thinking; individuals with problems in this area may have difficulty knowing, using, and monitoring their use of thinking and learning strategies, and learning from their mistakes.

Mild mental retardation A level of mental retardation that usually includes those with an IQ range of about 50 to 70.

Mixed hearing loss A type of hearing loss occurring when both a conductive and sensorineural hearing loss are present.

Moderate mental retardation A level of mental retardation that usually includes those with an IQ range of about 35 to 50.

Modifications Changes in policy that will support students with exceptionalities in learning.

Monocular A small telescope that enables a student to see print, pictures, diagrams, maps, and people.

Morphologic impairment An impairment in an individual's ability to use appropriate structure in oral language.

Morphology The rule system controlling the structure of words.

Motor excess A level of physical activity that is above expected levels for that age and cultural group.

Motor speech disorders Articulation disorders resulting from neurological damage, such as stroke or head injury.

Multipass A reading and comprehension strategy whereby students make three passes through content reading material: a survey, size-up, and sort-out pass.

Multiple intelligences The theory that there are many different types of intelligences, rather than a single, general factor common in all individuals.

Multisensory impairments Disabilities of both the visual and auditory kind in the same person.

Muscular dystrophy A progressive disease that is characterized by a weakening of the muscles.

Myelomeningocele A form of spina bifida where part of the spinal cord is included in the outpouching, which usually results in lower trunk and limb paralysis.

Natural consequences The use of consequences typically found in a child's environment as a positive or negative consequence.

Nearsightedness (myopia) The ability to clearly see objects up close but not at a distance.

Negative reinforcement The removal of an unpleasant consequence following a student's behaving or responding in the appropriate manner.

Neglect Situations in which a child is exposed to a substantial risk of harm.

Nondiscriminatory assessment A method of evaluating students that prevents discrimination on the basis of differences (e.g., cultural differences, gender differences, etc.).

Normalization The process of attempting to make life as normal as possible for persons with exceptionalities.

Normalization movement A widely held belief that all individuals, regardless of any disability, should have as normal an education and living arrangement as possible, as opposed to institutionalization.

Norm-referenced tests Evaluation procedures that are designed to enable the comparison of a child with a normative sample.

Nuclear family A reference to the modern family that is somewhat traditional in that there are two parents and children; however, both parents now generally work.

Omissions A speech production problem where individuals leave out sounds in their speech.

Ophthalmologist A medical doctor who specializes in the treatment of vision disorders and disorders of the eye.

Optometrist An individual who specializes in fitting eyeglasses to individuals with vision problems.

Orthomolecular therapy The use of dietary interventions to impact learning and behavioural disorders; research does not support these interventions.

Orthopedic impairment The U.S. disability category that includes children with impairments caused by congenital anomaly (e.g., clubfoot), disease (e.g., bone tuberculosis), and other causes (e.g., cerebral palsy, amputations, etc.).

Other health impaired (OHI) The U.S. disability category that includes children with health problems that can result in eligibility for special education and related services.

Otitis media An inflammation of the area behind the eardrum or the middle ear typically associated with fluid buildup; the fluid may or may not be infected.

Peer tutoring An instructional technique that uses children to teach other children a variety of skills.

Phonation The process of putting speech sounds together to form words and sentences.

Phonemic awareness An understanding that words are composed of sound segments.

Phonologic impairment An impairment in an individual's ability to follow the rules that govern the formation of words and sentences from sounds.

Phonology The rule system that governs the individual and combined sounds of a language.

Physical abuse The treatment of children in inappropriate physical ways that are illegal and can lead to disabilities and even death.

Physical disabilities A variety of impairments related to health problems, such as spina bifida, cerebral palsy, and polio.

Placement The physical environment in which a student is educated.

Portfolio assessment A method of evaluating children that considers their work, in addition to their performance on tests.

Positive behaviour support A collaborative assessment-based process used to develop individualized interventions for individuals with challenging behaviour. Support plans encompass all educational methods that can be used to teach, strengthen, and expand the positive behaviour of individuals.

Positive reinforcement Affirmative, pleasant consequences that are given to an individual in recognition of an appropriate behaviour or response.

Prader-Willi syndrome A rare syndrome, caused by a problem with the fifteenth chromosome, that leaves an individual with mild intellectual disabilities and an obsession with eating.

Pragmatics The relationships among language, perception, and cognition; the system controlling language function.

Prenatal Occurring prior to the birth of a child, during the approximately nine months of gestation.

Preventive discipline A method of behaviour management where emphasis is placed on preventing behaviour problems rather than reacting to them.

Primary disabilities Disabilities that a child is born with (i.e., visual impairment).

Processing problems The primary problems experienced by students classified as having a learning disability, including thinking, memory, and organization.

Profound mental retardation The lowest level of functioning in the traditional classification system for individuals with intellectual disabilities, representing an IQ range below 20.

Psychostimulants The most commonly prescribed medications for attention deficit/hyperactivity disorder.

Psychotic behaviour Ways of conduct indicative of a serious mental illness, such as schizophrenia.

Punishment The application of something that is unpleasant to a child after an inappropriate behaviour; the least-desired behaviour management method available.

Pure-tone audiometry One of the methods used to evaluate hearing loss and hearing capabilities of individuals.

Receptive language Language that is received and decoded or interpreted.

Reinforcement The process of providing consequences, positive or negative, following a particular behaviour or response.

Relative isolation The phase prior to the 1970s during which students with exceptionalities were served either outside public schools or in isolated settings within them.

Remediation The offering of special aid or attention to learners who are struggling in a certain area.

Residential programs The way in which many children with intellectual disabilities and/or sensory deficits were taught prior to the normalization movement.

Residual hearing Amount of hearing remaining after hearing loss; generally relates to a profound hearing loss.

Resilience The ability to thrive despite risk.

Resonance Tone of voice that is affected by air coming out of the nose—either too much air or not enough—resulting in hypernasality or hyponasality.

Resource room A special education classroom where students go for brief periods during the day for specific help in problem areas.

Response cost A behaviour management technique where rewards or reinforcements are taken away from students who do not exhibit appropriate behaviours.

Rett syndrome A genetic disorder almost exclusively present in females. Young girls develop typically until sometime between 6 and 18 months of age, at which point difficulties with speech and motor skills, repetitive hand movements, seizures, and motor control problems appear.

Secondary disabilities Disabilities that develop over time that are the result of a mismatch between the individual and his or her environment (e.g., social or mental health problems).

Self-determination Making students more active participants in designing their educational experiences and monitoring their own success (i.e., by teaching self-awareness and self-advocacy skills).

Self-evaluation A method that students can use to assess their own behaviours or work.

Self-injurious behaviours Behaviours exhibited by an individual that result in harm to that person, such as head banging.

Self-instruction Various techniques that students can use to teach themselves.

Self-management A cognitive strategy that helps individuals with attention or behaviour problems to manage their own problems.

Self-monitoring A cognitive strategy where students keep track of and record information about their own behaviours.

Self-paced instruction In this model for serving students who are classified as gifted and/or talented, students move through a curriculum at their own pace.

Self-regulation The ability to appropriately adapt one's behaviour to an environment or situation.

Self-reinforcement A cognitive strategy where students affirm themselves for appropriate behaviours.

Semantics The system in a language that governs content, intent, and meanings of spoken and written words.

Sensorineural hearing loss A type of hearing loss that affects the inner ear or cochlea.

Sensory impairment A disability affecting either the visual or auditory abilities.

Sequential phonics program Intervention program that follows a specified sequence of normal phonics development.

Severe mental retardation A level of intellectual disability pertaining to an IQ range of approximately 20 to 35.

Sexual abuse A form of abuse involving unwanted sexual activity (e.g., fondling, intercourse, indecent exposure).

Snellen chart The chart used by schools and others to screen individuals for visual problems.

Social competence The ability to use social skills properly in appropriate contexts.

Social skills Any number of skills that facilitate an individual's successful participation in a group.

Socialized aggression A form of behavioural disorder affecting children whose inappropriate behaviours are acceptable in a group setting.

Speech The vocal production of language that is the easiest, fastest, and most efficient means of communicating.

Speech disabilities Any number of disorders affecting an individual's ability to communicate orally.

Speech disorders Impairments of voice, articulation, and fluency.

Speech-language pathologist A professional who works with students who experience speech and/or language problems.

Spina bifida A physical disability that results in the spinal column not closing properly, leaving an exposed spinal cord.

Splinter skills Skills that an individual with a severe disability, such as autism, possesses that are beyond explanation.

Strategy A skill that is taught to students to give them the ability to deal with instructional content and social situations on their own.

Stuttering A disorder of speech fluency that results in a person's expressive language being difficult to understand due to breaks and repetitions in speech.

Subject-matter acceleration In this system of providing accommodations for students classified as gifted and/or talented, students move through a particular subject area at an increased rate.

Substance abuse The practice of using illegal or inappropriate substances, such as alcohol, cocaine, or inhalants.

Substitutions A speech production problem characterized by the practice of substituting one sound for another.

Supported education The model of teaching used when students with exceptionalities are included in general education classes with the supports necessary for them to achieve success.

Syntax Various rules of grammar that relate to the endings of words and the order of words in sentences.

Talented The second component to the category of gifted and/or talented that includes children who excel in various arts and nonacademic areas.

Team teaching The utilization of more than one professional or paraprofessional who actually co-teach classes of students or lessons.

Testing The component of the assessment process where specific questions are asked of an individual and a response is recorded.

Time out A behaviour management technique where the student is isolated from receiving reinforcement.

Tinted glasses Glasses with certain colour tints that have been used with persons with learning disabilities to correct reading problems; research data do not support their use.

Tourette syndrome A disorder that results in behaviour tics and inappropriate vocalizations, such as shouting cuss words.

Trainable mentally retarded (TMR) A term frequently used in schools to identify students with IQ ranges of 30 to 50.

Transition The process of moving students from one setting to another, such as preschool programs to Kindergarten, elementary school to junior high school, and high school to work.

Traumatic brain injury (TBI) A disability category that results from an injury to the brain, causing a student to have significant problems in school.

Validity The evidence collected to support appropriate inferences, uses, and consequences that result from an assessment.

Verbal apraxia A disorder of the nervous system, not due to muscular weakness or paralysis, affecting a person's ability to sequence and say sounds, syllables, and words.

Vestibular dysfunction medication A controversial therapy for treating dyslexia.

Vision therapy A controversial way to treat individuals with learning disabilities. It is based on the theory that the disabilities are caused by visual defects.

Voice disorders Speech production disorders that typically affect the pitch, loudness, and/or quality of the sounds being produced.

Vulnerable A term used to refer to children who are experiencing an episode of poor developmental outcomes.

Whole language A language arts curricular approach that focuses on teaching language arts as a whole, including written, reading, and oral language skills.

Whole language method Development in areas such as phonics is thought to occur naturally within a wider language context; the teacher teaches specific needed skills through mini-lessons.

References

Abbott, M.W., Walton, C., & Greenwood, C.R. (2002). Phonemic awareness in kindergarten and first grade. *Teaching Exceptional Children, 34*(4), 20–26.

Acrey, C., Johnstone, C., & Milligan, C. (2005). Using universal design to unlock the potential for academic achievement of at-risk learners. *Teaching Exceptional Children, 38*(2), 22–31.

Agnew, C.M., Nystul, B., & Conner, L.A. (1998). Seizure disorders: An alternative explanation for students' inattention. *Professional School Counselor, 2,* 54–59.

Alberta Education. (2006). Individualized program planning. Retrieved from http://education.alberta.ca/admin/special/resources/ipp.aspx.

Alberta Learning. (2004). *Special education definitions 2004/2005.* Edmonton, AB: Author.

Alberta Learning. (2004). *Teaching students with fetal alcohol spectrum disorder: Building strengths, creating hope.* Edmonton, AB: Author.

Algozzine, B., Browder, D., Karvonen, M., Test, D.W., & Wood, W.M. (2001). Effects of interventions to promote self determination for individuals with disabilities. *Review of Educational Research, 71,* 219–277.

Algozzine, R., Serna, L., & Patton, J.R. (2001). *Childhood behavior disorders: Applied research and educational practices* (2nd ed.). Austin, TX: Pro Ed.

Allsopp, D.H., Santos, K. E., & Linn, R. (2000). Collaborating to teach pro-social skills. *Intervention in School and Clinic, 33,* 142–147.

American Academy of Ophthalmology. (1984). Policy statement. *Learning disabilities, dyslexia, and vision.* San Francisco: Author.

American Association on Mental Retardation. (1992). *Mental retardation: Definition, classification, and systems of supports* (9th ed.). Washington, DC: Author.

American Association on Mental Retardation. (2002). *Mental retardation: Definition, classification, and systems of supports* (10th ed.). Washington, DC: Author.

American Humane. (2003). *Protecting children: Child abuse and neglect fact sheets.* Retrieved October 19, 2007, from www.americanhumane.org/site/pageServer?pagename=pc_facts_info.

American Psychiatric Association. (2000). *Diagnostic and statistical manual of mental disorders (DSM-IV-TR)* (4th ed. rev.). Washington, DC: Author.

American Speech-Language-Hearing Association. (n.d.). *Speech and language disorders and diseases.* Retrieved from www.asha.org/public/speech/disorders.

American Speech-Language Hearing Association (ASHA). (2007). Stuttering: Assessment and diagnosis. Retrieved March 28, 2007 from www.asha.org/public/speech/disorders/stutter/AssessDiag.htm.

American Speech-Language-Hearing Association. (1982). Definitions: Communicative disorders and variations. *ASHA, 24,* 949–950.

American Speech-Language-Hearing Association. (1995, March). Position statement: Facilitated communication. *ASHA, 37* (Suppl. 14), 22.

American Speech-Language-Hearing Association. (2002). *Communication facts: Incidence and prevalence of communication disorders and hearing loss in children—2002 edition.* Retrieved June 29, 2002, from http://professional.asha.org/resources/factsheets/children.cfm. Rockville, MD: Author.

American Speech-Language-Hearing Association. (2004a). *Introduction to augmentative and alternative communication.* Retrieved August 2004, from ASHA website: www.asha.org/public/speech/disorders/Augmentative-and-Alternative.htm.

American Speech-Language-Hearing Association. (2004b). *Types of hearing loss.* Retrieved August 2004, from ASHA website: www.asha.org.

American Speech-Language-Hearing Association. (2004c). Technical report: Cochlear implants. *ASHA Supplement, 24,* in press.

American Speech-Language-Hearing Association. (2004d). *Traumatic brain injury.* Retrieved December 2004, from ASHA website: www.asha.org.

American Speech-Language-Hearing Association, Ad Hoc Committee on Service Delivery in Schools. (1993). Definitions of communication disorders and variations. *ASHA, 35* (Suppl. 10), 40–41.

Amerson, M.J. (1999). Helping children with visual and motor impairments make the most of their visual abilities. *Review, 31,* 17–20.

Anthony, S. (1972). *The discovery of death in childhood and after.* New York: Basic Books.

Archer, A., & Gleason, M. (2002). *Skills for school success: Book 5.* North Billerica, MA: Curriculum Associates, Inc.

Archer, A., Gleason, M., & Vachon, V. (2003). Decoding and fluency foundation skills for struggling readers. *Learning Disabilities Quarterly, 26,* 89–101.

Aseltine, R., & DeMartino, R. (2004). An outcome evaluation of the SOS Suicide Prevention program. *American Journal of Public Health, 94,* 446–451.

At-risk youth in crisis: A handbook for collaboration between schools and social services. (1991). Albany, OR: Linn-Benton Education Service Digest.

Austin, J.F. (1992). Involving noncustodial parents in their student's education. *NASSP Bulletin, 76,* 49–54.

Austin, V.L. (2003). Pharmacological interventions for students with ADD. *Intervention in School and Clinic, 38*(5), 289–296.

Autism Society of America. (n.d.) *Defining autism.* Retrieved December 2004, from Autism Society of America website: www.autism-society.org.

Autism Society of Canada. (n.d.). *Research into prevalence.* Retrieved December 7, 2006, from www.autismsocietycanada.ca/asd_research/research_prevalence/index_e.html.

Autism Treatment Services of Canada. (2006, February). *What is autism?* Retrieved December 7, 2006, from www.autism.ca/whataut.htm.

Ayvazoglu, N.R., Oh, H., & Kozub, F. M J. (2006). Explaining physical activity in children with visual impairments: A family systems approach. *Exceptional Children, 72,* 235–248.

Babkie, A.M. (2006). Be proactive in managing classroom behavior. *Intervention in School and Clinic, 41*(3), 184–187.

Babkie, A.M., & Provost, M.C. (2002). Select, write, and use metacognition strategies in the classroom. *Intervention, 37,* 172–175.

Baker, S.B., & Rogosky-Grassi, M.A. (1993). Access to school. In F. L. Rowlley-Kelly & D. H. Reigel (Eds.), *Teaching the students with spina bifida* (pp. 31–70). Baltimore, MD: Brookes.

Baren, M. (2000). *Hyperactivity and attention disorders in children: A guide for parents.* San Ramon, CA: Health Information Network.

Barkley, R.A. (1997). *Defiant children: A clinician's manual for assessment and parent training.* New York: Guildord Press.

Barkley, R.A. (2010). *Attention deficit hyperactivity disorder in adults: The latest assessment and treatment strategies.* Sudbury, MA: Jones and Bartlett Publishers.

Barkley, R.A (2006). *Attention deficit hyperactivity disorder: A handbook for diagnosis and treatment (3rd ed).* New York: Guilford Press.

Barkley, R.A. (1999–2000). *ADHD in children and adolescents.* Fairhope, AL: Institute for Continuing Education.

Barnhill, G.P. (2006). *Right address. . . wrong planet: Children with autism spectrum disorder becoming adults.* Shawnee, KS: Autism Asperger Publishing Co.

Barr, R.D., & Parrett, W.H. (1995). *Hope at last for at-risk youth.* Boston: Allyn and Bacon.

Barr, R.D., & Parrett, W.H. (2001). *Hope fulfilled for at-risk and violent youth: K–12 programs that work* (2nd ed.). Boston: Allyn and Bacon.

Barrish, H.H., Saunders, M., & Wolf, M.M. (1969). Good-behavior game: Effects of individual contingencies for group consequences on disruptive behavior in a classroom. *Journal of Applied Behavior Analysis, 2,* 119–124.

Bau, A.M. (1999). Providing culturally competent services to visually impaired persons. *Journal of Visual Impairment & Blindness, 93,* 291–297.

Beirne-Smith, M. (1989a). A systematic approach for teaching notetaking skills to students with mild learning handicaps. *Academic Therapy, 24,* 425–437.

Beirne-Smith, M. (1989b). Teaching note-taking skills. *Academic Therapy, 24,* 452–458.

Bélanger, J., & Gagné, F. (2006). Estimating the size of the gifted/talented population from multiple identification criteria. *Journal for the Education of the Gifted, 30*(2), 131–281.

Bender, W.N. (1998). *Learning disabilities: Characteristics, identification, and teaching strategies* (3rd ed.). Scarborough, ON: Allyn and Bacon.

Bender, W.N. (2001). *Learning disabilities: Characteristics, identification, and teaching strategies* (4th ed.). Boston: Allyn and Bacon.

Bender, W.N. (2003). *Relational discipline: Strategies for in-your-face kids.* Boston: Allyn and Bacon.

Benner, G.J., Nelson, J.R., & Epstein, M.H. (2002). The language skills of children with emotional and behavioral disorders: A review of the literature. *Journal of Emotional and Behavioral Disorders, 10*(1), 43–59.

Bergland, M., & Hoffbauer, D. (1996). New opportunities for students with traumatic brain injury: Transition to postsecondary education. *Teaching Exceptional Children, 28,* 54–57.

Berry, V. S. (1995). Communication strategies for fully inclusive classrooms. In B. Rittenhouse & J. Dancer (Eds.), *The full inclusion of persons with disabilities in American society* (pp. 57–65). Levin, New Zealand: National Training Resource Centre.

Best, S.J. (2006a). Health impairments and infectious diseases. In S.J. Best, K.W. Heller, & J.L. Bigge (Eds.), *Teaching individuals with physical or multiple disabilities* (5th ed., pp. 59–85). Columbus, OH: Pearson/Merrill.

Best, S.J. (2006b). Physical disabilities. In S.J. Best, K.W. Heller, & J.L. Bigge (Eds.), *Teaching individuals with physical or multiple disabilities* (5th ed., pp. 31–58). Columbus, OH: Pearson/Merrill.

Best, S.J., & Bigge, J.L. (2006). Cerebral palsy. In S.J. Best, K.W. Heller, & J.L. Bigge (Eds.), *Teaching individuals with physical or multiple disabilities* (5th ed., pp. 87–109). Columbus, OH: Pearson/Merrill.

Biklen, D. (1990). Communication unbound: Autism and praxis. *Harvard Educational Review, 60*(3), 291–314.

Blenk, K. (1995). *Making school inclusion work: A guide to everyday practices.* Cambridge, MA: Brookline Books.

Bolt, S.E., & Thurlow, M.L. (2004). Five of the most frequently allowed testing accommodations in state policy: Synthesis of research. *Remedial and Special Education, 25,* 141–152.

Bos, C.S., & Vaughn, S. (2002). *Strategies for teaching students with learning and behavior problems* (5th ed.). Boston: Allyn and Bacon.

Bosman, A.M.T., Gompel, M., Vervloed, M.P.J., & van Bon, W.H.J. (2006). Low vision affects the reading process quantitatively but not qualitatively. *Journal of Special Education, 39*(4), 208–220.

Bowman, B. T. (1994). The challenge of diversity. *Phi Delta Kappan, 76,* 218–224.

Brandes, J.A. (2005). Partner with parents. *Intervention in School and Clinic, 41,* 52–54.

Breeding, M., Stone, C., & Riley, K. (n.d.). *LINC: Language in the classroom.* Unpublished manuscript. Abilene, TX: Abilene Independent School District.

British Columbia Ministry of Education. (2002, August). *Special education services: A manual of policies, procedures, and guidelines.* Retrieved December 2004, from B.C. Ministry of Education website: www.bced.gov.bc.ca.

British Columbia Ministry of Education. (2009). *Individual education planning for students with special needs: A resource guide for teachers.* Retrieved from www.bced.gov.bc.ca/specialed/docs/iepssn.pdf.

British Columbia Ministry of Education, Special Education Branch. (1995). *Special education services: A manual of policies, procedures and guidelines.* Victoria: Author.

Brody, J., & Good, T. (1986). Teacher behavior and student achievement. In M. C. Wittrock (Ed.), *Handbook of research on teaching* (pp. 328–375). New York: Macmillan.

Browder, D., & Snell, M.E. (1988). Assessment of individuals with severe disabilities. In M.E. Snell (Ed.), *Severe disabilities.* Columbus, OH: Merrill.

Brown, J., Cohen, P., Johnson, J.G., & Salzinger, S. (1998). A longitudinal analysis of risk factors for child maltreatment: Findings of a 17-year prospective study of officially recorded and self-reported child abuse and neglect. *Child Abuse & Neglect, 22,* 1065–1078.

Brown, M. R., Higgins, K., & Paulsen, K. (2003). Adolescent alienation: What is it and what can educators do about it? *Intervention in School and Clinic, 39*(1), 3–9.

Broun, L., & Umbarger, G. (2005). *Considerations on the use of medications with people who have autism spectrum disorder.* Position Paper. Division on Developmental Disabilities.

Bryan, T., Burstein, K., & Ergul, C. (2004). The social-emotional side of learning disabilities: A science-based presentation of the art. *Learning Disabilities Quarterly, 27*(1), 45–51.

Buck, G.H., Bursuck, W.D., Polloway, E.A., Nelson, J., Jayanthi, M., & Whitehouse, F.A. (1996). Homework-related communication problems: Perspectives of special educators. *Journal of Emotional and Behavioral Disorders, 4,* 105–113.

Bullock, L. (1992). *Exceptionalities in children and youth.* Boston: Allyn and Bacon.

Burns, B.J., Hoagwood, K., & Maultsby, L.T. (1999). Improving outcomes for children and adolescents with serious emotional and behavioral disorders: Current and future directions. In M.H. Epstein, K. Kutash, & A. Duchnowski (Eds.), *Outcomes for children and youth with behavioral and emotional disorders in their families: Programs and evaluation of best practices* (pp. 685–707). Austin, TX: Pro-Ed.

Buros Institute at the University of Nebraska. (n.d.). Mental measurement yearbook. Retrieved from http://web.ebscohost.com/ehost/search?vid=1&hid=104&sid=4e0b0b05-ad16-4f55-a757-a96b1f734269%40sessionmgr114.

Bursuck, W., Munk, D., & Olson, M. (1999). The fairness of report card grading adaptations: What do students with and without disabilities think? *Remedial and Special Education, 20,* 84–92, 105.

Bursuck, W.D., Polloway, E.A., Plante, L., Epstein, M.H., Jayanthi, M., & McConeghy, J. (1996). Report card grading and adaptations: A national survey of classroom practices. *Exceptional Children, 62,* 301–318.

Canadian Association for Community Living. (n.d.a). *Adult learning, training and employment.* Retrieved April 2005, from CACL website: www.cacl.ca/english/priorityresouces/altemployment/index.html.

Canadian Association for Community Living. (n.d.b). *Some definitions.* Retrieved April 2005, from CACL website: www.cacl.ca/english/aboutus/definitions.html.

Canadian Association of the Deaf (CAD). (2002). *Definition of deaf.* Retrieved August 2004, from CAD website: www.cad.ca.

Canadian Association of Speech-Language Pathologists and Audiologists (CASLPA). (2004). *Fact sheet: SLP's and AUD's—who we are and what we do?* Retrieved August 2004, from CASLPA website: www.caslpa.ca.

Canadian Association of Speech-Language Pathologists and Audiologists (CASLPA). (2005). *Fact sheet: Speech, language and hearing.* Retrieved from www.caslpa.ca.

Canadian National Institute for the Blind. (1999). *National consultation on the crisis in vision loss.* Toronto: Author.

Carbone, E. (2001). Arranging the classroom with an eye (and ear) to students with ADHD. *Teaching Exceptional Children, 34,* 72–81.

Carpenter, S.L., & McKee-Higgins, E. (1996). Behavior management in inclusive classrooms. *Remedial and Special Education, 17,* 195–203.

Carr, E.G., Dozier, C.L., & Patel, M.R. (2002). Treatment of automatic resistance to extinction. *Research in Developmental Disabilities, 23,* 61–78.

Cassidy, V.M., & Stanton, J.E. (1959). An investigation of factors involved in the education placement of mentally retarded children: A study of differences between children in regular and special classes in Ohio. Columbus, OH: Ohio State University. (ERIC Document Reproduction Service No. ED 002752).

Cavkaytar, A. & Pollard, E. (2009). Effectiveness of parent and therapist collaboration program (PTCP) for teaching self-care and domestic skills to individuals with autism. *Education and Traning in Developmental Disabilities, 44*(3), 381-395.

Cawley, J. (1984). *Developmental teaching of mathematics for the learning disabled.* Austin, TX: Pro-Ed.

Cawley, J., & Foley, J.F. (2001). Enhancing the quality of math for students with learning disabilities. *Learning Disabilities: A Multidisciplinary Journal, 11,* 47–59.

Chalfant, J.C., & Van Dusen Pysh, R.L. (1993). Teacher assistance teams: Implications for the gifted. In C.J. Maker (Ed.), *Critical issues in gifted education: Vol 3. Programs for the gifted in regular classrooms* (pp. 32–48). Austin, TX: Pro-Ed.

Chalmers, L. (1991). Classroom modifications for the mainstreamed student with mild handicaps. *Intervention in School and Clinic, 27*(1), 40–42, 51.

Chamberlain, S.P. (2005). Recognizing and responding to cultural differences in the education of culturally and linguistically diverse learners. *Intervention in School and Clinic, 40*(4), 195–211.

Chamberlain, S.P. (2006). An interview with Don Deshler: Perspectives on teaching students with learning disabilities. *Intervention in School and Clinic, 41*(5), 302–306.

Chan, A.S., Cheung, J., Leung, W.W., Cheung, R., & Chueng, M. (2005). Verbal expression and comprehension deficits in young children with autism. *Focus on Autism and Other Developmental Disabilities, 20*(2), 117–124.

Chase, P.A., Hall, J.W., & Werkhaven, J.A. (1996). Sensorineural hearing loss in children: Etiology and pathology. In F.N. Martin & J.G. Clark (Eds.), *Hearing care for children* (pp. 73–88). Boston: Allyn and Bacon.

Cheney, C.O. (1989). The systematic adaptation of instructional materials and techniques for problem learners. *Academic Therapy, 25,* 25–30.

Choudhury, N., & Benasich, A.A. (2003). A family aggregation study: the influence of family history and other risk factors on language development. *Journal of Speech Language, Hearing Research, 46*(2), 261–272.

Christenson, S.L., Ysseldyke, J.E., & Thurlow, M.L. (1989). Critical instructional factors for students with mild handicaps: An integrative review. *Remedial and Special Education, 10*(5), 21–31.

Chudley, A.E., Conry, J., Cook, J.L., Loock, C., Rosales, T., & LeBlanc, N. (2005). Fetal alcohol spectrum disorder: Canadian guidelines for diagnosis. *Canadian Medical Association Journal, 172* (5 suppl), S1–S21.

Clark, B. (1996). The need for a range of program options for gifted and talented students. In W. Stainback & S. Stainback (Eds.), *Contoversial issues confronting special education: Divergent perspectives* (2nd ed., pp. 57–68). Boston: Allyn and Bacon.

Clark, B. (2002). *Growing up gifted: Developing the potential of children at home and at school* (6th ed.). Upper Saddle River, NJ: Merrill/Prentice-Hall.

Clark, J.G., & Jaindl, M. (1996). Conductive hearing loss in children: Etiology and pathology. In F. N. Martin & J. G. Clark (Eds.), *Hearing care for children* (pp. 45–72). Boston: Allyn and Bacon.

Clarkson, W.P. (2003). Beautiful minds. *American School Board Journal, 190*(8), 24–28.

Clary, D.L., & Edwards, S. (1992). Spoken language. In E. A. Polloway, J. R. Patton, J. S. Payne, & R. A. Payne (Eds.), *Strategies for teaching learners with special needs* (4th ed., pp. 185–285). Columbus, OH: Merrill.

Clinkenbeard, P.R. (1991). Unfair expectations: A pilot study of middle school students' comparisons of gifted and regular classes. *Journal for the Education of the Gifted, 15,* 56–63.

Colangelo, N., & Davis, G.A. (Eds.). (2003). *Handbook of gifted education* (3rd ed.). Boston: Allyn and Bacon.

Coleman, L.J., & Cross, T.L. (2001). *Being gifted in school: An introduction to developing, guidance, and teaching.* Austin, TX: Pro-Ed.

Coleman, M.C., & Webber, J. (2002). Emotional and behavioral disorders: Theory and practice (4th ed.). Boston: Allyn and Bacon.

The Condition of Education. (1998). Washington, DC: Office of Educational Research and Improvement.

Connor, D. (2006). Stimulants. In R. Barkley (Ed.), *A handbook for diagnosis and treatment (3rd ed.)* (pp. 658-677). New York: Guildford.

Conroy, J. (1993). Classroom management: An expected view. In C.J. Maker (Ed.), *Critical issues in gifted education: Vol. 3. Programs for the gifted in regular classrooms* (pp. 227–257). Austin, TX: Pro-Ed.

Conte, R. (1991). Attention disorders. In B.Y.L. Wong (Ed.), *Learning about learning disabilities* (pp. 55–101). New York: Academic Press.

Cooper, H. (1989). *Homework.* White Plains, NY: Longman.

Copeland, S.R., Hughes, C., Carter, E.W., Guth, C., Presley, J.A., Williams, C.R., & Fowler, S.E. (2004). Increasing access to general education: Perspectives of participants in a high school peer support program. *Remedial and Special Education, 25*(6), 341–351.

Corn, A.L., Hatlen, P., Huebner, K.M., Ryan, F., & Siller, M.A. (1995). *The national agenda for the education of children and youths with visual impairments, including those with multiple disabilities.* New York: American Foundation for the Blind.

Cosden, M.A. (1990). Expanding the role of special education. *Teaching Exceptional Children, 22,* 4–6.

Council for Children with Behavioral Disorders. (2000, October). *Draft position paper on terminology and definition of emotional or behavioral disorders.* Reston, VA: Author. (A Division of the Council for Exceptional Children, 1920 Association Drive, Reston, VA. p. 2).

Council for Exceptional Children. (n.d.). Policy and advocacy: Testing. Retrieved from www.cec.sped.org/AM/Template.cfm?Section=Other_Policy_Resources&Template=/CM/ContentDisplay.cfm&ContentID=2521.

Council for Exceptional Children. (1997). Effective accommodations for students with exceptionalities. *CEC Today, 4*(3), 1, 9, 15.

Council for Exceptional Children. (1999). The hidden problem among students with exceptionalities—depression. *CEC Today, 5*(5), 1, 5, 15.

Craig, S., Hull, K., Haggart, A.G., & Crowder, E. (2001). Storytelling addressing the literacy needs of diverse learners. *Teaching Exceptional Children, 33*(5), 46–51.

Crane, L. (2002). Mental retardation: A community integration approach. Belmont, CA: Thomson Publishing.

Cross, T.L. (2005). Moving the discussion from pathology to context: An interview with Laurence J. Coleman. *Roeper Review, 28*(1), 5.

Cullinan, D., & Sabornie, E.J. (2004). Characteristics of emotional disturbance in middle and high school students. *Journal of Emotional and Behavioral Disorders, 12*(3), 157–167.

Cummings, C. (1983). *Managing to teach.* Edmonds, WA: Teaching Inc.

Cunningham, A.E., & Stanovich, K.E. (1997). Early reading acquisition and its relationship to reading ability ten years later. *Developmental Psychology, 33*, 934–945.

Dabkowski, D.M. (2004). Encouraging active parent participation in IEP team meetings. *Teaching Exceptional Children, 36*, 34–39.

Dagenais, P.A., Critz-Crosby, P., Fletcher, S.G., & McCutcheon, M.J. (1994). Comparing abilities of children with profound hearing impairments to learn consonants using electropalatography or traditional aural–oral techniques. *Journal of Speech and Hearing Research, 37*, 687–699.

Davies, P.W.S., & Joughin, C. (1993). Using stable isotopes to assess reduced physical activity of individuals with Prader-Willi syndrome. *American Journal on Mental Retardation, 98*, 349–353.

Davis, G.A., & Rimm, S.B. (1998). *Education of the gifted and talented* (4th ed.). Boston: Allyn and Bacon.

Davis, J. (1996). Two different flight plans: Advanced placement and gifted programs—different and necessary. *Gifted Child Today, 19*(2), 32–36, 50.

Davis, W.E. (1993). *At-risk children and educational reform: Implications for educators and schools in the year 2000 and beyond.* Orono, ME: College of Education, University of Maine.

Davis, W.E. (1995). Students at risk: Common myths and misconceptions. *The Journal of At-Risk Issues, 2*, 5–10.

Deiner, P.L. (1993). *Resources for teaching children with diverse abilities: Birth through eight.* Fort Worth, TX: Harcourt Brace Jovanovich.

Del Prete, T. (1996). Asset or albatross? The education and socialization of gifted students. *Gifted Child Today, 19*(2), 24–25, 44–49.

Deno, S.L., & Fuchs, L.S. (1987). Developing curriculum-based measurement systems for data-based special education problem-solving. *Focus on Exceptional Children, 19*(8), 1–16.

Desrochers, J. (1999). Vision problems—How teachers can help. *Young Children, 54*, 36–38.

Devlin, S.D., & Harber, M.M. (2004). Collaboration among parents and professionals with discrete trial training in the treatment for autism. *Education and Training in Developmental Disabilities, 39*, 291–300.

Dorn, L., & Allen, A. (1995). Helping low-achieving first-grade readers: A program combining reading recovery tutoring and small-group instruction. *Journal of School Research and Information, 13*, 16–24.

Dowdy, C. (1990). *Modifications for regular classes.* Unpublished manuscript, Alabama Program for Exceptional Children.

Dowdy, C.A., Patton, J.R., Smith, T.E.C., & Polloway, E.A. (1997). *Attention-deficit/hyperactivity disorder: A practical guide for teachers.* Austin, TX: Pro-Ed.

Dowdy, C.A., Patton, J.R., Smith, T.E.C., & Polloway, E. A. (1998). *Attention deficit/hyperactivity disorders in the classroom.* Austin, TX: Pro-Ed.

Downing, J.A. (2002). Individualized behavior contracts. *Intervention, 37*, 164–172.

Downing, J.E., & Chen, D. (2003). Using tactile strategies with students who are blind and have severe disabilities. *Teaching Exceptional Children, 36*, 56–61.

Doyle, W. (1986). Classroom organization and management. In M.C. Wittrock (Ed.), *Handbook of research and teaching* (3rd ed., pp. 392–431). New York: Macmillan.

Drasgow, E., Yell, M.L., & Robinson, T. (2001). Developing legally correct and educationally appropriate IEPs. *Remedial and Special Education, 22*, 359–373.

Dunn, L.M. (1968). Special education for the mildly handicapped: Is much of it justifiable? *Exceptional Children, 35*, 5–22.

Dworet, D., & Bennett, S. (2002). A view from the North. *Teaching Exceptional Children, 34*(5), 22-27.

Dworet, D.H., & Rathgeber, A.J. (1998). Confusion reigns: Definitions of behaviour exceptionalities in Canada. *Exceptionality Education Canada, 8*(1), 3–19.

Dyches, T. (1998). The effectiveness of switch training on communication of children with autism and severe disabilities. *Focus on Autism and Other Developmental Disabilities, 13*, 151–162.

Easterbrooks, S.R. (1999). *Adapting regular classrooms for children who are deaf/hard of hearing.* Paper presented to the Council for Exceptional Children convention, Minneapolis, MN.

Eaves, R.C. (1992). Autism. In P.J. McLaughlin and P. Wehman (Eds.), *Developmental disabilities* (pp. 68–80). Boston: Andover Medical Publishers.

Edwards, C. (1996). Educational management of children with hearing loss. In F.N. Martin & J.G. Clark (Eds.), *Hearing care for children* (pp. 303–315). Boston: Allyn and Bacon.

Egel, A.L. (1989). Finding the right educational program. In M.D. Powers (Ed.), *Children with autism: A parent's guide.* New York: Woodbine House.

Ehlers, V.L., & Ruffin, M. (1990). The Missouri project—Parents as teachers. *Focus on Exceptional Children, 23,* 1–14.

Elders, J. (2002). Keynote address. 57th Annual Conference of the Association for Supervision and Curriculum Development, San Antonio, TX.

Elizer, E., & Kauffman, M. (1983). Factors influencing the severity of childhood bereavement reactions. *American Journal of Orthopsychiatry, 53,* 393–415.

Elksnin, L.K., Bryant, D.P., Gartland, D., King-Sears, M., Rosenberg, M.S., Scanlon, D., Strosnider, R., & Wilson, R. (2001). LD summit: Important issues for the field of learning disabilities. *Learning Disability Quarterly, 24,* 297–305.

Ellenwood, A.E., & Felt, D. (1989). Attention-deficit/hyperactivity disorder: Management and intervention approaches for the classroom teacher. *LD Forum, 15,* 15–17.

Emery, R.E. (1989). Family violence. *American Psychologist, 44,* 321–327.

Engelmann, S., & Carnine, D. (1982). *Theory of instruction.* New York: Irvington.

Epstein, M.H. (1999). The development and the validation of a scale to assess the emotional and behavioral strengths of children—adolescents. *Remedial and Special Education, 20,* 258–262.

Epstein, M.H., & Charma, J. (1998). *Behavioral and emotional rating scale: A strength-based approach to assessment.* Austin, TX: Pro-Ed.

Epstein, M.H., Polloway, E.A., Bursuck, W., Jayanthi, M., & McConeghy, J. (1996). Recommendations for effective homework practices. Manuscript in preparation.

Erickson, J.G. (1992, April). *Communication disorders in multicultural populations.* Paper presented at the Texas Speech-Language-Hearing Association Annual Convention, San Antonio, TX.

Etscheidt, S.K. (2006). Progress monitoring: Legal issues and recommendations for IEP teams. *Teaching Exceptional Children, 38,* 56–60.

Etscheidt, S.K., & Bartlett, L. (1999). The IDEA amendments: A four-step approach for determining supplementary aids and services. *Exceptional Children, 65,* 163–174.

Evertson, C.M., Emmer, E.T., & Worsham, M.E. (2006). *Classroom management for elementary teachers* (7th ed.). Boston: Allyn and Bacon.

Faraone, S.V., & Doyle, A.E. (2001). The nature and heritability of attention-deficit/hyperactivity disorder. *Child and Adolescent Psychiatric Clinics of North America, 10,* 299–316.

Favazza, P.C., Phillipsen, L., & Kumar, P. (2000). Measuring and promoting acceptance of young children with disabilities. *Exceptional Children, 66,* 491–508.

Federico, M.A., Herrold, W.G. Jr., & Venn, J. (1999). Helpful tips for successful inclusion. *Teaching Exceptional Children, 32*(1), 76–82.

Feldhusen, H.J. (1993a). Individualized teaching of the gifted in regular classrooms. In C.J. Maker (Ed.), *Critical issues in gifted education: Vol. 3. Programs for the gifted in regular classrooms* (pp. 263–273). Austin, TX: Pro-Ed.

Feldhusen, H.J. (1993b). Synthesis of research on gifted youth. *Educational Leadership, 22,* 6–11.

Feldhusen, J.F. (1998). Programs for the gifted few or talent development for the many. *Phi Delta Kappan, 79*(10), 735–738.

Felner, R., Ginter, M., Boike, M., & Cowan, E. (1981). Parental death or divorce and the school adjustment of young children. *American Journal of Community Psychology, 9,* 181–191.

Feng, Y., Crosbie, J., Wigg, K., Pathare, T., Ickowicz, A., Schachar, R., Tannock, R., Roberts, W., Malone. M., Swanson, J., Kennedy, J.L., & Barr, C.L. (2005). The SNAP25 gene as a susceptibility gene contributing to attention-deficit hyperactivity disorder. *Molecular Psychiatry, 10,* 998–1005.

Ferguson, D.L. (1995). The real challenge of inclusion: Confessions of a "rabid inclusionist." *Phi Delta Kappan, 77,* 281–287.

Fiore, T.A., Becker, E.A., & Nerro, R.C. (1993). Educational interventions for students with attention deficit disorder. *Exceptional Children, 60,* 163–173.

Flexer, C. (1999). *Facilitating hearing and listening in young children* (2nd ed.). San Diego, CA: Singular Publishing.

Flick, G.L. (1998). Managing AD/HD in the classroom minus medication. *Education Digest, 63*(9), 50–56.

Fombonne, E. (2003a). Modern views of autism. *Canadian Journal of Psychiatry, 48*(8), 503–505.

Fombonne, E. (2003b). Epidemiology of autism and other pervasive developmental disorders: An update. *Journal of Autism Developmental Disorders, 33,* 365–381.

Fombonne, E. (2005). Epidemiology of autistic disorder and other pervasive developmental disorders. *Journal of Clinical Psychiatry, 66,* 3–8.

Fombonne, E., Zakarian, R., Bennett, A., Meng, L., & McLean-Haywood, D. (2006). Pervasive developmental disorders in Montreal, Quebec, Canada: Prevalence and links with immunization. *Pediatrics, 118*(1), 139–150.

Foorman, B.R., & Torgesen, J. (2001). Critical elements of classroom and small group instruction promoting reading success in all children. *Research and Practice, 16,* 203–212.

Forness, S.R. (1999). Stimulant medication revisited: Effective treatment of children with attention deficit disorder. *Journal of Emotional and Behavior Problems, 7,* 230–233.

Forness, S.R., & Kavale, K.A. (1988). Planning for the needs of children with serious emotional disturbance: The National Mental Health and Special Education Coalition. *Behavior Disorders, 13*, 127–133.

Forness, S.R., Walker, H.M., & Kavale, K.A. (2003). Psychiatric disorders and treatments. *Teaching Exceptional Children, 36*(2), 42–49.

Foster-Johnson, L., & Dunlap, G. (1993). Using functional assessment to develop effective, individualized interventions for challenging behaviors. *Teaching Exceptional Children, 56*, 44–52.

Fowler, M. (1992). *C.H.A.D.D. educators manual: An in-depth look at attention deficit disorder for an educational perspective.* Fairfax, VA: CASET Associates, Ltd.

Fox, P., & Emerson, E. (2001). Socially valid outcomes of intervention for people with MR and challenging behavior: Views of different stakeholders. *Journal of Positive Behavior Interventions, 3*(3), 183–189.

Fraenkel, J.R., & Wallen, N.E. (2000). *How to design & evaluate research in education* (4th ed.). Toronto, ON: McGraw-Hill.

Friedman, D., & Scaduto, J.J. (1995). Let's do lunch. *Teaching Exceptional Children, 28*, 22–26.

Friend, M., Bursuck, W., & Hutchinson, N. (1998). *Including exceptional students: A practical guide for classroom teachers.* Scarborough, ON: Allyn and Bacon.

Friend, M.F., & Bursuck, W.D. (2002). *Including students with special needs: A practical guide for classroom teachers* (3rd ed.) Boston: Allyn and Bacon.

Friend, M., & Cook, L. (2009). *Interactions: Collaboration skills for school professionals.* Upper Saddle River, NJ: Prentice Hall.

Fritzell, B. (1996). Voice disorders and occupations. *Logopedics, Phoniatrics, and Vocology, 21*, 7–12.

Fuchs, D. (2003). Assessing responsiveness to intervention: Conceptual and technical issues. *Learning Disabilities Research & Practice, 18*, 172–186.;

Fuchs, D., & Fuchs, L.S. (1994–1995). Sometimes separate is better. *Educational Leadership, 52*, 22–24.

Fuchs, L.S., & Fuchs, D. (2001). Helping teachers formulate sound test accommodation decisions for students with learning disabilities. *Learning Disability Research and Practice, 16*(3), 174–181.

Fuchs, D., Fuchs, L.S., McMaster, K.L., Yen, L., & Svenson, E. (2004). Nonresponders: How to find them? How to help them? What do they mean for special education? *Teaching Exceptional Children, 37*, 72–77.

Fuchs, D., Mock, D., Morgan, P.L., & Young, C.L. (2003). Responsiveness-to-intervention: Definitions, evidence, and implications for the learning disabilities construct. *Learning Disabilities Research and Practice, 18*(3), 157–171.

Furner, J.M., Yahya, N., & Duffy, M.A. (2005). Teach mathematics: Strategies to reach all students. *Intervention in School and Clinic, 41*(1), 16–23.

Gable, R.A., Arllen, N.L., & Hendrickson, J.M. (1994). Use of students with emotional/behavioural disorders as behavior change agents. *Education and Treatment of Children, 17*, 267–276.

Gallagher, J.J., & Gallagher, S.A. (1994). *Teaching the gifted child* (4th ed.). Boston: Allyn and Bacon.

Garcia, S.B., & Guerra, P.L. (2004). Deconstructing deficit thinking: Working with educators to create more equitable learning environments. *Education and Urban Society, 36*(2), 150–168.

Garcia, J.G., Krankowski, T.K., & Jones, L.L. (1998). Collaboration intervention for assisting students with acquired brain injury. *Professional School Counselor, 2*, 33–38.

Gardner, H. (1983). *Frames of mind: The theory of multiple intelligences.* New York: Basic Books.

Gardner, H., & Hatch, T. (1989). Multiple intelligences go to school: Educational implications of the theory of multiple intelligences. *Educational Researcher, 18*(8), 4–9.

Gargiulo, R.M. (1990). Child abuse and neglect: An overview. In R.L. Goldman & R.M. Gargiulo (Eds.), *Children at risk* (pp. 1–35). Austin, TX: Pro-Ed.

Garrick Duhaney, L.M. (2000). Culturally sensitive strategies for violence prevention. *Multicultural Education, 7*(4), 10–17.

Gartin, B.C., & Murdick, N.L. (2005). IDEA 2004: The IEP. *Remedial and Special Education, 26*(6), 327–331.

Gartland, D. (1994). Content area reading: Lessons from the specialists. *LD Forum, 19*(3), 19–22.

Gay, I. (2003). The teacher makes it more explainable. *Reading Teacher, 56*(8), 812–814.

Gay, Lesbian, and Straight Education Network (GLSEN). (2005). *GLSEN's national school climate survey.* Washington, DC: Author.

Geneva Centre for Autism. (2004). *Fact sheet—autism.* Retrieved December 2004, from Geneva Centre website: www.autism.net.

Gersh, E.S. (1991). What is cerebral palsy? In E. Geralis (Ed.), *Children with cerebral palsy: A parents' guide.* New York: Woodbine House.

Gersten, R., Jordan, N.C., & Flojo, J.R. (2005). Early identification and intervention for students with math difficulties. *Journal of Learning Disabilities, 38*(4), 293–304.

Getch, Y.Q., & Neuhart-Pritchett, S. (1999). Children with asthma: Strategies for educators. *Teaching Exceptional Children, 31*, 30–36.

Gibb, G.S., & Dyches, T.T. (2000). *Guide to writing quality individualized educational programs.* Boston: Allyn and Bacon.

Giangreco, M.F., Edelman, S.W., Broer, S.M., & Doyle, M.B. (2001). Paraprofessional support of students with disabilities: Literature from the past decade. *Exceptional Children, 68*, 45–63.

Goin, R.P., & Myers, B.J. (2004). Characteristics of infantile autism: Moving toward earlier detection. *Focus on Autism & Other Developmental Disabilities, 19*(1), 5–12.

Gomez, C.R., & Baird, S. (2005). Identifying early indicators for autism in self-regulated difficulties. *Journal of Autism and Other Developmental Disabilities, 20*(2), 106–116.

Goree, K. (1996). Making the most out of inclusive setting. *Gifted Child Today, 19*(2), 22–23, 43.

Government of Canada. (2009). *The chief public health officer's report on the state of public health in Canada 2009: Growing up well—priorities for a healthy future.* Ottawa, ON: Author. Retrieved from http://public health.gc.ca/CPHOreport.

Government of Newfoundland and Labrador. (2003). *Teaching students with autism spectrum disorders.* St. John's, NL: Author.

Graham, S. (1992). Helping students with LD progress as writers. *Intervention in School and Clinic, 27*, 134–144.

Graham, S., Harris, K.R., & MacArthur, C. (2006) Cognitive strategy instruction. In C. MacArthur, S. Graham, & J. Ditgerald (Eds.), *Handbook for writing research* (pp. 187–207). New York: Guildford.

Grant, J. (1993). Hearing-impaired children from Mexican-American homes. *Volta Review, 95*(5), 212–218.

Greenbaum, P.E., Dedrick, R.F., Friedman, R.M., Kutash, K., Brown, E.C., Lardieri, S.P., & Pugh, A.M. (1998). National adolescent and child treatment study (NACTS): Outcomes for children with serious emotional behavioral disturbance. In M.H. Epstein, K. Kutash, & A. Duchnowski (Eds.), *Outcomes for children and youth with emotional and behavioral disorders and their families: Programs and evaluation of best practices* (pp. 21–54). Austin, TX: Pro-Ed.

Greer, J.V. (1991). At-risk students in the fast lanes: Let them through. *Exceptional Children, 57*, 390–391.

Gregory, R.J. (2004). Psychological testing: History, principles, and applications (4th ed.). Boston: Pearson.

Grosenick, J.K., George, N.L., George, M.P., & Lewis, T.J. (1991). Public school services for behaviorally disordered students: Program practices in the 1980s. *Behavioral Disorders, 16*, 87–96.

Grossman, H.J. (1983). *Classification in mental retardation.* Washington, DC: American Association on Mental Deficiency.

Guterman, B.R. (1995). The validity of categorical learning disabilities services: The consumer's view. *Exceptional Children, 62*, 111–124.

Guyer, B. (2000). Reaching and teaching the adolescent. In B. D. Guyer (Ed.), *ADHD: Achieving success in school and in life.* Boston: Allyn and Bacon.

Hall, B.J., Oyer, H.J., & Haas, H.J. (2001). Speech, language, and hearing disorders: A guide for the teacher (3rd ed.). Boston: Allyn and Bacon.

Hall, T.E., Wolfe, P.S., & Bollig, A.A. (2003). The home-to-school notebook: An effective communication strategy for students with severe disabilities. *Teaching Exceptional Children, 36*, 68–73.

Hallahan, D.P., & Kauffman, J.M. (1991). *Exceptional children: Introduction to special education* (5th ed.). Boston: Allyn and Bacon.

Hallahan, D.P., & Kauffman, J.M. (1995). *The illusion of full inclusion.* Austin, TX: Pro-Ed.

Hallahan, D.P., & Kauffman, J.M. (1997). *Exceptional learners: Introduction to special education* (7th ed.). Boston: Allyn and Bacon.

Hallahan, D.P., & Kauffman, J.M. (2000). *Exceptional children: Introduction to special education* (8th ed.). Boston: Allyn and Bacon.

Hallahan, D.P., & Kauffman, J.M. (2006). *Exceptional children: Introduction to special education* (10th ed.). Boston: Allyn and Bacon.

Hallahan, D.P., Lloyd, J.W., Kauffman, J.M., Weiss, M.P., & Martinez, E.A. (2005). *Learning disabilities: Foundations, characteristics, and effective teaching* (3rd ed.). Boston: Allyn and Bacon.

Hallahan, D.P., Lloyd, J.W., & Stoller, L. (1982). *Improving attention with self-monitoring: A manual for teachers.* Charlottesville, VA: University of Virginia Press.

Halvorsen, A.T., & Neary, T. (2001). *Building inclusive schools: Tools and strategies for success.* Boston: Allyn and Bacon.

Hammerness, P.G. (2009). *Biographies of disease: ADHD.* Westport, CT: Greenwood Press.

Hammill, D. (2004). What we know about correlates of reading. *Exceptional Children, 70*(4), 453–468.

Hammill, D.D., & Larsen, S.C. (1974). The effectiveness of psycholinguistic training. *Exceptional Children, 41*, 5–14.

Hansen, C.R. (1992). What is Tourette syndrome? In T. Haerle (Ed.), *Children with Tourette syndrome: A parents' guide* (pp. 1–25). Rockville, MD: Woodbine House.

Hardman, M.L., Drew, C.J., Egan, M.W., & Wolf, B. (1993). *Human exceptionality: Society, school, and family* (4th ed.). Boston: Allyn and Bacon.

Harniss, M.K., & Epstein, M.H. (2005). Strength-based assessment in children's mental health. In M.H. Epstein, K. Kutash, & A.J. Duchnowski (Eds.), *Outcomes for children and youth with emotional and behavioral disorders and their families* (2nd ed., pp. 125–141). Austin, TX: Pro-Ed.

Harwell, J.M. (1989). *Learning disabilities handbook.* West Nyack, NY: Center for Applied Research in Education.

Haynes, W.O., & Pindzola, R.H. (1998). *Diagnosis and evaluation in speech pathology* (5th ed). Engelwood Cliffs, NJ: Prentice Hall.

Hazel, J.S., Schumaker, J.B., Shelon, J., & Sherman, J.A. (1982). Application of a group training program in social skills to learning disabled and non-learning disabled youth. *Learning Disability Quarterly, 5*, 398–408.

Health Canada. (2006). Fetal alcohol spectrum disorder. Ottawa, ON: Author. Retrieved December 7, 2006, from www.hc-sc. gc.ca/iyh-vsv/alt_formats/cmcd-dcmc/pdf/ fasd-etcaf_e.pdf.

Heath, N.L., & McLean-Heywood, D. (1999). Research highlights: A clinic school partnership program for including students with behavioral problems. In J. Andrews & J. Lupart (Eds.), *The inclusive classroom, instructor's manual*. Toronto: ITP Nelson.

Heflin, L.J., & Simpson, R. (1998). The interventions for children and youth with autism: Prudent choices in a world of extraordinary claims and promises: Part II. *Focus on Autism and Other Developmental Disabilities, 13*, 212–220.

Heiligenstein, E., Conyers, L.M., Berns, A.R., & Miller, M.A. (1998). Preliminary normative data on DSM-IV attention deficit hyperactivity disorder in college students. *Journal of American College Health, 46*(4), 185–188.

Heinrich, S.R. (1999). Visually impaired students can use the internet. *NASSP Bulletin, 83*, 26–29.

Heller, K.A., et al. (Eds.). (2000). *International handbook of giftedness and talent* (2nd ed., pp. 695–702). Kidlington, Oxford: Elsevier Science.

Heller, K.W., Alberto, P.A., Forney, P.E., & Schwartzman, M.N. (1996). *Understanding physical, sensory, and health impairments*. Pacific Grove, CA: Brooks Publishing Co.

Heward, W.L. (2003). *Exceptional children: An introduction to special education* (7th ed.). Upper Saddle, NJ: Merrill.

Hietsch, D.G. (1986). Father involvement: No moms allowed. *Teaching Exceptional Children, 18*, 258–260.

Hill, D. (1991). Tasting failure: Thoughts of an at-risk learner. *Phi Delta Kappan, 73*, 308–310.

Hiller, J.F. (1990). Setting up a classroom-based language instruction program: One clinician's experience. *Texas Journal of Audiology and Speech Pathology, 16*(2), 12–13.

Hilton, A. (1990). Parental reactions to having a disabled child. Paper presented at annual International Conference of the Council for Exceptional Children.

Hobbs, T., & Westling, D.L. (1998). Promoting successful inclusion. *Teaching Exceptional Children, 34*, 10–14.

Hoida, J.A., & McDougal, S.E. (1998). Fostering a positive school environment for students with cancer. *NASSP Bulletin, 82*, 59–72.

Holcomb, D., Lira, J., Kingery, P.M., Smith, D.W., Lane, D., & Goodway, J. (1998). Evaluation of jump into action: A program to reduce the risk of non–insulin-dependent diabetes mellitus in school children on the Texas–Mexico border. *Journal of School Health, 68*, 282–287.

Homme, L. (1969). *How to use contingency contracting in the classroom*. Champaign, IL: Research Press.

Hooper, C.R. (2004). Treatment of voice disorders in children. *Language, Speech, and Hearing Services in Schools, 35*, 320–326. Hoover, J.J., & Patton, J.R. (2005). Curriculum

adaptations for students with learning and behavior problems. Austin, TX: PRO.ED.

Hoover, J.J., & Patton, J.R. (2008). The role of special educators in a multitiered instructional system. Intervention in School and Clinic, 43, 195-202. Hoover, J.J. (1990). Curriculum adaptations: A five-step process for classroom implementation. *Academic Therapy, 25*, 407–416.

Horner, R.H. (2000). Positive behavior supports. In M.L. Wehmeyer & J.R. Patton (Eds.), *Mental retardation in the 21st century* (pp. 181–196). Austin, TX: Pro-Ed.

Hou, F., Milan, A., & Wong, I. (2006). Learning disabilities and child altruism, anxiety, and aggression. *Canadian Social Trends, 81*, 16-22. Retrieved January 2008 from www.statcan.ca/english/freepub/11-008-XIE/2006001/PDF/disabilities_81.pdf.

Howell, R.W., Evans, C.T., & Gardiner, R.W. (1997). Medication in the classroom: A hard pill to swallow? *Teaching Exceptional Children, 29*, 58–61.

Hoy, C., & Gregg, N. (1994). *Assessment: The special educator's role*. Pacific Grove, CA: Brooks/Cole.

Huff, C.R. (1999). *Comparison of criminal behaviors of youth gangs and at-risk youth*. Washington, DC: Department of Justice National Institute of Justice.

Hughes, C., Copeland, S.R., Guth, C., Rung, L.L., Hwang, B., Kleeb, G., & Strong, M. (2001). General education students' perspectives on their involvement in a high school peer buddy program. *Education and Training in Mental Retardation and Developmental Disabilities, 36*, 343–355.

Hume, K., Bellini, L., & Pratt, R. (2005). The usage and perceived outcomes of early intervention and early childhood programs for young children with autism. *Topics in Early Childhood Education, 25*(4), 195–207.

Hunt, P., Doering, K., & Hirose-Hatae, A. (2001). Across-program collaboration to support students with and without disabilities in general education classrooms. *Journal of the Association for Persons with Severe Handicaps, 26*, 240–256.

Hunt, P., Hirose-Hatae, A., & Doering, K. (2000). "Communication" is what I think everyone is talking about. *Remedial and Special Education, 21*, 305–317.

Hutton, A.M., & Caron, S.L. (2005). Experiences of families with children with autism in rural New England. *Focus on Autism and Other Developmental Disabilities, 20*, 180–189.

Huure, T.M., Komulainen, E.J., & Aro, H.M. (1999). Social support and self-esteem among adolescents with visual impairments. *Journal of Visual Impairment & Blindness, 93*, 326–337.

Hux, K., & Hackley, C. (1996). Mild traumatic brain injury. *Intervention in School and Clinic, 31*, 158–165.

Individuals with Disabilities Education Act. (2004). Washington, DC: U.S. Government Printing Office.

Idol, L. (1983). *Special educator's consultation handbook*. Austin, TX: Pro-Ed.

International Dyslexia Association (IDA). (2002). *What is dyslexia?* Author: www.interdys.org.

Iovannone, R., Dunlap, G., Huber, H., & Kincaid, D. (2003). Educational practices for students with autism spectrum disorders. *Focus on Autism & Other Developmental Disabilities, 18*(3), 150–165.

Iskowitz, M. (1998). Psychosocial issues. *ADVANCE for Speech-Language Pathologists and Audiologists, 36,* 14–15.

Jaquish, C., & Stella, M.A. (1986). Helping special students move from elementary to secondary school. *Counterpoint, 7*(1), 1.

Jayanthi, M., Nelson, J.S., Sawyer, V., Bursuck, W.D., & Epstein, M.H. (1995). Homework-communication problems among parents, general education, and special education teachers: An exploratory study. *Remedial and Special Education, 16*(2), 102–116.

Jenkins, J., & O'Connor, R. (2001). *Early identification and intervention for young children with reading/learning disabilities.* Paper presented at the 2001 LD Summit: Building a Foundation for the Future. Available online from http://www.air.org/ldsummit.

Jenkins, J.R., & Heinen, A. (1989). Students' preferences for service delivery: Pull-out, in-class, or integrated models. *Exceptional Children, 55,* 516–523.

Jerger, J., & Musiek, F. (2000). Report of the consensus conference on the diagnosis of auditory processing disorders in school-aged children. *Journal of the American Academy of Audiology, 11*(9), 467–474.

Jessiman, S.M. (2003). Speech and language services using telehealth technology in remote and underserviced areas. *Journal of Speech-Language Pathology and Audiology, 27*(1), 45–51.

Johnson, A. (2001). How to use thinking skills to differentiate curricula for gifted and highly creative students. *Gifted Child Today, 24*(4), 58–63.

Johnson, D.J. (1999). The language of instruction. *Learning Disabilities: A Multidisciplinary Journal, 9*(2), 1–7.

Johnson, G., Johnson, R.L., & Jefferson-Aker, C.R. (2001). HIV/AIDS prevention: Effective instructional strategies for adolescents with mild mental retardation. *Teaching Exceptional Children, 33,* 28–32.

Johnson, L.J., Pugach, M.C., & Devlin, S. (1990). Professional collaboration. *Teaching Exceptional Children, 22,* 9–11.

Jones, V.F., & Jones, L.S. (2001). *Comprehensive classroom management* (6th ed.). Boston: Allyn and Bacon.

Jones, V., & Jones, L. (2007). *Comprehensive classroom management*(8th ed.). Boston: Allyn and Bacon.

Kaderavek, J., & Pakulski, L. (2002). Minimal hearing loss is not minimal. *Teaching Exceptional Children, 34,* 14–18.

Kamps, D., Leonard, B., Vernon, S., Dugan, E., Delquadri, J., Gershon, B., Wade, L., & Folk, L. (1992). Teaching social skills to students with autism to increase peer interactions in an integrated first-grade classroom. *Journal of Applied Behavior Analysis, 25,* 281–288.

Kaplan, P. (1996). *Pathways for exceptional children: School, home, and culture.* St. Paul, MN: West Publishing.

Kataoka, J. (1987). *An example of integrating literature.* Unpublished manuscript.

Kauffman, J.M, & Landrum, T.J. (2009a). *Characteristics of emotional and behavioural disorders of children and youth (9th ed.).* Upper Saddle River, NJ: Merrill.

Kauffman, J.M, & Landrum, T.J. (2009b). Politics, civil rights, and disproportional identification of students with emotional and behavioral disorders. *Exceptionality, 17,* 177-188.

Kauffman, J.M., & Landrum, T.J. (2006). *Children and youth with emotional and behavioral disorders: A history of their education.* Austin, TX: Pro-Ed.

Kauffman, J.M., Lloyd, J.W., Baker, J., & Riedel, T.M. (1995). Inclusion of all students with emotional or behavioral disorders? Let's think again. *Phi Delta Kappan,* 542–546.

Kavale, K.A. (2001). *Discovering models in the identification of learning disabilities. Executive summary.* Washington, DC: LD Summit.

Kavale, K.A., & Forness, S.R. (1999). The future of research and practice in behaviour disorders. *Journal of Behaviour Disorders, 24,* 305–318.

Kavale, K.A., & Forness, S.R. (2000). History, rhetoric, and reality: Analysis of the inclusion debate. *Remedial and Special Education, 21,* 279–296.

Kavale, K.A., & Mostert, M.P. (2004). Social skills interventions for individuals with learning disabilities. *Learning Disabilities Quarterly, 27*(1), 31–43.

Keith, B., & Lenz, B. (2004). Creating school-wide conditions for high quality learning strategies classroom. *Intervention, 41*(5), 261–268.

Keller, W.D., & Tillery, K.L. (2002). Reliable differential diagnosis and effective management of auditory processing and attention deficit hyperactivity disorders. *Seminars in Hearing, 23*(4), 337–347.

Kerr, L., Delaney, B., Clarke, S., Dunlap, G., Childs, K. (2001). Improving the classroom behavior of students with emotional and behavioral disorders using individualized curricular modifications. *Journal of Emotional and Behavioral Disorders, 9,* 239–247.

Kerrin, R.G. (1996). Collaboration: Working with the speech-language pathologist. *Intervention in School and Clinic, 32*(1), 56–59.

King-Sears, M.E. (2001). Three steps for gaining access to the general education curriculum for learners with disabilities. *Intervention in School and Clinic, 37,* 67–76.

King-Sears, M.E., & Bradley, D. (1995). Classwide peer tutoring: Heterogeneous instruction in general education classrooms. *Preventing School Failure, 40,* 29–36.

Kirk, S.A. (1962). *Educating exceptional children*. Boston: Houghton Mifflin.

Kirk, S.A., Gallagher, J.J., & Anastasiow, N.J. (1993). *Educating exceptional children* (7th ed.). Boston: Houghton Mifflin.

Kirsten, I. (1981). *The Oakland picture dictionary*. Wauconda, IL: Don Johnston.

Kitano, M.K. (1993). Critique of Feldhusen's "individualized teaching of the gifted in regular classrooms." In C.J. Maker (Ed.), *Critical issues in gifted education: Vol. 3. Programs for the gifted in regular classrooms* (pp. 274–281). Austin, TX: Pro-Ed.

Klassen, R. (2002). A question of calibration: A review of the self-efficacy beliefs of students with learning disabilities. *Learning Disabilities Quarterly, 25,* 88–102.

Kohn, A. (1996). *Beyond discipline: From compliance to community*. Washington, DC: Association for Supervision and Curriculum Development.

Kollins, S.H., Barkley, R.A., & DuPaul, G.J. (2001). Use and management of medications for children diagnosed with attention deficit hyperactivity disorder (ADHD). *Focus on Exceptional Children, 33*(5), 1–23.

Korinek, L., Walther-Thomas, C., McLaughlin, V.L., & Williams, B.T. (1999). Creating classroom communities and networks for student support. *Intervention in School and Clinic, 35*(1), 3–8.

Kortering, L.J. (2009). School completion issues in special education. *Exceptionality, 17,* 1-4.

Kovacs-Burns, K., & Gordon, G.L. (2010). Analyzing the impact of disability legislation in Canada and the United States. *Journal of Disability Policy Studies, 20*(4), 205–218.

Kroeger, S.D., & Kouche, B. (2006). Using peer-assisted learning strategies to increase response to intervention in inclusive middle math settings. *Teaching Exceptional Children, 38*(5), 6–13.

Kully, D. (2000). Telehealth in speech pathology—applications to the treatment of stuttering. *Journal of Telemedicine and Telecare, 6,* S2: 39–41.

Lahey, M. (1988). *Language disorders and language development*. New York: Macmillan.

Lambert, M.A., & Nowacek, J. (2006). Help high school students improve their study skills. *Intervention in School and Clinic, 41*(4), 241–243.

Lambros, K.M., Ward, S.L., Bocian, K.M., MacMillan, D.L., & Gresham, F.M. (1998). Behavioral profiles of children at-risk for emotional and behavioral disorders: Implications for assessment and classification. *Focus on Exceptional Children, 30*(5), 1–16.

Lang, L. (1998). Allergy linked to common ear infection. *ADVANCE for Speech-Language Pathologists and Audiologists, 36,* 8–9.

Lavoie, R. (Writer). (1989). *How difficult can this be? Understanding learning disabilities: The F.A.T. city workshop* [Video]. (Available from PBS Video, 1320 Braddock Place, Alexandria, VA 22314).

Learning Disabilities Association of Canada (LDAC). (1987). *LDAC definition of learning disabilities*. Ottawa, ON: Author.

Learning Disabilities Association of Canada (LDAC). (2002). *Official definition of learning disabilities*. Ottawa, ON: Author.

Learning Disabilities Association of Canada (LDAC). (n.d.). *Prevalence of learning disabilities*. Retrieved from www.ldac-taac.ca/learn-more/prevalence-of-lds/prevalance-of-learning-disabilities.html.

Lee, S.H., Palmer, S.B., Turnbull, A.P., & Wehmeyer, M.L. (2006). A model for parent–teacher collaboration to promote self-determination in young children with disabilities. *Teaching Exceptional Children, 38,* 36–41.

Lenz, B.K., Deshler, D.D., & Kissam, B.R. (2004). *Teaching content to all: Evidence-based inclusive practices in middle and secondary schools*. Boston: Allyn and Bacon.

Leo, J. (2002, January/February). American preschoolers on Ritalin. *Society, 39,* 52–60.

Lerner, J.W. (2000). *Learning disabilities: Theories, diagnosis, and teaching strategies* (4th ed.) Boston: Houghton Mifflin.

Lewis, T.J., & Sugai, G. (1999). Effective behavior support: A systems approach to proactive school-wide management. *Focus on Exceptional Children, 31*(6), 1–24.

Lloyd, J.W., Forness, S.R., & Kavale, K.A. (1998). Some methods are more effective than others. *Intervention in School and Clinic, 33,* 195–200.

Lloyd, J.W., Landrum, T., & Hallahan, D.P. (1991). Self-monitoring applications for classroom intervention. In G. Stoner, M.R. Shinn, & H.M. Walker (Eds.), *Interventions for achievement and behavior problems* (pp. 201–213). Washington, DC: NASP.

Locke, M.N., Banken, L.L., & Mahone, T.E. (1994). *Adapting early childhood curriculum for children with special needs*. New York: Merrill.

Loehr, J. (2002). *Read the picture stories for articulation* (2nd ed.). Austin, TX: Pro-Ed.

Lopez, R., & MacKenzie, J. (1993). A learning center approach to individualized instruction for gifted students. In C.J. Maker (Ed.), *Critical issues in gifted education: Vol. 3. Programs for the gifted in regular classrooms* (pp. 282–295). Austin, TX: Pro-Ed.

Luckasson, R., Borthwick-Duffy, S., Buntinx, W.H.E., Coulter, D.L., Craig, E.M., Reeve, A., Schalock, R.L., Snell, M.E., Spitalnik, D.M., Spreat, S., Tass, M.J. (2002). *Mental retardation: Definition, classification and systems of supports* (10th ed.). Washington, DC: American Association on Mental Retardation.

Luckasson, R., Coulter, D., Polloway, E.A., Reiss, S., Schalock, R., Snell, M., Spitalnik, D., & Stark, J. (1992). *Mental retardation: Definition, classification and systems of supports*. Washington, DC: American Association on Mental Retardation.

Luckasson, R., Schalock, R., Snell, M., & Spitalnik, D. (1996). The 1992 AAMR definition and preschool children: Response from the committee on terminology and classification. *Mental Retardation, 34*, 247–253.

Luthar, S.S., Cicchetti, D., & Becker, B. (2000). The construct of resilience: A critical evaluation and guidelines for future work. *Child Development, 71*(3), 543–562.

Lyon, G.R., Fletcher, J.M., Shaywitz, S.E., Shaywitz, B.A., Torgesen, J.K., Wood, F.B., Schulte, A., & Olson, R. (2001). Rethinking learning disabilities. In C.E. Finn, A. J. Rotherham, & C.R. Hokanson, Jr. (Eds.), *Rethinking special education for a new century* (pp. 259–287). Washington, DC: Thomas B. Fordham Foundation.

Lytle, R.K., & Bordin, J. (2001). Enhancing the IEP team: Strategies for parents and professionals. *Teaching Exceptional Children, 33*, 40–44.

MacMillan, D.L., Gresham, F.M., & Siperstein, G.N. (1993). Conceptual and psychometric concerns about the 1992 AAMR definition of mental retardation. *American Journal of Mental Retardation, 98*, 325–335.

MacMillan, D.L., & Siperstein, G.N. (2001). *Learning disabilities as operationally defined by schools.* Paper presented at the 2001 LD Summit: Building a Foundation for the Future. Washington, DC.

Madaus, J. (2006). Employment outcomes of university graduates with learning disabilities. *Learning Disabilities Quarterly, 29*, 19–30.

Maheady, L., Harper, G.F., & Mallette, B. (2001). Peer-mediated instruction and interventions and students with mild disabilities. *Remedial and Special Education, 22*, 4–14.

Maheady, L., Harper, G., & Mallette, B. (2003). Preparing pre-service teachers to implement class wide peer tutoring. *Teacher Education and Special Education, 27*(4), 408–418.

Maker, C.J. (1993). Gifted students in the regular education classroom: What practices are defensible and feasible? In C.J. Maker (Ed.), *Critical issues in gifted education: Vol. 3. Programs for the gifted in regular classrooms* (pp. 413–436). Austin, TX: Pro-Ed.

Makkar, R., Gomez, L., Wigg, K.G., Ickowicz, A., Pathare, T., Tannock, R., Malone, M., Kennedy, J.L., Schachar, R., & Barr, C.L. (2007). The gene for synapsin III and attention-deficit hyperactivity disorder. *Psychiatric Genetics, 17*, 109–112.

Malott, R.W., Whaley, D.L., & Malott, M.E. (1997). *Elementary principles of behavior* (3rd ed.). Upper Saddle River, NJ: Prentice-Hall.

Manitoba Education, Training, and Youth. (2001). *Towards inclusion: Tapping hidden strengths: Planning for students who are alcohol-affected.* Winnipeg, MB: Author.

Marchant, J.M. (1992). Deaf-blind handicapping conditions. In P.J. McLaughlin & P. Wehman (Eds.), *Developmental disabilities* (pp. 113–123). Boston: Andover Press.

Marschark, M., Lang, H.G., & Albertini, J.A. (2002). *Educating deaf students: From research to practice.* London: Oxford University Press.

Martini, R., Heath, N.L., & Missiunia, C. (1999). A North American analysis of the relationship between learning disabilities and developmental coordination disorder. *International Journal of Special Education, 14*, 46–58.

Masten, A.S. (2001). Ordinary magic: Resilience processes in development. *American Psychologist, 56*(3), 227–238.

Masters, L.F., Mori, B.A., & Mori, A.A. (1999). *Teaching secondary students with mild learning and behavior problems.* Austin, TX: Pro-Ed.

Mastropieri, M.A., & Scruggs, T.E. (1993). *A practical guide for teaching science to students with special needs in inclusive settings.* Austin, TX: Pro-Ed.

Mastropieri, M.A., & Scruggs, T.E. (2001). Promoting inclusion in secondary classrooms. *Learning Disability Quarterly, 24*, 265–274.

Mastropieri, M.A., Scruggs, T.E., & Graetz, J.E. (2003). Reading comprehension instruction for secondary students: Challenges for struggling students and teachers. *Learning Disabilities Quarterly, 26*(2), 103–116.

Mathes, P., & Torgesen, J. (1998, November). *Early reading basics: Strategies for teaching reading to primary-grade students who are at risk for reading and learning disabilities.* Paper presented at the Annual Council for Learning Disabilities Conference, Albuquerque, NM.

Matthews, D.J., & Foster, J.F. (2005). A dynamic scaffolding model of teacher development: The gifted education consultant as catalyst for change. *Gifted Child Quarterly, 49*(3), 222–230.

Mayer, C., Akamatsu, C.T., & Stewart, D. (2002). A model for effective practice: Dialogic inquiry with students who are deaf. *Exceptional Children, 68*(4), 485–502.

McAnally, P.L., Rose, S., & Quigley, S.P. (1999). *Reading practices with deaf learners.* Austin, TX: Pro-Ed.

McCardle, P., Cooper, J., Houle, G.R., Karp, N., & Paul-Brown, D. (2001). Next steps in research and practice. *Learning Disabilities Research and Practice, 16*(4), 250–254.

McConaughy, S.H., & Wadsworth, M.E. (2000). Life history reports of young adults previously referred for mental health services. *Journal of Emotional and Behavioral Disorders, 8*, 202–215.

McConnell, J. (1999). Parents, adolescents, and career planning for visually impaired students. *Journal of Visual Impairment & Blindness, 93*, 498–515.

McConnell, K. (2001). Placement. In R. Algozzine, L. Serna, & J.R. Patton (Eds.), *Childhood behavior disorders: Applied research and educational practice* (pp. 309–330). Austin, TX: Pro-Ed.

McConnell, K., Patton, J.R., & Polloway, E.A. (2006). *BIP-III.* Austin, TX: Pro-Ed.

McConnell, K., Ryser, G., & Patton, J.R. (2002a). *Practical ideas that really work for disruptive, defiant, and difficult students: Preschool through grade 4.* Austin, TX: Pro-Ed.

McConnell, K., Ryser, G., & Patton, J.R. (2002b). *Practical ideas that really work for disruptive, defiant, and difficult students: Grades 5 through 12.* Austin, TX: Pro-Ed.

McConnell, M.E., Hilvitz, P.B., & Cox, C.J. (1998). Functional assessment: A systematic process for assessment and intervention in general and special education classrooms. *Intervention in School and Clinic, 34,* 10–20.

McDevitt, T.M. (1990). Encouraging young children's listening. *Academic Therapy, 25,* 569–577.

McDonnell, J.J., Hardman, M.L., McDonnell, A.P., & Kiefer-O'Donnell, R. (1995). *An introduction to persons with severe disabilities.* Boston: Allyn and Bacon.

McDougall, D. (1998). Research on self-management techniques used by students with disabilities in general education settings: A descriptive review. *Remedial and Special Education, 19,* 310–320.

McEvoy, A., & Welker, R. (2000). Antisocial behavior and academic failures and school climate: A critical review. *Journal of Emotional and Behavior Disorders, 8,* 24–33.

McEwan, E.K. (2006). *How to survive and thrive in the first three weeks of school.* Thousand Oaks, CA: Corwin Press.

McGinty, A.S., & Justice, L.M. (2006). Classroom-based versus pullout speech-language intervention: A review of the experimental evidence. *EBP Briefs, 1*(1), 1–25.

McGrail, L. (1998). Modifying regular classroom curricula for high ability students. *Gifted Child Today, 21,* 36–39.

McKamey, E.S. (1991). Storytelling for children with learning disabilities: A first-hand account. *Teaching Exceptional Children, 23,* 46–48.

McKeever, P. (1983). Siblings of chronically ill children: A literature review with implications for research and practice. *American Journal of Orthopsychiatry, 53,* 209–217.

McLesky, J., Henry, D., & Hodges, D. (1999). Inclusion: What progress is being made across disability categories? *Teaching Exceptional Children, 31,* 60–64.

McLoughlin, J.A., & Lewis, R.B. (2000). *Assessing special students* (5th ed.). Columbus, OH: Merrill.

McMaster, K.N., & Fuchs, D. (2002). Effects of cooperative learning on the academic achievement of students with learning disabilities. *Learning Disabilities Research and Practice, 17,* 107–117.

McMillan, J.H., Hellsten, L.M., & Klinger, D.A. (2011). *Classroom assessment: Principles and practice for effective standards-based instruction (Canadian edition).* Toronto: Pearson Canada.

McNamara, J.K., & Wong, B. (2003). Memory for everyday information in students with learning disabilities. *Journal of Learning Disabilities, 36*(5), 394–406.

McNeill, J.H., & Fowler, S.A. (1996). Using story reading to encourage children's conversations. *Teaching Exceptional Children, 28*(2), 43–47.

McPartland, J.M., & Slavin, R.E. (1990). *Policy perspectives increasing achievement of at-risk students at each grade level.* Washington, DC: U.S. Department of Education.

Meadan, H., & Monda-Amaya, L. (2008). Collaboration to promote social competence for students with mild disabilities in the general education classroom: A structure for providing social support. *Intervention in School and Clinic, 43*(3), 158–67.

Mercer, C.D. (1997). *Students with learning disabilities* (5th ed.). New York: Merrill.

Meyer, D. (2001). Meeting the unique concerns of brothers and sisters of children with special needs. *Insight, 51,* 28–32.

Mihalas, S., Morse, W.C., Allsopp, D.H., & McHatton, P.A. (2009). Cultivating caring relationships between teachers and secondary students with emotional and behavioral disorders: Implications for research and practice. *Remedial and Special Education, 30,* 108–125.

Miller, R.J. (1995). Preparing for adult life: Teaching students their rights and responsibilities. *CEC Today, 1*(7), 12.

Miller, S.P., Mercer, C.D., & Dillon, A.S. (1992). CSA: Acquiring and retaining math skills. *Intervention in School and Clinic, 28,* 105–110.

Minnesota Department of Education. (2003). Introduction to auditory processing disorders. Retrieved August 2004, from http://education.state.mn.us/content/059872.pdf.

Mirman, N.J. (1991). Reflections on educating the gifted child. *G/C/T, 14,* 57–60.

Montgomery, J.R., & Herer, G.R. (1994). Future watch: Our schools in the 21st century. *Language, Speech, and Hearing Services in the Schools, 25,* 130–135.

Montgomery, W. (2001). Creating culturally responsive, inclusive classrooms. *Teaching Exceptional Children, 33,* 4–9.

Moores, D. (2001). Educating the deaf: Psychology, principles, and practices (6th ed.). Columbus, OH: Merrill.

Morgan, S.R. (1994a). *At-risk youth in crises: A team approach in the schools* (2nd ed.). Austin, TX: Pro-Ed.

Morgan, S. (1994b). *Children in crisis: A team approach in the schools* (2nd ed.). Austin, TX: Pro-Ed.

Moriarty, D. (1967). *The loss of loved ones.* Springfield, IL: Charles C. Thomas.

Morris, S. (2002). Promoting social skills among students with nonverbal learning disabilities. *Teaching Exceptional Children, 34,* 66–70.

Morrison, G.S. (1997). *Teaching in America.* Boston: Allyn and Bacon.

Munk, D.D., & Bursuck, W.D. (2001). Preliminary findings on personalized grading plans for middle school students with learning disabilities. *Exceptional Children, 67,* 211–234.

Munk, D.D., Bursuck, W.D., Epstein, M.H., Jayanthi, M., Nelson, J., & Polloway, E.A. (2001). Homework communication problems: Perspectives of special and general education parents. *Reading and Writing Quarterly, 17,* 189–203.

Murray, C., & Greenberg, M.T. (2006). Examining the importance of social relationships and social contexts in the lives of children with high incidence disabilities. *Journal of Special Education, 39*(4), 220–233.

Musselwhite, C.R. (1987). Augmentative communication. In E. T. McDonald (Ed.), *Treating cerebral palsy: For clinicians by clinicians* (pp. 209–238). Austin, TX: Pro-Ed.

Myles, B.S., & Simpson, R.L. (2002). Asperger syndrome: An overview of characteristics. *Focus on Autism and Other Developmental Disabilities, 17*(3), 132–138.

Naremore, R.C. (1980). Language disorders in children. In T. J. Hixon, L. D. Shriberg, & J. H. Saxman (Eds.), *Introduction to communication disorders* (pp. 111–132). Englewood Cliffs, NJ: Prentice-Hall.

National Heart, Lung, and Blood Institute. (1998). How asthma friendly is your school? *Journal of School Health, 68,* 167–168.

National Institutes of Health. (2000). Consensus and development conference statement: Diagnosis and treatment of attention-deficit/hyperactivity disorder. *Journal of the American Academy of Child and Adolescent Psychiatry, 39*(2), 182–193.

National Joint Committee on Learning Disabilities. (2005, June). Responsiveness to intervention and learning disabilities: A report prepared by the National Joint Committee on Learning Disabilities. *Learning Disabilities Quarterly, 28,* 249–260.

National study on inclusion: Overview and summary report. (1995). *National Center on Educational Restructuring Inclusion, 2,* 1–8.

Nelson, J.R., Benner, G.J, Neill, S., & Stage, S.A. (2006). Interrelationships among language skills, externalizing behaviour, and academic fluency and their impact on the academic skills of students with ED. *Journal of Emotional and Behavioural Disorders, 14*(4), pp. 209–216.

Nelson, J.R., Benner, G.J., & Cheney, D. (2005). An investigation of the language skills of students with emotional disturbance served in public schools. *Journal of Special Education, 39*(2), 97–105.

Nelson, J.S., Jayanthi, M., Epstein, M.H. & Bursuck, W.D. (2000). Using the nominal work technique for homework communication decisions. *Remedial & Special Education, 23*(6), 379–386.

Nelson, L.G.L., Summers, J.A., & Turnbull, A.P. (2004) Boundaries in family-professional relationships. *Remedial and Special Education, 25,* 153–165.

Nessner, K. (1990, Winter). Children with disabilities. *Canadian Social Trends,* 18–20.

Newman, L., Wagner, M., Cameto, R., & Knokey, A. (2009). *The post-high school outcomes of youth with disabilities up to 4 years after high school: A report from the National Longitudinal Transition Study-2 (NLTS2)* (NCSER 2009-3017). Washington, DC: U. S. Government Printing Office.

Northern, J.L., & Downs, M.P. (2002). *Hearing in children* (5th ed.). Philadelphia, PA: Lippincott Williams & Wilkins.

Norwich, B. (1999). The connotation of special education labels for professionals in the field. *British Journal of Special Education, 26*(4), 179–183.

Nowacek, E.J., & McShane, E. (1993). Spoken language. In E.A. Polloway & J.R. Patton (Eds.), *Strategies for teaching learners with special needs* (5th ed., pp. 183–205). Columbus, OH: Merrill.

Oakland, T., & Rossen, E. (2005). A 21st-century model for identifying students for gifted and talented programs in light of conditions: An emphasis on race and ethnicity. *Gifted Child Today, 28*(4), 56–63.

O'Brien, J., Forest, M., Snow, J.E., & Hasbury, D. (1989). *Action for inclusion: How to improve schools by welcoming children with special needs into regular classrooms.* Toronto, ON: Frontier College Press.

Odom, S.L., Brown, W.H., & Frey, T. (2003). Evidence-based practices for young children with autism. *Focus on Autism and Other Developmental Disabilities, 18*(3), 166–175.

Olson, J.L., & Platt, J.M. (1996). *Teaching children and adolescents with special needs* (2nd ed). Englewood Cliffs, NJ: Merrill.

Orr, T.J., Myles, B.S., & Carlson, J.R. (1998). The impact of rhythmic entertainment on a person with autism. *Focus on Autism and Other Developmental Disabilities, 13,* 163–166.

Owens, R.E. (2008). *Language development: An introduction* (7th ed.). Boston: Allyn & Bacon.

Palmer, D.S., Fuller, K., Arora, T., & Nelson, M. (2001). Taking sides: Parent views on inclusion for their children with severe disabilities. *Exceptional Children, 67,* 467–484.

Pandiani, J.A., Schacht, L.M., & Banks, S.M. (2001). After children's services: A longitudinal study of significant life events. *Journal of Emotional and Behavioral Disorders, 9,* 131–138.

Parke, B.N. (1989). *Gifted students in regular classrooms.* Boston: Allyn and Bacon.

Patton, J.R., Blackburn, J., & Fad, K. (2001). *Focus on exceptional children* (8th ed.). Columbus, OH: Merrill.

Patton, J.R., & Cronin, M.E. (1993). *Life skills, instruction for all students with disabilities.* Austin, TX: Pro-Ed.

Patton, J.R., & Dunn, C.R. (1998). *Transition from school to adult life for students with special needs: Basic concepts and recommended practices.* Austin, TX: Pro-Ed.

Patton, J.R., Jayanthi, M., & Polloway, E.A. (2001). Home-school collaboration about homework. *Reading and Writing Quarterly, 17,* 227–242.

Patton, J.R., Polloway, E.A., & Smith, T.E.C. (2000). Educating students with mild mental retardation. In M.L. Wehmeyer & J.R. Patton (Eds.), *Mental retardation in the 21st century.* Austin, TX: Pro-Ed.

Patton, J.R., Polloway, E.A., Smith, T.E.C., Edgar, E., Clark, G.M., & Lee, S. (1996). Individuals with mild mental retardation: Postsecondary outcomes and implications for educational policy. *Education and Training in Mental Retardation and Developmental Disabilities, 31,* 77–85.

Pearpoint, J., Forest, M., & O'Brien, J. (1996). MAPs, circles of friends, and PATH. In S. Stainback & W. Stainback (Eds.), *Inclusion: A guide for educators* (pp. 67–86). Baltimore, MD: Brookes.

Peebles-Wilkins, W. (2006). Evidence-based suicide prevention. *Children & Schools, 28*, 195-196.

Pemberton, J.B. (2003). Communicating academic progress as an integral part of assessment. *Teaching Exceptional Children, 35*, 16–20.

Pemberton, J.B., Rademacher, J.A., Tyler-Wood, T., & Careijo, M.V. (2006). Aligning assessments with state curricular standards. *Intervention, 41*(5), 283–289.

Pfiffner, L., & Barkley, R. (1991). Educational placement and classroom management. In R. Barkley (Ed.), *Attention deficit hyperactivity disorder: A handbook for diagnosis and treatment* (pp. 498–539). New York: Guilford.

Pierangelo, R., & Giuliani, G. (2006). *Learning disabilities: A practical approach to foundations, assessment, diagnosis, and teaching*. Boston: Allyn and Bacon.

Pierce, C. (1994). Importance of classroom climate for at-risk learners. *Journal of Educational Research, 88*, 37–44.

Plummer, D.L. (1995). Serving the needs of gifted children from a multicultural perspective. In J.L. Genshaft, M. Bireley, & C.L. Hollinger (Eds.), *Serving gifted and talented students: A resource for school personnel* (pp. 285–300). Austin, TX: Pro-Ed.

Pocock, A., Lambros, S., Karvonen, M., Test, D.W., Algozzine, B., Wood, W., & Martin, J.S. (2002). Successful strategies for promoting self-advocacy among students with learning disabilities: The LEAD Group. *Intervention in School and Clinic, 37*(4), 209–216.

Podemski, R.S., Marsh, G.E., Smith, T.E.C., & Price, B.J. (1995). *Comprehensive administration of special education*. Columbus, OH: Merrill.

Polloway, E.A. (1997). Developmental principles of the Luckasson et al. AAMR definition: A retrospective. *Education and Training in Mental Retardation and Developmental Disabilities, 32*, 174–178.

Polloway, E.A., Bursuck, W., Jayanthi, M., Epstein, M., & Nelson, J. (1996). Treatment acceptability: Determining appropriate interventions within inclusive classrooms. *Intervention in School and Clinic, 31*, 133–144.

Polloway, E.A., Epstein, M.H., & Bursuck, W.D. (2002). Homework for students with learning disabilities. *Reading and Writing Quarterly, 17*, 181–187.

Polloway, E.A., Epstein, M.H., Bursuck, W.D., Jayanthi, M., & Cumblad, C. (1994). Homework practices of general education teachers. *Journal of Learning Disabilities, 27*, 500–509.

Polloway, E.A., & Jones-Wilson, L. (1992). Principles of assessment and instruction. In E.A. Polloway & T.E.C. Smith (Eds.), *Language instruction for students with disabilities* (pp. 87–120). Denver, CO: Love Publishing.

Polloway, E.A., Lubin, J., Smith, J.D. & Patton, J.R. (2010). *Mild intellectual disabilities: Legacies and trends in concepts and educational practices. Education and Training in Developmental Disabilities*.

Polloway, E.A., Miller, L., & Smith, T.E.C. (2003). *Language instruction for students with disabilities* (3rd ed.). Denver: Love.

Polloway, E.A., & Patton, J.R. (1993). *Strategies for teaching learners with special needs* (5th ed.). Columbus, OH: Merrill/Macmillan.

Polloway, E.A., & Patton, J.R. (1997). *Strategies for teaching learners with special needs* (6th ed.). Columbus, OH: Merrill.

Polloway, E.A., Patton, J.R., & Nelson, M. (2010). Intellectual disabilities. In Hallahan, D.P., Kauffman, J.M., & Pullen, P. (Eds.), *Handbook of special education*. New York: Routledge.

Polloway, E.A., Patton, J.R., & Serna, L. (2001). *Strategies for teaching learners with special needs* (7th ed.). Columbus, OH: Merrill.

Polloway, E.A., Patton, J.R., & Serna, L. (2008). *Strategies for teaching learners with special needs* (9th ed.). Columbus, OH: Merrill.

Polloway, E.A., Patton, J.R., Smith, J.D., & Roderique, T.W. (1992). Issues in program design for elementary students with mild retardation: Emphasis on curriculum development. *Education and Training in Mental Retardation, 27*, 142–150.

Polloway, E.A., Smith, J.D., & Antoine, K. (2010). Biological aspects and the promise of prevention. In Beirne-Smith, M.E. et al. (Eds.), *Intellectual disabilities* (8th Ed.). Columbus, OH: Pearson.

Polloway, E.A., Smith, J.D., Chamberlain, J., Denning, C., & Smith, T.E.C. (1999). Levels of deficit vs. levels of support in mental retardation classification. *Education and Training in Mental Retardation and Development Disabilities, 34*, 48–59.

Polloway, E.A., Smith, J.D., Patton, J.R., & Smith, T.E.C. (1996). Historic changes in mental retardation and developmental disabilities. *Education and Training in Mental Retardation and Developmental Disabilities, 31*, 3–12.

Prater, M.A., Joy, R., Chilman, B., Temple, J., & Miller, S.R. (1991). Self-monitoring of on-task behavior by adolescents with learning disabilities. *Learning Disability Quarterly, 14*, 164–177.

Prestia, K. (2003). Tourette's syndrome: Characteristics and interventions. *Intervention in School & Clinic, 39*(2), 67–71.

Prince Edward Island Education. (2001). *Minister's Directive No. MD 2001-08*. Retrieved April 2005 from Prince Edward Island Education website: www.gov.pe.ca/educ/index.php3?number=76715.

Public Health Agency of Canada. (2005). Early hearing and communication development: Canadian working group on childhood hearing (CWGCH) resource document. Ottawa, Ontario: Author. Retrieved January 18, 2007, from www.phac-aspc.gc.ca/rhs-ssg/index.html.

Pugach, M.C., & Warger, C.L. (2001). Curriculum matters. *Remedial and Special Education, 22*, 194–196.

Pugh, K.R., Mencl, W.E., Jenner, A.R., Lee, J.R., Katz, L., Frost, S.J., Shaywitz, S.E., & Shaywitz, B.A. (2001). Neuroimaging studies of reading development and reading disability. *Learning Disabilities Research and Practice, 16*(4), 240–249.

Quay, H., & Peterson, D. (1987). *Revised behavior problem checklist.* Coral Gables, FL: University of Miami.

Quinn, M.M., Kavale, K.A., Mathur, S.R., Rutherford, R.B., Jr., & Forness, S.R. (1999). A meta-analysis of social skill interventions for students with emotional and behavioral disorders. *Journal of Emotional and Behavioral Disorders, 7*, 54–64.

Raskind, M.H., Goldberg, R.J., Higgins, E.L., & Herman, K.L. (2002). Teaching life success to students with learning disabilities: Lessons learned from a 20-year study. *Intervention in Schools and Clinic, 37*(4), 201–208.

Raskind, W.W. (2001). Current understanding of the genetic basis of reading and spelling differences. *Learning Disabilities Quarterly, 24*, 141–157.

Ratner, V.L., & Harris, L.R. (1994). *Understanding language disabilities: The impact of language.* Eau Claire, WI: Thinking Publications.

Reeve, R.E. (1990). ADHD: Facts and fallacies. *Intervention in School and Clinic, 26*, 71–78.

Reid, R., & Nelson, J.R. (2002). The utility, acceptability, and practicality of functional behavioral assessment for students with high-incidence problem behaviors. *Remedial and Special Education, 23*, 15–23.

Reis, S.M. (1989). Reflections on policy affecting the education of gifted and talented students. *American Psychologist, 44*, 399–408.

Reis, S.M. (2001). External barriers experienced by gifted and talented girls. *Gifted Children Today, 24*, 31–36.

Reis, S.M., & Schack, G.D. (1993). Differentiating products for the gifted and talented: The encouragement of independent learning. In C.J. Maker (Ed.), *Critical issues in gifted education: Vol. 3. Programs for the gifted in regular classrooms* (pp. 161–186). Austin, TX: Pro-Ed.

Renzulli, J.S. (1979). *What makes giftedness: A reexamination of the definition of the gifted and talented.* Ventura, CA: Ventura County Superintendent of Schools Office.

Renzulli, J.S., & Reis, S.M. (1997). The schoolwide enrichment model: New directions for developing high-end learning. In N. Colangelo & G.A. Davis (Eds.), *Handbook of gifted education* (2nd ed.). Boston: Allyn and Bacon.

Renzulli, J.S., Reis, S.M., & Smith, L.M. (1981). *The revolving door identification model.* Wethersfield, CT: Creative Learning Press.

Reynolds, C.T., & Salend, S.J. (1990). Teacher-directed and student-mediated textbook comprehension strategies. *Academic Therapy, 25*, 417–427.

Richards, T.L. (2001). Functional magnetic resonance imaging and spectroscopic imaging of the brain: Application of fMRI and fMRS to reading disabilities and education. *Learning Disabilities Quarterly, 24*(3), 189–203.

Rieck, W.A., & Wadsworth, D.E. (1999). Foreign exchange: An inclusion strategy. *Intervention, 35*, 22–28.

Riley, T. (1999). The role of advocacy: Creating change for gifted children throughout the world. *Gifted Child Today, 22*, 44–47.

Roach, V. (1995). Supporting inclusion: Beyond the rhetoric. *Phi Delta Kappan, 77*, 295–299.

Roberts, C., Ingram, C., & Harris, C. (1992). The effect of special versus regular classroom programming on higher cognitive processes of intermediate elementary aged gifted and average ability students. *Journal of the Education of the Gifted, 15*, 332–343.

Roberts, G., & Nanson, J. (2001). *Best practices: Fetal alcohol syndrome/fetal alcohol effects and the effects of other substance use during pregnancy.* Ottawa, ON: Health Canada.

Robin, S.S., & Johnson, E.O. (1996). Attitude and peer cross pressure: Adolescent drug and alcohol use. *Journal of Drug Education, 26*, 69–99.

Robinson, C.S., Manchetti, B.M., & Torgesen, J.K. (2002). Toward a two-factor theory of one type of mathematics disability. *Learning Disabilities Research and Practice, 17*, 81–89.

Robinson, L.M., Skaer, T.L., Sclar, D.A., & Galin, R.S. (2002). Is attention deficit hyperactivity disorder increasing among girls in the U.S.? *CNS Drugs, 16*, 129–137.

Robinson, S.M., Braxdale, C.T., & Colson, S.E. (1988). Preparing dysfunctional learners to enter junior high school: A transitional curriculum. *Focus on Exceptional Children, 18*(4), 1–12.

Rock, E.E., Rosenberg, M.S., & Carran, D.T. (1995). Variables affecting the reintegation rate of students with serious emotional disturbance. *Exceptional Children, 6*, 254–268.

Roeher Institute of Canada. (1996). *Disability, community and society: Exploring the links.* North York, ON: Author.

Rooney, K. (1993). *Attention deficit hyperactivity disorder: A videotape program.* Richmond, VA: State Department of Education.

Roseberry-McKibbin, C., & Brice, A. (2002). Choice of language instruction: One or two? *Teaching Exceptional Children, 33*, 10–16.

Roseberry-McKibbin, C., & O'Hanlon, L. (2005). Nonbiased assessment of English language learners: A tutorial. *Communication Disorders Quarterly, 26*(3), 178–185.

Rosenberg, M.S., O'Shea, L., & O'Shea, D.J. (1991). *Student teacher to master teacher: A handbook for preservice and beginning teachers of students with mild and moderate handicaps.* New York: Macmillan.

Rosenberg, M.S., Wilson, R., Maheady, L., & Sindelar, P. (1992). *Educating students with behavior disorders.* Boston: Allyn and Bacon.

Rosenshine, B., & Stevens, R. (1986). Teaching functions. In M. Wittrock (Ed.), *Handbook of research on teaching* (3rd ed., pp. 376–391). New York: Macmillan.

Ross, S.M., Smith, L.J., Casey, J., & Slavin, R.E. (1995). Increasing the academic success of disadvantaged children: An examination of alternative early intervention programs. *American Educational Research Journal, 32,* 773–800.

Rosselli, H. (1993). Process differentiation for gifted learners in the regular classroom: Teaching to everyone's needs. In C.J. Maker (Ed.), *Critical issues in gifted education: Vol. 3. Programs for the gifted in regular classrooms* (pp. 139–155). Austin, TX: Pro-Ed.

Rotter, K. (2006). Creating instructional materials for all pupils: Try COLA. *Intervention in School and Clinic, 41*(5), 273–282.

Ruble, L.A., & Dalrymple, M.J. (2002). COMPASS: A parent–teacher collaboration model for students with autism. *Focus on Autism and Other Developmental Disabilities, 17,* 76–83.

Sabatino, D.A. (1987). Preventive discipline as a practice in special education. *Teaching Exceptional Children, 19,* 8–11.

Sabornie, E.J., Cullinan, D., Osborne, S.S., & Brock, L.B. (2005). Intellectual, academic, and behavioral functioning of students with high-incidence disabilities: A cross-categorical meta-analysis. *Exceptional Children, 72*(1), 47–64.

Sacks, S., Wolffe, B.A., & Tierney, F. (1998). Lifestyles of students with visual impairments: Preliminary studies of social networks. *Exceptional Children, 64,* 63–78.

Safford, P.L., & Safford, E.J. (1998). Visions of the special class. *Remedial and Special Education, 19,* 229–238.

Safran, J.S. (2002). A practical guide to research on Asperger's syndrome. *Intervention in School and Clinic, 37,* 283–293.

Salend, S.J. (1990). *Effective mainstreaming.* New York: Macmillan.

Salend, S.J. (1994). *Effective mainstreaming: Creating inclusive classrooms* (2nd ed.). Columbus, OH: Merrill/Prentice-Hall.

Salend, S.J. (1999). Facilitating friendships among diverse students. *Intervention in School and Clinic, 35,* 9–15.

Salend, S.J. (2000). Parental perceptions of inclusive placement. *Remedial and Special Education, 21,* 121–128.

Salend, S.J. (2010). *Creating inclusive classrooms: Effective and reflective practices* (7th ed.). Columbus, OH: Prentice Hall.

Salend, S.J. (2001). *Creating inclusive classrooms: Effective and reflective practices* (4th ed.). Columbus, OH: Merrill/Prentice Hall.

Salend, S.J. (2004). Fostering inclusive values in children: What families can do. *Teaching Exceptional Children, 37*(1), 64–69.

Salend, S.J., & Duhaney, L.M.G. (1999). The impact of inclusion on students with and without disabilities and their education. *Remedial and Special Education, 20,* 114–126.

Salend, S.J., & Duhaney, L.M.G. (2002). Grading students in inclusive settings. *Teaching Exceptional Children, 34*(3), 8–15.

Salvia, J., & Ysseldyke, J.E. (2004). *Assessment in special and inclusive education* (9th ed.). Houghton Mifflin.

Sander, E.K. (1972). When are speech sounds learned? *Journal of Speech and Hearing Disorders, 37,* 62.

Sansoti, F.J., Powell-Smith, K.A., & Kincaid, D. (2004). A research synthesis of social story interventions for children with autism. *Journal of Autism and Other Developmental Disabilities, 19*(4), 194–204.

Santrock, J.W., & Warshak, R.A. (1979). Father custody and social development in boys and girls. *Journal of Social Issues, 35,* 112–125.

Sargent, L.R. (1991). *Social skills for school and community.* Reston, VA: CEC-MR.

Sargent, L.R. (1998). *Social skills for school and community: Systematic instruction for children and youth with cognitive delays.* Virginia: CEC publication.

Saskatchewan Learning. (2000). *Directions for diversity: Enhancing supports to children and youth with diverse needs.* Regina, SK: Author.

Saskatchewan Learning. (2004). *Planning for students with fetal alcohol syndrome disorder: A guide for educators.* Regina, SK: Author.

Saskatchewan Learning. (2001). *Creating opportunities for students with intellectual or multiple disabilities.* Regina, SK: Author.

Saskatchewan Learning. (2005, September). *Funding and documentation 2005–06: A Guide for School Divisions.* Author.

Savage, R.C. (1988). Introduction to educational issues for students who have suffered traumatic brain injury. In R.C. Savage & G.F. Wolcott (Eds.), *An educator's manual: What educators need to know about students with traumatic brain injury.* Southborough, MA: National Head Injury Foundation.

Scanlon, D., & Melland, D.F. (2002). Academic and participant profiles of school-age drop-outs with and without disabilities. *Exceptional Children, 68,* 239–258.

Schaffner, C.B., & Buswell, B.E. (1996). Ten critical elements for creating inclusive and effective school communities. In S. Stainback & W. Stainback (Eds.), *Inclusion: A guide for educators* (pp. 49–65). Baltimore, MD: Brookes.

Scahill, L., & Schwab-Stone, M. (2000). Epidemiology of ADHD in school-age children. *Child and Adolescent Psychiatric Clinics of North America, 9,* 541–555.

Schalock, R.L., Stark, J.A., Snell, M.E., Coulter, D.L., Polloway, E.A., Luckasson, R., Reiss, S., & Spitalnik, D.M. (1994). Changing conceptualizations of and definition of mental retardation: Implications for the field. *Mental Retardation, 32,* 181–193.

Schall, C. (2002). A consumer's guide to monitoring medication for individuals with ASD. *Focus on Autism and Other Developmental Disabilities, 17,* 228–235.

Scheuerman, B., & Webber, J. (2002). *Autism: Teaching does make a difference.* Belmont, CA: Wadsworth.

Scheffler, R., Hinshaw, S., Modrek, S., & Levine, P. (2007) The Global market for adhd medications. *Health Affairs, 26*(2), 450–457.

Schiever, S.W. (1993). Differentiating the learning environment for gifted students. In C.J. Maker (Ed.), *Critical issues in gifted education: Vol. 3. Programs for the gifted in regular classrooms* (pp. 201–214). Austin, TX: Pro-Ed.

Schleichkorn, J. (1993). *Coping with cerebral palsy: Answers to questions parents often ask* (2nd ed.). Austin: TX: Pro-Ed.

Schloss, P., Schloss, A., & Shloss, C.N. (2007). *Instructional methods for secondary students with learning and behavior problems.* Boston: Allyn and Bacon.

Schuck, S.E.B, & Crinella, F.M. (2005). Why children with adhd do not have low IQs. *Journal of Learning Disabilities, 38*(3), pp. 262–280.

Schumaker, J.B., Deshler, D.D., Nolan, S., Clark, F.L., Alley, G.R., & Warren, M.M. (1981). *Error monitoring strategy: A learning strategy for improving academic performance of LD adolescents.* (Research Report No. 32). Lawrence, KS: University of Kansas IRLD.

Schumm, J.S., & Strickler, K. (1991). Guidelines for adapting content area textbooks: Keeping teachers and students content. *Intervention in School and Clinic, 27*, 79–84.

Schwartz, S.E., & Karge, B.D. (1996). *Human diversity: A guide for understanding* (2nd ed.). New York: McGraw-Hill.

Schwean, V.L., Saklofske, D.H., Shatz, E., & Falk, L.K. (1996). Achieving supportive integration for children with behavioral disorders in Canada: Multiple paths to realization. *Canadian Journal of Special Education, 11*, 33–50.

Scott, T.M., & Nelson, M.C. (1998). Confusion and failure in facilitating generalized social responding in the school setting: Sometimes 2 + 2 = 5. *Behavioral Disorders, 23*, 264–275.

Scruggs, T.E., & Mastropieri, M.A. (1994). Successful mainstreaming in elementary science classes: A qualitative study of three reputational cases. *American Educational Research Journal, 31*, 785–811.

Scruggs, T.E., & Mastropieri, M.A. (1996). Teacher perceptions of mainstreaming/inclusion, 1958–1995: A research synthesis. *Exceptional Children, 63*, 59–74.

Scruggs, T.E., & Mastropieri, M.A. (2000). The effectiveness of mnemonic instruction for students with learning and behavior problems: An update and research synthesis. *Journal of Behavioral Education, 10*, 163–173.

Searcy, S., & Meadows, N.B. (1994). The impact of social structures on friendship development for children with behavior disorders. *Education and Treatment of Children, 17*, 255–268.

Seeley, K. (1995). Classwide peer tutoring. Unpublished manuscript, Lynchburg College (VA).

Seery, M.E., Davis, P.M., & Johnson, L.J. (2000). Seeing eye to eye: Are parents and professionals in agreement about the benefits of preschool inclusion? *Remedial and Special Education, 21*, 368–378.

Sexton, D., Snyder, P., Wolfe, B., Lobman, M., Stricklin, S., & Akers, P. (1996). Early intervention inservice training strategies: Perceptions and suggestions from the field. *Exceptional Children, 62*, 485–496.

Shaner, M.Y. (1991). Talented teachers for talented students. *G/C/T, 22*, 14–15.

Shanker, A. (1994–1995). Educating students in special programs. *Educational Leadership, 52*, 43–47.

Shanley, R. (1993). Becoming content with content. In C. J. Maker (Ed.), *Critical issues in gifted education: Vol. 1. Defensible programs for the gifted* (pp. 43–89). Austin, TX: Pro-Ed.

Shapiro, E.S., DuPaul, G.J., & Bradley-Klug, K.L. (1998). Self-management as a strategy to improve the classroom behavior of adolescents with ADHD. *Journal of Learning Disabilities, 31*, 545–555.

Sharpe, W. (2008). *he abcs of school success: ips, checklists, strategies for equipping your child.* rand Rapids, MI: Revel.

Sileo, T.W., Sileo, A.P., & Prater, M.A. (1996). Parent and professional partnerships in special education: Multicultural considerations. *Intervention in School & Clinic, 31*, 145–153.

Silver, L.B. (1995). Controversial therapies. *Journal of Child Neurology, 10* (suppl. 1), 96–100.

Silver, L.B. (2000). Alternative treatment for ADHD. In B.P. Guyer (Ed.), *ADHD: Achieving success in school and in life.* Boston: Allyn and Bacon.

Silver, L.B. (2003, September/October). Another claim of a treatment for learning disabilities. Should you consider it? *LDA Newsbriefs*, pp. 4, 12.

Silverman, A.B., Reinherz, H.Z., & Giaconia, R.M. (1996). The long-term sequelae of child and adolescent abuse: A longitudinal community study. *Child Abuse and Neglect, 20*, 709–723.

Silverthorn, K.H., & Hornak, J.E. (1993). Beneficial effects of exercise on aerobic capacity and body composition in adults with Prader-Willi syndrome. *American Journal on Mental Retardation, 97*, 654–658.

Simmons, D., Fuchs, D., Hodge, J., & Mathes, P. (1994). Importance of instructional complexity and role reciprocity to classwide peer tutoring. *Learning Disabilities Research and Practice, 9*, 203–212.

Simpson, R. (2001). ABA and students with autism spectrum disorders. *Focus on Autism and Developmental Disabilities, 16*, 68–71.

Simpson, R. (2004). Evidence-based practices and students with autism spectrum disorder. *Journal of Autism and Other Developmental Disabilities, 20*(3), 140–149.

Sitlingon, P.L., & Frank. A.C. (1998). *Follow-up studies: A practical handbook.* Austin, TX: Pro-Ed.

Skotko, B.G., Koppenhaver, D.A., & Erickson, K.A. (2004). Parent reading behaviors and communication outcomes in girls with Rett syndrome. *Exceptional Children, 70,* 145–166.

Sladeczek, I.E., Madden, L., Illsley, S.D., Finn, C., & August, P. (2006). American and Canadian perceptions of the acceptability of conjoint behavioural consultation. *School Psychology International, 27*(1) 57–77.

Slavin, R.E. (1987). *What research says to the teacher on cooperative learning: Student teams* (2nd ed.). Washington, DC: National Education Association.

Slicker, E.K., & Palmer, D.J. (1993). Mentoring at-risk high school students: Evaluation of a school-based program. *The School Counselor, 40,* 327–334.

Smith, C.R. (2004). *Learning disabilities: The interaction of students and their environments.* Boston: Allyn and Bacon.

Smith, D.D., & Luckasson, R. (1992). *Introduction to special education: Teaching in an age of challenge.* Boston: Allyn and Bacon.

Smith, D.D., & Luckasson, R. (1995/1998). *Introduction to special education: Teaching in an age of challenge.* Boston: Allyn and Bacon.

Smith, D.D., & Rivera, D.P. (1995). Discipline in special and regular education. *Focus on Exceptional Children, 27*(5), 1–14.

Smith, G., & Smith, D. (1989). Schoolwide study skills program: The key to mainstreaming. *Teaching Exceptional Children, 21,* 20–23.

Smith, J.D. (1994). The revised AAMR definition of mental retardation: The MRDD position. *Education and Training in Mental Retardation and Developmental Disabilities, 29,* 179–183.

Smith, J.D. (1995). Inclusive school environments and students with disabilities in South Carolina: The issues, the status, the needs. *Occasional Papers, 1,* 1–5.

Smith, T.E.C. (1990). *Introduction to education* (2nd ed.). St. Paul, MN: West Publishing.

Smith, T.E.C. (2002). Section 504: Basic requirements for schools. *Intervention in School and Clinic, 37,* 2–6.

Smith, T.E.C., & Dowdy, C.A. (1992). Future-based assessment and intervention and mental retardation. *Education and Training in Mental Retardation, 27,* 23–31.

Smith, T.E.C., Dowdy, C.A., Polloway, E.A., & Blalock, G. (1997). *Children and adults with learning disabilities.* Boston: Allyn and Bacon.

Smith, T.E.C., Finn, D.M., & Dowdy, C.A. (1993). *Teaching students with mild disabilities.* Ft. Worth, TX: Harcourt Brace Jovanovich.

Smith, T.E.C., Gartin, B.C., Murdick, N.L., & Hilton, A. (2006). *Families and children with special needs.* Columbus, OH: Merrill.

Smith, T.E.C., & Hendricks, M.D. (1995). *Prader-Willi syndrome: Practical considerations for educators.* Little Rock: Ozark Learning.

Smith, T.E.C., & Hilton, A. (1994). Program design for students with mental retardation. *Education and training in mental retardation and developmental disabilities, 29,* 3–8.

Smith, T., Polloway, E.A., Smith, J.D., & Patton, J.R. (2007). Self-determination for persons with developmental disabilities: Ethical considerations for teachers. *Education and Training in Developmental Disabilities, 42,* 144–151.

Smith, T.E.C., Price, B.J., & Marsh, G.E. (1986). *Mildly handicapped children and adults.* St. Paul, MN: West Publishing.

Smith, T.J., & Adams G. (2006). The effects of comorbidity AD/HD and learning disabilities on parent-reported behavioral and academic outcomes in children. *Learning Disabilities Quarterly, 29*(2), 17–21.

Smith, W.J., & Foster, W.F. (1996). *Equal educational opportunity for students with disabilities.* Montreal, PQ: McGill University, Office of Research on Educational Policy.

Smutny, J.F., Walker, S.Y., & Meckstroth, E.A. (1997). *Teaching young gifted children in the regular classroom: Identifying, nurturing, and challenging ages 4–9.* Minneapolis, MN: Free Spirit.

Snell, M., & Drake, G.P. (1994). Replacing cascades with supported education. *Journal of Special Education, 27,* 393–409.

Sokol, R.J., Delaney-Black, V., & Nordstrom, B. (2003). Fetal alcohol spectrum disorder. *Journal of the American Medical Association, 290*(22), 2996–2999.

Solomon, C.R., & Serres, F. (1999). Effects of parental verbal aggression on children's self-esteem and school marks. *Child Abuse & Neglect, 23,* 339–351.

Southern, W.T., & Jones, E.D. (1991). Academic acceleration: Background and issues. In W.T. Southern & E.D. Jones (Eds.), *Academic acceleration of gifted children* (pp. 1–17). New York: Teachers College Press.

Stainback, S., Stainback, W., East, K., & Sapon-Shevin, M. (1994). A commentary on inclusion and the development of a positive self-identity by people with disabilities. *Exceptional Children, 60,* 486–490.

Stainback, W., & Stainback, S. (1984). A rationale for the merger of special and regular education. *Exceptional Children, 51,* 102–111.

Stainback, W., Stainback, S., & Bunch, G. (1989). A rationale for the merger of regular and special education. In S. Stainback et al. (Eds.), *Educating all students in the mainstream of regular education* (pp. 15–26). Baltimore, MD, England: Paul H. Brookes Publishing.

Stainback, W., Stainback, S., & Stefanich, G. (1996). Learning together in inclusive classrooms: What about the curriculum? *Teaching Exceptional Children, 28,* 17.

Stainback, W.C., Stainback, S., & Wehman, P. (1997). Toward full inclusion into general education. In P. Wehman (Ed.), *Exceptional individuals in school, community, and work* (pp. 531–557). Austin, TX: Pro-Ed.

Stanovich, K.E. (2005). The future mistake: Will discrepancy measurement continue to make the learning disabilities field a pseudoscience. *Learning Disabilities Quarterly, 23,* 103–106.

Statistics Canada. (2001a). A profile of disability in Canada, 2001. Ottawa, ON: Statistics Canada. Retrieved May 31, 2007, from www.statcan.ca/english/freepub/89-577-XIE/pdf/89-577-XIE01001.pdf.

Statistics Canada. (2001b). Profile of Canadian families and households: Diversification continues. Ottawa, ON: Statistics Canada. Retrieved May 31, 2007, from www12.statcan.ca/english/census01/products/analytic/companion/fam/pdf/96F0030XIE2001003.pdf.

Statistics Canada. 2002). *profile of disability in Canada, 2001.* ttawa, ON: Author. Retrieved January 2008 from www.statcan.ca/english/freepub/89-577-XIE/89-577-XIE2001001.pdf.

Statistics Canada. (2005). *Family violence in Canada: A statistical profile.* Ottawa, ON: Statistics Canada.

Stewart, D.A., & Kluwin, T.N. (2001). *Teaching deaf and hard of hearing students.* Boston: Allyn and Bacon.

Strichart, S.S. & Mangrum, C.T. (2010). *Study skills for learning disabled and struggling students: Grades 6–12.* Upper Saddle River, NJ: Pearson.

Strichart, S.S., & Mangrum, C.T. (2002). *Teaching learning strategies and study skills to students with learning disabilities, attention deficit disorders, or special needs* (3rd ed.). Boston: Allyn and Bacon.

Summers, J.A., Hoffman, L., Marquis, J., Turnbull, K.A., Poston, D., & Nelson, L.L. (2005). Measuring the quality of family-professional partnerships in special education services. *Exceptional Children, 72,* 65–81.

Swanson, H.L. (2000). Are working memory differences in readings with learning disabilities hard to change? *Journal of Learning Disabilities, 33,* 551–566.

Tabassam, W., & Grainger, J. (2002). Self-concept, attributional style, and self-efficacy beliefs of students with learning disabilities with and without ADHD. *Learning Disabilities Quarterly, 25,* 141–151.

Tankersley, M. (1995). A group-oriented management program: A review of research on the good behavior game and implications for teachers. *Preventing School Failure, 40,* 19–28.

Tannenbaum, A.J. (1997). The meaning and making of giftedness. In N. Colangelo & G.A. Davis (Eds.), *Handbook of gifted education* (2nd ed.). Boston: Allyn and Bacon.

Tavzel, C.S., & Staff of LinguiSystems. (1987). *Blooming recipes.* East Moline, IL: LinguiSystems.

Taylor, R.L. (2000). *Assessment of individuals with mental retardation.* San Diego: Singular.

Taylor, R.L., Richards, S.B., & Brady, M.P. (2005). *Mental retardation: Historical perspectives, current practices, and future directions.* Boston: Allyn and Bacon.

Tennant, C., Bebbington, P.R., & Hurry, J. (1980). Parental death in childhood and risk of adult depressive disorders: A review. *Psychological Medicine, 10,* 289–299.

Test, D.W., Fowler, C.H., Wood, W.M., Brewer, D.M., & Eddy, S. (2005). *Remedial and Special Education, 26*(1), 42–54.

Thomas, P.J., & Carmack, F.F. (1993). Language: The foundation of learning. In J.S. Choate (Ed.), *Successful mainstreaming: Proven ways to detect and correct special needs* (pp. 148–173). Boston: Allyn and Bacon.

Tirosh, E., & Canby, J. (1993). Autism with hyperlexia: A distinct syndrome? *American Journal on Mental Retardation, 98,* 84–92.

Toliver-Weddington, G., & Erickson, J.G. (1992). Suggestions for using standardized tests with minority children. In J. G. Erickson (Ed.), *Communication disorders in multicultural populations* (1992, April). Paper presented at Texas Speech-Language-Hearing Association Annual Convention, San Antonio, TX.

Torres, I., & Corn, A.L. (1990). *When you have a visually handicapped child in your classroom: Suggestions for teachers.* New York: American Foundation for the Blind.

Trad, P.V. (1999). Assessing the patterns that prevent teenage pregnancy. *Adolescence, 34,* 221–238.

Tryon, P.A., Mayes, S.D., Rhodes, R.L., & Waldo, M. (2006). Can Asperger's disorder be differentiated from autism using DSM-IV criteria? *Focus on Autism and Other Developmental Disabilities, 21*(1), 2–6.

Tsal, Y., Shalev, L., & Mevorach, C. (2005). The diversity of attention deficits in ADHD: The prevalence of four cognitive factors in ADHD versus controls. *Journal of Learning Disabilities, 38*(2), 142–157.

Turnbull, H.R., Pereira, L., & Blue-Banning, M. (2000). Teachers as friendship facilitators. *Teaching Exceptional Children, 32,* 66–70.

U.S. Department of Education. (1991, September 16). *Memorandum: Clarification of policy to address the needs of children with attention deficit disorders within general and/or special education.* Washington, DC: Author.

U.S. Department of Education. (1993). *15th annual report to Congress on the implementation of IDEA.* Washington, DC: Author.

U.S. Department of Education. (1995). *17th annual report to Congress on the implementation of IDEA.* Washington, DC: Author.

U.S. Department of Education. (1998). *Safe and smart: Making the after-school hours work for kids.* Washington, DC: Author.

U.S. Department of Education. (1999). *The condition of education, 1998.* Washington, DC: Author.

U.S. Department of Education. (2002). *24th annual report to Congress on the implementation of the Individuals with Disabilities Education Act.* Washington, DC: Author.

U.S. Department of Education. (2006). *28th annual report to Congress on the implementation of the Individuals with Disabilities Education Act.* Washington, DC: Author.

US Department of Education (2009). *29th annual report to Congress on the implementation of the individuals with disabilities education act*. Washington, DC: Author.

U.S. Department of Health and Human Services. (2003). *Helping the student with diabetes succeed*. National Diabetes Education Program.

U.S. Office of Education (USOE). (1977). Assistance to states for education of handicapped children: Procedures for evaluating specific learning disabilities. *Federal Register, 42*, 65082–65085.

Van Eerdewegh, M.M., Bieri, M.D., Parrilla, R.H., & Clayton, P.J. (1982). The bereaved child. *British Journal of Psychiatry, 140*, 23–29.

van Garderen, D., & Whittaker, C., (2006). Planning different multicultural instruction in secondary classes. *Teaching Exceptional Children, 44*, 12–15.

Van Laarhoven, T., Coutinho, M., Van Laarhoven-Myers, T., & Repp, A.C. (1999). Assessment of the student instructional setting, and curriculum to support successful integration. In M.J. Coutinho & A.C. Repp (Eds.), *Inclusion: The integration of students with disabilities*. Belmont, CA: Wadsworth Publishing.

VanTassel-Baska, J. (1989). Appropriate curriculum for gifted learners. *Educational Leadership, 47*, 13–15.

VanTassel-Baska, J. (1998). *Gifted and talented learners*. Denver: Love.

VanTassel-Baska, J., Patton, J., & Prillaman, D. (1989). Disadvantaged gifted learners at-risk for educational attention. *Focus on Exceptional Children, 22*(3), 1–16.

Vaughn, C., & Long, W. (1999). Surrender to win: How adolescent drug and alcohol users change their lives. *Adolescence, 34*, 9–22.

Vaughn, S., & Fuchs, L.S. (2003). Redefining learning disabilities as inadequate response to instruction: The promise and potential problems. *Learning Disabilities Research & Practice, 18*, 137–146.

Vaughn, S., Gersten, R., & Chard, D.J. (2000). The underlying message in learning disabilities intervention research: Findings from research synthesis. *Exceptional Children, 67*, 99–114.

Voltz, D., Brazil, N., & Ford, A. (2001). What matters most in inclusive education. *Intervention in School and Clinic, 37*, 23–30.

Wadsworth, D.E., & Knight, D. (1999). Preparing the classroom for students with speech, physical, and health needs. *Intervention in School and Clinic, 34*, 170–175.

Wagner, M., Kutash, K., Duchnowski, A.J., Epstein, M.H., & Sumi, W.C. (2005). The children and youth we serve: A national picture of the characteristics of students with emotional disturbances receiving special education. *Journal of Emotional and Behavioural Disorders, 13*(2), 79–96.

Walberg, H.J. (1991). Does homework help? *School Community Journal, 1*(1), 13–15.

Walker, B. (1993, January). *Multicultural issues in education: An introduction*. Paper presented at Cypress–Fairbanks Independent School District In-Service, Cypress, TX.

Walker, J.E., & Shea, T.M. (1995). *Behavior management: A practical approach for educators* (6th ed.). Columbus, OH: Merrill.

Wallace, G., Cohen, S., & Polloway, E.A. (1987). *Language arts: Teaching exceptional children*. Austin, TX: Pro-Ed.

Walther-Thomas, C., Korinek, L., McLaughlin, V.L., & Williams, B.T. (2000). *Collaboration for inclusive education*. Boston: Allyn and Bacon.

Wang, M.C., & Birch, J.W. (1984). Effective special education in regular classes. *Exceptional Children, 52*, 36–49.

Wang, M.C., Reynolds, M.C., & Walberg, H.J. (1994–1995). Serving students at the margins. *Educational Leadership, 52*, 12–17.

Warren, D. (1994). *Blindness in children*. Cambridge, MA: Cambridge University Press.

Waterman, B.B. (1994). Assessing children for the presence of a disability. *NICHY News Digest, 4*(1), Washington, DC: U.S. Government Printing Office.

Wayman, K., Lynch, E., & Hanson, M. (1990). Home-based early childhood services: Cultural sensitivity in a family systems approach. *Topics in Early Childhood Special Education, 10*(4), 65–66.

Webber, J. (1997). Responsible inclusion: Key components for success. In P. Zionts (Ed.), *Effective inclusion of students with behavior and learning problems*. Austin, TX: Pro-Ed.

Weber, K. (1994). *Special education in Canadian schools*. Thornhill, ON: Highland Press.

Weber, K., & Bennett, S. (1999). *Special education in Ontario schools*. Don Mills, ON: Highland Press.

Wehby, J.H., Symons, F.J., Canale, J.A., & Go, F.J. (1998). Teaching practices in classrooms for students with emotional and behavioral disorders: Discrepancies between recommendations and observations. *Behavioral Disorders, 24*, 51–56.

Wehman, P. (Ed.). (1997). *Exceptional individuals in school, community, and work*. Austin, TX: Pro-Ed.

Wehmeyer, M. (1993). Self-determination as an educational outcome. *Impact, 6*(4), 16–17, 26.

Wehmeyer, M. (1994). Perceptions of self-determination and psychological empowerment of adolescents with mental retardation. *Education and Training in Mental Retardation and Developmental Disabilities, 29*, 9–21.

Wehmeyer, M.L. (2006). Universal design for learning, access to the general education curriculum, and students with mild mental retardation. *Exceptionality, 14*, 225–235.

Wehmeyer, M.L., Lattin, D., & Agram, M. (2001). Achieving access to the general education curriculum for students with mental retardation: A curriculum decision-making model. *Education and Training in Mental Retardation and Developmental Disabilities, 36*, 327–342.

Wehmeyer, M.L., Morningstar, M., & Husted, D. (1999). *Family involvement in transition planning and implementation*. Austin, TX: Pro-Ed.

Weinbender, M.L.M., & Rossignol, A.M. (1996). Lifestyle and risk of premature sexual activity in a high school population of Seventh-Day Adventists: Valuegenesis 1989. *Adolescence, 31*, 265–275.

West, G.K. (1986). *Parenting without guilt.* Springfield, IL: Thomas.

West, G.K. (1994, Nov. 10). Discipline that works: Part 1. *The News and Daily Advance.*

West, G.K. (2002). Parent education programs and benefits for parents of children with disabilities. Unpublished manuscript, Lynchburg College in Lynchburg, VA.

Westling, D.L., Herzog, M.J., Cooper-Duffy, K., Prohn, K., & Ray, M. (2006). The teacher support program: A proposed resource for the special education profession and an initial validation. *Remedial and Special Education, 27*(3), 136–147.

Westling, D.L., & Koorland, M.A. (1988). *The special educator's handbook.* Boston: Allyn and Bacon.

Weston, D., Ludolph, P., Misle, B., Ruffins, S., & Block, J. (1990). Physical and sexual abuse in adolescent girls with borderline personality disorder. *American Journal of Orthopsychiatry, 60*, 55–66.

Weyandt, L.L. (2001). *An ADHD primer.* Boston: Allyn and Bacon.

Wicks-Nelson, R., & Israel, A.C. (1991). *Behavior disorders of childhood.* Englewood Cliffs, NJ: Prentice-Hall.

Wiener, J. (2004). Do peer relationships foster behavioural adjustment in children with learning disabilities? *Learning Disability Quarterly, 27*, 21–30.

Wiig, E.H. (1986). Language disabilities in school-age children and youth. In G.H. Shames & E.H. Wiig (Eds.), *Human communication disorders* (2nd ed., pp. 331–383). Columbus, OH: Merrill.

Wiig, E.H., & Semel, E. (1984). *Language assessment and intervention for the learning disabled* (2nd ed.). Columbus, OH: Merrill.

Wilens, T.E., Biederman, J., & Spencer, T.J. (2002). Attention deficit/hyperactivity disorder across the lifespan. *Annual Review of Medicine, 53*, 113–131.

Williams, M.A., & Macmillan, R.B. (2005). Litigation in special education: From placement to programming. *Education Law Journal, 15*(1), 31–59.

Williams, R.J., Odaibo, F.S., & McGee, J.M. (1999). Incidence of fetal alcohol syndrome in northeastern Manitoba. *Canadian Journal of Public Health, 90*(3), 192–194.

Willms, J.D. (Ed.). (2002). *Vulnerable children: Findings from Canada's national longitudinal survey of children and youth.* Edmonton, AB: University of Alberta Press.

Winebrenner, S. (2000). Gifted students need an education, too. *Educational Leadership, 58*(1), 52–57.

Winocur, S.L., & Mauer, P.A. (1997). Critical thinking and gifted students: Using IMPACT to improve teaching and learning. In N. Colangelo and G.A. Davis (Eds.), *Handbook of gifted education* (2nd ed., pp. 308–317). Boston: Allyn and Bacon.

Winzer, M. (1999). *Children with exceptionalities in Canadian classrooms* (5th ed.). Scarborough, ON: Prentice-Hall Canada.

Wolfe, P.S. (1997). Deaf-blindness. In P. Wehman (Ed.), *Exceptional individuals* (pp. 357–381). Austin, TX: Pro-Ed.

Wolfe, P.S., & Hall, T.E. (2003). Making inclusion a reality for students with severe disabilities. *Teaching Exceptional Children, 35*, 56–61.

Wolfensberger, W. (1972). Voluntary citizen advocacy in the human services. *Canada's Mental Health, 20*(2), 14–18.

Wong, B.Y.L. (Ed.). (2004). *Learning about learning disabilities* (3rd ed.). San Diego, CA: Elsevier Academic Press.

Wong, B. (1996). *The ABCs of learning disabilities.* San Diego, CA: Academic Press.

Wood, D.K., & Frank, A.R. (2000). Using memory-enhancing strategies to learn multiplication facts. *Teaching Exceptional Children, 32*, 78–82.

Wood, J.W. (1996). *Adapting instruction for mainstreamed and at-risk students* (3rd ed.). New York: Merrill.

Woronov, T. (1996). Assistive technology for literacy produces impressive results for the disabled. In E. Miller & R. Tovey (Eds.), *Inclusion and special education* (pp. 9–11). Cambridge, MA: Harvard Educational Letter.

Wurst, D., Jones, D., & Luckner, J. (2005). Promoting literacy development with students who are deaf, hard-of-hearing, and hearing. *Teaching Exceptional Children, 37*, 56–60.

Ylvisaker, T., Szekeres, N., Hartwick, R., & Tworek, L.L. (1994). Collaboration in preparation for personal injury suits after TBI. *Topics in Language Disorders, 15*, 1–20.

Young, G., & Gerber, P.J. (1998). Learning disabilities and poverty: Moving towards a new understanding of learning disabilities as a public health and economic-risk issue. *Learning Disabilities, 9*, 1–6.

Young, M.E., Kersten, L., & Werch, T. (1996). Evaluation of patient-child drug education program. *Journal of Drug Education, 26*, 57–68.

Ysseldyke, J.E., & Olsen, K. (1999). Putting alternative assessments into practice: What to measure and possible sources of data. *Exceptional Children, 65*, 175–185.

Zabel, R.H., & Zabel, M.K. (1996). *Classroom management in context.* Boston: Houghton Mifflin.

Zentall, S. (2006). *ADHD and education: Foundations, characteristics, methods, and collaboration.* Upper Saddle River, NJ: Merrill Prentice Hall.

Zhang, D. (2001). Self-determination and inclusion: Are students with mild mental retardation more self-determined in regular classrooms? *Education and Training in Mental Retardation and Developmental Disabilities, 36*(4), 357–362.

Zirkel, P.A. (2002). The autism case law: Administrative and judicial rulings. *Focus on Autism & Other Developmental Disabilities, 17*(2), 84–94.

Name Index

Hall, T.E., 28, 43, 409, 410
Hall, 294, 295
Hallahan, D.P., 6, 11, 85, 86, 91, 94, 235, 239, 260, 334
Haller, 227
Halvorsen, A.T., 36
Hamaguchi, P.A., 68
Hammerness, P.G., 123, 124, 126–131
Hammill, D.D., 14, 94–95, 96, 100
Hanks, 232
Hanson, M., 71
Harber, M.M., 416
Harper, G.F., 39, 360
Harper, 179
Harrington, 104
Harris, K.R., 103
Harris, L.R., 67
Hartwick, R., 243
Hasbury, D., 3
Hatch, T., 262, 263
Haynes, W.O., 49
Heath, N.L., 92
Hebig, Kim, 310
Heflin, L.J., 208
Heinen, A., 29
Heller, K.A., 250, 260
Heller, K.W., 246
Hellsten, L.M., 15, 19
Hendren, 212
Hendricks, M.D., 253
Hendrickson, J.M., 172
Herman, K.L., 93, 110
Herrold, W.G. Jr., 34
Hess, 113
Heward, W.L., 49, 55
Higgins, E.L., 93, 110
Higgins, K., 362, 379
Hilton, A., 39, 45
Hinshaw, S., 134
Hokanson, C.R. Jr., 93
Holcomb, D. et al., 248
Homme, L., 326
Hooper, C.R., 56
Hoover, J.J., 110, 189, 190, 343, 344, 345, 364
Hornak, J.E., 253
Horner, R.H., 328–329
Hou, F., 85
Houle, G.R., 97
Hourcade, J.J., 43
Huber, H., 210
Huff, C.R., 291
Hughes, C. et al., 195
Hughes, R., 324

Hull, K., 97
Hume, K., 209
Humes, 113
Hunt, P. et al., 34
Hutchison, D.R., 354
Hutton, A.M., 402, 404
Huurre, T.M., 239

I

Idol, L., 30, 326
Illsey, S.D., 175
Iovannone, R., 210

J

Jaffe, P., 324
Jaindl, M., 227
Jakobson, 142
Jayanthi, M., 109, 192, 367, 412, 418
Jefferson-Aker, C.R., 251
Jenkins, J.R., 29, 94
Jessiman, S.M., 79
Jitendra, A., 405
Johnson, D.J., 107
Johnson, G., 251
Johnson, J.G., 298
Johnson, L.J., 34
Johnson, R.L., 251
Johnson, S., 243
Johnstone, C., 345–346
Jones, D., 231
Jones, E.D., 273–274
Jones, L.S., 37, 39, 40, 41, 314, 316, 340
Jones, 314
Jones, V.F., 37, 39, 40, 41, 314, 316, 340
Jordan, N.C., 102
Joughin, C., 253
Justice, L.M., 61

K

Kaderavek, J., 223, 224, 227
Kalachnik, TTT et al., 212
Kanner, L., 199
Kaplan, P., 162
Kaplan, S.N., 278
Karge, B.D., 39
Karp, N., 97
Kataoka, J., 278
Kauffman, J.M., 6, 11, 153, 156, 157, 169, 172, 204, 235, 239, 260
Kavale, K.A., 29, 33, 93, 106, 169, 209
Keith, B., 396
Keller, W.D., 226

Kerr, L., 168
Keyser-Marcus, L., 243
Kikas, 142
Kincaid, D., 210
King-Sears, M.E., 34
Kirk, S.A., 83
Kissam, B.R., 100, 145
Kitano, M.K., 278
Klassen, R., 86
Klein, D.M., 403
Klinger, D.A., 15, 19
Kluwin, T.N., 227, 231
Kollins, S.H. et al., 134
Komulainen, E.J., 239
Koorland, M.A., 414
Korinek, L., 24, 38, 39
Kortering, L.J., 161
Kouche, B., 360
Kovacs-Burns, K., 3
Kozub, F.M.J., 234, 237
Kroeger, S.D., 360
Kully, D., 79
Kumar, P., 37, 38

L

Lahey, M., 61
Lambert, M.A., 394
Landrum, T.J., 153, 156, 157, 168, 169
Lang, H.G., 231
Larsen, S.C., 96
Lattin, D., 34, 190
Lavoie, R., 41
Lazure, 3
LeBlanc, N., 214
Lee, S.H., 416
Lenz, B.K., 100, 145–380, 385, 387, 395, 396
Lerner, J.W., 106, 109
Leung, W.W., 204
Levin, 317, 336, 338
Levine, P., 134
Lewis, R.B., 15
Lewis, T.J., 171, 172
Lewis, 296
Li, 232
Linn, R., 42, 90, 144, 145
Lipsey, 93
Lloyd, J.W., 334
Loehr, J., 59–60
Long, W., 301, 302
Loock, C., 214
Lowrey, K.A., 210
Lubin, J., 179

Luckasson, R., 55, 180, 181
Luckner, J., 231
Luthar, S.S., 305
Lynch, E., 71
Lyon, G.R. et al., 7, 88, 92, 94–98
Lytle, R.K., 21

M

MacArthur, C., 103
MacMillan, D.L., 93, 94
Madaus, J., 110, 382
Madden, L., 175
Maheady, L., 39, 360
Makkar, R. et al., 124
Male, M., 282
Mallette, B., 39, 360
Malmgren, K.W., 44
Malott, M.E., 163
Malott, R.W., 163
Manchetti, B.M., 89
Mangrum, C.T., 145
Marschark, M., 231
Martin, 212
Martini, R., 92
Marzano, 313
Masten, A.S., 305
Masters, L.F., 373–374
Mastropieri, M.A., 36, 37, 40, 41, 91,
    102, 106
Mathes, P., 92–93, 360
Mathur, S.R., 169
Matthews, D.J., 287
Mayer, C., 223
Mayer-Johnson, 76
Mayes, S.D., 8, 202–203
McCardle, P., 97
McCart, Sue, 218
McConaughy, S.H., 161
McConnell, K., 156, 163, 166
McDevitt, T.M., 363
McEvoy, A., 158
McEwan, E.K., 316, 321
McGee, J.M., 214
McGinty, A.S., 61
McGrew, 191
McLaughlin, V., 24, 39
McLaughlin-Cheng, E., 206
McLean-Haywood, D., 204
McLoughlin, J.A., 15
McMaster, K.N., 93, 361
McMillan, J.H., 15, 19
McNamara, J.K., 91
McNeill, J.H., 69

McPartland, J.M., 292
McReynolds, 52
McShane, E., 67
Meadan, H., 42
Melland, D.F., 161
Melloy, G., 327
Meng, L., 204
Merasty, Heather, 138
Mercer, A.R., 97, 117, 376
Mercer, C.D., 351, 376
Mercer, 94
Merrill, R.M. et al., 57
Mevorach, C., 125
Meyer, D., 406
Mihalas, S. et al., 160, 165, 167
Milan, A., 85
Miller, L., 223, 347, 348
Miller, R.J., 188
Miller, S.P., 351
Milligan, C., 345–346
Missiunia, C., 92
Mock, D., 93, 95
Modrek, S., 134
Monda-Amaya, L., 42
Montgomery, 227
Montgomery, W., 400
Moores, D., 227
Morgan, P.L., 93, 95
Morgan, S.R., 305
Mori, A.A., 373–374
Mori, B.A., 373–374
Morris, S., 90, 105
Morrison, G.S., 304, 305, 306
Mostert, M.P., 106
Munk, D.D., 369, 391, 408, 416, 418
Murdick, N.L., 21
Murray, C., 37
Myers, B.J., 203
Myles, B.S., 204

N

Nanson, J., 215
Neary, T., 36
Neihart, 282
Nelson, J.R., 159–160, 168, 171
Nelson, J.S. et al., 393
Nelson, L.G.L. et al., 408
Nelson, M., 34, 292
Nelson, 192
Nerro, R.C., 333
Newman, L. et al., 161
Nolan, 336, 338
Nordstrom, B., 214

Northern, J.L., 224, 226
Nowacek, J., 67, 394

O

Oakland, T., 267
Obiakor, F.E., 207
O'Brien, J., 3, 43
O'Connor, R., 94
Odaibo, F.S., 214
Odom, S.L. et al., 211
Oh, H., 234, 237
Olsen, K., 13, 15
Olson, J.L., 104
Orr, T.J., 204
Osmond, Cordell, 408
Owens, R.E., 64
Oyer, H.J., 56

P

Pakulski, L., 223, 224, 227
Palmer, D.J., 309
Palmer, D.S., 34
Pandiani, J.A., 161
Parrett, W.H., 9, 291, 306, 307, 308, 309
Patton, J.R., 4, 19, 23, 88, 105, 110, 135,
    136, 140, 144, 156, 160, 167, 186,
    188, 189, 190, 192, 271, 292, 315,
    334, 343, 344, 345, 346, 352, 354,
    367, 375, 412, 418
Paul-Brown, D., 97
Paulsen, K., 379
Pearpoint, J., 43
Peebles-Wilkins, W., 303–304
Pemberton, J.B., 344–345, 408
Pereira, L., 38
Perske, R., 194
Peterson, D., 155
Pfiffner, L., 335
Phillipsen, L., 37, 38
Piaget, J., 97
Pierangelo, R., 144
Pinzola, R.H., 49
Platt, J.M., 104
Pocock, A. et al., 109
Podemski, R.S. et al., 30, 41
Pollard, E., 43
Polloway, E.A., 4, 7, 23, 88, 105, 135,
    136, 140, 144, 156, 179, 186, 189,
    192, 223, 292, 293, 295, 315, 334,
    346, 347, 348, 352, 354, 362, 367,
    375, 389, 412, 418
Prater, M.A., 402
Pratt, R., 209

Pressley, M., 102
Prestia, K., 255, 256
Provost, M.C., 145
Pugach, M.C., 39
Pugh, K.R. et al., 86
Pullen, 94

Q

Quay, H., 155
Quinn, M.M., 169

R

Rademacher, J.A., 344–345
Rankin-Erickson, J.L., 102
Ranta, 200
Raskind, M.H., 93, 110
Raskind, W.W., 86
Ratner, V.L., 67
Reeve, R.E., 144
Reid, R., 168
Reid, 159, 160
Reinherz, H.Z., 300
Reis, S.M., 262, 279, 285
Remenda, Jeanne, 188
Renzulli, J.S., 262, 263, 279
Repp, A.C., 39
Rett, A., 201
Reynolds, C.T., 364
Reynolds, M.C., 31
Rhodes, R.L., 8, 203
Richards, S.B., 7
Richards, T.L., 86
Rieck, W.A., 34
Rimm, S.B., 260
Roberts, G., 215
Roberts, 3, 93
Robinson, C.S., 89
Robinson, G.A., 354
Robinson, T., 210
Rock, M.L., 381
Rohena, 131
Rosales, T., 214
Roseberry-McKibbin, C., 71
Rosenberg, M.S., 322
Rossen, E., 267
Rossignol, A.M., 302
Rotherham, J., 93
Rothstein, 157
Rotter, K., 391, 392
Roy, 205
Ruble, L.A., 208, 213
Ruffin, M., 416
Rutherford, R.B. Jr., 169
Ryan, 143

S

Sabatino, D.A., 170
Sabornie, E.J., 158–159, 160, 379
Safford, E.J., 29
Safford, P.L., 29
Safran, J.S., 201, 206
Salend, S.J., 28, 34, 37, 44, 131, 143,
    361, 364, 367, 369, 390
Salvia, J., 11, 12, 235
Salzinger, S., 298
Sander, E.K., 53, 55
Sanford, J.P., 337
Sansosti, F.J. et al., 211
Santamaría, L.J., 10
Santos, K.E., 42, 90, 144, 145
Saunders, M., 329
Savage, R.C., 8
Scanlon, D., 161
Schacht, L.M., 161
Schack, G.D., 285
Schalock, R.L. et al., 180
Scheffler, R., 134
Scheuermann, B., 198, 204, 205
Schloss, A., 379, 382, 386
Schloss, C.N., 379, 382, 386
Schloss, P., 379, 382, 386
Schneider, 90
Scholes, 395
Schuck, S.E.B., 123
Schumaker, J.B. et al., 395
Schumm, J.S., 113, 364
Schwartz, D., 270
Schwartz, S.E., 39
Schwartzman, M.N., 246, 250
Scott, S., 18
Scruggs, T.E., 36, 37, 40, 41, 91, 102
Seeley, K., 360
Seery, M.E., 34
Semel, E., 64
Serna, L., 23, 88, 105, 136, 140, 160, 167,
    315, 346, 352
Serres, F., 299
Sexton, D. et al., 306
Shalev, L., 125
Shanker, A., 29
Shanley, R., 279, 282
Shapiro, E.S., 333
Sharpe, W., 146
Shaw, 382
Shea, T.M., 170, 410
Sherron-Targett, P., 243
Sileo, A.P., 402
Sileo, T.W., 402
Silver, L.B., 96, 111, 112

Silverthorn, K.H., 253
Simpson, R., 198, 204, 208, 212
Siperstein, G.N., 93, 94
Skoto, B.G. et al., 416
Sladeczek, I.E., 175
Slavin, R.E., 292
Slicker, E.K., 309
Sliverman, A.B., 300
Smedley, T.M., 362
Smith, C.R., 313, 316, 320
Smith, D.D., 55
Smith, J.D., 4, 33, 189, 295
Smith, L., 279
Smith, T., 189
Smith, T.E.C., 4, 7, 30, 33, 39, 45, 135,
    186, 223, 253, 262, 293, 334, 347,
    348, 405
Smith, T.J., 91
Smith, 143
Smith, W.J., 21
Snell, M., 40
Snow, J.E., 3
Snyder, 93
Sokol, R.J., 214
Solomon, C.R., 299
Soto, G. et al., 76
Southern, W.T., 273, 274
Spinelli, 244
Stainback, S., 2, 33, 40
Stainback, W., 2, 33, 40
Stanovich, K.E., 92, 98
Sternberg, R.J., 262
Steuernagel, 200
Stewart, D.A., 223, 227, 231
Stoller, L., 334
Strichart, S.S., 145
Strickler, K., 113, 364
Sudweeks, R.R., 207
Sugai, G., 171, 172
Summers, J.A. et al., 407
Svenson, E., 93
Swain, 104
Swanson, H.L., 84
Symons, F.J., 168
Szekeres, N., 243

T

Tabassam, W., 90, 105
Tannenbaum, A.J., 262
Tannock, R., 124
Taylor, R.L., 7, 15
Taylor, 293
Tessier, A., 403
Test, D.W. et al., 383, 384

Subject Index

ChatPC, 77
childhood cancer, 245–246
childhood disintegrative disorder (CDD), 202
circle of friends, 44, 194
class transitions, 336–337
classroom, general education
    see also classroom, special education
    belonging to, 4
    EBD, 144–145, 167–168
    effectiveness, 40
    gifted and talented students, 270–272
    hearing impairments, 229
    intellectual disabilities, 188–190
    secondary school students, 375–384
    setting for students with exceptionalities, 29
    visual impairments, 236
classroom, special education
    see also classroom, general education
    approach, 29–31
    benefits, 30
    disadvantages, 31
    diversity of students, 31
    resource room model, 31–33
classroom arrangement
    AD/HD, 139
    elementary school, 366
    for language disorders, 70
    in organization and management, 321–323
classroom observation, in ecological inventory, 17
classroom organization and management
    accessibility, 323
    for AD/HD, 135–139
    arrangements, 321–323
    class transitions, 336–337
    concepts, 314
    cultural considerations, 317
    definition, 314
    factors affecting dynamics, 317–319
    gifted and talented students, 275–278
    grouping, 336–338
    guiding principles, 316
    instructional dimension, 336–338
    lesson plans, 338
    models, 314–316
    physical component, 321–323
    procedural component, 319–321
    psychosocial component, 317–319
    rules in, 319–320
    scheduling, 336–337
    success of, 40

teachers' organizational dimension, 339–340
    technological aids, 338, 340
classroom rules, 136–170, 319–320
classroom teachers. *See* teachers
classwide peer tutoring (CWPT), 360
co-operative learning, in elementary school, 359–361
co-operative teaching. *See* collaboration
co-teaching, 43
cognition difficulties, 91
cognitive differences, 116–117
cognitive model, 97
COLA checklist, 391, 392
collaboration
    see also communication
    in AD/HD, 149
    description, 43
    for EBD, 144
    in elementary school, 359
    family and school personnel, 149, 407
    general education and special education teachers, 32, 41–43, 378
    for language disorders, 71
    speech-language pathologists and teachers, 77–78
    students and teachers, 380
    and support of personnel, 36–37, 41–45
    teams for success, 41–42
    types of, 43–44
Coller, Chad, 285
Committee on Goals 2000 and the Inclusion of Students with Disabilities, 345
communication
    see also collaboration
    definition, 49
    as a disability, 49
    language and, 49
    parents and personnel, 408–413
    style and cultures, 72–73
    variations, 50
communication disorders
    see also language disorders; speech disorders
    behaviours related to, 66–67
    definitions, 49–50
    future trends, 78–79
    identification and assessment, 50
    inclusive classrooms enhancement, 77–78
    prevalence and causes, 50

social problems and, 48
    types, 49–50
communicative difference, 50
community, sense of, and social acceptance, 36–38, 117–118, 286
community-based instruction, 355
community-building skills, for teachers, 146–147
comprehensive curriculum, 346
computation. *See* mathematics and computation
computers and technology
    see also technology
    learning disabilities and, 104, 114–115
conductive hearing loss, 224
Constitution Act (1982), 3
constructionist model, 97
content, of language, 63
contingencies for classroom behaviour, 326–327
contingency plans, in secondary school, 385–386
continuum of services model, 33–34
contracts, 140–141, 326–327
conversation difficulties, 89–90
coordination problems, 92, 116
COPS strategy, 395
Corkett, Dr. Julie, 380
Council for Children with Behaviour Disorders, 33–34
Council for Exceptional Children (CEC), 33–34, 39
creativity, 263
criterion-referenced assessments, 15
culture
    see also diversity; language differences; multiculturalism
    in classroom organization and management, 317
    communication style and, 72–73
    factors in assessment, 73
    families and, 399–400
curriculum-based assessments, 15
cystic fibrosis, 247–248

D

daily report cards, 415
data collection, for assessment, 12–13
deaf, 50, 223–224
    see also hearing impairments
death, 297–298

exams preparation, in secondary school,
381–382
exceptionalities. *See* students with
exceptionalities
expressive language, 61–62

F

fairness, 40–41
families
see also parents
in 21st century, 400
adaptation to ASD, 207
challenges to having children with
exceptionalities, 402–404
classroom dynamics factors, 318–319
collaboration with school personnel,
400–407
culture and, 399–400
death in, and at risk students,
297–298
direct instructional support, 415–416
home-based intervention, 415–418
home visits to, 412
homework support, 416–417
involvement in education, 398–399,
400, 404–406, 414–418
reinforcement provision, 415
siblings of children with
exceptionalities, 404–406
single parents and at risk students,
295–297
support principles, 401
Family Network for Deaf Children,
33–34
fetal alcohol spectrum disorders (FASD)
cause, 215
characteristics, 216
concepts, 214
definition, 214–215
identification, 215
interventions, 216–218
overview, 8–9
Sue McCart profile, 218
Fetal alcohol syndrome (FAS), 8
First Step to Success program, 166
flexibility, instructional, 41, 45
fluency, description, 57
fluency disorders
definition, 50, 57
emergence, 57
identification, 57–58
stuttering, 57
types, 57

form, in language, 63
formal assessment, 13–14
The Fourth R Project, 324–325
friendship, 44
full inclusion, 33
functional behavioural assessment
(FBA), in EBD, 163–165

G

games playing, through language
improvements, 69–70
Gaudet, Danielle, 285
Gay, Lesbian, and Straight Education
Network (GLSEN), 302–303
general education classroom. *See*
classroom, general education
Geneva Centre for Autism, 199
gifted and talented students
acceleration options, 273,
278, 279
career development, 282
Chad Coller and Danielle Gaudet
profiles, 285
characteristics, 264–266
classroom management, 275–278
concepts, 260–261
creativity, 263
curricula goals, 270
curriculum and instruction
considerations, 278–282
curriculum compacting, 278, 279
definition, 261–262
differentiated programming, 269–270,
272–282
enrichment options, 273–275
Gardner and Hatch's model, 262
general education classroom, 270–271
identification, assessment, and
eligibility, 267–269
inclusion, 286
labelling, 260–261
misconceptions about, 260
multicultural issues, 267, 269, 270
overview, 9
personnel needs to deal with, 271
placement options, 272–273
prevalence and origins, 264
programming approaches, 273–275
Renzulli's three-ring conception,
262, 263
Romeo and Juliet play, 278–279, 282
sense of community and social
acceptance, 286

social-emotional considerations,
282–286
special grouping practice, 275
Sternberg's theory, 262
strategies for curriculum and
instruction, 269–275
teacher supports, 287
girls, with AD/HD, 124
GLBT (Gay, Lesbian, Bisexual, or
Transgendered) students, 302–304
goals, in IEPs, 22–24
Grabowski, Cassandra, 358
grading practices, 367–369, 390–391
grouping, 336–338
guardians. *See* parents

H

hard of hearing, 50, 223–224
see also hearing impairments
head injury. *See* traumatic brain injury
health problems and physical disabilities,
244–255
hearing disorder, definition, 50
hearing impairments
assistive listening devices, 231
audiologists and, 228
auditory processing disorder, 226
Cassandra Grabowski profile, 358
characteristics, 227, 228
classification, 224–226
classroom adaptations and
accommodations, 229–232
concepts, 223
conductive hearing loss, 224
definition, 223–224
identification, assessment, and
eligibility, 227–229
otitis media, 224
overview, 222
prevalence and causes, 227
sensorineural hearing loss, 224
strategies for curriculum and
instruction, 229–230
technology, 231–232
hearing loss, 224–226
Hebig, Kim, 310
high school. *See* secondary school
HIV and AIDS, 251–252
home-based intervention, 415–418
home-to-school notebook,
409–410
home visits to family, 412
homelessness, 294–295

homework
    elementary school, 366–367
    family support, 416–417
    organization, 144–146
    practices for success, 389–390
    secondary school, 387–390
Hospital for Sick Children, 124
hyperactivity. *See* attention deficit/
    hyperactivity disorder
hyperglycemia and hypoglycemia, 250
hyperkinetic disorders. *See* attention
    deficit/hyperactivity disorder

I

IEPs. *See* individualized education
    programs
inclusion
    AD/HD, 146–150
    advantages, 31, 34
    authors' position on, 419
    classroom teachers role, 35–36
    concept, 36
    continuum of services model, 33–34
    curricular needs, 39–40
    disadvantages, 34–35
    EBD, 144–145, 166–168
    effectiveness, 45
    elementary school, 343–358, 359
    enhancement methods, 36
    evolution of, 3–4
    full inclusion model, 33
    gifted and talented students, 286
    intellectual disabilities, 190–191,
        193–194
    model description, 33–34
    problems with, 30
    setting for, 29
    special education teachers and
        personnel role, 35
    success features, 36–45
    visual impairments, 240–241
independent living preparation,
    381–383
individual student support plan (ISSP).
    See individualized education
    programs
individualized education programs (IEPs)
    evaluation in, 24
    intent and concept, 21, 22
    key components, 22–24
    parents' involvement, 413–414
    sample, 25
    steps leading to, 11

    teachers and, 21, 22, 24
    team, 21–22
individualized program plan (IPP). *See*
    individualized education programs
Individuals with Disabilities Education Act
    (IDEA) (1990), 2
Individuals with Disabilities Education Act
    (IDEA) (2004), 83–84, 92, 122,
    200, 207
informal assessment, 14–16
information gathering, for assessment,
    12–13
Institute of Medicine, 204
integration, 3–4, 36
    see also inclusion
intellectual disabilities
    challenges and goals for general
        education, 188–190
    characteristics, 182–183, 192
    classification, 181–182
    classroom adaptations and
        accommodations, 192–196
    definition, 178, 179–180
    identification, assessment, and
        eligibility, 185
    inclusion and, 190–191, 193–194
    intellectual functioning and, 179–180
    Jeanne Remenda profile, 188
    prevalence and causes, 182–183
    self-determination, 188–189
    transition considerations, 186–187
intellectual disability, overview, 7
International Classification of Diseases
    (ICD-10), 123
International Dyslexia Association, 112
isolation of students, 4

J

junior high school, 64, 354
juvenile deliquency, 304–305
juvenile diabetes, 249–250

K

key words, as teaching tool, 145

L

labelling of people, 5, 153, 260–261
language
    communication and, 49
    considerations, 49
    content, 63
    deficits in EBD, 159–160

    definition, 61
    development, 62
    dimensions, 63–64
    diversity and AD/HD, 130–131
    expressive, 61–62
    form, 63
    hearing impairments and, 223
    learning disabilities and, 89–90,
        95–96, 107–108, 113–115
    morphology, 63
    phonology, 63
    receptive, 61–62
    syntax, 63
    use, 63–64
language differences, 71–78
    augmentative and alternative
        communication, 74–77
    communication style and, 72–73
    description, 71
    electronic communication aids, 77
    ELLs and, 71–72
    multicultural considerations, 73, 74
    nonautomated devices, 74–76
    observation considerations, 74
language disorders, 61–71
    see also communication disorders;
        speech disorders
    adaptations and accommodations,
        64–71
    behaviours related to, 66–67
    causes, 64
    classroom arrangement and, 70
    of content, 50
    definition, 49–50
    development, 62
    of form, 50
    of function, 50
    impact and remediation, 61
    indicators, 64
    music and games for, 69–70
    older students and, 70–71
    problems related to, 67
    process writing and, 71
    specific language impairment, 64
    speech-language pathologist and, 71
    story reading and storytelling, 69, 71
learning difficulties, and EBD, 165
learning disabilities
    see also learning strategies for
        curriculum and instruction
    academic difficulties and, 87–89,
        113–115
    behavioural model, 97
    characteristics in students, 86–92

learning disabilities (*continued*)
    classroom adaptations, 112–117
    cognitive differences, 116–117
    cognitive model, 97
    computers and technology, 104, 114–115
    cultural and linguistic diversity, 95–96
    definition, 83–85
    developmental model, 97
    discrepancy concept, 92
    distinguishing, 82, 83
    dyslexia, 88, 111–112
    identification, assessment, and eligibility, 92–95
    language difficulties and, 89–90, 107–108, 113–115
    learning strategies, 100–102, 109, 110
    listening skills, 104
    mathematics, 88–89, 102, 103
    metacognition and, 91–92, 116
    orthomolecular therapy, 111–112
    overview, 7
    perception, 116
    phonemic awareness, 100
    preschool students, 94–95
    prevalence and causes, 85–86
    reading and, 87–88, 100, 102, 107
    responsiveness-to-intervention model, 92–93, 95–96
    self-determination, 109
    sense of community and social acceptance, 117–118
    social-emotional problems, 90–91, 115–116
    social interactions, 104–106
    sound blending activity, 98
    spoken language, 103–104
    strengths and needs in children, 87
    teachers and, 109–110
    vision therapy, 112
    whole language method, 100
    writing, 89, 102, 103
Learning Disabilities Association of Canada (LDAC), 7–8, 33–34, 84–85, 92
learning strategies for curriculum and instruction, 96–112
    AD/HD, 144–146
    adults, 110
    approaches overview, 96–97
    controversial and nontraditional approaches, 110–112
    elementary school, 98–106

preschool services, 97–98
secondary school, 106–110, 380–381, 394–395
traditional approaches, 97
lesson plans, 338, 384–385, 386
LGBT (Lesbian, Gay, Bisexual, or Transgendered) students, 302–304
life skills, 189, 354
Lightwriter SL35, 77
linguistic problems, and language disorders, 67
listening, 89, 104, 361–362
low vision, definition, 233

M

mainstreaming, 4–36
management. *See* classroom organization and management
mathematics and computation
    elementary school, 349–351, 352
    learning disabilities, 88–89, 102, 103
McCart, Sue, 218
medication and medical intervention
    AD/HD, 131–135
    ASD, 211–212
    EBD, 174
memory difficulties, learning disabilities and, 91
mental health personnel, for EBD, 144
Mental Measurements Yearbook, 13
mentor programs, for at-risk students, 309–310
Merasty, Heather, 138
metacognition difficulties, and learning disabilities, 91–92, 116
middle school, 64, 354
modification
    see also accommodation; adaptation
    definition, 29, 385
    secondary school, 377, 384–388
    supports and, 40–41
morphology, 63
motor skills and coordination problems, 92, 116
motor speech disorder, definition, 52
multiculturalism
    see also culture; diversity
    ASD and, 207
    EBD considerations, 173
    gifted and talented students, 267, 269, 270
    language differences and, 73, 74
    at risk students, 292, 293

multisensory impairments, 248
    see also hearing impairments; visual impairments
multitiered model of curriculum, 345
muscular dystrophy, 252–253
music, 44, 69–70

N

National Institute of Mental Retardation, 4
National Institutes of Health (NIH), 121
National Longitudinal Survey of Children and Youth (NLSCY), 85, 155–156
neglect, of at-risk students, 298–301
neurological research, and learning disabilities, 85–86
nonautomated devices, for language differences, 74–76
nondiscriminatory assessment, 19–20
normalization movement, 2, 31
Northwest Territories, 6
note taking skills, 363

O

observation, for assessment, 12–13
"One Million Children: A National Study of Canadian Children with Emotional and Learning Disorders" (Roberts and Lazure), 3
Ontario, 6, 324–325
oral expression difficulties, 89
oral presentations, in elementary school, 362–363
Organisation for Economic Co-operation and Development (OECD), 156
organization. *See* classroom organization and management
orthomolecular therapy, 111–112
orthopedic impairments, overview, 8
Osmond, Cordell, 408
otitis media, 224
output communication aids, 77

P

paraprofessionals and paraeducators, 43
parents
    see also families
    acceptance of children with exceptionalities, 402–404
    collaboration with teachers for AD/HD, 149

common questions of, 414
communication with, 408–413
conferences with teachers, 413–414
education of, 406–407
home-to-school notebook and,
    409–410
IEPs and, 21, 413–414
inclusion, support of, 34–35
involvement in education, 398–399,
    400, 404–406, 418
observations, 411
single parents and at risk students,
    295–297
websites to learn about
    exceptionalities, 399
words and language to use with,
    409–411
partial fetal alcohol syndrome (pFAS), 8
passports, 415
Peer Assisted Learning Strategies
    (PALS), 360
peer-mediated strategies, 326–327
peers
    interactions through
        paraprofessionals, 44
    support systems, 43, 44
    tutoring in elementary school,
        359–360
"people first" language, 5
perception, and learning disabilities,
    92, 116
performance, in IEPs, 22
personal program plan (PPP). See
    individualized education programs
personnel. See special education teachers
    and personnel; teachers
philosophy of education, teachers and
    personnel, 38–39
phonation disorders, 55
phonemic awareness, 100
phonological disorder, definition, 52
phonological system and errors, 52–55
phonology, 63
physical abuse, 299
physical disabilities and health problems,
    244–255
pitch disorders, 55–56
placement, definition, 28
portfolio assessment, 13, 15
positive behaviour supports (PBS), for
    EBD, 171–172
positive reinforcement of classroom
    behaviour, 325–326
post-secondary training, 382

poverty, in at-risk students, 292–294
Prader-Willi syndrome, 253
pragmatics difficulties, 89–90
pregnancies, in at-risk students, 302
prejudice. See bias
preschool students, 94–95, 97–98, 353–354
primary school. See elementary school
Prince Edward Island, 6
problem solving, in elementary
    school, 351
Professional Group for Attention and
    Related Disorders (PGARD), 146
program, definition, 28
program planning, assessment and, 12
psychostimulants, for AD/HD, 132
punishment techniques, 330–332

R

rating scales, for assessment, 13
Read the Picture Stories for Articulation
    (Loehr), 59–60
reading
    basal series, 347
    comprehension, 349
    deficits in EBD, 160
    direct instruction, 347
    elementary school, 346–348, 363–364
    learning disabilities, 87–88,
        100, 102, 107
    stories, for language disorders, 69
    whole language, 347
    word recognition and, 348
receptive language, 61–62
recollection, for assessment, 13
referral, 11, 12
reinforcement, 325–326, 329, 415
relational discipline, 324
Remenda, Jeanne, 188
reprimands, 331
residential programs, 3
resilience, 163, 305
resonance disorders, 56
resource room model, 31–33
response cost procedures, 331–332
responsiveness-to-intervention (RTI)
    model, 92–93, 95
Rett syndrome, 201–202
Ritalin, 132, 174
rules in classroom, 136–170, 319–320

S

Saskatchewan, 6, 50, 154
scheduling, 336–337

school district representative, in IEPs, 21
science teaching, for hearing
    impaired, 231
scores, 13, 14
screening, and assessment, 12
SCROL strategy, 395
seating arrangement, 322
    see also classroom arrangement
secondary school
    adaptations, accommodations, and
        modifications, 377, 384–388
    challenges at, 373–374
    content preparation, 380–381
    contingency plans, 386
    counselling for daily crises, 379
    curricula considerations, 374–375
    employment preparation, 383, 384
    exams preparation, 380–382
    general education teachers, 376–378
    grading practices, 390–391
    homework, 387–390
    independent living preparation,
        381–383
    language impairment indicators, 64
    learning strategies, 380–381, 393–396
    lesson plans, 384–385, 386
    personnel roles, 376–383
    post-secondary training and, 382
    programs to meet students' needs and
        demands, 375
    special education teachers, 378–383
    strategies for curriculum and
        instruction, 106–110
    success strategies in general education
        classes, 383–385
    teachers' self-evaluation, 378
    testing, 391–393
    transition from elementary school,
        354–355
seizures, epileptic, 250–251
self-contained education classes, 29–31
self-determination, 188–189, 416
Self-Determined Learning Model of
    Support (SDLMS), 416
self-efficacy, 380
self-instruction and behaviour, 334–335
self-management, 144–211, 213,
    333–335
self-monitoring of behaviour, 334
self-regulation, 144, 380
sensorineural hearing loss, 224
sensory impairments, 8, 222
    see also hearing impairments; visual
        impairments

seriously emotionally disturbed (SED), 153
  see also emotional or behavioural disorders
settings for special education
  resource room model, 31–33
  self-contained education classes, 29–31
  students with exceptionalities, 29
  towards inclusion, 33
sexual abuse, 299–300
siblings, 404–406
single education program, emergence, 33
single-parent homes, and at-risk students, 295–297
Snellen chart, 235
social acceptance. See community, sense of, and social acceptance
social-emotional problems
  communication disorders and, 67
  gifted and talented students, 282–286
  learning disabilities and adaptation, 90, 115–116
  for visual impairments, 239–240
social interactions, and learning disabilities, 104–106
social skills, 146–169, 352–353
social stories, for ASD, 211
socio-economic status, in at-risk students, 292–294
sound blending activity, 98
speaking difficulties, 89
  see also speech disorders
special education classroom. See classroom, special education
special education services. See special needs and services
special education teachers and personnel
  see also teachers
  collaboration with classroom teachers, 32, 41–43, 378
  communication with parents, 408–413
  Cordell Osmond profile, 408
  Dr. Julie Corkett profile, 380
  for EBD, 144
  family collaboration and involvement, 400–401, 407
  Heather Merasty profile, 138
  home visits to family, 412
  interactions in classroom organization and management, 339
  philosophy of education, 38–39
  in resource room model, 32

role in inclusion, 35, 37–38
secondary school, 377–383
in specialized classrooms approach, 29–30
students' support and collaboration, 36–37, 41–45, 380
words and language to use with parents, 409–411
special grouping practice, for gifted and talented students, 275
special needs and services
  development, 3–4
  historical changes, 4
  identification, 10–11
  students and, 5
specialized equipement, 323
specific language impairment (SLI), 64
speech, communication and, 49
  see also language
speech disorders, 50–61
  see also communication disorders; language disorders
  of articulation, 52–55
  classroom adaptations and accommodations, 59–61
  definition, 49–50
  of fluency, 57–58
  overview, 8–9
  self-monitoring by students, 59
  strategies for learning, 60–61
  of voice, 55–57
  work with peers or parents, 59–60
speech-language pathologists
  collaboration with teachers, 77–78
  language disorders and, 71
  services and intervention, 78–79
  Sharon Bond profile, 78
spina bifida, 253–255
spoken language, and learning disabilities, 103–104
standards of learning curriculum, 344–345
stereotyping, 5, 153, 261
storytelling, 69, 71
strengths-based assessments, for EBD, 162–163
student-team achievement division (STAD), 361
students with exceptionalities
  categories, 6–9
  classroom dynamics factors, 317–318
  collaboration with teachers, 380
  curricular needs, 39–40
  definition and description, 6–9

historical changes, 4
in provinces and territories, 6
setting for education, 29
in success of inclusion, 38
study skills, secondary school, 393–394
stuttering, 57
substance abuse, in at-risk students, 301–302
suicide, 159
supports and supported education
  ASD, 208
  concept and benefits, 40–41
  gifted and talented students, 287
  hearing impairments, 230
  intellectual disabilities and, 190
  principles for families, 400–401
  for visual impairments, 241
syntax, 63

T

talented students. See gifted and talented students
teacher aides, 43
teacher assistance teams, 43
teachers
  see also special education teachers and personnel
  AD/HD adaptation and accommodation, 141–143
  articulation and phonological errors, 53–55
  assessment role, 11–12, 20–21
  classroom dynamics factors, 318
  classroom organization and management, 339–340
  collaboration with parents for AD/HD, 149
  collaboration with special education teachers, 32, 41–43, 378
  collaboration with speech-language professionals, 77–78
  collaboration with students, 380
  common questions from parents, 414
  communication skills and style, 72–73, 318
  community-building skills, 146–147
  conferences with parents, 413–414
  diversity of student needs, 4
  EBD and, 144–145
  functions, 35–36
  gifted and talented students, 271–272, 287
  identification of special needs, 10–11
  IEPs and, 21, 22, 24